MW00365701

FEARLESS WOMEN

Books by Elizabeth Cobbs

NONFICTION

The Hello Girls: America's First Women Soldiers

American Umpire

All You Need Is Love: The Peace Corps and the Spirit of the 1960s

The Rich Neighbor Policy: Rockefeller and Kaiser in Brazil

Major Problems in American History

FICTION

The Tubman Command: A Novel

The Hamilton Affair: A Novel

Broken Promises: A Novel of the Civil War

FEARLESS WOMEN

FEMINIST PATRIOTS FROM ABIGAIL ADAMS TO BEYONCÉ

Elizabeth Cobbs

THE BELKNAP PRESS OF HARVARD UNIVERSITY PRESS

CAMBRIDGE, MASSACHUSETTS | LONDON, ENGLAND 2023

Printed in the United States of America

First printing

Library of Congress Cataloging-in-Publication Data

Names: Cobbs, Elizabeth, author.
Title: Fearless women: feminist patriots from Abigail Adams to Beyoncé / Elizabeth Cobbs.
Description: Cambridge, Massachusetts : The Belknap Press of Harvard University Press, 2023. | Includes bibliographical references and index.
Identifiers: LCCN 2022031732 | ISBN 9780674258488 (cloth)
Subjects: LCSH: Women's rights—United States—History. | Feminism—United States—History. | Feminists—United States—History. | Feminists—United States—Biography. | Equality—United States—History.
Classification: LCC HQ1236.5.U6 C635 2023 | DDC 305.420973—dc23/eng/20220707
LC record available at https://lccn.loc.gov/2022031732

For Bertha Lopez,
with thanks for her loving care of my children, and the children of countless other working parents. Women like her make the world go.

Contents

FEARLESS WOMEN

Prologue

> The fundamental purpose of feminism is that women should have equal opportunity and equal rights with every other citizen.
>
> FIRST LADY ELEANOR ROOSEVELT, 1935

THREE GOOD FRIENDS—all women professors—told me when I started writing this book that they do not consider themselves feminists. I wondered why. One earned a substantial living at a public college that had integrated by gender only a few decades earlier. Another boasted of being the first female full professor of economics at a famous Ivy League university. Yet another had achieved renown in the study of war, a field dominated by men. All had benefited from and contributed to the dogged effort to dismantle barriers. Yet each separately confided that she was not one of *them*. Meaning, as they all explained, a difficult person with extreme views.

"What's in a name?" Juliet asks in *Romeo and Juliet.* "A rose by any other name would smell as sweet." This book unpacks the storehouse of US history to reclaim a word that, while it describes a basic political value, is also one that many shy away from, or even recoil at, in the belief that it applies to someone else. Someone they may not like.

Accused on the right of being a subversive cult of man-haters, and on the left of being racist and transphobic, "feminism" may be irredeemably tarnished. But this is our only universal word for the global effort to achieve equality between the sexes. Admitting the obstacles, I hope in this book to pop the growing myth that those who fought for equal rights were a cliquish band of bourgeois white women whose sole preoccupation was combating patriarchy, thereby "further dispossessing the most marginal," in the words of one academic.[1]

The courageous, loving, embattled women profiled here show that this was actually a broad social movement, sparked by the American Revolution's claim that "All men are created equal." They were a wildly diverse group who came from every corner of the land: rich and poor, Black and white, liberal and conservative, male and female, Hispanic and Asian American, immigrant and native.

Many devoted their lives to the cause, but millions more advanced equality with their feet, challenging the nation to live up to its own bold claim. Some, like Angelina Grimké and Mary Church Terrell, asked for a voice in the political process—a goal then considered repulsively radical. Others wanted a piece of America's shiniest economic promise. Ann Marie Riebe yearned for a ranch in the North Dakota Badlands, and Muriel Siebert dreamed of a seat on the New York Stock Exchange. Still others bravely fought for mere survival. Yvonne Swan asked only for the right to defend her life and her children from a predator. In every generation, such women advanced the nation's highest hopes and best interests.

Feminist values spread. A study in 2020 found that average citizens of thirty-four nations valued gender parity above regular elections, and that 91 percent of Americans considered it "very important for women to have the same rights as men." Those results would have astounded Susan B. Anthony, Harriet Jacobs, Frances Perkins, Abigail Adams, and Elizabeth Packard. Yet women of a later generation, such as Beyoncé Knowles-Carter and Gretchen Carlson, would have nodded in recognition. We owe this transformation to those who demanded an education, fought to own property, insisted on being heard, showed they were as capable as men of running government, and made it clear that a woman's body belongs to herself and not to her father, husband, or boss. Not even to her child—though on this last point, some disagreed.[2]

Sexual equality inspired ambivalence. Pointing to the Bible, Koran, Torah, Vedas, or Analects of Confucius, many thought that giving rights to women would undermine their sacred roles as wives and mothers. Others worried about unintended downstream effects. The concern that gender equality would disturb the natural order reaches back to 1776, when Abigail Adams asked her husband John to "remember the ladies" as he wrote the laws for the new nation—and he refused, for fear that it might unleash chaos.

Gender hierarchy felt organic to most people until quite recently. Authoritative voices praised female deference as sexually attractive, morally virtuous, and socially practical. At the time of the Revolution, a woman was an extension of her husband with no legal existence of her own. Every penny in her pocket and hour of her day belonged to him. By 2021, few people could conceive of such radical dispossession—though, as gymnast Simone Biles made clear in her testimony before the US Senate the same year, many still fight for protection from the powerful. Even so, her presence reflected the rights that previous generations had won: rights to an education, to speak publicly, to lobby legislatures, to vote, to earn a living, to enjoy the benefits of the Constitution, to compete, and to be physically safe. "All men would be tyrants if they could," Abigail Adams reminded her husband in 1776, deliberately using the Founders' own explanation for revolt against one-man rule.

+++

I ARGUE THAT the explanation for the steady gains in women's rights lies in the country's origins. The language of the Revolution, borrowed from Europe and returned to the world in more potent form, gave observant—and sometimes desperate—women a handle on social problems that others scarcely perceived, along with a tool for addressing them. The United States coalesced around an explicit set of ambitious objectives drawn from the Enlightenment. First among them was the ideal of equality, a noble goal to which no other large government then aspired. This ideal became a template that made it easy to recognize the many ways in which the nation failed to realize its promise, spurring citizens to action. Arguments for subordination never stood up well against the founding principle of equality, which became a battering ram against hierarchies of all types.

Americans are inundated to this day by evidence of the nation's shortcomings. Yet it is equally important to be reminded of how we worked together to get things right. People grow by practicing good habits, not just reviewing mistakes. This book begins with a king as the head of government. It concludes with a woman of color as vice president. How might we explain this arc? *Fearless Women* explores how those who called themselves feminists, and many who did not, tried to improve their country. The life stories of these individuals, and others who joined them, show that the long quest for equality—what I have come to call "patriotic feminism"—helped make the nation what it is today.

It is common to think of women's history as a side story to the grand narrative of US history. As if it is something that pairs well with the main dish. I ask readers to reconceive of feminism as one of the principal themes in America's story—comparable in influence to the Industrial Revolution, the Civil War, or the Great Depression.

I use the term "feminist" as neither a compliment nor an insult, but to capture the experiences of people who fought for their own rights or those of others. The litmus test used in this book is whether or not someone subscribed to the belief that women and men are entitled to equal dignity and opportunity. By this broad definition, most Americans today are feminists and have been for several generations. Some argue for narrower definitions—like environmentalist Rebecca Clarren, who suggested in 2013 that feminists must oppose fracking, or Linda Sarsour, a Palestinian American organizer who declared in 2017 that feminism is incompatible with support for Israel—but I believe that doing so is historically inaccurate and politically coercive.[3]

Some feminists were racists, just as some civil rights activists were sexists. Some endorsed the Equal Rights Amendment, while others opposed it. Some supported access to abortion, others fought it. Feminists could be nuns or atheists, cattle ranchers or vegetarians, developers or environmentalists, soldiers or pacifists, beauty queens or pageant picketers, Republicans or Democrats. Some were even anti-feminists, meaning they pressed for equality in one arena while opposing it in another. These women were not uniformly appealing—some were downright obnoxious—but we are indebted to them for the opportunities we take for granted.

I call them patriotic, another loaded term at which some will take offense. By this, I simply mean that those who exerted themselves on behalf of gender equality saw themselves as helping the United States achieve its own goals, a perspective that fueled their confidence and improved their success. It is easy for people today to recognize patriotism in the rousing speeches of Angelina Grimké, Susan B. Anthony, or Mary Church Terrell, but we must remember that they were considered troublemakers in their own time. I hope to help contemporary readers recognize the call to national service in the words of more recent champions like Chicana activist Martha Cotera and singer-songwriter Beyoncé Knowles-Carter.

Feminists played a major role in laying the nation's milestones: public education for all, the abolition of slavery, an inclusive electorate, a social safety net, wider access to the benefits of economic progress, and the redefinition of marriage as a romantic partnership between equals. In every epoch, devoted women and men championed the promise of greater opportunity, even though they often disagreed vehemently on strategy and the scope of reform, which widened over time. Some reaped more benefits than others, as is true of any social change. Activists in other countries did not advocate for women's rights as an expression of American values, naturally enough, but *Fearless Women* is about feminism on these shores.

According to the *Oxford English Dictionary,* the original meaning of "patriot," dating to the 1570s, is a "person who loves his or her country, *esp.* one who is ready to support its freedoms and rights and to defend it against enemies or detractors." In American usage after the 1770s, the word acquired a second meaning, namely, "a member of a resistance movement, a freedom fighter." Two centuries later, in the 1980s, "patriot" assumed yet another guise, sometimes referring to opponents of government regulation who claimed the word for "right-wing libertarian political and militia groups." Today, many think a patriot is someone who parades in red, white, and blue, but this is like expecting all good mothers to wear aprons. Some do, but plenty more would not know where to buy one.[4]

In this book, I use "patriot" in its original sense, to mean someone who has a love of country and a willingness to defend national values. This is not the same as chauvinistic nationalism. World history offers many examples of patriotism twisted into nefarious shape to justify violence and repression, but that is not its only shape. From Abigail Adams to Beyoncé, many felt the nation could do better, and they were not shy about expressing it. As First Lady Claudia "Lady Bird" Johnson said, "The clash of ideas is the sound of freedom." Patriot, like patriarchy, comes from the Greek *patris* and Latin *patria,* meaning fatherland. The feminists in this book claimed that the United States belonged equally to mothers. This land was their land, too.[5]

Some thought they asked too much. John Adams compared his wife to a member of the insolent riff-raff, one of the "renegadoes." The House Un-American Activities Committee interrogated only one member of Franklin D. Roosevelt's cabinet: the first woman to serve at that level, former suffragist Frances Perkins. Yet far from tearing down the nation, women such as these hoped to complete the structure framed in 1776.

I do not link feminism and patriotism frivolously. Success arose from appeals to national values. Measures aimed at greater equality were hard to keep down indefinitely when pursued by reformers steeped in Fourth of July traditions. This was Susan B. Anthony's insight. "With such women consecrating their lives, failure is impossible," she predicted in her last speech. "Wild heresies" would one day become "fashionable orthodoxies." Indeed, behavior that one generation rejected as immoral—such as women attending school, speaking publicly, casting a ballot, wearing trousers, using birth control, or pursuing a career—often seemed admirable to the next. The most traditional Americans eventually came to view equality between the sexes as congruent with the country's purpose. People who did not call themselves feminists began living feminist-inspired lives, though partisanship ensnared the word in the 1980s, when Phyllis Schlafly appropriated the language of patriotism to defeat the Equal Rights Amendment.[6]

As scandalous propositions became humdrum practices, the tools used to bring about this transformation were obscured. My goal is to excavate them. Each generation, building upon the last, tended to forget how awful were the conditions that prompted reform and how controversial was the fight. This made it easy to judge women who advocated for change as harpies rather than heroines. Those wives and daughters who did not experience the dilemmas that concerned reformers sometimes viewed their project with skepticism. As Olive Logan reflected in the 1880s, she felt so immune from the problems that riled Susan B. Anthony that joining the crusade "was as far removed from my thoughts as becoming a female gymnast and whirling upon a trapeze." Only when she learned that others were not as fortunate did her feelings change.[7]

Men and women—and people who do not identify with either gender—shall always grapple with how best to love, support, and protect one another as the stakes for personal well-being are high. In every generation, handfuls of Americans have advanced the conversation into unexplored territory, feeling their way toward a better future. My goal in this book is to give voice to these pathbreakers, as well as to those who believe that feminism points only toward ruin.

+++

A WORD ABOUT THE STRUCTURE OF THIS BOOK. Historians have written numerous tomes that emphasize organizations and policy, but we do not yet have a survey showing how the quest for gender equality reshaped individual lives from 1776 to the present. *Fearless Women* relies on personal accounts. It covers a longer period than most, and readers inspired to learn more may want to delve into the books cited in the notes to explore the literature on feminism both within and outside the United States.

This book is not encyclopedic. My aim is to provide a broad, yet intimate account that helps readers imagine what it was like to live through these momentous changes. Specialists will recognize that much of this immense story is not included, and casual readers may wonder why I did not discuss their favorite suffragist, author, lawmaker, athlete, or girl band, and why I did not include representatives of every possible demographic. I hope they will ultimately be grateful that the book they hold is a few hundred pages rather than a thousand.

Each chapter features two women whose lives reveal important turns on the path to equality. Their stories show that each generation improved society in identifiable ways even while struggling with issues they could not resolve, just as we do. To chart progress, I spotlight a key development in each period, typically championed by the first individual. For example, Chapter 1, "The Right to Learn," reveals that the Revolutionary generation grappled with whether or not to educate girls, a question that preoccupied Abigail Adams and led to support for the first Ladies Academies. It also describes the consequences of oppressive marriage laws through my secondary character, Abigail Bailey, as a way to show why some were ultimately unsatisfied with educational reform alone. It would be several more lifetimes before the laws that harmed Abigail Bailey and her children were rewritten.

Chapter 2, "The Right to Speak," carries us forward to the next generation, in which educated women pioneered the novel practice of speaking publicly, advanced by Angelina Grimké, the lead character in this chapter. The companion biography features Harriet Jacobs, who faced the more extreme problem of slavery's assault on women's bodies. Jacobs lived to see slavery end, but the double standard of morality that complicated her life took much longer to change. Successive chapters show how each generation that followed obtained ever more rights, generally revealed through the life of my lead character, while the companion biography illuminates the ongoing struggle against some stubborn impediment. The contrast between the two people—between what was achieved and the problems that remained—explains why feminists kept expanding their goals.

Despite gains, it is important to note that changes in human behavior never align precisely with dates. To give an example, Chapter 4 focuses on "The Right to Vote," even though, by then, suffragists had already campaigned for fifty years. The Nineteenth Amendment would be named for Susan B. Anthony, the heroine of Chapter 3, but she died without seeing victory. Through the story of Mary Church Terrell, a prominent Black suffragist, Chapter 4 shows instead that the fight for a federal amendment to the Constitution came to a successful conclusion between 1900 and 1920, though many women like her still could not vote for another forty years. The secondary character in this chapter is Rosa Cavalleri, a laundrywoman with little interest in suffrage whose life reveals why reproductive rights emerged as a major feminist concern. Most of the secondary characters in this book experienced a dilemma to which reformers did not yet have solutions. Some of these problems exist to this day. The combination of two biographies allows readers to see how particular issues came to a boil—and were resolved—while others continued to simmer.

Each chapter covers a time span that historians recognize as having its own peculiar characteristics, like Reconstruction or the Great Depression. Some epochs are short, others longer. Most people lived across several, so some of the dates in each chapter fall outside those indicated by the chapter title. Frances Perkins, for example, was born before and died after the New Deal, in which she played a starring role. I ask readers to accept that none of my biographical subjects took her first or last breath on cue. Some events inevitably took place outside the era in which any given character had maximum impact.

Readers will further note that I often use first names. This is not to diminish major figures, but out of respect for gendered naming patterns. Most women changed their surnames upon marriage, giving them more than one surname during their lifetime. Their first names were their one permanent marker of identity. Tellingly, some women entertainers and politicians today use first names exclusively, as if to say, this is *me.* I use first names to acknowledge this freighted history, and to minimize confusion between family members. For this literary device I ask readers' indulgence.

Mindful that no one individual can represent any era, I have chosen my characters carefully. The first person in each chapter is someone who objected to an injustice that was often outside her personal experience, but which she felt compelled to address as a civic-minded individual. This first person is the face of feminism, so to speak. While I have selected individuals who made notable contributions, I could easily have picked others. A few are obvious, but not everyone profiled here would be considered the "top feminist" of her era, if there was such a person. I have deliberately chosen leaders from various regions, ethnic communities, and class backgrounds. Documenting the process by which feminism entered everyday life requires some choices that may surprise readers who think they know the usual suspects. For example, the chapter on the 1960s and 1970s focuses on Martha Cotera. Gloria Steinem garnered more headlines, but Cotera extended feminism's reach among Hispanics, the nation's most rapidly growing population group.

The second biography features someone who helps us see why we should care. Women's rights advocates continually faced the accusation that they made mountains out of molehills. Government was mostly fair, employers mostly reasonable, husbands mostly kind. Why the fuss? My secondary biographies spotlight people who did not start out as reformers. They were survivors who prevailed against harrowing odds. Their eye-opening biographies reveal why, when presented with specific life histories, men and women often found themselves more sympathetic than they expected to be toward people whose suffering seemed incommensurate with America's vision of itself. Over time, Americans changed their laws, institutions, and customs accordingly, though not without serious misgivings and pushback.

For these secondary characters, I often rely on memoirs. Historians know that such sources are not ideal. Most people cannot recall precise dates or conversations years later. They are trapped inside their own perspective, which changes as time sharpens or dulls certain feelings about the past. But scholars are trained to work with what they have. Few of these were people whom the press followed around, because women were not generally considered historically important. As of 2022, the Pulitzer Prize in History had been awarded only once in 106 years to a book on women's history—and even then on the stereotypical subject of midwifery. Almost none of my subjects recorded her own experiences day by day, and some literally could not. The memoirs used in this book, whether the recollections of an enslaved mother, an illiterate immigrant stuck in an arranged marriage, or a woman involuntarily incarcerated in an insane asylum by her husband, are like scrolls discovered centuries after a civilization has crumbled: incomplete, but priceless. I have tried to mitigate the limitations of these testimonies by examining them alongside other sources.

Some of the terms used here would have puzzled those within its pages. Words mutate from generation to generation. "Democratic" had a pejorative connotation during America's revolutionary years, when the favored word was "republican." Nevertheless, Americans today trace their democracy to the Revolution. I encourage readers to think similarly about feminism, even though the term was invented in France in the late nineteenth century and arrived in the United States just before World War I. Like scholar Nancy Cott, I do not limit it to one "specific historical time." Applying it to someone like Abigail Adams or Susan B. Anthony allows us to chart the genealogy of an evolving idea. In this respect, I also use Chimamanda Ngozi Adichie's commonsense definition of a feminist as anyone whose actions reinforced what we today identify as "equal rights for men and women." She explains, "My great grandmother did not know the word feminist, but it doesn't mean she wasn't one." The label feels anachronistic until we recognize that it is a new term for something old—in the way that "racist," coined around 1935, and "sexist," coined around 1969, are applied to earlier periods. Susan B. Anthony used "colorphobia" and "sexphobia."[8]

Readers may challenge this definition, preferring one with strong exclusions. Some religious groups preach that a good Christian (Jewish, Muslim, Hindu) woman cannot be a feminist. Political groups also impose limits. Phyllis Schlafly wrote in 2014 that the feminist movement was only "about power for the female left." Some leftists implicitly seemed to agree. Organizers of the 2017 Women's March on Washington asked people who opposed abortion not to participate in the show of disapproval over Donald Trump's election. Some activists trace feminism to Friedrich Engels's 1884 Marxist analysis of women's subordination (thirty-six years after Seneca

Falls). Yet history convinces me that the quest for equality, in a variety of flavors, has inspired people across the political spectrum for almost three centuries, much like republicanism. As the unthinkable idea of equality became a common value, it became common property, not subject to eminent domain by any one faction. An individual might be a "bad feminist," as Roxane Gay disarmingly puts it, but a feminist nonetheless, since humans are complex.[9]

Readers should draw their own conclusions about the past and future. The aim here is to provide information useful for forming them. In my twenties I edited a national feminist newspaper and helped run a women's center in Southern California. I left that work behind in the early 1980s when I went to graduate school, where I specialized in US foreign relations. I have waited many years, and written eight other books, to ensure that I had adequate distance. While never perfectly realized, objectivity is my goal as a historian.[10]

My three friends worry that the quest for gender equality can be divisive. The furor accompanying the reversal of *Roe v. Wade* in 2022 proves they have cause for concern. Yet *Fearless Women* endeavors to show that, on balance, this journey has actually defined Americans and even united them. Reformers expressed an aspiration to liberty and justice for all that pricked the nation's conscience and goaded its development. Like democracy, a term of scorn in 1776 that is admired today, feminism gives us a common language if we do not run from the word.

Our story begins with two patriots, both named Abigail.

CHAPTER I

The Right to Learn

1776–1800
Abigail Adams and Abigail Bailey

Why should a woman not be allowed to pronounce the word *I*?

THEODOR GOTTLIEB VON HIPPEL, 1793

ONE ENJOYED NEARLY EVERY BLESSING a woman could hope for. The other suffered nearly every blow a woman could endure. One stood up to tyranny in government, the other to a tyrant in the flesh. The pair never met, although they lived only two hundred miles apart. Neither went so far as to suggest that women existed for themselves, not merely to serve their families, but they were among the earliest American citizens to resist injustice based on gender.

Abigail Adams, a Massachusetts mother of four with a warm sense of humor, served as First Lady to John Adams, forged a friendship with Thomas Jefferson, and wrote more than two thousand invaluable letters documenting the early republic. What sparked her passion for women's rights, given all that she had? Abigail Bailey of New Hampshire enjoyed the respect of her community as a pious churchgoer while her husband won the admiration of fellow soldiers in the War of Independence. What lack of rights compelled this Abigail to flee her husband and race hundreds of miles on horseback to save her children?

Even God Despises a Nag

When John Adams first met the young Abigail Smith, nine years his junior, he was not impressed. Nabby, as she was then known, and her older sister Mary, nicknamed Polly, spoke their minds far too freely to meet his approval. "Polly and Nabby are Wits," he carped to his diary in the summer of 1759. He compared the Smith girls unfavorably to a demure young woman he considered "fond" and "candid." His teeming brain analyzed expressions even as he jotted them down. "Fondness is doting Love," he explained. "Candor is a Disposition to palliate faults and Mistakes, to put the best Construction upon Words and Actions, and to forgive Injuries." By this definition, the Smith girls were "Not fond, not frank, not candid."[1]

Yet Abigail's wittiness turned out to be unexpectedly alluring, and John grew to appreciate her jaunty repartee. When he began courting her three years later, shortly after she turned eighteen, he discovered an intellect as unfettered as his own.

Abigail Smith was fortunate to have parents who encouraged her to cultivate her mind. Her mother came from a family that, unlike many in colonial New England, respected widows enough to let them manage property. Her father was a benevolent parson who settled his wife and four children on a picturesque estate in Weymouth, a small town three miles across a breezy ocean inlet from Braintree, where the Adams family owned a humbler farm. A watercolor from the era shows vegetable gardens running from the porch of the spacious two-story home down to a white picket fence. Fat cows, whose milk Abigail learned to churn into butter, graze peacefully alongside a large barn.[2]

Born in 1744, Abigail was a high-spirited child who described her girlhood as wild and giddy. Her maternal grandmother indulgently reminded the nervous parents that, as Plutarch had observed, "wild colts make the best Horses." Abigail never attended school, but her mother taught her to read. It wasn't long before her father opened his private library to her, to satisfy her curiosity. Abigail's spiky handwriting and inventive spelling reflected a lack of formal education, but she devoured the classics as she matured into a short young woman with a pointed chin and keen eyes that seemed to observe the world ironically. John wooed Abigail by bringing her books to read. She gave him ardent kisses in return. The two fell in love and married in 1764.

John became Abigail's dearest friend. "My anxiety for your welfare will never leave me but with my parting Breath," she wrote when they were separated during the Revolution, which disrupted their quiet life twelve years into marriage. "Tis of more importance to me than all this World contains." By then she had given birth to five children, one of whom they had buried at thirteen months, as was heartbreakingly common in that era.[3]

Abigail Adams accepted the prevailing conviction that God had fashioned women mostly to serve men and their offspring. According to Genesis, God devised woman to be man's helper. As Abigail later wrote her younger sister Betsy, "the all wise creator made woman an help meet for Man and she who fails in those Duties; does not answer the end of her creation."[4]

Law reinforced this well-established Christian belief, also expressed in other religions. Under British statutes applicable in the Thirteen Colonies, a young man's legal standing improved on the day of his nuptials. He escaped the patriarchal control of his father and became a patriarch himself. But a girl's legal standing shrank. In the words of William Blackstone, whose 1765 *Commentaries* on law guided attorneys like the young John Adams, "the very being or legal existence of the woman is suspended during the marriage, or at least is incorporated and consolidated into that of the husband: under whose wing, protection and *cover,* she performs everything." The legal term for this system was "coverture."[5]

Coverture made wives into legal shadows, sewn to their husbands' feet. A woman took a man's name, and in return, all of her possessions became his. The children she "gave" him became his sole property. So-called dower rights provided a wife with limited use of whatever she brought into marriage, but she could not give it away because it belonged to "his" children upon her death. If he died first, she had lifetime use of one-third of the estate. This meant that a widow had no legal right to continue to live in her own home, unless his heirs—her own offspring—granted permission. For English aristocrats, this generally meant removal to a smaller "dower house," but for most women it meant a room in the home of one of her children.

Disqualified from owning property under British law, wives were not entitled to leave wills. They had nothing to bestow. Nor could they enter into legal contracts or serve on a jury. Women were not allowed to sign the

Mayflower Compact, and Plymouth's first governor, William Bradford, excluded them from government "as both reason and nature teacheth they should be." A husband could hire his wife out as a servant, beat her as he saw fit, and, in Blackstone's words, "restrain a wife of her liberty, in case of any gross misbehavior." A wife even had trouble committing a crime, since she was presumed to be acting on her husband's command when in his presence.[6]

In the happiest of marriages, to a kind man who efficiently managed family affairs, coverture posed few obvious problems. But husbands who mismanaged family finances or abused their wives and children could wreak havoc. The wealthiest families sometimes arranged prenuptial trusts to shield an heiress's resources, but these were rare and brides were expected to acquiesce to their husband's authority. A noncompliant woman was considered improper and unattractive. Puritan minister John Winthrop preached in 1645 that "A true wife counts her subjection [as] her honor and her freedom." To Winthrop, God himself despised a nag.[7]

The Value of Female Ignorance

Newspaper columns, popular books, and etiquette guides offered advice to wives. Echoing the Bible, they portrayed service as life's key purpose. James Fordyce's 1765 *Sermons to a Young Woman,* which Abigail Adams recommended to her sister, explained that women were "manifestly intended to be . . . softer companions who, by nameless delightful sympathies and endearments, might improve our pleasures and soothe our pains, to lighten the load of domestic cares, and thereby leave us more leisure for rougher labours or severer studies." As a character from a story in Benjamin Franklin's *Pennsylvania Gazette* told his wife, "'Tis your duty to help make me able."[8]

Most literature suggested that a limited education should suffice. "Be cautious in displaying your good sense," John Gregory warned in 1774 in *A Father's Legacy to His Daughters.* "If you happen to have any learning, keep it a profound secret, especially from the men, who generally look with a jealous and malignant eye on a woman of great parts and cultivated understanding." A virtuous woman held her tongue and masked her native quickness. She shared in conversation with her eyes alone, not "uttering a syllable," John Gregory counseled. John Adams concurred. He wrote to Abigail in 1775 that he was impressed upon meeting John Hancock's new wife to find that she behaved "with perfect modesty" and was "totally silent, as a Lady ought to be."[9]

Jean-Jacques Rousseau, whose works John Adams commended to Abigail, gave one of the fullest justifications for keeping women ignorant. Rousseau waxed poetic about the virtues of family life, though he would eventually deposit in an orphanage every one of the five children he fathered with his illiterate laundrymaid—as was his prerogative and not hers. Families were the building blocks of a stable society, he reflected. Woman's labor cemented the home and her subservience made it harmonious. "If woman is made to please man and to be subjugated to man, she ought to make herself pleasing to him rather than to provoke him," Rousseau wrote in *Émile,* his 1762 treatise on education. A girl's training should match her role, because the "male is only a male now and again," while a female was "always" and nothing but "a female." For her own happiness, a girl should be "trained to bear the yoke from the first" in order not to "feel it."[10]

Doctors concurred. French physician Pierre Jean Georges Cabanis warned that women's "cerebral pulp" was too soft to withstand serious study without making them into "ambiguous beings . . . who are, properly speaking, of neither sex." One Dr. Moreau asserted that the uterus, since it was an internal organ, suffused a woman's experience of reality. As an external organ, the penis exerted less control over a man's thoughts. (A dubious proposition.) In the parlance of the day, females were "the Sex," meaning that their reproductive function was the most important thing about them. They performed nature's greatest miracle, creating another human being. "Nature has given women so much power," English writer Samuel Johnson quipped, "that the law has wisely given them little."[11]

Men of letters confided to each other that it was important to deceive women about the unfairness of this exchange. "We can hardly shew them too much respect, or pay them too much deference," suggested David Fordyce, "that we may conceal, and, in some degree, compensate to them the superiority which nature has given us over them." Lord Chesterfield wrote to his son that he must "with the utmost care, conceal and never seem to know" the fact that females were gullible nincompoops for whom "no flattery is either too high or too low."[12]

Some men objected. Daniel Defoe, author of *Robinson Crusoe,* wrote in 1697 that he could not believe "God Almighty ever made so delicate, so joyous creatures, and furnished them with such charms, so agreeable and delightful to mankind; with souls capable of the same accomplishments with men; and all to be only stewards of our houses, cooks, and slaves." Defoe suggested that academies should be created to give women a liberal education, though none yet existed. Satirist Jonathan Swift, author of *Gulliver's Travels,* urged young women in 1723 to cultivate their intelligence, "without which it is impossible to acquire or preserve the friendship and esteem of a wise man" who wanted "a true friend through every stage of his life." John Adams enjoyed just such a partnership with Abigail.[13]

For women of the era, it took extraordinary strength to swim against the tide. Abigail Adams scrutinized the books of leading thinkers for encouraging words, and stubbornly insisted, as she put it, that females "inherit an Eaqual Share of curiosity with the other Sex."[14] She pointed out to a friend that James Fordyce acknowledged "the most conscientious Men, are in general those who have the greatest regard for women of reputation and talents." Despite views that raise hackles today, Enlightenment writers represented new ways of thinking, Abigail believed.[15]

Indeed, depictions of women as vain but pleasant dimwits were, in some respects, a genuine improvement. Holding the King James Bible in church every Sunday, Abigail would have read Saint Paul's older condemnation of women. For Eve's crime in the Garden of Eden, she and all her daughters had forever forfeited their right to speak in church. "Let the woman learn in silence with all subjection," Saint Paul wrote in the first century, advancing an interpretation of God's will not ascribed to Christ himself. "I suffer not a woman to teach, nor to usurp authority over the man, but to be in silence."[16]

Female guilt was deeply embedded in the writings of the church fathers, who described women as the wicked, polluted, sexually insatiable daughters of Eve, whom God deservedly punished with the agony of childbirth. "You are the Devil's gateway," accused Tertullian, the influential third-century theologian. For decency, every virgin should cloak her sinful face with a veil. Plainly clothed married women ought to wear self-abnegation like a cross. In the sixth century, Saint Jerome called woman an "atrocity," the cause of war, lust, and murder.[17]

Protestantism created more space for individual religious convictions, but Martin Luther and John Calvin still embraced Saint Paul's view.

"Women are not created for any other purpose than to serve man and to be his assistant in producing children," Luther sermonized in 1527. Eve had fatefully wished "to become clever," plucking from the tree of knowledge—an act for which God punished her, and the generations that followed her, by requiring women to "keep silence in the churches." Knowledge in a woman was dangerous. Calvin described them as "an accessory of man," destined to submit to his rule. Instigator of the world's misery, Eve had passed God's "curse of the woman" to her daughters in perpetuity.[18]

Enlightenment thinkers thus softened the superstitions that had prompted the hanging, burning, beheading, and drowning of up to half a million "witches," almost exclusively women past childbearing age. The writings of the *philosophes* were generous compared with the fifteenth-century *Malleus Maleficarum,* endorsed by Pope Innocent VIII, which declared that "witchcraft is chiefly found in women" because it "comes from carnal lust, which is in woman insatiable."[19]

Abigail Adams indulged a bit of wishful thinking about what she might have done had she been born a man. "Had nature formed me of the other Sex," she wrote her cousin Isaac Smith, "I should certainly have been a rover." But "the many Dangers we are subject too [*sic*] from your Sex, renders it almost impossible for a Single Lady to travel without injury to her character."[20]

Her emphasis on character is telling. Rape was the only crime for which a sufferer was presumed responsible. No one believed that a man who handed his wallet to a thief actually wanted to, but in the words of historian Sharon Block, only "a woman's willingness to lose her life instead of her chastity proved that the incident was an attempted rape rather than a consensual encounter." In court cases of the era, even victims agreed that submission amounted to consent. As a Pennsylvania servant—beaten so badly that her arm was immobilized—reluctantly admitted when cross-examined in a 1789 rape trial, "I struggled each time, but consented at last." Victims were imprisoned by language itself, which gave them no other word than "consent" to indicate acceptance of facts to which alternatives did not exist.[21]

Bawdy literature blurred the line further by portraying sex as a game in which women resisted while sporting men strove to overcome their defenses. According to Block, most people assumed that truly virtuous women somehow controlled "all sexual uses of their bodies," regardless of the violence directed against them.[22]

Abigail Adams simply accepted that solo exploration was impossible, and set aside the "great inclination" to travel that she had felt since childhood. A woman must remain by the hearth. "Instead of visiting other Countries," she wrote to her cousin with a sigh that reverberates three centuries later, women must "content themselves with seeing but a very small part of their own." Lucky ones might read books about faraway places if their fathers or husbands allowed them.[23]

Abigail nonetheless found fulfillment in marriage. When a sixth pregnancy swelled her apron, she wrote John to tell him, with amusement, that their puzzled young son had said, "I never saw any body grow so fat as you do." John was affectionate and kind, and their marriage was filled with laughter and conversation. She wrote to him that woman had "no earthly happiness eaquel to that of being tenderly beloved by her dearest Friend."[24]

Under a Patriarch's Thumb

Born in 1746, two years after Abigail Adams, Abigail Abbot of New Hampshire accepted the same traditions. "While I lived with my parents, I esteemed it my happiness to be in subjection to them," she recalled in one of the rare published memoirs left by an American woman of the period. As she contemplated marriage, she "thought it must be a still greater benefit to be under the aid of a judicious companion, who would rule well his own house." Abigail's words echoed those of Saint Paul, who preached that a man should "ruleth well his own house." Like many devout New Englanders, she studied her Bible so closely that it flavored her writing and structured her thoughts.[25]

Protestantism fostered literacy to diminish reliance on clergy. Abigail Abbot may have learned to read at home, or perhaps at a "Dame" school, the colonial equivalent of preschool, where motherly caretakers offered instruction. Her parents may even have sent her to a village elementary, though she made no mention of her education in her memoir. In 1647, Massachusetts Bay Colony had passed the first law requiring towns to provide schools that taught writing and basic numeracy to all children, male and female, free or enslaved—though guardians had no obligation to send them. Larger settlements provided Latin grammar schools, offering courses in Latin and upper-level subjects like science and mathematics. Girls sometimes attended the elementary grades, but the higher ones were reserved for young men, making knowledge of Latin a potent symbol of gender differences.[26]

A committed Calvinist, Abigail heard a sermon at eighteen from a fiery evangelist, one Reverend Peter Powers, who convinced her that she was "a guilty and very filthy creature." She took to heart that she was "vile," a word she used repeatedly. As a teenager, she joined Reverend Powers's tiny church as one of fifteen followers. She accepted that redemption required her to submit to whatever "all-wise" God imposed. Bible stories of heroic men who kept faith amid cruel trials, from Job on his sickbed to Daniel in the lion's den, fired her imagination. Acquaintances described her as a tall, "very comely" young woman with piercing eyes. Slender, she must have possessed the toughness of the river willow, whose canes New Englanders bent into chairs strong enough to bear a man's weight.[27]

Abigail married at twenty-two, a typical age for a New England bride, hoping for a fond partner but prepared to revere her husband under all circumstances, aware as she was of her own "infirmities and failings." She may not have known Asa Bailey long, since she said nothing about his background in her memoir. In eighteenth-century America, suitors generally approached prospective wives through their parents. Courtship had not yet acquired the private, romantic gloss it would in the next century. However their acquaintanceship unfolded, Abigail assumed that happiness would ensue if she embraced her husband's wishes. The Lord meant for woman to please man, and she was determined to do so.[28]

Faster than she could have anticipated, Asa let her know that pleasing him would not be easy. Within a month, he showed that he felt entitled to hurl angry words, make arbitrary demands, and even resort to blows. A harsh, haughty man, he was quick to blame and eager to chastise. Abigail had never seen her parents utter an angry word. Her childhood had been sunny and peaceful. Now she realized that for the remainder of her days she must "expect hard and cruel treatment." It was God's divine plan, she saw, "to try me with afflictions." To save her soul, she must sacrifice her self.[29]

When she was alone, the newlywed wept and pored over the Bible. The Good Book suggested that she return abuse with kindness. She resolved to confide in Asa as if he were her truest friend in the hope of softening his heart. She convinced herself that he cared for her but suffered from man's natural sinfulness, compounded by a difficult personality. Her faith would make him a better Christian and kinder husband. It was better for her to "suffer wrong than do wrong."[30]

Asa Bailey was eager to share her bed when he was not angry and Abigail desired his "tender affections." The marriage settled into a pattern. Abigail found she could palliate her husband's volatility for "weeks together" if she trod carefully. Despite his troubling propensities, she came to feel "the tenderest affection for him as my head and husband." He was father to her children, and kept her focused on the "hard labour" of rearing them. Birth control implemented through abstinence or withdrawal was a man's decision in this era. As one Massachusetts man said in his defense against a paternity lawsuit in 1771, "I fucked her once, but minded my pullbacks."[31]

Asa Bailey was not so mindful. Abigail bore seventeen children in twenty-two years. As a study of colonial Pennsylvania showed, women between the childbearing ages of fifteen and forty-five were forty times more likely to die than men, even during wartime. Fortunately, Abigail Bailey survived to tell her story.

Men Are What They Are by Education

Men were quicker than women to question patriarchy. In fact, it was an Enlightenment philosopher's attack on the notion that one man should rank above all others that gave Abigail Adams a new vocabulary. According to the *Oxford English Dictionary,* "equal" was first used as a personal adjective around 1526, soon after Martin Luther sparked the Reformation that undermined the authority of the *Papa* (Italian for "Father") across western Europe. In the next century, English philosopher John Locke used the term in his famous justification for sovereignty of the people.[32]

Locke's immediate goal was to justify his own treason. A spindly, brainy bachelor with the profile of Ichabod Crane, he escaped England in 1683 to avoid imprisonment for complicity in plots to assassinate a king hostile to Parliament and friendly to Catholics. In 1688, he returned home from Holland on a royal yacht with new, more compliant Protestant monarchs who were installed in what the English call the "Glorious Revolution."

King William and Queen Mary accepted Parliament's new "Bill of Rights," which curbed royal power and strengthened the people's ability to have a say in government via their representatives in Parliament.

Locke spelled out the rationale in his 1689 tract *Two Treatises of Government.* The second treatise is remembered best, because it has shaped democratic government since. In it, Locke asserted that kings ruled not by divine right but by leave of their subjects, whose God-given ability to reason entitled them to decide whether a government was capable of protecting their "life, liberty, and property." If an informed people decided that their monarch had failed, Locke wrote, they "might as often and innocently change their governors as they do their physicians."[33]

In his first, less famous treatise, Locke targeted patriarchy, specifically the *Patriarcha* of Sir Robert Filmer. Published in 1680, *Patriarcha; or, The Natural Power of Kings* was then the fullest English-language articulation of the divine right of kings. It denounced "the supposed natural equality and freedom of mankind" as a ridiculous notion that contradicted Holy Scripture. Filmer was himself responding to the suggestion by a priest of the Catholic Counter-Reformation that "power is derived from the people." The priest had asserted that because the Catholic pope no longer anointed some governments (Protestant ones), "The people make the king, who otherwise would be a private individual like the rest of men, naturally free and equal."[34]

Filmer rejected this as papist nonsense. He considered patriarchy essential to God's plan for the universe. God the Father ruled the heavens. On earth, kings ruled. In individual households, fathers ruled their children, wives, and servants. God intended some men to command and everyone else to obey. A baronet, Filmer argued that only hereditary rule guaranteed liberty. Average men did not want, need, or deserve responsibility for making decisions. They had liberty enough under benevolent kings—like wives in relation to husbands and servants in relation to masters. Allowing unequipped men to choose their rulers served "only to destroy liberty." It recklessly ignored that "the desire of liberty was the first cause of the fall of Adam."[35]

Yet God was merciful, Filmer believed. He had given Adam absolute command over his own children, which passed to Adam's male descendants. Biblical patriarchs even had the right to kill disobedient offspring. In time, groups of families joined together as distinct nations. Kings descended from Adam's bloodline became fathers "over many families." As patriarch of his country, each ruler delegated "to every subordinate and inferior father, and to their children, their rights and privileges."[36]

To secure an argument for rule of the people, John Locke had to demolish Filmer's paradigm. In his first treatise, he charged that the book *Patriarcha* offered naught but "chains for all mankind," and served only to "persuade all men that they are slaves, and ought to be so." Men were self-evidently born free and equal, Locke asserted, and could meet life's challenges if taught to think and allowed to do so. Francis Bacon, René Descartes, Isaac Newton, and other stars of the Scientific Revolution had lit the way.[37]

The Enlightenment opened a new chapter in the ancient debate over which mattered most in human development: nature or nurture. Thinkers of the seventeenth and eighteenth centuries bet on nurture. They believed that what generally limited men was ignorance, not low birth. As Locke put it, "Men . . . are what they are, good or evil, useful or not, by education. It is that which makes the great difference in mankind." With schooling, men of every race could make something of themselves—and should. The duty to improve oneself, and one's country thereby, distinguished man from "his cattle."[38]

British jurist William Blackstone echoed Locke in 1770, asserting that every man "should pursue his own true and substantial happiness" according to God's wish. In 1776, economist Adam Smith argued that free men acting in their own self-interest increased a nation's prosperity. Men might choose to act altruistically, but they were entitled to elbow to the front of the marketplace, if they wished. Thomas Jefferson married Blackstone to Locke that same year in the opening line of the American Declaration of Independence, which proclaimed man's inalienable right to "life, liberty, and the pursuit of happiness."

Jefferson's declaration reflected the colonists' complaint that Parliament had violated their rights by unilaterally imposing new taxes, including one on tea. At the time, colonists were not allowed to elect representatives to the House of Commons. Although Parliament had levied the taxes to meet the cost of defending the colonies, settlers believed that they should not forfeit the input they had won in the Glorious Revolution simply because they had sailed across the ocean.

Instead of backing the colonists, King George III unwisely sided with Parliament. Rebels retaliated by pitching the empire's hated tea—the "weed of slavery," Abigail Adams angrily called it—into Boston harbor. The king sent Redcoats to Massachusetts, and colonists fired from behind trees, rocks, and buildings in the opening salvos of the American Revolution.

British immigrant Thomas Paine stoked the insurrection with his 1776 pamphlet *Common Sense,* rejecting George III's claim to be the "Father of His People." No true father could "unfeelingly hear of the slaughter" of his children or "composedly sleep with their blood upon his soul," Paine wrote. George III's patriarchal status was false. Authority did not derive from biology or blood. It was a function to be assigned depending on how well a man served other men.[39]

If no *man* was innately superior, then perhaps no woman was innately inferior, Abigail Adams began to reason. For a nimble mind, the leap was not far. And if education made the man, might it not make the woman? The seeds of equality that had germinated in Europe took root in America in ways that even the most enthusiastic cultivators of liberty never foresaw. One caught unawares was John Adams.

All Men Would Be Tyrants

In 1772, John Adams bought a second residence to be closer to his Boston law practice. The family lived there until John joined the Continental Congress in Philadelphia. At that point Abigail moved back to their two-bedroom saltbox in Braintree with the children, shooing John away in August 1774 with the reassurance that she could handle their small farm, even though she was the one who would hear the tramp of boots and jingle of guns if Redcoats came down the old coastal road from Boston to Plymouth. It would be almost ten years before the couple would live together again for any length of time. She teased him that he had made her into Penelope from Homer's *Odyssey,* fending off dangerous suitors while he roamed the seas.[40]

Abigail bore the brunt of family responsibilities as Massachusetts came under siege. The lone protector of four children, the eldest only nine, she wore a brave face for them, though she confided to her friend Mercy Otis Warren, "My heart beats at every whistle I hear, and I dare not openly express my fears." It did not take her long to identify with the revolutionary cause. "Is it not better to die the last of British freemen than live the first of British slaves?" she wrote Warren. Strikingly, Abigail adopted a nom de guerre in April 1775. She began signing her letters "Portia" after the wife of Brutus, leader of the plot to assassinate Caesar once he became a dictator. Historically, Portia symbolized a willingness to withstand torture for a noble cause, and a woman's loyalty to a righteous husband.[41]

In June 1775, more than a thousand revolutionary troops snuck onto the high ground of a Boston peninsula overlooking Charlestown, the area's oldest settlement, and began building fortifications for artillery. His Majesty's ships in the harbor interrupted their plan. On June 17, British general William Howe began a heavy naval bombardment of the rebels' elevated position and the village below.

"The decisive day is come on which the fate of America depends," Abigail wrote John. She climbed a windy promontory in Braintree with young John Quincy to watch the shelling fourteen miles away. Black smoke roiled the skies. The explosions sounded close. Unable to eat or sleep, she and the children trembled through the night. Abigail learned that the family's doctor, president of the Massachusetts Provincial Congress, had taken a fatal bullet to the head. Still the battle raged. On the second day, the Redcoats marched uphill in suicidal formation to wipe out the last defenders, winning the Battle of Bunker Hill at the cost of half their men. Historic Charlestown—homes, churches, and wharves—lay in charred ruins below.[42]

British troops occupied the city with a "spirit of malice and revenge," Abigail wrote John. An officer confiscated the Adams's Boston residence, threw out the furnishings, and heaped supplies of coal and salt in the rooms. Out in the countryside, Abigail tried to keep her family safe, fearful that soldiers might haul them to town or drive them "from the sea coasts to seek shelter in the wilderness." John Quincy later recalled that he and his siblings lived a year in "unintermitted danger" under their mother's watch.[43]

Abigail helped panicked refugees, nursed civilians and soldiers, and answered correspondence that arrived for John. She forwarded sensitive information on Boston under martial law and offered hospitality to rebel officers, including George Washington. She fought dysentery and smallpox epidemics that killed John's brother and sent her own mother to an early grave. To provide, she spun thread, sewed clothing, baked bread, sold goods for cash, and recruited scarce hands to plow the fields. To keep up John's spirits, she relayed tidbits of their children's loving prattle. He wrote frequently to express his gratitude.

In March 1776, British troops finally evacuated Boston to regroup in Canada for a wider war. Two weeks later, Abigail thought she might request something in return. She reached for her pen, perhaps sitting in John's downstairs law office, close to the kitchen where she might have had chowder on to boil. The British retreat had lifted her spirits. It made her bold.

Abigail's husband had personally nominated George Washington of Virginia as commander in chief of the Continental Army and he would soon persuade Thomas Jefferson to draft the Declaration of Independence. He had penned the country's first foreign policy and would give the principal speech in support of the resolution for separation from England. He had had a hand in every major task of the Continental Congress. In a position to write new laws, John Adams was not just any husband receiving a letter from his wife, as both knew.

Abigail had come to the conclusion that freedom was indivisible. Shielded from the pressures to compromise under which John labored in Congress, she foresaw the Revolution's most radical implications. She had previously written that Black people have "as good a right to freedom as we," and she began this new missive by questioning whether the slave states would prove as steady under fire as Massachusetts since the passion for liberty could hardly "be equally strong in the breasts of those who have been accustomed to deprive their fellow creatures of theirs." Then she pushed further. Declaring her hope that the Continental Congress would move rapidly toward formal independence, she added a "by the way" (a segue doubtless familiar to many husbands). "By the way," she wrote, "in the new Code of Laws which I suppose it will be necessary for you to make I desire you would Remember the Ladies."

Employing a phrase used by critics of monarchy, she wrote "all men would be tyrants if they could," a sentiment she knew John shared because it was the argument for constitutional limits. "Why, then, not put it out of the power of the vicious and lawless to use us with cruelty and indignity with impunity?"

Historians do not know what cruelties Abigail Adams had seen men exact during her thirty-one years. Her own marriage was good, yet the troubles of other women must have made an impression on her. She hastened to add that most husbands were not this way, of course. Good men "abhor those customs which treat us only as the vassals of your Sex."[44]

Abigail may have felt some trepidation. She archly teased that she and other ladies would otherwise "foment a Rebellion, and will not hold ourselves bound by any Laws in which we have no voice, or Representation"—using the precise terminology of the rebels in Boston and Philadelphia. Would her husband take the threat as a joke, or recognize that she was at least half serious? Abigail knew that John admired female self-effacement. He had written only four months earlier to praise John Hancock's docile bride. When Abigail had directed their son's Latin tutor to teach their daughter as well, John had reminded his wife that their girl, "by Reason of her sex, requires a different education." John also wrote to the ten-year-old, named Abigail for her mother, that "it is scarcely reputable for young Ladies to understand Greek and Latin."[45]

Abigail sent John four more letters while she awaited an answer to her request. The first emphasized how much she still needed him. "I really am cumbered about many things and scarcely know which way to turn myself," she wrote. "I miss my partner." Her fourth letter took a submissive tone. John had not replied to her previous request for a copy of the newly published *Lord Chesterfield's Letters to His Son* (scandalous for its cynical advice about seducing women, whom Chesterfield portrayed as "children of a larger growth"). He normally sent whatever books Abigail requested if he believed they would contribute to her "improvement." Since he had not done so, she would submit "intirely to your judgement." She sent news of military intelligence from Halifax and, in the same letter, pointed out that a group of gentlemen in Cambridge thought it "highly proper" that a committee of three ladies, herself included, should interrogate the "Torys Ladies" in the wake of the British evacuation.[46]

With mail hampered by war and distance, Abigail finally received John's reply a month after she had put her letter in the post. He respectfully answered her questions about southern readiness and the declaration of independence. Virginia and North Carolina had made provisions for a robust defense of the coast, he explained. They would fight for freedom despite their "Aristocratical turn." And independence would be announced soon. But as to her request that he remember the ladies in drafting the new code of laws, he wrote mockingly, "I cannot but laugh." He had heard that students, apprentices, Indians, and slaves had grown insolent as a result of the Revolution, which had "loosened the bands of Government" wherever it touched. "But your Letter was the first Intimation that another Tribe more numerous and powerful than all the rest were grown discontented."[47]

He fell back on the cliché that women already ruled the world with their wiles. "We know better than to repeal our Masculine systems," John told his wife, which "are little more than Theory." If women gained any more power, they would subject men altogether "to the Despotism of the Petticoat," and General Washington and "all our brave heroes" would be forced to rally. John may have realized that he risked insulting Abigail by calling women a "tribe," and he acknowledged his words were coarse. "But you are so saucy, I wont blot it out." He pointed a finger at the British for encouraging every species of complainer to harass Congress, from bigots and "landjobbers" to Irish Roman Catholics and "Scotch Renegadoes." And now, at last, the weaker sex. His words were joking, but the implication clear. Her demands bordered on disloyal.[48]

A subtle tactician, John Adams understood the wisdom of deflecting threats nonchalantly. He actually took Abigail's request far more seriously than he let on. The next month, in May 1776, John received a letter from James Sullivan, one of those engaged in implementing Adams's recommendation that every colony write its own constitution to formalize its sovereignty. Sullivan pointed out that anyone who had "the least acquaintance with true Republican principles" must admit that "a very great number of the people" had been wrongly excluded from local assemblies in the past. "Rich and poor alike" should enjoy representation, he believed.[49]

John replied in a tone different from the one he had taken with his wife. He agreed "in Theory" that the consent of the governed was the only moral basis for government. "But to what an Extent Shall We carry this principle?" Great were the dangers in opening the floodgates. "There will be no end of it," John Adams warned. After all, "Whence arises the Right of Men to govern women, without their consent?" The objection that women were not politically experienced, or adept at soldiering, applied to many men. Since there was no indisputable basis for a male monopoly on power, it could be challenged. "Depend upon it, sir," he cautioned, "Women will demand a vote." Adams, of course, knew one who had already threatened a rebellion if women did not receive "Representation."[50]

The first draft of the state constitution explicitly wrote women out of government. Men at the convention conceded that females were capable of reason, but the "delicacy of their minds, their retired mode of life, and various domestic duties" precluded the worldly exposure "necessary to qualify them for electors." These were the very arguments that Adams had warned were flimsy. Subsequent drafts of the constitution avoided mentioning women altogether. The final version flatly proclaimed that every "male person" with an annual income of three pounds was entitled to vote in local elections.[51]

Abigail Adams did not fail to notice as Massachusetts and most other colonies silently excluded women from democratic governance. She later protested to her husband that in the world's freest country, legislatures obliged women "to submit to those Laws which are imposed on us."[52]

Charles Brockden Brown of Philadelphia, a rare critic of misogyny, gave the female protagonist of his 1798 novel, *Alcuin,* the line that lawmakers "thought as little of comprehending us in their code of liberty, as if we were dogs or sheep." Through "Mrs. Carter," he pointed out that representation for women "was quietly discarded, without leaving behind the slightest consciousness of inconsistency or injustice." Mrs. Carter criticized men for forcing a woman into servility: "She will be most applauded when she smiles with most perseverance on her oppressor, and, when, with the undistinguishing attachment of a dog, no caprice or cruelty shall be able to estrange her affection."[53]

There was one exception to the new state constitutions. New Jersey erected no gender barriers, even while the other twelve stipulated that electors be male. Surrounded by states that ignored the full implications of republicanism—non-monarchical, democratic government—the middle colony simply stipulated that an estate worth fifty pounds was the only qualification. Not sex or race.

Single women of means met this criterion since they, unlike wives, could own property. For thirty-one years, unmarried women cast their ballots. Political parties courted their votes, and New Jersey law referred to electors as "he or she." An anonymous 1790 petition in the *Burlington Advertiser,* titled "The Humble Address of Ten Thousand Federal Maids," promised that in exchange for the right to run for office, too, they would gladly serve in the military. This trial balloon was soon punctured. Both single women and free Blacks in New Jersey lost the right to vote in 1807, when politicians rewrote the state constitution to eliminate voters whom they thought would not reliably support their parties. Voter suppression triumphed.[54]

Until then, Abigail Adams looked on New Jersey with envy. As she commented to her sister Mary in 1797 about a candidate they both liked, "if our State constitution had been equally liberal with that of New Jersey and admitted females to a vote, I should have certainly exercised it in his behalf."[55]

This was long after the sting of John's reply had faded. In May of 1776, Abigail Adams did not trust her tongue. She dashed off a letter to Mercy Otis Warren in nearby Plymouth, telling her about the letter John had sent. Colonial law gave men unlimited power to abuse their wives, Abigail reminded Warren. But in response to the "List of Female Grievances which I transmitted," John had said "he cannot but Laugh at My Extraordinary Code of Laws." His ridicule must have hurt. Her idealistic husband would not stand up for women.[56]

Abigail waited ten days to write John. She began by saying how much she missed "the companion of my youth, and the Friend of my Heart." She admitted she had not written promptly because "I have not felt in a humour to entertain you. If I had taken up my pen perhaps some unbecomeing invective might have fallen from it." Abigail discussed conditions in Boston, and asked again about independence. Then, sandwiched between less controversial subjects, she returned to her preoccupation. "I can not say that I think you have been very generous to the Ladies," she protested, "for whilst you are proclaiming peace and good will to Men, Emancipating all Nations, you insist upon retaining an absolute power over Wives."[57]

Abigail spoke of all women yet she, too, was a wife under a man's power. Suasion was her only recourse. In a paraphrase of Alexander Pope's misogynistic poem "Epistle to a Lady on the Characters of Women," infamous for its claim that "Most women have no Characters at all," she reminded him that the duplicitous techniques that men permitted women, the only ones they had, were beneath any person of virtue. Male intransigence meant that women possessed only the prerogative to manipulate: to "charm by accepting, by submitting sway; Yet have our Humour most when we obey." During the darkest months of British occupation, Abigail had ended her letters with "Adieu" or "Your Ever Faithful Friend." Now, for the first time in eight months, she signed and then drew a black line under her name of defiance, Portia.[58]

Perhaps the future First Lady was letting her husband know that she did not intend to give up, but also that she would fight beside him. When

British troops threatened Congress a few months later, insensitive acquaintances in Boston and Braintree passed along rumors of John's death "with as little sensibility as a stock or a stone." Abigail assured John that she was with him in every twist of fate: "I never close my Eyes at night till I have been to Philadelphia, and my first visit in the morning is there." Unless—no, *until*—they won the war, no other question mattered. When the enemy routed George Washington from New York in August 1776, Abigail begged John not to despair. If Britain defeated their army, Congress would find a patriotic "Race of Amazons" behind them.[59]

Abuse and the Limits of the Law

Abigail Bailey experienced the Revolution differently from her neighbor in Massachusetts. For her, war was a blessing. The Revolution made Asa Bailey a man of substance. He proved a perfect fit for military leadership, won a major's commission, and was "celebrated as an active and good officer at the head of his regiment." Other men sought his advice and he "became a leading man in the town." Public service also helped dispel a scandal that had tainted his name.[60]

A few years before the war, Asa had twice propositioned servants in their household. The first time it happened, Abigail blamed the employee, who clung to her job. Domestic service was virtually the only economic option available to women outside the family. The position provided food and shelter, though female servants drew wages far below those of male laborers. In neighboring Massachusetts, women's wages were 60 percent less than men's, by law. Asa resisted Abigail's request that he fire the maid, though he eventually tired of the conflict (or girl) and yielded.[61]

Then, while the colonies reeled from Parliament's tax on tea, Abigail learned that Asa had preyed on yet another young servant. Her husband "fell into a passion" when confronted. He shut himself in their bedroom all day, leaving Abigail to do the work of the family while he watched darkly from the window as she went outside to milk the cow in the summer twilight. Goosebumps must have swept her arms. She had a sudden premonition that his anger had turned deadly. As she pulled on the cow's warm udders, she beseeched God not to add murder to Asa's crimes.[62]

Convinced that she must submit to the Lord's will regardless, Abigail carried the full pail indoors. When she braved a closed door to check on her husband, she found him thrashing on their bed, apparently conscience-stricken. Asa confessed that he had plotted to kill her, but then had recalled the "terrors of the law." He admitted to pressuring the servant for sex, promised that nothing had happened, and pledged to alter his ways. Abigail hoped that he might now "prove a child of God." Their life entered a peaceful phase for nearly a year until, to Abigail's mortification, the servant testified before a grand jury that Asa had violently attacked her. He confessed only to plying her with flattery. It was her word against his. No charges were filed.[63]

The Revolution thus came at an opportune juncture. Military service took Major Asa Bailey away, and his wife ran the farm. When he returned, he acquired a better spread of two hundred acres, plentifully stocked with cattle, horses, and sheep. Yet success failed to sweeten the veteran's sour temper. He verbally abused his wife whenever she questioned him. Abigail blamed herself, still longing for his good opinion "as a hungry child longs for the breast."[64]

In 1788, Asa began to talk of relocating to the Ohio River Valley. The new United States had doubled its territory by virtue of a spectacular peace treaty with Great Britain, negotiated by John Adams, Benjamin Franklin, and John Jay. Asa traveled west to explore the raw wilderness, then returned to uproot the family. Neither Abigail nor the children wished to move, but none protested as "never were more pains taken to please the head of a family." All deferred to the patriarchal "sovereign" who had always been so "severe and hard" that his children "stood in the greatest fear of him," Abigail wrote.[65]

Asa announced that he would travel ahead to make arrangements, and take one of their daughters, his "favorite," to cook for him. He said he wished to become more "pleasing and familiar" to the girl to prepare for the journey. Abigail kept her daughter's name out of her later memoir, but she described the ways in which Asa began cornering the girl at her spinning wheel, fawning, flattering, and telling stories. Abigail sometimes noticed tears on her daughter's cheeks. Horror crept over her. When she tried to distract Asa, he grew suspicious and started monitoring communications between the girl and other members of the family. Abigail herself was pregnant again, for the fourteenth or fifteenth time, and Asa no longer sought her bed.[66]

Finally, Abigail "found it impossible to annihilate evident facts." Preying on servants had invited public censure. Her husband had turned to a safer target.[67]

Like other patriarchs in the Early Republic who committed rape, Asa used beatings in order to prevail when charm didn't work. He began to find excuses to punish their daughter, and vowed that he wished her "dead, and buried." Sometimes he hit her with a thick rod; other times with a stick used to drive animals. Brooding at the hearth one cold morning with the smallest children gathered round for warmth, Asa called for the girl. She came quickly, but not quickly enough to suit him. Eyes glittering dangerously, Asa grabbed a horsewhip to teach her "that when he called her, she should come to him." He rained blows on her face and hands. When she bent double to protect her head, he laid the whip to her back. Abigail and the other children cowered. "It seemed as though the poor girl must now be destroyed under his furious hand," she thought. Sir Robert Filmer, author of *Patriarcha,* would have attested that biblical precedent allowed this treatment.[68]

Abigail recorded these events with a degree of detail she did not use when cataloging Asa's acts toward herself. She appears to have seen his ruthlessness more clearly when it was turned on someone else. Even so, she did nothing. To the wider world, it would seem that Asa was within his legal rights, though Abigail was now convinced he had exceeded them by exploiting the child sexually. Pregnant with twins, she felt a profound anguish, yet also considered herself powerless. Responsible for more than a dozen mouths and accustomed to obedience, she was stunned and fearful.

Abigail questioned her daughter in private, but the battered girl mutely refused to confirm her mother's suspicions. Abigail began to resent her even though she knew the child was blameless. After Abigail gave birth to twins, she finally confronted her husband, who again denied any wrongdoing.

Asa grew brash. He taunted Abigail that she had no proof. Reporting him would be futile anyway. "He wished to know whether I had considered how difficult it would be for me to do any such thing against him," she later recalled, "as I was under his legal control; and he could overrule all my plans as he pleased." When Abigail continued to object, Asa tried apologizing, perhaps because the charge was so grave. He denied the worst, but promised to curb his temper. Summoning the patience for which God had loved Job, Abigail gave her husband another chance.[69]

She also recognized that Asa was largely correct. Incest was a capital offense in New Hampshire and proving it was difficult. Prosecution also traumatized the victim. In 1789, the year the US Constitution went into effect, Abigail's daughter left home to live with an aunt and uncle when she turned eighteen. She finally told Abigail the truth, but "overwhelmed with shame and grief," refused to testify publicly that she had been raped. Had the girl done so, the court might have punished her, too.[70]

The rare eighteenth-century trial where a daughter was brave enough to testify against an abusive father sometimes resulted in her being convicted of incest, even if she had endured beatings and death threats before "consenting." Victims faced the possibility of a public whipping, the letter "I" stitched onto their blouses for the rest of their lives, and even hanging if they had delayed reporting the assault. A minor's case was also easily compromised by the fact that pedophiles often did not need to resort to physical force. The commandment to obey could paralyze a child's defensive capacity when an adult in authority assumed that use of a child's body was his privilege. "Who has a better right," asked one James Weller of Massachusetts with a laugh, when questioned in a 1783 lawsuit about his sexual relations with his stepdaughter.[71]

Abigail Bailey could not fathom why a man with an honorable reputation and a thriving estate would risk everything. Historians cannot know what roused Asa's inner demons, but the law that gave "unlimited power to the Husband to use his wife ill," in Abigail Adams's words, egged on those demons and made his wife into an accomplice. Anything that threatened him and his estate also threatened her and her dependent brood. The time never seemed right to bring Asa's abuse to the attention of outside authorities. The Bible commanded Abigail to obey, as she reminded herself again and again. God in His wisdom had given her this cross to bear.[72]

Her legal options were certainly poor. New England courts rarely granted divorces, and the children, including all underage daughters, would go to Asa as his property even if she obtained one. So she opted for private measures. Once the eighteen-year-old had finally confirmed Abigail's suspicions, she packed her husband's clothes, threatened him with exposure, and watched him ride away.

A month later Asa slunk back, pleading for forgiveness. Dismayed, but with no tools beyond persuasion, Abigail again asked him to leave. He consented, but kept putting it off. She still had no legal right to deny him the use of her body, and he "tarried" long enough that Abigail found herself pregnant yet again.[73]

Asa finally departed, but returned several months later. This time he took away two sons to hire out for cash in distant towns, an act that Abigail had no authority to resist though she feared she would never again see her boys, one of whom was sickly. Still, she trusted that God would provide the relief that the law did not, and keep Asa away. Again, she stayed the course He had set with His own hand.[74]

Republican Motherhood and Education for Girls

Abigail Adams may have been the first American woman to request legal reform, but she was not alone in her commitment to patriotic ideals. Women throughout the colonies stepped into the shoes of men who went to the battlefront. A few slipped into their trousers, too, grabbed a gun, and joined the fight. Wives had always shouldered greater duties in wartime, but this revolt was different. Rather than a conflict between professional armies, it was a citizen's war and thus one of the first to mobilize a whole society.[75]

Growing literacy raised political consciousness. Documents executed with signatures rather than X's indicate that white women had slowly caught up with men in their ability to read during the eighteenth century, probably as a consequence of the colonies' increasing wealth. In 1740, roughly 40 percent of New England women could scribble their names. By 1760, approximately 60 percent could, compared with nearly 100 percent of men. Then, during the Revolution, basic literacy shot up to 80 percent or more for white women, exposing many to thrilling debates in newspapers and broadsides.[76]

Patriotic fervor soared, and husbands and fathers urged women to side with their cause. As buyers of household goods, women had power to make boycotts stick. In 1774, one unusual group of fifty-one women in the port town of Edenton, North Carolina, gathered at the shoreline behind the county courthouse. Ten months after the more famous Boston

Tea Party, they tossed their tea into Edenton Bay and signed a set of "Resolves" boycotting English imports. The Edenton activists did not demand rights for women but, edging beyond their sphere, did claim a duty "not only to our near and dear . . . but to ourselves."[77]

Male loyalists ridiculed them. A cartoon in the London *Morning Chronicle* showed the "patriotic ladies" signing their declaration while a dog urinates on the floor and licks the face of a forlorn baby. The spoof depicted revolutionary women as neglecting their domestic duties, even though a boycott actually required them to weave their own cloth and devise substitute beverages. Consistent with the belief that assertive women were unfeminine, they were shown with double chins, big ears, and dour expressions, all except for a solitary pretty girl in whose ear a lecher whispers subversion. A colonist who saw the cartoon while traveling in London compared the ladies to Amazons, and feigned terror at the "dreadful consequences" should they try to crush men into "Atoms, by their Omnipotency." He urged his brother back home to forward more of the amusing details.[78]

Patriots gave women a warmer reception, perhaps because they proved effective fundraisers. In 1780, a so-called Ladies Association of Philadelphia collected an astounding $300,000 by knocking on the doors of 1,400 households. At George Washington's request, they used the money to purchase linen that they sewed into uniforms, thereby contributing their skilled labor, too. "Patriotic Sisters" in New Jersey, Maryland, and Virginia formed similar associations.[79]

Although most women who supported the Revolution did not seek social equality, a consensus began to evolve in the 1780s around a girl's right to an education, couched in terms of rendering service to the nation. Book learning would better qualify future mothers to rear virtuous sons for the infant republic. In historian Linda Kerber's words, a new ideology of "Republican Motherhood" gave every woman "a significant political role, though she played it in the home."[80]

The state of education in the colonies was a subject of grave concern to John Adams. Five months after he quashed Abigail's hope of legal reform, he wrote her that Boston's sons must become more knowledgeable. "New England must produce the Heroes, the statesmen, the Philosophers, or America will make no great Figure for some Time," John told Abigail.[81]

She shot back that some "would laugh at me," but if America hoped "to have Heroes, Statesmen, and Philosophers, we should have learned women." Her husband deplored the education of America's sons, yet its daughters "experience the want of it" every day. When the couple had decided to tutor their offspring at home—considering the village primary school too rough—John had shown his confidence in Abigail's ability to teach not only reading, but also geography and geometry. He knew that the knowledge gleaned from her father's library had been foundational.[82]

Abigail would not let the matter rest. Two years later she complained again about the "trifling narrow contracted" schooling of American daughters. The neglect of girls' minds bothered her immensely. "You need not be told how much female Education is neglected," she wrote her husband in 1778, "nor how fashonable it has been to ridicule Female learning." Abigail wrote her cousin John Thaxter the same spring, saying, "I cannot sometimes help suspecting that this Neglect arises in some measure from an ungenerous jealosy of rivals near the Throne—but I quit the subject or it will run away with my pen."[83]

Abigail Adams did not believe that education should merely equip mothers to teach their children. Knowledge benefited the individual herself. In 1784, she traveled to Britain to join John at a diplomatic post awarded him after the Revolution, finally indulging her yearning to be a rover. From there she wrote to her sister Mary, marveling that scientific lectures in London were "like going into a Beautiful Country, which I never saw before, a Country which our American Females are not permitted to visit or inspect." Men believed that women should make the household their sole province, yet "surely as rational Beings, our reason might with propriety receive the highest possible cultivation." Far from making women unattractive, knowledge made a person more beautiful, she wrote, "for wisdom says Solomon maketh the face to shine."[84]

The Young Ladies Academy of Philadelphia

Abigail was not the only American patriot angry over the state of women's education. Essayist Judith Sargent Murray of nearby Gloucester privately wrote her cousin in 1777 that Rousseau's prescriptions for women were so "abominable" and "humiliating to our sex" that "I shall never forgive him." Thirteen years later, in 1790, she published an essay in *Massachusetts Magazine* titled "On the Equality of the Sexes" that began by criticizing "the lordly sex" for declaring women imbeciles while robbing "us of the power t'improve." Murray attributed women's lesser abilities to their stunted education. "Is it reasonable that a candidate for immortality, for the joys of heaven, an intelligent being . . . should at present be so degraded, as to be allowed no other ideas, than those which are suggested by the mechanism of a pudding, of the sewing seams of a garment?"[85]

Some men agreed. A group of Pennsylvanians had taken the first steps by establishing the Young Ladies Academy of Philadelphia on cobblestoned Cherry Street during the same muggy summer of 1787 that delegates five blocks away sweated over the fabric of the US Constitution. John Poor, a Harvard graduate and aspiring educator, invited one hundred girls to earn diplomas for upper-level studies that included geography, history, astronomy, mathematics, philosophy, and oratory—though not yet Latin. He hired graduates of Yale and Princeton to instruct the young women. John Poor may have found inspiration in the same revolutionary ideals as Abigail Adams, though he left behind no explanation beyond his model school.[86]

Fortunately, another man did. Abigail and John Adams's close friend Benjamin Rush, former surgeon general of the Continental Army, addressed students and trustees a month after the Young Ladies Academy opened. Rush wrapped women's education in the flag. He acknowledged that his opinions were "contrary to general prejudice," but he was of the view that monarchy's overthrow required new ways of thinking. Women needed to be able to instruct "their sons in the principles of liberty," he opined. No more finishing schools that taught little more than painting, dancing, and music. New secondary institutions like the Young Ladies Academy must "make ornamental accomplishments, yield to principles and knowledge, in the education of our women." Rush considered it the logical outcome of 1776. "I know that the elevation of the female mind . . . is considered by some men as unfriendly to the domestic character of a woman," he told his audience, but such views fell into the same category of elitist thought that resisted education for the poor. They were "the prejudice of little minds."[87]

Historians debate whether the American Revolution was socially conservative or progressive. Yet had it done nothing more than proclaim female education compatible with marriage, it might be called radical. Erudite women had dotted ancient and medieval history, and left their mark on the Renaissance, but most were wildly wealthy or married to God. In historian Gerda Lerner's phrasing, there was no accepted route for average women "to lead a 'normal' woman's life and also to think." The Revolution of 1776 pointed a path—still faint—to the junction of women's rights and conventional marriage. The success of Abigail and John Adams's own union suggested that intellectual equality actually improved romantic relationships.[88]

Most families did not yet have enough money to educate older daughters, but the idea spread. Ladies academies were not called high schools—that phrase did not arise until the middle of the next century—but they typically offered instruction through the teenage years. Soon after the Young Ladies Academy opened in Philadelphia, Scottish immigrant Isabella Graham started a similar school in New York City. In 1792, Sarah Pierce founded Litchfield Female Academy in Connecticut, which later counted Harriet Beecher Stowe among its graduates. In 1798, Judith Sargent Murray congratulated America's "fair country-women, on the happy revolution which the past few years has made in her favour." They had won an "inestimable" prize, she believed. "Female academies are every where establishing," Murray wrote, "and right pleasant is the appellation to my ear." Schools varied widely in ambition, but nonetheless offered a more substantial education than before. Graduates often became teachers who brought learning to the next generation. Access was not extended to enslaved children, then about one-fifth of the nation's girls and boys, but improvements in education accelerated the takeoff of the Industrial Revolution.[89]

Historians sometimes paint Republican Motherhood as another example of female self-sacrifice. Benjamin Rush's comments are taken as proof that he advocated schooling mostly to help women develop their sons' potential. This is true, but it undersells Rush. "To be the mistress of a family is *one of the great ends* of a woman's being," he asserted, implying that a woman might entertain other purposes as well.[90]

This wording sounds oblique today, but it emboldened students. In a 1793 speech, graduate Priscilla Mason saluted trustees "in the name of myself and sisters" for rescuing woman from "despotic man," who in his own self-interest had kept her ignorant. "Being the stronger party, they early seized the scepter and the sword; with these they gave laws to society; they denied women the advantage of a liberal education"—all so they could maintain "the power and preeminence they had usurped."

Mason complimented male trustees for proving that a "liberal way of thinking begins to prevail."[91]

She believed that women should be allowed to use their learning outside the home as well. "The Church, the Bar, and the Senate are shut against us," Mason pointed out, blasting Saint Paul as "contemptible" for acting on personal prejudice when he ordered females "to keep silence in the Church." Women should preach, litigate, and govern. "I am assured there is nothing in our Constitution or laws to prohibit it," she insisted. The trustees may have squirmed in their seats, but they nonetheless printed the fiery oration in a compendium designed to acquaint "neighboring states" with the first government-chartered female academy in the United States or, they proudly asserted, "perhaps in the world."[92]

Most imaginations did not stretch as far as Priscilla Mason's. Only the year before, valedictorian Molly Wallace had urged classmates at the trustees' closing ceremony never to forget that they had enjoyed opportunities "which thousands of our sex are denied." Nonetheless, she accepted this was her last public address, since speaking in front of men was otherwise "absolutely unsuitable, and should always be carefully avoided." Wallace's comments reveal that equality bloomed tentatively and withered easily. In New Jersey, men had given the vote to women who never asked for it. Thirty-one years later, they took it away without provoking complaint. Ancient customs underwritten by reproductive differences took generations to change, even after a revolution as successful as America's.[93]

Women's Rights Sail the Sea

The link between women's rights and republicanism was borne out by yet another revolt. During the summer of 1789, poor harvests turned Europe's largest nation into a political time bomb. Unlike the American colonies, where disaffection built slowly over a decade, anger flared quickly in France. While the grievances were old, revolutionaries borrowed a new sense of possibility from the American conflict.

Historians sometimes date the emergence of the modern political values of equality, democracy, and feminism to the French Revolution. As one recent survey of world history puts it, "the entire political history of the world since 1789" is traceable to France. Yet this ignores American precedents. It was nineteen-year-old Marquis de Lafayette who joined the foreign army of forty-five-year-old George Washington, not the reverse. The young marquis asked his wife Adrienne to be "a good American" during his absence, by which he meant a defender of liberty. They named their firstborn son Georges Washington. When the marquis returned home in 1785, he hung a copy of the US Bill of Rights alongside an empty frame, which he hoped in the future would "contain a similar document for France."[94]

In August 1789, a month after Parisians stormed the Bastille, the National Assembly issued "A Declaration of the Rights of Man and of the Citizen." Lafayette penned it with Thomas Jefferson, then living in Paris, at his elbow. Its first article proclaimed, "Men are born and remain free and equal in rights." The second article guaranteed the right to "liberty, property, security, and resistance to oppression." No one initially thought that these privileges would pertain to women, but women would demand them.[95]

French women had a long history of "flour wars"—protests over bread shortages. In October 1789, a young woman began beating a drum in the market one morning, crying out against hunger. Female peddlers, fishwives, and shopkeepers clustered around. Milling around and then marching through the streets of Paris, they called to others peering from their kitchen windows. The growing mob surged toward city hall, the Hôtel de Ville. There they challenged Lafayette and other officials for failing to compel King Louis XVI to sign the Declaration of the Rights of Man and of the Citizen two months earlier. They called the men cowards, seized their weapons, and swept back into the streets to find the king, twelve miles away at Versailles.[96]

Thunderclouds opened overhead. The women's heavy skirts were soon soaking wet as pelting rain turned Paris's streets into a slurry of mud and manure. Tugging cannons and carrying pikes, clubs, and swords, a throng of five thousand trudged through the downpour. Arriving at the palace, they threatened the gates until the king granted an audience to a small delegation. He signed the declaration and promised better food supplies, but the volatile crowd dragged him back to Paris the next day to make good on his commitments. Market women had captured the king of France.[97]

Some on that same rainy Monday surged into the adjoining National Assembly. Wives and mothers took delegates' chairs, raised their hands, and upbraided reformers for ignoring the grain shortage. One plopped down in the president's seat. Their brashness alarmed delegates. Followers of Rousseau associated "individual freedom" with males, and "social cohesion" with females. Man was "I"; woman, "we." Women who demanded the individual rights guaranteed by the Declaration of the Rights of Man appeared to threaten the family.[98]

The march on Versailles nonetheless prompted conversations about female education. Earlier that year (two years after the opening of the Young Ladies Academy in Philadelphia), a public petition to the French king from "Women of the Third Estate" had formally requested schooling for girls. "Do not raise us as if we were destined for the pleasures of the harem," it pleaded. Following the October march, an anonymous newspaper article cited women's valor at Versailles as proof that they should be freed from "slavery." Yet another pamphlet demanded female participation in the judiciary, legislature, and military. One wild proposal in the National Assembly would have declared: "All the privileges of the male sex are entirely and irrevocably abolished throughout France. . . . The feminine sex will always enjoy the same liberty, advantages, rights, and honors as does the masculine sex."[99]

The Marquis de Condorcet, a philosopher and mathematician, took up the cause after the assembly defined women as "passive" members of the nation "who contribute nothing to the maintenance of the public establishment." In his 1790 essay "On the Admission of Women to the Rights of Citizenship," Condorcet wrote that women were so accustomed to violations of their rights that "no one thinks of reclaiming them, or is even conscious that they have suffered any injustice." Meanwhile, those "tranquilly depriving one-half of the human race of the right of taking part in the formation of laws" suffered no twinges of conscience. In his view, it was time to overturn this state of affairs and grant women full civil rights.[100]

In December of 1790, before the Revolution turned murderous, Etta Palm d'Aelders addressed a society known as Friends of Truth on "The Injustice of the Laws in Favor of Men, at the Expense of Women." A Dutch baroness drawn to Paris by events, she argued that husbands wrote the laws for their own benefit, often forcing wives "into the humiliating necessity of winning over the cantankerous and ferocious character of a man, who . . . has become our master." Her description easily fit Abigail Bailey.[101]

The next year, Olympe de Gouges, a playwright who had dramatized the crimes of African slavery, distributed the first public manifesto on women's rights. She modeled her "Declaration of the Rights of Woman and of the Female Citizen" on the earlier "Declaration of the Rights of Man," which had itself been modeled after the US Declaration of Independence. Women had "natural, inalienable, and sacred rights, " wrote de Gouges, the daughter of a French butcher. She asked rhetorically: "Man, are you capable of being just?" De Gouges suspected the answer was no. Although she had persuaded the national theater to perform two of her plays, officials had repeatedly delayed production. One told her, "I like pretty women; I like them even better when they are easy to seduce; but I dislike seeing them anywhere but at home." A popular actor commented ominously, "Madame de Gouges is one of those women to whom one feels like giving razor blades as a present, who through their pretensions lose the charming qualities of their sex."[102]

De Gouges was undaunted. The 1791 declaration of the rights of women, published at her own expense, proclaimed the rights to education, property, and freedom of speech. Tragically, in retrospect, she observed that since "Woman has the right to mount the scaffold; she must also have that of mounting the Rostrum."[103]

Other women sought the right to self-defense. Lafayette's declaration had asserted the right to resist "oppression," echoing the Second Amendment of the US Constitution, which allowed citizens "to bear arms." In March 1792, a chocolate maker who formed a Society of Revolutionary Republican Women presented a petition to establish a women's militia. With the power of three hundred signatures it declared, "We want only to defend ourselves as you do." As Pauline Léon told the legislature, "You cannot refuse . . . unless you pretend that the Declaration of Rights does not apply to women and that they should let their throats be cut, without the right to defend themselves."[104]

Unfortunately, throat-cutting became the norm. As the Revolution turned bloody, women became targets along with men. Marie Antoinette faced the guillotine in October 1793. And when the Marquis de Lafayette fled France, he left his family behind, assuming that women would be safe. Instead, guards placed his wife Adrienne under house arrest, then imprisoned her nine months later. Her sister, mother, and seventy-year-old grandmother soon lost their lives to the guillotine. Elizabeth Monroe, the wife of American minister James Monroe, saved Adrienne only by insisting that the Frenchwoman was a friend of the United States, then France's ally.

In November 1793, Olympe de Gouges walked to the scaffold with a "calm and serene" expression, according to one eyewitness who thought that "such courage and beauty had never been seen before." The Jacobin faction charged the forty-five-year-old mother with being too favorable toward the queen, whom she had defended against accusations that the queen was responsible for all the nation's maladies. After the executioner dropped his blade on Olympe de Gouges's exposed neck, a leading newspaper gloated, "the law has punished this conspirator for having forgotten the virtues that suit her sex."[105]

Pierre Gaspard Chaumette, an instigator of the Reign of Terror, cited the execution a few months later as a way to frighten women who had shown up to a public meeting wearing the red cap of liberty. "Since when are women allowed to renounce their sex?" he asked, objecting to their attire. "And since when is it the custom to abandon the sacred duties of their households and the cradles of their children to enter the public sphere, the rostrum of the Assembly and Senate, the ranks of our armies, in order to perform duties assigned to men alone?" Chaumette told them to remember "the impudent Olympe de Gouges . . . whose head fell beneath the avenging knife of the law."[106]

The French Revolution silenced feminism. Condorcet perished in jail under suspicious circumstances, and Etta Palm d'Aelders died soon after her release from prison. Chocolate-maker Pauline Léon survived a short imprisonment, but the legislature outlawed her Society of Revolutionary Republican Women in October 1793. Sadly, other women facilitated the crackdown. When Pauline Léon led a campaign to control food prices, female vendors rebelled.

The National Convention used the vendors' complaint to denounce all women as hysterical. (The term comes from *hystera,* Greek for uterus.) It ruled that "Women are disposed by their constitution to an overexcitation which would be deadly in public affairs." One deputy accused the activists of being "adventurous women, errant cavaliers, emancipated girls, female grenadiers." In November 1793, with only a single dissenting vote, the National Convention outlawed all women's organizations. Two years later, in 1795, the male legislators who had guillotined thousands of innocents decreed women too volatile to be allowed in public: "all women should retire . . . into their respective homes." Groups of five or more congregating publicly would be arrested.[107]

A Disciple of Wollstonecraft

Both Abigail and John Adams were horrified by the violence in France. Their perspectives diverged, however, on the most famous European declaration of women's rights. Mary Wollstonecraft's *Vindication of the Rights of Woman,* first published in 1792, brought into the public domain ideas that Abigail had expressed privately sixteen years earlier. The work reinforced her views and possibly pricked John's conscience.[108]

As founder of a small primary school for girls, Mary Wollstonecraft had supported her younger brothers and sisters after their father's descent into alcoholism. Inspired by the early days of the French Revolution, and part of a coterie of British liberals, Wollstonecraft penned *A Vindication of the Rights of Man* in 1790 to foil criticisms of republicanism generally. Published to wide praise, the anonymous first edition sold out in three weeks. She placed her self-evidently female name on the second edition, shocking some readers but ensuring her renown.[109]

Two years later, disgusted by French proposals to exclude girls from public education, Wollstonecraft published *A Vindication of the Rights of Woman* with the help of a publisher for whom she worked as a translator. Women were inherently no less brainy, sensible, or moral than men, she argued. They were *trained* to be empty-headed. Wollstonecraft echoed Condorcet, de Gouges, and d'Aelders. She channeled Judith Sargent Murray's 1790 essay "On the Equality of the Sexes" and English historian Catharine Macaulay's *Letters on Education,* also written in 1790, which boldly proclaimed "there is but one rule of right for the conduct of human beings."[110]

In 1792, Wollstonecraft combined the yearnings of the era with insights she had expressed in an earlier etiquette guide, *Thoughts on the Education of Daughters* (1787), in which she had urged girls to swap "the whole tribe of beauty-washes" for "a mind-illumined face." In *Vindication,* she condemned "men of genius" who were more inclined to train women as "alluring mistresses than . . . rational human beings." She criticized women for succumbing to their flattery. "The understanding of the sex has been so bubbled by this specious homage, that the civilized women of the present century, with a few exceptions, are anxious only to inspire love, when they ought . . . by their abilities and virtues exact respect." Wollstonecraft stopped short of recommending changes to the law, yet like John Locke she depicted patriarchy as a human institution, not one divinely ordained.[111]

The 482-page *Vindication* far exceeded the personal letters and one-page manifestos that preceded it. Its unflinching demand for "JUSTICE for one-half of the human race" planted the flag of feminism. Then, like so many women in the era before birth control, Mary Wollstonecraft perished in childbirth.[112]

Historians do not know when Abigail Adams first picked up the *Vindication,* but her younger sister Betsy wrote her in December 1793, pleading to borrow the recently published book. "I wish you would be so kind as to lend me the Rights of Women—the first opportunity," Betsy asked. John wrote three weeks later expressing concern that their son Thomas tended to fritter away his time with young ladies, from whom "nothing is learned." Then his brain darted to the implication of his words. "Pardon me! Disciple of Woolstoncroft!" he teased, adding suggestively that he preferred speaking with ladies "one at a time and alone rather than in company" so as not to waste his day.[113]

Beautiful Abigail. The exception to the rule.

Love must have kept her from crumpling John's letter. When Abigail's cousin had earlier sent news about the honor paid to British historian Catharine Macaulay, whose life supposedly proved that "once in every Age" a woman might approach the genius of men, Abigail had asked why they "cannot do justice to one Lady, but at the expence of the whole Sex?"[114]

Wollstonecraft's *Vindication* infiltrated popular consciousness. When Elias Boudinot, a friend of Alexander Hamilton, addressed an admiring crowd of New Jersey women voters on the Fourth of July in 1793, he noted, "The Rights of Women are no longer strange sounds to an American ear; they are now heard as familiar terms in every part of the United States." By 1811, seven hundred miles away in Kentucky, a Lexington newspaper printed a letter from a disgruntled teacher who suggested, "As Thomas Paine has given the public his sentiments of the Rights of Man, and Mary Woolstonecraft [*sic*] on the Rights of Women, permit me through the medium of your very useful newspaper, to offer a few remarks on the *Wrongs of Schoolmasters.*"[115]

Not everyone admired Wollstonecraft, of course. Hannah More, an English gentlewoman, established a tradition of anti-feminism that continues to today. A writer educated at home by her schoolmaster father, she was a complicated individual: one who opposed slavery but criticized republican government, and someone who counted herself among a group of intellectual women known as the "bluestockings" even though she considered women inferior to men. Abigail Adams herself sometimes quoted Hannah More, whose poetry she read.

More believed that most women should be educated only in reading, sewing, and the Bible. She resolutely opposed teaching lower-class women how to write. For women of her own background who attended finishing schools to learn social graces, she recommended heavy doses of religion along with a dash of John Locke to make them good mothers. Female assertiveness horrified her. Her *Strictures on the Modern System of Female Education,* published seven years after Wollstonecraft's *Vindication,* asserted that "the imposing term *rights* has been produced . . . with a view not only to rekindle in the minds of women a presumptuous vanity dishonorable to their sex, but . . . to excite in their hearts an impious discontent with the post God has assigned them in this world." Political rights subverted women's "true interests," which were to preserve the differences "stamped by the hand of the Creator" that made them appealing to "the stronger sex."[116]

More herself had resolved not to marry after a disastrous engagement at twenty-two. Her older suitor kept putting off the date, and after six years, the betrothal was canceled. Her fiancé gave her a lifetime income, no strings attached. At the time, a woman could sue a man for "breach of promise," which may have affected his decision. Hannah More was thus immune to the mortal hazards and financial powerlessness of a wife. Even so, she considered motherhood the proper focus of women's attention. Those who pursued science, philosophy, or public influence were simply "bad imitators" of men. "Is it not then more wise as well as more honorable to move contentedly in the plain path which Providence has obviously marked out to the sex?" she asked.[117]

Hannah More refused to read Mary Wollstonecraft, who was on the opposite end of the English political spectrum, which had divided first over the American Revolution and then, more bitterly, over the French. She admitted to essayist Horace Walpole—famous for denouncing Wollstonecraft as a "hyena in petticoats"—that she had been "much pestered to read the 'Rights of Women,' but am invincibly resolved not to do it." She tartly assured the earl that "there is perhaps no animal so much indebted to subordination for its good behavior as woman."[118]

Hannah More set a precedent that would be adopted by later generations of anti-feminists, who accepted some components of feminism while balking at others. More established a town school that taught poorer girls to read, even though she opposed higher education. Women were too "unstable and capricious," in her view, to participate in serious institutions. To show that she practiced what she preached, Hannah More declined membership in the Royal Society of Literature, saying, "I consider the circumstance of sex alone a disqualification."[119]

Abigail Adams, meanwhile, continued to seek confirmation for her ideals. In 1795, she read yet another book on gender inequality, this one by the reverend John Bennett. First published in England, Bennett's *Strictures on Female Education* surveyed two thousand years of human history to show that women had been an "injured and persecuted sex," simultaneously "courted and despised" by men. The answer, Bennett asserted, was an education that would empower them.[120]

"You may be sure Bennet is a favorite writer with me for two reasons," Abigail Adams wrote John. "He is ingenious enough, to acknowledge and point out the more than Egyptian Bondage, to which the Female Sex, have been subjugated, from the earliest ages." Her husband, then vice president, would soon run for the presidency. Greater attention had been "paid to the Education of Females in America, within these last fifteen years than for a whole century before," she wrote him, but "much yet remains to be done."[121]

Education for girls had indeed won some measure of acceptance. Only a few weeks earlier, John had written Abigail from Philadelphia about a "female commencement" he planned to attend, presumably at the Young Ladies Academy, though he did not say. He promised to send "my dearest friend" all the details, but later reported that the US Senate had deliberated late into the evening, and he "was therefore disappointed." Nonetheless, he reported, First Lady Martha Washington, the entire House of Representatives, and a host of local luminaries had carved out the time to watch eight young women deliver their speeches and receive their diplomas.[122]

Eight female high-school graduates. In its own way, a revolution.

Naturally, not everyone took part in such changes. Academies charged fees, and most parents gave little thought to any education beyond reading and writing. Thomas Jefferson admitted after his presidency in a letter to Nathaniel Burwell, a dignitary who wanted Jefferson's advice on establishing schools for girls in Virginia, that "a plan of female education has never been a subject of systematic contemplation with me." When his own motherless girls were young, he had bought them lessons in music, dancing, drawing, and French. He had told them that they should learn to dress well. "Nothing is so disgusting to men as a want of cleanliness and delicacy in women," he lectured his eldest in 1783. Fortunately for her, when they moved to Paris he enrolled her in a boarding school where nuns taught a fuller curriculum. Once grown, Martha Jefferson did better by her own offspring.[123]

As Abigail Adams neared the end of life, the "disciple of Woolstoncroft" was prompted to an act of defiance. When her last sister died, she penned a will. Legally, every coin in her purse and dress in her trunk belonged to John, but this did not stop her from instructing that, upon her death, a portion of his estate should be divided among her female relatives. Abigail excluded male family members, except her surviving sons. Two years later, in 1818, she caught typhus. Watching his wife of fifty-four years writhe with the fatal fever, John remarked, "I wish I could lay down beside her and die too." Unable to do so, he honored her last will and testament instead.[124]

A Mother's Desperate Gamble

In New Hampshire, Abigail Bailey glimpsed an end to her own ordeal the year that *A Vindication of the Rights of Woman* entered print. After an eight-month absence, Asa returned to sell the family property, claiming that he would divide assets with his estranged wife. Abigail hardly knew whether to believe him, but he went about the negotiations so decisively that she began to have faith, unaware that anything he "gave" her would remain his by law since she had no separate legal existence. Asa informed Abigail of a bid he had received for the farm. There was one catch. She must go with him on a three-day ride in winter weather to meet the buyer and receive her portion. Asa promised to collect one of their absent sons along the way.

Desperate to "be released from him forever," as she recounted, Abigail left the younger children with the older ones. On the second day of the journey, Abigail was briefly reunited with her son, but Asa changed his mind about bringing the boy. They set off again alone, their sleigh churning through the deep snowdrifts of the Green Mountains. Abigail's anxiety grew. Two more days passed. Then another two. Acting the man of the world, Asa told Abigail she was "foolish" to question their slow progress. Travel took time.[125]

At last, passing some marker known only to him, he "threw off the mask" and boasted that they had crossed into New York, whose laws were "far more suitable to govern women such as you." He told her that New York would allow him to sell her if he wished. (Not true.) If she managed to escape, he could advertise her as a runaway and forbid anyone from helping her. (Absolutely true.) Regardless of how much she cried out, she would "never return home again."[126]

Abigail knew little of her rights, only that she was now entirely in her husband's power and, worse, many people would assume she endorsed his plans. "I well knew the appearances against me (if I did not soon return) must be exceedingly dark," she later wrote. Asa played on his wife's fear and ignorance, telling her that former neighbors considered her criminally complicit for being "too favorable to him, after it was believed he had committed such abominable crimes."[127]

They traveled west through unfamiliar landscapes. As the weather warmed, they switched to horseback, forded swollen rivers, and stumbled in deepening mud. Whenever they encountered strangers, Asa ordered her to smile. Seventeen days after they had left New Hampshire, the pair dragged into the rough village of Unadilla, where smallpox was rampant. Abigail fell ill from a live inoculation and nearly died. She slowly recovered in a half-finished hut and began plotting what seemed an impossible escape. She had never ventured even twenty miles alone, "and this was 270 miles, among strangers." The couple had only one horse. She had but "two thirds of a dollar in money."[128]

When Asa mentioned that he intended to return to New Hampshire to complete the sale of his land, Abigail saw her chance. She pretended curiosity about the towns he would pass through and lulled him into writing down their names. Asa left a month later. By a stroke of good fortune, he set out on foot, leaving the horse behind. Fearful of overtaking him and being discovered, Abigail waited two weeks before setting off.

Still weak from smallpox, she mounted the horse and steered it onto the path. People stared at her as she passed towns and fields, perplexed to see a woman alone. When one suspicious farmer suggested that she had "more courage than [good] conduct," Abigail "felt my hair rise on my head"—but then he offered food and shelter. Abigail sold buttons from her sleeves and a pair of shoe buckles, for which kindly buyers offered more than they were worth. A farmwife said she "appeared like a person in trouble." Finding her way through forests, fording rivers, and ascending the Green Mountains that separated her from her children, Abigail clung to her religious faith. Two weeks after she saddled her husband's horse in Ohio, she knocked on the door of her brother's home in Vermont, across the river from New Hampshire. He and another brother went with her to confront Asa Bailey and demand a settlement. Asa affected surprise, but then threatened to sue her brothers for "harboring" a runaway wife.[129]

Abigail went to the local authority and "swore the peace," leading to Asa's temporary arrest. In a last cruel maneuver, he hired an accomplice, a man he called Captain White, another military veteran perhaps, to load the couple's children into a cart and haul them away to disperse among strangers. Abigail and one of her brothers rushed to an attorney who regretfully informed them that "he knew of no authority" by which Abigail could get her children back. Any father had "a right to move his children where he should think best, and the wife had no right by law to take them away from him." The attorney was sympathetic. Like other good men, he wanted to help, but women simply had no rights. All seemed lost until he added that there was no statute against female trickery.[130]

"I then and ever understood that trusting in God implies the due use of all proper means," Abigail later wrote. So she wrote a letter to Captain White, hoping to bluff him into thinking she actually could sue. Abigail's brother overtook White on horseback to deliver the missive and warn that if he "wished to avoid trouble" he had better turn around. The man yielded and the children "leaped for joy, as though they had been released from captivity." With the children safe, Abigail and her brother threatened Asa that they would ask the court to send him across the river to New Hampshire, where incest was a hanging offense. He finally broke. Under the watchful gaze of other men, Asa split the estate. The attorney and sheriff waived their normal fees.[131]

Twenty-five years after Abigail merged her legal identity with her husband, she obtained a divorce. Her husband "gave" her most of their children, but took the three oldest boys, exercising his patriarchal privileges to the last. Abigail initially rented a cottage, though her financial settlement did not go far and she eventually had to indenture the youngest children to local families and become a servant herself. In later years she lived with her grown children.[132]

When Abigail Bailey died of pneumonia in 1815, her memoir was discovered among her papers. Her pastor, who corroborated the story with neighbors, facilitated its publication to show readers that they could rely on God through the worst experiences. Later generations would wonder why a woman could not rely on the law, too.

+++

WEDDED TO A MAN who honored his wife, Abigail Adams stood tall enough to glimpse horizons denied her sex. Wedded to a rapist who took advantage of the tyranny that coverture allowed, Abigail Bailey was brought so low as to see only her husband's boots. The Massachusetts revolutionary clamored for change, while the New Hampshire Puritan struggled for survival. Even so, Abigail Bailey defended herself and her children when coverture failed to keep them safe, and chronicled her experience for the edification of future generations.

The American Revolution led to new laws that aimed to protect weaker men from more powerful ones. One of its animating ideas, that every person has the right to climb from degradation to dignity, would prove irresistible to both sexes. When presented as a way to make mothers better tutors for future leaders, female learning was elevated to virtue and ignorance demoted to vice. Law continued to deprive women of autonomy in marriage, but the journey had begun. Girls' access to education—the precious prerogative that distinguished humans from their cattle—was the first step. The right to speak publicly about what they had learned would be the next.

CHAPTER 2

The Right to Speak

1800–1865
Angelina Grimké and Harriet Jacobs

How long O Lord how long wilt thou [allow] the foot of the oppressor to stand on the neck of the Slave.

ANGELINA GRIMKÉ, 1829

IN THE EARLY YEARS of the nineteenth century, the spread of education accompanied a wave of religious revivalism that spurred concern about social issues. Citizens of the young republic began to confront the myriad ways in which their rhetoric failed to match reality. Nowhere was this more apparent than in the case of slavery. Most suppressed their disquiet at the vision of chained families in the land of the free, but a tiny group of abolitionists demanded that fellow citizens stop, look, and change. This next struggle to fulfill America's promise again triggered calls for women's rights. Pioneering a new theory of citizenship, Black and white women demanded the right to speak publicly against slavery.

Angelina Grimké and Harriet Jacobs stumbled onto this path as Southern women from vastly different backgrounds. Born in the Carolinas eight years and three hundred miles apart, they grew up surrounded by violence. Decapitated heads figured in the landscapes of their childhoods, although this sight was not as common as fathers strapped to whipping posts and mothers prodded onto auction blocks.

Angelina was the child of wealthy South Carolina planters whose involvement in benevolent organizations after the Revolution gave her a glimpse of how women might exercise a role outside the home. She turned to protest in order to be a better Christian. Harriet Jacobs was the daughter of North Carolina slaves privileged enough to spare her much hardship during the first six years of her life—a reprieve that may have given her the strength that she needed later to hide in a dark crawl space for seven years, entombed alive while awaiting a chance to free herself and her children.

The Great Awakening of Angelina Grimké

From a young age, Angelina Grimké had felt there was "a work before me to which all my other duties & trials were only preparatory," even though she was "nothing but a woman." The problem, she admitted on the first page of the diary she began at twenty-two, was that she had no idea what that work could be. All she knew was that she must listen closely to "the small still voice of Jesus in my heart." The month before her twenty-third birthday, the debutante tore up her novels, pulled the bows off her shoes, and ripped the lace from her bonnet. Friends reproached her for dressing conspicuously plainly. It hardly seemed Christian.[1]

Born in 1805, Angelina had come late into her parents' lives, the fourteenth child of a couple whose wealth was derived from multiple plantations on Charleston's periphery. The family's stylish mansion in town, cooled by sea breezes, was stuffed with strong personalities: an idealistic father to whom all deferred as a war hero and state supreme court justice, a socialite mother whose family boasted two governors, brilliant older brothers who went to Yale to become lawyers and doctors, charming older sisters who attracted favorable matches. It would have been easy to go along. But Angelina tended to speak awkward truths, perhaps because as the last of fourteen she either had to stand out or be utterly forgotten.

Devout parishioners of the local Episcopal church, the Grimkés required everyone in the household to say prayers together daily. Tall, with intense blue eyes and curly chestnut hair, Angelina surprised her parents around age twelve by refusing to be confirmed. Her father was ill and her mother, whose affection Angelina craved though the two clashed, must have been the one to whom the bishop spoke. Angelina had told him that she would not recite the vows because she could not fulfill all of them. The bishop explained that the text was simply an outward "form," to which she replied that swearing to it then would "be acting a lie."[2]

Angelina finally acquiesced, only to frustrate her family again at twenty-one when she joined the Presbyterian church, a less hierarchical sect. There, the impassioned young woman taught a Sunday school class that attracted 150 children. She also organized a prayer group attended by twenty other young women whom she told to remove the rings from their fingers and flowers from their hats. When one worried whether it was still holy to cultivate geraniums, Angelina replied that she had "no time for such things." Charitable activities consumed her time.[3]

Angelina's parents were involved in philanthropy, too. After the Revolution, to promote the public good in a country of limited government, Americans formed fire brigades, turnpike companies, temperance groups, libraries, peace societies, anti-vice organizations, orphanages, and countless other private groups. In New England, charities proliferated from a few dozen in the 1780s to nearly two thousand by 1820. Bemused Europeans found it curious. Alexis de Tocqueville famously remarked that unlike other nationalities, "Americans of all ages, all conditions, and all dispositions constantly form associations." To Angelina's mother, Polly, that meant the Ladies Benevolent Society of Charleston, founded in 1813 to aid the sick, and to her father, John, the Society of the Cincinnati, a veterans' organization started by George Washington.[4]

For women, this opened a door to a wider world beyond the home. When girls began going to school, their mothers began going to meetings. Isabella Graham of New York incorporated the first women's benevolent association in 1802 with the help of Elizabeth Schuyler, Alexander Hamilton's wife. Ridicule turned to approval as the organization helped impoverished widows. The Boston Female Asylum, incorporated the following year, drew criticism for giving public roles to "frail feeble woman" in violation of "the design of her creation," but here, too, opposition subsided as organizers rescued abandoned girls.[5]

Such groups gave married women legal powers outside their homes that they did not enjoy within them. By the 1810s, they were raising money, buying property, making investments, and negotiating contracts that they could not legally sign on their own behalf, but could execute as "directoresses" of organizations. They justified their participation as an expression of patriotic and Christian values. Members acquired experience "in investigating the condition of their needy sisters . . . and in mobilizing for action," one historian writes. Angelina Grimké took their existence for granted, having accompanied her mother to the Ladies Benevolent Society from a young age. Yet Presbyterianism along with her various charitable activities soon proved disappointing to the ardent girl, and she searched for a stronger faith.[6]

Angelina's restlessness reflected the fervor of the post-revolutionary generation. In the 1820s and 1830s, spiritual revivals swept the country as evangelical ministers encouraged Americans to rely on emotional conversion experiences ("seeing the light") for personal salvation. In a period known to historians as the Second Great Awakening, preachers multiplied in number four times faster than the rest of the population. The most zealous, particularly Methodists and Baptists, lured adherents from more traditional denominations. Angelina had company in abandoning the church of her childhood. In outdoor camp meetings and overflowing village chapels, preachers exhorted the flock to help the young republic fulfill its destiny of bringing about a new millennium. Combined with America's associational impulse, this religiosity inspired thousands of new "moral enterprises" to address ancient sins and novel needs.[7]

The Second Great Awakening's leading doctrine was "perfectionism," which held that any devout person could win God's mercy. Perfectionism fit the nation's optimistic mood after the War of 1812, and it touched most sects to one degree or another, eclipsing the gloomy predestination of John Calvin, who had emphasized man's limitless depravity and the Lord's limited charity. It encouraged young women like Angelina Grimké to think they could change the world.[8]

Charles Grandison Finney, a minister who created a sensation when he built the nation's first mega-church in New York City, holding more than two thousand worshipers, best articulated the yearning that drove evangelicals toward reform. Finney acknowledged that sinners sometimes did wrong things because "the sinfulness of it was not apparent to their minds." But ignorance would not excuse them forever. "True Christian consistency," he preached, "consists in holding our minds open to receive the rays of truth from every quarter and in changing our . . . practice as often and as fast as we can obtain further information." Once enlightened, moral persons must root out their flaws.[9]

Angelina Grimké found hope in this can-do theology, which reached her as early as 1828. "I do feel astonished that so many Christians reject the doctrine of Perfection," the young woman scrawled in her diary. Once she had concluded that Presbyterians were not perfectionist enough, she decided to continue her spiritual quest elsewhere. Again, she felt the sting of disapproval. "The whole christian community are looking at me with amasement," she confided. Angelina's family was less surprised. "Though we considered her views entirely irrational," one sister observed, "yet so absolute was her sense of duty, her superiority to public sentiment, and her moral courage, that . . . we all came to look upon her with a feeling of awe."[10]

Angelina turned to the Quaker faith, to which her sister Sarah, older by thirteen years, had already converted. The pair had an unusual relationship. Sarah, the sixth of the Grimkés' children, had been frustrated by the limited education available to her as a girl. Her Oxford-educated father allowed her to take private lessons along with an older brother, but he barred her from learning Latin. Even her brother ridiculed the notion. This may be why she took "an almost malicious satisfaction," as she said, in secretly teaching her enslaved maidservant to read despite the law forbidding it. When John Grimké discovered his daughter's crime, he swore he would beat the servant if Sarah persisted. Foiled again, she became depressed. When Angelina was born, Sarah asked her parents' permission to act as godmother. Her parents agreed, apparently to give her a project, and the baby called Sarah "Mother." They remained close as Angelina matured.[11]

Sarah first encountered Quakerism in 1819, when she accompanied their dying father to Philadelphia to seek medical advice. Two years later she moved there to pursue a faith that South Carolinians considered freakish because of Quakers' distinctive dress, archaic use of "thee," silent worship, and egalitarian principles. The family was shocked by Sarah's conversion, but Angelina was intrigued. It led her to Charleston's tiny Quaker congregation, comprised of two bickering old men. In 1828, Angelina sailed north to Philadelphia for the summer to visit Sarah. She returned home a convert to Quaker beliefs, including the sinfulness of slavery.[12]

At some earlier point Angelina had decided never to own a slave, though she never explained why in her diary. She had attended Charleston Seminary, a primary school for wealthy girls. (The city did not offer girls a secondary education until 1856, when Charleston opened its first public high school.) Angelina had been taught that God condoned slavery. Yet she felt sick when she passed the Work House on Magazine Street, the city-run punishment facility where, for set prices, guards beat enslaved men, women, and children until they could "scarcely walk." She fainted at school one morning when a small boy limped into her classroom with blood crusted on the back of his legs. Sarah, too, was repelled by slavery. She could never forget the slit ears and pulled teeth of captured runaways, maimed to make them more identifiable to bounty hunters, or the grisly head on a pike she spied from her coach one day, posted to warn others against seeking freedom.[13]

North and South, most white Americans accepted the biblical justification for slavery. While the institution of slavery was acknowledged as harsh, it was not yet widely judged as wrong. The Revolution had strengthened the Bible's authority for many citizens, who could read for themselves that God had given slaves to Abraham and other patriarchs. In Timothy 1, Saint Paul had instructed those "under the yoke" to honor their masters. A literal interpretation of the Bible counseled acceptance of one's fate, whether master or slave.[14]

Black Americans viewed the scriptures differently. Forbidden to read by law, most enslaved preachers hewed to the spirit rather than the letter of the Bible, knowing that Jews had fled slavery in Egypt and that the meek were supposed to inherit the earth. The rare literate preacher was more likely to cite a different passage from Saint Paul, namely, Galatians 3:28: "There is neither Jew nor Greek, there is neither bond nor free, there is neither male nor female: for ye are all one in Christ Jesus."[15]

Organized into autonomous congregations called "meetings," Quakers were religious outliers whom others considered fanatics. The Philadelphia meeting to which Sarah Grimké belonged had banned members, known as Friends, from owning slaves since before the Revolution. It presented the first petition to Congress against slavery in 1790. In response, one congressman from South Carolina reminded colleagues that the Constitution was based on compromise: "We took each other with our mutual bad habits and respective evils, for better, for worse," he said. "The northern states adopted us with our slaves and we adopted them with their Quakers."[16]

The instant that Angelina returned to Charleston, she later recalled, "all the cruelty & unkindness & oppression which I had from infancy seen exercised towards these poor creatures came back to my mind with as much force as tho' it was only yesterday." Shocking observations piled up: a vicious beating that her brother Henry gave his manservant; servants made to sleep on the floor; wealthy friends' venom toward darker people; a frightened woman on the street begging for help as toughs dragged her to the deadly Work House.[17]

Angelina talked about the evils of slavery with whoever would listen, and experimented with different styles of delivery to reach their hearts (leaning her head on her brother's shoulder; sipping tea mildly with friends). To a friend who agreed she would never want to be a slave, Angelina quoted the Bible: "do unto others as thou wouldst they do unto thee." With her mother she was more blunt, whereupon Polly Grimké acidly reminded her that Angelina had previously insisted "nobody who wore a bow on their cap could go to heaven"—and now, nobody who owned slaves.[18]

Sometimes, she held her tongue. Angelina stood up calmly to a panel of Presbyterian elders who condemned her, wept privately at her own inadequacy, and resolved to behave in such a way that an "exact faithfulness in little things" would prepare her for "the future performance of greater." Disgusted family members urged her to return to Philadelphia and stop making them miserable. "None but those who learn from experience what it is to live in a land of Bondage can form any idea of the weight of exercise which is endured by those whose eyes are open to the enormities of Slavery," she wrote in her diary.[19]

Angelina achieved a small victory when her mother admitted that she had changed, "for when I look back & remember what I used to do & think nothing of, I shrink back with horror." Polly Grimké never freed any of her slaves, but she treated them less harshly. This seemed to be the best that Angelina could hope to accomplish at home. She sailed north in November 1829 to undertake the "high duties" she felt awaited her. She was twenty-four. The Quaker community would have no idea how to handle her either.[20]

A Girl Learns She Is a Slave

Since colonial times, slave status had passed from mother to child, never father to child. In 1662, Virginians became the first colony to adopt the doctrine of *partus sequitur ventrem,* meaning that slavery "followed" the womb. After a ban on importing slaves from Africa went into effect in 1808, impregnating enslaved American women became the only way to expand the population. Owners sometimes took the prerogative for themselves, turning their offspring into chattel. To this injury they added the insult "Jezebel," portraying Black mothers as harlots who welcomed their advances.[21]

Young Harriet Jacobs did not know this. Born in 1813, she lived with her family in a cottage behind the largest hotel in Edenton, North Carolina, only steps from the saltwater bay into which the ladies of the town had pitched their tea only a few decades earlier. Harriet's maternal grandmother, Molly Horniblow, worked at Horniblow's Tavern, which President James Monroe himself visited in 1819. Widely admired for her crackers and cakes, Molly probably cooked his food. The street in front of the hotel served as a gathering place for slave auctions.[22]

As in Charleston, Black Americans made up the majority of Edenton's population. Most labored on plantations, but a tiny percentage worked in town as artisans who earned money after the day's work was done or paid a monthly sum in exchange for the privilege of working independently. In effect, they rented themselves from their owners. Molly Horniblow and Harriet Jacobs's father, Elijah, who was a finish carpenter, were among these lucky few, and both saved their small profits with the hope of purchasing freedom. Harriet's mother Delilah died when her daughter was only six, but Harriet never forgot her mother's soft voice or final blessing.

Up to then, the family had "so fondly shielded" Harriet and her younger brother John that she had no inkling that she was legally enslaved—"a piece of merchandise, trusted to them for safe keeping, and liable to be demanded of them at any moment." Upon Delilah's death, the six-year-old learned that she was never more than a funeral or marriage away from catastrophe. Eavesdropping, she discovered that her self-sufficient mama had belonged to the tavern owner's ailing youngest daughter, which meant Harriet did, too.[23]

Life still smiled upon the child, but more weakly. Harriet had the good fortune to be owned by an unmarried woman with legal title to her own property. This meant that Harriet could hope to escape "one class of the evils that generally fall upon slaves," as she later delicately put it. Her mistress was also fond of Grandmother Molly, who had raised her. For the next six years, Harriet spent "happy days" as the companion of an invalid who taught her fine sewing, a skill that helped her escape outdoor work, and, in defiance of North Carolina law, to read and write.[24]

Luck ran out as she neared puberty. Harriet's father, Elijah, belonged to another unmarried woman, and when she wed, her new husband cancelled the arrangement by which Elijah worked in town, banishing him to a remote plantation where he died a few years later. The health of Harriet's own young mistress worsened, too. She willed her property to her mother, but the day she died, attended by her physician and brother-in-law James Norcom, someone scratched a single line at the bottom of the will. This unsigned amendment gave Harriet to James Norcom's baby daughter, placing the twelve-year-old in the physician's household.

Almost fifty at the time, James Norcom had troubled relationships with women. In private notes, he called females "the Heaven of my existence" and "bitterest of earthly curses." Handsome when young, with a high forehead and expressive eyes that conveyed sympathy and rage with equal fervency, Norcom thought that women could not resist his charms. When they did, he called them "demons incarnate." Norcom divorced his first wife for allegedly having sex with another man. He next married the eldest daughter of the owner of Horniblow's Tavern, a woman half his age.[25]

Harriet Jacobs was surprised to encounter "cold looks, cold words, and cold treatment" from the new mistress, pregnant with a seventh child, when she entered the mansion two blocks from the tavern. Mary Norcom knew that her husband sexually coerced slaves, and she had soured into a jealous tyrant who was especially cruel to the mother of any suspiciously light-skinned infant. When one hemorrhaged after delivering a "nearly white" baby, Harriet overheard Mrs. Norcom reprimanding the dying girl for being unchaste. "You suffer, do you?" she taunted. "You deserve it all, and more too."[26]

Slaveowners did not record their paternity of enslaved offspring, so historians do not know what percentage of newborns were conceived in this way. Anecdotal evidence suggests that such babies were common. Mary Boykin Chesnut, whose husband was a US senator from South Carolina, admitted that "the mulattos one sees in every family partly resemble the white children." Few wives acknowledged the truth. "Any lady is ready to tell you who is the father of all mulatto children in everybody's household but her own," Chesnut wrote in her diary. "Those, she seems to think, drop from the clouds." Harriet Jacobs's grandmother and father both had white fathers.[27]

Harriet became increasingly anxious. When an overseer brought a worker from one of Norcom's plantations to town one day, the twelve-year-old finally understood what was amiss. James Norcom ordered servants to tie the man's hands to a beam so his feet would not touch the ground. Once Norcom finished a leisurely supper, he beat the man so hard that Harriet covered her ears. The next morning, she spied a whip damp with blood, and heard that the man had chastised his wife for delivering a fair-skinned baby. A few months later, the doctor sold man, woman, and child. Harriet learned that the worst crime in the Norcom household was "for a slave to tell who was the father." Norcom had sired eleven enslaved children.[28]

Harriet realized then that she was fortunate to live in the same house as suspicious Mary Norcom rather than on an outlying plantation. But a mother of seven cannot see everything, nor could she hear the words that her husband whispered as Harriet turned fourteen. On a sunlit spring morning she never forgot, he told her for the first time, as she later recorded, "that I was made for his use, made to obey his command in *every* thing; that I was nothing but a slave."[29]

Norcom described Harriet as five feet four inches, with light skin and thick long hair that curled easily, though she sometimes wore it straight. "She speaks easily and fluently, and has an agreeable carriage," he wrote, meaning that she was articulate and graceful. Raised by parents who had made her feel free, the girl refused to yield to his suggestions. "Though one of God's most powerless creatures, I resolved never to be conquered." Thus began what Harriet called "the war of my life."[30]

Over the next year, she avoided being alone indoors with Norcom, though he shadowed her when she ran errands. More than three times her age, he promised pleasures that made her skin crawl. Sometimes he raged, trying to scare her into submission. He swore to kill her "if I was not as silent as the grave." Grandma Molly was Harriet's only living parent, and like most victims of child abuse, the girl was too humiliated to tell her religious grandmother "such impure things." Men like Norcom counted on shame to keep women quiet. Harriet also wanted to protect Molly, who she feared would protest so vehemently as to elicit retribution. Rumor had it that Molly had once chased a white man with a loaded pistol when he insulted her daughters.[31]

Molly Horniblow's nearby presence curbed Norcom's behavior. "It was lucky for me that I did not live on a distant plantation," Harriet recalled, "but in a town not so large that the inhabitants were ignorant of each other's affairs." Molly had purchased her own freedom and become a respected baker. Dr. Norcom's medical practice depended on his good reputation, so he "deemed it prudent to keep up some outward show of decency." Yet time was not on Harriet's side. Norcom warned that "there was a limit" to his patience.[32]

At fifteen, Harriet fell in love with a Black carpenter. The free young man proposed to first purchase, then marry her. When Norcom heard, he gave Harriet a blow that sent her reeling and threatened to kill her suitor. "How I despise you!" Harriet shot back. Heartbroken, she begged the carpenter to find a better life in the North.[33]

James Norcom began construction on a small house four miles outside Edenton. He informed the teenager that once it was finished, he would "make a lady" of her there. Harriet had long accepted that she must toil "from dawn to dark," but sexual degradation was one line she would not cross without being dragged. This, she knew, was the "perilous passage" in every slave girl's life.[34]

Harriet's inner world reflected the morality of her times, particularly the ideal of "True Womanhood." In antebellum America, as industrialization presented men with a kaleidoscope of new occupations off the farm, home was increasingly defined as a haven from the hurly-burly of the marketplace—the repository of morality and decency. Religious tracts, women's magazines, and the new girls' academies waxed eloquent on the role of "True Women" in maintaining its purity. One characteristic of such a woman, according to physician William Alcott, was "ignorance of evil." This meant that "well-educated young ladies" possessed little worldly knowledge, especially of sex. An unchaste girl was a "fallen angel," destined for the madhouse, brothel, or grave. No honorable woman could befriend her. No decent man wanted her. A respectable grandmother like Molly Horniblow would condemn her.[35]

This was "the abyss" that Harriet Jacobs now faced. Norcom's lurid propositions could not be unheard. Describing acts of which any virtuous girl was supposed to be unaware, Norcom compromised Harriet with words alone. "I wanted to keep myself pure," she wrote, "but I was struggling alone in the powerful grasp of the demon Slavery."[36]

Plantation mistresses considered the pedestal of True Womanhood wide enough only for themselves. As Mary Chesnut put it, no one "thinks any worse of a negro or mulatto woman for being a thing we can't name." Yet Harriet Jacobs inhabited the same moral universe and she yearned for respectability with the same ardor as others. "I became reckless in my despair," she wrote. "O, ye happy women, whose purity has been sheltered from childhood, . . . whose homes are protected by law, do not judge the poor desolate slave girl too severely!" Slavery rendered virtue "impossible," then judged its victims immoral.[37]

Help arrived in imperfect form. Samuel Sawyer stood higher on Edenton's social ladder than James Norcom. Rich, unmarried, and with a promising political career, he was not someone whom Norcom could afford to cross. Sawyer was in his late twenties when he approached fifteen-year-old Harriet in the lane with a friendly word, wooing her affections. She later reflected that there was "something akin to freedom in having a lover who has no control over you, except that which he gains by kindness and attachment." Becoming Sawyer's mistress brought her a limited reprieve from Norcom.[38]

Grandmother Molly was aghast. When she discovered that Harriet was pregnant, she told the girl never to come back. "You are a disgrace to your dead mother," she cried as she stripped Delilah's wedding ring from Harriet's finger. The girl left the house wretched and alone. A few days later, Harriet told Molly about Norcom's persecution and why she had accepted Sawyer, exchanging her virginity for protection. Molly refused to absolve her, but she eventually laid a hand on her head. "Poor child," she murmured. For the next five years Harriet kept up her liaison with Sawyer, who she felt treated her "honorably" given the circumstances.[39]

Norcom's wife pounced on the excuse of Harriet's pregnancy to turn her out of the house and make her return to Molly. Samuel Sawyer tried to purchase Harriet, but Norcom would not sell. The teenager went into premature labor. Mother and baby barely survived.

Once Harriet regained her strength, she felt happier. She was with her grandmother and had a little boy at her side. Harriet christened him Joseph for an uncle who had escaped to the North. Norcom often walked the two blocks from his residence to harangue or beat Harriet for her "ingratitude," and once to shear her hair to the scalp, but he no longer threatened to make her his concubine. A second child with Sawyer brought fresh grief when she learned that it was a girl. "Slavery is terrible for men; but it is far more terrible for women," Harriet reflected. She named her Louisa.[40]

Norcom sought ways to wreak his vengeance. In 1835, he ordered Harriet to prepare a mansion in the countryside that he had given to a newly married son. Norcom informed Harriet that he would fetch her children from town to "break" them to the cotton fields once the house was finished. Believing Norcom wanted to use her children to punish her, she decided to disappear in order to save them.[41]

A runaway slave risked torture and death. Advertisements in the Edenton newspaper sometimes offered a bounty for a head alone if it proved inconvenient for slave hunters to return the whole person. When Harriet was sixteen, an Edenton man she knew was decapitated, his body left to rot in the steaming sun near Horniblow's Tavern. She never forgot the stench of his corpse. Grandmother Molly begged Harriet to stay for the children. Expressing a premise of True Womanhood, she reminded Harriet, "Nobody respects a mother who forsakes her children." Historical surveys show that those who escaped slavery on the Underground Railroad were mostly single men.[42]

Harriet Jacobs decided she must flee, regardless of the risk to reputation or life. She paid a final visit to her children in the dead of night, when Norcom's son would not notice her absence. Harriet's touch startled her son awake. Rubbing away tears with his fist, five-year-old Joseph cried as if at a ghost, "They didn't cut your head off at the plantation, did they?"[43]

The week that Norcom's son brought his bride to the new residence, Harriet made her break. At half past midnight, she crept down two flights of stairs and eased open the front door. Rain fell in large, soft drops. No moon shone through the heavy clouds. Harriet fell to her knees to pray, then collected her courage and ran six miles in the dark to her grandmother's home, where she kissed her sleeping children.

Friends concealed her in nearby houses over the next several months while slave patrols ransacked Edenton. When a trader offered money for Harriet's children and her younger brother John, whom Norcom also owned, he sold the three in disgust, unaware it was a trick. Samuel Sawyer paid the trader and returned the children to Molly, their great-grandmother. To Harriet, this made every risk worthwhile. "The darkest cloud that hung over my life rolled away," she recalled. "Whatever slavery might do to me, it could not shackle my children." She had fulfilled the ideal of True Womanhood.[44]

Harriet Jacobs hid longest with Martha Hoskins Rombough Blount, a wealthy slave owner with ties to Edenton Tea Party signatories Anne Hoskins and Mary Blount. Blount did not condemn slavery, but she pitied Harriet. Something disturbed her conscience enough to risk hiding a runaway. The danger of discovery mounted, however, and a former apprentice of Harriet's father rowed her into the Great Dismal Swamp, a nearby marsh brimming with snakes. She waited in the underbrush while an uncle built a more permanent hiding spot.

A storage shed with a low pitched roof was attached to Molly Horniblow's house. Harriet's uncle installed floor-to-ceiling shelves in the back. Above the top shelf he hid a trap door leading to a small attic nine feet long, seven feet wide, and three feet high at the apex. After three days in the swamp, Harriet donned men's clothing, whisked through town at dusk, climbed the shelves like a ladder, and wiggled into the secret attic. Exhausted, she fell onto a mattress that Molly had laid on the floorboards and pulled a blanket over herself, dimly aware of mice scurrying across her feet. The chamber remained pitch black even after sunrise, but a sound she hadn't heard in days filtered through its thin walls. Tears wet Harriet's face when she recognized the voices of her children, playing outside.

"The air was stifling; the darkness total," she later wrote. She had only enough room to sit or crawl. After a few days she grazed her head against something she could not see and discovered a woodworking screw her uncle had forgotten. She rejoiced like "Robinson Crusoe . . . at finding such a treasure." Later, while the town slept, she drilled three rows of tiny holes in the wall facing the street. Then she chipped at the wood between them to make a peephole one-inch square. A whiff of fresh air greeted her, and she stayed up late to feel its cool trickle across her face. The next morning, Harriet pressed an eye to the hole to watch for her children, only to see James Norcom pass on the street below.[45]

From the age of twenty-one to twenty-eight, Harriet hid in her dark garret. Through seven broiling summers and seven freezing winters, she waited. Family risked their lives to pass food through the trapdoor and take her chamber pot down the makeshift stairs. When Norcom posted a reward for her capture, he warned that she could "read and write," never dreaming how Harriet would use her precious education against him.

An Outcast Discovers Other Outcasts

The North was not as liberating as Angelina Grimké had hoped. Sister Sarah belonged to the more conservative half of a sect divided over collaboration with non-Quakers, and the congregation she joined prized obedience to church discipline above what reformist Quakers called the "Inward Light of Christ." Sarah struggled to become a minister, a privilege granted to talented female speakers by the unusual sect, but she lacked self-confidence. Elders initially denied Angelina's application for membership because they thought she should return to Charleston to care for her aging mother. They relented only when Sarah spared Angelina the necessity by temporarily returning herself. To Angelina, the restrained Quaker meetings felt "lifeless."[46]

With a small inheritance from their father, Angelina and Sarah rented rooms from a widow. Angelina began to think about becoming a schoolteacher, and undertook a trip to Connecticut in 1831 to investigate the possibility of attending the renowned Hartford Female Seminary of Catharine Beecher, who enjoyed a favorable reputation as a teacher of teachers. Passing tidy white farmhouses "scattered like sheep upon the distant hills," Angelina rode into Hartford just as cannons announced the Fourth of July death of James Monroe, last of the Founding presidents.

The older, single, and then more famous sister of Harriet Beecher Stowe, author of *Uncle Tom's Cabin,* Catharine was one of the leading spokespersons for female education during the nineteenth century. Her seminary was one of the new ladies academies that spread outward from Philadelphia after the Revolution. By 1830, over 360 academies were offering girls a secondary-level education. Catharine Beecher supported the notion of establishing female colleges, too, although a farsighted man took the first step. Daniel Chandler of Georgia helped to establish the first degree-granting college for women, just as John Poor had founded the Philadelphia Young Ladies Academy.[47]

Numerous reformers believed that "universal education" was essential to democracy, most famously Horace Mann of Massachusetts. Primary and secondary schools multiplied, giving the nation the world's best-educated workforce just as industrialization took off. Daniel Chandler thought women should have access to higher education, too. In an 1834 speech in Athens, Georgia, he pointed out that "in our country there are 61 colleges, containing expensive philosophical and chemical apparatus, valuable cabinets of minerals, and libraries that embrace more than 300,000 volumes—and to the disgrace of the nation be it spoken, not one is dedicated to the cause of female education."[48]

Others took up the cause, and two years they later chartered Georgia Female College, subsequently renamed Wesleyan. A few legislators opposed it, saying "all a woman needs to know is how to read the New Testament," but more supported it. By 1870, single-sex colleges for women, a total of twelve, had sprung up in Tennessee, Ohio, Illinois, and New York. Most emphasized the liberal arts, but Mary Sharp College in Tennessee, named for a British abolitionist, taught trigonometry, chemistry, astronomy, and even Latin. Oberlin became the first coeducational college, allowing women to join men in 1837. Women's right to an equal education, championed by Abigail Adams and others, gained momentum. Despite Mary Wollstonecraft, it was still largely an American phenomenon. Britain did not open its first women's college until 1869, and women could not matriculate at German universities until the twentieth century.[49]

Catharine Beecher hoped to make women's colleges widely acceptable, so she conservatively suggested that they should train women for only two jobs: classroom teaching and "Domestic Economy," meaning cooking, cleaning, and childcare. Such colleges could help both wives and teachers become better at their jobs, she suggested. In the 1830s, a word of American origin entered the English lexicon: schoolmarm, meaning female teacher. Schoolmaster, the term for male teacher, was already six hundred years old.[50]

When Angelina Grimké arrived in Connecticut, Beecher advised her that "single women could be more useful" as teachers "than in any other way." She hoped to dispatch them westward to educate the country and reinforce the ideals that distinguished True Women from self-made men: "devotion and service to others, selflessness, and sacrifice." As one biographer notes, Beecher advocated self-denial "as the female equivalent" of male self-realization. Women achieved meaning through caregiving relationships, Beecher believed, while men derived it through their accomplishments in a competitive world. For wives, in the words of another historian, this meant "emptying oneself of one's own needs and taking on instead the task of filling the needs of others." For spinsters, it meant teaching and charity work. The "Cult of Single Blessedness," Rebecca Traister explains, was the nineteenth-century belief that unencumbered women made "perfect servants of god, family, and community."[51]

As she toured the school, Angelina took careful notes on Beecher's regimen of math, English, science, and just enough Latin "to understand the classification of language," which was all a girl needed. She enjoyed her visit to the training academy, despite awkward moments. She and a Quaker friend remained seated when others stood to pray, and "no doubt appeared like fools in their eyes." Her archaic dress led one Yankee to admit she "had never seen a Quaker before." Although being a "spectacle" made Angelina uncomfortable, a sense of humor saved her. When one young man became fixated on her curious Quaker bonnet, and asked to purchase it off her head, she joked about it with Catharine until, when they spied him later in a restaurant, she collapsed in a cathartic "fit of laughter which lasted full five minutes."[52]

Angelina returned to Philadelphia uplifted, only to find that Quaker elders felt "there was great danger" if she became a schoolteacher "in my throwing myself so entirely among Presbyterians." A young man who had seemed romantically interested stopped calling. Again, she wondered what she was doing and why.[53]

A different branch of Christian perfectionism drew her attention. In 1831, William Lloyd Garrison, a young Bostonian, began publishing the first American newspaper calling for the abolition of slavery as a betrayal of Christianity and the nation's patriotic ideals. *The Liberator* printed scathing reports of Southern violence and Northern complicity. Angelina was transfixed. She had long imagined herself "in the stead of the poor slaves," but had thought their rescue "utterly hopeless." Abolitionism seemed a prayer answered, a chance to help "oppressed & suffering fellow creatures," she wrote in May of 1834.

It was also terrifying. Abolitionists, denounced as purveyors of "insubordination, insurrection and massacre," were beaten in Massachusetts, New York, Ohio, Pennsylvania, and Tennessee. In August 1835, Boston's mayor presided over a hostile mass meeting at Faneuil Hall, where patriots had once planned the Tea Party. Two months later a lynch mob wrapped a noose around the neck of William Lloyd Garrison, who barely escaped. President Andrew Jackson urged Northern states to suppress the "wicked" reformers. In Philadelphia, rioters burned the homes of forty-five Black families. Yet what Angelina Grimké feared most was her own cowardice: "perhaps I may be just like Peter who was frightened into triple denial of his Master," she scribbled in her diary. Abolition expressed her deepest convictions. "I often feel as if I were ready to go to prison & to death in this cause of justice, mercy, & lov."[54]

Angelina read a plea in *The Liberator* in August 1835 for forbearance toward abolitionists who had refused to return "blow for blow." Impulsively, she reached for her pen and composed a letter to the most notorious man in America. "The ground upon which you stand is holy ground: never—never surrender it," she wrote William Lloyd Garrison. "If you surrender it, the hope of the slave is extinguished, and the chains of his servitude will be strengthened a hundred fold. But let no man take your crown," she continued with the swelling eloquence that would become her trademark, "and success is as certain as the rising of tomorrow's sun." Emancipation was "worth dying for," Angelina assured the perfect stranger. If martyrdom was required to end the suffering of "bleeding humanity," she wrote, "Let it come."[55]

The same year that Harriet Jacobs crawled into her dark attic, Angelina Grimké found her voice.

Three weeks later, an angry church elder gripping *The Liberator* pounded on Angelina's door. Garrison had printed the private letter. The Quaker community demanded that she retract it, but she refused. Even Sarah was displeased. She lectured that not only was it wrong to write the letter, but Angelina had disappointed her doubly by failing to withdraw it. Condemned on all sides, Angelina was "brought to the brink of despair" until she reflected that "human judges" were not the important ones.[56]

Angelina Grimké had unwittingly joined an informal anti-slavery sorority that reflected America's associational bent. Sixty female anti-slavery societies then dotted the North. Black women in Connecticut, Pennsylvania, and Massachusetts had organized independent societies in the early 1830s, as had white women in Boston, Cincinnati, and New York. Some groups were biracial. Four members of the Forten family, free women of color, had helped found the Philadelphia Female Anti-Slavery Society along with Quaker leader Lucretia Mott. "Free produce" stores encouraged consumers to boycott slave-made goods. Knitters and seamstresses donated items to street fairs where organizers raised money. The first American woman to address coed audiences about abolition was Maria Stewart, a free person of color who spoke in Boston in 1832 and 1833. Lydia Maria Child, famous for advice books and later remembered for her Thanksgiving poem "Over the River and through the Wood," published in 1833 a widely read *Appeal in Favor of That Class of Americans Called Africans.*[57]

Most groups employed the single political tool that the First Amendment gave every citizen: "to petition the government for a redress of grievances." In 1835, the national American Anti-Slavery Society developed a blank petition "To the Fathers and Rulers of Our Country" that women organizers used to collect tens of thousands of names. Signatories penned their names as "citizens," though they sometimes scratched out that word and wrote "ladies." One group justified its intrusion into politics as a defense of purity: "[we] plead for her [the female slave] as we would plead for ourselves, our mothers, and our daughters."[58]

Former president John Quincy Adams, Abigail's oldest son, now serving as a representative, introduced their petitions into Congress. He had internalized his mother's belief that Blacks "have as good a right to freedom as we," and his father's appreciation for determined women. Approximately 70 percent of the signatories on such petitions were female. The effort was so successful that slavery supporters passed a "Gag Rule" in 1836 banning such petitions, making abolitionism into a free speech issue.

Angelina Grimké left Philadelphia to stay with acquaintances in New Jersey, and ignored a request from the American Anti-Slavery Society to give parlor talks, fearful of incurring further disapproval. Her feeling for the cause deepened. When an acquaintance objected that abolition's time had not yet come, she replied, "If thou wert a slave, toiling in the fields of Carolina, I apprehend thou wouldst think the time had *fully* come." She decided she must do more. In August 1836, she composed an *Appeal to the Christian Women of the South* and submitted it to the American Anti-Slavery Society for publication, this time specifying that it should be published "with my name attached."[59]

She brought an original voice to the embattled cause. The first Southern white woman to publicly condemn slavery, Angelina urged her "Sisters in Christ" to ignore men's disapproval and do their patriotic duty. Women must act under "the good old doctrine of our forefathers who declared . . . that all men are created equal." She acknowledged that esteemed biblical patriarchs had once asked a bride price for daughters, but Southern behavior hardly compared. "Do the *fathers of the South ever sell their daughters*?" she asked. Gingerly approaching the unspeakable subject, she answered, "My heart beats and my hand trembles, as I write the awful affirmative, Yes!" White men sold their colored daughters, but "not as Jewish parents did, to be the wives . . . of the man who buys them, but to be the abject slaves of petty tyrants."[60]

The *Appeal* catapulted Angelina Grimké to infamy. She possessed rare credentials and a gift for prose. "Moral, like natural light," she wrote, "is so extremely subtle in its nature as to overleap all human barriers, and laugh at the puny efforts of man to control it." If Southerners built a wall to heaven, they could not shut out the light. Angelina addressed the old question of whether women could "be leaders of the people." She reminded readers that women had been leaders since Mary Magdalene. In this, she echoed Maria Stewart, who also cited Mary Magdalene when Black men discouraged her from public lecturing by calling it unladylike.[61]

The door to Angelina's past slammed shut. Charleston's mayor told her mother that Angelina would be arrested for sedition if she returned. The *Fayetteville Observer* of North Carolina ridiculed the thirty-six-page *Appeal* as a "silly" argument for "miscegenation" fit only for the flames.[62]

A window to the future swung open. The American Anti-Slavery Society renewed its invitation for Angelina to address other women. This time she accepted, and she made preparations to join the "Seventy," a biracial band of "Anti-Slavery Apostles" modeled on the Seventy Disciples of Christ from the Gospel of Luke. Henry Stanton, the future husband of Elizabeth Cady Stanton, and Theodore Weld, a former Oberlin student and a protégé of Charles Grandison Finney, would head the three-week training program in New York City. Angelina Grimké would be the only female apostle.

She approached Sarah for support. At the risk of expulsion from the congregation, Sarah agreed to join her. From the time their father had forbidden her to study Latin, Sarah had chafed against patriarchal restrictions, and her hope of becoming a minister had been conclusively dashed when the leading male elder, impatient at her halting speaking style, had recently told her to sit down.[63]

The pair attended the training, and in December 1836 gave their maiden speeches. Three hundred women attended. A man convened the assembly, then left to avoid violating the strong taboo that forbade women from speaking in front of men. The self-doubts that had plagued

Angelina as long as she could recall fell away. "After a moment," she wrote a friend, "I arose and spoke about forty minutes, feeling, I think, entirely unembarrassed."[64]

The sisters lectured around New York City for the next few months. It was there, in May 1837, that they attended the first national convention bringing together female anti-slavery associations. Lucretia Mott, a member of the liberal faction of Philadelphia Quakers, chaired the four-day meeting of seventy-one delegates. Angelina Grimké presented her draft of yet another essay, now aimed north of the Mason-Dixon Line, and the convention endorsed her original seventy-page pamphlet.

Appeal to the Women of the Nominally Free States applied the obligations of patriotic citizenship to women. "All moral beings have essentially the same rights and duties," Angelina boldly claimed, "whether they are male or female." She challenged those who would confine women to "the parlor and the nursery," asking, "Are we aliens because we are women? Are we bereft of citizenship because we are the mothers, wives, and daughters of a mighty people? Have women no country?" She touched once again on the subject of sexual exploitation, and the treatment of enslaved women "forcibly plundered of their virtue." Her wording made it plain that she considered virtue innate to all women. "They are our country women—they are our sisters," she wrote.[65]

On the second day of the convention, Angelina proposed a resolution from which Lucretia Mott later dated the official start of the movement for gender equality—namely, that all women should henceforth consider it their duty to act politically. Angelina moved that women ignore "the circumscribed limits with which corrupt custom and a perverted application of Scripture have encircled her." God meant for women to occupy a broader sphere: "to do all that she can by her voice, and her pen, and her purse, and the influence of her example, to overthrow the horrible system of American slavery."[66]

Angelina's motion passed after a warm debate, with "many members dissenting," according to Lucretia Mott. Elizabeth Cady Stanton and Susan B. Anthony later pointed to the convention as the first step toward "organized public action and the Woman Suffrage Movement, *per se*."[67]

After the convention, the Grimké sisters headed north to New England to embark on a regional speaking tour. Angelina proved to be an electric orator. Her openhearted description of her own homeland helped others visualize the plight of enslaved Americans as fellow human beings. Veteran abolitionists recognized the arrival of an unparalleled ally. Antislavery leader Wendell Phillips marveled at Angelina's "serene indifference to the judgment of those about her." She moved audiences to "painful silence and breathless interest," he noted. Lydia Maria Child observed that the young woman grew pale with stage fright before speaking, but this "passed quickly, and she went on to speak gloriously, strong in utter forgetfulness of herself, and in her own earnest faith—in every word she uttered." To Child, Angelina embodied "the greatest moral sublimity ever witnessed." She had a transparent sincerity. She was the match of any male speaker, and the superior of most.[68]

Wendell Phillips later recalled the events as a turning point in abolitionism, writing, "No man who remembers 1837 and its lowering clouds will deny that there was hardly any contribution to the anti-slavery movement greater or more impressive than the crusade of these Grimké sisters from South Carolina through the New England States." The pair not only made plain the "daily, hourly, ceaseless torture" of American slavery, but also blazed a new role for women. "Whatever it is morally right for a man to do, it is morally right for a woman to do," Angelina steadily claimed.[69]

The sisters reinforced one another, though Sarah's monotone made Angelina the star. Crowds grew. Four hundred people came to their first talk in Boston, then six hundred. A meeting in Salem, Massachusetts, attracted a thousand. Some women walked six or seven miles to listen. By the end of June, eight thousand New Englanders had heard the Southerners. By the end of July, another twelve thousand. The Grimkés' tour continued through October. It became impossible to keep out the curious men who pressed through the doors. "Promiscuous" audiences, as coed gatherings were called, became routine.

Notorious Women

The Grimké sisters might as well have grown two heads. Exercising one's voice in front of men betrayed every notion of True Womanhood. Congregationalist ministers of Massachusetts issued a "Pastoral Letter" urging local churches to close their halls to "any of that sex who so far forget themselves as to itinerate in the character of public lecturers and teachers." Such activists threatened "permanent injury" to other women by their example. "The power of woman is in her dependence, flowing from the consciousness of that weakness which God has given her for her protection," the ministers asserted. "But when she assumes the place and tone of man as a public reformer . . . her character becomes unnatural." They especially deplored discussion of that "which ought not to be named," or what Angelina called the "unspeakable indignities" perpetrated on "unconsenting" female slaves.[70]

The letter triggered alarms at the American Anti-Slavery Society. Abolitionism already polarized people. Why add to its difficulties? More than one of the Seventy cautioned the Grimkés against "forgetting the great and dreadful wrongs of the slave in a selfish crusade" to address the "paltry" grievances of women. Women's rights must not get in the way of antislavery. Abolitionism was already suffering from backlash, demonstrated most recently by Pennsylvania's decision to strip the franchise from free Black men, who had been voters since 1791.[71]

The sharpest rebuke came unexpectedly from Catharine Beecher. Like most Northerners, she opposed abolition, meaning an immediate end to slavery, favoring what was called gradualism. She considered abolitionists a menace, and believed that they should approach slaveholders "in a kind and respectful way with the hope of modifying their views and allaying their fears." Female abolitionists doubly horrified Beecher, and she castigated her former admirer in *An Essay on Slavery and Abolitionism, Addressed to Miss A. D. Grimké.* The pamphlet was released nationwide during the sisters' New England tour, leading Southern newspapers like the *Mississippi Free Trader* to praise Beecher for dispelling the "curse" of Angelina Grimké.[72]

Beecher's 152-page essay asserted that chivalry depended on "a woman's retaining her place as dependent and defenceless, and making no claims." Whatever rights she possessed were the "gifts" of men who loved her. The role of "combatant" in any political cause "throws her out of her appropriate sphere."[73]

Like most people at the time, Catharine Beecher believed that women should embrace their secondary status. She cautioned Angelina Grimké that learning, which allowed women to approach men "in intellectual elevation," would prove "a doubtful and dangerous blessing" if it encouraged trespass beyond the home or schoolhouse. With neither husband nor child to disprove her theories, Catharine Beecher claimed that a good woman could uplift any man and produce spotless offspring. She wrote that "the more intelligent a woman becomes, the more she can appreciate the wisdom of that ordinance that appointed her subordinate station, and the more her taste will conform to the . . . submission it involves." Sounding a great deal like Hannah More, Beecher caustically added, "An ignorant, a narrow-minded, or a stupid woman, cannot."[74]

Catharine Beecher's commentary struck most readers as reasonable. Public speaking was considered a male prerogative, and a woman who infringed on it must be desperate or deranged. The *New Hampshire Patriot* sneered, "not being able to obtain husbands, they think they may stand some chance for a negro." A few people took a more charitable view. One observed to William Lloyd Garrison that abolitionists are "said to be somewhat eccentric, and I am very much inclined to think they are." But, he added, "The cause of humanity very much depends on such eccentric men and women. God bless them!"[75]

Public criticism merely strengthened Angelina's convictions. She published a rebuttal, compiled into a booklet as *Letters to Catharine Beecher.* In it, she not only attacked slaveholding, but also defended women's rights as inalienable. "Woman's rights are not the gifts of man—no! nor the *gifts* of God. His gifts to her may be recalled at his good pleasure—but her *rights* are an integral part of her moral being." Echoing Abigail Adams, Angelina noted that women were "governed by laws *we* have no voice in framing." She reflected, "The investigation of the rights of the slave has led me to a better understanding of my own."[76]

Sarah Grimké bloomed, too, and found an eloquence on paper that eluded her at the podium. In 1837 she published a 128-page book that became, in the words of historian Gerda Lerner, the "first comprehensive feminist argument presented by an American woman, ten years before the Seneca Falls convention." *Letters on the Equality of the Sexes* ranged over every continent. Sarah emphasized gender equality as a goal unto itself, not just a tool for advancing abolition.[77]

She parsed the Bible. Eve bit the apple first, she conceded, but Adam bore no less responsibility for his actions. She plumbed popular attitudes, noting that many men would still "limit a woman's library to a Bible and cookery book." She examined law, noting that married women could not own property and their husbands could legally beat them. Borrowing from a recent tome by Lydia Maria Child on the *History of the Condition of*

Women (1835), which echoed the themes of the *Strictures on Female Education* admired by Abigail Adams years before, Sarah Grimké pointed out the myriad ways in which women were oppressed. In Siberia, they were "not allowed to step across the foot-prints of men"; in Burma, they could not enter a courtroom; in Muslim countries, "pigs, dogs, women and other impure animals" could not enter a mosque. History, Sarah Grimké concluded, "is wet with women's tears."[78]

Going beyond the persecution of African Americans, which arose at a specific time in a specific context, Sarah Grimké brought attention to the timeless subjection of women. In *Letters on the Equality of the Sexes,* she rejected Beecher's idea of groveling for privileges. "I ask no favors for my sex," Sarah Grimké explained. "All I ask of our brethren is, that they will take their feet from off our necks, and permit us to stand upright on that ground which God designed us to occupy."[79]

The Rights of Property

The Grimké sisters' views fit larger democratic trends that help explain why these arguments occurred to them and why others listened. Most men and women recognized the incompatibility between America's founding principle of equality and at least some of its inherited structures. In the 1810s and 1820s, property ownership was largely eliminated as a qualification for voting. State after state turned over the ballot to millions of poor white males. Class ceased to be a qualification. The electorate vastly expanded. So-called universal manhood suffrage—one man, one vote—made the continued exclusion of women all the more striking.[80]

Property laws came under scrutiny, too. Primogeniture was attacked as old-fashioned patriarchy at its most notorious. Under primogeniture, men were not born equal at all. First-born sons received entire estates that they passed intact to their own first-born sons. Land was unsellable and second sons were out of luck. Primogeniture had been most prevalent in the southern colonies, but even in the north, oldest sons customarily received twice the portion of younger brothers. Thomas Jefferson championed a state law in 1776 that released three-fourths of land in Tidewater Virginia from such restrictions. Across the United States, multigeniture gradually replaced primogeniture, meaning that all children (male and female) received equal portions unless a will specified otherwise. This resulted in further modifications to ensure that people with average learning could sell, buy, and manage property.[81]

Egalitarianism also gained traction in arenas that benefited women specifically. While Catharine Beecher and Angelina Grimké squared off, scattered conversations popped up about granting property rights to wives. New York State Assemblyman Thomas Hertell introduced an act in 1837 for the "Rights and Property of Married Women," arguing that women should be entitled to protection against "improvident, prodigal, intemperate and dissolute" husbands. American statutes had dispossessed them of the inalienable "right to *life, liberty,* and PROPERTY." Coverture, he suggested, was a relic of monarchical government.[82]

Hertell's bill failed, but it attracted the attention of other men who questioned the fairness of allowing husbands to spend their wives' inheritances. Sometimes they expressed this in the patriotic rhetoric of natural rights. In 1837, the *Cleveland Messenger* noted that the legislature should restore women's "original rights which 'the lords of creation' have taken from them." It opined, "There is, when examined[,] something so manifestly unjust and absurd in our laws on this subject, that we are astonished to think how long they existed, and how tamely they have been submitted to by the injured party." The *New-York Spectator* painted the United States as a potential world leader: "May our country be the first to do this justice toward the sex."[83]

Other advocates spoke the poetry of True Womanhood. They described property rights as a privilege to be bestowed on "lovely and devoted woman" by men charged with her care. The Washington *Globe* called for reform of property rights as a way to encircle a wife "with the guardianship to which she is entitled," encouraging her not to foolishly relinquish her inheritance out of her innate "kindness and generosity."[84]

An economic downturn that President Andrew Jackson triggered by killing the nation's central bank proved decisive. The Panic of 1837 drove a wave of legislation to prevent creditors from seizing married women's inheritances as payment for their husbands' debts. While reform sprang from economic considerations, this was the first time that female autonomy was proposed as a solution. Southern agricultural states took the lead, partly to avoid losing slaves to creditors. In 1839 Mississippi became the first state to allow married women to own property (slaves, particularly), though husbands retained the right to manage assets. Alabama, Arkansas, Florida,

Kentucky, and Maryland followed. Limited ownership rights for women became increasingly common all the way to the free state of Maine. Coverture weakened and women's rights crept into the law. One historian calls these initial changes "small islands in the vast ocean of the common law."[85]

Unable to get his bill passed in 1837, Thomas Hertell reintroduced it in 1848. New York passed the statute this time, becoming the first state to guarantee married women the right not only to own, but also to manage assets. By the time of the Civil War, fourteen states had granted wives some form of property, making this the most substantial gender equity legislation of the antebellum era, one advanced mostly by men. Elizabeth Cady Stanton later recalled that Hertell's 1848 bill inspired her to reflect that "if the men who make the laws were ready for some onward step, surely the women themselves should express some interest."[86]

Ernestine Rose, a Polish immigrant who had circulated the sole petition in support of Hertell's initial bill, noticed a dynamic that those who favored equity would experience repeatedly. Women told Ernestine that "they had rights enough; and the men said the women had too many rights already." But no sooner had property rights become legal than "all women said: 'Oh! that is right! We ought always to have had that!'" When rooted in democratic principles and expressed in patriotic language, shocking proposals appeared normal once they were on the books.[87]

Wage disparities came in for criticism, too. Eight hundred female mill workers in Lowell, Massachusetts, went on strike in February 1834 to defend their "unquestionable rights" when wages were cut. The *Boston Evening Transcript* reported that their leader "mounted a pump and made a flaming Mary Woolstonecroft [*sic*] speech on the rights of women and the iniquities of the 'monied aristocracy.'" The next year in Philadelphia, a public meeting on the "Rights of Women" brought together seamstresses, tailoresses, and binders to discuss the "oppression" that had left most "scarcely able to earn a miserable subsistence."[88]

Such protestors took for granted liberties that their mothers had not known, while criticizing the shortcomings of their own times. Mill girls enjoyed the new freedom to live semi-independently, and the wages they protested had narrowed the gap between male and female earnings. In 1815, before the spread of manufacturing, a woman who earned wages in agriculture or domestic service received roughly twenty-eight cents for every dollar a man earned. By 1850, she earned fifty cents to his dollar. Industrialization did more to equalize income than anything else until the passage of sex discrimination laws in the late twentieth century, according to economist Claudia Goldin. That still did not mean, however, that female wages provided an adequate living.[89]

Seneca Falls and the First Calls for Full Citizenship

Demands for the vote arose in this period as well, on both sides of the Atlantic, reflecting the transoceanic exchange of ideas. In London, liberalization of the electorate in 1832 to include men of modest property elicited a petition to give "equal, or very nearly equal" rights to both sexes. Instead, Parliament pointedly banned women from voting while enfranchising roughly 18 percent of adult men. Once again, the inclusion of some people made the exclusion of others more glaring. In New York in 1845, attorney Elisha Hurlbut published an essay explicitly advocating for female suffrage. "Government is the mere offspring of rights" that are inalienable, Hurlbut argued. As human beings, women inherently possess "the full rights of citizenship." Six women from New York followed up in 1846 with a petition for the vote as a right "ungenerously withheld."[90]

Legislative reforms helped spark the first women's rights convention. Three months after New York passed Thomas Hertell's 1848 bill, Lucretia Mott and Elizabeth Cady Stanton called a meeting in upstate New York to discuss "the condition of woman." The two had met eight years earlier, at a London convention of abolitionists where female delegates had been banished to the spectators' gallery. Lucretia Mott had long admired Wollstonecraft's *Vindication of the Rights of Woman.* To her surprise, roughly three hundred women and men turned up on a week's notice, eager to discuss gender equality. No one believed women capable of presiding over a "promiscuous" assembly, so Lucretia's husband chaired the gathering in Seneca Falls on July 19, 1848.[91]

Elizabeth Cady Stanton, a graduate of Troy Seminary, one of the first ladies academies, presented a "Declaration of Sentiments" that was modeled explicitly after the 1776 Declaration of Independence as a way to emphasize the patriotic character of its demands: "We hold these truths to be self-evident: that all men and women are created equal; that they are endowed by their Creator with certain inalienable rights." It pointed out that "the most ignorant and degraded men—both natives and foreigners," enjoyed rights that were denied educated American women. (In the nineteenth century, "degraded" connoted someone reduced in social rank, not necessarily someone depraved.) The convention passed Stanton's resolutions unanimously, with the exception of one that asserted women's "sacred right" to vote.[92]

A persuasive speech by Frederick Douglass, whose presence reflected the kinship between feminism and abolitionism, tipped the balance. The resolution that some feared would make the movement look ridiculous gained a small majority. Sixty-eight women and thirty-two men signed the final declaration.

State conventions followed over the next decade. Women predominated, but men shared leadership. The label "feminist" did not yet exist. Female participants generally called themselves "woman's rights advocates" during this era, while men like Douglass claimed the label "woman's rights man." The first national conclave in 1850 proclaimed, "The sexes should not, for any reason or by chance, take hostile attitudes towards each other . . . they should harmonize in opinion and co-operate in effort." Participants made plain that they were not anti-male.[93]

The movement nonetheless provoked reaction, just as Angelina Grimké's insistence on her right to plead "the cause of the slave woman" had roiled the anti-slavery crusade. As one preacher declared, "I will not sit in a meeting where the sorcery of woman's tongue is thrown around my heart . . . I will not submit to petticoat government, here, nor anywhere else." Trying to beat back female speech in church, a right that Quaker, Methodist, and some Baptist assemblies granted, one Congregational association declared that women should not even "open their lips, to utter any sounds audibly," aside from singing.[94]

One breaking point came in 1840, when William Lloyd Garrison proposed that a protégée of the Grimkés serve on the business committee of the American Anti-Slavery Society. Abby Kelley had attended Angelina and Sarah's lectures in Massachusetts, and Sarah had told her it was important for other women to "assert the right to speak in public" or it would never be accepted. Garrison's motion passed 557 to 440, but cleaved the movement down the middle. Abby Kelley embarked on a lecturing career that continued until the Civil War. When she became a mother, she told a disapproving friend who thought she should remain at home that she would continue touring "for the sake of mothers who are robbed of all their children."[95]

Harriet Jacobs's Escape

During the first weeks in the attic, Harriet Jacobs eagerly awaited rescue. Edenton was a port from which ships frequently sailed north. Sailors were often free men of color. A white captain might help a refugee for enough money, she thought. But few wished to court the hazards. Months passed. Then years.

Each season brought different torments. The pine roof wept turpentine onto Harriet's face in summer's merciless heat. Small red insects, "fine as a needle's point," attacked her arms. Autumn rains drenched her bedding, and leaky shingles could not be replaced lest someone glimpse her underneath. In winter, she developed inflammation in her unused joints, frostbite where her toes stuck out from the covers, and a pneumonia that almost took her life. In spring, the smell of new foliage drove her mad with the urge "to stretch my cramped limbs, to have room to stand erect, to feel the earth under my feet." She learned to be mute. A sneeze might alert passersby.[96]

The sight of her children in the street kept Harriet going. She found she could see enough to read or sew if she held a book or needle to the small shaft of light streaming through her peephole. At Christmas she made new clothes for the children, and had the joy of overhearing Joseph tell a neighborhood boy that Santa Claus was real. When the boy tattled that mothers put gifts in stockings, Joseph retorted that Santa had definitely brought the suit he was wearing, because his mother had been gone a long time.

A year into hiding, Harriet Jacobs learned that Samuel Sawyer had won a seat in the US Congress. Sawyer had no idea where she was, but she decided she must look her lover in the eye when he came to say goodbye to Molly and the children he had yet to free. For the first time in months, Harriet opened the trapdoor to creep down the shelves. Her muscles were so atrophied that her feet gave way when she reached the floor, so she crawled on hands and knees behind a barrel next to the shuttered window, attracting Sawyer's attention with a whisper as he passed. Shocked, he slipped inside the storeroom and assured Harriet that he would free their children. After he left, Harriet did not have the strength to climb back into her hole, and her alarmed uncle carried her up.

The threat of discovery stretched everyone's nerves. James Norcom stopped by frequently to snoop. When Harriet overheard him questioning the children in the street one day, she decided she must train his attention elsewhere. She sent for the friend who had rowed her into the swamp. She asked if he could get a northern newspaper and knew anyone who would take unposted letters north. He said he did know someone, then pulled a scrap from his pocket. He had just bought a cap wrapped in the *New York Herald.* Harriet scoured the paper for tidbits to improve her deceit. For the next six years, writing by the light of her peephole, she sent bogus correspondence to Norcom, mailed from Boston. She doubted he would dare go there, knowing it was a hotbed of anti-slavery. He stopped dropping by, and she began crawling down the shelves before dawn to exercise her limbs in the dark, readying herself to run.

Six years and eleven months after Harriet entered the garret, a sea captain agreed to smuggle her out for a price. Molly Horniblow's crackers and cakes bought her escape.

When the ship docked in Philadelphia in June 1842, the captain pointed Harriet to a "respectable-looking colored man." Reverend Jeremiah Durham belonged to the Vigilant Committee, an association whose members took turns shadowing the wharves to intercept refugees. While Durham waited, Harriet purchased a double veil, then a common article of women's clothing, to hide her face.[97]

Committee members offered to help Harriet book a passage to New York once she was rested. Philadelphia was the first city she had ever seen. The bustling town offered myriad wonders, including an artist's studio with portraits of people like Harriet. "I had never seen any paintings of colored people before, and they seemed to me beautiful," she recalled. Abolitionists who wanted to know her story came to meet her, and she was touched by "how careful they all were not to say any thing that might wound my feelings." One wrote to Lydia Maria Child that the young woman, shut up so long, could "hardly walk" yet presented one of the most remarkable cases of escape "you have ever seen."[98]

Before she left for New York, Harriet Jacobs learned not to discuss one aspect of her experience. Reverend Jeremiah Durham expressed surprise when she mentioned her children, because he "had taken me for a single woman." When she explained the circumstances, Durham advised Harriet not to tell others as "heartless people," white and Black, would treat her with "contempt." The warning left a new scar. An enslaved man might escape his past and become respectable, but a sexually compromised woman never could. The moral standards for men and women were different, and she carried the burden of being of both the "wrong" race and sex.[99]

In New York, Harriet was reunited with Joseph, now thirteen, and Louisa, nine, whom Samuel Sawyer had emancipated and sent north to live with one of his cousins. The Norcom family continued to hunt for Harriet. Eventually, she and the children moved to Boston for safety, where Joseph apprenticed himself to a printer. They lived with Harriet's younger brother John Jacobs, who had escaped earlier. Not wanting to lie about her history, Harriet mostly avoided abolitionist circles.

John felt differently. With nothing to hide, he became a lecturer for the American Anti-Slavery Society, often in company with Frederick Douglass. He encouraged Harriet to send Louisa to a ladies academy to become a teacher. In the winter of 1849, the girl packed her things to attend the Young Ladies Domestic Seminary in Clinton, New York, one of the few schools that accepted Black students. The night before Louisa's departure, Harriet forced out the words that she feared might destroy her daughter's love. Slavery had driven her to "a great sin." For the first time, Harriet admitted that Samuel Sawyer was the girl's father. Louisa hugged her and said she had already guessed.[100]

When Joseph left his apprenticeship and went to sea, Harriet followed her brother John to Rochester, New York. There he ran an anti-slavery bookstore upstairs from Frederick Douglass's *North Star* newspaper, whose masthead proclaimed, "Right is of no sex, truth is of no color." Harriet staffed the shop whenever John was on the road. Amy Post, a Quaker member of the Underground Railroad who had signed the Seneca Falls Declaration and convened the second women's rights convention in Rochester, offered her a place to stay. By happenstance, Harriet Jacobs had come to live with one member of the 1848 Seneca Falls convention and to work upstairs from another.

Harriet stayed with the Post family for nearly a year. Gradually she let down her guard. Amy Post heard Harriet's stories differently from

Reverend Durham. She understood that slavery had a particular meaning for women. Harriet broke down in tears repeatedly as her new friend listened. Amy Post encouraged Harriet to write about what had happened, and to say what women were not supposed to say. Harriet was horrified. She reminded Amy that "a woman can whisper her cruel wrongs in the ear of dear friend much easier than she can record them for the world to hear." Besides, Harriet was still in hiding.[101]

When Congress passed the Fugitive Slave Act in 1850, Harriet left Rochester for Manhattan, hoping to avoid bounty hunters amid the crowds. Gossip eventually reached her that James Norcom had died and left a measly estate. His heirs were determined to track her down. Learning by chance that they were nearby, Harriet fled north once again in a driving snowstorm. When Norcom's son-in-law knocked on the door of her New York residence in February of 1852, Harriet's employer, Cornelia Willis, paid $300 for her freedom (equivalent to $11,000 in 2022). Harriet Jacobs could walk a public street without a disguise for the first time since the age of twenty-one. She was thirty-eight.

Molly Horniblow lived long enough to learn of her granddaughter's emancipation, but died soon afterward. Her demise led Harriet to change her mind about telling her story. Public exposure could no longer humiliate Molly or endanger her. She had no idea how to write a book, but sat down every night to practice the skill taught to her by a granddaughter of the Edenton Resolves, a woman who for some reason felt that even an enslaved girl had a right to learn.

Harriet Jacobs struggled for four years to find a publisher. No one had ever printed a first-person account of the sexual exploitation of a Black woman, and editors had little interest in a manuscript that might both disgust white readers schooled in True Womanhood and alienate literate Blacks who were anxious to avoid criticism of their women. Amy Post wrote an appendix attesting to Harriet's "delicacy of feeling and purity of thought," but her endorsement was insufficient. The manuscript sat.

In 1860, Boston activist William Nell introduced Harriet to Lydia Maria Child. Nell had spoken at the Rochester convention convened by Amy Post, where he had thanked women for their zeal on "behalf of the oppressed class with which he stood identified." Frederick Douglass seconded these sentiments, saying that "he dared not claim a right which he would not concede to women." It was a feeling that many Black Americans shared. The National Convention of Colored Freedmen passed a motion soon thereafter stating, "We fully believe in the equality of the sexes." The sense of common cause had deepened to the point that by the 1850s the best-known abolitionists were women's rights activists, and vice versa. Their alliance was a gamble. Both risked losing supporters who could abide one set of reforms but not the other.[102]

Lydia Maria Child reviewed Harriet Jacobs's manuscript and reassured the novice that her book was "wonderfully good." She suggested only minor changes, and wrote a foreword. "I am well aware that many will accuse me of indecorum for presenting these pages to the public," she wrote, "for the experiences of this intelligent and much injured woman belong to a class which some call delicate subjects, and others indelicate." Child had seen hostile Bostonians mock Angelina Grimké as "Devil-ina" Grimké. She knew she risked her own reputation and career by vouching for Harriet Jacobs's account.[103]

Child's endorsement secured publication. *Incidents in the Life of a Slave Girl* appeared in January 1861, one month after North Carolina seceded from the Union. Harriet published it under the pseudonym Linda Brent. Some knew that Harriet Jacobs and Linda Brent were the same person, though it would take 126 years for historian Jean Fagin Yellin to establish it conclusively.

The first American woman to publish her experience of sexual predation felt unable to reveal her identity, knowing that many contemporaries would damn her as immoral. But while she hid behind a false name, she refused to excuse herself with "the plea of compulsion from a master; for it was not so." She had accepted Sawyer's offer "with deliberate calculation." Slavery had blighted her choices, so she made the best ones she could, though they still filled her with "sorrow and shame." The public forgave Harriet Jacobs when the ideals of True Womanhood did not allow her to forgive herself. She never married, but acquaintances respectfully addressed her as *Mrs.* Jacobs for the rest of her life.[104]

Abigail Bailey had exposed one man's corruption. Harriet Jacobs had exposed the corruption of an entire system founded on the unabashed appropriation of women's bodies. Her humble account of a heroic journey made *Incidents* one of the world's most powerful indictments of slavery. The *London Morning Star and Dial* recognized it as "the first personal narrative in which one of that sex upon whom chattel slavery falls with the deepest and darkest shadow has ever described her own bitter experience." The *Londonderry Standard* predicted that female readers would "rise in holy indignation."[105]

+++

ANGELINA GRIMKÉ had her greatest triumph when she became the first woman to address the Massachusetts legislature, shortly before her 1838 marriage to Theodore Weld. Afterward, she focused on the home, eager to disprove the myth that public speaking "ruined" women for domesticity. She wanted to show "that well regulated minds can with *equal ease* occupy high and low stations and find *true happiness in both.*" After giving birth to three children in five years and suffering a prolapsed uterus for which surgery was then unavailable, she mostly retired from the public eye, though she continued to encourage women who widened the path she had blazed.[106]

Intentionally or not, she participated in another trend as well. Angelina's mother had had fourteen children. In the mid-nineteenth century, millions of couples sought to limit family size through abstinence, coitus interruptus, or illicit (but not yet illegal) birth control devices such as condoms and sponges. In 1800, white American women had seven to eight children on average. By 1860, that number had declined to five. Black women still averaged eight, attesting to their limited options. No one can explain precisely why white families chose to have fewer children—a trend more pronounced in the North than the South—but the decline in family size accompanied rising education.[107]

Harriet Jacobs embraced public service. She wrote articles for *The Liberator* during the Civil War and volunteered in Black refugee camps that encircled the nation's capital. In 1864, she and Louisa established Virginia's first free primary school run by African American teachers, called the Jacobs School, in Alexandria, Virginia. As a rare educated woman of color, Louisa became headmistress of seventy-five students, one of the most exalted positions then open to any woman.

There is no evidence that Harriet Jacobs ever met the Grimkés, but their paths overlapped in the end. At Harriet's funeral in 1897, a preacher named Francis Grimké gave the eulogy. He was the son of Angelina's brother Henry, who had died in a typhoid epidemic in 1852 before emancipating the three boys he had had with an enslaved woman. Angelina discovered her nephews' existence after the Civil War, and she and Sarah helped pay for their educations. A respected Presbyterian minister by 1897, Francis Grimké described Harriet Jacobs as someone who rose above the common crowd like "peaks that shoot above the mountain range."[108]

The antebellum period introduced four new rights and customs: the freedom to form associations, inherit property, attend college, and—most controversially—speak up publicly. Few exercised these entitlements, but they existed. Women still had no claim to their earnings if they married, or their children if they wed, but they had begun to talk.

Enslaved American women had no rights whatsoever, and it was far from clear that the Civil War convulsing the nation would improve their plight.

CHAPTER 3

The Right to Lobby

1865–1900
Susan B. Anthony and Elizabeth Packard

The only fear you need have is the fear of not standing by the thing you believe to be right. Take your stand and hold it: then let come what will, and receive the blows like a good soldier.

SUSAN B. ANTHONY, 1906

ELEVEN STATES FORMED their own country in 1860. Confederate vice president Alexander Stephens explained that it rested "upon the great truth, that the negro is not equal to the white man; that slavery—subordination to the superior race—is his natural and normal condition." Abraham Lincoln announced that he would not "interfere with the institution of slavery where it exists," but opposed the Union's dissolution. One of his first acts was to suspend the right to trial before imprisonment, known as *habeas corpus,* to suppress the rebellion. He prophesied that the war would test whether "government of the people, by the people, for the people" would survive or "perish from the earth." Monarchies still dominated the globe. The collapse of America's body politic riveted international attention on the ultimate viability of democracy.[1]

It was a Quaker schoolteacher, Susan B. Anthony, who helped deliver the medicine that, if taken, would conclusively outlaw slavery, save the Union, and strengthen America's founding principles. Historian Eric Foner notes that the Thirteenth Amendment abolishing involuntary servitude "originated not with Lincoln but with a petition campaign organized by the Women's National Loyal League, an organization of abolitionist feminists headed by Susan B. Anthony and Elizabeth Cady Stanton." Even so, accusations of racism flew at them in the war's aftermath as reformers split over whether to put racial justice ahead of gender justice for the sake of expediency.[2]

Elizabeth Packard of Illinois, a mother of six, fought her own private war. Lincoln's suspension of habeas corpus had limited relevance since her husband could already lock her up without trial. Elizabeth Packard's story reveals the precariousness of freedom under the laws of coverture, even after women had gained limited property rights.

Susan B. Anthony and Elizabeth Packard both underwent courtroom trials for their convictions. Equipped with the education for which Abigail Adams had advocated, and the voice that Angelina Grimké had championed, they launched the next phase of the fight for equality, in which women began to lobby legislatures to change laws that deprived them of liberty and kept them from playing a role in a government that was supposedly of, by, and for the people.

A Modest Quaker Finds Her Calling

Born in 1820, the second of six children, Susan Brownell Anthony understood that life for the poor was precarious. When she turned eighteen, her father's business failed, and bankruptcy attorneys inventoried everything Daniel Anthony owned, from his home and struggling cotton mill down to his daughters' knickers. All of it, including Susan's underwear, was considered collateral. With no money for school, Susan quit the boarding academy she had attended in Philadelphia for only a year. The family moved to Hardscrabble, New York, a town that Charles Dickens might have named.[3]

By nineteenth-century standards, they were lucky. None of the daughters was forced to become a domestic servant. An uncle purchased the family's essentials at auction and returned them, along with a note payable over time. Daniel Anthony retained just enough money to open a sawmill. When that failed, he sank his remaining funds into a farm three miles from Rochester, which the Erie Canal had transformed into a boomtown.

Susan slept on the floor as they settled in. She had just enough education to obtain a teaching job to help clear her father's debts, and for the next eleven years she presided over one-room schoolhouses of squirrelly youngsters across upstate New York. Since female teachers received only one-quarter the pay of male teachers, she stretched her earnings by boarding with family and friends. Although she fretted about her lack of preparation, it turned out she had a knack for imparting information—and controlling unruly assemblies. Nary a playground bully escaped her eye.[4]

The pious Anthonys had instilled a strong sense of duty in their children. That meant living up to one's ideals, whether pleasant or not. When Daniel Anthony loaned an empty attic to a group of young people to do-si-do and sip non-alcoholic punch, Susan and her sisters watched longingly but stoically from their chairs, because Quakers did not dance or drink. Their mother Lucy was so eager to guard the girls' purity that she cut the pages on reproduction from the family's one medical book and never told them about the "Mysteries of Life."[5]

Lucy did lecture on reform, however. She and Daniel were members of the liberal wing of the Quaker faith, and they considered racism wrong. When a job took Susan to a town where conservative Quakers excluded Blacks from meetings, she wrote her parents indignantly, "What a lack of Christianity is this!" (Susan B. Anthony had a lifelong passion for dashes, underlines, and exclamation points.) She took tea with local African Americans, eager to show them "respect in this heathen land." On a trip down the Hudson, she overheard an abolitionist chastising a Louisianan, and it made her wish that she had the words to persuade Southerners to sever "the bonds of those poor degraded brethren."[6]

Yet she did not have much confidence in her rhetorical ability, and felt she needed to further cultivate her mind. During the winter of 1840 or 1841, she convinced a male cousin to teach her algebra. When a brother-in-law learned of her self-imposed task, he folded a criticism of her effort into a compliment of her excellent cream biscuits. "I'd rather see a woman make biscuits such as these than solve the knottiest problem in algebra," he said. "There is no reason," Susan replied, "why she should not be able to do both." The retort was typical. She often said things that sounded blunt in the moment, but later seemed like obvious common sense.[7]

What she would do once her father's debts were paid was not clear. Perhaps because of her upbringing, she thought a good person should do more than help her own family. In 1849, at the peak of her teaching career, she accepted an invitation to address the local Daughters of Temperance, an auxiliary of a men's group known as the Sons of Temperance.

Bans on alcohol and organizations to teach restraint first arose during the Second Great Awakening. Daniel Anthony had eschewed drink since the day he saw an alcoholic frozen to death in a ditch. At the local Daughters of Temperance meeting, Susan nervously read her first public speech aloud. As she later remarked, she hardly dared "say that my soul was my own without a paper in hand." Like Angelina Grimké, she urged women to do their civic duty and not confine "our influence to our home circle." She told them that "centering all our benevolent feelings on our own kindred . . . can never produce a desirable change in the Moral aspect of society."[8]

How a woman might actually change society was not self-evident. Her family expected that she would find a husband, and custom required teachers to quit once they did. Five-foot-five, with thoughtful gray eyes, superior cooking skills, a fondness for children, and lustrous brown braids at a time when a good head of hair was considered a woman's "crown of glory," Susan B. Anthony attracted at least three marriage proposals. Each took her by surprise. No suitor piqued her interest, and it mystified her that so many of her acquaintances were willing to give away their autonomy just to find a place beside a man given to whiskey, a widower with ten children, or a dolt who ignored her feelings.[9]

The plight of her favorite cousin, Margaret, brought home the risks. Susan boarded with Margaret's young family for two years when she accepted a post in Canajoharie, New York. The cousins enjoyed long talks and Margaret waited for Susan at the window each day after school. In preparation for a student performance at the schoolhouse one evening, Margaret affectionately wove Susan's thick braids into an elaborate updo.

A fourth pregnancy confined Margaret to bed toward the end of Susan's stay, and Susan cared for Margaret's every need. Margaret's husband assumed that Susan, as a spinster, would care for his children as well. Susan complied, but his presumption annoyed her, especially when he talked of leaving his wife in Susan's care to pursue his fortune in California, where gold had been discovered the year before, in 1848. When he complained one day of a headache, his pregnant wife reminded him that she had had one for several weeks. "Mine is a real head *ache,*" he replied, "yours is a sort of natural consequence."[10]

In the spring of 1849, Margaret's pregnancy took a turn for the worse. Susan was shocked at the anguish she endured in childbirth. Afterward, she nursed her cousin for seven weeks as Margaret slowly died. Susan had once joked that if she were a man, she would light out for California herself, but she returned to Rochester tired and heartbroken. Her father suggested that she run the farm as a reprieve from teaching, since he had taken a job in town.

For the next two years, Susan B. Anthony threw herself into cultivating, harvesting, and marketing. Because her mother was frail, she kept house, too, with energy that could have powered a lighthouse. With more leisure than before, she read novels and organized fundraisers for the Daughters of Temperance. She listened to her parents' stories about the second women's rights convention, held in Rochester two weeks after the meeting in Seneca Falls, and how they had added their names to the famous declaration of women's rights. She attended abolition meetings where she met her father's friend, Frederick Douglass, who sometimes invited her to his home for tea.[11]

Despite her sense of inadequacy at oratory, Susan began piping up when she felt that some plain point should be made. On the first occasion, in 1852, she rose to address a motion at an Albany conference to which the Sons of Temperance had invited the Daughters. Startled that a woman would wish to speak, the chair explained that a Daughter was expected to "listen and learn." Susan sailed out the door, feeling hot stares on her back. A few delegates followed, but most accepted that ladies should be silent in mixed gatherings. Susan sought out an old friend, Lydia Mott (a cousin of Lucretia Mott), who suggested that she convene her own temperance meeting. She did so a few days later, and the small group, sitting around a rickety church stove on a snowy night, decided to start a Women's State Temperance Society with an all-female group of officers. They were determined to stop "being seen and not heard."[12]

By then, Susan B. Anthony had met many of the period's renowned reformers, including Elizabeth Cady Stanton and Lucy Stone. She had much in common with the sweet-voiced Lucy, who came from a modest background and had lost a beloved sister to childbirth. Lucy Stone had also taught elementary school, earning her way through Oberlin College. Five years older and married, Elizabeth Cady Stanton resided on a higher social plane. As a granddaughter of the officer who had exposed Benedict Arnold's treason, and daughter of a US congressman, she felt as entitled as any patriot to hurl thunderbolts. Susan admired her extravagantly. The new Women's State Temperance Society elected Elizabeth Cady Stanton president. Susan B. Anthony became secretary, which meant that she pulled most of the workload, traveling to countless villages to organize chapters and show local women how to raise funds, call meetings, and petition door-to-door.[13]

In 1853, Susan tossed another firecracker into a crowd by becoming the first woman to speak at a New York educational convention. Direct and unpretentious, she had sat through previous annual meetings just as silently as the other schoolmarms who made up two-thirds of the audience, but she had promised herself not to do so again. Standing up and raising her hand, she waited for thirty minutes in front of five hundred people—knees trembling under her skirt—while the men debated whether or not to recognize her. The matter at hand was why teachers did not command as much respect as other professionals.

A small majority agreed at last that she should be allowed to speak, and she made her point. "Do you not see that so long as society says woman has not brains enough to be a doctor, lawyer, or minister, but has plenty to be a teacher," she said, "every man of you who condescends to teach, tacitly admits before all Israel and the sun that he has no more brains than a woman?" Heart pounding, she sat back down, too flustered to say more. Other women glared. "Did you ever see such a disgraceful performance?" she overheard one say. "I was never so ashamed of my sex."[14]

Such criticisms were tame in comparison with what would come. Year after year, Susan B. Anthony and other women who dared to speak publicly on temperance, education, women's rights, or—worst of all—abolition, faced loud hissing and catcalls of "shut up," "bow wow," "scum," and "get out." Reform audiences turned uglier yet when women bobbed their hair short in the early 1850s and adopted knee-length dresses over loose trousers, called bloomers, to make the point that dress should be more practical. (Skirts caught fire easily on open hearths where women cooked.) Men and boys heckled them on street corners. Newspapers harangued them as "hermaphrodites" who could not find husbands. After a couple of years, feminists gave up and switched back to floor-length dresses. William Lloyd Garrison reflected after one convention at which a woman was forced off stage by nonstop yelling, "I have seen many tumultuous meetings in my day, but on no occasion have I ever seen anything more disgraceful to our common humanity."[15]

For their part, male supporters were mocked as emasculated "male Betties" or, in the words of a critic from the *New York Courier,* "hen-pecked husbands, attenuated vegetarians, intemperate Abolitionists and sucking clergymen, who are afraid to say 'no' to a strong-minded woman." (The phrase "strong-minded" was perhaps the most common insult for an assertive woman during the nineteenth century.) Despite such ridicule, or perhaps because of it, many male abolitionists came to accept gender justice as inseparable from their work for racial reform.[16]

Friendships intensified between embattled activists. After 1852, Susan B. Anthony became a full-time volunteer on behalf of the great causes of the day, paying her expenses with the help of donations. She counted nearly all the prominent reformers of the era as dear friends, and stayed in their homes as she swept up and down the Eastern Seaboard taking petitions door to door, engaging printers, hiring halls, and addressing small audiences.

Throughout, she remained even-tempered and commonsensical. Her diary showed none of the angst that had troubled Angelina Grimké. She recorded the day's weather, her travel itinerary, political news, and expenses and receipts. (During one trip she noted that donations "from the time of leaving Albany" had been $22.57 compared with $114.46 in expenses.) She cheerfully recorded when strangers were "kind and polite" and described most conversations as "pleasant" and even "splendid." She became accustomed to public speaking but, in the belief that others had more talent, delighted in arranging tours for the most celebrated, who found her cajoling impossible to refuse. Boston abolitionist Wendell Phillips once teased: "She has been so modest, humble, ashamed, reluctant, apologetic, contrite, self-accusing, whenever, the last ten years, she has asked me to do anything, go anywhere, speak on any topic!!" Behind it all, he suspected, was superb "cunning."[17]

Susan B. Anthony campaigned almost every day, undaunted by snowstorms and heatwaves, traveling by sleigh, horse, railway car, and foot, and returning to Rochester only to replenish her small traveling kit. She braved at least three violent mobs, dodging rotten eggs and ignoring drawn knives. Other agitators were more emotionally compelling, such as Lucy Stone, more powerfully descriptive, like Sojourner Truth, more intellectually agile, such as Elizabeth Cady Stanton, and more socially eminent, like Lucretia Mott, but none was as indefatigable.

One of the few who did not marry, Susan B. Anthony became the coordinator on whom others relied. In 1856, the male leadership of the American Anti-Slavery Society offered her ten dollars a week to run its New York campaign while a mini civil war raged in Kansas between settlers who were for and against slavery. Bloodshed west of the Mississippi between 1854 and 1859 heightened abolitionism's notoriety. The movement depended more on Susan than "any other of our workers," explained Samuel May, secretary of the Anti-Slavery Society. "We need your earnestness, your practical talent, your energy and perseverance . . . your cheerfulness, your spirit—in short, yourself."[18]

She disappointed them only once. One freezing December afternoon, not long after Abraham Lincoln's 1860 election, she was visiting the store of a Quaker friend in Albany when a veiled woman entered the establishment. Uncovering her face, Phoebe Phelps explained that she was fleeing her husband Charles, president of the Massachusetts Senate. Senator Phelps had pushed his wife down a stairwell when she confronted him about an extramarital affair, and committed her to a frightening insane asylum for seventeen months. Since then, he had allowed her to visit their three children only infrequently.

Mrs. Phelps's brother took her into his home, but he had recently lost patience when she begged to see her thirteen-year-old daughter. "The child belongs by law to the father and it is your place to submit," he reminded her. Like his brother-in-law, he was a high government official allied with the Republican Party, and he cautioned, "If you make any more trouble about it we'll send you back to the asylum." Fearing reimprisonment, Phoebe Phelps kidnapped her daughter and sought refuge in the home of a friend. The family was hunting them, she explained, and they needed a safer hideout.[19]

Susan made discreet inquiries and found out that Phelps, a former schoolteacher, had described the situation accurately. She then met Phelps and her daughter, both disguised, at the Albany train station on Christmas Day. They reached New York City late that evening, and she walked the pair through the dark and snowy streets to find lodging. The first two inns would not accept female guests "unaccompanied by a gentleman," because it was believed that women traveling alone must be disreputable—perhaps even prostitutes. As it neared midnight, they reached a boardinghouse run by a friend who had divorced an abusive husband, but she told Susan that she would lose tenants if they discovered she was "harboring a runaway wife." In the wee hours, the clerk at a third inn threatened to call the police, whereupon Susan announced that they would wait in the lobby until the police arrived. The man relented and gave them an unheated room for the night. The next day, Susan finally found shelter for the mother and child with yet another friend, a woman writer. Ever active, she returned to Albany on the very next night train—the nineteenth-century version of a red eye.[20]

The state capital was small enough that the Phelps family soon guessed Susan had been complicit in the escape. The senator threatened her with arrest. For the next year, abolitionists fought her, too. Wendell Phillips claimed that she was harming their cause, and insisted "upon this woman returning to her relatives." William Lloyd Garrison sent a six-page letter defending Senator Phelps as an honorable man. He cornered Susan to lecture, "Don't you know that the law of Massachusetts gives the father the entire guardianship and control of the children?" For Susan, Garrison's appeal was hard to swallow, coming from one who had sworn to break every law to end slavery.[21]

She revered Phillips and Garrison, but stubbornly replied, "Trust me that as I ignore all law to help the slave, so will I ignore it all to protect an enslaved woman." Her father appeared to be the only abolitionist who, capable of seeing a Black man as fully human, could do the same for a woman. "Legally you are wrong, but morally you are right," Daniel Anthony reassured her. He advised her to put nothing incriminating on paper.[22]

A year later, while men bled on Virginia's battlefields, Senator Phelps's henchmen snatched his daughter from Sunday school in New York and took her back to Boston. Even with Susan's help, Phoebe Phelps had lost her battle. The law was stronger than either of them.

Another Crazy Wife

The same month that Susan B. Anthony helped Phoebe Phelps escape, Elizabeth Ware Packard contemplated the fragility of liberty for a married woman from inside the asylum to which her own husband had committed her. Born in 1816, Elizabeth had met her future husband at the age of ten, when he became an assistant to her father, a Calvinist preacher in Massachusetts. Red-haired and sober-minded, Theophilus Packard was fourteen years older, and she looked up to him as her father's protégé. He courted her a decade later, after she graduated from Amherst Female Seminary and became a schoolteacher. She quit her job upon marriage, as expected.

Sometime afterward, Elizabeth realized that the childhood origins of their acquaintance had conditioned her to become, as she wrote, "an unresisting victim to Mr. Packard's marital power." Her husband expected her to remain as malleable as she had been as a child. He provided her with a comfortable home but forbade any deviation from his will as they moved from Massachusetts to Iowa, and eventually Illinois, following his career. Across the years, Theophilus and the petite, five-foot-one-inch Elizabeth had five sons and one daughter.[23]

The strain of conformity brought her to a breaking point twenty-one years into marriage, when a deacon from their congregation in Manteno, Illinois—a grassy prairie town with a population of 861 souls—asked her to join an anemic Bible class that needed a shot of energy. The couple's relationship had shown cracks for some time. Theophilus's position as a Calvinist pastor required him to defend orthodoxy, but his wife enjoyed new ideas. One reason they had moved to Illinois was because he disapproved of her friends who espoused perfectionism. Then, despite his "grief and annoyance," as he wrote in his diary, she visited family back East, where she encountered spiritualists interested in communicating with the dead. On still another occasion, to his horror, she turned her back when he pulled out his Bible to quote for the hundredth time, "wives obey your husbands."[24]

With Elizabeth's curiosity and Theophilus's desire to keep her on a traditional path, the Bible class seemed like a good idea. Now forty-six, Elizabeth Packard was excited to discuss doctrines that had long puzzled her, specifically Calvinism's insistence on total human depravity. She did not consider herself corrupt, and felt that the public professions of wickedness expected in church were dishonest. Perfectionism appealed to her temperament. She believed that people were inherently good, even if, like the nation itself, they could be made better.

She asked for permission to attend the study group, which her husband granted. The deacon called on her at her first meeting and she did not hold back, though she must have known that her questions were likely to cause a stir. The lackluster group blazed to life. Membership jumped from six to forty-six, a conspicuous event in a small farm town like Manteno. Disturbed church elders replaced the deacon. Theophilus found himself in an awkward position when the new deacon showed up at his parsonage in the spring of 1860 and asked to speak privately.[25]

Anxious by nature, with a nervous stomach, Theophilus may have worried for his job. A man who could not control his wife was not considered much of a man. The family's moves had left him in debt, and the church's wealthiest benefactor wanted the congregation to follow a conservative line. After supper that evening, Theophilus extended his arms and asked Elizabeth to join him. She sat on his lap and clasped her arms around his neck, or so she recalled in a later memoir.[26]

He asked her to quit the Bible group. She agreed, and said she would tell the others that church leaders had asked her to resign. "No, wife, that won't do," Theophilus replied. She must say it was her idea. But that was dishonest, she pointed out.[27]

The conversation spiraled from there. In Elizabeth's mind, husbandly protection was the reward for wifely submission. When an unmarried woman gave a man all her power, he assumed the responsibility to defend her. Theophilus believed that a wife should adopt her husband's views. Elizabeth suggested that even wives had freedom of speech. Theophilus pushed her from his lap.

Next he pushed her from their home. Nineteenth-century law gave husbands the high cards in case of marital disagreement. America's young democracy had softened coverture laws, but change was halting. Wives in fourteen states could now keep an inheritance if they had one, but income belonged to husbands. In case of divorce, judges sometimes now granted custody to mothers if a child was especially young, yet paternal custody remained standard. A modern doctrine of "family privacy" subverted most inquiries into domestic violence. "Trivial complaints arising out of the domestic relationships" should not be adjudicated, one North Carolina court explained when exonerating a man who had whipped his wife "with a switch about the size of one of his fingers," since it was not as thick as his thumb. Jurists increasingly emphasized wifely obedience as an obligation of love rather than of coverture.[28]

Theophilus suggested that Elizabeth visit her brother on the other side of Chicago for a few months. She agreed, and asked for ten dollars to cover any doctor's bills that might arise for the children traveling with her. The money would come from a fund that Elizabeth's father, still living, had established on her behalf. Illinois did not enact its Married Women's Property Act until the next year, in 1861, so she had no say over the asset. Theophilus said he did not trust her with cash. Choosing her words carefully, she replied that in that case she would "rather" remain home. Red with anger, Theophilus declared that she had lost her last chance. "You shall go to an asylum!" he declared.[29]

Elizabeth could hardly believe her ears, but knowing her husband, she sought out a neighbor who professed to know Illinois statutes. The man assured her that habeas corpus required adjudication before imprisonment and no trial jury could possibly find her crazy. Elizabeth tried not to overreact as Theophilus's behavior became stranger.

First he stopped sleeping with her. Then he engaged a woman to assist with household chores, though he had previously not allowed Elizabeth to hire help. He began whispering to friends when they came to call. One of their middle sons, then thirteen, confided that his father had given him money to tell lies about her. Another son reported that he had been forbidden to speak with her. Soon thereafter Theophilus sent their eighteen-month-old baby to another family member, saying that Elizabeth needed rest. The baby clung to her neck but she had to let him go. The next evening, around midnight, she spied Theophilus packing her clothes.

Elizabeth woke to sounds on the front porch. Still in her nightgown, she hastily locked her bedroom door. Her husband had summoned a sheriff and two physicians, and dispatched the older children on errands. The sheriff forced the door. The doctors took her pulse and declared her insane. Elizabeth protested that she was a citizen with rights, to which Theophilus retorted, "while a married woman, you are a legal nonentity, without even a soul in law." His reply, almost an exact quote from Blackstone's *Commentaries,* revealed how deeply some continued to believe in coverture.[30]

Illinois allowed a husband to commit his wife without trial. Wives had no reciprocal privilege, reflecting the assumption that women were peculiarly prone to mental illness. Doctors warned that nondomestic activities threatened fragile brains designed primarily for childbearing. As an American physician wrote in 1870, it was "as if the Almighty, in creating the female sex, had taken the uterus and built up a woman around it." Failure to embrace one's role as a glorified incubator reflected—might even cause—

insanity. One particularly enterprising group of obstetricians in London cut off the clitorises of patients whose symptoms of madness included wanting sex. It made them more tractable, surgeons observed. A study of women in the Wisconsin state asylum between 1869 and 1872 listed "suppressed menses" and "domestic trouble" as the most common indications of mental illness, aside from "religious excitement."[31]

Theophilus may have genuinely considered his wife crazy. He described her self-assertion as proof, and decided to spirit her to the Illinois Asylum and Hospital for the Insane, two hundred miles away in Jacksonville. She did not go willingly. Elizabeth Packard informed her captors that she would not resist them, but also would not walk to her doom. They would have to carry her.

Astonished neighbors witnessed the men bodily move the middle-aged matron from her home to a horse-drawn lumber wagon. Word flashed from house to house. Elizabeth Packard was well liked, and a throng greeted the group at the station. Theophilus beseeched his wife to get down, saying, "You won't compel us to lift you out before such a large crowd, will you?" She maintained her poise despite a growing inward panic. "I shall let you show yourself to this crowd, just as you are—my persecutor, instead of my protector," she replied with dignity. Over the hubbub she spotted their thirteen-year-old with his hat pulled low. Perhaps for his sake, she asked her captors to lock their arms to make her a "saddle-seat" so her underclothes would not show. The men toted their prisoner from the wagon to the ladies' waiting room, then to a railway car once the train pulled in. Witnesses told the sheriff to release her, but he explained that he was following the law.[32]

The crowd swelled. Two more of Elizabeth's children arrived as the train whistle blew. The older one begged fruitlessly for help. The younger, only seven, chased the locomotive as it chugged away. When she could see him no longer, Elizabeth leaned her head against the seat in front of her and cried.

Ending Slavery in the Land of the Free

As the nation descended into war, Susan B. Anthony came to the conclusion that every gain women might make rested on quicksand until they had the vote. The powerful could otherwise bestow or waive privileges at whim.

"Men tell us they vote for us by proxy," she commented, but they often failed "to represent our true sentiments." Women needed to represent and defend themselves, she believed, just as men did. She did not consider suffrage a panacea for social problems, but a sine qua non for solving them.[33]

This point was driven home in 1862. Two years earlier, she had engineered a successful petition campaign to amend New York's Married Women's Property Act to allow shared guardianship of children, a provision that would have helped Phoebe Phelps. But when the reformers became distracted by the Civil War, conservative politicians restored full custody to fathers. There were no female legislators to protest. Susan B. Anthony felt sick. She wrote her friend Lydia Mott, saying, "Twenty thousand petitions rolled up for that—a hard year's work!—the law secured!—the echoes of our words of gratitude in the capitol have scarce died away, and now all is lost!"[34]

Still, the war consumed her energy for the next three years and, like women on both sides, she set aside other questions to contribute. Harriet Tubman, the former Underground Railroad conductor and a speaker at Boston women's rights meetings, commanded a team of military scouts during the war. Unknown numbers disguised themselves as common soldiers, including Loreta Velazquez of the Confederacy and Sarah Edmonds of the Union. Others treated wounds, passed military intelligence, and cut telegraph wires. Harriet and Louisa Jacobs, reunited after Louisa finished her teacher training, started their school for refugees.[35]

Most women gave practical help but a few organized politically. For Susan B. Anthony, that meant lobbying Congress to change the law. Abraham Lincoln declared most slaves free as of January 1, 1863, yet his Emancipation Proclamation was an executive order without any statutory basis. It freed only those in the states that had rebelled. Lincoln urged the four slave states still loyal to the Union, namely Delaware, Kentucky, Maryland, and Missouri, to liberate their own people, but all refused. Southerners dominated the Supreme Court and reformers worried they would overturn Lincoln's proclamation as unconstitutional. A large wing of "Peace" Democrats (Republicans called them "Copperheads") lobbied to guarantee slavery forever if Confederates would only rejoin the Union. The North had lost most of its initial battles, and British shipbuilders were busy constructing a navy for the Confederacy. The future of slavery remained an open question.[36]

One historian writes that Elizabeth Cady Stanton "never made eradication of slavery a priority," yet it was Stanton who dreamed up the patriotic broadside calling on Northern women to banish "the auction block—babies sold by the pound, and beautiful women for the vilest purposes"—from the nation's "sacred soil." Together, she and Susan B. Anthony founded the Women's National Loyal League, appealing to "daughters of the Revolution" to uphold the "birthright of freedom, and keep it a sacred trust for all coming generations." Susan convened the league's inaugural meeting on a hot, humid morning in New York City in May 1863. From the podium she presented resolutions on behalf of a business committee that she and Stanton had already formed, including a motion demanding equal protection for both "citizens of African descent" and women.[37]

Some conventioneers objected to that last word. They considered the mention of gender too controversial. Susan replied that justice was indivisible. "The great fundamental truth of democracy that was proclaimed by our Revolutionary fathers" belonged to everyone, she insisted. Angelina Grimké, now fifty-eight and mostly retired, spoke in agreement. The convention passed all of Susan B. Anthony's resolutions and set a goal of one million names on petitions to Congress. Watching from the audience, William Lloyd Garrison judged the meeting "a dead failure." Too much attention to women's rights, he thought.[38]

Abolitionists supported the campaign, though Susan had to poke, prod, and drag many who were otherwise engrossed by military events. She opened an office and recruited four biracial teams to drum up support throughout the Northeast. Soliciting money from merchants and preachers she knew, she paid the expenses for another team to tour the Midwest. She asked them to remind American women that, since they could not vote or enlist, their "only way to be a power in the government is through the exercise of this one, sacred, constitutional 'right of petition.'" Women must use their one tool "to the utmost."[39]

To cover rent, printing, and postage, she asked volunteers to collect a penny from each person who signed the league's petition. Within a year, the Women's National Loyal League had five thousand members and two thousand volunteers. A coordinating committee held weekly prayer meetings in New York City. When Susan B. Anthony traveled, she exhorted Elizabeth Cady Stanton, a busy mother of seven whose youngest was four, to get "down to the Office and see *exactly what* is *being done—don't allow us* to be *turned wholly* into a *praying machine.*"[40]

In spare moments, she wrote her sisters and mother, who were then deep in grief over Daniel Anthony's death the year before. Susan and her father had been discussing Lincoln's Emancipation Proclamation on a Sunday morning in 1862 when the apparently healthy sixty-eight-year-old doubled over in agony. He died two weeks later. Susan now sometimes walked down to the Hudson River after a long day to watch timber loaded onto ships. The smell of wood reminded her of his sawmill in Hardscrabble. "I doubt if there be any mortal who clings to loves with greater tenacity than I do," she wrote to sister Mary. It was a poignant confession for someone who chose never to marry, and who believed people should only do so for love. When asked once if women should propose marriage, she replied that they should not until they could support themselves economically. Otherwise, it would be like asking, "Please, sir, will you support me for the rest of my life?"[41]

Moments for herself were fleeting. Susan devoted herself to the Women's National Loyal League and its most essential supporter, Charles Sumner of Massachusetts, the leading abolitionist in the US Senate. Reinforcing the women's league, the American Anti-Slavery Society urged Sumner at the end of 1863 to introduce a constitutional amendment abolishing slavery. The senator agreed, so long as he received enough petitions.

Charles Sumner waited on Susan B. Anthony to provide them. For months, her office sent them by the thousands. In February 1864, two African American men ceremoniously carried the giant stacks into the Senate, and Sumner used the first one hundred thousand signatures to introduce the Thirteenth Amendment. The next month Susan B. Anthony sent twenty thousand more. She ultimately sent Charles Sumner almost four hundred thousand signatures. In April 1864, the Senate adopted the amendment abolishing slavery. A year-long fight in the House followed. In January 1865, Congress outlawed slavery.[42]

The great organizer closed her office and settled the books. After thousands in expenses, and more than three thousand dollars in penny donations, the league showed a deficit of $4.72. Susan B. Anthony paid the balance from her own pocket and left for Kansas to visit her brother. When a derailment delayed her train, she watched men pour from the cars in search of air and refreshment. Every woman onboard remained seated. The weight of custom settled on her shoulders. She paused, then stood to go in search of coffee, determined that respectability should not preclude freedom of movement. Once again, a small gesture sparked stares, though gawking bothered her less now and she found a mischievous delight in her "thick" and "dingy" cup of joe by the tracks.[43]

This was when Susan B. Anthony still enjoyed the admiration of her friends. A much harder stance awaited her as the Union turned from waging war to winning the peace.

+++

SUSAN STAYED EIGHT MONTHS IN KANSAS until word came, in May 1865, that William Lloyd Garrison had resigned from the Anti-Slavery Society, convinced that the Thirteenth Amendment meant his work was done. Wendell Phillips took over the postwar fight to secure full citizenship for African Americans. An old-line Bostonian, Phillips announced an expedient strategy that was at odds with the high moralism of previous years. The rights of women and Blacks must be divided. "Now is the Negro's hour," Phillips told the American Anti-Slavery Society. Elizabeth Cady Stanton hotly objected, "Do you believe the African race is composed entirely of males?"[44]

A month earlier, President Lincoln had expressed support for giving votes to Black men who were either military veterans or "very intelligent," meaning literate. But he also agreed to readmit Southern states regardless. Susan B. Anthony called it "the crime of crimes" to leave voteless former slaves at the mercy of armed ex-Confederates. John Wilkes Booth declared that Lincoln's outlook meant "nigger citizenship"—and killed him three days later.[45]

In August 1865, Susan B. Anthony boarded a train home to launch another petition drive, this time asking Congress to grant suffrage to emancipated slaves as well as "the only remaining class of disfranchised citizens," that is, the fifteen million women of the United States. In a companion letter to the *National Anti-Slavery Standard,* Elizabeth Cady Stanton objected that "women of the nation have done their uttermost for the last thirty years to secure freedom for the negro." Why should Black men now be elevated above all women? Stanton pointed out that they had the same capacity as their "Saxon compeers" to oppress women.[46]

These were treacherous waters given the nation's racist undertow, yet Stanton felt compelled to navigate them. Beginning with Abigail Adams, Stanton noted, patriots had long conceded that any man could become a tyrant if law permitted it. Stanton called illiterate former slaves "Sambo" and criticized their sudden superiority to Southern Black women who still had no right to their own "person, property, wages, and children." She simultaneously complimented Black veterans, and suggested that American women seize the opportunity "when the Constitutional door is open" to take "the strong arm and blue uniform of the black soldier to walk in by his side."[47]

Stanton kept up this argument for the next four years. Gradually it degenerated into damaging, white-hot outrage at what she called the "antislavery priesthood" of "supercilious boys" who insisted that anyone with a penis should receive the vote. To "Sambo" she added slurs against illiterate immigrants pouring in from Europe and Asia who would soon double the nation's population. Most states allowed non-citizens to vote. A man did not even need to be an American citizen, whereas a woman whose grandparent had been a hero of the Revolution—someone like her—had no say whatsoever. Referring to Irish, German, and Chinese immigrants, Stanton asked Americans to "Think of Patrick and Sambo and Hans and Yung Tung" making legislation for such women. She wrote on the eve of the amendment granting suffrage to Black males alone, "We object . . . we object . . . we object." Elevating one oppressed group over another tempted it to abuse others lower on the ladder, she believed.[48]

Frederick Douglass protested Stanton's use of "Sambo," but he did not disagree that men of all races could be oppressors. He had signed the 1848 Seneca Falls Declaration that denounced "ignorant and degraded men—both natives and foreigners"—for having greater rights than women. In 1860, he condemned "drunken Irishmen and ignorant Dutchmen." Robert Purvis, another eminent Black abolitionist, spoke up even more strongly for women. If anything, his daughter needed the vote more urgently than his son, Purvis said, articulating what a later generation called intersectionality. Since "she bore the double curse of sex and color," he said, "she should be protected first."[49]

Susan B. Anthony never stooped to public name-calling. She opposed efforts to drive apart movements that she believed should propel one another. It was she who suggested in 1866 that women's rights and anti-slavery organizations merge into a single American Equal Rights Association. The next year she recruited Sojourner Truth, a former slave whom Lincoln had received in the Oval Office, to address the first anniversary meeting. Truth called for female suffrage alongside Black male suffrage. Six feet tall, with a rich voice and magnetic persona, she told the convention that "There is a great stir about colored men getting their rights, but not a word about the colored women." Emancipation had effectively set Black men over Black women. She objected that "When the women come home, they ask for their money and take it all, and then scold because there is no food."[50]

Sojourner Truth had distilled family law precisely. States had begun granting women the right to their own wages in the 1860s, but all-male courts mostly refused to enforce the statutes. New York, for example, construed a wife's new right to keep her wages as meaning she could do so if her husband agreed. Judicial hostility undermined legislators' intent.[51]

A nurse who volunteered on the occupied Sea Islands of South Carolina during the Civil War reported that some Black women complained "our husbands treat us just as Old Massa used to, and whip us if they think we deserve it." She and Sojourner Truth both described how emancipation had given formerly enslaved men the same absolute entitlement to their wives' labor, bodies, and offspring that white men already possessed over their own wives. Many used this power judiciously, but the law allowed them to use it however they saw fit.[52]

Wendell Phillips's strategy fit the temper of the Republican Party, then the party of reform. Purists who had once given speeches on the social margins suddenly found themselves in bareknuckle matches over what was winnable. Utilizing his authority over a trust fund set up for women's rights by a generous donor, Phillips slowly tightened the spigot on Susan B. Anthony. Senator Charles Sumner now introduced her petitions with reluctance. Sumner told feminists he just could not conceive a way to keep "male" out of the Fourteenth Amendment, the proposal to grant full citizenship to former slaves.

Not all Republicans agreed. Thaddeus Stevens of Pennsylvania, a leader in the House of Representatives, opposed this divisive strategy. His first two drafts of the Fourteenth Amendment did not use the word "male." Stevens declared on the House floor, "I certainly shall never vote to insert the word 'male' or the word 'white' in the national constitution."[53]

Republicans found that abolition had put them at a disadvantage. The original Constitution had counted enslaved individuals as three-fifths of a person for the purpose of apportioning representation. Emancipation meant that readmitted Southern governments could now count Blacks as whole persons, deny them the vote, and actually increase their own seats in Congress. Republicans had acquired an instant incentive to enfranchise Black men. In June 1866, they passed the Fourteenth Amendment, declaring all native-born Americans "citizens" and guaranteeing them due process. This overturned the 1857 Supreme Court opinion in *Dred Scott* that Black Americans had "no rights which the white man was bound to respect." The amendment would also take some congressional seats from any state that denied the ballot to specific groups of "male inhabitants."

For the first time, the word "male" entered the Constitution.

Reformers Split into Camps

Susan B. Anthony sprang into action. Not only did the Fourteenth Amendment actively dispossess women, but it would allow states to exclude Black men from voting in exchange for losing a few seats in Congress. As she begged a Convention of Colored Citizens in New York City, they must fight a law that allowed states to exclude Black veterans. Frederick Douglass opposed the Fourteenth Amendment, too. Nonetheless, under Charles Sumner's leadership, it passed the Republican-dominated Congress in June 1866.[54]

Next, the individual states had to decide whether to enfranchise Black men—or accept that their representation in Congress would be proportionately reduced by the percentage of the male population disqualified from voting. Wendell Phillips asked Susan B. Anthony to help him overturn the property requirements that New York imposed solely on Black men. He explained that the vote for women of either race was a mere "intellectual theory" in comparison. Susan did not consider women's rights theoretical. Furious at his condescension, she retorted that she "would sooner cut off her right hand" than campaign for one group over the other.[55]

She returned to Kansas in 1867. A successful state campaign there might convince people like Sumner and Phillips that if reformers committed themselves firmly, both groups could win the franchise. Only a few Northern states allowed Blacks to vote. Kansas was not among them. There she organized a campaign to expand the electorate to include everyone. She reminded a coworker, "you have no right to say one word more for women than you do for the Negro." She had just come from New York, where she had traveled with Louisa Jacobs, among others. Louisa was "everything proper & right" in a speaker, Susan reported to their mutual friend Amy Post.[56]

Republicans in Kansas insisted on separate ballot measures for women and Black men. They found little to like about women's suffrage, since if women got the vote they would distribute themselves across the political spectrum, whereas new Black voters would clump around the party of Lincoln. They spread false reports of rivalry between Blacks and white women, and denounced feminists as "male women." Wendell Phillips refused to send funds. With no money for expenses, Susan B. Anthony failed to get famous speakers like Frederick Douglass and Henry Ward Beecher. At the end of her six-month campaign, George Francis Train, a wealthy Irish immigrant who supported women's suffrage, offered to accompany her for the last two weeks. Little did she know that Train had been recruited by Henry Blackwell, Lucy Stone's husband, who later regretted it but never admitted his role. This left Susan to shoulder the responsibility when Train, a Democrat, fanned anti-Black feeling among Irish railway workers. Still today, some historians denounce Susan B. Anthony as racist for associating with Train and accuse her of believing that white women were "racially superior," though there is no direct evidence for such a supposition and much that suggests otherwise. Roughly two-thirds of Kansans voted against both measures: women's suffrage *and* Black suffrage.[57]

This meant that one-third of voters thought differently. Some historians suggest that a better-funded campaign that combined the two measures might have produced universal suffrage in the bellwether state. Susan B. Anthony certainly thought so. She wrote a friend who had also canvassed the blistering prairie, "If but just one *popular* speaker—*man* from the *east had* gone through Kansas—and electrified the Republicans to rally to our side . . . the state might have been carried overwhelmingly." Instead, she could only lament "the listless do nothingness of the men we had always believed our best friends."[58]

Male reformers felt no embarrassment at collaborating with politicians who opposed gender equality, so long as they voted correctly on race. But they denounced Susan B. Anthony for accepting Train's help. The

Irishman complicated the matter further by writing Susan a check to start a feminist newspaper after the Kansas election. This led to the birth of *The Revolution* in 1868 with Susan as proprietor, meaning guarantor of the debts that accumulated rapidly when Train returned to Ireland. The paper declared itself nonpartisan, something that Republicans also found obnoxious. Susan knew that if women's suffrage were ever to pass Congress, it must still be ratified by the states, North and South. *The Revolution* declared that " if old Abolitionists and Slaveholders, Republicans and Democrats, Presbyterians and Universalists, Saints, Sinners and the Beecher family find themselves side by side in writing up the question of Woman Suffrage, they must pardon each other's differences on all other points." Overlooking differences after the Civil War was not likely, however.[59]

Anger about Kansas became enduring enmity in 1869, when Republicans passed the Fifteenth Amendment forbidding any state from denying citizens the right to vote "on account of race, color, or previous condition of servitude." States would no longer be allowed to decide for themselves whether or not to exclude people on the basis of race. But they could exclude people on the basis of sex—and all did.

The Fifteenth Amendment widened the growing divide until the American Equal Rights Association split in two. At its last meeting in May 1869, a thousand reformers pressed together to discuss ratification in Steinway Hall, New York's finest concert venue, where singer Jenny Lind, novelist Charles Dickens, and the city's famed philharmonic enchanted adoring crowds. Susan B. Anthony and Frederick Douglass had both opposed the Fourteenth Amendment, but they were split on the Fifteenth. Frederick Douglass urged adoption in response to the emergence of the Ku Klux Klan. "When women, because they are women, are hunted down . . . when they are dragged from their houses and hung upon lamp posts; when their children are torn from their arms," Douglass argued, "then they will have an urgency to obtain the ballot equal to our own."[60]

Unable to foresee the wave of lynchings that would engulf the South in coming years, Susan B. Anthony retorted that as outraged as they all were by the "hateful and mean prejudice" toward Blacks, she did not believe that men like Douglass would voluntarily change places with any woman. Debates about whose rights were more important had "no place" at the convention. "We have never brought them to the platform," she pointed out. Her next comment, however, showed a new willingness to go there.

She quoted Elizabeth Cady Stanton, who had argued that if others insisted on doling crumbs from the "loaf of justice," then the vote should be given first to the most "capable portion of the women," meaning those with an education. Some historians deem this prioritization racist, and many contemporaries called it selfish—a cardinal failing in any True Woman. It reflected Susan B. Anthony's experience. She believed that women would fight for those left behind, while men could not be trusted to make women their equals after they had pulled ahead.[61]

Frederick Douglass supported female suffrage more vigorously than most. Yet he also may have considered women's rights a theoretical good, at least to some extent. Retribution toward Black men occurred publicly. It was meant to be seen. Violence toward women, by contrast, occurred in private, and was intentionally hidden. Men who were not abusive, and women who were not abused, easily underestimated the problem. Douglass raised his hand to ask whether granting women the vote would really "change anything in respect to the nature of our sexes."[62]

Susan B. Anthony had a deep feeling for women's vulnerability, especially the poorest. She may have recalled when her underwear was listed as collateral or when she received quarter-pay as a schoolteacher. She may have pictured Phoebe Phelps, whose children had been torn from her arms. The vote would give women a fighting chance, she vehemently told the absorbed audience. She pointed out that "we have fugitive wives as they had fugitive slaves." Without the ballot, women would forever scrape for survival. She quoted Alexander Hamilton: "Give a man power over my substance and he has power over my whole being." She begged Douglass and the convention to oppose any amendment that privileged one group over another.[63]

The bonds of friendship snapped. Abolitionist Stephen Foster, husband of Abby Kelley, demanded Elizabeth Cady Stanton's resignation as president. He accused Susan B. Anthony, famously thrifty, of bilking the organization for money. Lucy Stone agreed that "Ku Kluxes here in the North in the shape of men take the children away from the mother," but she broke with her old friends to side with Frederick Douglass and her own husband, Henry Blackwell. Lucy Stone had pointedly kept her own name, but they were as one on this question. Poet Frances Harper, the sole Black woman whose comments were recorded, declared that if forced to pick, she must choose race first.[64]

The three-year-old American Equal Rights Association died that day. That evening, Susan B. Anthony and Elizabeth Cady Stanton met privately with a small group to form the *National* Woman Suffrage Association—and to campaign for all women, regardless of color. Lucy Stone retaliated by organizing the *American* Woman Suffrage Association six months later. In the end, Black men obtained the vote, though Southern states mostly subverted its implementation. The United States had inherited slavery. Jim Crow was its own creation. Female reformers of both races who might have resisted segregation remained voteless for another fifty years.

Susan B. Anthony was wrung out. In the early 1870s, her beloved newspaper went under. Since none of her married friends could legally contract a debt, she faced bills amounting to $10,000, equivalent to roughly $220,000 in the year 2022. She pleaded in vain with Charles Sumner to support a new campaign for the vote for "*women* black and white." She told him about seeking shelter for Phoebe Phelps on Christmas and finding no room at the inn. "I wish it were possible for your great, just nature to realize the indignities and injuries that even the *best known* of us women are subjected to," she wrote, noting that "the lowest of men love to manifest their superiority over women." Sumner never came around.[65]

Meanwhile, Elizabeth Cady Stanton became entranced with Victoria Woodhull, a glamorous one-woman publicity machine who campaigned for "free love" (no-fault divorce) while extorting money from former abolitionists to keep their extramarital affairs quiet. Twice divorced, Woodhull preached that she had "an inalienable constitutional, and natural right to love whom I may, to love as long or as short a period as I can, to change that love every day if I please." Muckraking journalists reveled in her story, which seemed to confirm that woman's rights advocates would destroy the family.[66]

When Woodhull tried to take over the May 1872 meeting of the National Woman Suffrage Association to start a new political party with herself as candidate for US president, Susan B. Anthony rapped her gavel and ruled the interloper out of order. Elizabeth Cady Stanton rebuked Susan as small-minded. Woodhull would not sit down, and in a later session called for a vote. Susan fruitlessly banged her gavel. Finally, when Woodhull would not stop talking, the Quaker schoolteacher descended the podium, strode from the auditorium, found the janitor, and told him to cut the gas lights.

As usual, it was Susan who had gone to the trouble of renting the hall. Class was over.[67]

Erect and strong at fifty-two but with gray strands wandering in her dark hair, Susan B. Anthony had arrived at a crossroads. She wondered if it might be the end of the road. In her diary, she scrawled, "I *never* was so *hurt with folly of Stanton.*" She told Martha Wright, a fellow Quaker, "I am thrown half off my own feet—really not knowing whether it is I who am gone stark mad or some other people." After decades of working for a pittance and scrimping even on food, Susan B. Anthony had not a single respectable dress nor one additional right. She stayed with her sister when in Rochester and with acquaintances when she was on the road. Journalists still attacked her as the quintessential ugly feminist. Old friends now scorned her, too. She clung to the belief that women's cause would prevail, but wondered if there was any further role for her. "I tell you, Mrs. Wright," she confided, "I am feeling today that *life doesn't pay.*"[68]

Prison for Wives

The Illinois Asylum and Hospital for the Insane had been open nine years when Elizabeth Packard climbed the stone steps on her husband's arm in June 1860. The intimidating, five-story building reflected the midcentury proliferation of state clinics for the mentally ill, which were typically situated on bucolic grounds to ease troubled minds.

An assistant superintendent took Elizabeth to an empty cell and showed Theophilus to comfortable guest quarters as twilight deepened. Unable to stop thinking of her children, Elizabeth hardly slept. The next morning she prevailed on an attendant for a washbowl and mirror. In the locked dining hall, she fiddled with her dry bread and boiled meat. After she returned to her cell, Theophilus entered with a distinguished-looking man who introduced himself as superintendent Andrew McFarland.

For the next two days, Theophilus played attentive husband. At the intake, he told Dr. McFarland that Elizabeth had never resisted his wishes "but now she seems strangely determined to have her own way, and it must be she is insane." McFarland initiated a pleasant conversation with Elizabeth about various topics, from politics to religion to his recent travels. She conversed in her normal way. McFarland appeared to understand that she was sane, but unbeknownst to her, he had already decided to accept her as a patient.[69]

The next day, Theophilus met his wife in a private reception room overlooking the front entrance. He guided her to a settee, explaining he hoped for "a pleasant interview" before they parted. Elizabeth looked at him in shock. It had not occurred to her that the fight was over. "Pleasant!" she exclaimed, "how could it be pleasant to leave me in such a place?" She thought of her eighteen-month-old and burst into tears. Theophilus assured her that someone would care for him. Elizabeth jumped to her feet. With a handkerchief to her streaming eyes, she began pacing. She pleaded not to be separated from her children. If he gave her the "one favor" of returning home, "my grateful, thankful heart will bless you forever." Theophilus remained silent. At last she looked him in the face. Stretched out on the couch, he was fast asleep.[70]

She shook him awake, and Theophilus left to say goodbye to McFarland. The superintendent later said he had never seen a man "so deeply afflicted, and even heartbroken." Elizabeth's impression was different. As Theophilus stepped lightly onto the asylum's outdoor portico, he caught her eye through the window. It was an intimate glance. The kind that couples of three decades share, when words are unnecessary. "He stopped to give me one look of satisfied delight," she noted.[71]

Neighbors who had witnessed the abduction petitioned McFarland. They hired a doctor who pronounced her "the sanest person I ever saw." Worried by Theophilus's descriptions of Elizabeth's lunacy, their eldest son came to see for himself. He found her "the same kind mother as ever." But Elizabeth was not the superintendent's only inmate. Numerous patients were similarly situated, and McFarland showed little interest in learning that another crazy wife was not.[72]

Most states allowed husbands to warehouse inconvenient wives. Men could be falsely committed as well, but not on the word of one person alone and without further evidence. Wives suffered involuntary confinement far more commonly than men or single women, perhaps because it was so easily accomplished.[73]

To reassure Elizabeth, McFarland rewarded her with a private room in a ward where other patients also appeared normal. He gave her access to books and to pen and paper, and even allowed her to go on shopping excursions and solo horseback rides. McFarland conducted therapy by shaking hands every day with each inmate, a procedure he called "laying on of hands." Elizabeth sensed he held hers a mite longer than others, and it restored her "crushed self-respect," as she wrote in a later memoir. Gradually she discovered that there were many patients who "had never shown any insanity while there, and these were almost uniformly married women." She realized that only those "cured" of disobedience were ever discharged.[74]

Four months into captivity, Elizabeth decided to express her concerns about "prisoners' rights" to McFarland. This temerity reflected her belief that any "pure spiritual woman" could reform a man. Inmates cautioned Elizabeth that she might "never see daylight again," but she did not believe McFarland capable of such treachery, at least toward her. In a lengthy letter, she described the cruelties she had seen "in the most expressive terms I could command." She sentimentally appealed to McFarland to become women's "protector and deliverer," rather than their tormentor. "The time for downtrodden and oppressed women to have their rights has come," she declared, wielding the vocabulary spread by reformers like Susan B. Anthony.[75]

Had Elizabeth Packard stopped there, all might have been well. But feeling empowered by True Womanhood, she offered to "forgive" McFarland if he repented and to "expose his criminal conduct publicly" if he did not. She took the precaution of sliding a copy in the backing of her mirror before she gave him the letter.[76]

Rights were naught but privileges, she learned once again.

Five days after he received her missive, McFarland marched Elizabeth to the most dangerous section of the hospital, a punishment for disobedient patients, male or female. Elizabeth smelled the noxious ward even before he turned the lock. Screaming, crying women swarmed the hall. Some sat in their own waste and "effluvia." Fetid puddles of urine shimmered in the light from the barred windows. Every patient was filthy. McFarland showed Elizabeth to a room with several other women, only a couple of whom were lucid enough to converse. He would leave her there a year.[77]

The superintendent withdrew the privilege of books and paper, which only increased her determination to record what she saw. She scrawled on food wrappers, and sewed them into the lining of her dresses. Missing her children, she mothered patients, coaxing them to sit still while she washed away layers of grime. Overworked attendants gave her baking soda that she mixed with hot water to scrub walls, floors, and patients' clothing.

Some days passed peacefully, others violently, as when an inmate of whom she was fond struck Elizabeth so hard that her glasses flew across the room and she was knocked unconscious. Another patient caught Elizabeth by the hair and dragged her from a chair. A third muttered death threats at suppertime. Elizabeth feared going to sleep. McFarland's wife, for whom she sewed dresses for no pay, eventually finagled her a single room. Elizabeth pushed her bed against the door.[78]

Worried that she might actually go crazy, as she had seen other inmates do once they lost hope, Elizabeth developed a routine. She began mornings with a cold-water sponge bath and what she called "gymnastics," exercises she must have previously taught schoolchildren. She organized prayer services, and to keep her mind sharp committed Shakespeare to memory when attendants read the bard aloud on quiet afternoons. Nights, when permitted, she attended dances between the men's and women's wards to avoid depression.[79]

Twice she slipped secret notes to visitors, only to have them turned over to McFarland. A third time she arranged to speak to the chaplain and assistant superintendent after church, but both men glanced away when McFarland pushed her and she tumbled to the ground. Looking up at the three officials, she had an epiphany. Male guardians who claimed to represent women did not. Their protection in return for obedience was a bad bargain. Women must defend themselves.

"I hardly knew whether I could rise or not, but when I saw the three men who ought to be my protectors . . . forsake me, I began to try my powers of self-dependence, and found I could not only raise myself, but could also stand alone too, without a man to lean upon!" Elizabeth got to her feet, whereupon McFarland ordered her to her cell. She replied she would never walk there again, and told orderlies to make a saddle-seat. Back in the ward she scribbled the incident in her secret record of inmate beatings, ice water submersions, food deprivation, and solitary confinement.[80]

In September 1862, while the Civil War raged, Elizabeth hit upon a new strategy. When McFarland arrived for daily inspection, she asked if she might share with the board of trustees the religious arguments that had led to her imprisonment. Perhaps worried that Elizabeth's neighbors might again press their objections, McFarland seized on this proposed meeting as a way to document her insanity. The Calvinist board would see for themselves how unreasonable she was.

Elizabeth prepared carefully. In an attractive white summer gown trimmed with blue ribbons from home, she entered the hearing on the arm of the doctor and demurely asked to be reminded when her ten-minute allotment was up. She presented a statement on religious philosophy, preapproved by McFarland, that was so novel that the trustees allowed her to continue an additional fifty minutes. Seeing that she had captivated them, she asked if she might read yet another statement McFarland had not seen. He objected, but the trustees overruled him, beguiled by the "playful, easy style and manner" of Elizabeth's delivery. She opened fire.[81]

Twenty years before journalist Nellie Bly created headlines with a similar account for Joseph Pulitzer's *New York World,* Elizabeth described the horrific conditions of the asylum. The astounded trustees listened closely. They promised to review her case at their next quarterly meeting. She thought she had brought them to her side.

After Elizabeth left the room, McFarland asked the trustees to release her immediately as untreatably insane. She was creating "discontent" among the inmates. The trustees put him off, so he laid another trap. He decided to indulge Elizabeth's "mania" by providing supplies he had previously withheld, telling her to go ahead with her declaration of patients' and women's rights. Even while presenting her case as an example of "moral insanity" at a national convention of asylum superintendents, McFarland transferred Elizabeth to a safer ward so that she could write uninterrupted. Unaware of his motives, she penned a manuscript calling for the repeal of laws that allowed a man to commit his wife without trial.[82]

Elizabeth Packard outfitted her demands in patriotic language. She claimed that, like Abraham Lincoln, she sought a more perfect Union. "I do not believe in divorce, the secession principle," she wrote, but neither did she wish to "expose myself to a life-long imprisonment, and the loss of all my property and children, and every other right as an American citizen." She made plain that she wanted only the guarantees promised under the Constitution.[83]

When the trustees discharged Elizabeth Packard in June 1863, she had a two-hundred-page manuscript exposing a system that made wives into legal nonentities "whose rights no one is bound to respect," she wrote, paraphrasing *Dred Scott.* McFarland released her to Theophilus, rather than on her own recognizance, whereupon Elizabeth again refused to walk. Asylum attendants locked arms to transport her—wearing her best hat and gloves—down three flights of stairs, across the entrance hall, and into the waiting carriage.[84]

Elizabeth's actions were melodramatic but not unwarranted. Her eldest son warned that Theophilus was now contemplating a Massachusetts hospital for her, though Theophilus deposited her with relatives a hundred miles from Manteno. It wasn't until she rallied residents to her side and a town committee collected thirty dollars to help her that she could return home. When she turned up, Theophilus ignored her as she hugged the children she had not seen in three years. The couple's only daughter, now thirteen, had done all the housework in her absence, and Theophilus forbade the overburdened girl to accept assistance. He allowed Elizabeth to move back into her bedroom, but denied her hot water or access to the linen closet. Not long after her arrival, Elizabeth found the closet keys in the lock and took them.

It must have had gotten on Theophilus's last nerve. After the keys went missing, he locked her in her room and screwed the windows shut. For the next six weeks, he admitted the children only to review their school lessons. On one occasion, as a special treat, he allowed them to polish the kitchen stove together. That same afternoon Elizabeth chanced upon a letter from an asylum a thousand miles away informing Theophilus that they would admit his wife for life "as a case of hopeless insanity." From the date, Elizabeth realized that he would spring his trap soon.[85]

She read and reread the awful letter. Then she penned a note and waited through the terrible night for morning, when a man she did not know passed on his daily walk. She motioned him closer, and fed the folded paper through a small gap in the double-hung windows. Whispering through the glass, she asked him to deliver it to a Mrs. A. C. Haslett, the "most efficient" woman she knew. The mystified stranger retreated down the path, pocketing Elizabeth's only hope.[86]

Voting while Female

Defeat just made Susan B. Anthony saltier. While exuberantly fond of family and prone to sign letters with "a great deal of love & a great many thanks," she could appear fierce. Susan took to wearing black after the failed experiment in dress reform. Like many in the nineteenth century, she did not smile for photographs, giving her the expression of the humorless farmwife in Grant Wood's *American Gothic*. When yet another male reformer accused her of some vague impropriety, she snapped in a letter to a friend, "He's a Jack___," adding, "you may supply the blank or not as you please." Asked about Horace Greeley, a Democratic nominee for the presidency, Susan did not mince words. She told the *Philadelphia Evening Telegraph* that Greeley was spineless even before the Civil War. "Three out of the four years he was a splendid abolitionist, but the year preceding a Presidential election he was always found to be weak in the back and shaky in the knees."[87]

She worked hard to place daylight between organized feminism and the nation's political parties. Women should not become captive to one party or the other, she now believed. She wrote colleagues that politicians should not be judged by their actions in the past, but by what they might accomplish for women in the future. Women should campaign for whoever would best serve them, a nonpartisan stance that most suffragists carried into the twentieth century.

In the presidential election of 1872, that still meant supporting Republicans, who, while they refused to give women's suffrage a plank at their convention, did manage a "splinter" that promised to treat women's requests "with respectful consideration." For Susan the election loomed large because of a new strategy blown in from the West, namely, the idea that women should just show up at the polls.[88]

In 1869, Virginia and Francis Minor, a Missouri activist and her lawyer husband, proposed what was called the "New Departure." They speculated that the Fourteenth Amendment, which asserted that no state could "deprive any person of life, liberty, or property, without due process of law," technically applied to women as well as men. The Minors reflected a spontaneous explosion in women's suffrage agitation after the Civil War, as Americans became more responsive to the idea. Susan kept meticulous notes on unauthorized voting by women in local and federal elections, including one time when two hundred Black women from North Carolina dressed up as men.

By 1870, individuals and small groups were testing Virginia Minor's hypothesis that the Fourteenth Amendment implicitly enfranchised adult women because it guaranteed due process to all citizens with regard to laws and privileges. Now they needed a favorable ruling from the US Supreme Court to confirm it. They found their opportunity in April 1871 when Frederick Douglass, who had returned to fighting for women's suffrage, accompanied sixty-one women to the District of Columbia registrar, who turned them away. A former Republican congressman from Ohio pressed their objection in the district's highest court, with his co-counsel arguing that "there is not in the Constitution one word that forbids Susan Anthony from being elected President of the United States at the next election if the people so will it." If they lost, they plotted an appeal to the US Supreme Court.[89]

No stunt could have spoken more to Susan B. Anthony's sense of political theater. Act like a free person and damn the consequences.

In November 1872, Susan and her three sisters strolled into a temporary voter registry in a barbershop in Rochester, New York. Three local officials were assisting with the registration, while two federal supervisors watched over the men's shoulders. Susan stepped confidently to the table and, according to one of the men, of an age to be Susan's son, "DEMANDED that we register them as voters." The registrars politely explained that they could not.[90]

Susan pulled out a copy of the Fourteenth Amendment, which she read aloud as if standing in front of a classroom. The men again declined. Susan retorted, "If you still refuse us our rights as citizens, I will bring charges against you in Criminal Court and I will sue each of you personally for large exemplary damages!" Still shouldering a $10,000 debt from her newspaper days, she bluffed that she had "any amount of money" to fry them in court.[91]

The men allowed the ladies to sign up. Afterward, Susan hurried to friends' homes, encouraged them to go immediately to the barber shop to sign up, too, and ducked into the office of an afternoon newspaper for a quick interview. When an evening paper called for the registrars' arrest, Susan rushed back to the barbershop to reassure the nice young men that she would personally pay any damages they might suffer (as she later did). Eleven other women registered in Susan's ward. The next day, women across Rochester's fourteen wards signed up. Nearly fifty got onto the voter rolls.[92]

Most did not cast a ballot. The day of the election, officials allowed only fifteen women to vote, four of them the Anthony sisters, who went to the polls at sunrise as the wintry landscape glimmered awake. Excited to her fingertips, Susan dashed a note to Elizabeth Cady Stanton. "Well I have been & gone & done it!!—positively voted the Republican ticket—strait—this A.M. at 7 o'clock." She chattily poured out the details, then closed, "I hope you voted too—affectionately—Susan B. Anthony."[93]

Other women across the nation attempted to cast ballots in the race that elected Ulysses S. Grant, but registrars turned away most, including Virginia Minor, who sued for being prohibited from exercising her rights. Only one individual suffered criminal prosecution.

Two weeks after the election, an apologetic federal marshal knocked on Susan B. Anthony's door in Rochester. He blushed as he explained that a warrant had been issued for Miss Anthony and the other fourteen who had voted. Susan asked to change into a suitable outfit, whereupon the officer suggested they meet at the courthouse. She replied, "Is that the way you arrest men?" He admitted it was not, and agreed to wait when she said she would not go unless escorted like any other suspect. Once she had finished dressing, Susan presented her wrists for handcuffs. The officer declined to put them on.[94]

The district attorney interviewed her along with the other women and the three male registrars. He arrested the women under a new antifraud statute that made it a crime to knowingly vote illegally. Susan replied that they believed the Fourteenth Amendment protected their rights, so they had not intentionally broken any law. The first hearing took place in the same room once used to interrogate Black prisoners under the Fugitive Slave Act. When the examiner asked Susan if she was a woman, she conceded she was. Mocking her gender, he queried the three registrars, "Was Miss Anthony dressed in the apparel of a woman and had she the appearance of a woman?" After a second hearing, the court ordered the fifteen women to post bail while awaiting the decision of a grand jury. All did with the exception of Susan B. Anthony, who calmly courted the prospect of a cell the day after Christmas. The federal marshal sent her home even though she notified him she intended to travel to Ohio, Indiana, and Illinois.[95]

The next week, twenty male grand jurors indicted Susan B. Anthony alone for "being then and there a person of the female sex" on the day she voted. Trial preparations consumed the next five months. The court doubled her bail from five hundred to a thousand dollars. Again she refused to pay, but her attorney posted bond without telling her, loathe to "see a lady I respected put into jail." Susan tried to cancel the transaction, concerned it would impede her chances of appealing to the US Supreme Court (as it later did), but the bailiff refused.[96]

In federal cases at the time, defendants were not allowed to testify. Women were barred from all juries. In anticipation of the trial, Susan B. Anthony traveled to each of the county's twenty-nine districts, determined to reach the male jury pool. No longer the bashful speaker convinced others had more to say, she boldly mounted each soapbox to deliver her lecture, "Is It a Crime for a U.S. Citizen to Vote?"

Newspapers from California to Georgia followed her case. A few expressed admiration and even fondness. "Susan in Trouble," read one headline in faraway Idaho, predicting that any attempt to imprison "the worthy matron" would expose the government to ridicule. Another emphasized the normalcy of her appearance. "Miss Anthony was fashionably dressed in black silk with demi-train, basque with flowing sleeves, heavily trimmed in black lace; ruffled white lace undersleeves and a broad, graceful lace collar; with a gold neck chain and pendant." The reporter added that "her abundant hair was brushed back and bound in a knot after the fashion of our grandmothers." The *Worcester Daily Spy* of Massachusetts observed, "She has argued her cause so well that almost the whole male population of the county has been converted to her views on the subject."[97]

Not all felt that way. The *Rochester Union* condemned her for perverting jurors, and urged the court to imprison her. The *Daily Graphic* of New York ran a front-page cartoon that depicted a snarling Susan B. Anthony with her hand on one hip. In it, she had the effrontery to wear Uncle Sam's own hat while America went topsy-turvy. A man in the background toted a bag of groceries as he conversed with another man, who held a baby to his shoulder. In the background, women attended a political rally.

The cartoon echoed a popular meme about the hazard of role-reversals. *The Spirit of Seventy-Six* was one example. A comedy written for amateur theatricals that went into fifteen editions between 1868 and the year of Susan's trial, the play by New England socialite Ariana Curtis depicted the romantic perils of a young businessman who returns from China after a long absence to find that feminists have won the vote. Comically ignorant women with names like Badger and Wolverine pontificate on politics. Husbands soothe infants while bachelors swat away obnoxious marriage proposals. Female soldiers stick parasols in the barrels of their rifles and female ship captains run aground while chatting at the wheel. The hero is saved by marriage to a lovely young thing who finds voting tiresome.[98]

Whether Americans considered women's rights absurd or inspiring, the subject was now inescapable. The worried US attorney in Rochester had no idea what sentiment would prevail in the jury room, so he requested a change of venue, granted on a Friday, to the adjoining county. The next Monday, Susan B. Anthony started canvassing the next county over, giving twenty-one public speeches in twenty-two days.[99]

The criminal trial finally convened on June 17, 1873, a pleasantly sunny day, on the second floor of a crowded court house in Canandaigua, New York. Atop its blue dome stood Justice, wearing her blindfold. Reporters and eminent citizens filled the seats of the courtroom, along with the other fourteen rebels, and former president Millard Fillmore watched from the gallery. Ward Hunt, the newest justice on the US Supreme Court, presided over the trial. Federal practice then required that the nine federal justices periodically hear cases in the nine circuit courts scattered across the nation. The clear-eyed, clean-shaven Ward Hunt had donned his new robes only a few months earlier. He was determined not to be made a fool by Susan B. Anthony.

Henry Seldon, a former lieutenant governor, took three hours to present Susan's case. He argued that "Miss Anthony" had simply acted on "the principles upon which our government is founded, and which lie at the basis of all just government." Namely, that "every citizen has a right to take part, upon equal terms with all other citizens." US Attorney Richard Crawley followed with a two-hour rejoinder. When Crawley finished, Justice Hunt took out an opinion he had penned aforehand. "Miss Anthony knew that she was a woman," Hunt read to a surprised audience, taken aback that neither attorney's argument would figure in the ruling. Each state had a perfect right to decide who may vote, Hunt continued, and New York had not enfranchised females. The Fourteenth and Fifteenth Amendments applied only to men of color. Hunt instructed the jury to find Susan B. Anthony "guilty of the offense charged." No other verdict would be entertained.[100]

Seldon objected that the jury must be allowed to deliberate. Hunt ignored him and told the clerk to record the verdict. Seldon asked for a poll of jury members, a right guaranteed even in less serious civil trials, but the judge again refused. Not a single juror had spoken, yet the clerk duly intoned "So say you all." Ward Hunt ordered Susan B. Anthony to return for sentencing.[101]

"The prisoner will stand up," he directed the next morning, after denying Henry Seldon's motion for a new hearing since the defendant had been "denied her right to a trial by a jury." Susan B. Anthony rose, as she had in teachers' conferences, temperance meetings, and railway cars. Justice Hunt asked perfunctorily, "Has the prisoner anything to say?"[102]

"Yes, your honor, I have many things to say," she answered, her gray eyes steely. "You have trampled underfoot every vital principle of our government."

Hunt moved to cut her off. "The court can not listen to a rehearsal of the arguments the prisoner's counsel has already consumed three hours in presenting."

"May it please your honor, I am not arguing the question but simply stating the reasons why . . . ," she continued undeterred, launching into a protest of taxation without representation, heedless of the Supreme Court justice craning forward in his seat.

Justice Hunt interrupted a long sentence about "life, liberty, property, and—"

Susan must have drawn a breath because he interjected more forcefully, "The court can not allow the prisoner to go on."

"But your honor will not deny me this one and only poor privilege of protest against this high-handed outrage," she said. "May it please the court to remember that since the day of my arrest last November, this is the first time that either myself or any person of my disfranchised class has been allowed a word of defense before judge or jury—"

"The prisoner must sit down; the Court cannot allow it," Hunt repeated in vain.

Susan B. Anthony had only just started. She gave the speech of her life, reminding the jury that only a decade earlier New Yorkers had risked six months in jail to "give a cup of cold water, a crust of bread, or a night's shelter to a panting refugee as he was tracking his way to Canada." Slaves had taken their freedom. "I have taken mine," Susan declared, "and mean to take it at every possible opportunity."

"The Court must insist," Ward Hunt blustered. "The court orders the prisoner to sit down. . . . It will not allow another word . . ."

She finally concluded: "failing, even, to get a trial by jury *not* of my peers—I ask not leniency at your hands—but rather the full rigors of the law!"

Susan B. Anthony sat down in the same instant that Hunt tried, once again, to make her. He immediately ordered her back to her feet. She stood. Miss Anthony, Ward Hunt declared, would pay a hundred dollars as well as the costs of the prosecution.

She quickly launched into an extended reply. "May it please your honor, I shall never pay a dollar of your unjust penalty."[103]

She never did pay the fine nor did the court choose to come after her, perhaps to defuse the issue. The Canandaigua trial capped reformers' efforts to achieve the vote during Reconstruction.

Democratic Party newspapers welcomed the verdict in *The United States v. Susan B. Anthony* as a refreshing reiteration of states' rights "that comes to us like good news from a far country." In 1875, the Supreme Court closed the book by ruling against Virginia Minor, too, rejecting her lawsuit against the St. Louis registrar. The Fourteenth Amendment did not imply suffrage for women, the Court opined in *Minor v. Happersett.* The Republican-led federal government withdrew Union troops from the South soon thereafter in exchange for support from key Democrats over disputed presidential electoral returns in Florida, Louisiana, and South Carolina. The infamous Compromise of 1877 ended efforts to protect the rights that Congress had so recently granted to African Americans.[104]

A handful of legislators continued to tout women's suffrage as a patriotic principle, keeping the proposal alive in Congress, just barely. Senator George Hoar's minority report of 1879 observed that "a hundred years of experience" had only strengthened democracy in the popular imagination: "This people are committed to the doctrine of universal Suffrage by their constitutions, their history, and their opinion." The vote for women must come.[105]

Susan B. Anthony campaigned for Hoar, and reminded one audience that only suffrage guaranteed respect. She pointed out that newspapers ridiculed "the lady teachers [who] asked that their pay should be made two-thirds of men," but when voting bricklayers struck for better wages, "every political newspaper advocated the increase, and some went so far as to say 'hang the capitalists.'"[106]

Legislative reform wilted even as Susan B. Anthony and Lucy Stone recruited members for their rival organizations. They faced opponents who now rejected women's suffrage not because it was untimely, but because female incompetence was timeless. Historian Francis Parkman helped develop these arguments. He argued in an influential 1879 essay that history had repeatedly proven that women with power—queens, royal consorts, and empresses—had an uninterrupted record of "meanness, jealousy, and inordinate vanity." Biologically, men and women were too different for equality to apply. "Whatever liberty the best civilization may accord to women," the respected scholar wrote, "they must always be subject to restrictions." Giving the vote to irrational womankind risked democracy's future. "Agitators," Parkman warned, "shall plunge us blindfold into the most reckless of all experiments" over "trivialities."[107]

On Trial for Freedom

Elizabeth Packard did not find her experience trivial. Lithographs show her perfectly composed at every heart-wrenching moment: posture straight, expression mild, her smooth dark tresses gathered at the nape of her neck. (She flattened her hair with sugar-water paste to obscure the gray.) But her pulse must have raced as she contemplated the latest threat. Fortunately, pillars of the community whom Theophilus scorned as "intermeddlers" convinced a judge to issue a writ of habeas corpus ordering him to bring Elizabeth to nearby Kankakee, Illinois, for a jury trial in January 1864 to evaluate her sanity. Habeas corpus now applied because Theophilus had bolted the windows and doors of the home, not imprisoned his wife in an approved government institution.[108]

Two hundred ladies and gentlemen jammed the county courthouse. Two physicians testified that Elizabeth was deranged over religion, though they refused to condemn her unreservedly. A third did not shy from declaring her "hopelessly" mad. He offered as proof the fact that she thought her husband wrong. He nailed the diagnosis by adding that she was susceptible to "agglutinating the polsynthetical ectoblasts of homogeneous asceticism," prompting guffaws among Elizabeth's supporters in the audience. Theophilus's family testified as well, focusing on unseemly behavior, such as serving guests baking powder biscuits instead of proper yeast bread.[109]

In Elizabeth's defense, neighbors testified to her normalcy and denounced Theophilus's ongoing efforts to imprison her. Three doctors praised her mental health. One noted she was "possessed of a good education," adding patriotically, "I pronounce her a sane woman, and wish we had a nation of such women." Her attorney argued that a wife did not have to be crazy to want to assert her own identity. Elizabeth was smart enough to be a "strong-minded" woman, he commented, but "native modesty" had saved her from this unfeminine error. Her conduct comported "strictly with the sphere usually occupied by woman," he emphasized, knowing that jurors favored compliant wives and, if Elizabeth later sued for divorce, judges granted alimony only to women of conventional virtue.[110]

On January 18, 1864, the fifth day of the trial, a jury of twelve men deliberated seven minutes. "We, the undersigned, Jurors in the case of Mrs. Elizabeth P. W. Packard . . . are satisfied that [she] is sane," they told the judge. Alongside news on the Civil War, the Kankakee *Gazette* editorialized that the doctors who declared her mad should be made to "suffer as she suffered, endure what she has endured."[111]

The verdict reflected the growing consensus that coverture reeked of medieval England. When Illinois had passed its first Married Women's Property Act three years earlier, a Chicago newspaper had called "the legal disabilities" of married women "heirlooms of the Mother Country." It continued, "Every father who has daughters feels that they need fuller protection in the enjoyment of the obvious right of life, liberty and happiness." Seven years later, when Illinois passed an act to guarantee women their own wages, another paper editorialized, "It is time that every vestige of the feudalism of the dark ages, which went on the assumption that men's wives were their slaves, was done away with." Another editor boasted of the state's leadership on "the rights of women." Although patriotic rhetoric overshot reality, these advances reflected a substantial transformation since 1776, when William Blackstone's *Commentaries* were unquestioned. Treating women as chattel increasingly seemed un-American.[112]

In Elizabeth Packard's case, vindication unfortunately produced no solution. Theophilus still had the right to commit her if she developed "symptoms." As the trial ended, he surreptitiously packed the children's clothing, rented out their house, and vanished aboard a train for Massachusetts, leaving her alone and penniless. A note invited her to follow him, but she understood that she risked institutionalization if she did.

Elizabeth's attorney advised her that only divorce could guarantee liberty or solvency. Otherwise, "whatever is yours is his—your property is his—your earnings are his—your children are his—and you are his." The words sunk deeply. Opposed to divorce as "a Bible woman," Elizabeth Packard embarked on a quest to improve the law itself. Coverture undermined family, she believed. Married women's lack of rights gave them no choice but secession if husbands abused them, and "secession is death to the Union—death to the principles of love and harmony which ought to bind the parts in one sacred whole."[113]

She began by publishing the book she had written. Walking door to door in Chicago to elicit subscriptions, she raised enough money to self-publish. The first edition sold six thousand copies. She used the proceeds to follow her husband to Massachusetts, where she campaigned for a "Personal Liberty Bill" to guarantee all mental patients access to the US postal system and the right to a psychiatric evaluation. Massachusetts amended its laws, and Elizabeth left to lobby other states. She continued publishing, and in time was reunited with her children, who never stopped believing in her sanity.

Over the next three decades, Elizabeth Packard waged campaigns in eleven states. In each capital she arranged appointments with leading public figures to solicit their support. Next she hired an attorney to draft a bill she convinced a lawmaker to introduce. Then she personally cornered every state legislator. She helped pass thirty-four bills nationwide. A Maine newspaper called her "the most successful lobbyist" of the session and reported that "her eloquence took the legislature by storm." The new statutes became known collectively as "Packard Laws." Historians credit Elizabeth Packard with initiating the movement to safeguard patients' rights.[114]

Illinois was one such state. There she consulted with a judge married to Myra Bradwell, who became famous when the US Supreme Court rejected her complaint against a law prohibiting women from becoming attorneys (*Bradwell v. Illinois,* 1873). With the help of James Bradwell, Elizabeth Packard persuaded the legislature to require mental institutions to grant female patients the same rights as male patients. A state committee investigated the Jacksonville asylum and identified eighteen staff members who had abused inmates, including one who testified that she had been taught "how long it was safe" to force patients' heads under water. McFarland resigned.[115]

Abraham Lincoln's widow was one beneficiary. When Mary Todd Lincoln's eldest son committed her to a private asylum in 1875, the depressed former First Lady used the Packard law of Illinois to defend her right to correspond with attorneys. None other than Andrew McFarland, now in private practice, lobbied for Mrs. Lincoln's continued institutionalization, but lawyers helped restore her liberty, enabling the former First Lady to live out her life at home. Securing mental patients' First Amendment right to correspondence with attorneys was Elizabeth Packard's tribute to the late president and his wife.[116]

Unlike Susan B. Anthony, Elizabeth Packard did not try to organize women. Instead, she organized men by warming cold Lockean arguments on the hearth of True Womanhood. "Let married women's inalienable rights be protected by the laws of our country," she urged. Legislators found her appeal to their manly benevolence irresistible.[117]

She pleaded indifference to women's suffrage. Men's protective instincts gave "more assurance of success in presenting these claims to a man legislature than to a woman legislature," she wrote in 1873. She looked for moments in private conversation when "manliness became . . . quickened into action." In Iowa she arrived just as local suffragists lost a bill. Politicians warned Elizabeth that they found feminists boring. They had been "button-holed already by the women longer than our patience can bear." She listened graciously, then moved legislators to tears with her emotional story. The men apologized for lumping her with ugly suffragists. Her "sensible" bill passed the Iowa assembly 78 to 1, and its senate 32 to 16.[118]

Elizabeth Packard presented herself as a conventional woman even while arguing for reforms that diminished gender inequality. To avoid impropriety, she declined "to go upon the platform as a public speaker," and held herself apart from other feminists. Unlike Susan B. Anthony, who believed women should "take" their freedom, Elizabeth Packard considered a demure request more effective. "We women are entirely dependent on your manliness for the enactment of laws for our protection," she assured legislators.[119]

Although the duo never met, they disagreed fundamentally on strategy. Women could not resort to arms to obtain their rights, as men did. They had to rely on persuasion since no "army" of women would ever take up guns. Consequently, activists often became divided over which tack would best convince brothers, fathers, husbands, and sons. Susan's bluntness alienated many, yet her arguments rested on the patriotic guarantees of the Declaration of Independence, which enhanced their durability. Elizabeth's personal charm, by contrast, involved deploying tropes of male generosity that were part of the problem. The approach flopped with her own husband and Dr. McFarland, but succeeded with legislators.

Gains won through sympathy were fleeting. Not every woman appeared equally deserving. Elizabeth soon discovered that laws required unbiased enforcement, but this was difficult to achieve. Elected officials responded to lobbyists. Jurists empowered for life and doctors ensconced in asylums interpreted new statutes conservatively. One group of trustees told her that they were simply waiting for the next crop of legislators to repeal her foolish law. Four years before her death in 1893, the Illinois legislature did precisely that. In following decades, some professional psychiatrists suggested that she was probably crazy after all.[120]

During the last quarter of the nineteenth century, the US Supreme Court gutted the three Reconstruction amendments in a series of interpretations that ranked states' rights above federal law, including *Minor v. Happersett, Bradwell v. Illinois,* and *The United States v. Susan B. Anthony.* In 1876, the Court held in *US v. Cruikshank* that only states could restrain private groups such as the Ku Klux Klan. Six years later, in the Civil Rights Cases of 1883, the Court ruled that federal authorities could not forbid segregation in private facilities. In *Plessy v. Ferguson,* in 1896, the Court allowed states to extend segregation to public facilities, including those related to transportation. At each turn, justices defined the Fourteenth and Fifteenth Amendments ever more narrowly, until they protected Blacks (and women) hardly at all. John Marshall Harlan was the lone dissenter, pointing out that such rulings undermined the victories achieved by the nation's deadliest war.[121]

The Packard Laws granting female patients the same due process as male patients never reached the Supreme Court. No one challenged their constitutionality. Had they, there is no reason to assume that the Court would have decided the Fourteenth Amendment applied to women. In most circumstances, the courts decided that women were a special case. Solving that problem would fall to a later generation.

+++

SUSAN B. ANTHONY FOCUSED on paying down her $10,000 debt after her conviction, while helping doomed state campaigns for women's suffrage. She kept the lights burning at annual meetings in Washington, spoke to Black and white audiences, and earned money by giving talks. Lecturers became popular after the Civil War on what was called the Chautauqua circuit—uncoordinated community lectures inspired by a utopian educational movement that sprang from a tiny, gingerbread town in upstate New York. Attitudes shifted. Once objects of "ridicule & scorn," suffragists could now earn a living by traveling and speaking, Susan wrote with amazement to a friend in 1871, especially when they were attractive and articulate.[122]

As she entered old age, Susan did not possess the first advantage, but she did have the second. Notoriety mellowed into celebrity. Newspapers pronounced her a "brave lady." Tickled audiences found the legendary Quaker "as young, enthusiastic, and impractical as she was thirty years ago." Journalists lavished praise when she honorably retired her debt. Journalist Mary Clemmer, a Washington insider, spoke of the guilt that Susan B. Anthony inspired in those who had benefited from reform without shouldering its burdens. Clemmer found her "sarcastic, funny and unconventional." Her jaw had "the resolute grip it would naturally get in a lifelong tussle to have its own way," and her large gray eyes "look straight at you." She possessed "no end of common sense, and lots of keen wit," but she was also "as affectionate and simple-minded as a child; a brave, noble woman, who has given her whole life to her highest convictions." Mary Clemmer admitted, "I like to look upon her at a safe and silent distance, where she cannot turn and rend me for my silence on 'the cause.'"[123]

In 1890, the daughters of Lucy Stone and Elizabeth Cady Stanton negotiated a merger of the organizations their mothers had started. Susan B. Anthony became president in 1892 of the combined National American Woman Suffrage Association (NAWSA). By then, numerous other nations had developed their own suffrage campaigns as representative government spread. Awestruck well-wishers greeted Susan warmly when she first crossed the Atlantic in 1883, and embraced her call for a coalition. In 1888, she organized the first meeting of the International Council of Women in Washington, DC. In 1899, Queen Victoria invited Susan B. Anthony to tea. British suffragist Emmeline Pankhurst was moved to civil disobedience as she contemplated "with sorrow and indignation that such a splendid worker for humanity was destined to die without seeing the hopes of her lifetime realised." Elizabeth Cady Stanton wrote, "From being the most ridiculed and mercilessly persecuted woman, Miss Anthony has become the most honored and respected in the nation."[124]

In 1904, the White House gave the eighty-four-year-old a reception. Susan took the prerogative of an elderly woman to lay a hand on Theodore Roosevelt's sleeve and ask him to support a federal amendment. "It is almost the last request I shall ever make of anybody," she cajoled. The dashing Republican half her age promised nothing. Two years later, she died at home in Rochester.[125]

When President Woodrow Wilson honored survivors of the Blue and the Gray in 1913, in a nostalgic reunion financed by the US Congress, slavery went unmentioned as the cause of the conflagration. Black veterans, who had composed 10 percent of Union soldiers, were not invited. Just as women's dreams had been bartered away for racial progress, civil rights had been bartered away for reconciliation between North and South. White men's valiant contributions to Emancipation would be long celebrated, but those of Black men and women of both races long ignored.[126]

Through lobbying, feminists had helped free four million enslaved Americans, improved rights for mental patients, and introduced proposals for women's suffrage in state assemblies nationwide. They had also learned the price of entangling their demands with other issues. What they had not done was win the vote. In the words of Elizabeth Cady Stanton's daughter, their work creaked along in "a rut worn deep and ever deeper."[127]

Whether American women would someday cast a ballot was far from certain.

CHAPTER 4

The Right to Vote

1900–1920
Mary Church Terrell and Rosa Cavalleri

By a miracle, the 19th Amendment has been ratified.

MARY CHURCH TERRELL, 1920

WORKING-CLASS WHITE MEN joined the electorate nearly unopposed, but Blacks and women fared differently, with women struggling longest for inclusion in the Constitution. When the Fifteenth Amendment came up for ratification, the country was primed to pass it. Union troops occupied the former Confederacy, and Republicans, who would benefit most, controlled the federal government. African Americans themselves were eager to secure more rights. States that had lost their seats in Congress due to insurrection had no choice but to ratify if they wanted back in the game. Passage was swift.

When it came time to vote on the Nineteenth Amendment, however, there was powerful resistance to overcome. Republicans and Democrats were trading Congress and the presidency back and forth, and neither party had much stake in women's suffrage. Southern states were determined to block any further expansion of suffrage, knowing that it would enfranchise more African Americans. And many women, North and South, opposed the vote. Obstacles to women's suffrage loomed higher than the Continental Divide.

Yet there were promising signs. Industrialization and immigration had turned many women into wage earners and some into social reformers, and both groups saw the vote as important. Between 1890 and 1900, four states granted the franchise to women. Even so, a federal amendment might not have materialized when it did but for two factors: the eruption of a world war that spurred democracy globally, and the tenacious advocacy of feminist leaders who parlayed international events to their advantage. Prominent among these leaders were Carrie Chapman Catt and Alice Paul, who stood at the helm of the two largest organizations. But it was Mary Church Terrell—dubbed "the feminine Demosthenes" after the legendary classical orator—whose personal story and career perhaps best illustrate the final battle for the Nineteenth Amendment.[1]

Mary Church Terrell built the first nationwide organization of African American women under the lengthening shadow of Jim Crow. Bridging the chasm between Black and white feminists who needed Southerners to endorse a federal amendment, she endured the sorrow of repeated stillbirths along the way. Even before this, the scholar of Greek and Latin had to decide whether America deserved her allegiance or whether, as a linguist comfortable in six countries, she should abandon a land whose moral compass appeared broken.[2]

One of millions of Italians who flocked to the nation, Rosa Cavalleri also coped with racial discrimination, as "race" was then defined. Even so, America delivered greater social equality than she had ever imagined. Spousal abuse and the suppression of information on reproduction nearly destroyed the young mother, but women who pioneered social work saved her. During these decades, the quest for women's rights took an institutional turn that went beyond the vote, and was expressed in service organizations to assist poorer Americans. In the end, Rosa Cavalleri found that becoming an American *woman* was more than just becoming an American.[3]

Historians call this the Progressive Era to describe the diverse attempts at reform, including a short-lived third party under Theodore Roosevelt known as the Progressive Party.[4] Other labels that surfaced for the first time were the "New Woman" and "Feminism," both of which conveyed, in one description of feminism, the "uncharted assertions and yearnings not expressed in palpable goals such as suffrage." This was a time when gender equality became a defining aspect of national identity. Globally, people began to think of the United States as a place that emboldened women even while it balked at giving them the vote.[5]

The Making of a New Woman

Mary Church Terrell was almost not born. Her expectant mother, normally a lighthearted soul, became so distraught that she tried to kill herself. No one knows what tipped Louisa Church of Memphis, Tennessee, toward self-destruction as her womb swelled with new life. Perhaps it was the thought of delivering a child into bondage.[6]

The Emancipation Proclamation did not apply in Tennessee when Mary drew her first breath in September 1863. Tennessee was exempt from Lincoln's punishment of states "in rebellion" because governor Andrew Johnson had thrown his support to the Union. It wasn't until two weeks before the 1864 election, when Lincoln would win a second term with the Tennessean as his new vice president, that Johnson abolished slavery by state proclamation. Mary Church Terrell never explicitly acknowledged the fact, but the timing suggests that she was enslaved the first year of her life.[7]

The notion was inconceivable to the sunny little person whose parents nicknamed her Mollie. Her mother and father, Louisa and Robert Church, did not talk about their former enslavement. Only quiet Grandmother Liza was willing to discuss the world before the Civil War.[8]

The first time that Mollie connected slavery with herself was at an elementary school in Ohio, where her parents had sent her for a better education than was available in Tennessee. She boarded with a white family who—such luck!—ran an ice cream parlor. As she was reciting a history passage with her classmates one morning, the teacher came to the Emancipation Proclamation and Mollie suddenly realized that she was the only one in the room to whom the lesson applied. Like most children, Mollie hated to stand out—she once refused to wear a velvet hat her mother sent for Christmas because no one else had one. Mortified by the lesson, she now understood that she belonged to a pariah group that had been "brutalized, degraded, and sold like animals." Slavery was not her family's fault, yet in that painful flash Mary Church experienced it as their shame.[9]

A blow that might have crippled a frailer child made Mollie stand straighter. She vowed to prove that she was the equal of anyone "whose forefathers had always been free," as she later recalled. Luckily, she excelled at school as "a sort of indoor sport." What she learned convinced her that all ancient peoples had endured oppression. God tested everyone.[10]

Her family's prosperity had previously shielded Mary Church from having to think much about the past. During Reconstruction, Louisa Church had started a hair salon on tony Courthouse Square in downtown Memphis to which white women flocked. Mollie's father, Robert, taught himself to read, opened a saloon, invested in real estate, and became the South's first Black millionaire. After the war, he resisted a lynch mob that left a bullet scar on the back of his skull, but he emphasized resilience rather than vulnerability to the child. With what later generations called movie-star looks, Robert Church mixed easily with whites. Young Mollie took it for granted that they "treated him, in general, as they did one another." When a white acquaintance challenged Robert to a horse race and lost, for example, the man paid his bet by taking Robert to dinner at a fine Memphis establishment.[11]

Robert Church did not owe this courtesy solely to his light complexion. Civility among well-to-do gentlemen flourished briefly after the war, until legislatures bent on revenge began passing the Jim Crow laws that excluded anyone with a single "drop" of so-called African blood from restaurants, schools, libraries, and railway cars. Opportunists fanned hatreds that grew hotter each decade, knocking aside Reconstruction statutes that had guaranteed access to all. Soon Southern institutions expelled even people with blue eyes and blond hair if it was discovered, in an environment of constant scrutiny, that they possessed any African heritage.

Mollie herself experienced this avalanche of hateful retaliation. In the early 1880s, she was invited to the inaugural of President James Garfield, accompanying Mississippi's Black US senator to the glittering ball at the Smithsonian. But by the late 1890s, she could not walk into her corner drugstore. She never forgot the day a Washington, DC, clerk informed her it was the last afternoon she could patronize his shop, as henceforth people of color were banned.[12]

By then, Mollie had lost the capacity for surprise. The first time a peer disparaged her race was in middle school. A gaggle of girls had clustered around a cloakroom mirror to compare attributes, praising one's student's long curls, another's rosebud mouth, a third's sparkling eyes. Pushing her arms though her coat and grabbing her hat, Mollie asked if she was pretty, too. The ringleader gave Mollie a haughty look, pointed a finger, and said, tauntingly, yes, Mollie was "pretty black."[13]

Giggles from other girls cut her to the quick. Their laughter died as she dropped her hat with nerveless fingers, "a pathetic little figure in that large room." After a tense pause, Mollie bent to pick up her headgear. Somehow, movement restored her courage. She straightened and shot back before dashing from the room, "I don't want my face to be white like yours and look like milk. I want it nice and dark just like it is."[14]

The insults of childhood smolder for years. Well into old age, Mollie cringed with embarrassment at that particular humiliation. But she also hammered the slight into a character lesson, deciding never to make fun of another person for his or her looks. Fortunately, such incidents felt rare at the schools her parents selected. The couple divorced when she was young, but remained deeply involved in raising their daughter. Louisa moved to New York where she established another salon, sending money for a German tutor in the conviction that Mollie should learn at least two foreign languages. And Robert Church paid Mollie's tuition at Oberlin College, which in the 1830s had become the first university to admit students without respect to race. Lucy Stone and Theodore Weld had been students.

In a memoir she wrote as an older woman, Mary Church Terrell asserted that during her time at Oberlin, outward expressions of "prejudice against colored students would not have been tolerated for one minute by those in authority." She may have played up the point to emphasize the contrast with later years, when Oberlin did tolerate discrimination as Jim Crow laws crowded out more humane sentiments. Yet it was also true that a spirit of equality persisted at least for a time where abolitionism once flourished, and Mollie thrived there.[15]

She had an aptitude for befriending people. Oberlin undergraduates nominated her "class poet" and selected her to represent them in literary debates. Girls pressed her to join clubs, and to sit with them in the dining hall. Mollie's instinct for fun contributed to her success. An excellent singer, guitarist, skater, swimmer, and tennis player, she especially loved to dance and did not care that snobs who wanted "to be classified as a highbrow" frowned upon it. "I would much rather dance any day or any night than eat," she said.[16]

An impressionable child when Susan B. Anthony came to fame, Mary Church supported the vote "with all my heart." At age sixteen, she penned a debate essay entitled "Resolved, There Should Be a Sixteenth Amendment to the Constitution Granting Suffrage to Women." She was a precocious example of what nineteenth-century writer Henry James dubbed the New Woman, or "girls [who] got on by themselves." More and more colleges now welcomed females, so that, by 1890, one-third of undergraduates and 17 percent of degree holders were women.[17]

As they became more numerous, women graduates exerted a subtle effect. States gradually rescinded laws that excluded them from the professions. Arabella Mansfield made history in 1869 when Iowa dropped its ban on women and licensed her, a college valedictorian, as America's first female attorney. In 1890, neighboring Illinois admitted to the bar Myra Bradwell—the woman whose appeal the Supreme Court had rejected seventeen years earlier, in 1873.[18]

Those who acted as if the pursuit of happiness was their birthright went from a vilified handful of aging "woman rights" advocates to a significant cross-section of the younger generation who thought of themselves as the trendy New Woman archetype reflected in books and magazines, including *College Girls,* a story collection published in 1894. Artist Charles Dana Gibson illustrated the book with his "Gibson girls": insouciant lasses ready to straddle a bicycle, solve a math problem, assemble a microscope, or tour the world solo, their beautiful locks famously piled high.[19]

In 1898, essayist Charlotte Perkins Gilman expressed the New Woman's instinctive rejection of patriarchal limits when she criticized traditionalists for allowing a girl only one way to succeed in life. "Wealth, power, social distinction, fame—not only these, but home and happiness, reputation, ease and pleasure, her bread and butter—all, must come to her through a small gold ring."[20]

Not so for Mary Church. She walked through every door that Oberlin opened. Many students still opted for the two-year "ladies" certificate instead of the four-year degree program recommended for men, but Mollie took the longer road. She enrolled as the only woman in a class of forty men studying classical languages. Friends warned that she would ruin her chances of finding a husband, because bachelors notoriously disliked women who knew more than they did. And "where," they asked, "will you find a colored man who has studied Greek?"[21]

Mollie preferred spinsterhood to a husband who wanted a sycophant. Had she been less youthful, brilliant, wealthy, or pretty, she might have felt differently. Yet other young Black women took similar stands, including one Lucia Knotts of Texas A&M Prairie View, a student who spurned her suitor until he dropped his demand that she quit college. Mollie Church became one of the "new educated women whose professional training was on a par with that of her male colleagues," in the words of one historian. Faculty supported her ambitions even when they could not shield her as a person of color. An admiring professor asked her to recite the *Iliad* for a distinguished guest, whereupon the visitor "expressed the greatest surprise imaginable, because, he said, he had thought the tongue of the African too thick to pronounce Greek correctly."[22]

Mollie graduated just as opportunities for women and previously enslaved Americans headed in opposite directions. She experienced this when classmates compared summer jobs available to coeds. Mollie thought "it would be a fine thing then to earn money with a lot of leisure on my hands." Three employers invited her to interview. All three cooled once they met her.[23]

Mollie described herself as moderately "swarthy." Northerners sometimes had to squint to determine her race. When one interviewer probed her about her "nationality," a euphemism for race, and she answered, "I am a colored girl," the employer appeared more shocked than if "I had told her I was a gorilla in human form." The interviewer admitted that she had never met an educated Black woman and "didn't know there were any in the world." All three employers told Mollie they could not hire her, for fear that other staff would quit to avoid the stain of association.[24]

During Mary Church's youth, orgies of violence terrorized Black communities and deepened white cowardice. Gory public spectacles became increasingly common. In 1892, a thousand witnesses watched a man burn at the stake in Texarkana. A month later, Mollie's childhood playmate Tom Moss, who offended a white grocer by starting a more successful store across the street, was tortured by a Memphis mob. The next year, ten thousand Texans watched another man burn alive. Between 1880 and 1940, public mobs murdered approximately 3,200 Black people. In 1901, the

United Daughters of the Confederacy commissioned a bronze statue of Nathan Bedford Forrest, founder of the Ku Klux Klan, for a park in Memphis. It gazed sternly down on strolling families until it was removed from display in 2017.[25]

When she completed her bachelor's degree, Mollie sought jobs in Black schools. But now gender presented an obstacle, raised by her own family. It turned out that her father expected his very own Southern belle to ornament the family's three-story mansion until she married. But "said daughter," Mollie noted, had imbibed the "Yankee's respect for work." Torn between the most important man in her life and her longing to join the wider world, she nervously accepted a teaching position at Ohio's Wilberforce University and left without telling him.[26]

Robert sent his daughter a single blistering letter and refused to answer any of hers. After a year, Mollie anxiously telegraphed that she would arrive home at dawn by train. When the locomotive puffed into Memphis, she stepped off the passenger car and onto the dim platform. Robert Church took his adored daughter into his arms. Gender expectations be damned.[27]

Mollie accepted a better position in Washington, DC, at a famed Black preparatory school established by Congress in 1870, the year that the Fifteenth Amendment had passed. There she taught classics alone rather than the jumble of subjects required at tiny Wilberforce. Her supervisor was one of the capital's most impressive young bachelors. Robert Terrell had waited tables at Harvard before becoming a student, graduating cum laude as the university's first African American valedictorian. Born into slavery and now head of a Latin department, he happened to admire young ladies who spoke Greek. They dated discreetly, but word got around. Robert Terrell's attentions were obvious enough that high-schoolers mischievously scrawled on the chalkboard, "Mr. Terrell . . . used to go to dances, but now he goes to Church."[28]

The New Woman was not ready to settle down, however. When Mollie's father offered her a chance to study abroad, she requested a leave of absence. From 1888 to 1890, she traveled through France, Switzerland, Germany, England, and Italy, becoming fluent in three additional languages while earning a master's degree through Oberlin. She experienced the euphoria of anyone who, formerly ostracized, finds herself feted.

Mary Church tasted the joy of not thinking about color. Opera houses, museums, pastry shops, fine restaurants, elite academies, and private homes opened their doors. Men bewitched by her erudition and beauty courted her. Friends in high school had teased that she "always had a boy tied to her apron strings," but now boys were serious. Three proposed marriage, one of them a baron who asked Robert Church for her hand.[29]

American tourists whom Mollie encountered sometimes tried to rile hotelkeepers against her, reporting that only "cranks" associated with Blacks back home. Europeans were astonished. One suggested that reports must be exaggerated because no "human being could object to another solely on account of the color of his skin." Mollie appreciated their dismay, though she noted that Europeans were not without prejudice, particularly against Jews. She also witnessed antipathy toward American girls—judged as too bold—and proudly told acquaintances about women's educational advantages in the United States. As a Black person, however, she could only confirm the disturbing rumors.[30]

She began to think about leaving behind the "humiliations, discriminations, and hardships" for a better life. Why not emigrate permanently to a more liberal country? Robert Terrell sent beguiling letters, but she had promised him nothing. Mollie found herself ruminating on the possibility as she strolled through Berlin one day. Then a flash of color caught her eye, and she looked up, startled to see the American flag snapping in the breeze. She had happened upon the US consulate.

A lump rose in her throat upon seeing the familiar red, white, and blue so far from her native shore. "Truly this is patriotism, and I am patriotic, after all," she thought as she blinked back tears, feeling both hurt and nostalgic. Racists had trampled the Fourteenth and Fifteenth Amendments. They had persecuted good people who had worked, fought, and died for the nation. They should not win.

"It is my country," Mary Church proclaimed aloud to the elegant German street as a sense of purpose overtook her. "I have a perfect right to love it and I will." She would go home.[31]

The Making of an Italian American

During the late nineteenth century, porous national borders turned the United States into a nation of immigrants, as steamships transported poorer Europeans to American cities and American innovations back to Old World villages. Rosa Cavalleri of Lombardy learned that the United States was a place that changed people. Paesani who returned were not as cowed as everyone else. "Those poor men from the village who go to America, they get smart," observed the women left behind. "They're not so afraid anymore."[32]

Rosa had little interest in abstract rights like the vote, but she was fascinated from afar by American opportunities and culture. In a memoir she later dictated to a Chicago reformer, she remarked that those Italians who returned from the United States no longer shied at inexplicable lightning storms, ghosts in dark cemeteries, poisonous night air, or the evil eye. They could read, count, and explain the natural phenomena that terrified villagers. Accustomed to a land where "all men were free and equal," they no longer feared "high people," shorthand for the rich. Rosa even heard that in America "the high people teach the poor people not to be afraid" instead of exploiting their timidity. "That's what America does for the poor," the old women of the village said. It set Rosa to wishing she might see America, too.[33]

Not that she could. Someone had deposited Rosa on a small turnstile cut into the wall of an orphanage on the day of her birth, turned the crank, and dropped her into a basket on the other side just like thousands before her. Since then, foster parents had made decisions for her. Eventually, a husband would choose where she lived. The world followed a strict order. "The boy and the girl, they were like the rich and the poor together," Rosa later recounted, "like the man and the woman, like the North Italian and the South Italian—the boy was so much higher than the girl."[34]

God had designed this hierarchy, just as he had ordained her arrival with a tag around the neck that read "Inez" at the orphanage in Milan, capital of Lombardy, in 1866 or 1867. No one could tell her which year, so she never learned her exact age. Fortunately, she had an omnipotent ally, Rosa believed, having arrived at the orphanage on the Purificazione di Maria, the day that Mary was made "clean" after the birth of Jesus.

Before baby Inez was big enough to press her palms in prayer, the Madonna appeared to intercede on her behalf: first when the newborn did not crack her head falling into the basket, then when a lactating mother who had lost her own baby accepted payment in exchange for milk, then again when a lonely old woman took the infant from the wet nurse after the milk ran dry, then when a barren wife agreed to adopt the busy toddler from the tired old woman in order to curry the Madonna's favor. This woman,

Inez's fourth and final mother, renamed the three-year-old "Rosa" after another orphan she once fostered. Mamma Lena and her husband lived in a tiny village eighteen miles outside Milan. They had just enough food for one more mouth.

The girl considered herself lucky. She had been blessed with a temperament that was affectionate enough, and face sweet enough, to melt hearts. Quick wits and hard work also helped. At five, Rosa raised silkworms. At six, Mamma Lena sent her to the local silk factory, where she proved so adept at tending the seventeen giant spools above her head that the supervisor hardly ever hit her.

Only once did the manager punch Rosa so hard that she stumbled and caught her braid in the rubber belt that drove the clanking machine. The belt whisked the child off her feet, yanking her by the hair toward the hungry gears. Again the Madonna intervened. In one lightning-fast rotation the machine miraculously spun her clear, unlike girls from whom it had stolen fingers or hands. "Sure it was the Madonna!" Rosa later said. "The Madonna is the best friend I have!" The Virgin guarded her even during sleep, Rosa believed, sparing her while she slumbered next to Mamma Lena's niece, who wasted away from the same tuberculosis that had slain her seven siblings.[35]

Rosa survived circumstances that drove millions of Italian men across the Atlantic: between 1890 and 1910, approximately 80 percent of Italian immigrants to the United States were male. Women typically stayed behind to care for the young, while men sent wages back. Children, too, earned pennies to help their families survive. Rosa's eight cents a week from her full-time job at the factory paid for the family's salt. America intrigued Rosa, but she was needed at home and could never have immigrated unless ordered to do so. Parents and husbands expected obedience.[36]

They valued ignorance, too. Rosa learned to read and write only a few words. Knowledge of reproduction was particularly forbidden. Rosa thought little about her body until a nun chastised her for maturing too quickly. "You're not eleven years old and you have such big breasts. . . . It's not nice—it's not modest," the nun told her. Rosa had never thought about her breasts, but now they made her ashamed as the nun took measurements for a gray dress to cover them.[37]

Another nun taught Rosa and her friends that Jesus had not been born from the sin between a man and woman. Rosa wondered what that sin could be, but was lectured that "Only the husband can tell a girl those things," and "A girl is not allowed to know until she is married." Such statements prompted Rosa to volunteer for the convent, but the nuns turned her down. Rosa's father was unknown. He might be a thief or worse. Her biological mother, Mamma Lena had discovered, was an actress, which everyone considered akin to a prostitute.[38]

Mamma Lena decided that Rosa should marry young. The girl liked to hug far too much in her estimation, and Mamma Lena told Rosa that she needed "an older man to make you meek and save you for heaven in the end." Mamma Lena chose Santino, a suspicious, taciturn man whom Rosa despised. She refused him, but Mamma Lena beat Rosa and withheld food until she capitulated. Even so, no one would tell Rosa what the husband "does to the woman when he has the matrimony with her." The deaf village priest failed to notice that Rosa did not answer "yes" during the nuptials.[39]

Beyond the secrets that Santino revealed on Rosa's wedding night, his behavior in subsequent months did not surprise her. He beat her mercilessly. Rosa already knew that husbands punished wives for infractions. A neighbor once paid the village doctor double the usual price to treat his wife's broken arm so he would not have to worry about the money when he broke the other. "The woman is made to be the servant of man," Mamma Lena's sister explained. "The man is the man and the woman must obey him, that's all." One time, Santino became so violent that Mamma Lena felt he might kill Rosa, and she pulled him off. Soon thereafter, a recruiter from America persuaded Santino to join a group leaving for the Missouri coal mines.[40]

A couple of months later, an eerie fluttering in Rosa's belly let her know she must be pregnant, though how "that baby got in there I couldn't understand." Nor would anyone tell her how it would get out. Would the baby burrow through her stomach like a silkworm emerging from the cocoon? Rosa prayed before bed each night that she would simply find it next to her in the morning. Labor failed to enlighten her. Because of Rosa's youth, doctors said, the fourteen- (or fifteen-) year-old nearly died as her body struggled for three days to give birth. She fainted repeatedly. When Rosa regained consciousness, the infant lay magically beside her.[41]

A year later, in 1884, she received a summons in the form of a boat ticket. Santino wanted her to come to Missouri. More than a half million

Italians would pour into the United States that year alone. The prospect of seeing Santino frightened Rosa, but Mamma Lena reminded her that even a bad husband had "the right to command." She ordered Rosa to leave the one-year-old boy with her and go to America.[42]

It may have been simple for Mamma Lena to endorse patriarchal traditions because her own life was not ruled by them. Her father had died young, so she had been at liberty to choose her husband. Considered a saint by the neighborhood women, he alone of the village men did not beat his wife. Ignorance of reproduction, too, did not affect her, since she adopted the offspring of other women.

Rosa reluctantly complied. When the day came to give away her precious baby, she pressed her lips to his fragrant hair, soft cheeks, and brown eyes, desperate to leave the imprint of her love. The village women comforted Rosa as Mamma Lena reached for the toddler. "You will get smart in America," they promised, "you will not be so poor."[43]

Whether Rosa would actually improve her financial situation was debatable, but it was certainly true that in America, she became smarter. There Rosa learned that a woman might say no.

One of "Our Own" in National Leadership

Twenty-eight-year-old Mary Church wanted Robert Terrell to know she would stand up for women's suffrage. The two dated after her return from Europe, and she felt his reaction would be a good test of their compatibility. Mollie attended her first national women's rights convocation in February 1891. Susan B. Anthony had organized the event, drawing together diverse organizations to form a National Council of Women. Some endorsed suffrage, but most had a different focus, including the Baptist Home Mission, Farmers' Alliance, National Christian League for the Promotion of Social Purity, and Woman's Christian Temperance Union.

Representatives met at Albaugh's Grand Opera House, a gaudy brick pile that was then Washington's largest theater. One speaker to whom Mollie may have paid particular attention was poet Frances Harper, the Black feminist who urged attendees to oppose the "fraud" disfranchising freed Southerners. Former Confederate states had largely voided the Fifteenth Amendment by layering on discriminatory poll taxes and literacy requirements that disqualified Black voters unable to explain the finer points of the state constitution to the satisfaction of hostile white registrars.[44]

As the meeting came to an end, a moderator asked anyone in favor of women's suffrage to stand. Rows of cautious faces gazed up at the speaker. Mary Church felt the audience stir uncomfortably. Most still hesitated to confess to such views even with old "Miss Anthony" gazing encouragingly over her wire-rimmed spectacles. Some may have wished to avoid implicating their organizations. A few ladies finally rose, including Mollie. "In the early 1890s it required a great deal of courage," she later reflected, "for a woman publicly to acknowledge before an audience that she believed in suffrage for her sex when she knew the majority did not."[45]

Robert Terrell, known as Berto, laughed when Mollie recounted the story. He teased his sweetheart that she had gone and done it this time, ruining her chances of finding a husband. Mollie may have slapped his hand—she certainly smiled—when she replied that she would "never be silly enough to marry a man who did not believe a woman had a right to administer the affairs of the Government under which she lived." Berto Terrell loved her precisely for her feisty integrity. Nothing amused him more than to watch a woman deflate the ego of some "narrow-minded, conceited, young coxcomb" who opposed the female vote. Berto chuckled and nudged Mollie at such moments. "There won't be a greasespot left, when she gets through with him," he liked to say. In Robert Terrell, the New Woman had found her New Man.[46]

The couple wed in October 1891. Forced to resign her teaching position upon her marriage, Mollie took up housekeeping, a decided challenge for a newlywed whose kitchen mishaps mimicked vaudeville. (She excelled at turning them into funny stories.) She also gave up a rare opportunity when Oberlin College offered her the position of registrar, which would have made her the highest-ranking Black official at any white university in the nation.

Mary Church Terrell could have either a job or a husband, but not both. Faced with this choice, half of the women who graduated from college in her generation never married. Mollie chose Berto, who showed his appreciation by encouraging her to lecture at the Bethel Literary Club, a rarified Black social club normally regaled by male luminaries, on "The Ethics of Woman Suffrage." Minutes do not survive, but the title suggests she argued that American values required full citizenship for women.[47]

Berto had meanwhile taken an administrative job with the Treasury Department under Republican president Benjamin Harrison and become a lawyer. He urged Mollie to explore other opportunities for self-fulfillment. Their mutual friend Lewis Douglass, son of Frederick Douglass, also chided her for wasting a university education on making slipcovers. He told her it would be a "big mistake" to forgo the public role for which she had been trained.[48]

Mollie was eager to start having children and soon conceived. In her third trimester, big with her first baby but still thinking about what she had witnessed at the National Council of Women, she joined a small group of Washington activists to start the Colored Women's League in June 1892. There were then no large coordinating bodies in the Black community, aside from church organizations, and this put the women at the forefront of a new trend. The Colored Women's League set up a host of local services, including a preschool, kindergarten, and penny savings bank. They invited women's groups from Nebraska to Rhode Island to become affiliates, determined to unite Black women nationwide.[49]

The Colored Women's League was an expression of Progressivism, the sprawling reform movement that attracted everyone from capitalists to socialists, suffragists to anti-suffragists, defenders of racial equality to advocates of Jim Crow. Ambitious Black women busied themselves in their corner of this big tent. Known for her own accomplishments as well as her husband's, Mary Church Terrell became a spokesperson. In 1893, she penned the first article on the Colored Women's League in *Ringwood's,* a journal of African American fashion.[50]

Married less than a year, Mollie was by then nursing a private sorrow instead of a child. Her pregnancy had triggered nephritis, which brought her to the brink of kidney failure, and she had aborted spontaneously. Berto had rushed his bleeding wife to the hospital, where she delivered a stillborn boy and fought for survival herself: the doctors warned Berto that she might not live and he telegraphed her parents, who took the first trains from Memphis and New York. Slowly, Mollie recovered. She and Berto grew closer as they consulted specialists in New York to see if they could attempt another pregnancy or must give up on having a child. For couples in this era without reliable birth control, avoiding child-bearing often meant terminating their sexual relationship. Fortunately for the Terrells, they were advised to try again.[51]

The loss of a child deepened Mollie's sense of urgency about reform. Consumed with grief, she happened one day upon a white friend in the street who offered condolences but wondered aloud "how any colored woman can make up her mind to become a mother," knowing the injustices the innocent child would face. Molly took no offense, but the blunt comment reminded her that her childhood friend Tom Moss had been slain during her second trimester. Tom had attended Mollie's wedding at her father's Memphis mansion, and she wondered if the shock she had felt at his murder had blighted the pregnancy.[52]

Mollie stepped up her involvement in anti-lynching activities. In addition to writing and speaking, she introduced journalist Ida B. Wells to Washington audiences. Wells also hailed from Memphis, and she mourned the death of Tom Moss, too. Wells's pioneering 1893 pamphlet, *Southern Horrors: Lynch Law in All Its Phases,* brought American crimes to international attention. The two women, born only a year apart, became friends.[53]

Mary Church Terrell remained committed to the Colored Women's League, which in 1894 was invited by Susan B. Anthony's organization to send delegates if the group could prove it constituted a national body. This welcoming gesture spurred the league to ask affiliates in other states to elect officers for a board. Meanwhile, in Boston, another group started its own national coalition in July 1895 under the leadership of newspaper publisher Josephine St. Pierre Ruffin. Suddenly, a Black women's movement appeared ready to take off, though possibly under competing organizations.

Ruffin's group used an international incident to attract support. A Missouri newspaperman named John Jacks had sent a letter to London's Anti-Lynching Committee, touting himself as a distinguished son of the South who knew the real story about "the 'downtrodden' race to which you seem so devoted." He advanced the lie that lynching was simply white men's chivalrous response to Black men's sexual assaults. Jacks told British reformers that, with rare exceptions, Black men were "wholly devoid of morality" and their wives were "natural liars and thieves."[54]

John Jacks's letter, whose contents were immediately publicized by the London group, provoked outrage. Men like him had long excused sexual predation by saying that Black women wanted it, and now they justified the murder of Black men as frontier-style justice even though most victims, men like Tom Moss, were never even accused of assault. Women and young children could be targets, too.

Aware that suffragists had split into two organizations after the Civil War, Ruffin's Boston coalition agreed to discuss a merger with the Colored Women's League, located in the nation's capital. Mary Church Terrell, the wife of a rare Black federal official and, according to Ida Wells, "the most highly educated woman we had in the race," was invited to the Boston meeting, but was unable to attend as she was again pregnant and was following a strict health regimen. Five months along, she followed events from home. She nonetheless honored a previous commitment when in the spring of 1895 she, along with a white woman, took her seat on the Washington, DC, Board of Education.[55]

Suffragists had long pressed for the inclusion of women on the school board. "For the first time since the government was founded," the *Washington Times* enthused, "the gentler sex is to be represented." One was to be white, the other Black. An article reprinted nationwide complimented both "well groomed" ladies for exhibiting none of the "eccentricities" of those women's rights advocates who allowed "domestic arrangements" to suffer.[56]

Newspapers praised Mollie particularly for not having sought "the friendship of any except her own race" when she attended Oberlin College—meaning, in the racist mindset of Jim Crow, that she had not imposed herself on whites (though in truth she had made many white friends). The first Black woman to serve on a school board anywhere, she now found herself dealing with parents of all backgrounds day and night. The only educator on the panel, she proved such an effective advocate that she was asked to serve two terms.[57]

Mary Church Terrell welcomed the work. It distracted her from the newest wound in her heart when, after a nine-month gestation, she delivered a second stillborn son. Again she was devastated. To lose a child at life's door was excruciating. She reminded herself that other mothers "have passed through this Gethsemane," and forced herself to carry on despite a crippling sorrow.[58]

The women's leagues from Boston and Washington finally met in the District of Columbia in 1896 to discuss combining their efforts. The setting was auspicious. Reverend Francis Grimké, Angelina Grimké's elderly nephew, gave his benediction at the historic Nineteenth Street Baptist

Church, the oldest Black congregation in the District, which was festooned with garlands for the occasion. Ladies waved white handkerchiefs in the "Chautauqua Salute" when military veteran Harriet Tubman took the stage to recount her service in the Civil War. The two coalitions could hardly have chosen a more unifying figure than "Mother Tubman" to bring them together.[59]

Margaret Washington, wife of Booker T. Washington (founder of the legendary Tuskegee Institute), called the sessions to order. Black women predominated, but interested whites attended, too. Delegates from eleven states and the District of Columbia selected a negotiating team to forge the merger. After a day-long parley on a rainy Tuesday, they elected Mary Church Terrell president of the combined federation, which was renamed the National Association of Colored Women. Mindful of the attacks on Black women's character, they had chosen someone who epitomized respectability with her polished manners, European education, and elite family.[60]

Yet Mollie owed others' trust principally to her ability to build bridges between different groups of people. Regional, economic, and philosophical rivalries divided Black women as they divided all others. She may have been the only attendee as comfortable in Boston as Berlin, as familiar with the North as the South, as easy with whites as with women of color. Superb diplomatic skills gave her an advantage over activists perceived as more abrasive, including Ida Wells (Wells-Barnett after her marriage).

When some delegates at the closing session complained that a Bostonian should have been selected instead of a Washingtonian, she listened patiently. Then, revealing her mettle, Mary Church Terrell reproved the dissidents "in language as classic as the vestal goddesses and with the eloquence of the sirens," according to a delighted reporter from the *Washington Bee*. She pointed out that backbiting hardly evinced "Christian charity." She asked, "Does this look like you want harmony?" The church erupted in grateful applause. Another reporter commented, "Mrs. Terrell knew her business and gave them all to understand it."[61]

Journalists declined to mention that she was in the second trimester of her third pregnancy. She and Berto were anxiously awaiting their baby's arrival. Four months later, Mollie delivered a full-term baby boy.

Black patients typically received treatment in segregated hospitals or segregated wings with substandard resources. Infant mortality was high everywhere in America. In 1900, about 16 percent of newborns died in the United States overall, and in crowded cities nearly one in four perished. The segregated hospital to which Berto brought Mollie had no incubator. Nestled in a makeshift device, the baby fought for life for two days after birth. Without medical records it is difficult to know whether he was inherently doomed or a casualty of inadequate care. Regardless, she later recalled that "every young thing stabbed my heart" after he died.[62]

Again Mary Church Terrell picked up the pieces. She served three terms as president of the National Association of Colored Women, competing with such distinguished candidates as Margaret Washington, Josephine St. Pierre Ruffin, and Ida Wells-Barnett, none of whom came close to winning the same number of votes. Unlike white women's organizations, which enjoyed an advantage in size and tended to specialize, the National Association of Colored Women felt impelled to address every issue. Affiliate clubs ran night schools, day nurseries, orphanages, old-age homes, and industrial training programs. They protested Jim Crow laws, advocated for enforcement of the Constitution, and encouraged women to pursue professional degrees.

As president, Mollie raised money for free kindergartens by writing a pamphlet on "The Progress of Colored Women." Each club, she implored, must "do for the little strays of the alleys what is not done by their mothers, who in many instances fall short of their duty, not because they are vicious and depraved, but because they are ignorant and poor." She reminded those women affluent enough to stay home of their responsibility to help, not judge, working mothers, consistent with the organization's motto, "Lifting as We Climb." In 1897, the organization had eighty-six affiliates. At its second convention in Chicago in 1899, representatives from two hundred affiliates joined three thousand spectators for a three-day marathon covering topics that ranged from prison reform to "the necessity of an equal moral standard for men and women."[63]

Chicago newspapers gushed with praise. "Of all the conventions that have met in this country this summer," a reporter for the *Chicago Daily News* declared, "there is none that has taken the business in hand with more good sense and judgment than the National Association of Colored Women." When Mollie's third term ended in 1901, she could look with pride on an organization that united Black women across the nation. They voted her honorary president for life. By 1924, the group had almost a hundred thousand members.[64]

During these same years, Mary Church Terrell was simultaneously connecting with white women. She believed that enduring progress could be achieved only through interracial cooperation. In February 1899, she signed up the National Association of Colored Women as a member of Susan B. Anthony's National Council of Women, at which she had stood anonymously only eight years earlier. That same summer, she accepted an invitation from Jane Addams to visit Hull House in Chicago.

Hull House was the pioneer settlement house in America, a new type of service organization on the vanguard of a movement to help the poor. The flood of immigrants, crowded into shabby housing and working for low wages in the cities, had raised awareness of the need for some kind of social safety net. Mollie and other officers of the National Association of Colored Women toured Hull House, "evincing great interest in every department," according to a reporter from the *Chicago Times-Herald.*[65]

The most remarkable moment came when the ladies placed napkins in their laps and tucked into lunch. Across much of the nation, Jim Crow customs forbade such simple things as people of different races sharing a meal. "The color line was given another good rub yesterday," the reporter noted, reflecting the liberal outlook of some Northern papers. Jane Addams and Mary Church Terrell later became colleagues on the boards of the National Association for the Advancement of Colored People (NAACP) in 1909, and the Women's International League for Peace and Freedom in 1915.[66]

By then, Mary Church Terrell was a household name in her own community and the nation's most prominent Black feminist. While she held to a pragmatic middle way, and did not press her organization to endorse suffrage until after her term ended, she nonetheless embodied the New Woman. Margaret Washington spoke for a more conservative set of African Americans when she contrasted Black women's hope for "status in the home" with white women's hope for "status in the affairs of men." Just as her husband justified separate spheres for the races, she endorsed separate spheres for women. Black women should be able to stay home with their children. Like many who had survived enslavement, Margaret was anxious to defend respectability. She extolled the True Woman.[67]

Booker T. Washington eventually cautioned Berto Terrell, whom he helped to obtain a judgeship under President Theodore Roosevelt, that his activist wife might be straying from respectability. By this standard, Mary Church Terrell had not been respectable for more than a decade. She had been active as a feminist since the mid-1890s, when she had raised her hand to attract Susan B. Anthony's attention at a meeting of the National American Women's Suffrage Association (NAWSA). Mollie had remarked then that she hoped the association would protest "the injustices of various kinds of which colored people are the victims."[68]

Always hopeful of drawing Black women into the overwhelmingly white movement, Susan asked, "Are you a member of this Association?" When Mollie replied she was not, the seventy-eight-year-old summoned the young woman forward and invited her to write a resolution, which Susan sent to the appropriate committee. In time, NAWSA asked local affiliates to protest state suppression of Black voters. Mollie later observed, "Thus began a delightful, helpful friendship." It was one that transformed her into an international sensation.[69]

Susan B. Anthony had promoted the country's most transcendent lecturers on its most incendiary topics for fifty years. She mentored new talent nonstop. But she also selected carefully, because inadequate speakers would only hurt the cause and themselves. She was especially mindful of the hurdles that Black orators faced after women from the former Confederacy began joining the suffrage movement. When Tuskegee teacher Adella Hunt Logan offered to speak at the NAWSA convention in 1898, Susan B. Anthony asked a friend for advice. Frances Harper had long performed magnificently, she pointed out, and "I do not shrink in the slightest from having a colored woman on the platform" even though such speakers made Southern delegates "hopping mad." But, she wrote, "I do very much shrink from having an incompetent one, so unless you really *know* that Miss Logan is one who would astonish the natives, just let her wait until she is more cultured and can do the colored race the greatest possible credit."[70]

Something in Mollie's manner convinced Susan B. Anthony to consider her closely. By 1898, Mary Church Terrell had accumulated credentials as a Washington school board member and president of the National Association of Colored Women. Yet she faced special challenges. White racists would criticize her as dark, while formerly enslaved people might feel she was too fair. To test her, Susan asked her to address a national meeting in Washington, DC, on "The Progress and Problems of Colored Women." She confided to her closest aide, "I only hope she is not too light to stand for the colored people."[71]

Mollie was exhilarated. She had watched Frederick Douglass speak at the National Council of Women in 1895 and had talked with him afterward, only hours before he died in his Washington home. Now it was her turn.

For the fourth time, she was visibly pregnant. As before, she did not shy from appearing in public, a departure from earlier generations when propriety compelled pregnant women to confine themselves to the home and some even wore special maternity corsets to mask their condition. Berto enthused to Robert Church that his daughter was "the only Colored woman invited to speak," in company with the famous "Susan B. Anthony, Elizabeth Cady Stanton, and Frances Willard," head of the Woman's Christian Temperance Union.[72]

Mollie's twenty-minute speech on the hopes and hardships of African American women electrified the audience. As the applause subsided, Susan B. Anthony told the crowd, "I am sure you have all been thrilled by what you have heard." Berto beamed with pride. He wrote his father-in-law that "Mollie immortalized herself last night before the Woman's Suffrage Convention." Women of both races "mounted the stage and fairly took her off her feet" at the end. "It was the greatest triumph of her life."[73]

Two months later, Mollie delivered a healthy baby girl in an unknown Northern hospital. Named for poet Phyllis Wheatly, the enslaved patriot who defended "freedom's cause" and was praised as a "genius" by George Washington, the baby became her parents' greatest delight. After three tragic deaths, a near-fatal brush with kidney failure, and experimental surgery for uterine cysts, Mollie finally had a child to love.[74]

At a subsequent suffragist convention, the program committee entrusted Mary Church Terrell with the keynote address. The organization wanted her to represent all women, not just women of color. They slated her to follow Isabella Beecher Hooker, the last surviving sister of Harriet Beecher Stowe. Mollie chose each word deliberately and "poured my very soul into everything I said." The rapt audience listened on a Friday evening in February 1900 as someone freed by the nation's bloodiest war articulated arguments first made by Abigail Adams.[75]

"The founders of this republic called heaven and earth to witness that it should be a government of the people, for the people, and by the people," Mollie said, employing the patriotic refrains of Lincoln's Gettysburg Address, "and yet the elective franchise is withheld from one half of the citizens, many of whom are intelligent, cultured and virtuous, while it is unstintingly bestowed upon the other, some of who are illiterate, debauched and vicious." Democracy denied no man in principle, regardless of his character. It empowered no woman, regardless of hers. Some historians consider Mary Church Terrell elitist for asserting that educated women deserved the vote more than uneducated men, but to her audience her words acknowledged a hurt that went deep. If democracy was a limited commodity, why should women with university degrees merit it least?[76]

Mollie acknowledged that some considered it unnatural for women to participate in politics. She countered that whenever "the world takes a step forward in progress some old custom falls dead at our feet." Advances in civilization required getting used to new things. "Nothing could be more unnatural than that a good woman should shirk her duty to the state, if it were possible for her to discharge it." Women were patriots, and voting a patriotic duty.[77]

The church rang as listeners interrupted her to applaud. At the end, they gave Mollie a standing ovation. *The Colored American* proudly dubbed her "the hit of the recent gathering of America's brainiest women." No other speaker "made a better impression for wisdom, happiness of expression and power of oratory than did our own Mary Church Terrell." A journalist for the *Boston Transcript* reported that suffragists had discovered "a woman of whom few present had heard, but whose address was one of the ablest and most brilliant." An editorial called it "the most striking and concise statement of the whole session." *The Colored American* declared Mary Church Terrell the female counterpart of Booker T. Washington.[78]

A national speaker's bureau recruited her the next year. In 1901, she began traveling the country, addressing both white and Black audiences. Wherever she went, she talked about the progress of her gender and race, and violations of the Thirteenth, Fourteenth, and Fifteenth Amendments. Some white Southerners welcomed her, from which she deduced that they had never heard a Black person speak "certain truths." Mollie missed Berto terribly, yet she wrote him, "I enjoy very much doing this kind of work because I really feel that I am putting the colored woman in a favorable light at least every time I address an audience of white people and every little bit helps."[79]

The ignorance of these white audiences flabbergasted her. Some Northerners refused to believe that Jim Crow laws had disfranchised most

Black men. A Harvard alumnus in New England cautioned her to "Walk softly, Mrs. Terrell, walk softly, when you declare that an amendment to the Constitution is so flagrantly violated as you claim it is." Possessed of a teacher's empathy, Mollie had no interest in making anyone feel stupid. With humor, tact, and a well-stocked repertoire of facts, she overturned misconceptions at high schools, benevolent organizations, and literary societies across the nation.[80]

By 1904, Mary Church Terrell's national prominence was such that the International Council of Women invited her to speak in Berlin. The organization was poised to undertake a global suffrage campaign. Mollie hesitated at the expense, but Berto insisted.

International conferences were a recent phenomenon, hastened by technological advancements. The first global political institution, the Permanent Court of Arbitration, had formed only five years earlier. Upon her arrival in Berlin, Mollie overheard excited chatter about "die Negerin" (the Negro woman) expected to address the assembly. Most of the world was under colonial rule, so the promise of a speech by a woman of color was intriguing. Although most Europeans failed to recognize Mollie's African ancestry when they met her, she quickly registered their complaint that American delegates neglected to speak foreign languages.

Mollie had not lived abroad in more than a decade. She asked feminist friends if she should risk a speech in her rusty German. One replied, "Well, Mary Church Terrell, if you can deliver an address before this Congress in German and don't do it, I think you are a fool in 57 varieties of languages."[81]

An aristocratic family opened its mansion to Mollie, and she holed up over the weekend to practice. An Austrian reporter polished her grammar. Three evenings later, in front of two thousand spectators at the lavish Berlin Philharmonic, Mary Church Terrell began with the statement, "If it had not been for the War of the Rebellion which resulted in victory for the Union forces in 1865, instead of addressing you as a free woman tonight, in all human probability I should be on some plantation in the southern states of my country, manacled body and soul." A German reporter rose from his seat and cried, "Die schame!" (The shame). When she finished, the applause was so prolonged that "she was forced to come forward and bow over and over again before she was permitted to take and keep her seat," an Ohio newspaper correspondent reported. The *Washington Post* declared that "the hit of the congress on the part of the American delegates was made by Mrs. Mary Church Terrell."[82]

Mollie gave a public eulogy in 1906 for Susan B. Anthony, who had delivered a eulogy at the funeral of Frederick Douglass in 1895. (Despite their disagreements, Douglass, Anthony, and Stanton remained cordial until their deaths, and Douglass featured portraits of both women prominently in his home.) Mollie expressed her empathy for the feminist abolitionist who had worked so hard to help others, only to suffer betrayal. It was "no wonder that Miss Anthony was wounded to the heart's core" when men "coolly advised her to wait for a more convenient season or refused absolutely to assist her." Mary Church Terrell refused to criticize Susan B. Anthony for turning her emphasis to gender justice, and urged Black Americans to honor her. Judge Robert Terrell felt similarly. In 1915, Berto told readers of W. E. B. Du Bois's magazine *The Crisis* that "what our fathers failed to do for these pioneers who did so much for our cause before and after the great war, let us do for those who are now leading the fight for woman suffrage."[83]

Not all Black leaders felt this way. Jim Crow had poisoned the landscape. Separatists like Marcus Garvey and his journalist wife, Amy Jacques Garvey, championed immigration back to a decolonized Africa. They considered it hopeless to cooperate with whites.[84]

Indeed, some Southerners openly advocated women's suffrage as a way of consolidating white supremacy. Kate Gordon of Louisiana, who opposed the federal amendment, endorsed state constitutional amendments to grant the vote to white women alone. Other Southern feminists organized against her baleful proposals, but their influence was limited. Rebecca Felton, a former slaveholder and the wife of a liberal Congressman from Georgia, advocated for both women's suffrage and the lynching of every "Black fiend who lays unholy and lustful hands on a white woman."[85]

As Jim Crow worsened, trust between Black and white suffragists became fragile in the North. After one 1917 suffrage conference in New York, a Black delegate charged white attendees with snubbing women of color. Other Black participants disagreed, believing they had been given a warm welcome. Black suffragists feared—and risked—being mistreated. Further complicating their position was the knowledge that even if a federal amendment passed, Southern racists would subvert it. In 1920, roughly 85 percent of African Americans resided in the former Confederacy. Under a Nineteenth Amendment, Black women might vote in South Dakota, where few lived, but certainly not in South Carolina. As late as World War II, only 4 percent of eligible Black adults in the South could vote.[86]

All of this was still in the future when Mollie returned from Europe in 1904. No suffrage amendment had been on the congressional docket for nearly twenty years, and anti-suffragists had established their own formidable organizations. Conservative opposition to votes even for white women remained strong.

Yet Mollie's world was bright. After a stopover in England, where celebrities like H. G. Wells and W. T. Stead entertained her at their palatial estates, she returned to her modest brick home in the segregated District of Columbia. Berto and her mother greeted her with proud smiles, though Phyllis must have been the first to rush into her arms. The six-year-old represented Mary Church Terrell's highest hopes: an America where her Black daughter could vote.[87]

New Choices in a New World

Castle Garden sat like a round pillbox at the tip of Manhattan. As the ship's tender bumped the dock in 1884, Rosa Cavalleri envied travelers whom officials ordered back to Italy on account of ill health. She had no choice but to drag her bundles up the pier and into the brick building that served as the nation's principal port of entry before Ellis Island opened eight years later. Rosa stuck close to those with whom she had spent the queasy ocean voyage below decks.

Some blinked at family they had not seen in years. A young man who had left Lombardy in wooden shoes now looked—"O Madonna!"—like "the president of the United States" with his white gloves and diamond stick pin. An Italian man with an impressively waxed mustache and shiny new cane rushed to greet Rosa's group. "A high man like that shaking hands with the poor!" she thought. "This was America for sure!" The man explained that although the paesani had already purchased train tickets, their departure for Missouri was not for another three days. They gave him their cash in exchange for lodging although, in truth, trains for the Midwest left twice a day. By the time the scoundrel finally escorted them to the depot, they had no money left. Taking her cue from the men, Rosa refused the food offered by sympathetic strangers, though she was impressed that, with their fancy "hats and everything," they rode in the same car as she did, "all equal and free together."[88]

The journey might have been exciting had each mile not brought Rosa closer to Santino. She transferred in St. Louis to the local train for Union, a tiny mining town fifty miles south. Rosa gripped her rosary tightly. "I must do what he wants, to not offend God and offend You," she prayed to the Madonna, "But You've got to help me!" When the conductor called their station, the immigrants piled out to meet a group of miners standing alongside two horse-drawn wagons.

A girl with whom Rosa had traveled nearly five thousand miles spied a long-lost cousin named Gionin. They greeted one another joyfully, laughing and talking over one another. Gionin introduced the young woman to the man she had come to marry—they had never met. The shy fiancés did not know what to say. The pair "just stood there getting red and red." Rosa did not see Santino. For a moment she thought she had forgotten his sour face. Then she spotted him studying her with "his half-closed eyes." Fear choked her throat as she climbed into the wagon.

The friendly Gionin took a seat beside her as the vehicle filled. The miners explained that she was to clean and cook for them. When she protested that Mamma Lena had always done the cooking, they laughed and vowed, "*Per l'amore del Dio* [for the love of God], don't worry about that. We will teach you!" Rosa tried not to watch Santino. The presence of the hearty miners quieted her dread as the wagon rumbled the three miles to camp.

Too soon, the wagon rolled into a bleak clearing with a cluster of shacks near a dark tunnel. Gionin pointed out the smaller shacks of the unmarried miners and the larger building that Rosa and Santino would share with another couple. Once inside, Rosa found two bedrooms behind a communal kitchen. Her eyes widened as the miners set out enough bread and butter "for a whole village!" Gionin, true to his word, taught her how to make coffee. After Rosa spread her sheets on the iron bedstead in one of the bedrooms, he found a nail and helped her position her crucifix above the pillows before leaving for his own shack.

Santino finally spoke. "Can't a man sleep with his own wife without God watching him from the wall?" he snarled. Rosa knew she was allowed to honor God ahead of her husband, so she made no move to take down the cross. Santino turned off the lamp.

In her memoir decades later, Rosa did not recount what came next. She simply said, "The things he did to me are too bad to tell!" The next morning she carried water from the spring and started a fire in the cookstove. Charged with arranging the miners' board, Gionin came back to show Rosa how to make their breakfast.

She cooked for a dozen men in subsequent months. When Santino beat her, the miners ignored the blows he rained on her. They knew better than to interfere with another man's wife, so they talked more loudly over supper. Gionin put his head in his hands. Rosa became friendly with Americans in town, where she bought groceries. To her amazement, they treated her "like I was as good as them." Miss Mabel, the store owner's unmarried daughter, called out whenever she walked through the door, "Here's Rosa!" Although Mabel and her father were "boss of the store and the post office," they taught Rosa a few words of English—and even allowed her to wait inside during winter rains, something she considered remarkable.

Rosa made a friend of the young mother who shared the adjoining bedroom. They grew especially close when both became pregnant. As Rosa later recalled, Domiana "was bigger than me." When Rosa revealed her ignorance about reproduction, Domiana explained "the husband planted a seed" from which babies grew. Domiana said she would knock on the wall at the start of her labor and Rosa should knock at the start of hers. Rosa worried about the lack of a doctor, since doctors had saved her the first time, but she did not ask Miss Mabel in town as it wasn't thinkable to mention such subjects to an unmarried woman.

One night Rosa heard a loud knock. She pulled on a skirt and rushed to the other chamber, dark but for a smoky lamp. Domiana's drunk husband had passed out. Domiana lay on the bed with a squalling newborn. Rose recoiled at the twisted purple cord linking child and mother. Domiana told Rosa to get a piece of string and pair of scissors she had laid out. When she told Rosa to cut the pulsing strand, Rosa protested, "I will kill you." Domiana begged her, then cried for the Madonna. Steeling herself, Rosa cut the cord and tied the string around the end. Domiana observed that Rosa now knew what to do, if by some ill fortune her own knock went unanswered.

Sure enough, no one was present when Rosa went into labor with her second child as she lugged a washtub into the Missouri sunshine on a Monday. Domiana's alcoholic husband had lost his job and the couple was gone. Rosa felt her strength vanish. In pain too intense to lift the sopping clothes, she stumbled indoors. She fetched the scissors and string, but agony overwhelmed her. She clutched the table to avoid collapse and labored to push out the baby. When the infant dropped, she cut the cord and lost consciousness.

A passing German neighbor noticed the empty laundry line. She knew Rosa hung the wash every Monday, so she went indoors to investigate. Rosa woke when the woman called her name. She turned her head toward the sound. The room went black again as she spied a naked newborn on the floor. It is not possible to know why Rosa lost consciousness during childbirth, but something was obviously not right.

When Rosa came to, another neighbor, an Italian, was swaddling the infant. She helped Rosa into bed and gave her the baby boy. She told Rosa to tell Santino to prepare the traditional dish of warm milk with bread and butter that Italian mothers ate after giving birth. Rosa waited until nightfall, growing hungry.

As she later told the story, Santino swore at the cold pots and pans when he arrived. He told Rosa that if she wanted something to eat "to get up and get it." The miners shot Santino dark looks, but nothing in their worldview permitted them to object to a man's decisions about "his" woman. They fixed their own meals that evening. Gionin sent his cousin back with food for Rosa.

Santino's abusiveness escalated. He slapped the baby when it cried. If Rosa was in the way, Santino struck them both. The miners at the nightly meals "sat silent, watching." One evening, Gionin could not take it anymore. After Santino stalked out, the miner jumped up from his card game and seized a sharp knife from a rack near the stove. Rosa tried to stop him, but he shook her off. "I am going to kill that man for you, Rosa! I am going to kill him!" he cried.

Rosa pleaded with Gionin not to sin against God or risk hanging. They agreed he should board elsewhere. After that, she saw Gionin only when men and women walked on opposite sides of the road to Sunday mass at the church four miles away. It comforted her to know that they heard the priest chant "the beautiful Latin words" at the same time.

Rosa inhabited a twilight between new and old. America offered a greater equality that she found appealing, but Italy offered stability. The relative merits of the two countries were irrelevant, however, since she had no choice—until she received a letter from Mamma Lena. Her adoptive mother wrote that Rosa's older son had become too much for her to watch. Rosa must come get him, if Santino would permit. To Rosa's surprise, her husband agreed. Santino wanted her to withdraw some savings he had at home.

Not until Rosa returned to Italy did she discover she had become an American. She wore a new hat when she and her infant boarded the train to St. Louis along with a tubercular countryman she had promised to shepherd home. She had never owned a hat and considered it empowering. When she got to the terminal in St. Louis, she marched to the ticket booth and asked how to transfer to New York. The clerk held up one finger, told her the train left in an hour, and pointed to a clock. "Think of that!" she marveled. "I had talked English to a strange man and he understood me." Her traveling companion gazed at her as if she was "something wonderful." Not accustomed to reading a clock, Rosa approached the agent some minutes later, and he assured her that the train was still coming. It still amazed her that "in America the poor can talk to anyone and ask what they want to know."

When their ship reached Italy, Rosa decided she could be brave there, too. At a transfer station, she asked the train conductor for help. "I didn't really need help but I wanted to ask for something," she later recalled. The conductor responded politely. Upon her arrival home, the whole village gathered in welcome. Young men climbed the bell tower to get a better look. Old women kissed Rosa's hand with respect "because I came from America and was wearing a hat and new shoes."

The real test came at the bank. Female customers had to wait until male customers completed their business. Like other village women, Rosa stood patiently as her feet grew tired. After a time she noticed chairs behind a railing. "Chairs for the high people," she realized. "But why," she asked herself, "should the high people have chairs and not the poor?"

Rosa's friends warned her that she would be arrested. A janitor tried to stop her. "Who gave you the permission to sit down?" he barked. Rosa smiled as she sank into the chair. "Myself," she said. She had money in the bank. That gave her "the right to use them, no?" The man scoffed, "You think you're smart because you come from America!" Rosa agreed. "In America the poor people . . . are not so stupid anymore," she replied.

When Rosa approached the teller's window, she spoke English to impress him, saying "If you please," followed by "How do you do. Thank-you. Good-bye." The teller had no idea what she was saying. He just smiled and arranged the transfer. The village women looked on "with their mouths hanging open."

The principle that "all men are created equal" allowed Rosa to assert herself in public settings. In private, she still took orders. Rosa considered staying on in Italy—allowing herself to dream about what *she* might want—then decided she had no legitimate choice but to return.

Upon arriving in Missouri with her two sons, Rosa learned why Santino had needed his savings. One evening after midnight, he told Rosa to get dressed. He wanted her to see a business he had purchased for five hundred dollars. Rosa climbed into the wagon with her boys, wondering why they were going out in the middle of the night, "but what he said I did, that was all." They came to a brightly lit house in the nearby woods. Men inside were laughing and joking. When Rosa entered, one threw his arms around her and pressed his body close. Horrified, she shoved him away. The insulted man asked in broken English, "Well, why for you come here, then?"

Rosa looked so mystified that the stranger explained they were in a whorehouse. Rosa glanced at Santino. He told her that the family would move into the brothel the next morning. Rosa did not have to have sex with customers if she did not "want to," but she must manage the business. She knew how to count and make change, and Santino did not. Rosa shouted, "Never! Never! I belong to God and the Madonna!"

Santino beat Rosa when they returned to their shack. Next, he used his fists on their little boys. Rosa caught him sharpening a razor. Santino vowed to kill her. For two nights she lit a small lamp next to her bed, petrified, staying awake to ward off an attack. She told herself that she had the right to disobey because a priest once said it was no sin to flout one's husband if he made her sin against God, and prostitution was certainly that.

The third morning, Rosa sought out Gionin's cousin. "Don't stay there and let him kill you," the woman pleaded. She said Gionin loved her. He would help if she asked.

Rosa found Gionin at the mine. He agreed that Santino would kill her if she did not leave. She hurried home to get a bag of pennies she had been hiding, and snuck her two boys onto the next railway car to Chicago, where Gionin had cousins. They detrained in Chicago just ahead of police, who had received a telegram from Santino demanding Rosa's arrest. Men still had the preeminent right to child custody, and wives owed husbands their labor in exchange for minimal room and board.[89]

Gionin's cousins found Rosa work taking in laundry. Gionin arrived himself a few days later and helped her find a room in a house shared by Norwegians and Italians. Rosa and her boys were there only a short while when a policeman showed up.

Rosa's hands were deep in a tub of dirty shirts, with one foot on her son's cradle, rocking him. The baby was sick. She did not know enough English to explain herself, but an elderly housemate pleaded with the officer. "Don't take her to jail," the man said. "She's an angel from heaven the way she works and takes care for her children." The policeman agreed not to arrest Rosa if she would come to court the following day.

"There I was, a young Italian girl with a shawl over my head, and I couldn't understand nothing," Rosa later recalled. Facing her in the Chicago courtroom, Santino told the judge she slept with other men. Rosa's elderly neighbor translated the judge's questions and her answers. Gionin and his cousins stood at the back of the chamber. In the end, Rosa's testimony and her neighbors' corroboration convinced the judge that Santino was at fault, not his wife. The magistrate told Santino to leave Chicago by sundown or face jail time—perhaps for perjury, though there is no way to find his record since Rosa did not reveal her previous surnames in her memoir. Gionin and his cousins escorted Santino to the train station with rocks in their pockets. American law had finally given them permission to follow their protective impulses. In Chicago, at least, a wife had some rights.[90]

Rosa never saw Santino again. He filed for divorce and remarried. His new wife reported him for assault, and he went to jail for twenty months. American courts increasingly convicted husbands for hitting their wives, especially if men were immigrant, poor, or Black. Violent partners from the middle or upper classes tended to receive greater clemency. Reformist groups like the Chicago Protective Agency were sometimes criticized for breaking up families if they defended the wives of such men, but attitudes were changing. To paraphrase Mary Church Terrell, Blackstone's law that men might "chastise" wives as they saw fit had fallen dead at Rosa Cavalleri's feet.[91]

Rosa was finally free to choose her residence and her spouse. She decided to stay in Chicago and marry Gionin. Had she not equated sexual ignorance with virtue, she might have lived happily ever after.

Lifting the Veil on Reproduction

Rosa and Gionin struggled to locate housing because "nobody would rent to Italians." Like the Irish before them, Italians were not considered fully white, meaning Anglo-Saxon. Books like Madison Grant's 1916 *Passing of the Great Race* typified the view that Europeans comprised different races, ranging from north to south, with "Nordics" being best. Southern and eastern Europeans were considered dangerous mongrels. This prejudice sometimes turned deadly: in 1891, a New Orleans mob had lynched and murdered eleven Italian Americans.

Forced into poor housing, the family nearly burned to death when the owner of a saloon over which they lived set it ablaze for insurance money. Gionin's employer offered a free apartment if Rosa would have sex with him, but unlike Santino, Gionin refused to pimp his wife. The family finally found decent housing, only to be ejected after a mysterious organization called Chicago Commons bought the building, planning "to teach the poor people good things," or so Rosa heard.[92]

Their next rental was a basement apartment near a maggot-infested garbage dump. It took on a foot of water whenever the skies opened. Gionin flung the filthy sludge out the door with a shovel. One morning, Rosa pounded on the door of their previous home. "On account of you people I had to get out from this home," she told the "nice young girl" in a red blouse who answered the door. "Last night I was drowned with the water, me and my children!"[93]

The woman from Chicago Commons followed Rosa back to the slum, where they found Gionin shoveling water. She promised action. By 6:00 p.m. she had negotiated rooms on a higher floor nearby and lent them the first month's rent. She wrangled a once-a-week job for Rosa scrubbing floors at the Commons. This was Rosa's first paid employment outside the home since the Milanese silk factory. It meant the family could eat when, sometime thereafter, Gionin temporarily accepted a job three hundred miles away.

Chicago Commons was a settlement house. It mimicked nearby Hull House, which suffragist Jane Addams had founded five years earlier. Addams sat on the boards of both organizations, which reflected a swelling egalitarian ethos in America and elsewhere. The first settlement was Toynbee Hall in England, from which she had drawn inspiration. When Rosa knocked on the door in 1894 or 1895, there were six in the United States. Within two decades, there were four hundred. College-educated "resident workers," mostly women, many suffragists, lived in the houses from which they operated services.

They aimed, as the Commons phrased it, to "cultivate human relationships across separating lines of race and language, condition and class, party and creed." Providing classes, clubs, kindergartens, and medical assistance to impoverished Chicagoans, they also lobbied city government to improve housing, remove garbage, and eliminate corruption. They invented the profession of social work. Chicago Commons started the first training program, later associated with the University of Chicago. College-educated women headed its faculty. One of their goals was to help immigrant girls navigate conflicts between "old-world customs" and American freedoms.[94]

Jane Addams thought the vote would help them, and by extension, the nation itself. She justified suffrage as essential to "municipal housekeeping." If women were to clean polluted neighborhoods, they needed the ballot. Italian Americans told Addams that "they would certainly vote for public washhouses if they ever had the chance to vote at all." The desire of immigrant women for a voice was "all so human, so spontaneous and so direct," she felt. When Illinois passed a state law in 1913 allowing women to vote for US president, the Commons immediately registered members of the Italian Mothers' Club, a club that Rosa Cavalleri had helped start. Yet Rosa never discussed suffrage in her memoir. What stood out to her was practical feminism: meaning, the "good ladies" who came to her when, once again, silence about sexuality nearly took her life.[95]

Settlement workers gave classes in maternal health, so it is somewhat surprising they did not notice when Rosa became pregnant, though she dressed in voluminous skirts and never mentioned her condition. It was normal for women to remain silent, and confused, when it came to sex.

Popular mythology held that virtuous women had no libido, and doctors had to reassure anxious patients that there was nothing wrong with them if they felt pleasurable sensations. Beyond this, a network of new federal and state laws had heightened the repressive atmosphere. Known as Comstock laws for Anthony Comstock, a religious activist who successfully lobbied Congress to seize even private letters with "obscene" information, they banned public distribution of materials on sex after the 1870s. Some states outlawed contraceptive devices as well. This move coincided with efforts by doctors to criminalize abortion, which had previously been legal until "quickening," usually around the fourth month.[96]

One Progressive appalled by the consequences was Margaret Sanger, a nurse who had watched a woman die from an abortion in 1912. The woman's physician had warned her that another pregnancy might be fatal, but he could not legally prescribe contraception. Two years later Sanger started *The Woman Rebel,* a newspaper in which she advocated "birth control," a term she coined. In 1917, she and her sister Ethel Byrne were arrested for distributing information at a birth control clinic they started in Brooklyn, the nation's first. The court did not allow Byrne to testify before shipping her to prison for thirty days, where she became the first American to mount a prison hunger strike.[97]

During this period, small families had become associated with modernity, with the birth rate falling from an average of seven children per woman in 1800 to four in 1900. But Americans still tended to assume that it was a husband's prerogative to decide when to have sex and whether to have children, and to limit conception by means of coitus interruptus, abstinence, or illegal condoms.

Feminists like Sanger insisted instead that fertility was something over which wives should have primary say, since they were the ones to take the mortal risks. As with the vote, they should represent themselves rather than relinquishing autonomy to another. Ignoring accusations of "free love" that had panicked their predecessors, reformers called birth control "self-ownership." Lawyer Crystal Eastman, a founder of the American Civil Liberties Union, commented in 1918 that whether or not feminists agreed on suffrage strategies, "we must all be followers of Margaret Sanger."[98]

Endorsed by the New York Federation of Women's Clubs, Sanger founded the American Birth Control League, and in 1928 published *Motherhood in Bondage,* a collection of letters from women around the nation seeking means of contraception, upon which, as Sanger put it, their "life, liberty and the pursuit of happiness" depended. *Motherhood in Bondage* broke the taboo around discussing reproduction. As one woman wrote, "One month before my thirteenth birthday, I became the mother of my first child, and now at the age of thirty I am the mother of eleven children, ten of them living, the youngest now seven years old." Others expressed sorrow at having to end sexual relations with their husbands to avoid death in childbirth. Sanger later changed her organization's name to Planned Parenthood.[99]

The idea of family planning arrived too late to help Rosa Cavalleri. She still had no choice about when or if to have children, and no sense that such subjects could even be discussed. She went into labor with her fourth or fifth child sometime around the turn of the century, when Gionin still worked in another state. It never occurred to her to tell the unmarried residents of the Commons, and she left work when contractions began. She sent her children to another family and climbed the stairs to her apartment alone. It was February. The temperature plunged to six degrees below zero. Hoarfrost lined the inside of her dim bedroom. Convinced she would die, Rosa begged the Madonna for help. Sometime after midnight she gave birth to a son, whom she wrapped in a thin undershirt. The next morning, a volunteer from the Commons happened by, looking for a different family. The woman apologized for knocking on the wrong door. "No, lady, you find the right place," Rosa cried desperately.[100]

The settlement worker lit a fire. Then she went for food and "all those little things the babies in America have." Another worker came and they stayed four nights. "They were high-up educated girls," Rosa marveled, yet they slept in her freezing apartment and used the public toilet on the sidewalk. "Why didn't you tell us before, Mis' Cavalleri, so we can help you?" they asked. No one had ever suggested that Rosa could talk about female mysteries. She considered them angels. "They were really, really friends!"

The baby did not survive. The frost had ruined his lungs. Rosa developed pneumonia and starting spitting blood. Again, the women intervened. They sent Rosa to a sanatorium and helped Gionin, who had returned, care for the other children. They secured a better apartment, defending her when yet another manager refused to rent to Italians.

Shortly thereafter, the Commons hired Rosa full-time. She became a mainstay. Her youngest children attended kindergarten at the Commons and she recruited neighbors for its women's clubs. When the Commons opened a summer camp, Rosa ran the kitchen, helping "Jew boys" and "Italian boys" learn to get along. When World War I broke out, she watched the director of the Commons register soldiers for the draft.

Rosa became adept at describing the inequalities of the Old World, and the hardships for immigrant women in the New. The staff invited her to meetings at Chicago Commons and Hull House, and classes at Northwestern University, to help wealthier Americans understand the need for reforms. A social worker transcribed her memoir. "I went everywhere," Rosa recounted. "I never said no." She had a marvelous way with words, perhaps the gift of her biological mother, who had once been maligned as immoral for appearing on stage. "I love so much the dramatics," Rosa said. In America, a woman could speak publicly without harm to her reputation.

It touched Rosa that Gionin loved her for it. "He was proud, how the people were enjoying to hear me tell."

Troubled Victories and the Art of the Possible

During the fiercest days of the suffrage campaign, volunteers for Alice Paul would ring Mollie by telephone, asking her to picket the White House. On those afternoons, even if snow on the ground meant she had to stand on hot bricks to avoid frostbite, she and Phyllis held signs and waved to federal officials as they streamed home after work. The Terrells were among the few African American faces in that small band.[101]

Some white feminists encouraged Black visibility and others discouraged it. Modern scholars often fault them for pursuing a "Southern strategy," meaning they "accepted the deteriorating racial climate in Congress as the situation within which they must work," in the moderate phrasing of Ellen DuBois. The premise of this critique is that feminists could have obtained the vote during the Jim Crow era with more ethical methods, or that winning a federal amendment was not worth the price of silence on racism.[102]

The amendment had long seemed unattainable. NAWSA mostly abandoned it after 1890, focusing on state campaigns. This changed when

Alice Paul and her friend Lucy Burns took over leadership of NAWSA's moribund Congressional Committee in 1912. They considered older leaders defeatist, and split off in 1914 to create a new organization, called the Congressional Union. This group, and eventually NAWSA, dedicated themselves to a federal amendment. The challenge was enormous. Even if Congress at last passed such a bill, it would face the challenge of ratification, another high hurdle since at least four former slave states would have to sign off. Like earlier reformers who had placated sexists by excluding women from the Fifteenth Amendment, feminists would have to placate racists or at least avoid sparking their wrath. They further understood that if women did get the vote, some would apply it to purposes with which they disagreed. That was the nature of democracy.

Suffrage organizations thus decided to follow the strategy of every sizeable institution in the United States—including labor unions, legislatures, corporations, newspapers, courts, universities, and the party of Abraham Lincoln—in refusing to confront Jim Crow. There was a difference, however. If they convinced segregationists to enfranchise all women, they would inscribe a non-racist, non-sexist law in the Constitution that nominally doubled the number of Black voters.

The victory of women's suffrage seems so flawed in retrospect that some find it hard to call it a success. Yet it was. Across the long reach of history, the Thirteenth, Fourteenth, Fifteenth, and Nineteenth Amendments gave US civil rights activists of the 1950s and 1960s a legal tool that was unavailable to people such as Black South Africans, whose constitution, like that of the former Confederacy, enshrined white supremacy.[103]

As a resident of Washington, DC, a resolutely Southern city wedged between segregated Maryland and Virginia, Mary Church Terrell accepted the necessity of partial victories. Her husband's livelihood depended on the willingness of the first Southern president since the Civil War to make an exception. Woodrow Wilson was born in Virginia in 1856, and grew up in Georgia at the onset of Jim Crow. Wooing the racist president became key to winning two battles close to Mollie's heart: saving Berto's career and securing women's suffrage.

On the recommendation of Booker T. Washington, Republican presidents, starting with Theodore Roosevelt in 1902, had repeatedly appointed Robert Terrell municipal court judge, making him the first African American judge in the District of Columbia. Since the Civil War,

Black people had occupied a variety of federal jobs. From postal clerks scattered across the country to diplomats fielded by the Department of State, nineteen thousand African Americans worked for the federal government in 1912, holding respectable jobs unavailable to them in the states on either side of the capital. Of these workers, those holding the top four posts, including Robert Terrell, constituted what some called the president's "Black cabinet."[104]

Southern congressmen opposed such appointments, but until the 1912 election they had never had sufficient votes to block them. Democrats swept the House and Senate that year, and their man in the White House, Woodrow Wilson, could implement none of his proposed reforms—from protection for child workers to autonomy for the recently colonized Philippines—without support from fellow Southern Democrats who wanted him to extend Jim Crow into the federal government. Wilson initially promised W. E. B. Du Bois and other Black leaders that he would be fair-minded, but he soon yielded to demands to treat African Americans like lepers, segregating federal toilets and lunchrooms and requiring clerks to work behind folding screens to avoid offending Americans of European descent. Black appointees found themselves unemployed when their terms ended. Within months of the inauguration, Wilson's administration had nearly eliminated Black officeholders. By 1916, only eight of the thirty-one most highly ranked appointees remained. No African American requiring Senate confirmation kept his job, with the exception of Robert Terrell.[105]

The most unabashed advocate of these racist measures was Senator James Vardaman of Mississippi. Newspapers from Alaska to Virginia reported that Vardaman had decided to make Robert Terrell the target of his campaign "to dedicate the Senate officially to approval of race prejudice," as one journalist put it. Vardaman was a populist who compared himself with Abraham Lincoln, spouted Thomas Jefferson, and hoped to ban Blacks from voting booths, juries, and public jobs. A former governor of Mississippi, he had previously advocated prison for anyone who married a person of another race and once proclaimed, "If it is necessary every Negro in the state [of Mississippi] will be lynched, it will be done to maintain white supremacy."[106]

As he fought to keep his job, Robert Terrell benefited from the support of Washington's legal community, which considered him one of its fairest jurists. At the urging of the all-white Bar Association, President Wilson nominated him for another four-year term despite Vardaman. Booker T. Washington arranged for prominent Black Democrats to buttonhole every senator on Berto's behalf, saying that he had "the happy faculty of making friends with all people of both races."[107]

Mollie agonized over Senator Vardaman's cruel campaign. Determined to document America's descent into bigotry, she saved cartoons from Southern newspapers that pictured her Harvard-graduate husband as a loathsome buffoon. Berto ignored the insults but they pierced Mollie, who swung between righteousness and despair. She wrote legislators, quizzed journalists, and paced the halls of Congress to lobby senators, one a fellow Oberlin alum.[108]

She needed to tread delicately, however. Her endorsement of women's rights and cooperation across factional divides within the Black community disadvantaged Berto, who faced not only his own enemies but also "the enemies of his wife," a member of the elite commented. Booker T. Washington had previously cautioned him that Mollie's choices might make it "harder for your friends to help you when the time comes." The collision between her activism and his career became especially perilous when James Vardaman decided to address women's suffrage the month before the Senate vote on Robert Terrell's reappointment.[109]

For the first time since 1887, Congress had allowed a women's suffrage bill to come to the floor, prompted by the first civil rights march to take place in the nation's capital. The day before Wilson's inauguration, Mollie and other members of the National Association of Colored Women had paraded alongside New York suffragists, hoisting the state banner in an unprecedented demonstration of five thousand women. Illinois delegates pressured Ida Wells-Barnett to walk behind them to appease Southerners, which she refused to do, but W. E. B. Du Bois noted that more enlightened suffragists largely prevailed. The day of the great event, he reported, "colored women marched . . . without let or hindrance." The headline from another Black newspaper read, "No color line existed in any part of it. Afro-American women proudly marched right by the side of the white sisters." Had she lived to see the day, Susan B. Anthony would have scattered exclamation points across the page.[110]

The bill brought before Congress in 1914 had been named in her honor. The Susan B. Anthony Amendment had little chance of obtaining the requisite two-thirds majority, but suffragists considered it a test of winds from the West. As the western territories formed governments, some gave women the vote, partly to attract settlers to the sparsely populated plains. In 1890, Wyoming became the first state to enfranchise women. Colorado followed in 1893, and Utah and Idaho in 1896. By 1914, women could also vote in Arizona, California, Kansas, Montana, Oregon, and Washington. Gradually, the West helped normalize the idea of women's suffrage as patriotic.[111]

Objections thawed. Forays of the New Woman into the professions and participation of immigrants in factory work brought women into public spaces. Anti-suffrage organizations still vociferously opposed female participation in government, but the impression began to grow that if women held jobs without losing their womanliness, perhaps they might vote without doing so. Journalist Samuel S. McClure, founder of *McClure's Magazine* and a pioneer of investigative journalism, predicted in 1914 that "the whole world will have it in ten years. It is the next step in democracy."[112]

Only a single senator on the snowy afternoon of March 19, 1914, felt impelled to denounce female suffrage as an anti-family measure when the amendment came up for discussion. A simple majority of the all-male Senate voted 35 to 34 in favor. (Twenty-six abstained.) Although the bill did not win the requisite two-thirds majority, a tipping point seemed imminent. One senator opined, "In 20 years, I believe, it will seem as strange that anyone opposed woman suffrage as it now seems that there ever was opposition to universal suffrage among men."[113]

The three-hour debate showed that racism had become the chief obstacle. Two weeks earlier, James Vardaman had added an amendment to the suffrage bill that threw its friends "into a panic," according to one observer. The Mississippian proposed trading Black male suffrage for women's suffrage. Hoping to nullify the Fifteenth Amendment, Vardaman proposed an addendum to the bill that would allow states to discriminate on any basis *except* sex. All other forms of discrimination would be tolerated. Vardaman asserted that the North's only goal in enfranchising former slaves had been to "humiliate the white people of the South." He had no problem with women's suffrage, especially if it restored state autonomy on racial questions.[114]

Historian Martha Jones has observed that Mary Church Terrell remained "uncharacteristically quiet" during these debates. Berto's confirmation remained in doubt, and she may have been keen to minimize attention to the Terrell name. Fortunately, the Senate voted down Vardaman's measure to limit the vote to white women, with 48 opposed, 19 in favor, and 28 too cautious to express an opinion. The next month, Northern senators forced a vote on Robert Terrell's reappointment, confirming him in executive session. As *The Shelby Republican,* an Indiana newspaper, observed, any other outcome would have signaled to the nation that, once again, "the South is in the saddle." Relief swept over Mollie, who felt she had endured a trial as great as "the Spanish Inquisition."[115]

Across the next four years, Carrie Chapman Catt, Susan B. Anthony's battle-hardened successor at NAWSA, and Alice Paul, head of what was now called the National Woman's Party, pressed for another vote in Congress. Mollie kept to her lecture schedule. Other suffragists worked on bills in state legislatures, which representatives consistently rejected. Women had not yet secured the franchise in a single Eastern Seaboard state. Both US senators from Massachusetts opposed the vote for women.

The superbly organized anti-suffrage movement erected some of the strongest roadblocks. Privy to the education and right to speak for which Abigail Adams and Angelina Grimké had campaigned, some of the nation's most idealistic women led the effort. Vassar graduate Josephine Jewell Dodge, founding president of the National Association Opposed to Woman Suffrage, had started New York's first nursery schools for working mothers, including women of color, and forged a federation of seven hundred affiliates to promote day care nationwide. A Progressive, Dodge sought to improve conditions for women without disturbing separate spheres. Voting would sully women, she believed, by forcing them to abandon the moral high ground for partisan swamps.[116]

Another vocal opponent of suffrage was Progressive journalist Ida Tarbell. The author of a famous muckraking exposé on Standard Oil, Tarbell faulted the American Revolution for the "strong yeast they put into the pot in '76." Liberty had given women ideas, prompting advances in education, and eventually, fostering envy of men's worldly occupations. Although Tarbell was a college graduate who never married, she thought other women should stay home. She praised John Adams's long-ago opposition to Abigail's request for political rights. What would become of America if women revised "nature's plan" for them? Tarbell's question was not trivial, and the answer not obvious. She pointed out that it was sometimes sensible to fear change.[117]

Massachusetts and New York boasted the most influential organizations against women's suffrage, and the so-called antis derailed multiple attempts to win the vote. The Massachusetts campaign of 1915 showed them at their most effective. As pro-suffrage sentiment reached new heights, anti-suffragists convinced legislators to put the measure to a vote. Speakers crisscrossed the state addressing county fairs, church picnics, labor meetings, and women's clubs. They presented slide shows at nickelodeons, ran ads in the Harvard College newspaper, printed Boston Red Sox schedules with anti-suffrage messages next to batting averages, and handed out yardsticks with the slogan "Measure the menace, do you want women on juries?" The male electorate rejected suffrage two to one.[118]

To antis, this proved that men could be trusted to act on women's behalf. They claimed that feminists had had "no connection whatever" with expanded educational opportunities, improvements in property laws, or growing access to the professions. Democracy and industrialization had accomplished those feats, and men had adjusted laws accordingly. "Most of the principal injustices of the law toward women have already been remedied by means of existing constitutional machinery," the president of the Massachusetts society declared, "and with regard to those which remain . . . we would rather trust to the curtesy and justice of men than seek to wrest advantages through the use of the ballot." Participation in government would shift "heavy burdens" onto women for which they were unsuited.[119]

Anti-feminist arguments echoed earlier ones supporting monarchy. Sir Robert Filmer had asserted three centuries earlier that men had liberty enough under the rule of benevolent aristocrats whose capacities were superior to their own. It was foolish to undermine the compact whereby the weak received protection from the strong.

This bargain was hard to justify indefinitely in a country where the principle of equality was practically the national religion, even when sinned against. In growing numbers, women were engaged in worldly activities. Even antis accepted many of the changes. "We desire the fullest possible development of the powers, energies, and opportunities of women," the president of the Massachusetts anti-suffrage society proclaimed. Public speaking and professional careers had become acceptable even if they were still uncommon. Yet traditionalists worried about where society was headed. If a woman's sphere kept expanding, it would eventually collide with man's. The ballot, they feared, would destroy both masculinity and femininity.[120]

The Last Push

The sixty-year impasse might have continued decades longer had World War I not made Woodrow Wilson the first US president to advocate for women's suffrage. Under the influence of the dignified Carrie Chapman Catt, Wilson had been slowly coming around to the proposition that, as one historian phrases it, "a normal, natural, kind, loving, and respectable person could be both a female and a political actor." When the United States entered the European war, Catt sacrificed her longstanding pacifism to support the president and win his favor, mobilizing women in a "second line of defense." Volunteers sold war bonds, made bandages, drove ambulances, and ran farms. The US Navy recruited women for the first time in March 1917, inducting eleven thousand volunteers. Wilson, a professor of government before he had entered politics, intuited that democracy was sailing in a new direction. "We feel the tide," he admitted to suffragists in 1916.[121]

The tide was moving fast. The Great War hastened constitutional movements around the world, again prompting calls for women's rights. The Romanov dynasty fell in February 1917. The next month, Russia's first female gynecologist, Poliksena Shishkina-lavein, led forty thousand women down the streets of St. Petersburg to demand the vote, which the new legislature gave them four months later. During the American and French revolutions, feminism had been a byproduct of republicanism; a century later, women's rights emerged front and center. British feminists won governmental support, too. Emmeline Pankhurst halted suffrage demonstrations until the war was won, and organized a "Right to Serve" march that showcased women's patriotic willingness to embrace the duties of citizenship. For the first time, the British Army inducted women. More than fifty thousand served in uniform, some under bombardment in France. In 1917, Parliament hammered out a bill that gave the vote to women and lower-class men. New Zealand and Australia granted women the vote even before the war.[122]

Wilson moved into the pro-suffrage camp as it became clear that, if the United States wanted to be perceived as a world leader, it could not lag behind on this issue. When the United States entered the war in 1917, Wilson quietly convinced the Democratic chair of the House Rules Committee to set up a subcommittee on women's suffrage. The Democratic

Party had long resisted a federal amendment as a violation of states' rights. In January 1918, the day after announcing his famous Fourteen Points for world peace, Wilson met with congressional allies to declare his support for the Susan B. Anthony Amendment. He never admitted that it would enfranchise more Black voters, but he privately acknowledged to Southern politicians that he knew an amendment would "embarrass" them.[123]

Historian Gary Gerstle describes Wilson as "timid, cold, practically indifferent to questions of racial justice." Fortunately, the president was bold and fevered about a Progressive world order. If votes for women would improve America's international image, he would accept a racially inclusive suffrage amendment—the only type that leading feminist organizations would endorse. The Susan B. Anthony Amendment contradicted Wilson's Jim Crow promises, but he accepted equally distasteful bargains with foreign allies to win agreement to the League of Nations.[124]

The president rationalized his reversal by pointing to international opinion and women's wartime service. The British House of Commons and House of Lords had both approved the new "Act for the Representation of the People." Wilson told shocked congressmen that "in view of the fact that Great Britain had granted the franchise to women and the general disposition among the Allies to recognize the patriotic services of women in the war against Germany, this country could do no less than follow that example." Like democracy itself, female suffrage was bigger than the United States. The vote was a simple act of "right and justice to the women of the country and of the world," Wilson proclaimed in January 1918. American women had worn the uniforms of the Navy and US Marines for nearly a year. Women would soon serve in the Army Signal Corps in France, some under bombardment, performing telephone jobs at which they outshone men. Two dozen nations preceded the United States in granting women the vote, including Germany. For two years, the president drove his reluctant party hard.[125]

Anti-suffragists considered Wilson's stance a betrayal. Their rhetoric flamed hotter. The national anti-suffrage organization replaced its top officers in June 1917, and they now painted feminism red. The word "feminism" had begun appearing in American newspapers only shortly before this moment. French suffragist Hubertine Auclert coined the term in the 1880s, and it reached the American scene around 1913, when activists suddenly took it up. The word spoke to a generation of young women eager to distinguish themselves as au courant. The "Woman Movement," the term identified with the nineteenth century, "has an old sound—it *is* old," one said. "But Feminism!" she gloried—that was new. Charlotte Perkins Gilman described "the Feminist" in terms suggestive of the New Woman, with overtones of Progressivism and modern secularism. "Here she comes, running, out of prison and off the pedestal; chains off, crown off, halo off, just a live woman."[126]

Anti-suffragists quickly latched onto the word and fused it with socialism. Some feminists were socialists, of course. Socialist parties endorsed women's suffrage and had achieved some popularity. Candidate Eugene Debs won 6 percent of the vote in the US presidential election of 1912. But the vast majority of advocates for women's rights were not socialists. The ever-cautious Carrie Chapman Catt excluded socialists from speakers' platforms after 1917, and declared NAWSA a "bourgeois movement with nothing radical about it." She explained that feminism was the term for the ongoing, worldwide quest for "human freedom," similar to the terms "enlightenment and democracy."[127]

Anti-suffragists ignored these distinctions. "Pacifist, socialist, feminist, suffragist are all parts of the same movement—a movement which weakens government, corrupts society and threatens the very existence of our great experiment in democracy," declared the National Association Opposed to Woman Suffrage. The group renamed its national magazine *The Woman Patriot,* suggesting that women's rights advocates were unpatriotic. In Massachusetts, anti-suffragists accused reformers of being un-American for ignoring the wishes of "normal" women. They depicted "Feminism" (with a capital F) as the harbinger of a world in which women prized individual fulfillment over family duty. Anti-suffragists considered feminists' supposed tolerance of romantic experimentation particularly dangerous. "The fiction of today is full of the disgusting experiences of young persons trying to find their ideal comrade," Lily Rice Foxcroft wrote in "Suffrage: A Step toward Feminism." The Russian Revolution further stoked fears of radicalism when Bolsheviks crushed the regime that liberal democrats had built on the ruins of the monarchy.[128]

Foreign events nonetheless worked largely in suffragists' favor, as Carrie Chapman Catt had predicted a decade earlier, when she told Congress that "Suffrage will ultimately triumph here as a result of its triumph in other countries." President Wilson said the same when he urged the

Senate to pass the bill in September 1918. "Are we alone to refuse the lesson?" he asked. "Are we alone to ask and take the utmost that our women can give—service and sacrifice of every kind—and still say we do not see what title that gives them?" If America balked, Wilson warned, it must "resign the leadership of liberal minds to others."[129]

The fight remained tough to the end. Suffragists did the heavy lifting, not the president, though his support was critical. Anti-suffragists and states' rights proponents hit back. Suffragists from every ethnic and religious background pressed hard. Mary Church Terrell and her daughter Phyllis, then nineteen, risked imprisonment along with other suffragists led by Alice Paul, whom police arrested for picketing the White House. Mollie kept the bridge open to Carrie Chapman Catt as well, ignoring the divide between competing organizations.[130]

One thing Mary Church Terrell did not do, and no Black woman could, was figure prominently in legislative lobbying, lest she attract greater opposition to the cause. She later noted that Woodrow Wilson was the only president between Benjamin Harrison and Herbert Hoover whom she had never met as a part of a delegation to the White House. The omnipresent threat of Southern backlash constrained interracial cooperation among suffragists, regardless of their personal views or relationships.[131]

The Senate voted down women's suffrage four times: in 1887, 1914, 1918, and February 1919. Then, on June 4, 1919, it finally approved the Susan B. Anthony Amendment.

Gone were the days when the Northeast led in revolutionary fervor. Henry Cabot Lodge of Massachusetts voted against the bill, as did senators from Connecticut, New York, Pennsylvania, and Vermont. William Borah, a famously liberal Progressive known as the "Lion of Idaho," opposed the amendment as complicating the racial issue that "Sphinxlike, inscrutable, and intractable" overshadowed national life.[132]

Segregationists provided the two-thirds majority. Senator Kenneth McKellar of Tennessee raised his hand in favor of the Susan B. Anthony Amendment, as did senators from Arkansas, Kentucky, Louisiana, and Texas. With their help, women's suffrage passed by two ayes. McKellar had previously declared on the floor of Congress, "Any person who really wants white supremacy in the South can not better guarantee it than by the enactment of this equal-suffrage resolution." Poll taxes and grandfather clauses had eliminated "the ignorant negro men vote, and they will eliminate the ignorant negro women vote," the Tennessean asserted. Not a single man in Congress stood up to contradict him.[133]

Carrie Chapman Catt, Alice Paul, and Mary Church Terrell did not have the luxury of allies who supported them for reasons with which they agreed. They could have an amendment with the help of unsavory allies or none at all, since either way, the same congressmen would retain office. As historian Ira Katznelson has observed with regard to Franklin Roosevelt's World War II alliance with Joseph Stalin, untainted partners did not exist.[134]

The bill now went to the states, where it faced an even higher hurdle. Three-fourths, not just two-thirds, had to approve. Hardworking suffragists fought the steep odds, and states began ratifying one by one. An unpredictable slugfest in Tennessee capped the seventy-year battle. Kate Gordon and her racist supporters lobbied representatives to reject the federal amendment as an affront to Jim Crow. They wanted a state bill instead that excluded Black women. Southern feminists who supported the inclusive federal amendment struck back. Men flipped their support from one to the other, back and forth. At a crucial moment, an influential senator denounced federal suffrage as an abomination invented by Yankee females of the "low neck and high skirt variety" who wanted "negro men" to marry white women.[135]

Illegal in thirty states, including Tennessee, intermarriage was the touchiest Jim Crow taboo. Carrie Chapman Catt issued a rebuttal from her Nashville hotel, calling the allegation "an absolute fabrication," and declaring intermarriage "an absolute crime against nature." Mary Church Terrell had mixed feelings herself. She recalled the scorn heaped on Frederick Douglass by both races when he wed a white woman after his first wife died, and it reinforced her belief that intermarriage was inadvisable even when legal. Historians do not know what she thought of Carrie Chapman Catt's statement, though scholars today criticize Catt for a lack of "moral fiber." Mollie considered Catt a personal ally without a hint of "race prejudice," and knew that her organization had long resisted efforts to insert white-only clauses into the Susan B. Anthony Amendment. She may have rationalized the statement as an unavoidable concession.[136]

At the end of a six-week debate, Tennessee approved the Nineteenth Amendment in August 1919 by a single vote, cast by a waffling representative whose widowed mother asked him to "be a good boy and help Mrs. Catt."

James Vardaman's home state of Mississippi did not ratify women's suffrage for another sixty-four years. The amendment entered the US Constitution nonetheless.[137]

Looking back on the journey from the Fourteenth Amendment to the Nineteenth, Carrie Chapman Catt commented:

> To get the word male in effect out of the constitution cost the women of the country fifty-two years of pause-less campaign thereafter. During that time they were forced to conduct fifty-six campaigns of referenda of male voters; 480 campaigns to get Legislatures to submit suffrage amendments to voters; 47 campaigns to get State constitutional conventions to write woman suffrage into State constitutions; 277 campaigns to get State party conventions to include woman suffrage planks; 30 campaigns to get presidential party conventions to adopt woman suffrage planks in party platforms, and 19 campaigns with 19 successive Congresses. . . . Young suffragists who helped forge the last links of that chain were not born when it began. Old suffragists who forged the first links were dead when it ended.[138]

Mary Church Terrell had been an important link in the chain of women's suffrage, making sure that Black women were represented in the struggle. Carrie Chapman Catt acknowledged as much in an article she penned for the Oberlin alumni magazine. Catt recalled hearing Terrell's first "gem" of a speech in 1898 and her incandescent oration in Berlin in 1904. "No one who heard her then ever forgot," Catt wrote in 1936. For decades, Mary Church Terrell had courageously served "her race and her sex."[139]

The pair were friendly into their seventies, with Catt addressing Mollie as "my dear Mrs. Terrell." The elder stateswoman urged her to publish a memoir, and they continued to share a commitment to world peace. Here, too, Mollie argued that tradition should not predetermine the future. Wives had once been told "the day would never dawn when gentlemen would not settle their 'affairs of honor' by duels." A century later, duels were obsolete.[140]

Alice Paul proved more disappointing. Her National Woman's Party awarded "Distinguished Service" medals to Mary Church Terrell and her daughter after suffrage passed, but she refused to campaign against

Southern voter suppression. Disheartened activists suggested that Alice Paul herself needed picketing. Mollie advised against it. She knew that defenders of one cause often avoided others to minimize dissension. When the National Woman's Party refused even to endorse birth control, Mollie recognized that Black women must seek allies elsewhere.[141]

She found them in the Republican Party. Southern states gutted the Nineteenth Amendment as they had the Fifteenth, but Northern states registered Black voters. After the World War, African Americans flooded out of the South in what historians call the Great Migration. The Republican Party hired Mollie to organize Black women for the 1920 presidential election and gave her a desk at their New York City headquarters. The club movement that Mollie had spearheaded proved an important resource. As one member observed, the work of the preceding twenty-five years had been "God's way of preparing us to assume this great task of citizenship."[142]

Mollie told Black audiences, "Every time you meet a woman, talk to her about going to the polls to vote." On a given day she might pack a toothbrush to catch a northbound train at 1:03 p.m., arrive in Rhode Island at 7:35 p.m., give a speech at 8:00 p.m., board a night boat to reach Manhattan by 7:00 a.m., answer correspondence at her office, then catch an 11:00 a.m. train to Delaware for another speech. She traveled up and down the East Coast as readily as other women climbed stairs, and remained prominent in politics over the ensuing decades, meeting with President Harry Truman, addressing the United Nations, and picketing segregated restaurants into her late eighties.[143]

The one thing she never did was cast a ballot. Not because she lived in the Jim Crow South, but because residents of the District of Columbia did not win the franchise until 1964, ten years after the death of Mary Church Terrell.[144]

+++

IN 1920, the United States forbade states to deny the vote on the basis of sex, trailing advances in Europe and Oceania. Although American feminists had figured prominently in international suffrage campaigns, federalism had given the states wide discretion to deny the ballot. After World War I, the nation caught up with the rest of the democratizing world.

Conservative women soon embraced voting, and helped to accelerate the Republican Party's rightward drift. The question for antis became how to use their ballots to restore men's authority over credulous women whom socialists and communists might bamboozle. Traditionalists could take comfort from the fact that husbands still retained significant control, women who married foreigners still lost their citizenship, and most states still would not seat women on juries. Birth control remained widely restricted and the Comstock laws stayed on the books. Working women like Rosa Cavalleri continued to occupy the lowest-paying jobs and face terrifying hazards during pregnancy and childbirth.[145]

Yet women could now go to school, speak publicly, own property, lobby Congress, and vote—at least according to the law. Reformers dedicated to the ideals of 1776 had built the ground floor of liberty.

CHAPTER 5

The Right to Earn

1920–1960

Frances Perkins and Ann Marie Riebe

Help Wanted—Female
STENOGRAPHER, Real Estate Office, monitor board;
$10, write fully. S.M., 450 Times.

Help Wanted—Male
ELEVATOR OPERATOR, age 45 up; no accent unless English;
high-class apartment; references; $80 month. 124 East 28th.

NEW YORK TIMES, 1933

IN 1920, the doors of government swung open at last. No one knew how many women would choose to walk through or what difference they might make. Frances Perkins joined the government at a time of peril. With tools that feminists had fashioned, including the vote and new methods for alleviating poverty, she helped knit the nation's safety net during a global economic freefall. The New Deal, shaped by her vision, set the framework for the nation's success for the coming century.[1]

A former settlement worker, Frances Perkins had prepared all her life for the opportunity. She had advocated for women's suffrage on wooden soapboxes, investigated factory fires killing immigrant workers, talked strikers into handing over cartons of dynamite, braved thugs who stalked young Black women, and served two wily governors as labor commissioner. Little scared her. Yet the night she accepted the job of secretary of labor—becoming the first woman in a presidential cabinet—she did something she never did publicly and rarely in private. She wept. Her husband was in a psychiatric hospital and her emotional daughter in high school. Frances carried the family's burdens alone. She cried herself to sleep that evening, then got up the next morning to fight for unemployment insurance, workers' compensation, a federal minimum wage, the forty-hour work week, and Social Security for the aged. Failing only at national health insurance, she helped the United States reconcile its industrialization with its humane values. For this, members of Congress tried to impeach her.

Ann Marie Riebe, another newly minted voter, but younger and more ordinary than Frances, was too preoccupied by economic challenges to give much thought to the opportunities created by the vote. A woman could not eat a ballot. Economic opportunity lagged behind the franchise, still limiting the freedom of fiercely independent girls like Ann to pursue paths besides marriage.

Ann lived on the harsh but beautiful Great Plains of North Dakota, where scorching heat turned fertile lands into barren waste in the 1930s, prompting her to write in her diary, "Talk about wind! Most of the scenery is in the air." The unprecedented drought that defined the Dust Bowl ravaged farms, livelihoods, and the earth itself. New federal policies promised to save—or destroy—everything her family had created. From the saddle of her horse, Ann withstood the winds of change that buffeted three generations, hanging on to her own dreams of the future as the gale threatened to snatch them away.[2]

The Great Depression and World War II overshadowed the struggle for gender equality. Activism receded as women turned political gains into strategies for helping the nation survive, and pressed for new laws that they hoped would protect women without limiting them. At a governmental and personal level, individuals like Frances Perkins and Ann Marie Riebe fought, compromised, and persisted, wrangling the best deals they could against epic odds.

A Feminist Recipe for Industrialization

Born in Massachusetts in 1880, Frances Perkins—Fannie on her birth certificate—considered Maine her real home. It shaped her notion of America. She spent summers there with her grandmother, near the oyster-studded estuary on the rocky coast where her ancestors had arrived in the

1750s. Cynthia Otis Perkins, Fannie's grandmother, was a descendant of the family that had produced James Otis, who popularized the phrase "taxation without representation is tyranny," and his sister Mercy Otis Warren, Abigail Adams's close friend. Her grandmother's cousin was Oliver Otis Howard, the Union general who lost his right arm at the Battle of Seven Pines, founded the Freedman's Bureau to help Americans who had been liberated from slavery, and started Howard University in Washington, DC, which was named after him. Fannie's grandmother filled her mind with US history, and the family's role in it.

Cynthia Otis Perkins also drilled Yankee values into the child, who grew up seeing herself as a Mainer, a member of a self-sufficient, uncomplaining, industrious, straightforward, patriotic breed with an itch for personal privacy. Frances developed a tough sense of duty, which to her meant doing whatever was right regardless of the consequences. "If somebody opens a door for you, my dear," her grandmother told her, "walk right in and do the best you can . . . for it means that it's the Lord's will for you."[3]

Not everyone would find such advice appealing. It would have been natural for Frances to settle into the comfortable life that her father provided as owner of a modest store. Instead, when missionaries explained that some children had "nothing to eat and no clothes," her stomach twisted in "vicarious physical agony." She must have seen her father reach into his pocket, just as she had seen her mother on other occasions hustle "clothing or a barrel of flour or the rent or a job" for a neighbor. She learned that parishioners should help the poor, though it mystified her why some failed to thrive in the "great and good civilization" that America had built.[4]

So bashful that she shied away from speaking to a librarian, Frances loved books, and in one of them she made an important discovery. *How the Other Half Lives* by Jacob Riis, a Danish immigrant, opened "a new world to me," she later said. With his grim photographs of boys sleeping next to trash heaps, children wrapping cigars in sweatshops, and hollow-faced families crowded into one-room apartments, Riis brought the misery wreaked by industrialization to middle- and upper-class readers in their easy chairs.[5]

One well-born reader was Theodore Roosevelt, an idealistic, thirty-something politician who sent Riis a note saying, "I have read your book, and I have come to help." Published in 1890, *How the Other Half Lives* set the agenda for a whole generation "who had a great passion for social justice," Frances recalled. Riis inspired her to seek similar books that brought her a "literary" understanding of poverty.[6]

She was lucky to have parents who believed in education and could afford to give her a good one. Around 1900, only 6 percent of Americans graduated from high school, and only 3 percent of girls went on to college. Frances did both. At Mount Holyoke College in Massachusetts, one of the prestigious women's schools known as the Seven Sisters, she majored in chemistry and physics. Her shyness faded, her wittiness sharpened, and her sociability blossomed—classmates even elected her president. An economics course continued her education about industrialization's darker side. She and other students visited factories where they interviewed workers and witnessed their difficult lives. In Frances's last year at Mount Holyoke, she sat through an enthralling guest lecture by a reformer whose example she swore to follow.[7]

An early resident of Hull House, reformer Florence Kelley believed that government should set uniform standards rather than abandon women to the whims of employers. In 1892, Kelley had surveyed Chicago slums for the Illinois Bureau of Labor Statistics. Zealous and indefatigable, with a crown of soft brown braids, she traipsed through tenement after tenement where seamstresses and their children hunched seven days a week sewing shirts and coats. Her feet swelled so badly, a friend observed, that "she sits with her feet in the washtub all the time she is not in the street." Florence Kelley investigated nearly a thousand sweatshops. She took legislators to the worst of them and convinced them to pass a bill limiting women's employment to eight hours a day, six days a week.[8]

The Supreme Court of Illinois struck the bill down as unconstitutional. Attitudes toward women had evolved since William Blackstone's declaration that a woman's legal existence ended with marriage. Illinois now insisted that, married or not, women were as capable as men of negotiating contracts. New York ruled against a similar law in 1907 that forbade work after dark. "An adult woman is in no sense a ward of the state," the state court ruled. "She has the same rights as a man and is entitled to enjoy, unmolested, her liberty of person and freedom to work for whom she pleases, where she pleases and as long as she pleases." Courts opposed any special status as a form of discrimination.[9]

Judges voided protective legislation for men as well, insisting that American men could stand up for themselves. Trade unions echoed the courts. They considered worker unity superior to government interference for obtaining employer concessions. Unlike union organizers across Europe, Americans opposed government regulation as socialistic. In the words of Samuel Gompers, head of the American Federation of Labor—which mostly excluded women, children, and African Americans—the very idea of workmen's compensation, government health insurance, or laws to establish maximum hours was an offense to "free-born citizens," and an insult to their "virility." Real men did not need government help.[10]

"The labor people opposed workman's compensation and practically every other piece of social legislation originally," Frances Perkins noted afterward. "Look to the union," the influential Gompers preached, though skilled workers who did not share his sex or race were rarely admitted. Women and Black workers organized their own unions, but they were small. And unskilled day laborers—the vast majority of working people—had no unions at all.[11]

When Frances Perkins heard Florence Kelley at Mount Holyoke, the question of whether government had the authority to do anything at all for workers, male or female, was still undecided. From what she could see, the poor had insufficient leverage. She believed that Progressives like Kelley, who also campaigned for women's suffrage, had a smarter strategy than men like Gompers. "I'd much rather get a law, than organize a union," Frances Perkins later remarked. The effects were more universal.[12]

Upon graduation, Frances boarded a train for New York City against the wishes of her parents, who had hoped she would marry. She wanted a job like Florence Kelley's. In New York, the head of one reform organization shook his head in amusement. The twenty-one-year-old needed more life experience, he counseled. Too self-respecting to whine, Frances joked to former classmates, "Well, nothing seemed to turn up for me, and I made up my mind that it was my mission to stay at home and make my family miserable."[13]

Frances taught school for two years, volunteering at a Worcester settlement house where she organized a social club for teenage working girls. She gained a literal understanding of the cost of poverty when a blade at a candy factory sliced off the hand of Mary Hogan, one of the members. The factory sent Hogan home. Frances frantically called a doctor to help her. Later, she also tried to collect money from the manufacturer, but to her horror she found that the amputee had no right to recompense for injury.

(New York passed a workmen's compensation law several years later.) A local minister shamed the company into sending Hogan a hundred dollars.[14]

The action of the village preacher echoed a time before towns grew into cities, and small businesses morphed into corporations with thousands of employees. After 1920, for the first time, more Americans lived in towns than in the countryside. Compared with people on farms, urbanites inhabited smaller dwellings. They had less food and their income was less reliable. The physical, economic, and emotional gap between wealthy and poor widened into a chasm. Mass industrialization and urbanization swamped old safety networks, which had been based on personal familiarity.[15]

Frances Perkins took a job at a girls academy near Chicago, the epicenter of the settlement movement. At twenty-five she started signing her name "Frances" instead of "Fannie," determined to make the world take her more seriously. In 1905 she registered as a volunteer with the Chicago Commons settlement house, where Rosa Cavalleri still worked as a janitor and cook. Frances volunteered at both the Commons and Hull House, helping nurses make rounds through the squalid neighborhoods. She carried water from street pumps to wash dirty houses and fretful children. When she was instructed to clean a drunk father who had vomited all over himself, Frances snapped in frustration, "Why don't you let him rot?" The nurse responded, "We have to straighten this family out."[16]

One Sunday afternoon Frances co-hosted a neighborhood social at Chicago Commons with the founder's son, a slim youth about her age. At a convenient moment, standing near a staircase that Rosa Cavalleri had undoubtedly mopped, she grilled her fellow volunteer: "What *is* the trouble? How *can* we cure this? Is it to go on forever, these people being so poor that we have to give out free milk, we have to have free nursing services, the babies die, there's nothing to do on a Sunday but get drunk?"

Frances had intense brown eyes. In photographs she often looked like she was waiting for an answer, and her fellow organizer must have felt the force of her attention as families chattering in different languages milled past. The young man slapped the handrail to the upper floors. "The only answer to this is the organization of all working people into trade unions," he said. Unions would make charity unnecessary.[17]

Frances recalled Worcester's iffy unions and the powerlessness of girls like Mary Hogan. She understood that many Progressives believed, as he did, that unions were the answer, but Florence Kelley's solution seemed more sensible: meticulous documentation of conditions, followed by lobbying. Women might be equal to men in theory, and workers to employers, but daily life suggested otherwise. They needed something more than voluntary unions.

Frances had also read a speech by the youngest US president ever to serve. Teddy Roosevelt was catapulted into the presidency after an anarchist killed President William McKinley in 1901. When elected in his own right, Roosevelt shared his thoughts at his 1905 inaugural. "Modern life is both complex and intense," the young Republican asserted, "and the tremendous changes wrought by the extraordinary industrial development of the last half century are felt in every fiber of our social and political being." America must practice "justice and generosity," and show that the "marvelous material well-being" generated by industrialization could benefit everyone.[18]

The words enchanted Frances. "This is it," she thought. "This is constructive. This is what can be done." Government should help.[19]

Frances Perkins decided that "by hook or by crook" she would get a job in social work. In 1907 she quit her well-paid teaching position and took an investigative job in Philadelphia that barely covered her rent. She pawned her watch whenever she ran out of money and retrieved it on paydays. Proud of her growing ability, she learned to "say something in five minutes" to solicit money for the kind of surveys that Florence Kelley had helped pioneer.[20]

Her job was to investigate sexual predators. White and Black pimps trolled the riverfront and railways looking for young immigrants. They posed as housing agents, then coerced unsuspecting women into prostitution. Frances had previously pictured immigrants as refugees fleeing impoverished regions of Europe, but when she found that another group had fled "miserable tenant farms" in the deep South, she hired two Black assistants. One was prominent in the African American settlement house movement. The other, a recent Cornell University graduate, was "a brave little girl" who paced the Philadelphia wharves after dark to intercept unaccompanied migrants—much as the Vigilant Committee had done for Harriet Jacobs in 1842. Pimps were not happy. One dark evening, Frances used her sharp umbrella to fend off a well-known thug, screaming his name to attract attention.[21]

The fearless twenty-seven-year-old impressed politicians, whose endorsement she courted. One said, "You've been a good girl. You've done your duty. We'll see you through." City hall passed ordinances to license lodging houses, and the police chief sent constables to patrol docks and depots. After that, she recalled, "girls weren't actually snatched off the platform and their last twenty-five dollars taken from them."[22]

Frances received less help from unions. It miffed her that most made no effort to organize women, and some actively excluded them. She discovered that "whatever the men got, they [women] got lower—in wages, in types of work, in privileges, in opportunities for employment." She became convinced, as she put it, that "women were the most exploited in this whole industrial picture." There was a lesson in that. If legislation started at the bottom, it might generate solutions for everyone above. Protection for female workers could be the driving wedge for all workers.[23]

Her thinking mirrored that of other feminists in the Progressive Movement, who were desperate to alleviate suffering and willing to barter equality for better living conditions. When the Philadelphia job ended, Frances took her résumé to New York City. There she found work with the legendary Florence Kelley, who charged her with lobbying for a state law to limit women's working hours. Kelley's group, the National Consumer Organization, had tried without success to pass the bill, but was encouraged by a new Supreme Court ruling the year before. *Muller v. Oregon* (1908) upheld the constitutionality of legislation protecting women as "a disabled class," to quote Felix Frankfurter, a Harvard professor who commented on the argument.[24]

The Court ruled that a woman's "physical structure and a proper discharge of her maternal functions—having in view not merely her own health, but the well-being of the race—justify legislation to protect her." It deemed adult women "wards of the state," whose liberty should be curbed to protect them from employers or their own poor choices. States could not touch men's working hours, but they could prohibit conditions that hampered women's reproductive role, whether or not those women desired children. Unrestricted freedom to pursue personal goals or "happiness," a patriotic guarantee, did not apply fully to women.[25]

Muller v. Oregon satisfied reformers who wanted relief and conservatives who believed that childbearing should remain a woman's highest priority. It defined reproduction as a social good for which women must pay as individuals. Men might live for themselves. Women must take precautions to preserve their usefulness to others.

The Supreme Court decision reinforced job segregation at the exact moment that mechanization made it easier for men and women to perform the same tasks, and increased everyone's dependence on wages. *Muller* legitimized "Help wanted" ads in newspapers that distinguished between men's and women's jobs. An unskilled man pushing elevator buttons might earn twice the pay of a trained typist hitting keys at sixty words per minute. Job ladders for women were shorter and education did not take them as far. Promotion was typically not an option. The longer that men and women stayed at a firm, the greater the gap between their wages.[26]

The downside of protective legislation like *Muller* was not yet apparent, however, and Frances Perkins fervently lobbied the Albany legislature for a fifty-four-hour week, pulling off an upset vote in 1912 that left the galleries ringing with applause and won her admirers among the cigar-chomping crowd. Florence Kelley threw her arms around her young friend when she heard the news.[27]

Frances's experiences in Chicago and Philadelphia had shaped her thinking about poverty. The experience in Albany brought her renown. Teddy Roosevelt, with whom she cultivated a correspondence, recommended her for a commission investigating the infamous Triangle Shirtwaist Fire that had sent 123 young women, ages fourteen to twenty-three, to agonizing deaths not far from fashionable Washington Square Park in New York City. One of those who had watched the trapped girls jump from the ten-story building was Frances herself, who had been visiting a friend around the corner. Roosevelt told sponsors that with Frances Perkins in charge, "You can't fail." Like Kelley before her, Frances took legislators to get a firsthand look at abysmal factories, "and from that look they never recovered," she observed. Under her leadership, the commission pushed through the first laws requiring automatic sprinklers in buildings over seven stories and banning smoking on crowded shopfloors. It established protocols for fire drills, occupancy limits, and emergency escapes that became a worldwide standard.[28]

Albany changed Frances's self-presentation, too. A woman in government appeared out of place, so she calculated ways to make men less uncomfortable. Realizing that legislators felt more trusting whenever they pictured her like their mother, she embraced the stereotype. From then on, she said, "I adopted the black dress with a bow of white at the throat as a kind of official uniform. It has always worked." On her head she wore a black tricorn, a three-cornered hat that subtly evoked the patriots of 1776 with their fifes and drums.[29]

Frances noticed that, fairly or not, the prettier outfits of many "good and intelligent women" did not "invite confidence in their common sense, integrity and kindly justice." Average in appearance, with remarkable eyes in an unremarkable face, she used plainness to her advantage. Fortunately, she had also met Paul Wilson, who liked her just as she was, sensible dress and all. "I adore and worship you, beloved, dearly beloved," he wrote before their 1913 marriage.[30]

Frances Perkins had had other admirers beguiled by her bright energy, including novelist Sinclair Lewis, who proposed marriage at the top of his lungs beneath her apartment window one warm summer night. A rich and dashing reformer, Paul Wilson succeeded where Lewis failed. Reflecting upon his ardent courtship, Frances confessed a painful vulnerability that she had never let anyone see. "Before you came into my life," she wrote him, letting down her Maine reserve, "it was a lonesome place—cold and raw and trembling except on the outside. . . . You stormed into my heart somehow and I could never let you go."[31]

Frances and Paul saw themselves as a modern couple with shared career ambitions. They purchased a brick townhouse with arched windows in Greenwich Village, an intimate Manhattan neighborhood of tangled streets that many feminists called home, and in which bohemian young New Yorkers cultivated relationships that allowed partners to thrive separately and together, bonded by sexual attraction and emotional honesty rather than economic need. A Colorado author of the era coined the term "companionate marriage" to describe the new romantic ideal.[32]

Paul Wilson encouraged Frances's dedication to women's suffrage, and she teamed up with another woman to give speeches on street corners to passersby, some of whom were hostile, but most of whom were friendly. The experience, she later recalled, "did more to make me truly at ease with everybody and fully democratic in my feeling about the roughest kind of people than anything else I ever did." She decided to keep her last name, "touched by feminist ideas" dating to Lucy Stone, who also kept her name.

A journalist tried to make a headline out of her decision, but she craftily redirected his attention. For private social occasions she accepted "Mrs. Paul Wilson."[33]

Frances wanted children even though it was still rare for a college-educated woman to have a career, a husband, *and* children. She must have been highly motivated and Paul particularly understanding. Of the women who rose professionally in this generation, 70 percent never became mothers, daunted by the obstacles. The couple gave up smoking and drinking to conceive.[34]

Despite their best efforts, tragedy crept into their lives. Pregnancy still carried deadly risks. At age thirty-five, Frances suffered a miscarriage. When she conceived again, she worked from bed. Then she developed pre-eclampsia, a perilous complication that can send a woman into fatal convulsions. She survived the dangerous caesarian, but their baby boy was stillborn. The grief-stricken couple conceived a third time. Frances finally had a healthy daughter, Susanna, in 1916. When their happiness seemed complete, Paul suffered a mental breakdown.

Unbeknownst to her, Paul Wilson had suffered from bipolar disorder since college. His moods now swung from ecstasy to rage. Unable to work, he lost his salary, then gambled away his inheritance. The couple gave up their home for a small flat. Frances hired attendants to restrain Paul when his anger turned physical. Instead of a supportive partner, he became an emotional and financial wreck. With a Mainer's penchant for understatement, Frances stoically called his illness "just one of the accidents of life." The lover who had breached her defenses was gone.[35]

For the next forty years, Frances devoted her earnings to Paul's care while protecting his privacy from curious friends and nosy reporters. (In 1943, when her federal salary was $15,000, she spent $6,000 on medical expenses and donated $1,500 to charities.) She lavished affection on Susanna, even as it became clear that Paul's condition was probably heritable. Psychologists of the era tended to blame wives if their husbands or children had mental problems, and some friends wondered if Frances's ambitions had damaged her family. Perhaps she wondered, too.[36]

Regardless, her job was their lifejacket. From 1918 onward, Frances was the primary provider. She gave up her hope of another child, and gradually accepted that Paul would not get better. Earlier she had feared being swallowed up by Paul's high-profile career; now her career took center stage. Fortuitously, when New York governor Al Smith decided to appoint a woman to the state's industrial commission in January 1919, he thought of Frances Perkins, whom he had seen in action.

Congress seemed likely to pass the Nineteenth Amendment. If women got the vote, they should help govern, Governor Smith believed, so he gambled and appointed one. Historically, the first women to attain public office had served in agencies dedicated to children, such as school boards. The first female presidential appointee, for example, was Julia Lathrop, whom William Taft named to the Children's Bureau in 1912. Al Smith upped the stakes by appointing a woman to the "man's job" of industrial regulation.[37]

Frances took a risk as well, exchanging a crusader's shiny armor for an insider's grubby coveralls. She worried that Florence Kelley might disapprove. Instead, Kelley burst into happy tears when Frances asked if government work would compromise their ideals. "Glory be to God," Kelley exclaimed. "I never thought I would live to see the day when someone that we had trained, who knew about industrial conditions, who cared about women, cared to have things right, would have the chance to be an administrative officer."[38]

For the next decade, Frances served two New York governors as their highest female appointee, adjudicating workers' injury claims, overseeing factory inspectors, and resolving strikes. When Franklin D. Roosevelt succeeded Al Smith as governor, and then became president in 1933, Teddy's ghost may have whispered in his ear. With Frances Perkins at his side, he couldn't fail.

Home on the Range

Sixteen-year-old Ann Marie Riebe recognized a fool a mile away. She pitied clever Aunt Nona for having picked one. Born in 1912, Ann knew she would not make the same mistake. She would never exchange independence for marriage, which obligated a woman to "please her husband and to champion his actions and opinions regardless of what she really thought," as she later observed. Aunt Nona's experience reinforced this conviction. Swinging onto her ornery stallion and cutting across the North Dakota prairie, Ann galloped twelve miles in August of 1928 to herd Nona's sheep while her aunt harvested hay alone in the hot sun.[39]

Nona's husband, a pool-playing bum whom Ann jokingly dubbed "the answer to the maiden's prayer," lumbered out of bed late to eat the breakfast his wife had prepared, wearing an expression so grouchy it was "wonderful to behold." Nona knew more about running a farm than most men, while her husband seemed capable only of running one into the ground. Ann must have shaken her head as she scribbled in her diary, "What man is ever willing to listen to a woman?"[40]

Like many young people in the Roaring Twenties, Ann felt the world was at a crossroads. Willa Cather famously observed that "the world broke in two in 1922 or thereabouts." Even on the family's remote ranch near the Canadian border, which electricity had not yet reached, she felt the tingle. Hand-cranked telephones arrived when she was still at the one-room schoolhouse. In high school, she drove her younger sister Ethel and brother Bud to class in the family's new Model T Ford. Talkies came to the movie house and films appeared in color. She knew she would live a different life than the older generation.[41]

When crops were good in 1927, Ann's father bought his wife a black silk outfit for special occasions. The young Ann wrote in her diary, "Here all women past forty wear black dresses for best." That would not be her. "When I get to be forty I'll wear a pink dress if I want to and never mind if the neighbors think I am trying to be young and frivolous." Ann's father made her change into "respectable" clothes for visits to town, though she preferred the trousers and boots she used for roping cattle. She declared, "When I grow up I'll wear all the pants I want to."[42]

The cowgirl probably never saw the flappers then scandalizing cities, but the definition of a flapper in a midwestern newspaper fit her perfectly. "Any real girl . . . who has the vitality of young womanhood, who feels pugilistically inclined when called the 'weaker sex,' who resents being put on a pedestal and worshipped from afar, who wants to get into things herself, is a flapper." Ann probably never saw any avowed feminists either, though their activities made it into North Dakota newspapers, and her behavior suggests she shared their goal of seeking "the admission of women to every activity."[43]

Ann Marie Riebe took for granted that she would grow up to be a voter—and she later volunteered for political campaigns—though she never commented on how that right had materialized. Certainly no one fussed over it, reflecting a popular sense that female suffrage had become unremarkable. The old unpleasantness could be forgotten. When Ann was eight years old, Congress received as a gift for the Capitol a statue of Susan B. Anthony, Elizabeth Cady Stanton, and Lucretia Mott emerging from a solid marble block, designed for placement near the statues of Jefferson, Jackson, Lincoln, and Washington, and such lesser figures such as James Garfield. The only female then in the rotunda was Pocahontas, of whom there were two depictions, including one in an improbably form-fitting white gown.

Jane Addams presided over the statue's 1921 dedication on the hundredth birthday of Susan B. Anthony. Speaker of the House Frederick Gillett called it "symbolic of a change of tremendous significance—the admission of women to our electorate as equal partners in the great business of government." Delegations from the forty-eight states laid bouquets at the white marble base. Newspapers carried the story. Then, two days later, someone mysteriously sanded the inscription off the statue, lugged it to the basement crypt where cleaning supplies were kept, and turned the three women, now nameless, to face the wall.[44]

Congress ignored requests to return the statue to the rotunda. "Feminists," an Iowa newspaper commented in 1928, "seemed to feel that its position was a slight on the sex." The Senate Library Committee said only that the inscription commending a "women's revolution" had been offensive. Journalists began calling the statue "three old ladies in a bathtub." It sat in the Capitol basement for the next seventy-six years. Gentlemen in Congress did not mind "giving" women the vote so long as they could forget the annoying old ladies who had won it.[45]

The suffrage fight was ancient history to Ann Marie Riebe. Yet the gifts of feminism showed in her father and mother's assumption that she would attend college and in her own hope for a career. A child of the region where women first voted, the young westerner believed that she could move any obstacle to which she put her shoulder. "I want to be a journalist," she told her diary as a high school senior, though she was willing to accept the humdrum fallback, once a mark of progress, "to teach school if nothing else." High school enrollment had shot from 8 percent of children when Frances Perkins was young to 29 percent in Ann Riebe's generation.[46]

Ann needed to win a scholarship first. In 1928, the family's fortunes took a hit. Ann's father had built one of the largest spreads in the county, which meant they shared a modest, four-bedroom house with two hired hands who roomed upstairs near the children. (Ann particularly enjoyed the arthritic cowpoke who could cuss "twenty minutes without repeating himself once.") Unlike many ranches, no portion was mortgaged. As a young man, Hugo Riebe had fed and clothed his widowed mother, paid off his father's debts, and put nine younger brothers and sisters through college, though he had to quit high school to do so. "Dad must have been as busy as a one-armed man saddling a bronco," Ann reflected. Not until age thirty-six could he afford to marry. When a freak hailstorm wiped out crops across North Dakota in July 1928, the Riebe family was in better shape than most. They had no debt. Still, times were lean and Ann worked to achieve high marks.[47]

She sought opportunities to earn money, too. In addition to milking eight cows at dawn and dusk, roping cattle that strayed from the herd, trimming wicks nightly on their kerosene lamps, sanitizing the forty gears of the mechanical milk separator twice a day, and helping her mother bake, cook, and haul water from the well, Ann raised hens for egg money. Her small savings grew comfortably enough at the bank in Kensal (population four hundred) that she figured she could splurge on a Royal typewriter for school, though it dinged her college fund by sixty dollars.[48]

Ann was lucky. Three weeks later, in November 1928, the town bank failed. Every penny on deposit vanished. The student association lost $124, with nothing to show for it. One teacher lost everything but fifteen cents and the debt for clothes she had just charged in Minneapolis. The wife of a destitute farmer saw two years' worth of earnings from cooking at other ranches disappear. At least Ann had the new typewriter with its stiff black and white keys.

"The whole community is pretty blue," she observed. Her father made light of the situation. "You better buy your shoes before I run out of money," he teased the aspiring writer he called "Doodler." Fortunately, he had purchased the winter's supply of coal, kerosene, flour, and sugar before the crash. Even so, their cushion felt thin and "Doodler" vowed not to take "Dad's money" for shoes.[49]

Ann's use of the phrase "Dad's money" reflected the laws of most states. The earnings of the ranch belonged solely to Hugo Riebe. As *Harvard Law Review* summarized in 1925, statutes had liberalized to the point where a wife could now keep earnings from employment by a "third person," but courts held that "her husband is still entitled to her labor in the home and perhaps in his business" in exchange for room and board. Unless they lived in one of the few community-property states, husbands had no obligation beyond this. Only 12 percent of married women worked for "third persons," and even cash that a woman earned by selling preserves from her kitchen was not legally hers.[50]

Ann decided her new typewriter could help. "Typewriters are as scarce in this town as people who can type," she noted. The school superintendent would pay her to type correspondence. Just another chore for her list.[51]

Rural banks in America, like the communities they served, had been fragile for a while. World War I had stimulated extraordinary demand. To turn wild grasslands into productive fields, new immigrants borrowed heavily between 1914 and 1918. Longer-term residents like Aunt Nona's husband made the same bet. When the war ended and European farms became productive again, American growers were stuck with the surplus. Agriculture entered a prolonged slump. Crop prices fell 50 percent and land values 20 percent. In the 1920s, nearly six thousand rural banks folded. On the Great Plains, an arid grassland stretching from the Canadian border to the Texas Panhandle, unpredictable weather heightened ranchers' vulnerability.[52]

"Since the July 1 hailstorm," Ann explained to her diary, "farmers have drawn out more than $50,000 and had nothing to put in." Like thousands of other institutions with small cash reserves, the Kensal bank closed when its coffers emptied. At sixteen, Ann did not worry. Her father would provide.[53]

Secure in her world, she often rode to visit her grandmother and two bachelor uncles a couple of miles away. The younger uncle operated the farm for his widowed mother, postponing marriage while building his own spread. The older one had sustained heart damage in the flu pandemic of 1918 and never recovered enough to live independently. Ann loved the horseback ride. When she delivered gifts on Christmas Eve, as she had done since age eight, the snow-covered hills gleamed magically. "Far away a coyote is howling in a silver world," she wrote at the end of 1928.[54]

Ann worked for the school district through spring. Lithe and pretty, with a quick tongue and bright hair gathered into a ponytail, she devised stratagems for handling men who wanted to monopolize her time. One day, while she was addressing three hundred letters after school, the principal "came into the office and gabbed so much I asked him to lick the stamps and envelopes," she jotted in her diary. "That shut him up and got the work done faster."[55]

Ann did not mind hard work. She minded people who did not work hard. She avoided criticizing her younger sister, but took note whenever Ethel dodged responsibility. It irked Ann that a healthy girl would use her gender to avoid earning money, milking cows, or learning to drive a car. Ethel wanted "good times and nice clothes."[56]

When summer came, Ann bought a hundred chicks to raise for sale. She got up before dawn and worked until dark alongside her six-foot-three-inch younger brother to train horses, mend fences, and help their father conserve on labor costs. The pair corralled untamed heifers when they needed cream. Range animals did not always cooperate. Ann laughed when brother Bud remarked after one particularly lively milking session, "That cow may be a mother, but she's no lady."[57]

Hail had ruined the Riebe crop in 1928, but 1929 was worse. Virtually no rain fell. Streams dried up like old bones. "Dad says it never happened before in his lifetime," Ann noted. She and her brother and father worked in 110 degree heat to glean what they could, stockpiling hay for their animals but with none left over to sell. Ann worked indoors, too, making soap from lye and baking pies and bread. After pressing the family's laundry with a flatiron, she went back outside to prop bundles of freshly cut wheat against one another to dry, forcing her arms to lift another heavy bundle even as she tired. Ann had a foot planted firmly on both sides of the family's gender divide.[58]

For all its challenges, the stark Stony Brook country, named for a nearby creek, moved her soul. The tender light at dawn, the song of the coyotes, the "distance-purpled" mountains, the undulating fields of blue flax flowers, the "flashing opal" of sunset over low hills—Ann Marie Riebe knew that whatever else life brought, she would always have the ranch, where work ensured independence.[59]

Others were not so fortunate. The father of her friend Edith had died. Afterward, Edith's mother "lost all her money in the bank failure." Her brother was forced to run the farm. Edith walked four miles to school on snowpack that reached the top of telephone poles in winter, unable to afford a room in town as the Riebe children did. Elderly neighbors lost farms to foreclosure, became indigent, and died of despair. Just after a blizzard in November 1929, Ann learned that North Dakota's financial troubles had spread. "There seems to be quite a furor in the country over a big stock market crash that wiped a lot of people out," she noted a year after she lost her own savings. "We are ahead of them."[60]

The first drop, on Black Thursday (October 24, 1929), knocked 11 percent off the New York stock market. Over the next three years, the nation's financial position plunged further and further. The failure of rural banks prompted runs on urban banks. The Dow Jones Stock Index fell more than 90 percent, from a high of 386 down to 40, and another five thousand banks closed, including the nation's largest. Investors lost $20 billion. The nation's gross domestic product declined by half. Unemployment soared. Deaths from heart attack increased. Aunt Nona's husband lost their farm to a bank and moved his family into a leaky shack with a warped floor.[61]

Ann's father hung onto the cattle he had raised to sell. Perhaps prices would improve. "Maybe next year we won't have to work so hard," Ann wrote, echoing farmers everywhere. "There may be plenty of rain and hay. Cattle prices may go up."[62]

At her parents' request, Ann waited to enroll in high school until Ethel could join her, and in May 1930, they graduated together. Ann used the money she earned from typing to purchase graduation shoes for her sister and herself. Two colleges offered scholarships. "Dad was beaming with pride," she reported to her diary, though she discounted the compliments she received after her valedictory speech on the class motto, "The one thing better than making a living is making a life." Ann wondered at their sincerity. "What in billy-blue-blazes do I know about making a life?"[63]

She ached to learn, though. Jamestown College, a small Presbyterian school thirty miles away, would prepare her as a journalist or teacher. Ann hoped to rebuild her savings over the summer to cover any additional costs, especially since her parents needed money for Ethel, who did not win a scholarship.

Without rain, the hot wind turned ugly, scattering oat and flax seeds before they could sprout. A neighbor planted his field twice. When the seed blew away the second time, he went fishing. "And Mama cried," his little girl told Ann. Dust coated the feathers of Ann's white chickens, and she locked their chicks in a shed for shelter. Not everyone was equally prudent. A hired man overworked one of the horses until it collapsed. Ann and her younger brother knelt in the dirt by the stricken animal. They put wet cloths on its brow and shooed away flies, but there was nothing they could do except stay "with him until he died so he would know he was loved and would not die alone."[64]

At eighteen, Ann remained stubbornly optimistic. She enjoyed training a new colt and went dancing with a boy named Vern. She stopped seeing him at the end of summer "because he was getting marriage ideas." Ann fell in love with college instead when she and Ethel arrived in September 1930. Vern continued writing "sappy letters," but Ann informed him she would "absolutely" not consider marriage. "If I ever marry," she confided to her diary, it would be to "a man with whom I can get someplace in this world."[65]

That was a secondary consideration, though. Ann Marie Riebe intended to spread her wings. She did not know that headwinds in the Dirty Thirties would make flight conditions chancy.

A New Deal for Women and Men (But Mostly Men)

Frances Perkins's father was a Republican, and as a settlement worker she had taken little interest in electoral races. One curmudgeon admitted that he had opposed her bill on the fifty-four-hour work week until he discovered that voters liked it. "Are you one of those women suffragists?" he growled. She stammered, "Yes, I am." He gave her a stare and said, "Well, I'm not, but if anybody ever gives them the vote, I hope you will remember that you would make a good Democrat."[66]

By 1933, politics were Frances's livelihood. She had served as top labor adviser to Governor Franklin D. Roosevelt, and a federal appointment seemed likely when he became president. But no woman had ever served at the cabinet level. Union officials considered the Department of Labor their fiefdom, and Frances had no stomach for the pillory such a job could easily become. Her fragile husband was in a psychiatric hospital, her daughter a volatile teenager. Frances called family "the greatest blessing anyone can have," but anguished over the vulnerability of her own.[67]

Competing with this was an exalted sense of duty—and opportunity. When the economy first broke down, Frances had encouraged Governor Roosevelt to consider state unemployment insurance, something that had never been tried. Roosevelt worried it would sap recipients' work ethic. Frances sailed to Britain with Susanna to study the system there and returned with a proposal to treat unemployment as an industrial problem, not a personal failing, so that individuals did not "suffer the total, crushing cost" of an uncontrollable event. According to this proposal, work stoppages would be treated like accidents, and employers would pay a tax to fund limited benefits for laid-off workers. Companies could pass this cost on to customers in slightly pricier goods. Roosevelt called a governors' conference to discuss the idea. No one yet thought in terms of federal involvement.[68]

Frances made herself into a national expert on unemployment. When Roosevelt ran for president, he asked her for a speech on why America needed social insurance. "We are going to construct a more inclusive society," Frances wrote. With his sharper instinct for vibrant language, Roosevelt translated it on radio as "We are going to make a country in which no one is left out."[69]

After he won, speculation flourished that Frances's boss would summon her to Washington. Letters flooded Roosevelt's office. Jane Addams, who had won the 1931 Nobel Peace Prize, wrote, "it is a wonderful coincidence that the woman best equipped for the post should have sat in the previous cabinet of the President of the United States." Felix Frankfurter, whom Roosevelt appointed to the Supreme Court, endorsed Frances, too, as did the founder of Filene's Department Store in Boston, who called her "the best equipped MAN for the job."[70]

Frances herself recommended that Roosevelt select someone "straight from the ranks" of the unions "to establish firmly the principle that *labor is in the President's Councils.*" She sent names. Roosevelt shot back, "Have considered your advice and disagree."[71]

Feminists pressured Frances to accept. She could advance their goals. Both Carrie Chapman Catt's League of Women Voters and Alice Paul's National Woman's Party supported the appointment. In charge of the female vote for the Democratic Party, former suffragist Mary Dewson told Frances that she should take the job because she owed it to all women, especially Florence Kelley, who had just died. Otherwise, "generations might pass" before another would be asked. When Roosevelt requested a meeting, Dewson lectured, "Don't be such a baby. Frances, you do the right thing. I'll murder you if you don't."[72]

Frances Perkins may have considered Roosevelt's own sacrifices. She had met him twenty years earlier. "I do remember—nobody who saw it will ever forget—how handsome Franklin Roosevelt was," Frances recalled. Six foot two, the athletic young patrician exuded grace and, with a tilt of his chin when he laughed, a touch of smugness. Frances judged him shallow. Then came polio, against which there was still no vaccine. Failing to kill the man, it left him in leg braces and a wheelchair.[73]

Frances considered humility "the greatest of virtues," and she knew that "if you can't learn it, God will teach you by humiliation." She had seen Roosevelt lurch uncertainly across public platforms or, worse, be carried in the arms of other men. With a hand to her throat the first time, Frances had watched him accept "the ultimate humility that comes from being helped physically." Roosevelt's hands shook with strain whenever he stood at a podium, holding on for strength and balance, yet he smiled infectiously. Frances softened. The man "asked for no quarter." How could she? Plus, as she later told Carrie Chapman Catt, she finally accepted that she had "a kind of duty to other women."[74]

If Roosevelt wanted what she did, she would endure anything. Nonetheless, Frances had her demands. She was fifty-two and abhorred prying reporters. She brought her list to his overrun brownstone on 65th Street on the cold night that he asked her to become secretary of labor.

The stakes were high. The week before, an immigrant critical of capitalism had shot at the president-elect, yelling, "Too many people are starving to death!" His bullet instead hit the mayor of Chicago, whom Roosevelt cradled until they got to the hospital where he died. (A female bystander wrestled the assassin to the ground.) The day before, the newly elected chancellor of Germany, Adolf Hitler, had met with leading industrialists to share his plan for solving the Great Depression. The next year, fascist leader Benito Mussolini of Italy promised every rural person "a clean and beautiful house." Whether democracies or dictatorships best helped the downtrodden was a question that commanded worldwide attention.[75]

Roosevelt and Frances Perkins both had a wicked sense of humor, and they joked about current events before he popped the question. Frances asked why he did not appoint a labor organizer. Roosevelt said he wanted to help all working people, not just the unionized. He wanted her to achieve for the nation what she had spearheaded in New York.

Frances pulled out her list. Nothing on it was radical, she believed. All of it had been tried by other democracies, some with great success, but she understood that Roosevelt might consider it unrealistic. "I won't hold you to this," she said, her brown eyes reassuring. "But I don't want to say yes to you unless you know what I'd like to do and are willing to have me go ahead and try."[76]

She described federal relief to the states, public works to generate jobs, and the prohibition of child labor. She also wanted a forty-hour work week and a minimum wage so that adults could earn enough to keep their children in school.

"Can that be done constitutionally?" Roosevelt asked.

Frances did not know, but she had learned from Felix Frankfurter that although the government could not tell corporations what to pay workers, it could set its own standards. Whether Washington bought pencils or airplanes, it could issue contracts for products made by people earning a decent wage, working decent hours. Businesses could decide not to bid, but most would participate. Better practices would be the result. Frances wanted nationwide unemployment insurance, too, and pensions for the elderly, one-third of whom leaned on family for survival.[77]

Roosevelt reminded her that he opposed giveaways. "You know, Frances, I don't believe in the dole and I never will." She explained that she had in mind a program of insurance, not charity.

The president-elect nodded approval. "I don't know how you'll do it," he said, "but it's all right. You have to invent the way to do these things. Don't expect too much help from me."

Frances asked for a day to consult her husband. Roosevelt looked up from his wheelchair as she stood to leave. Perhaps his chin tilted at the familiar jaunty angle. His expression was certainly bemused. "I suppose you are going to nag me about this forever," he said, referring to her list.[78]

Frances knew that he hoped she would, or he would not have offered her the job. "He wanted his conscience kept for him by somebody," she later observed. Wives, mothers, and temple priestesses had long played that role. Roosevelt could set aside his conscience when he felt he needed to, comforted that she was minding it.[79]

Frances visited the White Plains hospital campus in the countryside where her husband played tennis and received visitors on good days, though some still thought of the sanitarium by its earlier, more ominous name, the Bloomingdale Asylum for the Insane. Paul was in "a good, controlled mood," she found with relief. He did not sob or rant. He only declared that he would not move to "horrid" Washington. Paul's condition did not allow him to grasp that he was too ill to go, so Frances agreed that he should stay behind and promised to visit every weekend.[80]

Once she got home, she dissolved into tears. The agony of shyness, forgotten since childhood, reared up. Perhaps she also grieved again for the eager reformer her husband had once been. In a newspaper article praising Frances's appointment, a well-meaning Kansas journalist mentioned, "Frances Perkins' husband is in broken health and in a hospital." It was precisely the type of gossip that made her feel naked. Frances turned to her religious roots, which deepened. After moving to Washington, she often attended a women's retreat run by nuns at All Saints Convent near Baltimore.[81]

At her first White House meeting two weeks later, Frances selected a chair carefully. The men tried not to stare as she entered the room, but she knew they were studying her like a specimen. She felt them glance over when she looked down at her notes, so she kept her face a mask, reminding herself not to pipe up with any "bright ideas." Her strategy was "to give the impression of being a quiet, orderly woman who didn't buzz-buzz all the time, who didn't butt in where she wasn't wanted, who could be trusted not to be an embarrassment." She visualized herself as an observer "on the porch of a golf club, perhaps," as each man offered his observations.[82]

Roosevelt finally turned to her with "the encouraging smile of a brother who was interested in your being able to be successful." He amiably asked what she had in mind for the Labor Department, as if it were an everyday matter. The room tensed. In a neutral tone and with few words, Frances summarized her goal of temporary relief followed by permanent legislation. Cabinet members now stared openly. As she spoke, "every man in the room turned and looked at me very hard." Vice President John Nance Garner "stopped smoking, leaned forward, looked, looked, listened, looked, listened, looked, then sat back in his chair." A sigh went through the room.[83]

Vice President Garner told his wife Mariette afterward that Frances Perkins had spoken "plain and distinct" and then, fittingly, stopped. "I guess she's all right," he said. A Texan who attempted a run for office before women could vote, Mrs. Garner reported her husband's conclusion to Frances and the two women shared a laugh. "Mrs. Garner was a very witty woman," Frances recalled.[84]

Cabinet members had conducted an important test in an ongoing experiment. Democracy must grow to live, and women had earned a place at the table. Would men accept them? Would women comport themselves well? Those elected to rescue the United States from the Great Depression answered yes.

"The men in the cabinet, from the beginning, treated me as an equal and a colleague," Frances said. Roosevelt made sure they did not patronize. When Secretary of the Navy Claude Swanson hesitated to tell a certain story as there was "a lady present," Roosevelt encouraged him, saying, "Go on, Claude, she's dying to hear it."[85]

Outside the White House, sex segregation remained routine, especially in social situations where political wheels were greased. The Gridiron Club, the men-only press association, invited every cabinet member except the secretary of labor to its annual soirée the first month. To mitigate the slight that no man even noticed, Eleanor Roosevelt gave a dinner that night for Frances Perkins and Hattie Caraway, the first woman elected to the US Senate.[86]

The First Lady's gesture typified the outlook for which she became renowned. Eleanor Roosevelt was both an avowed feminist and a staunch supporter of Black civil rights. In 1933, she published *It's Up to the Women,* a popular guidebook in which she asserted, "In this present crisis it is going to be the women who will tip the scales and bring us safely out of it." They should be encouraged to participate, she believed. During her husband's years in office, the First Lady gave practical help to dozens who took important positions, a record of participation not repeated until the 1960s. The "New Deal political sisterhood," in the phrasing of biographer Joseph Lash, institutionalized social welfare reforms that women Progressives had advocated for three decades.[87]

The secretary of labor's first task was to evict her predecessor. On the morning that Frances Perkins arrived at the Department of Labor, the doorman asked for identification. "I'm Miss Perkins, the new Secretary of Labor," she replied.[88] The man blinked, said he recalled something in the newspaper about a lady secretary, and admitted her to the upper floors. There, a surprised Black receptionist gave her the only "ceremonial kind of greeting" she received. Another man said he would inquire if the secretary of labor was free. Once inside the office, Frances saw that papers still littered every surface. The outgoing official lounged at a large desk facing a portrait of himself. They spoke about the department for an hour or so, whereupon Frances suggested that the former secretary might wish to take an early lunch on his way home while the receptionist packed the office.[89]

In its first hundred days, the Roosevelt administration pioneered two major relief programs. Frances Perkins helped launch both. First was the Civilian Conservation Corps (CCC), Roosevelt's brainchild. He proposed sending men from breadlines in the big cities to work in the countryside, which had been troubled by hardships "almost beyond description."[90]

Though she little understood rural problems, Frances wondered if the plan was naïve. She asked what the men would do "when they got to the woods." Roosevelt replied that they could build dams and plant trees, introduce better farming practices, curb soil erosion, and protect wildlife. Frances pointed out that urbanites were not foresters. She reiterated, "Take those poor men off the breadlines and take them up to the Adirondacks and turn them loose?"[91]

Roosevelt told her to figure it out. She must convince Congress and recruit the men. Frances suggested that the Army run the camps because they had tents and trucks, and the Forest Service should select projects. Roosevelt endorsed her ideas enthusiastically. By her third week in office, Frances was the administration's star witness before Congress. An Associated Press journalist reported that she answered every objection "so effectively that there was rarely a retort." She even got laughs. Frances left the hearing aglow. She felt she had "jazzed it up well."[92]

In the cloakroom afterward, where congressmen lit up their cigars, some were not quite so respectful. One quipped that Frances had proved herself "an awful smart woman," but, he added, "I'd hate to be married to her."[93]

Frances Perkins roared at the crude comment when Ruby Black, a female reporter, repeated it to her privately. "You know, Ruby, it never occurred to me when I went up there that perhaps I could get a husband. It wasn't in my mind. How unfortunate I didn't think of it!" Like any seasoned politician, Frances could take a punch. Even so, she knew he had mocked her as sexually unappealing—the easiest insult. The jest made the rounds for years. Frances never responded, knowing she could not afford to appear sensitive since that, too, would supposedly prove women unfit for government.[94]

The other bandage was the Federal Emergency Relief Administration. A young friend, former social worker Harry Hopkins, contacted Frances with a design for a public works program, aware that she was keen to implement one. Frances hammered the pitch into shape and brought it to

Roosevelt, who agreed that Hopkins (whom he did not yet know well, but who would become the president's most influential adviser) should administer it. The program sent federal funds to state and local governments to build playgrounds, repair schools, build roads, lay sewers, create art, and even conduct oral history interviews of elderly Americans who had survived slavery.

Relief was temporary, however. As Frances told her old friend Felix Frankfurter, she had come to Washington to "work for God, F.D.R. and the millions of forgotten, plain, common working men." She wanted long-term solutions to the misery that was created when companies squeezed wages to beat rivals and fired people to match fluctuating demand for products.[95]

Other nations, particularly Britain and Germany, had already addressed these endemic hazards of industrialization. They provided all citizens with unemployment insurance, minimum wage guarantees, old age pensions, pregnancy leaves, child care assistance, and sickness benefits. One consequence was lower maternal and infant death rates. Countries with these social safety nets had had good results. When critics in 1881 called German Chancellor Otto Van Bismarck a socialist, the conservative prince retorted, "Call it socialism or whatever you like." European governments intended to preserve capitalism by mitigating the risks of industrialization for wage earners who could no longer grow their own food.[96]

Americans, by contrast, resisted intervention, especially by the federal government. This attitude dated to the country's founding, when state ratification conventions approved the Constitution by the slimmest of margins. Roosevelt himself made it plain that he wanted no handouts resembling charity. Whatever the architects of the New Deal built, it must rest on two pillars: avoiding Pyrrhic conflict with the states, and making workers feel that they had earned, rather than been given, social benefits.

Throughout her career, Frances Perkins had struck bargains that prioritized the many over the few. To pass the women's fifty-four-hour law, she agreed to exclude female cannery workers. A friend described Frances as "a half-loaf girl: take what you can get now and try for more later." Frances was a social worker first; a feminist second. "I was much more deeply touched by the problems of poverty," she said. She would use the opportunity that feminists had given her for the good of all Americans, even if it meant getting less for women in the short run.[97]

Her greatest accomplishments were the Social Security Act of 1935 and the Fair Labor Standards Act of 1938. Both helped hundreds of millions, but initially reinforced women's economic dependency and even discriminated against them.

In her second year, Frances nagged Roosevelt, as expected, telling him they had "probably our only chance in twenty-five years." She understood that one must catch a reform wave before it breaks. He appointed her chair of a committee charged with giving Americans "economic security," cradle to grave. The treasury and agriculture secretaries participated, along with Harry Hopkins and the US attorney general. Frances Perkins was the only one who attended every meeting. They drew from plans that Progressives, especially women in the settlement movement, had advocated for years. Working with lawyers and consultants, they addressed most of the items on Frances's list, with the exception of national health insurance, which the American Medical Association, in its zeal to protect doctors' incomes, called socialism. No one worked harder than Frances to develop the bill.[98]

Social Security was, in the view of the preeminent historian of the New Deal, the administration's "most durable and consequential reform." The committee accomplished it in fourteen months, with Frances working such long hours that her chauffer quit. Roosevelt set a deadline of Christmas for their report. When the small cabinet committee began to wrestle over the final recommendations, Frances invited them to her home in late December, put a bottle of Scotch on the table, and declared that no one could go home until they were done. She and Harry Hopkins delivered the report to Roosevelt on Christmas Eve, 1934. They spent the following months wheedling Congress.[99]

"The one person, in my opinion, above all others who was responsible for there being a Social Security program in the early 30s was Frances Perkins," said an assistant to Senator Robert Wagner, who sponsored the bill to the Senate. "I don't think that President Roosevelt had the remotest interest in a Social Security bill or program. He was simply pacifying Frances."[100] That assessment was not fair to Roosevelt, but he certainly relied on the plans that Frances and other settlement workers had developed.

The Social Security Act of 1935 sent money to disabled Americans, the indigent elderly, and single mothers. It funded health care for infants and pregnant women. Most famously, it created pensions and unemployment insurance funded by employee and employer taxes. Allies on the Supreme Court, particularly justices Louis Brandeis and Harlan Stone, had reminded Frances that the federal government had the authority to levy taxes, guiding her toward a bill they did not have to reject.[101]

The size of a person's monthly check depended on prior deductions from her or his paystub, matched by an employer's contribution. The deduction started at 1 percent of earnings in 1937. People with higher earnings paid more and took out more. Most European nations fashioned their safety nets differently, and people received benefits as citizens, not employees. Payments were pegged to need, not prior earnings. Frances Perkins's committee rejected this more generous alternative because of American antipathy to centralized government and welfare giveaways. She fought for what she could get, hoping to nudge the country in a better direction.[102]

Even so, many received nothing. To win over congressional skeptics and business opponents, the committee reluctantly added exemptions for farm laborers, household workers, government employees, and the staffs of hospitals, churches, and charities, with the hope of later including them. None of these workers or their employers contributed to Social Security.[103]

This included most African Americans, many of whom still worked on other people's farms or in other people's kitchens. Schoolteachers, nurses, and government clerks—typically female—also did not immediately benefit from Social Security. Nor did wives laboring at home. (In 1939, Congress increased workers' pensions to allow a supplement for wives, although if a woman outlived her husband she received only a fraction because, the government deemed, a widow could live more cheaply than a widower since she, unlike him supposedly, could cook her own meals.) The upshot, one historian notes, "was the exclusion of 55 percent of African-American workers, and 80 percent of all women workers, including more than 87 percent of wage-earning African American women." They received no unemployment insurance either.[104]

To add insult to injury, such workers effectively funded benefits for the others, since companies raised prices. An ineligible Black nurse buying orthopedic shoes, for example, would end up contributing to the pension of an eligible white male factory worker who stitched the soles.

Frances Perkins's second major achievement, the Fair Labor Standards Act, had discriminatory aspects, too. The 1938 law set a federal minimum wage, established the forty-hour-work week, and set the working age at sixteen. It helped few at first. To make sure the Supreme Court did not overrule it as unconstitutional, the Labor Department drafted the law so that it pertained only to people making goods that crossed state lines. Again guided by Court supporters, Frances relied on the fact that the federal government could regulate interstate commerce. Not long before, in *Adkins v. Children's Hospital* (1923), the Supreme Court had overruled a minimum wage for women in the District of Columbia, and Frances did not wish to repeat their defeat.

Getting past the Supreme Court was half the battle. She had to push the bill through Congress first. Unions and manufacturers attempted to load the bill with exemptions—from workers processing seaweed to dairymen churning butter. One version would have covered only 50,000 out of a population of 132 million. Frances Perkins tamped down as many exemptions as she could, but had to accept substantial limits to obtain a minimum wage for anybody at all. The new law again excluded occupations where women and African Americans clustered, including food service and retail sales. The Fair Labor Standards Act protected only 14 percent of working women compared with 39 percent of men. Nonetheless, Roosevelt deemed it the most important piece of New Deal legislation after Social Security.[105]

In the ensuing decades, most states passed local laws that matched and sometimes exceeded federal requirements. In 1966, Congress extended the federal minimum wage to nearly all workers, including most women, although as late as 2021 restaurants in sixteen states still paid servers only $2.13 an hour. No one system prevailed. Power sharing by the central government and fifty states made for a patchwork quilt of laws.[106]

What did broadly apply were protective regulations that limited women's working hours. In 1937, hourly maximums for women ranged from seven hours a day in Utah to eleven in Texas. Most states had something. From the 1920s through the 1960s, these regulations required businesses to distinguish between the sexes. Workplace improvements for male workers were called "fair standards," while those for females were called "protective."[107]

Feminists split over the way forward. Indeed, they disagreed over many things as an increasingly broad cross-section of women participated in government. Some became Republicans, others Democrats. Some joined third parties. Alice Paul's Woman's Party wanted to abolish protective legislation in favor of an Equal Rights Amendment. Yet other feminists, especially those who had campaigned for such laws—including members of Carrie Chapman Catt's League of Women Voters—considered the risks too great for women workers.

Disagreements over what made for a good or bad feminist echoed quarrels over tactics in other social movements, including civil rights and trade unionism. The term became less common as economic problems took center stage. In one national database, newspaper coverage of "feminism" plunged from 1,352 articles in 1930 to 382 in 1945. Frances Perkins took the side of reformers who opposed the Equal Rights Amendment, at least until Roosevelt ran for an unprecedented fourth term and his party endorsed it. The only major legislative gain for women's rights per se in this period was the Cable Act of 1922, which allowed American-born women who wed foreigners to keep their citizenship.[108]

Meanwhile, from the 1920s through the early 1950s, most office firms barred married women, as did most school districts. During the Great Depression, even the federal government discriminated against them. "Feminism hit a stone wall in America in 1932," a Texas newspaper announced. Renewed obstacles to female employment "makes marriage a girls' ideal and chief aim once more," the *Port Arthur News* commented.[109]

The movement faded to the point that, in 1949, French philosopher Simone de Beauvoir described feminism as a quarrel of "the last century." Freudian psychiatrists marginalized women who wanted lives outside the home as textbook cases of "penis envy," and maligned feminism as a "psychopathology" and "deep illness." Economic dependency remained a worldwide fact at midcentury. In America, it was woven into the safety net. With women less eligible than men for Social Security, unemployment insurance, and the minimum wage, a girl's best economic plan was to find a husband. Even this offered no guarantee, as Frances Perkins and Ann Marie Riebe's Aunt Nona could have attested.[110]

A photograph taken as Roosevelt signed the 1935 Social Security Act shows everyone but Frances smiling. Moments earlier, she had learned that

Paul had escaped the nurse she could barely afford and was wandering the city. When the flash bulbs stopped popping, she dashed to Union Station and caught the first train home.[111]

A Plague of Dust, Suitors, and "Government Geniuses"

Ann Marie Riebe tackled her coursework with dogged effort and dry humor. When a professor asked what she thought of a tough exam, she reassured him it was a masterpiece. "If he had asked what it was a masterpiece of, I'd told him that, too," she jotted in her diary.[112]

Ann needed high grades to retain her scholarship, so she applied herself even while complaining that "each prof thinks we have nothing to do but prepare for his course." She was too clever to protest; another student who did reaped the retort, "This is a college, not an amusement hall." Ann took Latin to improve her marketability as a future high school teacher, observing, "The things those old Romans said in their poetry would make one blush." Despite the levity, her goals were serious. When a Rural Sociology professor asked who intended to remain in the countryside, she alone raised her hand. "I can do some good there and make a worthwhile life for myself," she told her diary.[113]

To meet expenses, she worked at the school library. Her pay was low, hours terrible, and supervisor unsympathetic. But $14 for thirty-five hours of work felt like a pound of gold. News from home was bad. Ann's father had received only nine dollars for a 900-pound "canner" cow, meaning that the cow was so emaciated it was good only for canning. A friend had received just two dollars for a 350-pound hog, though his wife had to pay forty cents for a tin of ham that made only two dozen sandwiches. One neighbor could not even sell his pigs; the buyer said they were too skinny. So the rancher purchased fifty dollars' worth of feed and fattened them. The buyer paid him $51.60 for the lot. Another neighbor, a thirty-six-year-old farmer, found that 2,500 bushels of wheat brought only $2,500 with which to service his $11,000 debt. He died of a heart attack.[114]

As a girl, Ann especially appreciated cash. One schoolmate's father still opposed education for women and would not give his daughter a penny. The girl's mother, "though closely watched, sometimes manages to send Ruby a dollar or two." Ann's own father, Hugo Riebe, did his best to help his daughters financially and never abused his power over his wife, yet what Ann saw of the world strengthened her resolve to stand on her own feet.[115]

Ann's sister Ethel was different. She dropped out of Jamestown College, transferred to the more expensive state agricultural college, dropped out of that when she broke up with a boyfriend, transferred to the University of Illinois at Urbana, left it, went back to the agricultural college, decided it still was not right, then enrolled in a two-year teacher's college, the least demanding route. Although the sisters had started college at the same time, Ann finished first, got a job, and helped pay Ethel's college tuition for two more years. She also covered the hospital bill when her sister developed appendicitis. Throughout, Ethel bought new clothes with whatever spare cash she earned. After sopping up her own share of the college budget plus that of their younger brother Bud, Ethel finished school, taught one semester, and got married. The only explanation for the family's patience was that "Mama's heart is set on good educations for her children."[116]

The Riebes' insistence on giving all their children the same opportunity reflected an increasingly widespread acceptance of gender parity in education. Not all Americans felt the same, of course, but enough that by the 1930s women made up 40 percent of college graduates. Some girls failed to appreciate the opportunity. Ethel had Ann's affection but not her respect.[117]

This may not have mattered greatly in different times, but Ann graduated in 1934, the nadir of the worst North American drought in a thousand years. In weather "hot enough to wither a fence post," cattle starved, horses collapsed, dairy cows ran dry, and hens stopped laying. Ann's brother lost his prize heifer. "Somehow, to me, the look on his face when he shot Isabelle stood for this whole tragedy of a land laid waste, a way of life destroyed, and a boy's long struggle ending in despair," she wrote.[118]

Among the Riebe children, Ann alone envisioned a future in ranching. She, her father, and Bud rode their horses to the tallest hill one day where her father pointed out the features of the land. Speaking to Bud, he advised him to never give up the ranch's water rights, its most important asset. Bud had previously planned on attending agricultural college, but he took this moment to declare that he wanted to pursue civil engineering instead.

Looking over the land, the trio fell silent. Ann said nothing. She turned the terrible consequences over in her mind. Bud did not see the promise she did. "But what can a woman do?" Ann wondered. Gender roles had not yet changed enough to allow Hugo Riebe to imagine his daughter taking over the ranch, or for her to imagine asking.

"My country," she called the hills when they turned lavender in the evening and a golden mist covered the fields. But it was no longer clear that it would remain hers, especially as the winds turned fiercer.[119]

The drought took on biblical proportions as Ann waited to hear back on employment applications following graduation. Moisture in the soil evaporated to fifteen feet below the surface. Towering dust storms blew dirt hundreds of miles. Dust pneumonia killed babies and old people whose lungs filled with debris until they could not breathe. Some areas of the Great Plains lost 75 percent of their topsoil.[120]

Ann rode alongside fences to keep from losing her way during blackouts. Planting potatoes, she could hardly see her brother kneeling a few feet in front of her. They scrounged for dandelion weeds for salad until the garden came up, though it never did. Dirt infiltrated cupboards and closets, coating dishes that had to be cleaned before and after every meal. "Every room had to have dirt almost shoveled out of it before we could wash floors and furniture," she recorded. Morning and night, Ann, Ethel, and their mother repeated the exhausting cleanup.[121]

Help arrived when federal officials showed up in the summer of 1934, and Ann's Stony Brook country became a New Deal laboratory. She still had not found a job. Others did not dare give them up. The woman who supervised her student teaching explained that while she had hoped to wed, she could not. The school board would fire her since married women "have husbands to support them," even though her fiancé supported his widowed mother and could not afford another dependent. This meant that a high school job was out of the question for Ann, so she accepted an offer from a nearby elementary school.

The first New Deal officials the Riebe family encountered were surveyors. Army engineers were followed by the Biological Survey, trailed by the Missouri River Diversion Project. One group said the government planned to create a giant lake. The next said a game refuge. Yet another promised, Ann wrote ironically, "to put in a lot of trees to keep the wind from doing damage to the farms the other two outfits intend to eliminate."

She was not impressed. "Our bountiful and interfering government sometimes creates awful messes," she wrote. Perhaps repeating her Rural

Sociology teacher, Ann observed that the original homestead act had "broken lives and broken hearts" by encouraging settlement on unsustainably small parcels. Demand during World War I had prompted farmers to take out mortgages on "land which should never have been plowed," and failed to "protect them" from railroads that gouged farmers after prices fell. Her use of the word "protect" hinted at Ann's ambivalence. She believed that someone should regulate the vast network of interstate transport, but wanted no unintended consequences. It was a worthy goal but a historical impossibility.

Government buyers appeared. To Ann, they tunneled like weasels under the foundation of farm families' lives. They confirmed the plan of a wildlife refuge, for which the Department of the Interior needed land. Anxious to clear their books of bad debt, local banks sold repossessed acreage at a discount. A town physician who had no interest in his father's old ranch sold it for half price. Such sales set the value for everyone else. The government land agent knocked on doors, offering deals that barely allowed farmers to settle their debts. Families received an extra hundred dollars to skedaddle. Most bankrupt westerners got nothing, since the federal government could hardly turn all of the prairie into a wildlife refuge.

Ann watched through the kitchen window when the agent arrived at their home one Saturday. "In this country, when anyone drives in, you meet him at the gate with hand outstretched," she wrote, but when her father realized who the man was, he did not rise. Hugo Riebe owned every acre free and clear.

The diminutive man with a toothbrush mustache launched into his spiel about the wonder of the coming refuge. When that produced no results, he began a lecture about "submarginal land." Now Ann's father stood. All six-feet-four, work-hardened 250 pounds. Hugo Riebe's submarginal land had fed his family for generations. "You better go away before you make me mad," he warned. When the agent drove over to see Ann's grandmother, she switched off her hearing aid.

Ann admired their stance, but wondered if they should angle for the best price instead. Her brother did not want the land, and government engineers would wreck Stony Brook anyway. "Everything I loved will be gone," she worried. Her father said that if she "were a boy," he would consider starting over with her help in the North Dakota Badlands, but Ann could do anything on the ranch except be a boy.

Prospects seemed bleak. Once the government had bought the surrounding ranches, it could condemn theirs and compensate them at the going rate. Her uncle, not married at forty-two because he was still working his mother's spread while building his own, faced a worse threat. His mortgage was higher than the government's offer. If Washington forced him to sell, he would owe money on land that he no longer owned. Ann was twenty-two and funding her siblings' education. In an effort to shore up the family's situation, she bought a life insurance policy. That way, if anything happened to her, "the folks will have the money to plant me and help Bud and Ethel to the extent I could if alive."

Ann hated hearing the president on the radio, reassuring people in an East Coast accent that struck her ears as posh. "You are a fahmah, I am a fahmah," she mimicked. For her, "that rich man from Hyde Park was enough to turn a North Dakota farmer's stomach."

Still, she did not lose her sense of humor. When an agent from the Federal Emergency Relief Administration came to Ann's schoolhouse door one day, he noted the dust flying into the building as the children left for home. He inquired if it would do that all spring. "Probably," she said. "The northwest corner of Stutsman County has already blown in, but there are Foster and Wells Counties to come."

Ann enjoyed teaching. She found ways to help a disabled girl succeed, and refused to give up on one bright but antisocial boy. The board paid her fifty dollars and contributed a sack of coal. She bought all other school supplies from her own earnings, while saving for shoes she needed. The schoolhouse was more than a mile from home. When North Dakota's brutal winters dumped snow, she donned "all the clothes I own to keep warm" and trudged in twenty-below-zero temperatures to light the stove before class started. Parents said she was the best teacher their children had ever had.

A bevy of suitors pursued her, taking Ann to movies, dances, and roller skating. Even before she was out of college, one told her he would wait any length of time if she promised to marry him. She stopped seeing him, but found it harder to shuck a farmer who was as handsome as actor John Barrymore—though she told him she would if he brought up marriage again. The man was thirty-two and still supporting his widowed stepmother and five half-siblings. Like another suitor similarly burdened, he could not marry for a long time. His faraway expression was "the epitaph of dead dreams," Ann felt.

The year was 1934 and Frances Perkins's committee on economic security had just begun to meet. Not until 1938 would widows start receiving a federal subsidy so that older sons and daughters did not have to postpone their own lives.[122]

Ann's diary documents seven marriage proposals before she turned twenty-five. Family and friends said that a girl with her looks and brains could snag a millionaire. Ann had little interest. "I would lose my job immediately," she wrote. "Anyway, I don't want to get married, and that is that. A married woman loses all independence and any chance at a career of her own."[123]

Her social life became livelier with the arrival of the Civilian Conservation Corps. Ann had the skills of a stunt rider, and the two hundred young men hired to build the wildlife refuge admired her vastly as she herded cattle on weekends. When a city slicker asked if he could ride with her on the horse, "I told him to get a donkey—they would make a good pair."[124]

Only one man made any impression on Ann, a Harvard ornithologist brought in to manage the new Arrowwood Wildlife Refuge. Seth Low asked her to a dance, and on their first date, said he wanted to be her boyfriend. She agreed to date him over the summer, but warned she would be leaving come fall.

Ann felt that Kensal was her country no longer. "Government geniuses" had torn down neighbors' homes, ripped up improvements, fenced the range, and plowed firebreaks that "a blind man with his head down a well" could see were too narrow to stem any wildfire. She had her eye on a promising job in the Badlands, three hundred miles west. "Now is my chance," she told her diary. "I'm taking it."[125]

Blame the Woman

In 1936, Franklin D. Roosevelt carried every state except Vermont and Maine, winning the electoral college 523 to 8. Despite its shortcomings, the New Deal had triggered the landslide win. Unemployment had declined substantially. The Depression was far from over, but programs like Social Security promised a better future.

Nonetheless, federal activism provoked controversy. As the crisis ebbed, Frances Perkins became a target. She was easy to blame for anything that went wrong. Critics smeared New Deal officials as incompetents, traitors, socialists, and even agents of Satan—but in twelve years they attempted to impeach only one.

Union officials had resented Frances from the start. The president of the American Federation of Labor told the press in 1933, "Labor can never be reconciled to the selection made." A member of the seamen's union commented, "I guess us sailors, as well as bricklayers and miners, better get a powderpuff and lipstick to march in the inaugural parade."[126]

While unions rejected Frances Perkins, employers accused her of coddling them. New Dealers in Congress, particularly her old friend from Albany, Senator Robert Wagner, had passed legislation that guaranteed Americans the right to unionize. Membership exploded, growing from two million in 1933 to eight million in 1941. Testing their new strength, and responding to real needs, unions called innumerable strikes for better working conditions. Competition between the American Federation of Labor (AFL) and the new Congress of Industrial Organizations (CIO) made stoppages more frequent. As US secretary of labor, Frances had the thankless job of mediating such disputes.[127]

The press hounded her for comment. During one particularly controversial strike in 1937, a ringing telephone startled her awake at 2:00 a.m. Although she had found her disoriented husband when he wandered off two years earlier, disaster was never more than a call away. She always picked up the phone. Frances recognized the man on the other end as the nephew of the publisher of the *New York Times,* recently arrived in Washington. Voice froggy but mind sharp, she responded tolerantly instead of cutting off the journalist, reminding herself that she had once been young and impatient. He repaid her generosity with an article saying that the "strained" Miss Perkins seemed "on the verge of tears." Other newspapers embellished the story, one charging that Roosevelt had lectured her, when she came crying to him, "Frances, this is a democracy, not a tyranny of tears."[128]

Frances Perkins gritted her teeth. The journalist had implied that she was a hysterical woman staggered by a man's job. No reporter would suggest that a male cabinet member trembled with emotion. Until she left office in 1945, Frances heard repeatedly that if she were a "two-fisted male," there would be no strikes. Senator Harry Byrd of Virginia, a leader of the opposition to liberal legislation, urged the appointment of a man with "intestinal fortitude." The press turned on her with gendered language. *Tulsa World* called her "tender" toward communists; *Detroit Press* labeled her a "fussbudget"; and the *Asheville Citizen* denounced her as "a third-rate person bungling a first-rate job."[129]

Colleagues sometimes dismissed her, too. In the cabinet, she alone had the good sense to advise President Roosevelt against his disastrous attempt to expand the Supreme Court. Secretary of the Interior Harold Ickes, who tended to use the word "feminine" when describing men he did not like, wrote in his diary that her opposition was "to be expected of a woman," inclined as females were to "pussyfoot" around problems.[130]

Some conservatives who fulminated that the New Deal was a Jewish-Russian-Communist conspiracy went so far as to claim that Frances was secretly Jewish. One widely circulated graphic depicted a six-pointed Star of David with the name of a government official on each tip. Five of the six actually were Jews (Felix Frankfurter, Louis Brandeis, Henry Morgenthau, Edward Filene, and Bernard Baruch), but not Frances Perkins, the name most often in the news. "If I were a Jew, I would make no secret of it," she said. "On the contrary, I would be proud to acknowledge it." The rumor was nonsense but whispers continued.[131]

The worst came when an ambitious, thirty-six-year-old Texas Democrat became chair of a new committee charged with investigating subversion in government. Three weeks into the first public hearings of the House Un-American Activities Committee (HUAC), in what the Washington *Evening Star* called a "public orgy of red-baiting," Congressman Martin Dies threatened to impeach Labor Secretary Frances Perkins if she did not deport an Australian immigrant, Harry Bridges, for being a communist (though the man was not). Border patrol was then under the Labor Department.[132]

Frances had postponed Bridges's hearing while awaiting a Supreme Court decision on a similar case that might invalidate the charges against him. Congressman Dies lied to the press, saying "Perkins' own records show Bridges is a Communist, he has conspired riots and terrorism and he is deportable." Not only did the record say no such thing, but the labor secretary was simply following normal procedure.[133]

Dies accused Frances Perkins of flirting with high treason. His House Un-American Activities Committee laid the template for Senator Joseph McCarthy's attacks in the 1950s. McCarthy became more famous, but Dies pioneered the technique. Frances was his first high-level victim, perhaps because she made an inviting target as architect of the New Deal's signature legislation.

It was easy for some Americans to believe that communists had duped a woman. Bolsheviks were "sure to be found" in women's clubs, claimed a widely distributed chart that depicted feminism as a spiderweb of radical organizations preying on naïve female voters in order to turn all women into common sexual property. Congressman Dies told the press that "radical associates" whom Frances Perkins had brought into government had broadcast their "venom" of class hatred to secure passage "of certain legislation bearing their unmistakable imprint," meaning Social Security and the Fair Labor Standards Act. From Alaska to Florida, newspapers carried the accusation that Frances Perkins was using her cabinet position "to save Harry Bridges, a communist and alien leader."[134]

Frances normally took threats in stride. When police cordoned off a building to foil an attack her first month in office, she was more amused than worried. But HUAC's accusations prompted a type of hate mail that inflamed ancient prejudices. They painted her as a temptress who, like Eve, ruined good men. Some accused her of being Bridges's lover. Others claimed that they were married. Many questioned why Frances called herself "Miss Perkins," as if it were a ruse. "No decent Jewess would refuse to bear her husband's name, and a faithful Irish wife would scorn to masquerade as a maiden," one person wrote. "In the seclusion of your boudoir—free from the irritating influence of your lawful husband—sipping your cognac and sucking your cigaret, you may calmly reflect on the harm that your injudicious acts have done to President Roosevelt."[135]

She took the attack on her patriotism and morality hard. Visits to All Saints Convent became more frequent, and she began attending church every morning. "It seemed so manifestly unfair and improper," she later said, using terms from her Maine upbringing. When she read Dies's accusations, she could "hardly believe" a man educated at the University of Texas would make them, especially a Democrat from a Dust Bowl state to which the New Deal had devoted enormous effort.[136]

Over time she realized that his paranoia was genuine. Martin Dies echoed other white Southerners she sometimes met, "haunted by poverty and by social changes that had come with the abolition of slavery," who succumbed to "that awful longing for a scapegoat which runs through a good many parts of the human race." Of German heritage, Dies received support from the German American Bund, a pro-Nazi organization that spread conspiracy theories about immigrants and Jews.[137]

From September through December 1938, Dies attacked Frances Perkins relentlessly. She considered it a test of character, and reminded herself of "grandmother's dicta that all are to act as though nothing had happened." New England deportment kept her from retaliating in ways that "would have made me look silly and cheap."[138]

Friends in Congress refused to intercede, except for a few crusty Irishmen from her Albany days. "The Tammany Hall delegation, so help me God," she later said. "Nothing ever touched me so much in the world." One was Christy Sullivan, a sleepy backbencher. When Dies castigated Frances for disloyalty, Sullivan jumped to his feet and charged down the House aisle. "This woman comes from New York and we know her!" Sullivan shouted, waving a paper. "This is a good woman! You can't talk like that." A few pushed back on Dies's request for $150,000 to expand his investigation.[139]

In January 1939, the House Un-American Activities Committee introduced a resolution to impeach Frances Perkins. The motion was referred to the Judiciary Committee for investigation into whether she and two subordinates had abetted conspiracies to overthrow the government. She asked for a prompt public hearing, but the committee delayed its deliberations, then decided on a closed session.

Frances Perkins waited outside the committee's chamber on February 8, 1939, wearing a black dress and white bow. A clerk finally showed her and the lawyer for the Labor Department inside. The committee sat on a dais so high that Frances could see only their heads, dimly lit at the back of the large, empty hearing room. As she approached down the long aisle, Frances recalled a recent play about Joan of Arc walking to the stake after being condemned by the high clergy. Under her breath, she asked the lawyer if he remembered the scene. "Oh yes," he whispered. Frances broke into a soft laugh and he joined her, the two giggling like schoolchildren. Her anxiety lifted. As she took her seat, she recalled the high purpose that had always moved her.[140]

In a prepared speech, she explained the simple facts of the deportation case and reminded the all-male committee, "I have spent most of my adult life in the service of the people of my country . . . my record is an open book." Legislators replied with a mix of hostile accusations and polite queries that Frances spent the morning parrying. A month later, the Judiciary Committee reported that they had found no grounds for impeachment. House Resolution 67 was dismissed. The lunchroom at the Department of Labor cheered when Frances entered. Some employees cried openly. Frances smiled.[141]

Longing for a more private life, she offered Roosevelt her resignation when he won reelection in 1940 and 1944, but he rebuffed her both times. The world was at war. On the last occasion, shortly before his final meeting with Joseph Stalin and Winston Churchill at Yalta in 1945, Roosevelt begged her to stay. Frances Perkins decided she would "drop dead in her traces" before abandoning him.[142]

Headed for the Hills—or the Altar

In 1936, North Dakotans entered their ninth year of drought. It seemed to Ann that everyone who could had gassed up their jalopy and left—as John Steinbeck portrayed in his novel *The Grapes of Wrath.* The proportion of Americans living on farms declined precipitously, from 41 to 16 percent, between 1920 and 1945. Ann went for a moonlight ride to say goodbye to Stony Brook country. Her most recent boyfriend, the Harvard wildlife specialist, stormily complained about her taking a job elsewhere, but she was determined to leave.[143]

Ann wrote incredulously, "When I told him marriage for us is impossible, he said I didn't realize how much thought he had been giving it." Another beau had earlier insisted, "I'm going to make you care for me. We'll be married in the fall."[144]

Ann felt beaten up by what she called "a thousand petty discouragements," but one of the "many things I'm fed up with is men who get ideas of getting married." They never seemed to hear her say no. The 1920s slang for "wife"—a man's "ball and chain"—pictured marriage as a boon for women and a burden for men. Each of her suitors could not believe she would decline his offer. As to the head of the wildlife refuge, Ann guessed that he had many good qualities, but she thought he "would be a difficult man to live with." She signed her new teaching contract with a flourish.[145]

It took her to Sentinel Butte, North Dakota, on the western edge of the Badlands, a magical sandstone landscape striped pink and gold. Ann roomed with another teacher at the unheated town hotel. The women shared a bed for warmth, a practice that was common in hard times and without erotic implications. Ann's hotel had no plumbing. During winter, she made a forty-yard dash to the outdoor outhouse.

She loved her new position. Finally she had landed at a high school, where she taught public speaking, journalism, social science, Latin, typing, shorthand, physical education, and Girl Scouting in addition to core subjects. On weekends she rode, danced, hiked, and played Monopoly, a popular new game (invented by a woman) about capitalist booms and busts.

For once, Ann had help. The New Deal created a program called the National Youth Administration that gave jobs to older students so they could stay in school. The district assigned her two "NYA girls" to help her catalog the school library. They finished high school while she slept in on weekends. Ann campaigned in the 1936 election. She did not record her vote in her diary—her family was Republican—but the state chose Roosevelt.

Money remained tight. Her paycheck was often delayed. No longer supporting her sister, Ann sent every spare penny to her brother. The prior year, she had paid Ethel $50 a month from her $75 salary. That left her $21 for room and board, and $4 for clothing and life insurance. A hat cost $3.

Ornithologist Seth Low sent Ann an expensive radio when she moved to the Badlands. She could not afford the three-cent stamp for a thank you, and he took the train to see her. They quarreled when she again declined to marry him. Ann had just turned down another "wonderful guy" from the Badlands, knowing that a married woman "has no independence at all."

Ann never explained why independence meant so much to her. In her diary she criticized the "social dictum . . . that the only career for a woman was marriage and a confining life of housework and raising children." The word "confining" might have been the key. Ann liked the wind in her face. Although it tickled her vanity to receive yet another marriage proposal, this time from a newspaperman who told her she was a "witty, strong-minded, argumentative female" he could not live without, Ann balked at paying for companionship with her freedom.[146]

Journalist Dorothy Dix, whose daily advice column was carried by 273 newspapers, reflected the attitude that made Ann shudder. In 1939, a female reader suggested that perhaps wives should hold jobs. "The pioneer wife drove a wagon through a wilderness, felled trees, hewed timber, plowed oxen and did other work side by side with her man before there were office jobs for women," she noted. A modern husband might reasonably "expect as much assistance," and a wife's earnings could "save much friction in marriage." Dix disagreed. A wife who worked could not expect her husband to help clean the house or tolerate a "can-opener dinner." Her "best bet," Dix advised, was "bucking him up to do the best that is in him to do."[147]

Ann's parents meanwhile negotiated the price for their ranch, which represented three generations of work. The check for the sale took months to arrive, so they eked out a subsistence while waiting, reluctant to waste seed on a crop they might not harvest. Ann trained her gaze on the trail ahead. She knew the drought would break someday. Livestock prices would rise. Bud faced only one more year of college; then she could save for a ranch of her own. Until that time, teaching allowed her to make a difference. "If I can inspire them to keep on struggling, some of them will be successful," she wrote.[148]

A "wonderful stroke of luck" fell her way at last. The best in a decade. The proprietor of a Badlands curio shop offered Ann a summer job for thirty-two dollars a month plus room and board. It amused her to think how little work it required. "Pure velvet," she told her diary. She could save money, enjoy oodles of free time, and even wear dresses to work. Ann dropped the ironic tone she often used. "This is going to be a fun summer," she gushed. "I can hardly wait!"[149]

A month later, Ann received a letter from home. Her father had become too arthritic to ride a horse and her mother's varicose veins too painful for gardening. Ethel had married and Bud had landed a well-paid job. Ann must give up her summer job and fall teaching contract to care for the ranch until her parents moved to town. Perhaps she might reapply for jobs the following year.

"This is a round that will go on forever," Ann Marie Riebe thought as she scraped together the bus fare. At twenty-five, she felt her youth slipping away. "Somehow, I've got to get out!!" she raged to her diary as the bus rattled down the empty highway toward home. Only one alternative remained. She had beat the Depression and Dust Bowl, but she could not beat the system stacked against an unmarried woman. Ann closed her journal. She never wrote another line.

As a government naturalist, Seth Low made $3,156 a year. Ann earned $810, a quarter of his salary. Men's higher wages, unemployment insurance that excluded teachers, a Social Security pension system that favored males, and the family obligations of a spinster left her only one option. Ann Marie Riebe accepted Seth Low's ring.[150]

⁂

FIFTEEN HUNDRED MILES APART, college graduates Frances Perkins and Ann Marie Low both embraced the new possibilities bequeathed by previous generations of feminists, though neither found the road easy.

Frances Perkins helped the nation cope with the challenges of industrialization. A member of Britain's Parliament later called her "the most important woman in government in any democratic country in the first half of the twentieth century." It is hard to imagine anyone proving more abundantly than the shy girl from Maine that women could govern. After Roosevelt died of a brain hemorrhage, she worked as a civil service commissioner, relieved to exit the limelight. The fourth-longest serving cabinet member in US history—a testament to how much Roosevelt valued her—Frances made little effort to trumpet that fact. Her reputation faded, relegated to the basement of history like the three old ladies in a bathtub.[151]

Ann Marie Riebe's experience revealed the extent to which feminist values had spread, as well as how hard it was to implement them. The mother of two children, she followed her husband's career as he climbed, dutifully curbing her personality to fit his, since stunt riders and bird watchers were not a natural match. In 1938, she said goodbye to her brother Bud when he joined the Marines. Bud was the only one of his friends to return from World War II. He told Ann she had been "such a pretty girl," but marriage had aged her twenty years in eight. Seth Low served with the unit from General George Patton's Third Army that rescued the survivors of Buchenwald extermination camp in April 1945. The unit's photographers documented how Nazis treated people whom they considered biologically inferior. Next to piles of bones, women and men who looked like walking corpses described what had happened to those "who had not managed to escape to one of the democratic countries." Of the personnel in Seth Low's unit, 13 percent were uniformed nurses. They were the second generation of patriotic women in Army boots who had insisted on sharing men's hazardous duties, just as Ann had shared every dirty job on the ranch.[152]

Years after Seth died, Ann enrolled in a community college class in Arizona. Two female professors encouraged her to release her account of those years from which few emerged without scars. When the University of Nebraska printed *Dust Bowl Diary* in 1984, "Doodler" finally became a published writer, the author of a first-person account of America's most famous ecological disaster.

The Depression, World War II, and early Cold War eras appear traditional compared with the Progressive period. Yet during these decades, suffrage was normalized, and Americans accepted women in government in noticeable numbers. One of them, Representative Edith Nourse Rogers of Massachusetts, sponsored the bill that created the Women's Army Corps (WAC) in 1943. Black, white, Hispanic, and Asian American soldiers called WACs served from North Africa to the Philippines, fighting for a world in which people would not have to live in fear of conquest. Many women joined the labor force, boosting married women's participation from 12 percent to 24 percent. Hiring bans against wives faded. By the late 1950s, such prohibitions had mostly disappeared, dropped by employers convinced that a woman with bills to pay was a sure bet. If Ann Marie Riebe could have waited another twenty years, she would have had more options.[153]

Nonetheless, employers still advertised jobs by gender, and one-third of private firms used separate pay scales for men and women. Husbands were legally entitled to name the place of residence and wives were required to "conform thereto," in the phrasing of one Idaho statute. In half of the states, women now sat on juries on the same basis as men, but three still barred them completely. How—or if—Constitutional guarantees of equality applied to the female half of the population remained an open question in 1960.[154]

The next generation would try to answer it.

In 1766, two years into marriage, young Abigail Adams looks the picture of happiness—and intellectual curiosity. (Collection of the Massachusetts Historical Society)

British cartoonist Philip Dawe satirizes North Carolina patriots who declared a tea boycott in 1775. He depicts them swilling alcohol instead and ignoring a baby under the table. (Library of Congress Prints and Photographs Division, LC-USZ62-12711)

The only surviving portrait of Angelina Grimké reveals her seriousness, but not the bright charisma that mesmerized thousands. (Library of Congress Prints and Photographs Division, LC-USZ61-1609)

This only known photograph of Harriet Jacobs, taken three years before her death in 1897, suggests a woman at peace with herself and the world. (Wikimedia Commons)

Susan B. Anthony crisscrossed the country lobbying for the vote, but died without achieving her goal. This 1866 photograph shows her after her successful campaign to pass the Thirteenth Amendment abolishing slavery. (Rare Books, Special Collections & Preservation, River Campus Libraries / University of Rochester)

Enforcing the "Nonentity" Principle of Common Law for Married Women.

"I yield to reason everywhere—To despotism nowhere!" See page 245.

"Take Mrs. Packard up in your arms, and carry her to the 'bus!" See page 389.

This engraving depicts Elizabeth Packard's protest of the marriage laws that made wives into legal nonentities. Packard refused to walk to her cell in the insane asylum.

(Reproduced from E. P. W. Packard, *Modern Persecution; or, Insane Asylums Unveiled as Demonstrated by the Report of the Investigating Committee of the Legislature of Illinois* [New York: Pelletreau & Raynor, 1873])

THE DAILY GRAPHIC

AN ILLUSTRATED EVENING NEWSPAPER.

39 & 41 PARK PLACE.

VOL. I—NO. 81. | NEW YORK, THURSDAY, JUNE 5, 1873. | FIVE CENTS.

GRAPHIC STATUES, NO. 17—"THE WOMAN WHO DARED."

A dystopian cartoon shows the horrors that could follow if women like Susan B. Anthony were allowed to vote: men might carry babies, and women could become politically active. (Wikimedia Commons)

Mrs. Mary Church Terrell,

The Famous Platform Lecturer, and Member of School Board, Washington, D. C.

This noted lecturer spoke to crowded houses in Europe. She recently spoke in Marshall, Dallas, Fort Worth, Houston and New Orleans. She has inspired all who have heard her. She will lecture at the C. M. E. Church Tuesday night, May 5th, at 8:30 o'clock. Hear her.

ADMISSION, 25 CENTS.

An organizer of the first national coalition of Black women, Mary Church Terrell spoke worldwide on suffrage and the accomplishments of women after slavery. (Oberlin College Archives)

Laura Foster's 1912 anti-feminist cartoon in *Life* magazine suggests that the higher women climb, the unhappier they will become. The vote leads away from love.
(Library of Congress Prints and Photographs Division, LC-DIG-ppmsca-02940)

Italian immigrant Rosa Cavalleri tells stories of the old country at a settlement house in Chicago. Feminist social workers helped to save her life. (Chicago History Museum)

At a 1933 congressional committee, Frances Perkins presents her plans to rescue Americans from the Great Depression. (Granger Historical Picture Archive)

When Martin Dies of Texas requested lavish funding for his House Un-American Activities Committee in 1939, a cartoonist depicted his targets—including Frances Perkins—as humble street urchins. (Granger Historical Picture Archive)

North Dakota rancher Ann Marie Riebe did not want to marry because it meant surrendering her freedom. The Dustbowl stood in the way of her dreams. (Reproduced from *Dust Bowl Diary* by Ann Marie Low, by permission of the University of Nebraska Press. Copyright 1984 by the University of Nebraska Press.)

Feminism was a family affair for Martha and Juan Cotera. In 1970, they packed up their home and moved to south Texas to serve the *movimiento.* (AS-70-76114, Austin American-Statesman Photographic Morgue [AR.2014.039]. Austin History Center, Austin Public Library, Texas.)

In 1976, Yvonne Swan of the Sinixt Nation attended a fundraiser for her legal defense with musician Floyd Red Crow Westerman.
(Courtesy of Yvonne Swan)

Muriel Siebert grins at becoming the first woman to hold a seat on the New York Stock Exchange.
(Bettmann / Getty Images)

Phyllis Schlafly pressed the Republican Party to accept women as leaders, but opposed any further expansion of women's rights. (Library of Congress Prints and Photographs Division, LC-DIG-ds-00757)

Cartoonist Etta Hulme showed President Ronald Reagan—who renounced his earlier endorsement of the Equal Rights Amendment—courting Republican women with "Stop ERA" wine in 1981. The cartoon suggests they prefer "Legal Equality Ice Cream." (Courtesy Etta Hulme Papers, Special Collections, University of Texas at Arlington Libraries)

Beyoncé Knowles sang at the inaugurations of George W. Bush and Barack Obama. Here she performs the national anthem at the 2004 Super Bowl. (KMazur / WireImage / Getty Images)

Gymnasts Aly Raisman, Simone Biles, McKayla Maroney, and Maggie Nichols *(left to right)* support one another during a Senate hearing on the FBI's refusal to investigate sexual abuse. (Saul Loeb / Pool via AP)

CHAPTER 6

The Right to Equal Treatment

1960–1975

Martha Cotera and Yvonne Swan

Sex class is so deep as to be invisible. Or it may appear a superficial inequality, one that can be solved by merely a few reforms. . . . But the reaction of the common man, woman, and child—"*That*? Why you can't change *that*! You must be out of your mind"—is the closest to the truth.

SHULAMITH FIRESTONE, 1970

THE TWO-TIERED CLASSIFICATION that ranked males above females, and defined men's needs as normal and women's needs as unusual, had existed since time immemorial. In the 1960s, misfortunes long associated with the "weaker sex"—like pennilessness, uncontrolled pregnancies, domineering spouses, or vulnerability to assault—suddenly seemed like fixable social problems. At the time, the insight felt radical. Humanity had found a different pair of glasses.

A Mexican American activist from Texas, Martha Cotera, helped promote the recognition of "sexism," a new word that burst into public consciousness in 1969, attracting newspaper commentary in twenty states. *Parade* magazine, a Sunday insert carried by hundreds of newspapers, featured her on its cover nine years later as an exemplar of "woman power" beside Lady Bird Johnson and future Texas governor Ann Richards. Cotera was part of a cultural upwelling that brought feminism into the mainstream. Once people saw sexism, they typically saw it everywhere, to the annoyance of those who still could not see it at all.[1]

The American media made celebrities of a handful of activists like Gloria Steinem and Betty Friedan, fostering the myth that feminism was a white, middle-class phenomenon. This was an incorrect but unsurprising deduction at a time when the country was 85 percent white, although opponents exploited the stereotype to drive women apart.[2]

Diversity was actually the movement's greatest asset, lending feminism its reach. Pauli Murray, the pioneer of the legal doctrine that would give women full claim to the Constitution, was Black. Mexican American, Native American, and Asian American women raised their own demands. As one historian notes, "multiple feminist insurgencies" bloomed simultaneously. The dizzying array of groups sometimes disagreed sharply, yet they traveled in the same direction. Martha Cotera, an exuberant immigrant who applied for citizenship when her desire to vote for John Kennedy became "overwhelming," personified the grassroots organizers who invented domestic violence shelters, rape crisis hotlines, abortion clinics, women's credit unions, and sports leagues for girls. Among feminism's many faces, hers shone brightly.[3]

Like many, Martha worked primarily within her own ethnic group. During the Civil Rights Era, feminism resembled one of the Hindu goddesses whose limbs multiply while battling cosmic forces. The blurred, uncoordinated, overlapping arms of the multicultural women's movement occasionally whacked one another, but they collectively defended an emergent norm: females should be equal to males in all ways, and bottom-up institutions to help the most vulnerable were essential to making this happen.[4]

At the same time, top-down efforts by government activists focused on rewriting the law. The United States changes its laws in three ways: Constitutional amendment, legislative act, and case law, meaning the interpretation of statutes during courtroom trials to establish precedent. Women made significant legislative gains in this period, but courtroom victories reengineered the landscape, too. From Washington State to Washington, DC, feminist attorneys like Ruth Bader Ginsburg put the US Constitution on trial.

Two other such lawyers, Elizabeth Schneider and Nancy Stearns, did so as well when they defended Yvonne Swan Wanrow, a single mother from the Colville Indian Reservation who killed an accused rapist when he broke into her babysitter's house at dawn. The state of Washington sentenced her to twenty years for murder. Fighting a desperate battle against prosecutors determined to imprison her until her waist-long braids turned gray, Yvonne Swan Wanrow pleaded for the right to self-defense. Her case raised the question of whether courts could treat women and men the *same* while also recognizing that they *differ* in size, strength, and life experience. Attorneys who sought to help Yvonne argued that equal protection under the law required just that.

Her Mother's Helper

Martha Piña felt big from the time she was little. Born in 1938 in Chihuahua, the largest of Mexico's thirty-two states, she saw herself as part of a historical epic. Just outside her town lay the ghostly ruins of Paquimé, a Meso American settlement of two thousand rooms that had been abandoned seven centuries earlier. More recently, her grandparents had fought the dictatorship of Porfirio Díaz during the Revolution of 1910 and resisted the Catholic Church's hold on government by undergoing what they called a "political conversion" to Protestantism. Martha's grandmother still prayed over her rosary in private, but held her head high at the evangelical church on Sundays. Like Frances Perkins, Martha Piña grew up hearing about her family's dedication to liberty.[5]

But she felt big for another reason. She knew she must take care of her mother. Her father would not have given her the job at three-and-a-half if it was not something she could do.

Martha's two brothers had died abruptly in the summer of 1940, one after catching the heel of his small cowboy boot on a ladder and falling to his death, and the other of an unquenchable fever. Martha's bereaved mother, Altagracia, was eight months pregnant with a fourth child when her traumatized husband sold the family property and took the money, along with his wife's younger sister, to Tijuana, abandoning the twenty-one-year-old Altagracia, Martha, and the baby girl on the way.

In the fall of 1941, not long before the Japanese attack on Pearl Harbor, Martha held her mother's hand as they set off on a four-hundred-mile trek by carriage, train, and bus to Tijuana. When they reached the Pacific, tired female passengers took turns bathing in the sea behind a large white sheet. Martha helped hold the billowy cloth in the ocean breeze, convinced she was as tall and strong as the grown women.

At last they found her runaway father, and Altagracia convinced him to give her some of the proceeds from the sale of their property in Mexico. He accompanied them across the border to San Diego, where Martha saw him for the last time in her life. He said goodbye at the Spanish-tiled train depot before Altagracia and Martha boarded a train that would take them across the American Southwest and on home to Chihuahua. "Take care of your mom," he told her.[6]

Martha's grandparents welcomed them with the expectation that they would stay. But Altagracia refused to live under her parents' roof in a town that considered her a victim. Determined to give her daughters the educational opportunities she had not had, she moved them to El Paso, close enough to send them home to Mexico on school holidays and for aunts and uncles to babysit in a pinch. By day, Altagracia worked a factory job. At night she cooked in a restaurant in order to dress her girls "like little princesses," Martha later recalled, and so that she could rent a basement apartment in a safe neighborhood. Mexican American schoolchildren who resented immigrants called them basement rats. Altagracia remarried, but her second husband died of heart failure within six months.[7]

Bereaved, abandoned, and now widowed, Altagracia held on, determined to raise successful daughters. Photographs capture an expression of fierce, sober dignity. But it was hard. Martha knew that her mother cried nearly every day. It fired her with a thirst to vindicate the struggle of someone who persevered so nobly despite such a raw deal.[8]

Fortunately, Martha had a sunny disposition and iron will. At first, she wished she had been born a man. She admired the freedom of her grandfather, a preacher who traveled widely in northern Mexico and the American Southwest while her Grandmother Romanita managed not only a household with fourteen children, but also two farms and a candy factory in town.

Then Martha realized that the immense iron key ring at her abuela's waist, which opened all the locks, represented the source of their success. She decided to be like her grandmother. Women who earned money liberated everyone. Too many Mexican American men worked in manual labor to support a dozen children, while their wives worked only in the home. Latinas had the lowest rate of labor-force participation in the United States, behind Black and white women. From what Martha had seen in El Paso, men who took on "that horrible economic burden" alone often drank too much. "And then they beat you over it," she observed.[9]

Martha resolved to become strong. In junior high she made friends with a redheaded Irish American girl who taught her how to confront bullies, whether adults or kids. When a teacher told her a "C" was the best grade he ever gave a Mexican, Martha went to the principal. To develop her endurance, she hiked, played sports, and jitterbugged until she was out of breath at dance concerts at the County Coliseum given by Fats Domino, Elvis Presley, Chuck Berry, and Little Richard. Dancing to rock and roll bands admired worldwide, she felt she was really living. To improve her mind, Martha read constantly, especially biographies of Jane Addams. "She was my saint," Martha later said of the suffragist and settlement worker. "I wanted to be her."[10]

At twelve, she begged permission to use lipstick, not to attract boys but to look for work. Outlining her lips in a sophisticated shade, she convinced the Jewish owner of an El Paso shoe store that she was two years older than her actual age. Martha Piña began paying into Frances Perkins's Social Security plan in 1950. Her wages allowed Altagracia to quit night work. Older salespeople enjoyed the precocious child, including one who quietly advised Martha to leave her Minnie Mouse purse at home if she wanted to convince others she was fourteen. Martha fell hard for a heartthrob employee whom the storekeepers defended when he was later arrested at a gay bar, an experience that awakened a lifelong concern for homosexuals. During seven years at the store, Martha learned how to talk with all types of people—and get them to buy something.

Like many women who became feminists in this era, Martha Piña cared passionately about her mother while also vowing not to suffer her fate. High school advisers insisted that she take secretarial courses, but she also signed up for college preparatory classes. An ambitious writer, she became co-editor of the school newspaper along with her Irish American friend. Administrators suspended the incendiary duo when they endorsed Democratic presidential candidate Adlai Stevenson in 1956.[11]

Martha's verve reflected a charged political atmosphere. The world was processing the cruelties of World War II, and American teachers pursued what was called "intercultural education" during her elementary years. Its emphasis on human equality and respect provoked controversy. El Paso conservatives started a nationwide campaign to limit coverage of these subversive ideas in textbooks, but documents like the 1948 Universal Declaration of Human Rights still entered Texas classrooms. Spearheaded by Eleanor Roosevelt, the world-changing accord declared, "All human beings are born free and equal in dignity and rights . . . without distinction of any kind, such as race, colour, sex, language, religion, political or other opinion." Students would have gleaned that the United Nations opposed the kinds of prejudice they saw every day.[12]

In 1949, when Martha was eleven, papers across Texas blared the news that Senator Lyndon Johnson had brought the remains of US Army private Felix Longoria to Arlington National Cemetery after bigots in Three Rivers, Texas, had refused to bury the Mexican American war hero in the town's graveyard. In 1954, her mother talked about the Supreme Court decision in *Brown v. Board of Education,* which prohibited segregated schools of the type that were common across Texas. On her tiny salary, Altagracia donated new books to Black schools that only received used ones. Martha graduated with honors in 1957, the same year that neighboring Arkansas sent its National Guard to block Black teenagers from Little Rock High School. President Dwight Eisenhower reluctantly checkmated by countering with the 101st Airborne, generating headlines from El Paso to Moscow when US troops walked nine boys and girls through the school's front door. And in 1959, Martha joined the "Viva Kennedy" voter-registration drive, hoping to elect someone eager to improve America. "I think we can do better," John Kennedy said. "I think we are a great country, but we can be a greater country."[13]

Martha next enrolled full-time at the University of Texas at El Paso, a rare act for a Latina. Still helping her mother financially, she also took a full-time job at the city library. Eager to make herself indispensable, Martha organized the city's haphazard archive of 300,000 historical documents. The herculean task took four years, during which she self-trained as a professional bibliographer, a librarian who curates special collections. At the reference desk one afternoon, Martha helped a shy, dark-haired young man recently discharged from the US Air Force. They did not speak long, but something about Juan Cotera made her return the engagement ring she had accepted from another man. She spotted Juan again months later when he stood to give her his seat in a crowded classroom. Martha had a mischievous impulse to sit on his lap instead. They began dating.[14]

Martha wanted to avoid her mother's experience of marital disaster, so she waited to wed until after her graduation in 1963. She wanted to know for sure that Juan would be faithful and that he would argue with her about differences instead of feigning agreement until he had tied the knot. If Juan tried to boss her, she pushed back, determined to have a "totally modern" relationship. She did not want him to equate marriage with maid service. When Juan complained one day that his socks did not match, Martha suggested that he get pantyhose so they would not separate in the wash.[15]

Her impulses reflected a long-term social shift. Unlike college graduates in Frances Perkins and Ann Marie Riebe's generation, educated women now increasingly aimed to both marry and work. Whereas only half of female college graduates became mothers in the 1920s and 1930s, a full 80 percent did by the 1960s. Most quit their jobs while their children were young, but many resumed employment once the kids were in school. College graduates still clustered in teaching and earned less than men, but options had widened.[16]

The couple moved to Austin to allow Juan to study architecture at the prestigious University of Texas, where Martha experienced a different type of second-class status. El Paso's bilingual population had been nearly half Hispanic. In the state capital two hundred miles from the border, however, the people looked more like the rest of America, where Hispanics made up only 3 percent of the population. White landlords refused to rent to the Coteras unless they said they were foreigners, much like landlords in the segregated District of Colombia, who refused to rent apartments to local people of color while accepting diplomats from newly independent African nations at Kennedy's insistence. A satirical *Washington Post* cartoon in April 1961 captured the insult to local citizens perfectly: a restaurant manager reassures a waitress that she can serve a Black couple, saying, "It's alright to seat them. They're not Americans."[17]

Austin landlords considered Mexican Americans racially inferior and, equally objectionable, low class. The Coteras finally snagged an apartment after showing a landlord the silver and crystal wedding gifts they had received from Juan's wealthy Mexican parents. Martha gave birth to a daughter in 1964 and was hired to build a documents department for the Texas State Library. An executive salary allowed her to buy a Porsche for Juan as he completed his degree. But her interests went far beyond family and work.

After President Kennedy's shocking assassination in November 1963, social activism intensified. Lyndon Johnson pushed through legislation to outlaw racial discrimination, protect the environment, expand Social Security, and fight poverty—initiatives he called, collectively, the Great

Society. One was the Higher Education Act of 1965, which created financial aid to bring young people from minority and working-class backgrounds into college for the first time. College enrollments doubled from 3.7 million in 1960 to 7.8 million by 1969.[18]

Campus integration flushed racism to the surface. Many students of color had their first experience of being side by side with Anglos, most of whom were indifferent, though some were outright hostile. Martha mentored anxious newcomers. Her job at the Texas State Library placed her within a mile of the mushrooming university. She dashed between the two locations frequently while Juan completed his degree.

Ever a whirlwind, Martha became involved in 1964 with a Hispanic lobby that grew out of the Viva Kennedy clubs. She started a statewide network in 1965 to support Mexican American educational advancement, marched in farmworker protests in 1966, became involved with the new Mexican American Youth Organization in 1967, and tutored students who boycotted segregated high schools in 1968. Convinced that the University of Texas would never admit more than a tiny number of Mexican Americans, she and Juan renounced their comfortable life in Austin in 1969 to help start Colegio Jacinto Treviño, an experimental teacher's college in Mercedes, Texas, under accreditation from Antioch College. Living off savings, Martha began the school library while she and Juan completed master's degrees through Antioch's "University without Walls" program.[19]

By then the couple was deeply committed to the *movimiento,* the Spanish name for an inchoate, sprawling array of organizations from Colorado to California that rejected the moniker Mexican American in favor of Chicano, signifying identification with the Hispanic working class. Activists celebrated cultural traditions that they considered superior to those from Anglo civilization. As Lyndon Johnson removed governmental supports for Jim Crow—"Saint Lyndon," Martha called him years later—the spotlight on racism grew hotter and the chorus of outrage louder. Polls showed that the more discrimination declined, the more keenly its remaining vestiges were felt. The Chicano Movement chimed in with the Black Power, Puerto Rican, and American Indian movements to denounce racial brainwashing and assert a unique identity. Black, Brown, and Red were beautiful. They did not have to turn white in some giant American melting pot.[20]

For Chicanos this meant psychically reclaiming Aztlán, the mythological birthplace of the ancient Aztecs. Anything gringo, yanqui, or Anglo became suspect. "Chicanismo" was an alternative worldview that glorified the militant Aztec warrior and his loyal woman—and scorned female traitors who cooperated with whites as daughters of La Malinche, the indigenous mistress of Hernán Cortés, a Mexican version of Eve whose actions supposedly destroyed paradise. In the words of historian Ernesto Galarza, this cultural nationalism "privileged males and marginalized females," making for carefully prescribed roles. It condemned racism while enshrining sexism.[21]

A global move toward militancy compounded this trend. Third-world decolonization had generated two diametrically opposed philosophies of change. Mohandas Gandhi, a founder of independent India in 1947, touted nonviolent resistance as the best technique for advancing human rights. Martin Luther King Jr. epitomized the Gandhian approach in the United States. But Frantz Fanon, a theorist of the Algerian independence movement who was far younger than Gandhi, popularized the reverse. Fanon argued in his influential 1961 book *The Wretched of the Earth* that colonization had created an inferiority complex in men. (Women barely figured for Fanon.) He advocated violent resistance as the only way to recover one's dignity, rejecting nonviolence as bourgeois and effete. "At the individual level, violence is a cleansing force," he wrote. "The colonized man finds his freedom in and through violence."[22]

Fanon's views eclipsed those of Gandhi for young activists who looked upon Algerian, Cuban, and Vietnamese revolutionaries with admiration and a touch of envy. Chicano nationalists who read *The Wretched of the Earth* claimed brotherhood with the oppressed "in the jungles of Bolivia and Vietnam" and adopted the berets of Che Guevara, bandoliers of Emiliano Zapata, and clubs of Aztec warriors. Black Panthers who read Fanon photographed themselves with shotguns and carried automatic weapons into the California state capitol. Whites in the Weather Underground, a violent splinter group of the Students for a Democratic Society, donned denim shirts and built bombs. At the height of the period, these activists excoriated peaceful moderates as sell-outs to imperialism.[23]

Hypermasculinity sought its counterpart in docile femininity. Purveyors of Chicanismo extolled the long-suffering woman who obeyed her man, cooked his dinner, did the movement's menial work, and bore children to increase the Hispanic population. César Chávez of the United Farm Workers, a pacifist in the spirit of Gandhi, opposed birth control as a conspiracy to undermine Chicano power. "Smaller families would only diminish the numerical power of the poor," he told his followers. "The only solution is to make the minority much less of a minority and make the race multiply and progress." Elijah Muhammad, the leader of the Black Nation of Islam, similarly forbade birth control as "white man's tricknology."[24]

Martha Cotera disagreed that women should remain barefoot and pregnant. As a librarian, she knew that the much-ballyhooed Aztecs had brutalized other Indigenous groups. But the movement was her home and homes could be remodeled. She skipped the March 1969 Denver Youth Conference at which more than a thousand activists gathered from across the Southwest to adopt *El Plan Espiritual de Aztlán* (Spiritual Plan of Aztlán). She hoped the conference would build room for assertive Chicanas, but because she was juggling care of a four-year-old daughter, her job as a librarian, and a commitment to organize an independent third party, she did not have time to attend. She considered organizer Rodolfo "Corky" Gonzales a confirmed sexist, but assumed friends would hold a women's caucus. She hoped they would endorse the Equal Rights Amendment, popularly called the ERA.[25]

White, Black, and Hispanic feminists had recently instigated a new, but uncoordinated push to pass the decades-old ERA proposal. The Governor's Commission on the Status of Women, the Texas spin-off of a presidential commission established by John Kennedy, lobbied Austin to support the amendment and eliminate such double standards as Article 1220 of the Texas penal code, which pardoned any man who killed his wife's lover. Martha talked up the bill wherever she went. A conference in Houston had boosted her own consciousness the year before, in 1968. Although Chicanas did most of the legwork, none were invited to speak. When a group asked Martha to present their policy suggestions in an open session, and pushed her from the wings onto the stage, a young man tried to shout her off. "Go back home and wash the dishes," he cried. "What are you doing here?" he yelled.[26]

In that moment Martha suffered one of the many instances of harassment that female reformers encountered when they voiced their thoughts. In 1970, another Austin crowd booed seventy-three-year-old

Maria Hernandez, a renowned educational reformer. Men threatened by feminism had wielded ridicule ever since John Adams compared Abigail to a "Scotch renegado," but comments became increasingly vulgar as political rhetoric sharpened and as new men's magazines like *Playboy,* which placed photographs of nude women alongside highbrow articles on art and politics, legitimized cruder treatment.[27]

In 1969, a handful of white men heckled veteran activist Marilyn Salzman Webb at a conference of Students for a Democratic Society, with one yelling "take her off the stage and fuck her." Counterculture icon Abbie Hoffman joked, "The only alliance I would make with Women's Liberation is in bed." Roy Wilkins, head of the National Association for the Advancement of Colored People, founded by Mary Church Terrell among others, more politely lectured women organizers that they were "ignorant of the political process, should listen to their leaders, and just return home." Bayard Rustin blackballed speeches by female activists at the 1963 March on Washington where Martin Luther King Jr. gave his "I have a dream" speech, rejecting Pauli Murray, Rosa Parks, and Fannie Lou Hamer. Poet Amiri Baraka denounced women who resisted traditional roles as "devilishly influenced." Black Panther Eldridge Cleaver told co-eds at Stanford University that women could help the revolution by recruiting men with their "pussy power."[28]

One historian notes that some men used "racial pride rhetoric as a form of control." It took guts to challenge them. Cleaver's popular memoir *Soul on Ice* prompted Frances Beal and other members of the Student Non-Violent Coordinating Committee to organize a Women's Liberation caucus in 1968. Cleaver glorified rape as a way for Black men to recover their masculinity. Beal recalled her knees shaking at a meeting in Harlem where she challenged nationalists who preached that "the demand for women's rights was a white plot to divide the Black Liberation Movement, that abortion was genocide, and that women should be supporting the men's newfound 'manhood' by walking ten steps behind."[29]

Some women deflected hostility with flattery, hesitating to offend men they admired. The founders of the first Chicana newspaper glowingly dedicated the inaugural 1969 issue of *El Rebozo* (*The Shawl,* named for a traditional garment symbolic of modesty) to the inspiring "men of the Chicano movement." They complimented their brothers while gently admitting, "We have waited too long to say something."[30]

After the 1969 Denver Youth Conference, Martha Cotera received a phone call from her friend Enriqueta Vasquez, a former battered wife who was then publisher of the New Mexico journal *El Grito del Norte.* Vasquez had participated in the women's caucus where the majority approved a resolution calling for equality with men at home, at work, and in the movement. Prior to the general assembly, someone mysteriously replaced the majority resolution with a minority report that read, "It was the consensus of the group that the Chicana woman does not want to be liberated."[31]

Martha listened with dismay to Vasquez, who wrote afterward in *El Grito del Norte* that she "could have cried." The next year, in 1970, Robin Morgan reprinted the essay in the first anthology of women's liberation writings, *Sisterhood Is Powerful.* Meanwhile, a Chicana women's meeting at Stanford University also demurred, "We do not wish to join with the Anglo Woman's Liberation movement."[32]

Martha Cotera was fed up with accusations that feminism had no place in her community, a charge that Black and Indigenous women also confronted. She felt she had to prevent women's quest for equality from being painted white by critics. Her staunchest ally, Juan Cotera, agreed.

The Making of a Target

American law had long treated women as odd creatures, identical in their economic dependence, destiny as mothers, and need for male supervision. Until 1971, the Supreme Court judged women as a special class in response to every legal objection that doing so violated their Fourteenth Amendment right to equal treatment. When Susan B. Anthony and Virginia Minor tried to vote, courts ruled that being female disqualified them. In a myriad of ways afterward, the Supreme Court ruled that women, like children, could be excluded from a variety of adult roles. While the concept of "due process" meant the equal and fair application of the law to all citizens, the measure of "citizen" was implicitly male.

To courts, blanket restrictions on women seemed "natural, necessary, and benign," in the words of one scholar. In *Bradwell v. Illinois* (1873), the Court ruled that states could ban females from specific occupations. In *Minor v. Happersett* (1874), it decided that states could deny them the vote. In *Muller v. Oregon* (1908), it agreed that states could place limits on their work hours, and in *Goesaert v. Cleary* (1948) that states could require a male presence at work. In *Hoyt v. Florida,* in 1961, the Court declared that women did not have the same right as men to a jury of their peers. As attorney Ruth Bader Ginsburg remarked, prior to 1971 "the Supreme Court never saw a sex classification it didn't like."[33]

At the very same time, on criminal matters, courts held women to the exact same standards as men, resisting their perspective. For example, few judges understood that girls learned they were vulnerable targets of male assault the first time parents cautioned them to avoid adult men—and keep their legs firmly crossed at all times. Boys generally did not grow up with these warnings and their perceptions of safety did not form around them. When it came to the opposite sex, boys were generally encouraged to think like hunters, not prey. Courts exaggerated certain differences between men and women, while hardly acknowledging differences like this one at all.

Yvonne Swan was born in 1943 into the Sinixt Arrow Lakes Nation, following the matrilineal line of her mother, Lucy. She grew up in the northernmost reaches of Washington State, a region of blue lakes, gentle mountains, and tall ponderosa pine forests that soared straight to heaven. Bear cubs, deer, and friendly snakes peeped through the bushes looking for Yvonne, she thought, while bald eagles winged overhead. Indian lands surrounded her family's one-bedroom log cabin, tucked safely on the Colville Reservation that twelve nations called home. The most famous were the Nez Perce, once led by the legendary Chief Joseph, who evaded the US Army longer than anyone had ever thought possible. Yvonne's father Ted, a logger, hailed from Idaho, where his landless Chippewa-Cree and Assiniboine Sioux family had found refuge with the Coeur d'Alene people.

Although the reservation stretched farther than Yvonne could imagine, her mother taught her that the Canadian government had seized most of their tribal lands in the nineteenth century. Yvonne knew that it made her mother sad, and that it explained why Lucy spent so much time in the homes of elderly people urging them to resist any attempts by the American government to take more. Stirring a pot over the woodfire stove, Lucy would tell her daughter to value the land. An auntie would chime in, "You're Arrow Lakes, don't you forget. Arrow Lakes."[34]

Like Australia, Argentina, Canada, Chile, New Zealand, and a dozen other democracies established on Indigenous lands over the course of two centuries, the United States coveted native territories. It promised minimal goods and services in exchange for bountiful domains taken in innumerable shady deals and violent seizures. This spelled continuing hardship for Native peoples. The loss of fertile fields and virgin forests diminished economic opportunities permanently.

Over time, the United States tired of providing even limited compensation, or what Chippewa novelist Louise Erdrich later called "rent for use of the entire country." During the Cold War, Congress moved toward yet another unilateral solution: withdrawing federal recognition so that "socialistic" reservations could become private property. Lucy taught Yvonne that they must be vigilant against this new policy, ominously called "Termination," lest their remaining lands disappear. In 1953, Congress passed a law that began the process of voiding sovereignty for 110 tribes in eight states, denying building permits for hospitals and schools, and moving people off reservations. Lucy Swan worried that leaders of the Colville Reservation would not resist government officials who arrived with false promises of better lives in the city in exchange for signatures. The knowledge that Indians had lost before, and might again, sometimes filled Yvonne with dread.[35]

Mostly, however, she felt very brave. The seventh of eight children, Yvonne was dubbed the "bubbly" one in the family. Extroverted and cheerful, Yvonne walked right up to people she did not know, especially elders, with whom she liked to chat. At night she slipped from the bed she shared with four sisters to fetch her favorite fruit, red apples, from the dark cellar near the house. When others asked for a bite, she breezily told them to get their own and giggled at their reluctance. The outhouse held no terrors for her, and she walked the forest path alone after dark. The moon seemed a softer version of the sun. "Yvonne, she will do anything," her father would say with a laugh.[36]

She finally made fear's acquaintance when her devout parents sent her to Catholic boarding school in 1950 to avoid a risky winter commute to the public schoolhouse miles away. Although federal Indian education policy increasingly deemphasized boarding schools in favor of local ones, many children still went. Seven-year-old Yvonne found it disturbing. Some nuns brought a smile to her face, but others made her anxious when they swatted children who misbehaved. Older girls whispered ghost stories before bed, and teachers lectured about Eve's original sin, saying "since we were her children we had to suffer." Yvonne grew fearful of snakes when she learned that one had gotten humanity's ancient mother expelled from the Garden of Eden.[37]

She longed for her parents, whom she saw only during summers and at Christmas. One day in seventh grade she heard hammering and went outside to see the school carpenter, who reminded her of her father. The busy man nodded absently as she chattered from the stoop, until a nun appeared and led her inside with the warning, "You don't know what could happen." Over time, the bold child became shy. Only art projects buoyed her spirits. When a congenital defect required surgery on both knees and forced her parents to keep her home for a year, she rejoiced despite the scar tissue that prevented her from running fast thereafter.[38]

With strong features and a ready smile, Yvonne was sometimes told she was the prettiest of the five Swan sisters. It made her self-conscious, especially once men started staring. The first time, she and her mother were walking into a store when a strange drunk across the street began calling out "Yvonne," his speech slurred but unmistakable. She did not understand how he knew her name, which made his behavior more alarming. As she matured, men spoke as if she could not hear, saying, "I just want to sit and look at her." She began keeping her distance, "always looking around for the creepiest one." Inebriated men terrified her.[39]

An unlucky man might intuit that he was in sexual danger at some point during his lifetime. An unlucky woman might sense this more often than she could count. Yvonne was eventually assaulted by someone she knew and trusted. Like half of rapes documented decades later, it involved alcohol administered to impair self-defense.[40]

During high school, Yvonne's parents allowed her to enroll at a public institution only an hour away. Its mascot was the Colville Indians, although Yvonne was one of only two Indians to attend. Like many teenagers, she went driving with acquaintances after school one afternoon. The driver brought alcohol. A slight girl, Yvonne had too much to drink and blacked out. Someone took her home. The next day she noticed a strange discharge. A few weeks later she missed her period around the same time that her older brother walked into the house one afternoon, looked at her with loathing, and said in front of their mother, "Heard you got gang-banged."[41]

Yvonne knew from his tone that he considered it her fault. Embarrassment engulfed her. She felt dirty, guilty, and worthless, a devastating sensation that would not abate. A trip to the doctor revealed that she was not pregnant, but the rapists had given her a venereal disease. What the perpetrators probably considered a teenage prank triggered shame in Yvonne for the rest of her life.

Like most Americans, the Swans never reported the crime. Family, police, judges, and juries underestimated the prevalence of rape, and they faulted individual women for being in the wrong place at the wrong time. Prosecutors discouraged victims from taking cases to trial. Police officers did not collect forensic evidence until an activist developed a rape kit for hospitals in Chicago, a city whose police training manual at the time told officers, "Many rape complaints are not legitimate." Feminists did not begin addressing the problem until two decades after Yvonne's assault, in books like *The Politics of Rape* in 1974 and *Against Our Will* in 1975. They next widened their scope to condemn parental assaults of the type that Abigail Bailey's daughter had endured centuries earlier, beginning with *Kiss Daddy Goodnight* in 1978. Incest had until then been considered rare, occurring in one in a million families (0.001 percent). Scholarly studies soon discovered it was actually common, affecting more than 10 percent of families, the FBI reported.[42]

The first general surveys of rape did not occur until 1995, when shocked researchers at the Centers for Disease Control discovered that one in six American women had suffered forcible penetration during their lifetimes (compared with one in thirty-three men), more than half before age eighteen. Indians experienced the highest rate of attack, they found. Girls like Yvonne Swan were twice as likely to be sexually assaulted as those from other backgrounds.[43]

Yvonne married immediately after high school, certain she would otherwise be "an old maid" and fearing that no good man could want her, a phobia common among rape survivors. A white schoolmate's older brother had heard of her while he was in prison and insisted on meeting her when he got out. Jerry Wanrow pressed Yvonne to marry. His parents disliked her Indian heritage, but she said yes. Within a few years Jerry began beating Yvonne and they divorced. She now had two children. In 1966, still urging Indians to abandon reservations under the Termination program, the federal Bureau of Indian Affairs offered her tuition for a program in fashion design, a practical outlet for her love of art, and a one-way bus ticket to hilly San Francisco just as the clothing world exploded with new styles and colors in the mid-1960s. Yvonne felt her luck improving. With training, perhaps even a glamorous career, she could give her children a safer life.[44]

At the urging of the bureau agent, Yvonne left the toddlers with her parents until she got settled. Once she was away, Jerry Wanrow's prejudiced family falsely accused Yvonne's mother of being a drunk. The state welfare agency placed the children with white foster parents three hundred miles from the reservation. Yvonne fought for a year to get them back, finally bringing three-year-old Julie and four-year-old Darren to San Francisco in time to celebrate Christmas. The playful pair arrived just as the weather turned bitter.

On December 13, 1967, she bundled them up and walked downhill toward the bus stop, juggling bags and urging her little ones forward. Julie complained of a headache in the damp cold. Yvonne had had the children only three weeks and wished she could stay at home with them, but like any single parent she needed to work and relied on a helper she could afford. Licensed daycare was nearly unknown. In 1970, America's 11.6 million working mothers competed for 640,000 licensed openings nationwide. The untrained babysitter, whose apartment was near the bus stop, assured Yvonne that Julie would be fine once she warmed up.[45]

Yvonne's employer at the design firm called her to the telephone a few hours later. Over the phone, the babysitter told Yvonne that her daughter had gone into convulsions. Julie was dead. Yvonne numbly got in her employer's car and headed back to the apartment. Inside, Darren sat next to the lifeless girl with soft brown curls as if in some hideous nightmare. "I thought she was just pretending," the four-year-old said.[46]

The coroner declared the cause as encephalitis, but Yvonne felt responsible. Her children had been safe until she insisted on bringing them to a germ-ridden city so that she could better her prospects. Instead of faulting the social conditions that had endangered them all—rape and spousal abuse, racist child-welfare policies, a lack of infant care that disadvantaged female workers, and a federal initiative that drove a young Indian mother far from every social support—she denounced herself. Laudable in a man, perhaps, ambition in a woman suddenly seemed unforgivable to the grieving mother.

Yvonne returned north to be with Jerry Wanrow, hoping to make their relationship work. In Portland, Oregon, she conceived another little girl they named Yvette, but again he became physically abusive and after two years she left him for good. Later studies in the United States, Canada, Russia, England, and Wales would find that battered wives are at greatest risk of homicide immediately after separation or divorce, when violence often escalates. Yvonne's ex-husband broke into her apartment. She called the Portland police for help, but investigating officers expressed skepticism and she decided against pressing charges.[47]

Defeated, traumatized, and poor, Yvonne moved to Spokane to be near her youngest sister. In San Francisco, Yvonne had seen officers kicking an Indian on the ground and calling him Tonto (the name of a stereotypical Indian from a television show), but Spokane felt even more threatening. The town was 98 percent white, and the police always seemed to harass Indians whom she knew. Her neighborhood was sketchy. Living by herself, she bought a gun to protect the children. Yvonne took restaurant work, then started a secretarial course, but quit whenever Darren or Yvette developed a cold, panicked that she might lose another child. She accepted welfare checks from Aid to Families with Dependent Children, Frances Perkins's creation, until they felt better. To make herself feel better, she started drinking.[48]

Only twenty-eight, Yvonne felt life could hardly be more bleak. Then, one harrowing summer night, it became worse.

Building the Chicana Way

Martha Cotera confronted three obstacles to her goal of a united front: Chicanos, Chicanas, and white feminists. Reformers needed to pull together to create a better America, but Mexican American men saw no problem with their gender privileges, many Chicanas feared to complain, and most white women appeared to ignore their own advantages compared with Mexican Americans.

Martha's hope for change was not unique. A kaleidoscope of events after World War II had contributed to a widely held sense that society must reform fundamentally: from the revelation of the Nazi genocide to the birth of the United Nations, the postwar baby boom, the decolonization of Africa and Asia, the invention of television, the advent of rock and roll, the threat of nuclear annihilation, the expansion of universities, the rejection of "phoniness" in favor of authenticity, and the development of the birth control pill.

By the 1960s, American women had exercised the vote for forty years and entered the workforce in substantial numbers. In theory, they had a common interest in reducing barriers further, yet it was hard to bridge racial and class divides between them. White feminists who admired the Civil

Rights Movement aspired to work with minority groups, and some found opportunities for collaboration, but minority nationalism (and sometimes majority racism) spurred separation rather than unity. An informal consensus emerged that feminism should respect ethnic boundaries, with each group organizing its "own" community.[49]

In the midst of her busy life, Martha Cotera began digging into the question thrown at her in Houston, "What are you doing here?" Chicanas needed facts to reassure themselves and their families that feminism was a Mexican tradition. She realized, "I was the one person in the Texas movement that was the most, the best trained in research."[50]

What she found at the library convinced her that machismo was the foreign import, not feminism. She blamed sociologists for popularizing a stereotype of brutish Latinos and passive Latinas. Faulting white experts came easily, especially for an activist who at the time described herself as "anti-Anglo." For five years, Martha Cotera worked on a book to flip cultural nationalism on its head. Feminism epitomized patriotism, she would argue. It was the avenue to unity.[51]

In the midst of her scholarship she looked for ways to give help. At Jacinto Treviño college she noticed that radical professors infatuated with third-world communism preyed on young women. Spouting the sayings of Mao Zedong ("power grows out of the barrel of a gun") and packing pistols, swaggering educators invited impressionable undergraduates to parties emphasizing drugs and sex. Martha reported her fellow professors to the college with no effect, and she and Juan eventually quit in disgust.

In 1970, they moved to Crystal City, a hub of activism north of San Antonio where Martha directed the local public library and Juan created an urban renewal agency that helped Hispanic families claim homestead rights under Texas law. From there the couple helped organize the inaugural conference of La Raza Unida Party in San Antonio in 1971, where Martha (nine months pregnant with her second child, a boy) helped establish a separate women's caucus. She had noticed that Chicanas were expected to register voters door to door, monitor election codes, file government paperwork, and staff polling booths—even while being actively discouraged from leadership positions. The caucus would change this. Back in Crystal City, Martha also could not help but observe that the La Raza Unida founder used his prestige to secure college scholarships, but only for men. Again she complained, with no results.[52]

Chicanas elsewhere noted similar dynamics. A peer counselor in the new Educational Opportunity Program at California State University, Long Beach, noticed that male counselors used their status to impress incoming girls. Anna Nieto-Gómez felt that "it was a curse for a Chicana to be cute and beautiful because it left her very vulnerable." Over half of female students quit by their second year. "The pill was not yet widely available," Anna later recalled, "so for women the number one reason for dropping out was pregnancy either by the guys on the campus or by their old boyfriends in the community who didn't want them to go on to college."[53]

The US Supreme Court had only recently overruled state laws forbidding use of contraceptive devices by married couples. The female director of Planned Parenthood in Connecticut, Estelle Griswold, had fought her conviction for opening a clinic, and the liberal Warren Court decided in *Griswold v. Connecticut* (1965) that bans violated a constitutional right to privacy. The Supreme Court overruled prohibitions for unmarried people seven years later, in *Eisenstadt v. Baird* (1972).

At California State University, Long Beach, in the late 1960s, Anna Nieto-Gómez found herself shaken by calls from students who had inserted coat hangers or Coca-Cola bottles into their vaginas to induce miscarriage. "They were tiny little girls," convinced they would be "stoned" if they went home pregnant. A few years later, at San Diego State, a troupe of students performed a skit called "Chicana Goes to College." The parents in the play beg their daughter to get a job instead of going to university, warning her that "anything bad, ugly, awful, and dirty that happens to you will be because you brought it upon yourself." Anna Nieto-Gómez held girls' hands in emergency wards while they hemorrhaged. Doctors across the nation watched patients die of infection and organ failure. Not until *Roe v. Wade* eliminated bans on abortion in 1973 did such deaths decline. After *Roe,* fatalities from illegal procedures decreased by 89 percent.[54]

Anna started a women's group at Long Beach to talk about sexism. They directed students to doctors who provided safer illegal abortions. In 1971, they published three issues of *Hijas de Cuauhtémoc,* a newspaper named for a feminist organization that had played a role in the Mexican Revolution of 1910. Articles criticized men who called women *vendidas* (sell-outs) or *agringadas* (turncoats to gringoism) if they refused to help a revolutionary with his so-called needs. *Hijas* contextualized female oppression as the "result of policy, policy that could be changed."[55]

It was an idea that many Chicanas took up spontaneously. From Wisconsin westward, they met informally to share thoughts about the political causes of personal tragedies. In 1970, California activists established Comisión Femenil Mexicana "because women are not accepted as community leaders either by the Chicano movement or by the Anglo establishment." An Albuquerque undergraduate started a group called Las Chicanas in 1970 that told men it was time to stop using "dial-a-Chicana" whenever unglamorous tasks begged for attention. Women were not just "tortilla-makers, baby-producers." Chicanas at a farmworker's conference in Castroville, Texas, formed their own caucus in 1971. A movement poet described women's experience of being treated as nonentities who were good only for sex:

when we spoke
they let the moment pass and continued
as if nothing had been said,
Remember?[56]

Mexican American activities paralleled efforts by women from other backgrounds. Black activists who resented being told to have "babies for the revolution" started their own groups, including the Third World Women's Alliance, National Black Feminist Organization, and Combahee River Collective (named for Harriet Tubman's daring Civil War mission). They criticized the stereotype that all feminists were white and all Civil Rights activists male. The largest feminist organization, the National Organization for Women, founded by white, Black, and Hispanic women in 1966, had chapters from Florida to Hawaii. Women's studies programs proliferated as well. Two undergraduates and a professor at San Diego State University sat around a table in 1969 mapping the first such program. By 1975 there were 150 departments and research centers nationwide, and by 1990, there were 600.[57]

Americans in growing numbers entertained the possibility that sexism might be equivalent to racism, or at least somewhere on the same spectrum of unnecessary evils. Martha Cotera believed that every woman instinctively knew when she was being mistreated. People sometimes asked, as if inquiring about some exotic malady, "When did you turn feminist?" To this, she quipped that most girls could date their political consciousness to the first time that boys asked to compare "pipis."[58]

Martha used La Raza Unida to recruit women to stand for office. She herself ran for the state board of education, winning 28 percent of the vote. The party endorsed the Equal Rights Amendment, but she exhorted it to do more. Again and again she made the point that if La Raza Unida addressed issues like child care, female membership would double. In spring 1971, she applauded the decision of Chicana organizers at a Houston branch of the Young Women's Christian Association (YWCA) to hold a national conference. Planners sent invitations far and wide for the May event, which they called the "Conferencia de Mujeres por La Raza." Martha recruited women from South Texas, especially Crystal City, San Antonio, and Austin. She recruited Juan, too, who agreed to watch their young daughter from the sidelines. More instrumentally, Juan went to homes and workplaces reassuring wary husbands that the conference would be a good thing.

The response was overwhelming. More than six hundred people came from twenty-three states, though organizers had anticipated only a hundred and fifty. Sixteen women from Long Beach, California, jammed into two boat-like station wagons. Forty-four from San Diego hired a bus and settled in for the long ride. A florist, hair salon, barbershop, tortilla factory, cobbler, Mexicatessen, and candidate for city council bought ads for the conference booklet. Houston restaurants donated food.[59]

A PhD candidate in sociology at Arizona State University opened the conference with the promise that "togetherness can liberate Chicanas." Mothers who picked cotton to support their families and nuns from congregations serving the poor sat hip to hip with coeds in the YWCA gymnasium. The next day, Martha Cotera chaired one of nine breakout sessions that kept attendees on the edges of their folding chairs discussing sex, work, education, marriage, religion, child care, politics, Anglo feminism, and Chicana identity. The leader of a session on sexuality later recalled, "We talked about orgasms. We talked about masturbation. We talked about infidelity. We talked about virginity." The old taboo against discussing female sexuality went poof. So many women raised their hands that she could not call on everyone.[60]

One group circulated a survey to assess attitudes toward gender equality. They printed the results, revealing "88% agreed that a social double standard exists." When asked if the Chicano movement itself discriminated against women, 72 percent said "yes" while 28 percent voiced no opinion. Revealingly, none answered "no."[61]

Workshops debated resolutions for a national manifesto. Among other things, they called for "the right to legal abortions, the right to adequate child care, the right to contraceptive information and devices, the right to decide how many children they do or do not want to have." Any woman who wished for a large family should have one, but none should be "condemned to wash diapers and stay home" if she did not. On the last morning, participants came together for a Sunday plenary to vote on the resolutions.[62]

Martha Cotera was one of hundreds whose eyes widened when four young women from Los Angeles mounted the stage to seize the microphone. They proclaimed that the conference undermined Chicano solidarity. The gymnasium buzzed as they denounced planners for holding it at the YWCA, a facility run by "gavachas," pejorative slang for white women. One who described herself as a "campesina" ally of César Chávez sneered that the only thing that feminists talked about was "me, me, me. . . . Poor me." The group declared a walk-out, saying "our enemy is not with the macho but the gavacho [white man]."[63]

The Californians were members of a coed student club, Movimiento Estudiantil Chicano de Aztlán (MEChA), with chapters across the country. Club presidents from Southern California had met at UCLA weeks before the Houston event to persuade a small delegation to disrupt the conference. The club had paid their airfare from Los Angeles. One of the women later described the assignment as "a mission for us." She and her friends considered feminism "what white women do." Other Chicanas protested that the media had perpetuated a stereotype of "women's liberation people as karate-chopping, man-hating hippies," but it wasn't true.[64]

A quarter of the attendees trailed the protestors out of the building to a park across the street. Juan cried decades later when, at the fortieth reunion, he learned that one of their best friends had been among those intrigued enough to follow the saboteurs. The conference ended with so much animosity that the Houston organizers canceled their plan for an annual event. Factionalism of this type was not unusual during the explosive 1960s and 1970s. Relatively few organizations survived even when their reforms did. Such groups generally had a short life cycle, especially if they tended toward ideological purity.[65]

Still, to Martha Cotera, the Houston conference made plain that the record of Mexican feminism needed documentation. History showed that while Mexican American aspirations complemented those of white feminists, their goals were their own. In one of several exploratory essays published in movement forums, Martha indulged a popular antagonism toward assimilation, stressing that every Chicana "will meet head on any alien feminist movement which attempts to recruit her from her people," and she downplayed gender conflict within the movimiento itself, suggesting that women merely wished to participate on a higher level. Then she unleashed a barrage of facts about Mexican campaigns for gender equality, including the vote, won in 1959. "There has always been feminism in our ranks and there will continue to be as long as Chicanas live and breathe," she asserted. The charge that they were copying gringas was insulting. Mexican American women thought for themselves.[66]

By the mid-1970s, Martha had dug the foundations for a base of support among those who felt as she did. She never shied from what some called the "F" word. Instead, she applauded her people's "traditional feminist values," refusing to acknowledge tradition and feminism as oxymoronic. The fight against sexism was patriotic, not disloyal.[67]

She also built connections with the controversial gringas, aware that some Chicanos would view this as collaboration with the enemy. Following the Houston conference, Martha flew to Washington, DC, at the invitation of Secretary of Health, Education, and Welfare Elliot Richardson to ensure that minorities were "substantially represented" in new affirmative action programs for women. Martha was one of only eight Chicanas to be invited. The other seven came from the West Coast, leaving her to represent the rest of the country. The group took advantage of the occasion to organize a National Chicana Federation. Accustomed from her experience in libraries to wrangling with bureaucrats, Martha hoped to tap monies flowing from Great Society programs. The Californians soon won grants to produce such books as *Low Income Women Who Head Households* and *Every Woman's Right: The Right to Quality Education and Economic Independence.*[68]

Martha herself obtained funds to produce a volume on Chicanas from the Pre-Columbian Era to the present. Called *Profile of the Mexican American Woman* when it was in the form of a government report, Martha republished it as *Diosa y Hembra* (*Goddess and Female*) for use by Chicano and Chicana studies programs then spreading in universities. Written in neutral language, *Diosa* was a first attempt at a history of Mexican

American women. It planted the flag for a new academic field. The capital's leading newspaper, the *Austin American Statesman,* praised its "pint-size mover-and-shaker" author. Among other topics, Martha set the record straight on La Malinche, sold twice into slavery by her own people. Modern scholars considered the translator, diplomat, and yes, rape survivor, "totally justified in acting the way she did," Martha pointed out.[69]

She had more than facts to offer, however. She wanted readers to turn the world upside down and see it from an entirely fresh angle. Her effort paralleled that of other feminist thinkers. Shulamith Firestone, who grew up in an Orthodox Jewish household, daringly speculated that true equality would never be possible unless humanity found a way to conceive babies in test tubes and gestate them outside the womb. Perhaps anatomy otherwise was "destiny," as Sigmund Freud had so frustratingly suggested. Science fiction novelist Ursula Le Guin stretched readers' imaginations to a distant planet in *Left Hand of Darkness* (1969), where everyone was sometimes male, sometimes female. In a plot twist, Le Guin's narrator observed, "The king was pregnant." Firestone's and Le Guin's work challenged readers to consider how parenting might become more cooperative on earth, not just on faraway planets.[70]

Martha Cotera meanwhile worked to expand the Chicana presence in multiethnic coalitions. As of 1970, women held only 11 out of 535 seats in Congress. Shirley Chisholm, the first Black woman in Congress, and Bella Abzug, a Democratic representative from New York, led an effort to grow these numbers by forming a National Women's Political Caucus, joined by Black leaders Fannie Lou Hamer and Dorothy Height, writers Betty Friedan and Gloria Steinem, and Republican stalwarts Jill Ruckelshaus and Elly Peterson. Lobbies, including the old League of Women Voters and new National Organization for Women, increased their Washington presence, too.[71]

Martha resolved to cooperate with them while still attempting to distinguish herself from moderates she called "Mexi-gringos." Using the caucus technique pioneered at Chicano conferences to give women courage when men dominated, Martha brought women Hispanics together at meetings where white women dominated. She helped start the Texas branch of the National Women's Political Caucus in 1972 and a Chicana Caucus at the national level. When invited to present the Mexican American perspective at one multiethnic conference, she emptied both barrels.[72]

In Texas's teeming leftist community, Martha had eagerly worked with Anglo religious reformers, lesbian activists, union leaders, and journalists. But to her mind, higher-class white women who had been politically inert until feminism presented itself as a career opportunity were presumptuous newcomers. Their belief that they would liberate downtrodden Mexican American women left her steaming. Chicanas were "polished, battle-scarred veterans," she told the Texas Women's Political Caucus in March 1972. They had fought injustice long before these white women showed up.

"Help you we must," the fiery reformer admitted in the rough language of the Chicano Left, because "if you're screwed, we're screwed." But "look through our peepholes," Martha Cotera advised. Quit "playing hostesses" and issuing "tasteful memos" to men in power. Be ready to change everything. If white women wished to achieve real cooperation, "put yourselves on the line against racism," she harangued. If they would make that deep commitment, "no institution or practice—be it the job, the school, the home, or the bed—is beyond our grasp in this effort."[73]

As she noted later, "It is always easier to battle strangers than one's own family." Alienating women from the dominant ethnic group did not feel as risky as the prospect of alienating men from her own community. An anthropologist noted the same dynamic among Chicana playwrights, whose characters dismissed insensitive white feminists as "stupid Americans" while treating tone-deaf Chicanos as family in need of gentle reeducation.[74]

Activists from other ethnic communities experienced the same tug of loyalties. Some embraced collaboration with white women even while indulging in recriminations against them. It could make cooperation difficult. As one Black mother complained about a Brooklyn parents group, "you people get sucked in every time." She pointed out, "When black women are doing their thing by showing off and whites do their thing by accepting guilt, we're nowhere."[75]

Martha Cotera considered cooperation a matter of follow-through. Anglo members of the National Women's Political Caucus could easily demonstrate good faith by campaigning for candidates of La Raza Unida, she felt. Instead, they let her down almost immediately. Democrats and Republicans always voted for their own.

In races where no Chicanas appeared on the ticket, Martha sometimes stumped for white women, hoping to win their support on other issues. Ann Richards of Austin epitomized the worthless results, in Martha's view. In 1976, Martha campaigned hard for the Texas liberal with perfectly coifed blond hair, then running for office for the first time. Once elected county commissioner, Ann Richards failed to recommend Hispanics for judgeships. Martha accompanied a group of prominent men to her office. Direct as ever, Martha complained more vociferously than they. Ann Richards, renowned for bluntness too, finally slapped her desk, Texas-style. "Well, God damn it, Martha," she said. "You know I love your people!"

Martha shot back, "You know, God damn it, then. We don't need your love," she said. "We need you to appoint these judges!" Still Ann Richards did not come through.[76]

Working with men in the movimiento became easier over time. Cooperating with white feminists seemed harder. Indeed, all feminists faced the challenge of getting along with other women, especially after the United Nations declared 1975 "International Women's Year."

A Mother's Defense

It was hot in Spokane in August. Washington State had more than forty different types of mosquitoes, and Yvonne Wanrow's new babysitter must have found window screens helpful. A white single mother of three girls, Shirley Hooper certainly noticed the mysterious slash that had ruined the one in her bedroom. The landlord repaired the screen, but someone cut it again the next night. Frightened now, Hooper wondered if it was the man who had crouched in the dark near the front of her house a few days earlier. She lived in a rough, industrial section of Washington's second-largest city. Only a few homes dotted the neighborhood and she never felt entirely safe, especially after a doctor had diagnosed her seven-year-old daughter with a venereal disease six months earlier. Little Mildred never revealed who assaulted her. The mystery weighed on Hooper.

Yvonne Wanrow had no knowledge of this private tragedy when she dropped off Darren, then eight, and Yvette, only two, at Shirley Hooper's house on a Friday in 1972. Yvonne owned a car and Hooper did not, so she traded rides for babysitting. They were friends of a sort, linked by one of the sticky webs of modern life. Shirley's new boyfriend happened to be Yvonne's ex-brother-in-law, an Indigenous man previously married to her youngest sister, Angie.

Yvonne had a follow-up appointment for a fractured ankle. She had recently tripped and hit a coffee table, breaking the bone. She looked forward to hearing that she could put weight on it, the next phase in shedding the heavy cast that stretched from foot to knee.

Like many single mothers with little money, Yvonne had an old car. It broke down on the way to the clinic, so Yvonne called her other sister, Marcella, who gave her a ride to the appointment. Yvonne returned home in the late afternoon and was waiting by the phone to hear from a mechanic when Shirley Hooper rang around 6:00 p.m.

"Yvonne, the police are here," the babysitter blurted out. A sixty-year-old neighbor, William Wesler, had grabbed Yvonne's son and tried to pull him indoors. Darren broke free and ran back to Hooper's house, where the landlord was fixing the damaged screen. A tall man at six-foot-two, Wesler came to Shirley Hooper's front porch. "I didn't hurt the kid," Wesler said. "He fell. He fell." But Darren had a red mark on his arm and his bike was in the man's yard. The boy was clearly frightened.[77]

Worse, after the neighbor left, seven-year-old Mildred told her mother that Wesler was the man who had taken off her pants and assaulted her in his bedroom months before. The child had not said so previously because she was too afraid. As the landlord fixed the screen, he informed Hooper that Wesler had tried to molest the son of a previous tenant, for which, he believed, Wesler had spent time in the state mental hospital. When the landlord left, he stopped to check a non-functional porch light—and pointed out it was not broken. Someone tall enough to reach the bulb had unscrewed it. He suggested that Hooper keep a baseball bat close to defend herself.[78]

The landlord did not know of two additional allegations of sexual abuse against William Wesler, allegations that were never prosecuted because the underage victims were unable to recall the specific dates of the attacks, then a police requirement. One of the children's fathers had fired a gun at Wesler, and an officer had told Wesler he was lucky the man had not killed him. In a third case, Wesler served two days in jail for plying a child with cigarettes and alcohol. Like other private tragedies that once seemed unmentionable—illegal but ignored—child abuse did not figure in public conversation or medical journals until the mid-1960s, when a few states passed the first laws that facilitated reporting. In 1974, at the behest of Minnesota senator Walter Mondale, the federal government finally established a program to address child abuse.[79]

But it wasn't yet 1974. It was August 11, 1972, a Friday afternoon, when Shirley Hooper dialed the police, alarmed by what she had learned. The police officers took a statement from Shirley and her daughter but said they could do nothing further until she filed a complaint with the district attorney, whose office would reopen Monday morning. They suggested that she sprinkle flour outside her bedroom window to capture footprints in case someone slashed the screen again. She asked if she could use a gun to defend herself if anyone attempted to break in, whereupon they cautioned, "Wait until he gets in the house."[80]

Shirley Hooper was shaken when she telephoned Yvonne Wanrow. "Do you still have your gun?" she asked.[81]

The information washed over Yvonne: slashed screens, a dark porch, an accused rapist, her vulnerable child. A big man.

Yvonne admitted she still had the gun, but suggested that the babysitter and five children leave instead. "Shirley, I have just enough money for a cab," she said. "Come here. Spend the weekend. I'll go with you on Monday and we'll both file a complaint."[82]

But the babysitter insisted on staying put, so Yvonne grabbed milk for the children and a sixpack to calm her and Shirley. She took the gun she had test-fired only once. A sinus headache from earlier in the day came back as she climbed into the cab.

Darren showed Yvonne his bruise when she arrived, and explained that the man had offered to show him a cat. She and Shirley Hooper rehashed the events. Yvonne called her sister Angie, who came over with her husband and three young children. The four frightened adults kept vigil through the night, drinking beer. Yvonne used her crutches, afraid to step too heavily on the healing foot, still in a cast. Angie and her husband went outside occasionally to study Wesler's house, watching him drink with a friend through his kitchen window. Yvonne was scared to go with them. Out-of-control men terrified her. She kept the gun in the waistband of her summertime shorts.

As dawn neared, Yvonne's brother-in-law went outside again. Yvonne did not see him leave. She later learned that he had gone to tell William Wesler to stay away, and then walked around the side of the house with Wesler's companion to show him the screen that someone kept cutting.

When Yvonne realized that Angie's husband was gone, she looked out the front window and spied him with two men she did not recognize. Suddenly, the taller one came to the door. Shirley Hooper yelled, "I don't want that man in here!" But William Wesler stumbled into the room and approached the couch where Angie Michel's three-year-old son slept. "My, what a cute little boy," he said. Now Angie screamed. The toddler awoke and began to wail. Another child slept on the couch and yet another in a nearby crib.[83]

The room grew small. Yvonne felt like a bystander in a movie. She saw herself in the center of the room, though she stood closer to the porch. She glanced again through the front door but now did not see her brother-in-law. She, two other women, and eight small children were alone. When she turned around again, William Wesler was coming toward her. His spiky gray hair stood in a rigid crewcut. Startled, she looked up into eyes that seemed angry.

On crutches, Yvonne was ten inches shorter than Wesler. She weighed only 120 pounds. It had been decades since she could run fast. Wesler came so close that the gun met his shirt as she raised it. Yvonne heard a pop and then realized she had pulled the trigger. The man fell at her feet. A coroner later determined that Wesler's blood alcohol level had been 0.27, three times the legal limit to drive. Yvonne fired again and Wesler's companion entered the room in time to get hit in the right arm. Her brother-in-law was still outside. Everyone at the scene had slightly different perceptions of what had happened, as is normal with trauma. Wesler's companion said that Yvonne yelled threats as he fled. Yvonne could hardly remember him afterward.

Her shocked brain struggled to cope. Now weeping, she walked into Shirley Hooper's back bedroom and put the gun to her temple. She wanted it to be over.

"Think of your kids," came a voice inside, and she numbly laid the pistol on a bookcase.[84]

Shirley Hooper dialed 911, a new emergency service established in 1968 as part of Lyndon Johnson's Great Society reforms. The police dispatcher recorded the conversation. Hooper described the intruder, then Yvonne reported that she had shot two people. "We warned you—we told you guys," she said to the dispatcher. Her voice was level, but she urged the police to "hustle, hustle." The downed man was "in bad shape." The second man might come back "and shoot me," she repeatedly said. "There's a bunch of kids around here." Officers arrived shortly, arrested Yvonne, and booked her for felony murder of William Wesler and first-degree assault on his companion. They speculated that "revenge might have been the motive." With no prior arrests, Yvonne was released on bail after three nights in custody.[85]

Several days later, the free public defender leaned against his desk, looking down on Yvonne in a chair in his office, her leg still in the cast. He advised her to plead guilty. Sentencing would be quick. She could teach art to other Native women in prison. Yvonne told him she wanted a trial. "Yvonne," he said, "you know you're guilty."[86]

"But I don't *feel* guilty," she replied.[87]

Actually, her feelings were mixed. She did not regret shooting William Wesler, and yet she did. A man had died by her hand. When an officer first took her fingerprints, she had looked down in revulsion. She told him, "I wish you would cut my hand off," and burst out crying again. Was she guilty, as her attorney now said? She took his advice and pleaded guilty.[88]

Weeks later, awaiting her court date, she spoke over the phone with a nephew in San Diego. Get a different attorney, he told her. "Fight like an Indian."[89]

Yvonne had no idea what that might look like. She went to her Irish Catholic priest, who recommended a young attorney interested in civil rights who had never handled a murder charge but seemed like a fighter. Eugene Annis of Spokane took the case without mentioning payment. The first thing he did was change her plea to not guilty and persuade the prosecutor to switch the charge from first-degree murder, which carried the death penalty, to second degree. Second degree meant that the accused had no legitimate "excuse or justification" to take a life.[90]

This was the prosecutor's last merciful act. He intended to prove that Yvonne Wanrow had lured William Wesler into the house in order to kill him. Vigilantes must be punished, Donald Brockett told the jury a few months later. Europeans had "brought the gun" to the Americas, Yvonne recalled him lecturing her, and she had "no right to take the law into your own hands."[91]

The white prosecutor's allusion had special salience. American Indians had occupied the town of Wounded Knee in South Dakota two months earlier to protest federal policies that harmed Indigenous peoples. Two Indians were killed and fourteen people injured, including a marshal paralyzed by gunshot in a clash with federal law enforcement. The siege made headlines worldwide. It ended when Indians surrendered their weapons on May 8, 1973, the second day of Yvonne Wanrow's trial. Brockett tried to associate Yvonne with Native militancy. Eugene Annis advised his client not to wear Indian jewelry in court.

Yvonne's testimony remained consistent during the trial, but two key witnesses refined their stories. William Wesler's companion had told police that Yvonne invited him and Wesler into the house for a beer. He also gave conflicting descriptions of the event. The "drunk Indian woman" had fetched the gun from another room after they came in, he initially said, but also that it was already in her waistband. He now insisted, in a third version, that she had retrieved the gun after they entered and closed the front door to trap them. He testified that after Yvonne killed Wesler, she called out to him as he ran, "Come back here, I have another one for you."[92]

Shirley Hooper changed her story, too, perhaps under pressure from her boyfriend, Yvonne's ex-brother-in-law, who resented the Wanrow family and had bragged to Eugene Annis that Hooper would never cooperate. The babysitter now introduced information she had not previously mentioned. Shirley Hooper claimed that Yvonne had sworn to "fix" Wesler even before the shooting and said, "We are going to get it over with."[93]

At the end of the week-long trial, the judge instructed the jury not to consider anything that occurred before Wesler entered the house: not the damaged screens, disconnected lightbulb, attacks on children, or police refusal to investigate. Using the masculine gender to explain the law, the judge advised that defendants like Yvonne could be exonerated only if a "reasonable man" in the same situation would have considered "his" life in danger. If such a man had only "an ordinary battery" to fear, he must use his "naked hands" to repel the assault. A defendant was entitled to use a gun against an unarmed assailant only if "he" feared imminent death. The prosecutor alleged that Yvonne's "cool" tone on the telephone showed that nothing scared her. Self-defense did not apply. The 911 tape was given to the jury, though it was inadmissible under state law.[94]

The jury deliberated through Sunday, May 13, 1973. Richard Nixon had recently issued a proclamation honoring it as Mother's Day. "Today we are in the midst of a national movement to ensure equal rights for women," observed the Republican president, whose wife Pat publicly supported the ERA. It was a time to honor mothers, including those making contributions as working parents (although he vetoed a bipartisan measure funding child care). The Spokane jury returned a unanimous verdict of guilty that very day. Women on the jury wept.[95]

During sentencing, the judge allowed testimony on Native cultures that he had previously excluded. An expert testified that Indian peoples revered elders as wise, and a young mother who learned that an elder made a practice of harming children would be doubly alarmed. The prosecutor asked if that meant she "behaves basically like an animal."[96]

The Spokane judge sentenced Yvonne Wanrow to twenty years in prison for killing Wesler and wounding his companion. Yvonne did not doubt that racism had distorted justice. Only later did it occur to her that sexism, too, had influenced the verdict.

Building a Future

The antiauthoritarian ethos of 1960s activism peaked in the women's movement. Feminists wanted to be equal to one another, not just to men. Boundaries between leaders and followers vanished. Onlookers struggled to determine who was in charge. A sociologist observed that the media picked "stars" partly because the movement refused to select representatives. Activists often resented other women for a celebrity status they did not necessarily court.[97]

One such figure was writer Gloria Steinem, whose blue aviator glasses and chic miniskirts appealed to reporters though she was initially an awkward public speaker. Steinem's renown was sealed in 1971 when she started *Ms.* magazine with a cooperative team of six other women. More famous yet in the long run was the word "Ms." itself, a new honorific designed to eliminate competitive distinctions between married and unmarried women. The Government Printing Office started using "Ms." in official documents only two months later, as Americans seized on the term.

Martha Cotera navigated these choppy waters by publicizing the accomplishments of other Chicanas while playing down her own. "I" did not readily find her tongue and she usually substituted "we." The plural pronoun was an organizing strategy, feminist principle, and expression of Chicanismo. Mexican American feminists emphasized cooperative leadership even more than white women, whose individualistic leaders appeared to them to elbow forward. From what Chicanas could see, the majority community relied too much on "Big Mamas."[98]

In 1975, the new Johnson Presidential Library hosted a prominent, two-day symposium on "Women in Public Life." Lady Bird Johnson sat in the front row. Vice President Nelson Rockefeller gave a major address. Congresswoman Barbara Jordan, Gloria Steinem, and nearly every woman in Texas politics attended. Martha Cotera gave a ten-minute talk, bathed in the same limelight.

It infuriated her that no other Chicana had been invited to speak. She told the attentive audience of 1,500 people that she would take "whatever time is necessary" to describe *all* of the Mexican Americans who merited attention, and then read the names and qualifications of thirty, asking any of those present to stand. Martha spent half her speech acknowledging colleagues, and the other half telling whites to be more inclusive. It pained her to upset the bighearted First Lady, whom she liked, but she did not hold back. If necessary, she declared, Chicanas would wrest power not only from white and brown men, but from Anglo women, too, since when it came to equal opportunity they would clearly "get there first."[99]

Martha resisted acknowledging why she personally had been invited. After the event she admitted to a reporter, "Maybe the coordinators honestly don't know who our leadership is," adding, "we don't make ourselves visible." The organizers at the LBJ Library likely invited her because she was the foremost Mexican American feminist they knew, and one willing to enter alliances.[100]

A "Chicana Identity" conference the next week in Houston underscored the challenge. Martha Cotera gave the keynote address, urging attendees to stand proudly for feminism and embrace multiethnic coalitions. "Let's all get something going together," she exhorted. But other speakers disagreed. Two criticized white feminists as insensitive. One asserted, "Mexican American men are different from Anglo men," meaning they were not sexist, then added, "Whatever we will do in the Chicana movement will be through working closely with our men."[101]

Martha continued to win grants for innovative projects, such as guides for migrants picking crops state-to-state who needed to know where to enroll their children in school. She and Juan had brought their two children back to Austin, where Juan's career blossomed. He founded a leading architectural firm in a town where he once could not rent a house, helping to design the new airport and city hall. She started a nonprofit, the Chicana Research and Learning Center, to develop bibliographies for bilingual teachers and provide technical assistance to nonprofits. With money from the Department of Education, she wrote an assertiveness-training guide, *Doña Doormat No Está Aquí* (*Mrs. Doormat Doesn't Live Here*), which taught Chicanas to "identify their rights as human beings." After the University of Texas rejected Martha for a library job at the behest of Hispanic men irritated by feminist demands, Martha started a private company that published business directories. In 1976 Anna Nieto-Gómez had been squeezed out of academia, too, when professors in the Chicano Studies Program fired her from the faculty of California State University Northridge for calling them sexist.[102]

Martha approached eight friends to form an organization of Democrats, Republicans, and La Raza Unida members to remake Austin. It should have a neutral name, she believed. Texans needed permanent institutions that served everybody regardless of race, gender, or political affiliation. She asked each friend to call ten more. In 1974, they launched the Mexican American Business and Professional Women's Association with two hundred founding members. For the first time in her career, Martha did not defer to the movement's penchant for non-hierarchical leadership. She ran for president. She wanted too many things to tolerate self-defeating chaos.

Like Frances Perkins, Martha had a long list of demands: free birth control and abortions for the poor in Travis County, public transportation for the disabled and elderly, fair housing ordinances to prevent discrimination, programs to help mothers in prison see their children, better recreation for teens, parks on Austin's downtown lakefront, a twenty-four-hour rape crisis center, a shelter for battered spouses, a credit union for wives who were denied credit cards in their own names, a university program in Mexican American studies, and a $47 million dollar cultural center to showcase Texas's Hispanic heritage. In time, she got everything—except the credit union, which Anglo investors dropped at the last minute.

To develop public parklands, Martha worked especially closely with Lady Bird Johnson, whom she considered "an angel." They bonded as mothers, too. Years later, Martha would laugh about the time she asked the First Lady how her children were. Johnson closed her eyes and leaned against the rear of the elevator in which they were riding. "Tolerable," she drawled. Martha also appreciated First Lady Rosalynn Carter, who invited her to meet privately in Austin to discuss Chicana issues. President Jimmy

Carter subsequently named Martha to a national committee on women's rights.

Nonetheless, she continued to struggle with other high-profile white women who seemed deaf to the input of Chicanas. The problem came to a head in Houston in 1977 at a conference called by President Gerald Ford. Ford and his wife Betty strongly supported the ERA, which would prohibit sex discrimination "by the United States or any state." Following a UN-sponsored conference in Mexico City honoring International Women's Year, the president appointed a bipartisan commission to organize an American conference with the goal of forming "a more perfect union." As Ford said in one speech, echoing Abigail Adams's words to John when he was vice president, "much more needs to be done." Ford signed a bill that funded a series of state conferences to elect delegates and propose resolutions to a national conclave that would craft a national women's rights agenda. It was a stunning step forward.[103]

Republican moderate Jill Ruckelshaus, a mother of five, headed the president's group of advisers. In America's bicentennial year, she wrote him that "there exists a common misconception that the women's movement began in the 1960s." She linked feminism instead with the patriots of 1776. "The truth is that since the founding of our Nation there has been a strong impetus to gain a greater role for women than the narrow one prescribed for them by custom, tradition, and law." Ruckelshaus also considered women's rights a party tradition. The Republicans had endorsed the ERA before the Democrats.[104]

When Jimmy Carter beat Ford in the election that year, he invited Bella Abzug to take over the conference planning, despite warnings that replacing Ford's appointee, and the commissioners she had selected, would tarnish the conference's bipartisan appeal. First Lady Rosalynn Carter also opposed the appointment of Abzug, nicknamed "Battling Bella," for fear that the brassy New Yorker would alienate "the women at home." But the president listened to his specialist on women's issues, Midge Costanza, who endorsed Abzug. Costanza and Abzug prioritized diversity in the selection of new commissioners. Of those invited, 29 percent came from minority backgrounds, double the number on Ford's panel and almost twice the percentage in the population. Carter also made the first presidential appointment of an openly gay person, something that shocked many Americans.[105]

Martha Cotera followed the planning closely. She worried that Democrats had become cocky and were underestimating the opposition. Congress had passed the ERA easily in 1972, as well as Title IX, a law requiring schools that received federal money to provide equal educational opportunities for girls and boys, including in student sports. The US Supreme Court continued in a liberal trajectory, too, ruling in *Taylor v. Louisiana* (1975) that keeping women off juries violated the Constitution. Yet Martha sensed trouble ahead. Polls showed support for the ERA still high but declining.[106]

Martha raced out in front of the planning process, convinced that Chicanas must run harder than anyone else. Before Jimmy Carter even won, she submitted a hundred names for the Texas state commission. She heard nothing back, only vague rumors that prominent white feminists had no plans to invite any of them. Furious at what seemed a slight, Martha formed a Chicana advisory committee that started meeting weekly in December 1976 to advise a state planning group that had not yet even been named. Martha worried that white leaders would jeopardize the outcome by tolerating conservatives and excluding leftists. She feared that her own state might not endorse the ERA.[107]

In the end, a liberal Choctaw woman became chair of the Texas commission, and a Chicana became vice chair. Martha still worried that they were light on community activists and heavy on politicians—like Ann Richards and state representative Sarah Weddington, who had persuaded the Supreme Court in 1973 in *Roe v. Wade* that a pregnant woman should have the right to decide whether or not to carry a child. Martha considered such women schemers. Years later she admitted she did not have a politician's ability to "look at the big picture and love everybody." Temperamentally she was "an absolutist," she acknowledged, while Juan was better at compromise. She worried that upper-class women cared too little about the poor.[108]

Mutual suspicion was then common among reformers, who often viewed one another as insufficiently idealistic. What seemed like political overreach to one person could strike another as cowardly underreach. Midge Costanza deplored Rosalynn Carter's measured advocacy of the ERA, for example, even though others praised the First Lady for delivering ratification in Indiana. Perfectionism led easily to dogmatism, splitting reformers from one another and the mainstream.[109]

Conservatives did better at pulling together, filing nine lawsuits that attempted to halt federal funding of the women's conferences, and calling Republican Gerald Ford's initiative "a front for radicals and lesbians." Thousands of anti-feminists registered for the fifty state conventions.[110]

Using her mailing list of five thousand, Martha Cotera hoped to recruit hundreds of Chicanas and congenial white feminists for the Texas meeting to make sure they selected good delegates for the national meeting. She applied for funds from the state commission, which had a federal grant of $100,000, but the money never materialized despite what she took to be a verbal promise. She and Juan instead took ten thousand dollars from their life savings to fund printing, postage, travel, long-distance phone calls, and the expenses of organizers across the nation's second largest state. Martha self-published another book, *The Chicana Feminist,* and attended every meeting of the planning commission as an observer. To her, its members seemed "paralyzed by fear" of conservative criticism and unable to act decisively. She disdained their decision to invite quasi-religious groups like Women Who Want to Be Women to present alternative perspectives. One commissioner complained that Martha, though not a member, talked more than anyone else.[111]

Almost three thousand Texans showed up at the state convention, five times the number who had preregistered. From 212 nominees, participants elected 58 delegates to the Houston conference. Of them, 52 identified as pro-feminist and 6 as anti. Martha Cotera was one of those elected. She received 100 more votes than Ann Richards and 140 more than Sarah Weddington.[112]

The Choctaw chair of the state planning group said afterward, "Had the Chicanas not come—the Antis would have taken the delegates." The vice chair wrote more bluntly, "remember the name Martha Cotera; the energy, anger, stamina. If anyone deserves an award for the one who put it all together, kept it together, encouraged the disillusioned—give it to her."[113]

Neighboring Oklahoma had preregistered only two hundred people for their state conference, but a thousand churchgoers unexpectedly arrived on buses that morning. They voted down the proposed women's rights platform and swept every delegate. Conservative columnist James Kirkpatrick wrote afterward that "the troops of Bella Abzug got scalped" in "Indian country." Conservatives triumphed in twelve other states that summer. Mississippi elected an all-white delegation that included six men and the wife of the Grand Dragon of the state Ku Klux Klan.[114]

In November, female Olympic medalists, marathon winners, and high school athletes in blue and white T-shirts relayed a torch 1,600 miles from Seneca Falls, New York. First Ladies Rosalynn Carter, Betty Ford, and Lady Bird Johnson opened the festivities. Liberals, radicals, and conservatives jostled together. The Houston meeting featured the same dynamics as the state conferences, although supporters of women's rights predominated. Almost twenty thousand observers looked on as two thousand delegates discussed, then passed, a "National Plan of Action" that endorsed birth control and abortion, child care, lesbian rights, greater economic opportunity, and the ERA. The conference recorded its opposition to involuntary sterilization as well, an injustice that affected women of color particularly.[115]

Feminists thought they had arrived. They did not realize that antifeminists had, too.

Martha helped write the "Minority Women Resolution" for the final declaration. At the jammed sessions, Juan Cotera kept track of thirteen-year-old Maria wearing her "Uppity Women Unite" button. Six-year-old Juan Javier slung his mother's purse over his shoulder, keeping it safe. As Martha had always insisted, feminism brought families together. The solution to the challenges of marriage, she believed, was to make partners equal so that they pulled together, rather than apart, when life got hard.

An Indian Woman Is Not a "Reasonable Man"

After his election, President John Kennedy had asked a trusted campaigner what job she wanted. Esther Peterson, whose career went back to the days of Frances Perkins, asked him for directorship of the Women's Bureau of the Department of Labor. Soon thereafter Peterson convinced the president to establish a long-discussed commission on the status of women. Kennedy appointed eleven men and fifteen women, naming Eleanor Roosevelt chair. Even before their final report, Kennedy ordered federal agencies to stop advertising "Help Wanted" by gender. He also signed the Equal Pay Act, an amendment to Perkins's 1938 Fair Labor Standards Act, to ban gendered pay scales. States formed parallel commissions on the status of women. By 1967 there were fifty.[116]

Suffering from incurable tuberculosis, Eleanor Roosevelt recruited a protégée to help. She wanted Pauli Murray, the first African American to receive a doctorate in law from Yale, to fix a problem that had divided feminists since Alice Paul first proposed the ERA in 1923. Equality might be good in theory, but what if it voided protective legislation? How could women be both equal to—as well as different from—men? The First Lady wanted an answer.

Pauli Murray brought an unusual perspective to Kennedy's commission. She had enrolled at Yale because the chair of graduate studies at Harvard had written her that, based on her photograph, she was clearly "not of the sex entitled to be admitted to Harvard Law School." In New Haven, a landlord had informed her that he could not rent to "a colored person." Since childhood she had also felt that she was an "in between"—a person outwardly female and inwardly male—though this was one trait she could keep private.[117]

Murray possessed what law professor Kimberlé Crenshaw later called an "intersectional" perspective: a deep and personal understanding of how issues of race and gender overlapped. Mindful of *Brown v. Board of Education,* Murray advised Kennedy's committee that women should look for opportunities to convince the Supreme Court that Fourteenth Amendment guarantees of due process *did* pertain to them. Attitudes had changed enough that the courts might now recognize a parallel between Jim Crow and "Jane Crow," a term she invented. Blacks and women both suffered discrimination due to obvious but inconsequential physical characteristics, though males and females did differ from one another in a few important respects. The challenge was "to remove legal restrictions which are not grounded in biological and life-serving functions," Pauli Murray told the commission. Sex should become a "suspect classification" within the law, not an automatic one. Where gender did *not* apply, it should not be applied. Even where it *did* apply, sex should not subject women to unnecessarily "restrictive treatment."[118]

White women lawyers had for some time compared their situation with that of minorities, but courts had dismissed the analogy as frivolous. A Black legal scholar endorsed by the dying Eleanor Roosevelt had greater legitimacy. Equally important, Pauli Murray had come up with a new solution. She drew a subtle comparison that allowed women to fight gender discrimination without denying relevant physical differences. "I feel in my bones that you are making history," Esther Peterson told Murray, believing her strategy could offer a safer route to equality than the controversial ERA. The commission reported to Kennedy a month before his death that all they needed was a test case to bring to the Supreme Court.[119]

Ruth Bader Ginsburg, a law professor at Rutgers University, won that case nine years later. In *Reed v. Reed* (1971), she argued that gender must be interrogated as a "suspect" classification rather than accepted as a blanket classification. Laws and privileges should be gender-neutral unless there was some compelling reason for them to be gender-specific. Ginsburg listed Murray as co-counsel, and later said "we were standing on her shoulders." Ginsburg helped convince the US Supreme Court that an Idaho law that routinely named men as executors of estates violated an individual's right under the Fourteenth Amendment to due consideration of individual ability. Sally Reed had sued for the right to settle her deceased son's estate, a privilege that Idaho automatically awarded her former husband. Ginsburg argued that having a uterus had nothing to do with reading a contract. She won the first sex discrimination case in American history, a century after Susan B. Anthony had lost hers.[120]

In Washington, Yvonne Wanrow had an opposite, yet related, problem. A year after *Reed v. Reed,* the Spokane jury convicted Yvonne for not behaving like a "reasonable man." The court refused to acknowledge that a woman possessed any gender-specific disadvantage when it came to defending herself. Yvonne's attorney filed an appeal that allowed her to remain free on bail. Two years later, the Intermediate Court of Appeals ruled that the lower court had erred in *Washington v. Wanrow* by giving jurors the 911 tape. The Spokane prosecutor must try her again if he wished to pursue the case.

Yvonne knew he would. Struggling not to be overwhelmed by grief, she drank and contemplated suicide. Finally she prayed. Not long after her first trial, Yvonne had fallen in love with a singer associated with the American Indian Movement, Floyd Red Crow Westerman. The couple had a baby together. Through Westerman, she became involved with Native spiritualism. After fasting one day, she heard a voice say, "Indian people are the threshold to the Creator's heart." The phrase gave her a sense of responsibility. On July 4, 1974, Independence Day, she gave up alcohol permanently. Another elder told her that her daughter Julie was safe in another world, and that the sick man she had killed had forgiven her. The words gave Yvonne a sense of peace.[121]

She fought on. Her four sisters sewed Native-inspired clothes and gave fashion shows to raise money for her defense. While awaiting the Spokane prosecutor's next move, she followed the eight-month Wounded Knee trial, where New York defense attorney William Kunstler argued so aggressively that the judge had him physically expelled. Yvonne decided this was the lawyer she needed. When Westerman went to New York to give a concert, she borrowed money for a one-way ticket and asked him to introduce her.[122]

William Kunstler said he thought there might be some "women's issues" in her case. He directed Yvonne to two young feminists at his nonprofit firm, the Center for Constitutional Rights. Women's self-defense cases had recently gained prominence. Activist lawyers were then defending Joan Little, a twenty-year-old Black woman who in 1975 was facing the death penalty for killing a two-hundred-pound white jailor. Carrying an icepick, the North Carolina guard had removed his shoes in the hall outside her cell, in which the video camera was broken. Semen trailed down the dead man's leg. Joan Little claimed she had stabbed him with his own weapon in self-defense. Other prisoners testified that they, too, had been sexually assaulted by the jailor wielding an icepick. On the other side of the country, another legal team was defending farmworker Inez Garcia, convicted of murder for shooting a man after he had raped her. In Garcia's case, the judge instructed the jury to ignore all testimony about the rape and consider only testimony about the shooting. Feminist, lesbian, Black, and Chicano organizations picketed the trials.[123]

Kunstler's colleagues, Elizabeth Schneider and Nancy Stearns, impressed Yvonne with their transparency. Both were experienced litigators. Stearns had led a state-by-state fight against abortion restrictions, arguing in *Rhode Island v. Israel* that such restrictions violated the Nineteenth Amendment's guarantee of participation in the political process, since "abortion laws, in their real practical effects, deny the liberty, and equality[,] of women to participate in the wider world." Other litigators argued that such statutes violated the Thirteenth Amendment's ban on involuntary servitude, since there is "nothing more demanding upon the body and person of a woman than pregnancy, and the subsequent feeding and caring of an infant until it has reached maturity some eighteen years later."[124]

The lawyers explained Yvonne's choices rather than telling her what to do. Yvonne had often felt like "a dummy" around male counsel, but the pair treated her as their equal. Women lawyers were still rare, making up only 3 percent of attorneys, though the number of women attending law school grew tenfold between 1967 and 1977. Schneider and Stearns believed courts had a responsibility to consider that assault was riskier for women than for men. Failure to do so introduced gender bias into the law of self-defense. After talking with the lawyers, Yvonne met Harry Belafonte, a singer and civil rights activist who gave her money for the plane trip home.[125]

Other musicians also helped. When Yvonne told her story at a concert for the Wounded Knee defendants, Native singer Buffy Sainte-Marie, one of the nation's top songwriters, took Yvonne aside. She wrote a check and gave Yvonne the name of her Hollywood publicist. Feminist newspapers picked up the story, including *Ms.,* with its circulation of three million. Indigenous organizations spread the word, too.[126]

In September 1975, the Spokane prosecutor took his case to Washington's top court. Schneider and Stearns filed a response, arguing that men and women experienced threats differently. Girls were socialized to avoid physical confrontations. Research showed that most had no confidence in their ability to prevail in a hand-to-hand test of strength with men. Common experiences of rape and domestic violence made them fear, quite *reasonably,* as it were, for their very lives. Inadequate police protection reinforced their vulnerability.

Schneider and Stearns also took specific aim at the idea of proportional violence. A brawl between two men did not remotely resemble one between a large male aggressor and a small woman on crutches. Juries not given this information, or told what Yvonne knew about William Wesler prior to the shooting, would be unable to understand how her knowledge that he had previously assaulted children would affect her perception of danger.[127]

The supreme court of Washington State heard the case the following spring. Indian supporters beat drums outside the courthouse on February 23, 1976. With Schneider and Stearns beside her, Yvonne felt confident that she would win. After the hearing ended, while waiting upon the justices' lengthy deliberations, she testified at the International Tribunal on Crimes against Women held the next month in Belgium. Women there described how they had been subjected to genital mutilation, forced sterilization, jail sentences for abortion, sex trafficking, and banishment for divorce. It was a terrible time to be a woman—and a hopeful one.[128]

Had Yvonne seen inside the judges' chambers, she would not have been so optimistic. Her attorneys were considerably less confident than she. Not "in a million years" did Nancy Stearns, the more experienced of the pair, think the all-male, all-white court would accept their argument.[129]

It did not. Only one member of the state supreme court was persuaded, and he thought that racism would still circumvent a ruling in Yvonne's favor, despite the upswing in consciousness about sexism. Robert Utter saw anti-Indian sentiment all the time, and knew it heightened every obstacle. Over the next several months, he worked on his colleagues. He described the problem of violence against women and anti-Indian prejudice within their constituencies. One finally capitulated, agreeing, "You know, sometimes you've got to pull up your socks and be a judge." Utter eventually persuaded four others. In 1977, the majority upheld the appellate court's decision that the 911 tape had been inadmissible. A plurality opined that the lower court had erred in its instructions to the jury. Utter wrote for the group, "The impression created that a 5′4″ woman with a cast on her leg and using a crutch must, under the law, somehow repel an assault by a 6′2″ intoxicated man without employing weapons in her defense . . . constitutes a separate and distinct misstatement of the law and . . . violates the respondent's right to equal protection of the law."[130]

He added that the lower court's "persistent use of the masculine gender" to describe the female defendant undermined the jury's understanding of her perspective. Crucially, he continued, "The respondent was entitled to have the jury consider her actions in the light of her own perceptions of the situation, including those perceptions which were the product of our nation's 'long and unfortunate history of sex discrimination.'" The court ruling did not say that individuals should be entitled to interpret danger subjectively, but rather that an objective standard of conduct for a man in matters of safety was not necessarily the same as an objective standard for a woman. In other words, gender must be *investigated* to see when and where it applied. Women and men were equal, but they also had substantively different experiences in certain situations.[131]

Yvonne Wanrow's trial team soon found themselves inundated by new clients filing appeals from prison cells. Using *Washington v. Wanrow,* one feminist attorney created a practical workbook for "women's self-defense cases." She developed questions for prospective jurors, such as, for a man, "Have you ever arm-wrestled with a woman?" Or for a woman, "Have you ever arm-wrestled with a man" and "Have you ever won?" Lawyers appealed to common sense, backed by anatomical studies showing that women on average have 40 percent less upper-body strength than men due to their smaller muscle mass. Elizabeth Schneider wrote the book *Battered Women and Feminist Lawmaking.*[132]

Yvonne retook her maiden name. After emerging from the crucible, she wanted to become a Swan again. Her attorneys urged her to plead guilty to a lesser felony charge to avoid another encounter with the Spokane prosecutor, who could retry her so long as he did not make the same legal errors. Racism, they worried, still might prevent a fair verdict. Yvonne received five years' community service on the reservation, forfeiting the right to vote for the rest of her life. Freedom was worth it. She spoke at rallies on behalf of abused wives fighting murder convictions, became a court advocate for juveniles on the reservation, defended bears from sportsmen eager to open Indian lands to hunting, and wrote poetry. She called herself a feminist.

+++

AFTER THE HOUSTON CONFERENCE, Martha Cotera was ready for a break from battling fellow activists. She wanted to show the practical improvements that feminists could make. Calculating that collaboration with a bevy of prima donna activists would prove frustrating, she declined President Carter's offer to join his commission. It imploded anyway, when members challenged the president. Carter fired Abzug, demoted Costanza, and assigned Sarah Weddington to the downsized operation. Ronald Reagan defeated Jimmy Carter in the next election.

Martha Cotera had already achieved a remarkable goal: helping Mexican Americans accept gender equality as a legitimate aspiration that could improve rather than divide their community. In subsequent years, she applied herself to making a better Austin. With leaders like the Coteras, the city burgeoned. In 2021, *U.S. News and World Report* ranked the Texas capital fifth among the best places to live in America, praising its parks, affordable medical care, social equality, cultural vibrance, and economic growth.[133]

Martha and Juan Cotera also experienced one of the worst tragedies any couple could endure, perhaps reinforcing their belief that women must be free to choose or decline the profound responsibilities of parenthood. In 1997, the day after the couple celebrated Juan Javier's graduation from the University of Texas with a degree in political science, street thugs randomly executed their beloved twenty-five-year-old boy along with the son of an American astronaut. The assailants raped Juan's female companion and left her tied naked to a tree. Juan's parents opposed the death penalty for the violent teens knowing that their son believed, as posters of Gandhi cautioned, "an eye for an eye leaves the whole word blind."

Into her late seventies, Yvonne Swan admitted she was not sure she would ever get over what had happened to her. Martha Cotera lobbied government into her eighties, but her feelings must have echoed Yvonne's.

In the 1960s and 1970s, feminist lawyers established that constitutional guarantees applied fully to women. They had a right to equal treatment. Violence did not cease, but cases like *Washington v. Wanrow* strengthened women's right to self-defense. Community organizers meanwhile awakened the public's consciousness of misogyny and gave it a new name: sexism. They built new institutions and improved old ones.

These changes triggered others. Companies could no longer advertise jobs by gender or suspend employees for becoming pregnant. Feminist evangelicals declared Christianity and women's rights "inseparable," and touted slogans like "Jesus was a Feminist" and "Worship God, Not Your Husband." Even conservative evangelicals criticized the "male-dominated clergy system" and claimed that women had a right to lead churches in defiance of Saint Paul. Across the nation, women entered public life, energized by the conviction that they were as entitled as men to pursue a full life beyond the home. Most of the changes they made became uncontroversial.[134]

Reformers thought that America would now flourish as never before. By contrast, conservatives who were worried about moral dissipation believed that the time had come to reinforce conventional roles—or at least ensure that feminism did not alter them further.

CHAPTER 7

The Right to Compete

1975–2000
Phyllis Schlafly and Muriel Siebert

The Republican Party is carried on the shoulders of the women who do the work in the precincts, ringing doorbells, distributing literature, and doing all the tiresome, repetitious campaign tasks. Many men in the party frankly want to keep the women doing the menial work.

PHYLLIS SCHLAFLY, 1967

FEMINIST VALUES REDEFINED AMERICA. In 1970, polls showed that only 40 percent of Americans favored efforts to "strengthen and change women's status in society." By 1999, the figure had nearly doubled, to 75 percent. Thomas Jefferson proclaimed in his first inaugural address that certain bedrock beliefs united citizens despite their partisan differences. Centuries later, equality between the sexes had become one of them.[1]

Proof of this was the degree to which even critics supported the goal. Viewed this way, Phyllis Schlafly can be seen as a classic anti-feminist feminist. First, she demanded that her party include women as equals. Then she led the fight to stop the ERA and promote a new distinction between patriarchy in public and private: women should no longer take a back seat in politics, but within the home, a man must still be allowed to rule.

An early member of the ultraconservative John Birch Society, though she later denied it, Phyllis Schlafly used anti-feminism as first gear in her effort to drive the Republican Party rightward. For decades after the Civil War, feminists had avoided party affiliations to secure support from both sides. The League of Women Voters deliberately remained nonpartisan throughout the twentieth century. As a consequence, both Republicans and Democrats promoted the ERA until the early 1970s.[2]

Phyllis Schlafly rejected bipartisanship, fueling a trend toward vituperative political dialogue. While she benefited from past feminist gains, she caricatured further reforms as zealotry. Her political views paralleled those of Hannah More and Catharine Beecher, who had also considered reformers dangerous. Using Republican Party machinery to amplify her message at a time when religious values took center stage, she broadcast the same doomsday warnings that anti-suffragists had voiced sixty years earlier, but more loudly. Her success helps explain why, despite growing public support for the movement's goals, by 1999 only 26 percent of women called themselves feminists, and an increasing number of Americans viewed the label as an insult.[3]

Of course, most American women lived new lives without thinking too greatly about ideology. What interested them were opportunities. One of these was Muriel Siebert, a Jewish girl from Ohio with a bright, toothy smile who did not leave home until age twenty-six. Although she failed to graduate from the women's college to which her parents had sent her in the hope she would find a husband, Muriel adored numbers. They lit up a page. Numbers shone so brightly for her that she fought her way onto the New York Stock Exchange that Alexander Hamilton had helped establish two hundred years earlier.

A self-described "bleeding-heart Republican," Muriel Siebert used feminist gains to advance her own career and the financial wellbeing of ordinary people, including her widowed mother and disabled sister. Ironically, her biggest defeat stemmed from changes engineered by none other than Phyllis Schlafly. Nonetheless, she stood at the head of a new generation of women entering business, government, and sports on a wider basis. Most simply wanted to support themselves or their families, but some relished the new right to compete on a level playing field with men—like tennis star Billie Jean King, who beat Bobby Riggs in 1973 when he claimed no woman could defeat him.[4]

As barriers fell, women vied for success. Weathering both hostility and admiration, they became policemen, firemen, mailmen, milkmen, airmen, journeymen, brakemen, linemen, chairmen, and congressmen. Job titles changed. Asserting the right to test their wits in "the pursuit of happiness"—meaning fame, fortune, and worldly success—women found themselves competing more openly than ever before against not only men, but also one another.

A Model Daughter

To her doting parents, Phyllis Stewart was an angel straight from heaven. Her father, Bruce, a self-taught engineer, had waited until his mid-forties to start a family. At twenty-eight, his younger wife, Odile, documented every detail of their first daughter's arrival. In 1924, she sewed Phyllis's baptismal gown with fabric from her own First Communion dress. She made cards on the baby's behalf ("Love to dear daddy from your baby Phyllis") and recorded her first tooth, step, and word.[5]

Odile came from a distinguished family with old roots in St. Louis, Missouri. Her family's eminence guaranteed the baby's baptism in the city's mosaic-lined cathedral. Bruce Stewart rented a comfortable home for Odile and their two daughters until the Great Depression stole his livelihood in 1930. He was a has-been of fifty-one with no college degree when Westinghouse let him go without a pension, five years before Frances Perkins pushed through unemployment insurance. Not that Bruce Stewart would have applied. He considered the New Deal socialistic, and thought it more acceptable for wives to seek employment than for the government to assume new responsibilities. It was decades before some Republicans accepted federal benefits as "American," and even then a number argued that Social Security contributions should be voluntary. Bruce Stewart did not land another job until World War II. By then, his daughter Phyllis was nearly out of high school.[6]

Luckily, Odile had not one, but two college degrees. Forced from the dependent role she had anticipated, she went to work. "We had to eat," Phyllis later recalled, although Odile's ambition exceeded putting bread on the table. She ran the library at the St. Louis Art Museum six days a week, and on Sundays she helped out at the city's most elite Catholic school, the Academy of the Sacred Heart, in exchange for tuition. She sent her girls to the St. Louis Woman's Club, Junior League, and Girl Scouts, and when social occasions required formal gowns that exceeded her budget, Odile borrowed or made them. With her mother looking over her shoulder, Phyllis, from the age of six, wrote letters to the symphony asking for complimentary tickets, invariably granted. She learned polite persistence—in effect, how to beg.[7]

Yet Phyllis was fortunate. During the Great Depression, she had a stay-at-home father and a working mother with a superb education and unflinching work ethic. Odile kept the family in the middle class. Phyllis learned from her mother's experience that a girl had better get educated. As she later said, she knew she needed to "get myself trained to support myself, which my mother had done before me."[8]

With this attitude, combined with high intelligence and pleasing looks, the industrious girl thrived. "Phyllis took to school like most children take to the circus," her uncle later observed. Class valedictorian, she graduated with straight A's. A local women's college provided a scholarship, but Phyllis transferred to the more ambitious University of Washington. For tuition money, she took a night job at a munitions factory the same summer as the Battle of Midway. Phyllis donned pants, something most people still considered semi-scandalous but that the war helped to normalize. With war industries requiring trousers, women avoided the ridicule that bloomer-wearing feminists had endured in the 1850s. To sell American war bonds, Norman Rockwell painted Rosie the Riveter wearing denim overalls in 1943. Gender-neutral clothing symbolized patriotic service.[9]

The wartime boost in women's pay funded Phyllis's undergraduate education. She worked nights and studied by day, sleeping only a few hours. Unlike Rosie, who assembled machines, she tested guns. Dirty, dangerous, and at odds with traditional gender roles, the work of a gunner required test-firing as many as eight thousand machine gun rounds a shift. Phyllis earned five promotions. The experience—reinforced by classes in her major, political science—gave her a lifelong interest in weapons.

Ambitious and competitive, she set her sights on a master's from Harvard—which meant its sister college, Radcliffe. Harvard did not grant diplomas to women at the time, but had begun allowing them to attend some of the men's classes. Harvard professors taught the courses, and female students earned a Radcliffe degree. This anomaly did not register as a problem with Phyllis. "There was absolutely no discrimination," she later insisted, though a Harvard degree was more valuable. Different diplomas for women and men seemed natural to someone born in 1924, whose brilliance had already opened doors that many did not dream existed—or found still locked. Harvard Law School rejected Pauli Murray on account of sex in 1944, the same year that Phyllis first strolled Radcliffe's green quadrangle.[10]

In 1945, she took her master's degree to Washington, DC, where she worked for a year at a think tank that completed her intellectual journey. Phyllis happened upon a position at the American Enterprise Association, later renamed the American Enterprise Institute. The private organization funded academics who were critical of government expansion. Phyllis had gone to Washington with optimistic notions about the United Nations. She returned to St. Louis convinced that international cooperation was a chimera. She found herself agreeing with her father that "overregulation" was pushing America toward socialism.[11]

She also brought home an appetite for electioneering. Working side jobs to earn money, she talked her way into the campaign of Claude Bakewell, a Republican challenging a congressional incumbent. She answered phones, arranged appointments, and wrote snappy press releases charging that communists had "wormed their way into positions of power." She criticized Truman's economic policy as "spend and spend" even while condemning him as stingy. "The slogan of the present Administration with respect to veterans housing," she wrote, "is two families in every garage." Her delighted candidate won.[12]

After the election, Phyllis honed her writing skills on a monthly newsletter for a finance company into which she dropped critiques like "The Left Wing and the Bill of Rights" and "Our Defeat in China." Her interpretation of government policy anticipated that of Senator Joseph McCarthy, who became infamous a couple of years later for dark, unprovable accusations that communists were everywhere, a claim that President Harry Truman dubbed the "Big Lie."[13]

A conservative Catholic attorney impressed by an article calling a Democratic senator "a Socialist" dropped by to meet its author, and found to his surprise that the "guy" was a gal. At thirty-nine, Fred Schlafly considered himself a contented bachelor, but twenty-four-year-old Phyllis beguiled him. Like him, she was passionately opposed to "Godless" communism for both religious and political reasons. And her svelte figure made his head spin. He wrote, "I didn't believe in love at first sight so I took a second look. I gave her a look that you could have poured on a waffle." (Like Phyllis, Fred knew how to pack a phrase.) A modern couple, they kissed on the first date. Soon they exchanged vows near the altar where Phyllis had been baptized. Fred was entranced by her ambition. They moved across the river to the satellite suburb of Alton, Illinois, overlooking St. Louis and the broad Mississippi.[14]

Phyllis had chosen her husband carefully. She was able to do what her mother, who married a less well-established man, could not: spend as much time as she wished at home. At the height of the postwar baby boom, she had six children over fourteen years. Doctors of the era recommended formula, and up to 85 percent of infants were bottle-fed by two months. Phyllis resisted the modern trend and nursed every child for six months, perhaps in part because the church strictly forbade birth control, and breastfeeding suppressed ovulation. The seven women who in 1956 founded La Leche League, an organization devoted to the promotion of breastfeeding and "natural" motherhood, were all Catholic mothers from Illinois.[15]

As the Schlafly children grew, they sat down to dinner every night at 6:00 p.m. for a three-course meal that began with salad. Phyllis may have read the work of health reformers because she stocked the house with organic peanut butter, whole grain cereals, and raw milk. She rejected the 1950s infatuation with canned, frozen, and plastic-wrapped foods. White flour and sugar appeared only in birthday cakes. She set firm rules for behavior, too. Television was forbidden and her children were expected to get good grades—which they did. Alarmed by *Why Johnny Can't Read,* a critique of public education which came out in 1955, Phyllis taught her children to read herself.

For at least twenty-five years, a full-time African American housekeeper helped her manage the home. Fred's income allowed them to hire Willie Bea Reed, a local mother, to help cook and clean, freeing Phyllis to pursue outside activities. With her employer's encouragement, Willie Bea taught her own daughter to read using Phyllis's system of phonics, and helped keep an eye on the Schlafly children when their mother was busy. The burdens of parenthood were undoubtedly lighter for the woman with professional help than for the one providing it, who may have shared some of her modest salary with yet another caregiver, passing the work down the line with diminishing compensation.[16]

In 1952, when Phyllis Schlafly's first child was one year old, she decided to run for Congress. With Fred's encouragement, she campaigned as a housewife alarmed by corruption who believed that "women should get into politics and do something about it." She won the primary yet lost the election. For president, she preferred conservative nominee Robert Taft, but spoke not a word against her party's final candidate. President Dwight Eisenhower's policies proved considerably more moderate than she liked when the former Army general continued the New Deal and avoided conflict with the Soviet Union.[17]

The 1952 campaign made Phyllis a familiar figure. Organizations courted her as a magnetic speaker. With Fred as her financier, she became a leader in the Daughters of the American Revolution, United Way, and Illinois Federation of Women's Clubs. She built bridges to other religious groups by editing the newsletter of the National Conference of Christians and Jews. Nursing newborns at regular intervals, she took them to meetings where she found volunteers to babysit when she mounted the podium, decked out in pearls, her back straight, as she had practiced years before at the Academy of the Sacred Heart.

Phyllis thought that Americans underestimated the threat of communism. "We are engaged," she wrote in one of many articles for conservative newsletters, "in a life-or-death struggle with the criminal underground whose leaders confidently expect to destroy our Church, our country, our freedom, the institution of the family, and everything else we hold dear." To moderate Republicans, including Eisenhower, this phrasing bordered on hysteria. But Phyllis Schlafly was not alone in believing it. The most conservative Catholics exhibited a growing affinity with fundamentalist Protestants, Jews, and Muslims, who also resisted various modern trends.[18]

She became particularly well known for her opinions on military questions. Phyllis considered the United States foolishly interventionist, and criticized war in both Korea and Vietnam as a drain on resources better invested in weapons to scare Russia. In 1963, she testified before the US Senate Foreign Relations Committee against proposals to ban nuclear test explosions aboveground. She feared strategic weakness more than radioactive fallout.

In 1964, she achieved national fame when she self-published *A Choice Not an Echo,* a bestseller that helped Arizona senator Barry Goldwater, then considered an archconservative, to win the Republican nomination over Nelson Rockefeller. The book smeared moderate Republicans as secretive elites who accepted corrupt bipartisan compromises. It called for a grassroots rebellion against East Coast "kingmakers" and their "pro-Communist foreign policy." The National Federation of Republican Women elected Phyllis Schlafly vice president.[19]

With Fred's backing, she threw herself into the Goldwater campaign that birthed a new wing of the Republican Party. She lectured nationwide, rallied conventioneers, and collaborated on a documentary, all on a volunteer basis since the Goldwater campaign refused to hire her. She encouraged women's clubs to teach speechmaking, something that would have amazed Angelina Grimké, who had been ordered to remain silent by the conservatives of her own era. Phyllis's energy seemed "unlimited," according to historian Donald Critchlow. The Republican Party featured the Schlaflys in a television special where Fred read to their daughter in the background while the boys tossed a football. Phyllis, the picture of a modern woman, addressed the camera from behind a desk that hid the bump of her last pregnancy.[20]

Lyndon Johnson handily defeated Barry Goldwater, the candidate who seemed provocative even to many Republicans when he declared, "Extremism in the defense of liberty is no vice." Party leaders concluded after the lopsided election in which Goldwater lost by 22 percent that Republicans needed to recapture the liberal center, which was then the prevailing wisdom about how to score the presidency. Next they ran Richard Nixon, a moderate committed to avoiding nuclear war with the Soviet Union.[21]

Phyllis Schlafly, however, thought the party had simply not traveled far enough to the right. Alarmed Republicans began to consider her a liability. Even Goldwater kept his distance. When she ran for president of the National Federation of Republican Women in 1967, the party chair opposed her candidacy. Women's clubs had provided campaign workers since the passage of the Nineteenth Amendment, a fact that male leaders appreciated. A closed nominating body usually named a slate of officers for the women's auxiliary. Not in 1967. Phyllis Schlafly charged into the organization's Washington office to demand a spot on the predetermined ballot. Confrontation came easily to her. She crisscrossed the country giving three speeches a week.[22]

Moderates like Elly Peterson of Michigan, a friend of Governor George Romney (father of Mitt Romney), worried that the "nut fringe is beautifully organized." Phyllis's anxious neighbor in Alton, another Republican, declared that she could not support a "right-wing" propagandist who made charges "in a style so sweeping that it triggers the adrenalin and blanks the need to think." The Republican establishment moved the annual convention from California, a Schlafly stronghold, to the more neutral District of Columbia. For the first time since women started joining the party, delegates were divided. Regulars insinuated that someone with six children hardly had time to run an organization, to which Phyllis objected that the party was telling American mothers they could be "peons" but not leaders.[23]

Five thousand women jammed the convention hotel. Fred applauded from the audience. He liked to quip, "I regret that I have but one wife to give to my country." The *Washington Post* remarked, "Two GOP Rivals Unbutton Gloves." Both sides accused the other of dirty tricks. With the weight of party machinery behind the moderate candidate, Phyllis lost. Wearing a pink linen dress, she smiled graciously and told reporters that the voting machines had been rigged and the election "stolen."[24]

Phyllis particularly resented the heavy-handedness of male leaders. She argued for equality and insisted that women could play a more important role in the political life of the country. "The more we let their voices be heard in politics, the better off we are," the de facto feminist told the *Washington Post.* "Women should have a role beyond stuffing envelopes and stirring coffee."[25]

Female rivals agreed that women should have more input, but found Phyllis's aggressive style bruising. The newly elected president of the federation half-joked afterward, "I am very much inclined to agree with Margaret Mead the anthropologist, [that] women should not be drafte[d] for combat. They are too fierce."[26]

Three months later, Phyllis began self-publishing a newsletter, the *Phyllis Schlafly Report,* to express her opinions on national events. She mailed it to women who had supported her candidacy, including Ronald Reagan's daughter, Maureen. She also started a trust fund, later incorporated as the Eagle Forum, to accept donations that some followers had previously sent to Republican women's clubs.

The next year, in 1968, she organized an annual "political-action leadership conference" that one reporter thought resembled "guerrilla warfare." At the first meeting in a St. Louis hotel ballroom adorned with pink GOP elephant balloons and whimsical party favors, several hundred women from around the country gathered for three days to learn how to mount campaigns, hold press conferences, and testify to legislatures. In closed-door sessions, they discussed which scarves and makeup looked best on television, watched recordings of Phyllis Schlafly, and held mock debates. Their omnipresent hero exuded the glamour of Joan of Arc, ready to lead the troops, this time all-female. No detail was beneath her attention. Men of the press received gifts of after-shave lotion.[27]

Phyllis Schlafly's base was an evolving grassroots coalition of conservative Catholics, southern fundamentalists, Mormons, blue-collar workers, and suburban professionals. Some were renegade Republicans, others dissatisfied Democrats. All were passionately devoted to her. Her competitor at the National Federation of Republican Women denounced the extra-party activities as "subversion."[28]

In 1970 Phyllis ran one last time as a candidate of the Republican Party. Her rival for the US Congress, a former Marine, asked audiences if they thought his opponent should "stay home with her husband and six kids," to which they generally roared "Yes!"[29]

Phyllis refused to be daunted by his sexism. "My opponent says a woman's place is in the home," she told churchwomen, "but my husband replies that a woman's place is in the House—the US House of Representatives." Democrat Bella Abzug used a nearly identical line in her own bid for office that year. Endorsed by the *Chicago Tribune,* Phyllis lost the election by just seven percentage points.[30]

When reporters speculated that gender had hurt her chances, Phyllis said she simply considered 1970 a bad year for Republicans in Illinois. She also blamed "new voting machines" that favored Democrats, again implying that the returns were rigged. In her view, cabals of eastern elites, not misogyny, posed the greatest challenge. Her mother's role model and her own talent made her confident in competing against any man. "Some bigoted people" may have rejected her as a woman, she said, but others probably favored her. Equality was in the air. The *Daily Illini,* the University of Illinois student newspaper, ran news of Phyllis's loss above a half-page Air Force recruitment ad for the "True Woman" who wished to serve her nation on an "equal status with the men."[31]

Phyllis Schlafly believed there was no better time for women in politics. She made that very point two years later when she finally landed on an issue that commanded wide interest, and organized the largest populist campaign of the 1970s to kill the Equal Rights Amendment.

A Woman of Business

Competing with men on a level playing field was appealing to former grade-school yo-yo champion Muriel Siebert, born in 1928. The teaching and nursing emphasis of Flora Stone Mather, the women's college she entered at seventeen, made her yawn. She found history classes interesting, but they did not point toward a career. Then the Ohio native discovered a course at the affiliated men's school, Western Reserve University (later, Case Western Reserve). Like nearby Oberlin, Mary Church Terrell's alma mater, Western Reserve had originally welcomed female students, only to relegate them to a separate college in 1888. Women still took classes at the men's school on occasion, but they received their degrees from Mather, as Phyllis Schlafly had done at Radcliffe.

At Western Reserve, Muriel found a course on money that made her green eyes sparkle. So bright that her elementary school principal recommended she skip two grades, she aced the finance exams without doing homework. She must have raised her hand frequently, since the bemused instructor began calling her, the only woman in the lecture hall, "the delegate from Mather."[32]

Known as Mickie to family and friends, the gregarious blond did not mind the all-male environment. She had scads of male cousins because her Hungarian immigrant mother had been one of eleven children and her father one of five, so she always got along well with boys. And she adored competitive games of all types. Since childhood, Mickie had been a shark at yo-yo. She was not bad at ping pong, tennis, golf, bridge, or baccarat either. The unpretentious midwesterner liked to laugh and sing. She had a "low blues voice," or so she wrote on her college application. Classmates must have found her fun.[33]

Courses at the men's college failed to keep her in school, however. During Mickie's junior year, her father developed cancer, which was then considered incurable. Mickie's enthusiasm for finance evaporated. Only bridge, a card game played best by those able to calculate mathematical probabilities, took her mind off the slow, sad process of watching him die.

Betrayal made it more hellish. Her father, a dentist, leased office space from his brother, who was a wealthy doctor. When Mickie's unscrupulous uncle discovered that his brother was ill, he evicted the dying man and moved his own son, who had just completed dental school, into the practice. Mickie later joked that this was her "first experience with a hostile takeover," but she was devastated. "I just couldn't stand what was going on at home," she admitted. She began cutting classes and never went back to school.[34]

Eventually, financial circumstances forced her to think practically. The Sieberts were broke after years of expensive medical bills. Her father's five-thousand-dollar insurance policy paid for a formal burial, an important ritual in Jewish culture, but not much else. At age twenty-six, long after her classmates had graduated, Mickie left Cleveland in a rusty Studebaker with five hundred dollars, desperate to find a job that would allow her to send funds home to her mother, Margaret.

At the time, middle-class Americans generally kept their money in savings accounts at banks that paid a small return on deposits. The collapse during the Great Depression had sparked a New Deal reform to restore the trust of people like Ann Marie Low, who had seen their small savings vanish. Under the Glass-Steagall Act of 1933, banks were required to purchase insurance to reimburse clients in case of default, and were prohibited from using customer deposits to invest in stocks. Americans brought their money back to banks, which could only issue loans from which they, too, earned a small percentage. Banking became boring but safe.

Stockbrokers played a different game, risky and thrilling. There was no insurance. Stocks could lose all their value—or triple in a day. Brokerage commissions were high, so only the wealthiest had the pocket change to enter a market that, in theory, allowed the humblest citizen to purchase a piece of the economy. In 1952, only 4 percent of Americans owned stocks. A few firms dominated, generally run by white Protestant men from elite families. In the words of one historian, entry "depended on family, religious, and school connections."[35]

The Siebert family possessed none of the above. An anonymous Jewish woman without a degree, Mickie aimed her old Studebaker with balky hinges toward New York City's bright lights. She had visited once before, the only time in her life that she had traveled without her parents, on a lighthearted excursion with college girlfriends in a different life. Her older sister, working for a publisher in Manhattan, put Mickie up in her tiny studio and a cousin showed her around the gleaming United Nations, constructed four years earlier, where he had a job. Mickie inquired with the employment office but they needed only translators.

Then she recalled the tour bus that had stopped at the New York Stock Exchange on her prior visit. Looking down from the gallery on a heaving sea of suits, wooden floor awash in ticker tape, Mickie had enthused to her friends, "Now, *this* is exciting." Remembering the name Merrill Lynch, she submitted an application there. Again she was disappointed. The company had no place for a woman without a college education.[36]

The next day, Mickie applied to a smaller firm, Bache & Company. This time she lied. *Of course* she had finished her business degree. Bache gave her the choice of research analyst or accountant. Research paid less but sounded more fun. She took it. She and her sister secured a one-bedroom apartment up a freight elevator. Mickie used her first paycheck to buy a couch to sleep on from a discount emporium known as Foamland.[37]

Mickie's love of numbers flooded back. The job she had stumbled into required her to analyze the financial statements of companies in which Bache clients might want to buy stocks. Mickie's comprehension was instinctive, her memory nearly photographic. Budget reports told "a story," she later said, and she enjoyed the tales they told. She was also hungry for work. One harried senior analyst liked railroads and disliked the new airline companies, considering them unlikely to prosper. Mickie eagerly grabbed the fledgling airline industry when he dumped it on her. The same occurred with radio, television, and films. Few investors thought media would ever amount to much.

The numbers told Mickie a different story. She scrutinized financial statements, visited companies, attended trade luncheons, and read up on supply chains. She studied underlying costs and hidden sources of profit. She read *Civil Aeronautics Board Reports* under the hairdryer at the salon each week and fantasized about getting a pilot's license. Mickie was grateful for such interesting research. Only a handful of female analysts worked on Wall Street in the 1950s, and they were typically charged with industries considered girly, like food and cosmetics. Mickie's reports convinced Bache & Company that airlines and media were ready to take off. Clients who invested in the companies she suggested made spectacular returns, and Bache raked in the commissions. In two years, she doubled her weekly salary to $130 per week. It was still substantially less than what they paid any man.

Mickie Siebert later reflected in her memoirs that knowing she was underpaid gave her "gumption." Since every woman on Wall Street was underpaid, something else must have been at work as well. Perhaps it was the memory of her sick father being robbed of his livelihood by someone he trusted. As a child, Mickie had affectionately called her father's brother "Uncle Doc." Uncle Doc's cruelty may have stiffened her sense of right and wrong.[38]

Employers and economists typically justified pay inequity by saying that men needed more money than women. Paychecks should be considered a so-called family wage so that mothers who needed to care for children did not have to work. This rationale made sense, but had defects as well. Some men did not have wives or children. Some in finance came from rich families. Others—not on Wall Street, except as janitors—were paid so little that their wives had to work anyway. Sometimes wives supported husbands, not the other way around. And why did male stockbrokers in particular, who made a thousand times the average wage, need more than their female peers in order to support a family? A smart observer might have pointed out that compensation according to "need" was a communist, not a free-market, argument.

Mickie began to think about her options when famed World War I fighter pilot Eddie Rickenbacker happened to visit one day to explain Eastern Airlines' plan for expansion. At a board meeting, Mickie asked questions about a footnote she had spotted in his report. Senior partners swiveled and woolly eyebrows went up at the young researcher in the back. The delegate from Mather appeared to have no fear.

Mickie believed that Eastern Airlines, and thus its stock, were more valuable than they appeared. She knew that airlines' profitability seemed marginal because they faced the upfront cost of expensive planes. Calculating from three different depreciation schedules in the report, Mickie thought the company's cash flow was stronger than it looked. She wanted to verify her assumptions so she could recommend the stock to clients. Rickenbacker chuckled at the astute inquiry, then offered her a job.

Mickie found Wall Street too exhilarating to abandon, so she privately asked Rickenbacker to introduce her instead to other brokerages. Personnel directors at two firms explained that they hired women only as secretaries. Their "girls" were required to wear hats and white gloves in company elevators, like in church. They explained that female staff could hardly accompany colleagues on business trips or take clients to dinner at all-male supper clubs. A third brokerage offered her a job but withdrew the contract just as her present boss discovered that she was scouting around. Bache & Company fired her that day.

Muriel Siebert started over. In 1958, she sent out her résumé without getting a single nibble. She asked a placement bureau to mail it out with the initials "M. F. Siebert," rather than her first name, to cloak her female identity. A company replied immediately and Mickie showed up for the interview with her best smile. Impressed once they met her, Shields & Company started Mickie at a salary 30 percent higher than her previous position had offered. Once again she proved her savvy, attracting clients and becoming one of the company's best analysts. Customers hung on her advice.

After a successful year, Mickie's salary remained unchanged. A colleague, aware that the company paid men with the same duties $20,000 a year instead of the $9,500 that Mickie received, reached out to management. To make her "happy," senior partners offered to increase her salary to $12,500, which was still well below what everyone else was paid. Again she began looking around and was fired when the firm found out.[39]

It is not surprising that both companies fired her. They paid staff to develop knowledge and personal relationships. No brokerage wanted that to walk away, so they punished attempts to do so. Old-line firms had an especially paternalistic attitude, expecting lifelong loyalty from employees in return for being part of the family. In the case of women, this bargain had a midcentury design. Brokerages expected female experts on money to gratefully accept half pay. Shields gave the accounts she had developed to other employees.

A small brokerage firm, Stearns & Company, approached her at last, attracted by her reputation as an innovator. Mickie specialized in giving expert advice to institutions managing large pension funds at the very moment that pensions became common for American workers after World War II. This gave financial institutions more money than ever to invest, but they had to be careful not to lose people's retirements. Mickie demonstrated an uncanny ability to read trends in product development and a sensitivity to the need for stable earnings. She was among the first to push investment in Boeing when it built the innovative 737 jet, and to recommend Kodak when it invented a camera that developed pictures instantly. Stearns made her a partner, which meant she finally earned commissions on sales.

Her integrity drew a following. She would advise investors against purchasing a stock even if doing so cost her a commission. One day she called up a banker she did not know at Chase Manhattan after she learned he had offered to sell stocks that her clients might wish to purchase. Mickie advised him against doing so. From depreciation schedules, she had deduced that the company was undervalued and would soon rise in price. She did not want to exploit his ignorance. He took her advice and decided not to sell. Afterward, a member of Chase Manhattan's investment committee asked, "Who is this Siebert, God?"[40]

Not all brokers exercised the same ethics. Mickie left Stearns when she discovered shady dealings that bordered on illegal. Once again, the abrupt departure clouded her employment record. For the fourth time, she found herself looking for a job, with "no welcome mat rolled out." This time, however, she had the good fortune to touch a piece of history that brought her luck—and her first mentor.[41]

Since arriving in New York, Mickie had volunteered at the Henry Street Settlement House, the New York equivalent of the Chicago Commons. Like the female Progressives who saved Rosa Cavalleri, Mickie spent her spare time volunteering to help inner-city children, teaching games like ping-pong and assisting with the annual Christmas fundraiser. Her interest in social issues extended back to high school, and she empathized with immigrants who had left everything behind. She felt grateful to the nation for taking them in. All but two of her Hungarian relatives had been murdered in the Holocaust, and Mickie never forgot her mother's bleak expression when she took the phone call after the war. Mickie was deeply "pro-American," a friend later recalled. She wanted to give back.[42]

At Henry Street she met another young volunteer whose father had started his own small brokerage. He recommended her to his father. "She's clean as a whistle," he told David Finkle, "and these firms are being unfair to her."[43]

Finkle took a liking to the determined young woman who struck him as smart but naïve. He offered her a larger salary and a higher commission, and took the time to teach her that the big money came not from clever analysis or one-off deals, but from representing both sides in a transaction—buyers as well as sellers. When Mickie enthused about a two-thousand-dollar commission from her first sale, he shrugged. "That's shit," he said. Had she handled both sides, she would have doubled the amount. When she had sellers, she should find buyers, and vice versa. "You come sit here next to me," the avuncular man said, and picked up the phone. Confidence was key.

"I got this block of XYZ stock," he told a bigwig at one investment company, she later recalled. "I don't know shit from pound cake about the earnings. All I know is it sells for twenty dollars, and it pays a dollar and a half dividend. You'll take the block?"[44]

Mickie's heart raced whenever she lifted the phone. The person on the other end had millions, and she felt self-conscious. David Finkle taught her that, when speaking with brokers, "every other word had to be a four letter word." The swaggering traders of Wall Street respected profanity. She must speak their language, which had a gendered twang. They would relax and do business with someone who acted like them. When she asked her boss on what pretext she should call a particular trader, he said, "Aw, I don't give a fuck, just call him."[45]

After several years of working for Finkle, then for a slightly larger firm, Mickie decided to aim for one of the major investment houses. The "big guns" represented the pinnacle of her profession, and she was as eager to win as she had been during her first bridge tournament on the way to grand master.[46]

Mickie was already earning close to a quarter of a million dollars a year, a royal sum but still well below the takings of male rivals. She invited a client to lunch one day in 1967 and asked which large Wall Street house would give her the same opportunities as a man. She knew that none had female partners. Bigger firms had approached Mickie about working for a better salary, but no commission.

He snorted. "Don't be ridiculous," he said. "There is *nowhere* you can go."[47]

The experience of women who entered Wall Street afterward confirmed his pessimism. The gender gap narrowed less in finance than elsewhere. By the end of the twentieth century, across all jobs, American women generally earned 75 percent of what men did. On Wall Street, by contrast, they took home a measly 60 percent of their male peers' salary, not because salaries were unequal, but because subjective evaluations determined year-end bonuses. As one scholar notes, at the end of the century the gap between bonuses for male and female professionals with identical financial performance averaged "an astounding $223,368."[48]

Mickie's friend suggested she start her own company. "Buy a seat on the Stock Exchange and work for yourself," he advised. "Don't *you* be ridiculous," she said. "There are no women on the Exchange."[49]

The New York Stock Exchange, commonly known as the NYSE, had exactly 1,366 seats, all held by named individuals. Most seat holders were allied with companies that sent trades through them. They alone could buy and sell on the tumultuous auction floor that had first mesmerized Mickie. There were other small exchanges around the country, including the American Stock Exchange, which had two female members, but 80 percent of all trades went through the NYSE. The biggest, fanciest, wealthiest corporations sold their shares there. Blue chips, traders called them.[50]

Mickie Siebert thought her friend was crazy, but then recalled the recent Civil Rights Act of 1964 that had prohibited sex discrimination. Perhaps it applied. Mickie studied the constitution of the NYSE. Nowhere did it actually say women could not own a seat. Then she worried that *she* was crazy, or at least abnormal.

Being a good New Yorker, Mickie consulted a psychiatrist. She had come of age when women eager to succeed outside the home were sometimes told they had penis envy. Unable to accept their natural limitations, they wanted to be men. In the 1940s and 1950s, some psychiatrists attributed sexual "frigidity" to female overeducation, which they said worsened penis envy. Mickie may have worried that her career aspirations suggested a budding neurosis. Her psychiatrist concluded each session by asking for stock tips. At the end of the sixth, he pronounced her a healthy individual who just enjoyed a challenge.[51]

It took Mickie six months to muster her courage to buy a seat on the NYSE. Finally she approached John Mulcahy, the official who handled the sale of seats. She had rehearsed an elaborate speech but froze when she stepped into his office. The grandiloquent phrases she had committed to memory vanished. She drew a shallow breath and blurted, "Can I buy a seat, or is this just a country club?"[52]

Mulcahy came from a Brooklyn Irish family. A military veteran who had worked his way through law school selling train tickets at Grand Central, he confirmed that the law now protected women's rights: "We can't turn you down for nonbusiness reasons, on the basis of sex, or you could sue every member of the board of governors."[53]

Not that the board would encourage her. She needed two sponsors, and the men she asked came up with weak excuses to say no. One fessed up, "Holy shit, Mickie, I won't have a friend left." The chair of the NYSE board of governors groused to another colleague, "We don't want her, but we think we have to take her." Others said, "we've never had a woman apply. No one would *dare* to apply."[54]

Opposition piqued her stubbornness. Mickie wrote the exchange a personal check for $89,000 as a deposit and filed her application. She recalled the Studebaker that had brought her to New York. The driver's door tended to stick. Sometimes she had had to plant both feet on it to get out. It was a metaphor for life. "When you hit a closed door and it doesn't budge, just rear back and kick it in," she thought. A sense of the unfairness to other women struck her as well. "Hold it open so others can follow you," she told herself.[55]

Mickie Siebert finally obtained two sponsors, "brave soldiers" who were asked about "Miss Siebert's personal life," questions not raised about male candidates. A purpose of the New York Stock Exchange was to guarantee brokers' reputations, and at the time, a woman's reputation had an unwritten sexual component. The exchange also required her to obtain a special bank guarantee not demanded of male applicants, even though she had already arranged for a loan of $300,000 to cover the balance of the cost. It was then common practice to require a husband's signature on a wife's credit-card application, and they may have thought that Mickie's word alone was not good enough. She started waking up at night, worrying.[56]

If denied, she would look foolish to image-conscious colleagues on Wall Street. She might be judged a shrew for barging in where unwanted. What if she lost her job again while trying to go into business for herself? Her elderly mother required increasingly expensive care. Pessimists noted that the New York Stock Exchange did not even have a women's bathroom—nor did it intend to install one.[57]

Most men dragged their feet to do the right thing, but a few hurried. A banker from Chase Manhattan who recalled when Mickie had warned them against selling low spoke up for her on the exchange. The admiring head of a pension fund also intervened. One of the toughest traders on Wall Street bragged that he enjoyed placing orders with her—and going home at night to tell his daughter. Slowly, the market came around. The seat was approved.

In December 1967, Muriel Siebert, age thirty-eight, who had arrived in New York with a mere five hundred bucks, paid $445,000 to integrate the New York Stock Exchange by gender. Men who purchased seats the same day received ornate scrolls for framing. Mickie got a handshake. Amused newspaper editors from New York to Alaska touted the arrival of "executives in skirts." Posing as a compliment, one snide commentary read, "Miss Muriel Siebert, of New York City, is one of those rare women who is bored when talking about herself." Mickie's mother would have preferred a wedding announcement. Bewildered, the Hungarian immigrant asked, "What am I going to tell my friends?"[58]

The newest member of the NYSE took French champagne to co-workers at her old firm, then went home to collapse. She had a quiet dinner alone. For the next ten years, she remained the only woman among 1,365 men.

Muriel Siebert was one of a generation of "firsts" who climbed over barriers in business, government, and sports. Legislators had rewritten the rules, but pioneers like Mickie braved the game. Many onlookers thrilled to the results, considering them the logical expression of the nation's values. When asked what he thought of his new colleague, one male stockbroker patriotically quipped to the *New York Times,* "God bless America. I think it's great."[59]

STOP-ping the Equal Rights Amendment

In 1971, when Phyllis Schlafly's youngest daughter, Anne, was seven, a friend invited the Illinois matron to Connecticut to debate the ERA. Phyllis asked if she could speak on missiles instead. Domestic issues did not interest her. She considered feminists "selfish and misguided," but their amendment harmless.[60]

Phyllis bobbed in the mainstream in this respect. President Nixon and his vice president, Spiro Agnew, were both ERA supporters. In his 1972 report to Congress, Nixon promised that his administration would "continue its strong efforts to open equal opportunities for women, recognizing that women are often denied such opportunities today." Alabama governor George Wallace and Senator Strom Thurmond of South Carolina, racial segregationists who normally reviled liberalism, had good things to say, too. Legal equality across gender lines had become a safe subject. In 1972, the Senate passed the ERA by 84 to 8. When Phyllis Schlafly thought about the ERA at all, she considered it "something between innocuous and mildly helpful."[61]

Bigger problems commanded her attention. Richard Nixon had followed through on détente with Soviet Russia. "The delusion that America can be defended by treaties instead of by weapons," she told readers of her newsletter, "is the most persistent and pernicious of all liberal fallacies." Treaties were America's "obituary" (though they had thus far prevented a commonly predicted World War III). When Nixon traveled to mainland China to restore diplomatic relations, she objected, "Civilized people don't dine with murderers and criminals. Communists have liquidated 20 million Chinese." She considered Nixon a liberal sell-out and shuddered to think of his reelection.[62]

Her Connecticut friend was insistent, however. Phyllis protested, "I don't even know which side I'm on," but the New Englander promised that she *would* know, once she had read the ERA.[63]

The amendment was brief. Its first clause stated that government could not abridge "equality of rights" on the basis of sex. A dozen states from Alaska to New Hampshire had adopted similar laws. Utah's law dated to 1896. Legal rights, it read, "shall not be denied or abridged on the basis of sex." The statute had never raised a ripple because Utah's conservative courts refused to enforce it.

In contrast, Illinois, where Phyllis lived, had a brand new statute. A 1970 amendment to the state constitution guaranteed "equal protection" under the law. Illinois courts enforced it rigorously. Using the legal principle of "strict scrutiny," courts required state government to err on the side of treating males and females equally unless the relevance of gender could be demonstrated. Phyllis and conservatives like Senator Sam Ervin of North Carolina, one of the lone votes against the federal amendment, considered the Illinois law reasonable.[64]

As she studied the federal proposal, Phyllis found herself reacting differently. It seemed a bottomless pit of horrors—a "Pandora's box of trouble for women." The ERA's second clause gave Congress the power to enforce the amendment across state boundaries. Phyllis had grown up in the segregated South. She stood firmly for states' rights. Illinois and Utah might do what they wanted, she thought, but the federal government should have no oversight.[65]

The ERA would also mandate that the one federal activity Phyllis did endorse—national defense—be held to nondiscriminatory principles. She worried that women might become subject to the draft. Washington seemed to have an unquenchable fascination for foreign sideshows, and American women could be caught in the crossfire. Phyllis realized that the ERA might also threaten protective labor legislation.

These concerns were neither trivial nor novel. What one historian calls "the other women's movement," which included Frances Perkins and Eleanor Roosevelt, had long opposed the Equal Rights Amendment. Mary Anderson, head of the Women's Bureau of the Department of Labor through 1944, considered it a "narrow" measure promising "doctrinaire equality" without "social justice." Esther Peterson felt the same, and had steered Kennedy's Commission on the Status of Women away from the ERA. She reluctantly changed her mind around the same time that Phyllis Schlafly changed hers, heading in the opposite direction. Organized labor continued to resist. The clothing workers' union declared that repealing protective legislation "would discriminate against the many for a few." The AFL-CIO thought the amendment privileged salaried workers. Congressional passage in 1972 brought unionists around. Recognizing that they were out of step, the AFL-CIO endorsed the ERA in 1973. The clothing workers yielded in 1974.[66]

Feminist lawyers liked the amendment. Ruth Bader Ginsburg argued that only an ERA could trigger reconsideration of thousands of discriminatory laws that litigants must otherwise challenge one by one, from an Arizona statute that prohibited women from becoming governor to a Wisconsin law that forbade women from cutting men's hair. Protective laws could be extended to males rather than withdrawn from females. Neither sex need lose "a genuine benefit they now enjoy," Ginsburg argued in 1973.[67]

Phyllis's complacency was shattered. Galvanized when the amendment went to the states for ratification, she founded STOP ERA in October 1972. (STOP stood for "Stop Taking Our Privileges.") Years of organizing bore fruit. Phyllis had a ready-made group of trained volunteers. She now tapped into their resentments over Supreme Court rulings that had banned school prayer, legalized abortion, and widened access to pornography. Domestic issues moved to the top of her agenda. From six in the morning to midnight, she wrote speeches and returned calls.[68]

Phyllis Schlafly could rally a thousand women in a day. Unlike liberals who balked at hierarchy, she coordinated her troops with the panache of a symphony conductor. In her home state, she recruited fifty-nine female "chairmen" for the state's fifty-nine districts. Under them were twenty-thousand volunteers who delivered anti-ERA materials along with fragrant loaves of banana bread to legislators. Feminine politeness was their calling card. In television interviews, Phyllis smiled before, during, and after every point. She had the face of a Madonna and the instincts of a ninja.[69]

Most important, she wielded the language of women's rights like nunchucks. Phyllis Schlafly never suggested turning the clock back to before 1964; instead she tried to make sure it did not tick forward. She emphasized that all sensible Americans wanted "more job employment opportunities for women, equal pay for equal work, appointments of women to high positions, admitting more women to medical schools, and other desirable objectives which all women favor." But they should not have to worry about changes ahead. Had the ERA contained a provision retaining protective labor legislation she would have supported it, she said, although her suspicion of federalism sheds some doubt.[70]

Phyllis Schlafly conceded that professional women, higher on the economic pyramid than most, still suffered discrimination. "We support your efforts to eliminate all injustices," she wrote. But a solution already existed, namely the Civil Rights Act of 1964 and Equal Employment Opportunity Act of 1972. As one of her lieutenants elaborated, citing Ruth Bader Ginsburg in *Reed v. Reed,* "the Supreme Court increasingly uses the 14th amendment to repeal laws which unfairly discriminate against women."[71]

To anyone of conservative disposition, cautious at a time of extraordinary change, such arguments made sense. Legal scholar Mary Frances Berry, who served as President Carter's assistant secretary for Health, Education, and Welfare, wrote that earlier efforts to amend the Constitution had had to convince citizens that "a societal problem existed that had not been remedied by the courts, legislatures, or the Congress, and which could be solved only if the Constitution were changed." Slavery, for example. By the measure of history, "ERA approval was problematic at best and defeat predictable."[72]

To achieve ratification, ERA proponents would have to persuade thirty-eight state legislatures of its wisdom. Phyllis Schlafly had to sow doubt in only thirteen. STOP ERA could point to the successes of women's liberation itself to disprove the claim that constitutional change was essential.

She did not stop there, however. She wanted converts to grassroots conservatism generally. Using simple, direct language, she praised the desire of most women to marry, raise children, and stay home if they could. She pointed out truths that reformers downplayed, such as the fact that the majority of women did not want to work the overtime required to become a corporate titan. They had more maternal drive than competitive drive. She simultaneously reveled in exaggeration, insisting that feminists wanted to expel mothers from the home and place children in Soviet-style daycare. The modern American woman had a beautiful life. "Past injustices" were simply that. As a writer for the Copley News Service reported in 1976, "she admits that in some point in the past women faced prejudices in jobs and pay. But not so today."[73]

Partisan to her core, Phyllis Schlafly was not trying to find common ground with opponents. She wanted to crush them. Deriding them as "libbers," she courted polarization to vanquish moderates. In this sense, she was opportunistic. Other conservative women had opposed sex education in schools and bans on classroom prayer for a decade. Phyllis had finally stopped reading *Janes Yearbook,* the annual survey of military weaponry, long enough to notice.

Public relations techniques polished over decades served her well. By the mid-1970s, Americans were weary of conflict. Defeat in Vietnam, runaway inflation, escalating divorce rates, college protests, high interest on home loans, and rising unemployment had shaken the nation's confidence. Five months before the 1977 International Women's Year Conference in Houston, Phyllis Schlafly published *The Power of the Positive Woman.*

Adorned by a jacket photograph of herself with a Coca-Cola smile, the book characterized feminists as negative whiners trapped in their "dog-in-the-manger, chip-on-the shoulder" dogma. Cheerful women like herself, by contrast, found biological differences uplifting. They appreciated men taking care of them. Equality in the home was incompatible with happiness, Phyllis wrote. Patriarchal domestic roles had "a valid and enduring purpose." In public debates, she enjoyed thanking her husband Fred for his permission to attend. "I like to say that," she explained to her biographer with a twinkle, "because I know it irritates the women's libbers more than anything else."[74]

Followers absorbed her rhetorical strategies. A Missouri opponent of the ERA commented that Phyllis Schlafly gave younger conservatives "the tools and information to accomplish great things." An admirer in Oklahoma said, "I learned how to turn a hostile question into the one you want to answer, how to get your message across in a radio or TV interview in soundbite sections."[75]

Conservatives wanted to disarm complaints that they were merely out-of-date. In 1973, self-help author Marabel Morgan had published *The Total Woman,* a book that advised Christian women to mold their personalities around their husbands. "It is only when a woman surrenders her life to her husband, reveres and worships him, and is willing to serve him, that she becomes really beautiful to him," Morgan claimed, using biblical stories to illustrate conventions that had once discouraged Ann Marie Low. The reward for submission, Morgan promised, was "sizzling" sex, emotional intimacy, and well-adjusted children.[76]

The Total Woman soared to the bestseller list as American women, hoping for answers to the mysteries of modern life—which baffled men, too—struggled to decide whether equality improved or destroyed relationships. The twentieth-century ideal of marriage as a companionate relationship, rather than an economic one, had upped the costs of emotional friction. States began passing no-fault divorce laws that allowed either partner to dissolve a union without proving the other guilty of misbehavior. California Governor Ronald Reagan, himself the object of a messy divorce, signed the first in 1969. Divorce rates increased from roughly 15 percent of marriages in 1970 to nearly half by the year 2000, with women filing more commonly than men. Marabel Morgan touted wifely submission as a small price for curing such discord.[77]

Not all conservative women agreed. Rosemary Thomson, Phyllis Schlafly's collaborator in the Eagle Forum, considered Morgan dangerous. Male or female, Americans tended to value individualism. "ERA proponents will use the book to 'prove' that all of us opposing the 27th amendment are mindless slaves to chauvinist husbands," she wrote in her own 1978 book, *The Price of LIBerty* (a play on the pejorative nickname "Lib" or "Libber" for a women's liberation activist). Even God recognized that modern women should be freer than their predecessors, Thomson believed. She told Eagle Forum followers, "In His protective will, women are free to become all He intended, including developing creative talents which may lead to careers in or out of the home." This included politics. She reassured them that having small children was "no excuse" not to campaign.[78]

More frequently, however, Phyllis Schlafly fed women's anxieties about change. She suggested that husbands might use the ERA to force wives to work. The morally "evil" amendment would wipe away homemakers' "legal right" to be full-time wives, something Phyllis assumed that all families could afford. Indeed, women might even be required to support a "lazy husband," something she assumed none already did. The divorced would suffer, too. The ERA would "abolish a woman's rights to child support and alimony," she said flatly, and daughters would "absolutely and positively be subjected to the draft." Phyllis had no proof of any of these propositions, some of which were unlikely, but who could say? No one knew with certainty what greater equality might bring. Thomas Jefferson had not known.[79]

Conservatives were not the only Americans to hanker after tradition. One historian points out that women in the Black nationalist Nation of Islam eagerly exchanged individual autonomy for the "promise of patriarchy," hoping that men would defend them from exploitation and poverty. Female converts to Islam during the later twentieth century reckoned that if patriarchy—"an ideology of liberation through subordination"—could deliver all that, it was worth it. Leaders exhorted male converts to protect women as "our most valuable property."[80]

Next to Phyllis Schlafly, ERA spokeswomen sometimes appeared ill-mannered and defensive. She used gendered insults of the type that feminists eschewed, and against which they had little defense. Phyllis called them "shrill," "aggressive," "yapping," "straggly-haired," "sharp-tongued," and "high-pitched." She denounced them as elitist frauds who thought they were superior to normal people.[81]

Most of her targets were women with fewer decades of political experience than she. Many rejected cosmetics and genteel decorum, and embraced the bohemian norms of the counterculture. They believed that women should not just smile regardless of the sexism they endured. Women might not be able to prevent assault, for example, but they no longer had to laugh along with men's jokes about it—like the old jest about a woman's response to the chase: "Don't! Stop. Don't. Stop! . . . Don't stop, don't stop, don't stop." Phyllis accused feminists of being shrews, and her multiplying attacks drove them to distraction. Her steel-plated gentility and unshakable claim of God's favor only made things worse.

Some tried to be fair. Karen DeCrow, president of the National Organization for Women, cordially jousted with Phyllis Schlafly on numerous public occasions. She told her biographer, "I think that what Phyllis is doing is absolutely dreadful. Yet I admire her." DeCrow explained that she was "everything you should raise your daughter to be" in the way of assertive. "She's an extremely liberated woman," DeCrow added. "She sets out to do something and she does it. To me, that's liberation."[82]

Others took the bait that Phyllis dangled. Betty Friedan infamously exploded during a 1973 debate in Indiana, saying "I'd like to burn you at the stake." Phyllis coolly replied, "I'm glad you said that, because that just shows that the intemperate, agitating proponents of ERA are so intolerant of the views of other people that they want to burn us at the stake." Florynce Kennedy, co-founder of the National Black Feminist Organization, told a Miami radio station in 1974, "I just don't see why some people don't hit Phyllis Schlafly in the mouth." No woman did, although a male demonstrator struck Schlafly in the face with an apple pie at a Republican luncheon in 1980.[83]

Such attacks built sympathy. They seemed to prove Phyllis Schlafly's claim that "bitter" feminists offered "no happy role models," though she was well aware of the less astringent feminism of Betty Ford, Rosalynn Carter, and Lady Bird Johnson, all shining portraits of personal fulfillment and wifely duty. Phyllis threw accusations like spaghetti against a wall. She wanted to make feminism "an epithet" that stuck.[84]

The bipartisan consensus dimmed. Legislators who had previously worried that they risked votes by not supporting the Equal Rights Amendment now fretted that constituents would penalize them if they did. Public support had been strong until Phyllis Schlafly's campaign. Gallup polls in 1974 showed that 74 percent of Americans favored the measure, including most small-town residents and low-income workers. When presented as a restatement of the nation's patriotic creed, the Equal Rights Amendment excited admiration. But when characterized as an attack on families, it caused apprehension. "Something fundamental about being a woman and a man seemed threatened—woman's place, man's place, child's place as the ideal even when not the reality," one historian notes. "The mere possibility, without a probable reality," was enough to give Americans pause.[85]

Fear of the unknown is universal, but some feel it more intensely than others. From the 1960s through the 1990s, scientists noted in multiple studies that psychological traits paralleled political divisions. Research showed a key variable was enjoyment or dislike of new things. Some people gravitated toward novelty, others toward the familiar. Some snapped up the newest technology, others waited to make sure it would not explode. Phyllis Schlafly told constituents that the ERA was a ticking timebomb, and many believed her.[86]

By 1980, she and other conservatives had driven approval of the ERA down twenty-two points, from 74 to 52 percent. Spooked women opposed the ERA in greater numbers than men. Approval among religious fundamentalists dropped ten points, from 63 to 53 percent. More than 50 percent of housewives still supported the ERA, but politicians abandoned the amendment. Republican nominee Ronald Reagan renounced his former support of the ERA even while promising to appoint the first female member of the US Supreme Court. By then, such acts could be portrayed as congruous (although Phyllis snubbed Justice Sandra Day O'Connor, saying, "It's obvious that she got the job because she's a woman"). Americans could support equality and still pretend it was disconnected from feminism. Phyllis's coalition grew and the country reddened. Oklahoma, a Democratic stronghold since statehood eighty years earlier, became unshakably Republican by 1982.[87]

In 1977, ratification stalled at thirty-five states, three short of the total needed. Indiana was the last, ten months before a counter-demonstration that Phyllis helped to organize against the Houston conference to celebrate International Women's Year. President Carter persuaded Congress to grant an extension of the ratification period, but the amendment expired in 1982 without any further takers. The ERA was dead unless, like Frankenstein (or Sleeping Beauty), a later generation restored it to life.

Phyllis Schlafly's influence did not wane as the ERA fizzled. Instead, victory gave her the momentum to complete her transformation of the Republican Party.

A Real SOB (Superintendent of Banking)

Conscious that all eyes were glued on the first woman of Wall Street—and eager to spot mistakes—Mickie Siebert gloried in the challenge. She bought a memo pad for her desk. "When I'm right, no one remembers," it read. "When I'm wrong, no one forgets." Previously, she had tried to blend in. Now she wanted to stand out. Finance should get used to women, she believed. "None of that unisex 'dress for success' nonsense with the little bowtie at the neck of a dark jacket," she wrote in a later memoir, unwittingly describing the first woman in a presidential cabinet, when female executives were rarer than Hawaiian shirts on Wall Street. She splurged on purple designer pantsuits and bought a silver Mercedes—the newest model. She called a friend acquainted with the company's German president, saying, "I think the first woman member of the Stock Exchange should have the first 350SL that comes into this country." He agreed.[88]

She did not yet have access to private clubs where some of the biggest deals went down, although the Union League Club, founded by Republicans during the Civil War, gave Mickie special permission to attend a luncheon one day. The concierge reminded her to enter through the kitchen and come up the back stairs since women were not allowed in elevators. The club boasted four traditions: "no women, no dogs, no reporters and no Democrats."[89]

She designated a representative to execute orders in her name, as did most seat holders on the exchange. The NYSE still did not have facilities for women and she had assured the men who granted her a seat (but not a toilet seat) that she did not intend to spend her days pacing its hallowed floor. Her business model required private time with clients. But when she got her first really big order, she decided to tread the famous wooden boards herself.

It was October 1969. "High time," she thought, for a woman to execute a deal on the exchange. The *New York Times* treated it like a fashion show, reporting that she filed the order wearing two-inch alligator heels. She played it up intentionally. Brokers normally wrote orders on white memo pads. Mickie had pink ones.[90]

Yet she recognized that image meant nothing without performance. A $300,000 debt swung over her head (equivalent to $2.3 million in 2022), enough to make any gambler swallow. Most people hesitated to trust a woman to fly a jet, much less handle millions, so she aimed to give better service than her competitors. She concentrated on pension funds, dug into new trends that more complacent brokers ignored, and arranged bond deals for companies seeking loans. In one, Mickie initiated a consortium with larger brokers on behalf of a trucking company. The deal was worth a lot, but she walked away when the lead partner, who explained that no Wall Street firm would tolerate a woman's name ahead of theirs, wrote her name last on the contract. Even so, she quadrupled her income the first year, from $250,000 to $1,000,000. Owning her own firm paid handsomely.[91]

It also gave her freedom to address two matters close to her heart: female vulnerability and the nation's financial interests. Her fame brought women to the door as soon as she put out a sign. Some were housewives who had to beg their husbands for money; others were single mothers who could not pay the rent or widows whose advisers wanted to put their inheritances into risky stocks that earned high commissions, instead of stable bonds. Even before Mickie bought a seat on the exchange, she had volunteered her time to educate such women. In 1961, she spoke at the male-only Harvard Club, where women visitors were shunted through a "Ladies Entrance." The *New York Times* reported that housewives and widows crowded the room.[92]

Mickie now paid for a survey of 137 women's colleges. Why did women have to get a day pass to the Harvard Club for simple information? Come to think of it, why had she needed to audit classes at Western Reserve? The survey revealed that more than half of women's colleges offered no courses on finance. College administrators explained that business was "not a proper subject for ladies."[93]

Mickie Siebert urged clients to become financially literate. Over the next four decades, she donated 30 percent of her income to a variety of programs to improve financial education, and started the Muriel F. Siebert Foundation to distribute materials to middle and high school students that explained how to create a budget, establish credit, pay taxes, and set financial goals. Schools widely adopted the curricula.[94]

As she told the US Securities and Exchange Commission (SEC), the federal regulatory agency, finance was "largely incomprehensible" to most Americans. Exploiting consumers' naïveté, companies collected the highest fees from the poorest people. Women who started their own businesses typically used credit cards for startup costs. Ignorant of business loans, they paid twice the interest rate their rivals did. Everywhere Mickie turned, she found people unaware of how America's financial institutions worked and how they might invest their money.[95]

She leapt at the opportunity to democratize the system itself. For two centuries, the exchange had required all brokers to charge the same fees. Prices were fixed. During Gerald Ford's presidency, however, Congress passed two laws that exposed stockbrokers, for the first time, to the same competitive pressures as grocers selling milk. The first law required pension managers to pay the lowest commission available, rather than doing business with whichever stockbroker they admired. Since commissions were fixed, this meant nothing until, a year later, Congress passed a second law that eliminated price fixing.[96]

As of May 1, 1975, Wall Street brokers could legally undercut one another. Horrified financiers dubbed it May Day. Most balked, hoping to maintain informal price fixing through peer pressure. Not Mickie. She knew that if she lowered her prices, pension managers would have to come to her, and they could then lower the prices they charged the elderly. It had long disturbed her that she made more in one afternoon than her father did "standing on his feet for a year as a dentist." Price fixing affronted her patriotism. She thought that Wall Street itself should have to cope with the free-market pressures it had long touted as "the American way."[97]

At opening bell on May Day, Muriel Siebert & Company became the first Wall Street titan to challenge what economists called "the oldest cartel of modern times." Laying everything on the line, Mickie unilaterally cut prices in half for institutional clients, and soon for retail clients. Elite firms retaliated by spreading rumors that her company was going under, trying to scare her clients. Bear Stearns stopped clearing her orders and Citibank froze her out. Mickie reduced her staffing by half to stay afloat.

She reached out to average people who had never purchased stocks. She advertised the route she walked to work in the morning, and listed her personal number in the free directory that the telephone company put on New York doorsteps. She distributed yo-yos to remind novices that the market always came back up after it went down. Within a couple of years, Siebert & Company was thriving again, and other discount brokers had emerged. In time, elite companies discounted their services, too. The cost of entering the market plunged. By the turn of the century, the proportion of Americans invested in the stock market had climbed from 4 percent to more than half.[98]

Mickie's prominence led reformers to seek her out, and in the early 1970s she found herself drawn into a network of feminists that included Bella Abzug, Gloria Steinem, Betty Friedan, Ann Richards, and Jane Macon, San Antonio's first female city attorney. They ate good take-out and drank wine at her spacious apartment at River House, near the United Nations, where Secretary of State Henry Kissinger also had a residence.

In 1974, Mickie became a founder of the Women's Forum of New York, prompted by a friend who asserted, "We have to start the equivalent of an old boys' network." A sizable number of women occupied top positions in government and industry for the first time in US history. Eleanor Holmes Norton, a Black civil rights activist and city commissioner who represented forty-six female employees in a 1970 discrimination lawsuit against *Newsweek* for barring female reporters, became a founder, too. Organizers told one another they needed to come to "terms" with power rather than avoiding hierarchy, and use it to solve such problems as the extra burden carried by female wage earners who accepted primary responsibility for childcare or elder care. Over the next four decades, affiliates sprung up in thirty-three countries, and became known collectively as the International Women's Forum.[99]

Mickie drew back when it came to overt protest, however. Sales were her meat and potatoes. She literally could not afford to alienate Americans more traditional than she. This constraint tempered her self-presentation. When asked why she had not yet married, she replied lightly, "It's either been the right man at the wrong time, or the wrong man at the right time." She reassured the reporter that she still had hopes. "I'm definitely not one of those male-hating career women you run into," she said in a 1974 article. Like Phyllis Schlafly, Mickie made a point of insisting that she was a lady, and often handed her own corporate card to a male staff member to pay the tab in a restaurant. She said she was not a "formal feminist," leaving open what an informal feminist might be.[100]

Watching her step, Mickie rarely stumbled when negotiating new gender mores. She did trip, however, when nominated as the first female superintendent of banking for New York. In the spring of 1977, Democratic governor Hugh Carey fulfilled a campaign promise to appoint more women. He said that everyone suggested Mickie. With her stockbroker's sense of humor, it tickled her that the acronym for superintendent of banking was SOB. She thought the job sounded fabulous. The superintendent oversaw state-chartered institutions within the largest, wildest financial community in the world. She would be banker to the planet.

The timing was not good, however. Mickie's mother had been paralyzed by a stroke and lost a leg to blood clots. Mickie could hear her sweet, optimistic mother singing down the corridor of the hospital whenever she visited, and she hesitated to talk about the job offer. Margaret's twenty-four-hour care cost nearly $250,000 a year. The government salary would be $47,000. Meanwhile, Mickie's older sister Elaine had developed severe mental health problems, and sometimes disappeared to live on the street. Frantic with worry, she would have to go looking, and she began paying Elaine's expenses to keep her sister safe.

Without informing Margaret, Mickie decided to undergo the state confirmation hearing that would determine whether or not the job was really hers. She learned that a reporter was trying to stir up opposition. The man had disliked her ever since she had caught him leaking information that she had given him in confidence—and then denied doing so. At the hearing in Albany, she addressed the issue immediately. "You're going to have to excuse my language," she apologized, "but I called him a fucking liar to his face." The legislators burst out laughing.[101]

They confirmed Mickie almost unanimously. The exception was a man who bristled when, in response to his question about the background of her employees—a new line of inquiry after President Richard Nixon created "affirmative action" to fight union resistance to racial minorities—Mickie referred to one staff member as a "Black girl." The African American politician objected. "Most people in the forefront of the women's movement don't use that word," he said—meaning girl, not Black, though he may have resented the two in combination.[102]

Profanity was now acceptable in arenas where "girl" raised hackles. Under the spotlight, middle-aged Mickie awkwardly ad-libbed, "I'm still flattered when *I'm* called a girl." The senator voted against her confirmation. It was a sign of a war over symbols that would divide reformers in coming decades.[103]

Margaret Siebert died four days after Mickie took the new job, unaware that her unmarried daughter had become the most financially powerful woman in the world.

Mickie Siebert agreed to serve for two years, but the governor, pleased at her performance, later talked her into five. She shepherded the state and nation through numerous shocks, including the Iranian hostage crisis of 1979, when the new fundamentalist government (which also lowered the marriage age for girls to nine) allowed a mob to kidnap fifty-four Americans from the US embassy. As SOB, Mickie had defended the right of Iranians to establish banks in the state of New York. Now she called the US State Department and alerted the undersecretary that they might try to transfer their money home, leaving behind only their debts. A few days later, Iran's foreign minister announced his intent to withdraw all deposits, as she had predicted. President Jimmy Carter froze Iranian assets and Mickie's waiting staff descended on the banks' Manhattan offices. "Boss," her deputy told her, "you've got brass boobs."[104]

Mickie's government service cost her literally millions. Her company survived, but stagnated under a lackluster trustee. Still, the experience was worth the price, she felt, and it got her to thinking. She had seen the government solve enormous problems, only to bog down over small ones. The penalty for fuzzy thinking on Wall Street was "swift and painful," she reflected. She could not understand how American "government operated in such a fog, with such circular reasoning."[105]

New Yorkers had never sent a woman to the US Senate. In 1982, Muriel Siebert decided to campaign as a bleeding-heart Republican.

Anti-Feminism Becomes the New Anti-Federalism

By the time of Ronald Reagan's 1980 election, Phyllis Schlafly had shown her party a new way. The ultraright no longer needed to rely so heavily on the specter of communism. Feminism was the new bogeymen: just as un-American and closer to home. Baptist televangelist Pat Robertson, an eventual contender for the Republican presidential nomination, called feminism "a socialist, anti-family political movement that encourages women to leave their husbands, kill their children, practice witchcraft, destroy capitalism and become lesbians." In 1991, rightwing radio host Rush Limbaugh took to calling them "feminazis."[106]

Phyllis had pioneered hyperbolic attacks on rivals since her first campaign. Now she redirected conservatives' focus away from communism and racial segregation toward the family—a useful switch as the Cold War ended and Jim Crow was outlawed. Her populist criticisms of eastern "kingmakers" helped transform the Republican Party from one associated with the establishment to one imbued with anti-establishment fervor. In one of history's more surprising developments, Democrats and Republicans switched places in the wake of the Civil Rights Movement. Abraham Lincoln's pro-Union, federalist party became the party of state rights.

The movement was bigger than Phyllis Schlafly, yet one of her principal contributions was to unite groups that normally avoided each another, including Catholics and Baptists, through single-focus issues like abortion. She taught followers to tolerate one another in the service of a higher purpose: "Although they might be sitting next to someone who might not be saved, we could nevertheless work together on behalf of a social / political goal we all shared." Through Eagle Forum affiliates, she kept pressure on moderate Republicans to adopt increasingly conservative stands on abortion, childcare, the ERA, and her old favorite, national defense.[107]

Meanwhile, she lambasted any new reform. She opposed tax deductions for childcare, and laws that made it easier for married women to obtain credit cards, on the basis that they incentivized mothers to accept paid employment. She criticized the federal Pregnancy Discrimination Act of 1978 for advancing the "feminist goal of driving all wives out of the home." She argued that female soldiers who got pregnant should be discharged, and that pregnant private employees should voluntarily resign. In 1981, she testified against new sexual harassment regulations. "Virtuous women are seldom accosted," she told a committee chaired by Republican Senator Orrin Hatch of Utah. "A non-virtuous woman gives off body language that invites sexual advances." Phyllis may have reinforced the committee chair's prejudices. Senator Hatch would later question Anita Hill's truthfulness in 1991, and Christine Blasey Ford's integrity in 2018, when they accused Supreme Court nominees of sexual harassment.[108]

Urged on by televangelists like Jerry Falwell of Virginia and James Robison of Texas, as well as voter-mobilization groups like the Christian Coalition, religious fundamentalists flocked to the polls. Employing the rhetoric that Phyllis Schlafly had perfected, Republican candidates gained on Democratic rivals.[109]

Historically, American politics have been characterized by alternating periods in which one party largely commands the House, Senate, and presidency. After the Civil War, Lincoln's party had mostly dominated across seven decades. Beginning with the Great Depression, Roosevelt's party largely controlled the next six decades. As the Cold War ended, the Republican party once again became ascendant. Beginning in 1994, conservative Republicans dominated Congress over the next three decades, making "family values" their central issue. Phyllis Schlafly could claim some of the credit, and did. In the words of historian Robert Self, "the liberal left lost political purchase on the mythology of the family." According to Donald Critchlow, "gender played an essential role in the triumph of the Right."[110]

To convince followers that feminists were villains, Phyllis Schlafly had to separate them from earlier reformers whose accomplishments had allowed her to attend school, speak publicly, lobby legislators, cast a ballot, and pursue interests outside the home. Her denunciations gradually became more extreme. In the 1960s, she equated suffragists with George Washington and Thomas Jefferson. In the 1970s, she asserted that women's liberation was an outgrowth not of suffragism but "the history of radicalism." In the 1990s, she characterized "mean-spirited" feminists as advocates of "Big Brother Government." By the 2010s, when the eighty-something activist was still publishing, she claimed feminism was actually a form of Marxism. "Feminists want people to think feminism began with the nineteenth century suffragettes, but it didn't," Phyllis wrote. "In fact, the two groups have nothing in common."[111]

Feminism's communistic plot would have surprised stockbroker Mickie Siebert. The disconnect between suffrage and feminism would have astounded Alice Paul, who had penned the ERA in 1923. Feminism was a spectrum, of course, with a left wing that included people like Martha Cotera, but there were innumerable moderates as well, many of them proud Republicans. While there was no such thing as a standard-issue feminist, creating a scapegoat required Phyllis to pretend otherwise.[112]

Inflammatory rhetoric—by Phyllis and other polemicists—helped spark the rise of violent, anti-government fringe groups. In 1996, a domestic terrorist murdered 168 people, including nineteen children at day care, when he bombed a federal building in Oklahoma. Two decades later, Phyllis Schlafly endorsed the candidacy of Donald Trump, whose false claim that the 2020 election was "stolen" prompted an assault on the US Capitol. Ironically, one of those who died that day was a female military veteran shot while breaking into the House chamber. Feminists like Edith Nourse Rogers had secured her right to serve.

Despite all this, Phyllis Schlafly failed to stop the overall trend of increased approval for gender equality. While activists keenly felt the criticisms leveled against them, as journalist Susan Faludi expressed in her 1991 bestseller *Backlash: The Undeclared War against American Women,* the news was mostly positive. Pollsters found that support for "the social, political, and economic equality of the sexes" was high between 1980 and 1999. Black feminists made particularly strong gains. Overall, African Americans supported "the women's movement" at a higher rate than did whites (73 percent compared with 66 percent in a 1998 survey).[113] By 2004, 74 percent of voters in Republican red states supported an "equal women's role," hardly different from the 78 percent in Democratic blue states. This roughly equaled the percentage of Americans who could correctly identify England as the country from which the United States had become independent in 1776.[114]

The principle of gender equality had entered the American creed. In her own staunch defense of women's right to compete politically, Phyllis Schlafly had advanced feminism. Still, she never used the word without making it sound like a slur.

Banking on the Senate

Muriel Siebert had a rosier outlook on American government, which she considered capable of positive leadership. In 1982, only one in a hundred senators was a woman: Nancy Kassebaum, a liberal Republican from Kansas. Mickie decided Kassebaum needed "some sisterhood."[115]

Her years as superintendent had convinced her that the banking laws needed improvement and that most lawmakers had little idea how. Some did not even care. She lumped first-term senator Patrick Moynihan, a Democrat, in that category after he refused to help her save a group of struggling banks when she came to see him as SOB. Moynihan told her to call on a Republican for sympathy. She later admitted in her memoir that she "*hated*" him for it. She had loyally served a Democratic governor. To Mickie, the good of the people came before politics. Anything else was despicable.[116]

When Moynihan's Republican challenger had to pull out of the next race, a door popped open. Mickie resigned from government and rented a ballroom the next day at the new Helmsley Palace, an exquisite hotel in midtown Manhattan, to announce her candidacy. New York had a long history of liberal Republicans. William Seward, friend of Harriet Tubman and Lincoln's secretary of state, had been New York's first Republican senator. More recently, New York governor Nelson Rockefeller had led the party's liberal wing. Rockefeller was well known for his support of gay rights, Black colleges, services for the poor, and access to abortion.[117]

Mickie Siebert recruited Malcolm Wilson, Rockefeller's former lieutenant governor, to introduce her that sunny morning in May 1982. Arrangements were hurried. Even the taxi was late, and when she dashed into the ballroom, she saw that her banner had not arrived at all. Only "Siebert for Senate" balloons decorated the space, giving the impression of a children's birthday party. The lectern, too, was made for someone taller. The other leading Republican in the primary was six-foot-six.

Malcolm Wilson told the press that the businesswoman brought "a unique set of qualifications," including twenty-two years on Wall Street and five in state government. She was "a female version of Horatio Alger," Wilson enthused, referring to a nineteenth-century author whose novels had immortalized the trope of ragged but honest urchins rising to wealth though hard work.[118]

The five-foot-three candidate approached the lectern, kicked off her high heels, and stepped onto a milk crate that someone had hustled from the hotel kitchen and covered with a cloth napkin. Photographers captured her in her nylons. She pledged that New Yorkers would find her "very conservative fiscally and probably quite liberal in terms of people and human rights." She praised balanced budgets and investment in new technologies, things she had valued since her earliest years as an analyst. She added that she supported the Equal Rights Amendment and a woman's right to abortion. New York then had four major parties: Republican, Democratic, Conservative, and Right-to-Life. Election law allowed candidates to appear on more than one ticket. Mickie said she would seek the Republican and Conservative nominations, but not Right-to-Life.[119]

She might as well have kicked a beehive with her stockinged foot. In the ten years since *Roe v. Wade,* abortion had become the nation's angriest issue. More than 80 percent of public hospitals still refused to terminate pregnancies, and small private clinics performed most services. Antiabortion activists bombed twenty-six clinics between 1977 and 1984. In the next decade, three physicians were gunned down, targeted by a right-wing fringe campaign that called for "justifiable homicide" and printed "Wanted" posters with doctors' photographs, phone numbers, and home addresses.[120]

Under pressure from Catholics in particular, states had passed dozens of regulations restricting access to abortion, mimicking the Comstock laws a century earlier. Women in twelve states struggled to obtain the procedure at all. Republican Gerald Ford vetoed a bill sponsored by Catholic congressman Henry Hyde that prohibited federal funding of abortion for poor women after 1976, but Congress overruled him. Allied with Phyllis Schlafly, President Reagan cut funding for all types of family planning, including birth control, by 25 percent in his first year in office and started a trend of appointing antiabortion jurists to the Supreme Court.[121]

Mickie spoke for most Republicans. Polls showed that more Republicans than Democrats supported legal abortion, and that the majority of citizens supported abortion with some restrictions. Nevertheless, New York's Conservative Party pleaded with Mickie to at least pretend to reconsider, given the vehemence of splinter groups. But she refused to compromise on what she considered "reproductive freedom." It especially bothered her that low-income women without travel funds or private health insurance had the fewest options. Conservatives sought to deny abortion even "to a twelve-year-old who had been raped by her stepfather," she noted. The Conservative Party responded by nominating a Catholic former assemblywoman with little name recognition outside Brooklyn.[122]

Mickie disliked negative campaigning. In business, bad-mouthing others paid no dividends. She talked up her own ideas and refused to criticize either the Brooklyn candidate or her other competitor, a former US attorney named Whitney Seymour. Both she and Seymour were well known. (Mickie's reputation extended internationally, because she had resisted foreign takeovers of established New York banks.) One of the two was expected to win the Republican nomination and challenge the wily, well-funded Moynihan.[123]

Polls showed Mickie far ahead. Then, two days before the vote, a last-minute pamphlet that called Mickie a "baby killer" reached New York Republicans. It criticized Whitney Seymour for opposing school prayer, and declared the election a race between "two liberals and a Reagan Republican." Mickie found the flyer when she returned home from a Jewish New Year celebration. It was too late to mail a rebuttal. The Brooklyn antiabortion candidate had illegally violated a provision of New York's electoral laws, but the damage was done.[124]

Primaries normally attract the most dedicated partisans. In this case, highly motivated voters selected the inexperienced Brooklyn Catholic to challenge Moynihan. He easily defeated her by the biggest margin in state history.[125]

Mickie Siebert wrote to President Reagan a few months later. She doubted he would read her letter, but felt she must try to reach him. For the first time since 1920, elections showed a gender gap, with women more likely to vote Democratic and men more likely to vote Republican. "For the first time in thirty years of voting, I have a deep conflict between being a woman and voting Republican," she told her party leader. "I do not believe your close advisors are sensitive enough to today's women and their very legitimate concerns."[126]

She would never know how many Republican women she might have kept in the fold or Democrats she might have wooed had her name appeared on the ballot. In 1982, conservatives spoiled the chances of their party's most competitive candidate.

+++

MOST OF PHYLLIS SCHLAFLY'S six children had children of their own. Her first-born did not. John stood by his mother's side at the 2004 Republican convention when she advocated a constitutional ban on gay marriage. Phyllis had first criticized homosexual unions in *The Power of the Positive Woman,* writing that "NOW is for prolesbian legislation giving perverts the same legal rights as husbands and wives."[127]

It is hard to know how this felt to John Schlafly, who was gay. Still living with his parents, he commented to the press in 1992 that homosexuality was not a choice. Phyllis directed the spotlight onto herself and called newspaper coverage of his sexual orientation "a political hit on me." She asked rhetorically, "Does every child do what you want them to do?"[128]

She made a valid point. Not everyone did what others did. Freedom meant they did not have to.

First Lady Barbara Bush spoke for Republican moderates, many loathe to express their opinions for fear of reprisal, when she said during her husband's failed reelection campaign that abortion and homosexuality were "personal things" that should be left out of party platforms. "I don't think that's healthy for the country when anyone thinks their morals are better than anyone else's," she said.[129]

Mickie Siebert had blown $400,000 on her own failed campaign. She could afford it. In coming decades she rebuilt the fortune that she then willed to charity after her death. "Giving back is more than an obligation," she wrote. "It's a privilege." Case Western Reserve University awarded her an honorary doctorate and she established a fund to encourage pro-choice women to run as Republicans. She had two long-term romantic relationships with men in the business community, Larry Levine and Howard Levy, but never married. The New York Stock Exchange eventually named an auditorium Siebert Hall, the first room in the historic building to honor an individual. She even got a toilet.[130]

Two years after Mickie joined the NYSE, a trader had shown her a hidden women's bathroom on the first floor of the Exchange, installed during the Korean War when females were temporarily allowed to deliver messages. But the seventh-floor dining club still had none when Mickie invited a group of female business executives to lunch in 1987. European guests who asked to use the facilities expressed shock when directed to a different floor. "Such a thing would never happen in a civilized country like France or Italy," they said.[131]

The indignities that Muriel Siebert had borne gracefully hit her all at once. She called the chairman of the NYSE and threatened to order a giant plastic port-a-potty for the club, to arrive in a few days. He must have dialed a plumber. On February 9, 1987, women got their own bathroom.

Everyday life had come to approximate the 1873 cartoon lampooning Susan B. Anthony. Men sometimes carried babies. Women sometimes attended political rallies without them. Most Americans considered this normal. So did much of the world. Pope John Paul II issued a "Letter to Women" in anticipation of another UN Conference on Women, set for Beijing in 1995. His tone differed markedly from that of Phyllis Schlafly, his fellow Catholic. The pontiff condemned sexual violence, unequal pay, and the lack of support for working women. He explicitly praised "women's liberation," and lauded those who had battled sexism since the time of Christ: "I cannot fail to express my admiration for those women of good will who have devoted their lives to defending the dignity of womanhood by fighting for their basic social, economic and political rights, demonstrating courageous initiative at a time when this was considered extremely inappropriate . . . and even a sin!" He liked to call himself the "feminist Pope."[132]

Muriel Siebert believed that "equality will come only when women who gain power . . . begin to use it on behalf of other women." As a Jewish woman touched by the Holocaust, she admired progress. She wanted to unite citizens around constructive goals.[133]

Phyllis Schlafly mistrusted progress and rejected consensus. "I've never been bipartisan," she wrote in the last year of her life. When he stepped down from office, George Washington had warned about the tendency of parties to "misrepresent the opinions and aims" of rivals. Cruel taunts would "render alien to each other those who ought to be bound by fraternal affection." Democracy required "uniform vigilance to prevent its bursting into a flame," he believed. In her sweeping review of American history, Jill Lepore reflects, "If the wrenching polarization that would later bring the Republic to the brink of a civil war has a leading engineer, that engineer was Schlafly."[134]

She had company, of course. Self-identified feminists on the Left dissed those in the middle. De facto feminists on the Right insisted that the label had nothing to do with them. Both inflamed antagonisms.

In the quarter century after second-wave feminists institutionalized equal rights, American women flexed their right to compete at work, in sports, and on the campaign trail. Yet there was more to life than the public arena. Mothers still assumed greater responsibility than fathers for raising children, and government did little to help them balance this work with paid employment. Families struggled under heavy daycare costs. While governments across Europe and Asia invested in subsidized childcare and maternal leaves of up to one year, mothers in America received minimal paid leave, if any, to care for newborns and infants. Children often did not receive the attention they needed. Women remained grossly underrepresented in government, and sexual harassment was widely condoned. Americans also wrestled over new social practices. How should men treat women, and women treat men, going forward? How should women treat one another? As the world entered the next millennium, a third wave of feminism reignited interest in such questions.

CHAPTER 8

The Right to Physical Safety

2000 TO THE PRESENT
Beyoncé Knowles-Carter and the Women of #MeToo

I am proud of my representation of this Nation through gymnastics. . . . And I believe without a doubt that the circumstances that led to my abuse and allowed it to continue, are directly the result of the fact that the organizations created by Congress to oversee and protect me as an athlete . . . failed to do their jobs.

SIMONE BILES, 2021

PEOPLE GROWING UP in the 2000s had every reason to conclude that sex discrimination was over. From its peak use in 1975, the phrase faded for thirty-five years. Then, suddenly, "sex discrimination" reappeared around 2010. Articles peppered the *New York Times* and other newspapers. By 2020, mentions of gender inequality nearly equaled their frequency at the height of the second wave. Reformers had vastly improved laws and institutions, but it seemed the nation had saved some of the toughest challenges for last, particularly sexual harassment and rape. Standing on the foundation built by preceding generations, Americans were in a stronger position to tackle them.[1]

One woman literally "performed" this generation's vision of feminism. Singer-songwriter Beyoncé Knowles built a career around the themes of how men should treat women, women should treat one another, and girls should treat themselves. Speaking to millions, she promoted—and still promotes—female autonomy, self-respect, and solidarity, as well as equality within marriage.

The superstar also challenged the stereotypes that had led many citizens to equivocate, "I am not a feminist, but . . ." From her electronic pulpit, Beyoncé defied leftist accusations that feminism represents only white women and rightist accusations that it is un-American. Once hesitant to use the F-word, the African American performer emblazoned "Feminist" across the backdrop of her 2013 world concert tour and explained, "I love being a woman and a friend to other women."[2]

By 2021, Beyoncé had earned more Grammy Awards than the Beatles, Lady Gaga, Queen, and Madonna combined. More Grammys than any performer in the history of the prize. In a testament to her image as a model American, she headlined the inaugurals of both George W. Bush and Barack Obama, and sang the national anthem at the Super Bowl. Her family suffered from the same problems as many, and the question for her was how a twenty-first-century woman should cope with them. Scholars praised her answer as a blueprint for recovery for women "when their worlds fall apart."[3]

Not everyone was a fan. One icon of second-wave feminism, bell hooks, characterized Beyoncé as a "terrorist" and a purveyor of "fantasy feminism." Other guardians of the brand have objected that true feminists reject capitalist "wealth and power"—and keep their spangly shorts to an acceptable length. No pop star could fulfill such standards, though some—like Madonna, Lady Gaga, and Taylor Swift—have appeared to weather fewer assaults on their feminist credentials.[4]

This debate has highlighted the continuing controversy over feminism as a label, even if gender equality has become a widely accepted goal. Some conservatives reject the label as strenuously as ever, undermining their own efforts to defend sexual decency. And some leftists have refused to share it, upending their own efforts to unite American women around the social justice issues they hold dear. Beyoncé resisted such dichotomies. She took her message to every corner of the land, reaching across class, partisan, racial, religious, and regional divides to express her vision—and sell albums.

And then there was the issue that sparked so much press coverage after 2010. While Beyoncé bared her soul and her marriage, women around the country began, at first one by one, but soon in a tidal wave of testimonies, to make public their experiences of sexual harassment and rape, shining a spotlight on a problem that every generation had grappled with since Abigail Bailey threatened her husband with exposure and extricated herself from his abusive embrace. Americans once again found themselves shocked at the harms of sexism, as survivors spontaneously launched the #MeToo campaign of 2017. Dedicated women and men, journalists especially, dug deep to uncover abuse in sports, at work, and in private life.

Their effectiveness came from a bountiful harvest of evidence that assault and misconduct were still shockingly common, and reached as high as the presidency. Why did some men consider these practices acceptable? Why did so many Americans look the other way? The public airing of such questions helped to de-normalize abusive behavior. Once again, a new generation moved the nation closer to its founding aspirations.

In the spirit of #MeToo, this aspect of the chapter departs from our previous pattern. Instead of featuring a single person, it highlights several. The first story follows a woman who was raped in her home. The second spotlights two women who were harassed at work. The third channels the voices of hundreds of girls assaulted while pursuing a sport they loved. One biography alone cannot explain why so many Americans of this era concluded that sexual abuse, long stomached, must be decisively addressed. As *New York* magazine observed in 2014, individual tales had failed to move the nation. Only "the sheer volume of seeing them together, reading them together," prompted change. The cascade of similar stories from dissimilar settings renewed Americans' commitment to justice for all. Because—they believed—women have a right to safety at home, work, and play. Everyone does.[5]

Girl Power Meets Girl Drama

Introverts sometimes make great performers. A microphone can be a license to open up publicly in ways that might not otherwise feel comfortable to a reticent person. A shy child may experience the stage as a place where she can be the star of her dreams until the curtain cloaks her once again. Born in Houston in 1981, Beyoncé Knowles grew up in the shadow of two strong personalities in a rocky marriage. Her mother Tina, née Celestina Beyoncé, was articulate and flamboyant. Childhood friends in Texas said she was a "firecracker" in any group. The green-eyed Creole came of age during the second wave of feminism, and was told that "there were no limits to what a woman could do."[6]

Beyoncé's father, Mathew, had a rougher upbringing. His Alabama family was poor. His parents fought over money, and he started work early. Mathew Knowles belonged to the generation of African American children who integrated hostile white schools after *Brown v. Board of Education.* He courted friends through sports, music, and scholastics, and eventually won a college scholarship. When the couple met in the 1970s, each was impressed by the other's big personality. It was ironic that their little girl was so shy.

By the time Beyoncé entered kindergarten, both parents had demanding careers. Tina applied for a small business loan to open her own hair salon. Mathew sold equipment for Xerox. The successful duo bought an elegant two-story home in a middle-class, integrated Houston neighborhood graced with towering oaks covered in Spanish moss. Yet Tina felt insecure. Mathew was compulsively unfaithful. She sometimes took Beyoncé and her younger sister, Solange, to the salon. To teach the rewards of work, Tina paid them to sweep cuttings from the floor.

Beyoncé had inherited her mother's flossy hair, her father's brown eyes, and both parents' intensity. Their sociability left little imprint. She later remembered herself as the shy kid who trained her gaze on the ground at recess, unsure what to say. "I would just smile and be quiet," she later recalled. She made an easy target. Students poked fun at her uncommon first name, and some assumed that her light complexion and long hair meant she was "stuck-up." Ambivalence about European physical traits within the African American community—what Mathew Knowles and others called "colorism"—created tension. Tina felt bad when little Beyoncé told her, "I wish I was darker." The child literally kept her head down, developing a stoop.[7]

Like many girls insecure about their appearance, Beyoncé wore baggy pants and oversized shirts. She was particularly intimidated by girls who might "beat me up or talk bad about me," so she twisted her hair into a bun to avoid their noticing its length. Her fears were well founded. The film *Mean Girls,* written by Tina Fey in 2004, depicted an old dynamic that claimed new attention during Beyoncé's childhood in the 1980s. Regardless of race and class, some girls climbed to popularity on the backs of other girls. They reserved their worst aggression for their own sex, and used put-downs of those outside their circle to heighten their status. Such girls seemed unable to compete without making it personal. Loathe to interact on such terms, Beyoncé withdrew. She allowed few classmates to really know her.[8]

Fortunately, Beyoncé knew herself. She had bopped around the house to music since she was a toddler in white cowboy boots. When she was in first grade, she told her mother that the teacher had taught them a song. Tina wiped her hands and sat down to listen. The six-year-old launched into a stirring rendition complete with dramatic expression and impromptu dance steps. Tina's eyes widened in delight. Perhaps her daughter had a whiff of a firecracker after all. "My goodness, this is really . . . *something,"* she recalled thinking. Seeing her mother's reaction, Beyoncé realized she loved singing for her mom. "It was a rush," she later said.[9]

To encourage Beyoncé to make friends, her parents signed her up for singing and dancing lessons affiliated with the local school. The instructor told the seven-year-old to stop slouching, but also pointed out that she brought "something special" to the art. She urged Beyoncé to enter a school talent show and coached her in John Lennon's "Imagine," stretching the bashful girl's imagination about a better world.[10]

On the big night, Beyoncé watched the crowd settle into their plastic yellow seats as the auditorium filled with parents. She wondered how she could face them, but when she stepped onto the stage, her fears vanished. She felt more in control than anywhere she had ever been. Beyoncé saw her parents' mouths "open in amazement." Tina and Mathew Knowles clapped loudly at the end, and on the ride home Beyoncé feigned sleep to enjoy their happy whispers.[11]

A video from the following year, when Beyoncé began entering local talent contests, explains their reaction. Still available on the internet, the grainy film shows a Houston dignitary introducing a young girl in a sequined pinafore. Dressed as Dorothy from the musical *The Wiz,* the child is sober. When the music starts, her face brightens and her voice soars to an adult register as she toe-taps across the floor. The child's age registers only at the end when she briefly loses her spot in a final, sparkly twirl. Beyoncé disliked the scrutiny that came with such "glorified beauty pageants," as she later called them, but she tolerated it to qualify for the talent portion.[12]

Young Beyoncé was right to be wary of the pageant industry. An Atlantic City entrepreneur established the tradition in 1920 with a "Miss America Scholarship Pageant" to lure customers to his seaside hotel after

Labor Day. He lent respectability to the parade of skimpy bathing suits by linking it with the feminist-inspired pursuit of a college education. Naming the winner "Miss America" wrapped voyeurism in patriotism. A Miss USA / Miss Universe organization later owned by Donald Trump split off from the Atlantic City franchise in 1952. Analysts found that winners averaged five feet six, weighed 119 pounds, and had brown eyes. Their ancestors hailed from Europe until Vanessa Williams became the first African American to win in 1984. Even Italians had once been considered too dark. The Miss USA organization disqualified contestants who stuffed their bras, while the Miss America organizers winked at padding. Neither prohibited plastic surgery.[13]

By the time Beyoncé entered her first talent contest, toddlers were being groomed for perfection. Some appeared to enjoy it, but Beyoncé noticed others with "makeup caked all over their little faces" who seemed sad. Twenty-five years later, she sang that being "pretty hurts" when competitions "shine the light on whatever's worst."[14]

As a cosmetologist, Tina relished hair and costume design, and Mathew wanted his reserved daughter to find a hobby. But Beyoncé drove the process. She felt "free" on stage, like "a totally different person," she later said. If someone performed better, she analyzed the other girl's approach afterward. Not until she had thirty trophies did her parents begin to take her passion as seriously as she. Hesitant but excited, her father finally said after a year, "Maybe you really could be successful at a career in music!" Beyonce's parents warned her that she would have to work hard—but it turned out they had to race to keep up.[15]

A break came when two Black Houstonians decided to try their hand at the music business. Entrepreneurs Denise Seals and Deborah Laday admired successful boy bands. In 1990 they formed a management company, placed ads in the *Houston Chronicle,* and auditioned more than one hundred girls for a DJ act, a hip-hop group named "Destiny," and a singing ensemble called "Girls Tyme." Beyonce's instructor called to recommend her, saying she had to be seen to be believed. The entrepreneurs selected the eight-year-old as the youngest of three lead singers, impressed not only by her talent, but also her leadership. The persistent pipsqueak was soon teaching other girls their parts.[16]

Girls Tyme debuted in June 1990 at Prairie View A&M University, Texas's formerly all-Black college. The Houston-area campus had integrated in 1963, at the same time that the main campus, in College Station, was desegregated. Girls Tyme charmed the audience, leading to other local gigs. Beyoncé was its most eager member. When Tina Knowles tried to excuse her daughter from performing after a long family trip, she found herself handing over the telephone to Beyoncé, who pleaded, "But I ain't too tired to sing my part, Miss Deborah. So please come get me, okay?"[17]

Costs soon overran expenses. After only six months, her parents arrived one afternoon to find an eviction notice on the office door. The two entrepreneurs bequeathed leadership of the effort to a third newbie, who started her own talent agency using money from a settlement after a drunk driver killed her husband. Big-hearted Andretta Tillman, who also earned a living at the local power company, became the girls' principal manager. Tillman dismissed the least accomplished performers and combined the three acts. The only singer to survive the cuts was Beyoncé, who was joined by two new vocalists and two dancers.

The preteens bonded immediately. For Beyoncé, their affection had special meaning. Her sister was almost five years younger. While the others had chums at school and church, shy Beyoncé did not. Now she had four instant best friends, all crazy about the same thing. The nine-year-old could hardly wait for daily rehearsal. She had found her place and girls to share it. In spare moments she began writing songs.[18]

Andretta Tillman hired an assistant, paid for voice lessons, and coached the children herself. She selected a girl two years older than Beyoncé as lead singer. In 1991, Tillman secured a slot for Girls Tyme at a California meeting of music producers, and the young Texans excitedly took their first plane trip. Afterward, a Bay Area studio that had once produced Stevie Wonder invited Girls Tyme to record a demo tape. Tillman could afford plane fare for only two band members, so she took the lead singer and Beyoncé. Tina Knowles wept at the airport, but Beyoncé, all of ten, reassured her, "I'm fine, Momma. I want to go!"[19]

In California, the studio found that the lead singer struggled with the syncopation of a tune written especially for Girls Tyme. At the end of a frustrating hour, Tillman's assistant asked Beyoncé, who seemed fidgety, if she thought she could do better. "Yes, Mr. Kenny," she replied. "I sure do." Andretta Tillman reluctantly swapped the younger singer for the older one. Within minutes, Beyoncé had mastered the piece. One of the adults commented, "It was like listening to a young, female Michael Jackson." The studio sent the tape to rock legend Prince.[20]

Like Beyoncé's first instructor, professionals recognized that the hardworking child brought "something special." She absorbed improvements immediately, and her mezzo-soprano voice had a soulful energy. As a dancer, she demonstrated a kinetic quality, known to choreographers as musicality, that captured the eye. Beyoncé's verve tended to make "other girls look like they're not working as hard," one coach noted. At ten, the precocious child probably did not altogether intend to eclipse her new friends, but she did, with troubling consequences for their relationships.[21]

The band underwent several transformations on the way to becoming Destiny's Child, the group that launched Beyoncé as a star. When Andretta Tillman returned to Texas with the two singers in 1991, and played the tape for their parents, everyone realized that Beyoncé had replaced the lead vocalist. The other girl's mother tried not to overreact, but brash Mathew Knowles did not hesitate to remark, "I've actually been thinking for awhile that Beyoncé was the standout." Tina shushed him, but he protested, "Hey, I'm not saying anything that everyone here doesn't already know."[22]

Over the next several years, Mathew exercised increasing leadership. He became co-manager with Andretta Tillman in 1992, then sole manager. Once he sensed his daughter's potential, he quit his well-paid job. Tina Knowles fashioned the girls' costumes and styled their hair to give each a different look: one with silky black tresses, another with spiky purple highlights, a third with red streaks, and Beyoncé with long blond waves. The family risked everything, including their Houston home, which they eventually forfeited after filing for bankruptcy in 1995. Andretta Tillman sank her savings into the ensemble, too. A lender repossessed her car.

Show business is notoriously capricious. Artists routinely lose out to others scarcely more talented. Mathew Knowles was arrogant, but he was also a loving father who wanted control "over how this plays out for my daughter." Andretta Tillman suffered from severe lupus, an illness from which she died before the release of Destiny Child's first song. After the group's rise to stardom, Tillman's sons sued for a greater percentage of earnings, believing that Mathew had pressured their mother into relinquishing more authority than necessary, and the court awarded a settlement of $1.25 million to reflect her contribution.[23]

Mathew Knowles brought business savvy and a good ear for musical trends to the enterprise. For five years he pushed the group in front of producers, scouted opportunities, negotiated, and pressed the girls to train harder. Unlike Andretta Tillman, he retained the original performers, although the mother of the older singer withdrew her daughter. The four remaining girls became Destiny's Child. Beyoncé was fifteen when their first single, "Killing Time," hit the airwaves in 1997 on the soundtrack for the film *Men in Black,* starring Will Smith and Tommy Lee Jones. The film's success lifted the album to number one on *Billboard*'s Top 200 and it sold three million copies. The girls' own first album arrived six months later.

Beyoncé remembered hearing their first solo hit, "No, No, No," on the radio as she turned into a school parking lot to pick up her little sister. Solange dropped her bookbag and ran to the car as the music poured through the window. "This was unbelievable to us," Beyoncé recalled. "To find that after all that hard work, it just happens sort of overnight." The song jumped to fourth on the pop chart. She had just turned sixteen.[24]

Teenage drama lurked around the bend. Two members of Destiny's Child grew to resent the attention that journalists increasingly lavished on Beyoncé, as well as production decisions that appeared to favor her. When Kelly Rowland's single mother moved to another state, Kelly moved in with the Knowles family. She and Beyoncé, closer than most sisters, shared a bedroom they decorated with Mickey Mouse paraphernalia. They gradually realized that the other singers, their best friends for most of a decade, were quietly fuming.

With her southern manners and fear of conflict, Beyoncé played peacemaker. A bandmate described her as "the type of person who, even if you raise your voice, she'll keep calm." A self-described "people-pleaser," Beyoncé worked to keep her world together. She credited other band members as co-writers, guaranteeing them an equal portion of royalties though she wrote most of the lyrics and melodies. She typically sang lead, yet she also made sure others had solos, and challenged her father whenever she thought he promoted her unduly. But she could not prevent the ensemble's implosion. In the annals of pop, eight years was actually a decent run.[25]

At the end of 1999, as the two other girls turned eighteen, they unilaterally turned up the heat. Without consulting Beyoncé or Kelly, they engaged a lawyer to dismiss Mathew as their manager, even while insisting they wished to remain in Destiny's Child. They had miscalculated badly. As the band's owner, Mathew accepted their decision to fire him, then replaced them with two other singers.

Beyoncé took the anger of the other girls hard. For weeks she retreated to her bedroom, and spent hours praying at the United Methodist Church to which the devout family belonged. At last she poured her disappointment into a letter, reminding her estranged friends of her efforts to make everyone shine, holding "their hands in the studio if they wanted me to" and losing her childhood home to cover their startup costs. The more she sacrificed, the more they sulked, she felt. Beyoncé did not use the term co-dependent, but her words evoked the problem in which one person's over-compensation reinforces another's laziness. Working eleven-hour days, she had also recorded vocals, coached, and produced final mixes. "I've never complained when I was working my butt off in the studio . . . when the two of you were sleeping or on your phones eighty percent of the time," she now said. They criticized Mathew, but Beyoncé thought they actually begrudged her. Her prose was stiff, perhaps from hurt. "I feel that the two of you did not enjoy my presence," she concluded.[26]

Barely eighteen, Beyoncé struggled to understand why anyone could turn spiteful when God gave "everyone his or her own gifts." She reflected, "I've learned that when you're nice to people who envy you, they dislike you more, which is frightening." The former band members sued, and Beyoncé and Kelly Rowland paid them $850,000 to drop the case. Fans took sides, making private wounds the subject of public gossip. "I swore that Beyoncé was the cause and refused to buy any more Destiny's Child albums," one later wrote. She simply did not believe "the pretty, light-skinned, affluent, superstar black girl could really love other black girls."[27]

Still the drama was not over. Five months later, in July 2000, one of the two new singers complained about Mathew's management, and petulantly boycotted a major concert tour by not showing up for an international flight, a move guaranteed to embarrass the others. Beyoncé borrowed a cell phone at the gate and pleaded with her to get a cab, but she could not sway her. She finally rang off, saying politely but definitively, "May God bless you. *Goodbye*!" Beyoncé, Kelly Rowland, and Michelle Williams boarded the flight to Australia, scrambling to rearrange the vocals, choreography, and staging for a concert two days later. When the trio accomplished the feat with flair, they were finally launched.[28]

Beyoncé poured her confusion into songwriting, which she called "my therapy." For her, words felt "more powerful when I sing them than when I speak them." In one of several hits she penned for Destiny's Child the next year, she proclaimed that women needed to treat one another better. In "Survivor," the trio announced that they would not compromise their "Christianity" to "hate on" others, "cause my Mama taught me better than that." The music video showed them shipwrecked on a deserted island. Picking themselves up, they traded gowns for skins and camouflage, and like a team of commandos blazed a path through the jungle. Each singer had a solo, with Beyoncé on lead. "I'm a survivor, I'm not gon' give up," she sang. "You thought I'd be weak without you, but I'm stronger . . . I'm gon' work harder." From that point onward, the trio avoided discussing former band members. "We are not the type of girls who gossip or blame anyone," Rowland insisted.[29]

That same year, in 2001, fellow Texan George W. Bush invited Destiny's Child to perform at the inauguration, an honor Beyoncé earned again in 2009 and 2013. The fast-rising group scored their first Grammy nomination for "Say My Name," which lectured a philandering boyfriend to be honest. Another hit, "Independent Women, Pt. One," told "ladies" to vote for going "fifty-fifty in relationships" regardless of the work required. "Depend on no one else to give you what you want," Beyoncé sang. Learn to be self-supporting, she encouraged fans. Released as the theme song for *Charlie's Angels,* a film about female detectives based on the long-running 1970s television show, "Independent Women" captured number one on *Billboard*'s Hot 100 chart for eleven weeks. Beyoncé wrote both songs. She was nineteen.

The *New York Times* pronounced Destiny's Child "in tune with the New Feminism." Music critic Ann Powers commented that Beyoncé, "an unusually authoritative teenage star," and her "lieutenants," had taken on "the predicaments of womanhood with the determination of warriors." Their appeal sprang from "seriousness, not charm," and they sang as openly about religious faith as about child sexual abuse ("It's not your fault, young girl / Don't cry, you're beautiful"). They were complicated and imperfect, Powers observed, but "that's where the real women live."[30]

For some, Beyoncé embodied the modern feminist ideal that women could be both sexy and wholesome, carnal and moral. With their low-cut shirts and high-cut skirts, Destiny's Child stood for a younger generation's understanding of women's rights. They refused to be intimidated by old insults like "bitch" and "slut." Female sexuality should not have to be cloaked under a burka. For young Black women especially, the message defied two centuries of ugly insults. "Destiny's Child is sexy, but don't get it twisted," Beyoncé said. "We're not *bad* girls."[31]

Andi Zeisler, co-founder of *Bitch* magazine in 1996, claimed that her generation had more interest in female rock bands than second-wave theorists. "Pop culture is a critical locus of feminism," Zeisler later told the *New York Times.* Confident in the equality secured by the previous generation, younger women embraced what some called "lipstick feminism," meaning the right to cultivate physical beauty without being denigrated by older reformers or harassed by men. Feminist punk bands, announcing a "Riot Grrrl" Movement, went the other way, matching delicate dresses with clunky shoes, dying their hair pink or black, shouting into the microphone, and mocking sexism. One "manifesta" demanded in 2000 that the older generation "truly listen to girls, even when they reveal that they actually like Barbie."[32]

In other words, girls had a right to pursue happiness, or, as singer Cyndi Lauper put it, to have fun. The artist who was forced out of her home at seventeen by a peeping stepfather sang in 1983, "Some boys take a beautiful girl / And hide her away from the rest of the world / I want to be the one to walk in the sun / Oh girls, they want to have fun." Lauper, Madonna, and other songwriters inspired by feminist values felt that women should stop apologizing for seeking self-fulfillment. Mary Wollstonecraft had once advised them to swap "the whole tribe of beauty-washes" for "a mind-illumined face." This generation insisted they could have both.[33]

Author Veronica Chambers, a rookie editor for *Newsweek* at the time, recalled that "Independent Women" by Destiny's Child was a "game changer." Beyoncé, shown at the head of a corporate boardroom in the first scene of the music video, "was everything I—and every young woman I knew—wanted to be: glamorous, in charge, with her best girls by her side." For Chambers, the performance expanded her vision of what "might a Black girl be in this world."[34]

One thing a Black girl might be was a champion of female solidarity. No more mean girls. She might also show that positive, polite women could achieve equality with powerful men, including one's own father.

Rape: Unsafe at Home

The first "unalienable right" set down in America's Declaration of Independence was the right to life. Patriots employed John Locke's contract theory of government to justify revolution: rulers who failed to protect citizens physically forfeited their legitimacy. Yet at the outset of the twenty-first century, women had cause to wonder about the commitment of their own government to this founding principle. Their lives were often not safe, and officials responsible for protecting them seemed not to care.

Rebecca Walker, the daughter of Pulitzer-winning novelist Alice Walker, coined the phrase "third-wave feminism" in a 1992 essay for *Ms.* magazine. She had been stunned by the skepticism with which an all-male Senate Judiciary Committee greeted law professor Anita Hill's testimony during confirmation hearings for Clarence Thomas. Thomas had been Hill's supervisor at two government agencies. Following an FBI investigation, she reluctantly agreed to describe his sordid campaign to convince her to have sex with him. "How reliable is your testimony?" Senator Arlen Specter of Pennsylvania badgered. Senator Howell Heflin of Alabama asked, "Are you a scorned woman?" A journalist for *American Spectator* mocked Hill as "a bit nutty and a bit slutty." In effect, the committee judged Hill a liar. Rebecca Walker pleaded with her generation to rebel against a system that was still so stacked against women.[35]

Even worse than tolerance of workplace harassment was a deliberate passivity toward rape, as a Detroit prosecutor discovered when he chanced upon thousands of cardboard boxes in an old police warehouse in 2009. "What are those?" he asked the officer escorting him through the facility. Dust furred the lids of the oldest of the boxes, which were stacked in long rows on steel shelves.[36]

Rape kits, his guide answered. For thirty years, officers had sent the kits, unopened, to the warehouse. Many contained the DNA of criminals, some serial rapists. All contained the pubic hair, blood, saliva, and photographs of traumatized victims who had been civic-minded enough to allow nurses to collect evidence from every surface and orifice of their bodies.[37]

The man contacted his boss, Kym Worthy. The first African American to act as Detroit's chief prosecutor, Worthy had been raped herself decades earlier in Indiana, attacked while jogging at night. She had not had the nerve to call the police or to endure the grueling four-hour exam. Now she knew her reluctance had been immaterial. The unopened kits in Detroit's police warehouse numbered 11,431. A national audit soon found that Arizona had six thousand unprocessed kits, Oklahoma had seven thousand, North Carolina had nine thousand, California had fourteen thousand, and so on. Those were only the ones catalogued in the databases. Gross negligence in one jurisdiction could be explained by individual carelessness, but spread across the nation, it meant that American authorities were not committed to deterring or prosecuting rape.[38]

The news shattered expectations. The development of rape crisis centers, police sensitivity programs, and "rape shield statutes" preventing the interrogation of victims about their prior sexual history—not to mention the evidentiary kits themselves—had led many to believe that real progress had been made. At the start of the millennium, it became clear this was illusory.

In the most appalling cases, courts penalized victims for false reporting, because authorities were convinced, as one Idaho sheriff told a television station in 2016, that "the majority of our rapes—not to say we don't have rapes, we do—but the majority of our rapes that are called in, are actual consensual sex." Prosecutors ignored "imperfect victims" whose profile did not match a soccer mom. Americans were not alone. In 2006, a British police surgeon blithely pronounced that 90 percent of rape allegations were untrue.[39]

False reports did occur, as with any crime, including robbery and fraud. Famously, rape charges against three lacrosse players at Duke University were dropped in 2007 when an unscrupulous prosecutor withheld information favorable to the students. But research showed this was atypical. False reports of rape were rare, and overeager prosecutors rarer yet. Surveys in the United States and Britain found that 92 to 98 percent of rape victims reported truthfully, yet their cases vanished at each step of the judicial process. Cops dropped them, and then prosecutors dropped them, until hardly any victim received justice. Between 2010 and 2014, barely more than 1 percent of cases went to trial.[40]

Marie, a white girl from Washington State identified publicly only by her middle name, became the face of the problem. Her experience brought to light the failings of a system that most people thought had been fixed when two reporters broke her story, which was later turned into the Netflix miniseries *Unbelievable.*

The attack occurred in 2008, just after Marie turned eighteen and while she still had braces on her teeth. Having survived a nightmarish childhood, Marie felt like she finally had a shot at a normal life. She did not remember attending kindergarten, though she did recall "being hungry and eating dog food," according to a social worker. She had met her father only once. Her mother had left her with adult boyfriends who sexually assaulted her. At seven, she was taken into protective custody, medicated for depression, and began rolling through more than a dozen foster families.[41]

When Marie reached tenth grade, her foster family lost its license, so she entered a two-week placement near Seattle with a woman who befriended her. Afterward, she lived with a social worker until she reached the age of majority. Those two guardians remained in her life when she moved into her first apartment, which was subsidized by a state program for homeless teens. Marie got her learner's permit to drive and a job at Costco.

She had been in the new apartment only a few weeks when a man who would become a serial rapist made her his first victim. Marc O'Leary had struggled to repress disturbing fantasies of assaulting women since the age of five. There seemed to be no way to get help, or make the thoughts go away. A military veteran enamored of pornography, he enjoyed reconnaissance—"hunting," he called it—and he broke into Marie's apartment twice to familiarize himself with the floorplan. The morning she awoke to find him standing over her with a butcher's knife, he chastised her for leaving a sliding glass door unlocked. It became part of his routine: telling victims they had not done enough to protect themselves. "You should know better," he told Marie, shifting the blame onto her. He told a later survivor, "You're not a bad person. But you left your window open."[42]

O'Leary tied Marie's wrists with her own shoelaces, raped her, and took souvenir photographs, including one of her tagged like meat with her new learner's permit positioned across her torso. Two months later, he raped his second victim, a sixty-three-year-old in another Seattle suburb whom he again bound with her own shoelaces.

Marie had not reported the assaults she had suffered before the age of seven, but she remembered them, and decided to stand up for herself this time to make sure "nobody else got hurt." She wanted to help police find the man. When O'Leary left, Marie cut the restraints from her lacerated wrists and called for help.[43]

Trauma scrambles memory. The brain seeks to protect itself from terror, and victims express shock in idiosyncratic ways. Some act preternaturally calm. Others respond hysterically. Memories of the event can arise at unusual moments and arrange themselves in a new order. The day Marie was raped, she told her story four times on one hour's sleep. She had a headache and her wrists throbbed, but she patiently endured the grueling rape kit exam. Police officers asked her to write her account, too. Afterward, she called her former foster mothers. One came to console Marie, who cried briefly but spoke with detachment.

The woman found Marie's manner strange and the events too bizarre to be believed. Why would a rapist use shoelaces instead of rope? Why would he take photographs? Had Marie let someone snap nude pictures and then constructed a cover story in case they were posted on the internet? Marie's other foster mother had the same reaction when the girl shared the news in a flat voice. This woman had been assaulted herself years before. When she had finally informed someone, she had wept profusely. Wasn't that typical? The women did not know that victims' responses vary widely, and that people who have endured previous assaults are sometimes especially composed. They know how to lock away their emotions in an effort to act normal under freakish pressures.

The foster mothers had met Marie through a system built to help hurt children. They wondered if some psychological pathology had motivated her report. The neglect she had suffered became a demerit against her credibility. The rape-kit exam documented abrasions on Marie's wrists and labia, but the women did not have this information. The professionals did.

Marie's town of Lynnwood, Washington, had no sexual assault unit. The officers who took her case had minimal experience with rape because the vast majority of victims never reported the crime. Officers failed to dust for fingerprints on the front door, though Marie told them that her attacker had exited through it. They canvassed the neighborhood to determine if anyone had spotted the intruder, but stopped when they received a call the next day from one of Marie's foster mothers, expressing doubts.

In the course of twenty-four hours, the officers turned from investigating a rape to investigating Marie. Three days later they picked her up for questioning. To a teenager, the next question was obvious. She asked, "Am I in trouble?" To them, her inquiry was as good as an admission of guilt.[44]

Two detectives grilled her mercilessly, not telling Marie that she could have an attorney. They said her foster mother disbelieved the report. They alleged that her former boyfriend was also suspicious, though he had indicated no such thing. They pointed out small inconsistencies in the five accounts she had given the first day and said that the rape kit did not support her allegations, though it did. They used a technique common in police procedure, which was to scare a suspect into confessing a crime by pretending to have information. Twice her age, the men insisted that she had made the whole thing up. At last Marie cracked. She agreed she had lied.

The adults' behavior corroborated studies begun in the 1990s. Many criminologists wondered why feminist reforms had not yielded robust conviction rates. It was a worldwide problem. As one group of researchers noted in 2010, "In Canada, as in Australia, the United States and a number of other countries (e.g., New Zealand, Scotland, and England and Wales), the attrition of sexual assault cases, at all stages of the criminal justice system, is alarmingly high." Few cases reached courtrooms. Investigators identified the main roadblock as "rape myths" that served to "deny and justify male aggression towards women."[45]

Rape myths were habits of disbelief that eviscerated the right to safety. They included assumptions about what constituted assault (a male who attacked a female and left obvious wounds), which victims had genuinely resisted (chaste females with stereotypically feminine traits, especially if they were white and middle class), and which complainants were credible (those who sobbed or spoke "in a trembling voice"). Criminologists knew that objective data refuted every single rape myth. Sexual assault happened to a wide variety of individuals, including men and transgender people, and victims processed trauma differently. Unfortunately, those who were calm had the least chance of being believed. Jurors and criminal justice officials had scripts in their head about what rape looked like, and judged victims accordingly. These heuristics—mental shortcuts—resulted in persistently incorrect deductions.[46]

At first, Marie felt better. She went to the public bathroom and washed her hands. As she described it, she "flipped the switch" that allowed her not to experience pain. The detectives told Marie to tell counselors at her complex that she had fibbed. A couple of days later she returned to the station to recant her confession, but now the officers threatened to revoke her subsidized housing. She offered to take a polygraph. One retorted that if she failed the test, "I will book you into jail." Again the eighteen-year-old capitulated, but the men decided she needed a sterner lesson. Three weeks later, Marie received a summons for "false reporting." If convicted, she could spend a year in jail.[47]

On the advice of a court-appointed attorney, she repeated at trial the falsehood the police wanted. The judge levied a fine of $500 and sentenced her to probation. Word got around town. Marie endured hateful internet posts calling her a liar and slut. She lost her job, friends, and the motivation to work. The police department destroyed her rape kit as false evidence. It likely contained the only complete DNA proof of Marc O'Leary's forthcoming crime spree. He had been a nervous novice with Marie. In subsequent attacks he forced his victims to shower to remove all bodily residue.

Marie's case was horrific but not unusual. Between 2008 and 2015, forty-seven women called the police in her hometown to report a rape. Officers dismissed ten of the cases (20 percent) as unfounded and not worth investigating, five times the national average.[48]

Miscarriages of justice elsewhere confirmed that the problem was serious and widespread. In Wisconsin a legally blind woman was raped at knifepoint in her home in 1997. Because she suffered from depression, police questioned both whether she was actually blind and whether she had actually been assaulted. The officer said he knew who committed the crime. "You did," he told her, and charged her with obstruction of justice. In New York, a girl raped on her sixteenth birthday was booked for false reporting when hospital tests revealed that she was two weeks pregnant. Police assumed she was trying to whitewash her own conduct. And in 2004, officers in Pennsylvania jailed a gas station attendant who was robbed and raped at gunpoint, booking her for theft and false reporting when they discovered money missing from the cash register. In all three cases, indisputable evidence exonerated the women, but only after they had been publicly shamed.[49]

In 2011, two years after Marie's conviction, the Lynnwood police commander knocked on her door. He reimbursed her five-hundred-dollar fine and explained that detectives in Colorado had arrested a suspect accused of violently assaulting four women. When Colorado officers located the man, they found photographs of his victims, including one of a young woman with a learner's permit on her naked torso. The name, address, and face were hers.

The two detectives who caught Marc O'Leary watched him receive a prison sentence of 327 years. The two journalists who broke the story won the 2016 Pulitzer Prize for Explanatory Reporting. Netflix announced that 32 million households streamed the 2019 award-winning *Unbelievable* within the first month. Marie married, had two children, and found a job driving long-haul trucks. She received a settlement of $150,000 from the police department. Scarred but vindicated, she built the normal life she had always wanted.[50]

Marie's story was one piece of an emerging picture. A variety of new reports were beginning to suggest that despite the progress that had been made, women and girls in America still faced grave dangers.

The Beyoncé Effect: Independence, Positivity, and Equality

With her busy career, Beyoncé dated only two men: her high school boyfriend and the man she married in 2008, Shawn "Jay-Z" Carter, a fellow musician. Jay-Z had been abandoned at age eleven by a father who later died of alcoholism. His mother, a lesbian who pretended to be straight to protect her four children, had been the family's sole support. When Beyoncé expressed frustration at her father's overbearing ways, Jay-Z told her, "I *wish* I'd had a father like Mathew Knowles." He reminded her of the time she got a bad tattoo and Mathew offered to get a matching one if it would make her feel better.[51]

A fatherless boy naturally admires a man who stands by his child. As Beyoncé matured, however, she grappled with how to love the man who had made her a star but diminished the women who were closest to her. Andretta Tillman, Denise Seals, and Deborah Laday had all found Mathew Knowles difficult. Her bandmates had quit over his domineering ways. Worse, Mathew betrayed Tina repeatedly with other women. "I grew up seeing my mother trying to please," Beyoncé said. She wondered if she should strike out on her own.[52]

From the start, autonomy had been a leitmotif in Beyonce's lyrics, one of three feminist themes that expressed her generation's point of view. Female independence was primary: women must make their own way. Second was what younger feminists called "body positivity": one must love one's physical self regardless of social expectations. Third was fidelity: men and women should commit equally.[53]

Beyoncé touted independence as one of ten life lessons for young women. In the words of Destiny's Child, "Don't let guys get up in your business. Be an independent woman." Prior to the song for *Charlie's Angels,* Beyoncé wrote "Bills, Bills, Bills" (1999). Nominated for a "Best R&B Performance by a Group" Grammy Award, the song criticized moochers who ran up their girlfriends' cellphone bills and borrowed their credit cards.[54]

Honoring Tina Knowles, the music video took place in a beauty shop, evoking a spirit of autonomy as heady as the ammonia in a perm. A "triflin', good for nothing brother" was no match for these women, styling one another's locks and rolling their eyes under the dryer. The lyrics underscored the girls' sense of responsibility for their own financial futures. Beyoncé penned the line, rhymed with triflin' brother, "Oh silly me, why haven't I found another?" A self-respecting woman would not tolerate a user. Beyoncé was proud when she learned that "Bills, Bills Bills" was a hit among young Japanese women, who thought it made self-support look "cool."[55]

"Independent Woman," released the next year, further advanced the theme. Susan B. Anthony had once quoted Alexander Hamilton to explain why economic dependence made wives vulnerable to abuse: "Give a man power over my substance and he has power over my whole being." In 2001, Beyoncé sang, "Try to control me boy, you get dismissed / Pay my own fun, oh and I pay my own bills."[56]

She repeated the mantra of autonomy in her 2008 solo hit "Single Ladies," winning a Grammy for Song of the Year. The female protagonist wants to marry, but her partner won't commit. She rejects his attitude of entitlement, knowing her options and worth: "I got gloss on my lips, a man on my hips . . . I can care less what you think / I need no permission, did I mention." Economically self-sufficient, she cannot be bought. Like Frances Perkins a century earlier, she wants a companion, not a handout.[57]

In 2010 Beyoncé wrote "Run the World (Girls)." The video showed a group of female dancers stopping a gang of male thugs. "I'm repping for the girls who taking over the world," Beyoncé sings; "Help me raise a glass for the college grads." She compliments "all the men that respect what I do," pointing out that good men appreciate women who are "strong enough to bear the children" and get back to running the world the next day.[58]

Beyonce's songs were a mélange of tradition and change. Her "Single Ladies" protagonist challenged her fickle lover to "say I'm the one you own," a turn of phrase guaranteed to trip feminist alarms. The desire for belonging appears to belie the desire for autonomy. In "Run the World," Beyoncé sang "Hope you still like me," suggesting that even powerful girls want male approval.

Such lyrics led some to question whether the songwriter could really call herself a feminist. One pundit wrote that Beyoncé offered women little more than a "banal brand of beginner feminism" expressed in "inoffensive pro-girl" anthems that failed "to challenge trenchant gender ideals." Yet the critique itself was problematic. Were "beginner feminists" not cool enough for professional ones? Should inoffensive "pro-girl" anthems aim to be offensive instead? Must heterosexual women reject the "gender ideal" of marriage to win approval from self-satisfied censors?[59]

Beyoncé's success sprang precisely from her embrace of contradictions. People want different things at different times, even if they do not ever wish to be exploited. Audiences related to her longing for both autonomy and connection, self-reliance and interdependence. The artist magnified this message on her fifth world tour in 2013. Recently married, Beyoncé called it the "Mrs. Carter Show." She projected "Feminist" across the stage backdrop and hired a group of women back-up musicians whom she named the Suga Mamas. Beyoncé was not subtle: a feminist could adopt her husband's name if she wished. Choice, not conformity, was the definition of liberation.[60]

Some critics considered the tour title retrograde, and again questioned the authenticity of her feminism. Documentary filmmaker Aisha Simmons thought racial expectations played a role. "If Beyoncé were white, she would definitely be called a feminist," Simmons commented to *Ms.* magazine in 2013. White observers wanted Black women to be cardboard cutouts of badass fighters, not complex human beings. When normal longings and frailties surfaced, "you don't get to be the face of feminism."[61]

The 2013 music video for "Pretty Hurts" advanced the second theme: body positivity. Beyoncé despised the harm wreaked by arbitrary standards of beauty. The video showed contenders in a pageant giving one another dirty looks and literally clawing for advantage. Beyoncé's character endures bulimia, isolation, and despair. "Perfection is a disease of a nation," she sings. "It's the soul that needs surgery," not women. At the end, Beyoncé smashes the trophies she spent her childhood accumulating.[62]

The singer was not just critical of old beauty standards; she proposed new ones. Unlike other members of Destiny's Child, she accumulated pounds easily and had to exercise rigorously to achieve her goals. That said, she loved her body and wanted other young women to feel the same. Mathew Knowles said "Hell, no" when told his daughter intended to record a song about her "big butt," but she insisted on the title "Bootylicious."[63]

She told a co-producer, "My whole thing is that it doesn't matter if you're a full-figured girl or what your body looks like, you should be proud of it." She wanted women to know they did not have to be skinny to be attractive. "You can have a little jelly," she explained. "Just wear it proudly." In 2001, "Bootylicious" soared to number one. Listeners thrilled to the message. Challenging people to accept women for who they are, Beyoncé playfully teased, "I don't think you're ready for this jelly . . . cause my body too bootylicious for ya, babe."[64]

But for all her celebration of natural beauty, Beyoncé was not immune to the pressure of idealized standards. Despite Tina's objections, she decided to undergo plastic surgery in her early twenties to enlarge her breasts. She decided they looked better on camera that way, telling a friend, "Bigger boobs are sexy." It was her choice, but the kind of choice that some feminists would criticize and tabloids obsess over.[65]

Beyoncé gave fans a fuller view of her dimensions sixteen years later when she performed at the 2017 Grammys. Carrying twins, she asked the audience, "Do you remember being born?" Wearing a filmy sheath that clung to a swollen abdomen that women like Rosa Cavalleri had once hidden, the proudly pregnant performer asked, "Are you thankful for the hips that cracked, the deep velvet of your mother, and her mother, and her mother?" Generations of women had risked their lives, battling eclampsia, hemorrhage, sepsis, and breech births. She wanted people to appreciate that.[66]

Beyonce's most famous song in praise of the female form, and the most edgy, was "Flawless" in 2013. It demanded respect not only for women's bodies, but also for the singer herself. Beyoncé had reaped scorn for her marriage to Jay-Z, twelve years older and with his own shelf of Grammys. Some fans considered her his underling. One dismissed Beyoncé for the singer's supposed effort "to reinvent herself as, chiefly, a wife and mother" and her "longstanding valorization of female domesticity." Beyoncé got pushback in Houston also. In "Flawless" she rhymed "H-Town bitches" with "vicious."[67]

In the first section of the three-part video, Beyoncé upbraided other women. "I took some time to live my life / But don't think I'm just his little wife / Don't get it twisted, get it twisted / This is my shit, bow down, bitches!" The use of "bitches" was unusual for the southerner who habitually addressed women as ladies. Younger feminists had reclaimed the word, but it still stung. Fans debated whether she was being a mean girl or confronting mean girls. Whatever the case, the lyrics implied that women were not delicate sylphs. They were bitches responsible for their actions—full human beings—and strong enough to take criticism.[68]

In the second section of "Flawless," Beyoncé inserted a voiceover from the TED Talk by Chimamanda Ngozi Adichie that would become the basis for Adichie's best-selling book *We Should All Be Feminists*. "We teach girls to shrink themselves," Adichie began, evoking a dynamic familiar to the Texas schoolgirl who once studied her shoes. Beyoncé vocalizes softly as Adichie continues: "We raise girls to see each other as competitors, not for jobs or for accomplishments, which I think can be a good thing, but for the attention of men." Adichie adds, "We teach girls that they cannot be sexual beings in the ways boys are," and in a bridge to the final section, asserts that a feminist is a "person who believes in the social, political, and economic equality of the sexes."[69]

The last section of the song was another anthem to body positivity. Beyoncé exhorted listeners to repeat after her: "We flawless, ladies tell 'em / I woke up like this." Perhaps to explain the song's beginning, she added, "My Daddy taught me how to love my haters / My sister told me I should speak my mind."[70]

Lastly, Beyoncé considered fidelity an expression of equality. As a Bible-loving southerner, she took aim at the custom of female self-abnegation praised in country western songs like Tammy Wynette's 1968 hit "Stand by Your Man," which encouraged wives to forgive dalliances, "'Cause after all, he's just a man." On her first solo album in 2003, she tackled the theme head-on. "I can't believe I fell for your schemes," the protagonist laments in "Me, Myself, and I," berating herself for thinking that her boyfriend would treat her differently than he had treated other women. She does not beg him to change. That is his responsibility. Autonomy is her solution. "I took a vow that from now on / I'm gon' be my own best friend," she sings, determined to get the treatment she deserves.[71]

The theme of infidelity appeared again on her second solo album, in 2006. In "Irreplaceable," which topped the charts for ten weeks, the protagonist tells her lover to put "everything you own in the box to the left" as he leaves. When he threatens her, saying that she won't find another man, she coolly replies, "You must not know 'bout me / I could have another you in a minute / Matter fact he'll be here in a minute, baby." The singer echoes the beautician in "Bills, Bills Bills," who remarks about one worthless "brother"—"Oh silly me, why haven't I found another?"[72]

In a music video for her third album, Beyoncé equates infidelity with sexist double standards. In "If I Were a Boy," she is dressed as a police officer who dashes out the door without tasting the breakfast her husband has cooked and jumps into a patrol car with a handsome partner. "If I were a boy, even for a day," she sings, she would "drink beer with the guys / And chase after girls . . . and I'd never get confronted for it / 'Cause they'd stick up for me." She would do what she liked while her husband followed the rules. When the faithful spouse in the video spots his wife nuzzling her partner in a bar, the roles reverse again. It turns out that Beyoncé has been the one watching her husband jump into a patrol car with a sexy colleague. The singer predicts that someday "You'll wish you were a better man."[73]

The same year that she released "If I Were a Boy," Beyoncé's father rented a house in California for his mistress. Within months, this mistress and another woman both gave birth to children by him. Her mother filed for divorce. Beyoncé had recently started her own company, named Parkwood for the home the family had lost on Parkwood Drive in Houston. Her entrepreneurship gave her choices when an audit suggested that Mathew Knowles had mismanaged, or possibly stolen, some of her funds. In 2011, she cut contractual ties with her father. "He is my father for life, and I love my dad dearly," she said in an official statement.[74]

Media outlets from Billboard to the BBC dissected the news. Beyoncé gained some measure of peace by refusing to discuss family matters with the press. Since childhood, she had felt most in control holding her own microphone. Two years later, in a 2013 documentary that she directed herself, *Life Is But a Dream,* she looked into the camera on her laptop, wearing a simple T-shirt and no makeup. "I'm feeling very empty because of my relationship with my dad," she said, her expression tentative. She glanced away. "I feel like my soul has been tarnished," she said. She "needed boundaries."[75]

In 2014, in her role as president of her own company, Beyoncé joined with Facebook executive Sheryl Sandberg and former secretary of state Condoleezza Rice in a Girl Scout campaign to ban "bossy," a label sometimes used to disparage girls and discourage them from exerting leadership. The internet video featured prominent women explaining how they had been told to act more demurely as children. It gave Beyoncé the last word. "I'm not bossy," she stated, "I'm the boss." That same year, she penned an essay for the opening pages of a report on the status of women compiled by Maria Shriver, President Kennedy's niece. "We need to stop buying into the myth about gender equality," Beyoncé wrote. It had not yet been accomplished. "We have to teach our boys the rules of equality and respect so that, as they grow up," she emphasized, "gender equality becomes a natural way of life."[76]

The next year, Beyoncé faced a personal crisis that forced her to do precisely that.

Harassment: Unsafe at Work

Muriel Siebert had made enough money to start her own company, but most women who benefited from new career choices worked for someone else. The law of the land now prohibited job discrimination, something that would have wowed Ann Marie Riebe, but the integration of women into the workplace proved tricky. Some men retaliated in ways both subtle and obvious.

The federal government issued its first set of guidelines defining workplace harassment in the 1980s. The problem gained notoriety in the 1990s as a result of Bill Clinton's extramarital affairs, Senator Bob Packwood's resignation after groping female employees, and a scandal that erupted when the US Navy was exposed for hazing rituals that included assaults on female sailors. Yet the new laws remained weakly enforced. Celebrity and wealth shielded some of the worst offenders. Women who reported assaults often found themselves socially ostracized and barred from further employment.[77]

Sexual harassment on the job burned like a low-grade fever until the second decade of the new millennium. That's when a rash of cases ignited a movement known as #MeToo, spurred by Hollywood actresses who thought that, with attitudes shifting, they might fight abuse without becoming pariahs. Republicans and Democrats found themselves united on the issue. The turnaround of opinion was rapid. Within little more than a year it came to seem abnormal, rather than normal, for a powerful man to demand sexual favors.

With poetic justice, a former Miss America helped touch off this newest wave of protest. Gretchen Carlson had a sturdy platform from which to withstand the ensuing misogynistic backlash. Accusations of radicalism or personal disappointment did not stick easily. Carlson, a registered independent with conservative views and a Fox News anchor, took on Roger Ailes, the chair and CEO of Fox News, not knowing whose career would fall first. Megyn Kelly, another anchor, rallied "an underground army of women" in support.[78]

Gretchen Carlson was born in 1966 and grew up in Anoka, Minnesota. (Anoka was also the hometown of public-radio host Garrison Keillor, a genial humorist who made the modest lifestyle of its Scandinavian American settlers famous—until he became infamous in the wake of #MeToo.) Gretchen's family blended liberal and conservative viewpoints. Her progressive grandfather, a Lutheran preacher, had a profound influence on her, as did her Republican grandmother. Gretchen grew up with a deep religious faith. "The church was a second home to me," she wrote in *Getting Real,* the autobiography published a year before she herself got real with the American public.[79]

When she turned six, the energetic, competitive child—short for her age—begged for piano lessons. An instructor examined her small hands and suggested violin. Gretchen fell in love the moment she slid her fingers down the strings. "It felt familiar and right to me," she later wrote, "a way to express my personality and emotions . . . that I could control." Her aptitude was apparent. Gretchen became a student of the state's top violin instructor at age seven. At ten, she was selected to perform for the great violinist Isaac Stern. At eleven, she won an orchestra seat in the Aspen Music Festival. But the pace was grueling. As she approached college, she turned down a Julliard scholarship and escaped to Stanford.[80]

During a junior year abroad at Oxford, Gretchen received a call from her mother suggesting that she enter the Miss America pageant. First prize meant a $30,000 scholarship. The director had announced a campaign to rehabilitate the old institution, long criticized by feminists. The next winner would be a "socially responsible achiever whose message to women all over the world is that in American society a woman can do or be anything she wants." Gretchen liked that idea.[81]

She took a one-year leave from Stanford to prepare. The dean complained that it was "absolutely the most ridiculous thing" she had ever heard, but approved the request. Gretchen attacked her goal with ferocity, exercising, studying, and practicing violin eight hours a day. She avoided talking about the pageant, aware that many considered it "a crass objectification of women." Eighty thousand women competed each year. According to the statistics, Miss America was tall, thin, and intellectually bland. Gretchen was only five foot three. One of the judges later wrote that he considered the devout contestant, at 108 pounds, a "Miss Piggy" who was far too much of a "God-Clutcher" to win. But Gretchen placed her faith in the violin. Talent counted for the greatest number of points. In September 1988, she won with a bravura classical performance.[82]

Gretchen spent the next year fulfilling her public relations duties and, in her own mind, blowing up stereotypes. As she wrote in 1989 for *Parade* magazine, the experience strengthened her love of the country and its values. She wanted to inspire Americans with a new ideal of female accomplishment, one symbolized by "talent and professional aspirations." No woman should be "just a body."[83]

Gretchen returned to Stanford with a new career goal: broadcast journalism. She took a class in Feminist Studies and wrote about the objectification of Miss America. The professor gave her an "A" and made no comment on the paper, perhaps unsure whether to applaud or criticize. Finding a job after graduation proved challenging. The pageant title did not impress most employers, who assumed she must be dumb despite graduating summa cum laude. Those it did impress were worse. One New York executive grabbed her in the back of a limousine and forced his tongue down her throat. In Los Angeles, another shoved her head into his crotch. She was humiliated, but worried that no one would believe her if she reported the incidents.[84]

These traumatic experiences made her wonder, "How many other women had this happened to? And if we all said nothing, what does that mean?" She felt ashamed and powerless. The two "high-profile predators," as she later called them, seemed "just too powerful" to challenge. She finally got a break when the manager of a station a thousand miles from home agreed to watch her tape. He judged her on the basis of talent and offered her a job. Soon she was one of his star reporters.[85]

When she was alone with a cameraman one day, returning from a remote rural location, he told her he liked grazing his hand against her breasts whenever he attached microphones. She felt terrified, and sick at being thought responsible. Worried for her job, she did not report the incident. But the news director sensed that she was upset and she confided in him. The cameraman was let go.

A woman in the public eye easily became a target in a way that few men experienced. Gretchen became terrified when a stalker mailed her an engagement ring, told the police they were a couple, and violated restraining orders. She took a job in another state partly to evade him, and continued her professional climb.

Some of the hazards she encountered affected few women, but in many ways her experience was common. A study of federal employees between 1989 and 1990 found that 42 percent of women had experienced some form of sexual harassment in the preceding twenty-four months. A 1991 study by the National Council for Research on Women estimated that half of all female workers in both the public and private sectors would have to fend off sexual advances at some point in their career. Corporations started developing guidelines to avoid lawsuits for negligence, and a federal circuit court ruled in 1993 that sexual harassment must be evaluated on the basis of how a "reasonable woman," not a man, would assess the threat.[86]

Yet harassment failed to subside. A 2016 *Harvard Business Review* report found that three-quarters of women interviewed had experienced putdowns or advances. In especially "masculine" work cultures, some men used "subjugation of women as a way to relate to other men and prove their masculinity, while reinforcing women's lower status," researchers found. Alpha males treated women as spoils in their wars against one another, bragging about how many they had had. Women who worked in construction or high tech reported the highest rates of harassment. Service occupations could also be hazardous. A Canadian study found that nurses suffered "more acts of violence than police officers or prison guards."[87]

In 1997, Gretchen Carlson married a sports agent who supported her career and shared the work of parenting. They moved to New York from Ohio when Gretchen landed a job as a correspondent with CBS, producing stories for the *Evening News with Dan Rather.* On September 11, 2001, after terrorists flew planes into the World Trade Center, Gretchen proved her mettle when, on assignment from CBS, she braved the burning rubble, standing in front of the ruins and inhaling fumes. Her impressed bosses eventually gave her an anchor slot on their Saturday *Early Show.* In 2006, she finally won her dream job: host of a daily news program. The new boss encouraged her to talk on camera about being Miss America. CBS had deleted it from her résumé, but Roger Ailes of Fox News liked the title.[88]

Ailes had been a media adviser to Republican candidates since Richard Nixon, and head of Fox since 1996. Emphasizing opinion over facts, he had cultivated a profitable fan base by stoking an us-versus-them mentality. A master of symbols, he titled the company website "Fox Nation," equating the country with his own television network. He claimed red, white, and blue as his colors, and patriotism as his brand. To Ailes, politics was a game of capture the flag.

Gretchen soon learned that he also nurtured a sexist work culture. Ailes had a policy of settling harassment lawsuits by paying off victims. He barred female reporters from wearing trousers and ordered glass-topped tables so viewers could ogle their legs. Male commentators bantered on air about the pushiness of modern dames. In 2014, when Fox anchor Kimberly Guilfoyle reported that the first female fighter pilot from United Arab Emirates had executed an important bombing mission in a jet named "Lady Liberty," her two co-hosts smirked. One joked that after the pilot landed her jet, "she couldn't park it." The other asked if the mission meant Emirates now had "boobs on the ground." Nonplussed, Guilfoyle barely objected.[89]

Gretchen Carlson had a similar moment when Brian Kilmeade, one of her two co-hosts, mocked the US Navy Band for admitting female musicians. "Women are everywhere now," he complained with a smile on live television in 2012. "We're letting them play golf and tennis now. It's out of control." But Gretchen was fed up with her co-anchors' sexist digs, including continual on-air references to her as "hot," "a babe," and "a skirt." Her other co-host, Steve Doocy, sometimes pulled on her arm to quiet her, a controlling gesture inconceivable toward another man. This time, in

2012, the veteran journalist with more hard news experience than either of her co-hosts stood up when Kilmeade called women "out of control" and, still smiling, walked off the set.[90]

Her protest walked the line between playful and serious. A Fox News anchor could not afford to look like an angry feminist. The label was an electric fence around women at the network. Anyone who got too close risked being burned. Employees' fear of being called a feminist helped foil resistance to what one producer later called the "sexualized nature" of the newsroom.[91]

Gretchen Carlson complained privately to Ailes, meeting with him at least half a dozen times to discuss her co-hosts. Ailes told her to stop being a "man hater" and learn how to "get along with the boys." A year after her walkout, he demoted her to a mid-afternoon show at reduced pay. For years he had propositioned her sexually. He now told her that her problems would go away if she would just yield. His advance did not surprise her. She had long deflected such moves. But in 2014, she began plotting a counterattack.[92]

Gretchen knew that Ailes used video cameras to surveille employees. Famously suspicious, Ailes had a double door on his office and kept handguns in the desk. She decided to use her iPhone to record their conversations in his inner sanctum. For more than a year, she stealthily captured the ugly comments. On one occasion he told her, "I think you and I should have had a sexual relationship a long time ago, and then you'd be good and better and I'd be good and better." Another time he wheedled, "I'm sure you can do sweet nothings when you want to."[93]

Roger Ailes had worked in television since the 1960s. He justified his predatory behavior as normal by telling prospects, "That's how all these men in media and politics work." When women objected, he made threats like "No girls get a job here unless they're cooperative." He pulled out his genitals in front of one sixteen-year-old and told her, "Kiss them." He ordered another woman to don a garter belt and videotaped the private fashion show to blackmail her. He told some they had to sexually service his friends, too. As a political consultant, he told a woman applying for a job with the Republican National Committee, "If you want to play with the big boys you have to lay with the big boys." When questioned about one woman who reported his abuse, Ailes dismissed her as a "militant feminist."[94]

Gretchen began taping Ailes at around the same time she wrote her autobiography. In *Getting Real* she discussed the harassment she had suffered as a young woman, and her regret about not reporting it, but she made no mention of Ailes's behavior. Instead, she described her boss as "sharp and inscrutable" and claimed they had a "real connection." She may have praised him to allay his paranoia while gathering evidence. Regardless, he grew tired of her stalling and declined to renew her contract. She lost her job on June 23, 2016.[95]

Gretchen consulted lawyers who specialized in sexual harassment, a growing branch of the law. They advised her that she could not sue for employment discrimination because of a clause, common in contracts, that required arbitration. Ailes had used such clauses to suppress sexual harassment complaints against Bill O'Reilly, the network's biggest star. The attorneys suggested that she sue Roger Ailes personally once he gave her cause. On July 6, 2016, two weeks after her contract was cancelled, Gretchen Carlson nervously did what no one had done before. At the risk of not working in television ever again, she pushed Ailes's abuse into the open without realizing that she was about to catch a turning tide.

Opposition to rape and sexual harassment had swelled. Two years before, allegations against Bill Cosby finally undid a defense that the actor had maintained successfully since the 1960s, despite allegedly drugging and raping nearly fifty women, many of whom came to him for jobs. Black comedian Hannibal Buress broke the logjam by denouncing the senior actor who had perfected the guise of righteous citizen.

In California, where Cosby worked, the legislature responded in 2016 by eliminating the ten-year statute of limitations on rape. A number of other states doubled or tripled the amount of time victims had to report. The same week, due to yet another high-profile case, California redefined sexual assault on an unconscious person as forcible rape. Previously, the law did not define that crime as violent, since assaulting a drugged individual required no force.[96]

The 2016 presidential campaign also helped Gretchen's case. For the first time since women got the vote, one of their number had scored the nomination of a major party. A self-described feminist, Hillary Clinton ran against a man who liked to brag about his sexual prowess. The contrast between them roiled sentiment nationwide.

Donald Trump presented himself as a man of the people. He appealed to an anti-government strain in American culture as old as the Whiskey Rebellion of 1794, when men who thought they were defending the nation's values threatened George Washington's government with violence. Trump reveled in defamation, and his insults attracted voters who equated aggression with honesty, a confusion encouraged by Fox News. The candidate ridiculed women who questioned him, and adopted the persona of a tough guy willing to speak truths that weaker men avoided out of political correctness. As he told *Rolling Stone* about Republican rival Carly Fiorina, "She's a woman and I'm not s'posedta say bad things." Trump pointed with mock horror to her image. But, "*Look* at that face!" he told the reporter. "Would anyone *vote* for that?"[97]

The Republican candidate's behavior was unusual. No candidate had ever openly insulted women. Politicians historically had taken the opposite tack of gentlemanly politeness, assuming that public discourse was supposed to be civil. No one could altogether explain why the reverse approach worked for Trump, but then no one had tried it—until Fox News popularized belligerence.

Public discomfort at Trump's violation of social norms became acute the month before Gretchen Carlson filed her lawsuit. In May 2016, sexual harassment allegations surfaced when the *New York Times* published a research piece on Trump's propensity to kiss strangers on the lips, grope women he met, shame Miss USA contestants about their weight, and praise his daughter's "hotness." Fox News threw cold water on the allegations. Celebrity host Bill O'Reilly targeted *Times* female reporter Megan Twohey, who had co-written the article with a male colleague. "The problem," O'Reilly told viewers, "is Megan Twohey is a feminist."[98]

Feminist-baiting worked so well that O'Reilly and many others, including Roger Ailes, failed to anticipate that at least some women at Fox were angry enough to brave the label and risk their livelihood. Megyn Kelly, a lawyer turned journalist and the star of her own evening show, became the key mover. Kelly recognized Roger Ailes's modus operandi as she read the charges that Gretchen had filed. The boss had propositioned her, too, ten years earlier. She had wondered at the time if Ailes was a serial abuser, he was "so brazen about it," but a supervisor swore that no one else had complained. Kelly had since met only one other victim, though she had promised herself she would come forward if she learned of others. Even so, she hesitated, having recently tangled with another bully.[99]

As one of the anchors of a presidential debate in the fall of 2015, Megyn Kelly had asked Donald Trump about his descriptions of women as "fat pigs, dogs, slobs, and disgusting animals." Trump deflected her question, then repaid her that night by unleashing a barrage of comments on Twitter about "#CrazyMegyn." The media spread the story, and far right outlets like Breitbart would not let it go. Trump later alleged that Kelly had "blood coming out of her *wherever*" during the debate, implying that she was menstruating and thus mentally unstable, a diagnosis harkening back to Elizabeth Packard's days in the asylum.[100]

Trump's tweets unleashed his most ardent fans. For months, his supporters dished Kelly a relentless diet of "You're a real cunt," "Fuck off, you slut," and "Twisted bitch." The presidential candidate retweeted calls for violence: "We can gut her," read one. The abuse stopped only after Kelly solicited a personal interview with Trump. He agreed, perhaps calculating the value of a primetime slot watched by millions eager to see a grudge match. Kelly steeled her nerves, but when she stepped into his New York office, Trump opened his arms for a hug. He had decided the torture was over. He gave a pleasant interview and stopped harassing her online.[101]

Kelly now faced another potential ordeal. Ailes was pressuring everyone in the company to declare that he was not an abuser. But once a lawyer, always a lawyer—Megyn Kelly refused to tell a lie she might have to repeat in court. She remained quiet even as Ailes planted stories that she was trying to improve her brand with "a feminist moment." His power seemed impregnable.[102]

Kelly had discussed feminism publicly on earlier occasions, distancing herself from the term. Earlier that year she had explained to television host Stephen Colbert that she felt it had been "co-opted by some people who don't want you in their club unless you see certain women's issues the way they see them." She admired the accomplishments of the second wave, she said, but did not think of herself as a feminist. Some of Colbert's fans booed. Kelly later protested, "We need more women in this sisterhood tent, not less. Who gives a damn what label we use so long as we are living a life that supports women?"[103]

One morning, Megyn Kelly looked at her daughter, age four, playing outside. As she gazed out the window, she realized her daughter deserved a mother who would say, "This man will not do this to another woman at Fox News. Ever." She called the other person whom Ailes had harassed, and they secretly spread the word to others who might have had a similar experience. Cautiously, they built what Kelly called "an underground army of women." Fox employees contacted her to report that it had happened to them. She dialed the owner of the company, Lachlan Murdoch, to tell him she had something to say.[104]

Unemployed, Gretchen Carlson watched from the sidelines in disbelief. Two weeks after she filed suit, Roger Ailes lost his career. The company issued her an apology and a check for $20 million. They gave him a severance package of $40 million. The outcome was far from equitable. Both forfeited their jobs, but he got twice the payout.

Yet partial victories can be transformative. The so-called Most Powerful Man in News had suffered a rebuke. The precedent stunned onlookers. As one reporter noted, "Giants, we learned, actually *could* fall." The next year, in 2017, *New York Times* reporter Megan Twohey published another exposé, this time about a liberal mogul. Allegations of rape against filmmaker Harvey Weinstein, for which he was later sentenced to prison, sparked the #MeToo Movement. The spontaneous internet campaign began when actress Alyssa Milano tweeted a phrase that community activist Tarana Burke had coined years earlier to encourage women to report assault. Within twelve months, more than two hundred prominent men (and three women) across the nation had been discharged for harassment.[105]

Social media thrives on snap judgments, and some Americans worried that vigilantism would overtake due process. The nation had wrestled with mob mentalities since its founding, and no form of lynching was a credit to democracy. Denunciations of men for awkward romantic passes vied with charges of criminal assault for attention on the internet. Political hacks highlighted the misdeeds of those whom they disliked and ignored the offenses of their favorites. Yet the accused had rights. Companies weighed the potential for wrongful termination lawsuits before picking sides. And, undeniably, far fewer victims came forward than the actual number who had been harmed.

To Gretchen Carlson, the floodgates seemed to open on her doorstep. A deluge of email arrived from women. They came from "virtually every profession and walk of life," she noted, and they reminded her how inconsolable she had been the first time a man assaulted her. Women now had jobs everywhere, but were not completely safe anywhere. She published the self-help book *Be Fierce,* campaigned against arbitration clauses that voided employees' rights, and testified to the US Congress. When she became chair of the Miss America Organization in 2018, the pageant rebranded itself as "Miss America 2.0" and dropped the swimsuit competition.[106]

Gretchen Carlson once wrote that although the National Organization for Women "never invited me to play on their team . . . no one feels as strongly as I do about equality for women." Her comment alluded to a possessiveness on the Left that could be as intense as the aversion on the Right. Gretchen Carlson struggled for street cred with some activists. Even so, few could deny that this particular beauty queen had been a warrior for women.[107]

Man's Redemption

Beyoncé Knowles and Jay-Z Carter kept their 2008 wedding ceremony small. Her mother and his grandmother cooked for forty guests. The only over-the-top opulence consisted of sixty thousand white orchids flown in from Thailand and draped throughout Jay-Z's Manhattan apartment. The couple did not announce their union for six months, to shield their sacred vows from the idly curious.

Critics had long accused feminists of disliking marriage. Some did, but most did not. Journalist Evette Dionne noted that for "Black women, who were once forbidden from getting hitched in America, a union can be an act of agency." Marriage was a symbol of freedom. Philosopher Lindsey Stewart pointed out that Black artists often felt pressured to limit their repertoire to protest and tragedy, but a person who found love was a winner, not a loser. Stewart observed that Harriet Jacobs had been the first Black writer to identify the "kinship between sexual love and freedom." Liberty meant the pursuit of happiness.[108]

For Beyoncé Knowles-Carter, marriage expressed her faith in the possibility of an equal commitment between women and men. She had ended the relationship with her first boyfriend over his infidelity. While Jay-Z had had many liaisons before marriage, she believed him when he promised to cherish her alone.

To all appearances, they had a perfect marriage. Beyoncé miscarried their first baby, but she gave birth in 2012 to a little girl. She reported that they both changed diapers, and Jay-Z agreed that the most important part of parenting was to spend time with one's children. Nannies filled in when the parents worked. Together, they were worth a billion dollars, roughly half her earnings and half his. Then, before their daughter's second birthday, a security camera in a hotel elevator captured a video, leaked to the press, that spelled trouble. The couple was leaving a benefit for

New York's Metropolitan Museum along with Beyoncé's sister. Jay-Z sported a white tuxedo, Beyoncé a floor-length Givenchy ballgown. Solange wore a short peach tunic that proved the more practical choice.[109]

When the elevator doors closed, Solange confronted Jay-Z. Whatever he said in response did not appease her. In the silent footage, she lobbed a punch at her brother-in-law, who deflected the blow. A bodyguard pulled Solange away, but she wriggled free and punched again. When the bodyguard lifted the twenty-six-year-old off her feet, pinning her arms, she kicked with her feet. Beyoncé looked on, pulling the hem of her beaded gown away from the brawl while Jay-Z dodged Solange's peach stilettos. When the doors opened, television cameras greeted the composed trio as they exited. Solange's face was a stoic mask. Beyoncé smiled faintly. Jay-Z followed the women toward a limousine, but the bodyguard directed him to another vehicle.[110]

The footage soon became public, and the family issued a short response to the "unfortunate incident" that read, "Jay and Solange each assume their share of responsibility for what happened." The statement did not disclose the cause of the fight, other than "families have problems and we're no different."[111]

The closest thing the world got to an explanation came two years later. In May 2016, Beyoncé released her sixth album, *Lemonade.* The title evoked the old proverb that when life gives you lemons, make lemonade. Again, Beyoncé used music as therapy. Should she tell the father of her children to put his things to the left, as in the song "Irreplaceable," or find some way to help them both? In *Lemonade* she chose to put him on trial. The exposure must have been excruciating. Anyone who thinks that reporting an abuser in one's family is easy has never done so.

One song on the album was "Sorry," perhaps the strongest condemnation of a philanderer ever to roll off a woman's pen. The video opens with Beyoncé sitting on a bus with other women who are wearing Yoruba body paint, evoking the universality of her problem. They sway in unison as the singer recites lines adapted from the poetry of Somali British author Warsan Shire:

> So what are you going to say at my funeral, now that
> you have killed me?
> Here lies the body of the love of my life, whose heart I
> broke without a gun to my head

Here lies the mother of my children, both living and
dead.
Rest in peace, my true love, who I took for granted.[112]

Only women appeared in the video, which celebrated female solidarity at the same time as it condemned male disloyalty. Tennis champion Serena Williams played the protagonist's companion, looking sternly into the camera as her best girl lolls weakly in a chair. Later, back on the bus and looking stronger, Beyoncé laughs with her companions, telling them to put their "middle fingers up" since "Big homie better grow up."[113]

Neither "Sorry" nor any other song mentioned Jay-Z. Yet the association was explicit. Jay-Z called himself "Big Homie" on his own records. The lyrics referenced commercial products he had famously endorsed, including a cognac that Beyoncé expropriates for her party bus. The album did not simply damn the accused. It showed a path to redemption. Set within the imagery of antebellum slavery, the African diaspora, modern ghettos, and the Black Lives Matter movement, *Lemonade*'s twelve songs progressed from denial to confrontation to forgiveness. One music-streaming service called it "a conceptual project based on every woman's journey of self-knowledge and healing." An entertainment critic described Beyoncé's magnum opus as "complex, mind-boggling, and ethereal." A musicologist dubbed it "a prodigious feminist manifesto."[114]

Lemonade fueled a new academic field calling itself Beyoncé Studies. Professors at Cornell, Rutgers, University of Texas, University of South Carolina, Arizona State, and University of Copenhagen offered classes to accompany books like *The Beyoncé Effect* (2016), *Queen Bey* (2019), *The Lemonade Reader* (2019), and *Beyoncé in the World* (2021). They charted the contributions of a woman who, to them, stood for all the Black female performers long ranked below Black men and white women. They refused to watch her be consigned to the list of those who, in the words of one scholar, had been "overlooked and understudied, and their legacies lauded far too late."[115]

The person who approached *Lemonade* with the greatest seriousness was Jay-Z Carter. A year after his wife's album, he released his own, titled *4:44*. The opening track was "Kill Jay-Z," expressing his determination to squash the insecure false ego that led him to harm his family, friends, and "the baddest girl in the world." The streetwise rapper chided himself, saying, "This 'fuck everybody' attitude ain't natural." In the title song,

"4:44," Jay-Z chronicled the ways in which he had acted selfishly. "I seen the innocence leave your eyes / I still mourn its death," he sang, apologizing not only to her but also "to all the women whom I toyed with your emotions."[116]

Approximately 1.7 million people downloaded Beyoncé's indictment. An even greater number downloaded her husband's act of contrition. Jay-Z discussed his infidelity with the *New York Times* and late-night host David Letterman. He acknowledged the role of therapy in helping him crack the shell of ghetto "toughness" he had acquired as a boy in order to hide his fears. "The hardest thing is seeing pain on someone's face that you caused, and then have to deal with yourself," he admitted. Jay-Z discussed his mother's years in the closet as a lesbian and his relief at her freedom.[117]

The public learned that the couple had used the creative process to work through the trauma, as Beyoncé's last songs on *Lemonade* showed. In "All Night," the penultimate track, the lovers reunite when the female protagonist finds "the truth beneath your lies." She tells him, "I've seen your scars and kissed your crime." She decides to "give you some time to prove that I can trust you again." Love, she believes, can conquer pride.

The internet responded with its usual hyperbole. Some thought Beyoncé should prove her feminism by divorcing her husband. Others praised the singer for not leaving him behind. Carmen Perez, an advocate for troubled children of the type Jay-Z had once been, heralded Beyoncé for modeling "a type of feminism that says, I can both challenge and uplift the men in my community." Other feminists of color, including Mary Church Terrell and Martha Cotera, would have agreed. The challenges they faced were intersectional and the solutions must be, too. It was a model for all women and men, all people, regardless of background.[118]

Beyoncé wrote for *Vogue* in 2018, "I come from a lineage of broken male-female relationships, abuse of power, and mistrust." She added, "Only when I saw that clearly was I able to resolve those conflicts in my own relationship. Connecting to the past and knowing our history makes us both bruised and beautiful."[119]

She took the same attitude toward her country. America was bruised and beautiful, too. For example, one might hold the nation responsible for racism while still loving it, she explained. Her goal was to write songs and invent choreographies "that hopefully will change the nation." It was the next generation's version of patriotic feminism.[120]

Child Abuse: Unsafe at Play

The young women facing the panel of senators in September 2021 had come from four sides of the country to testify: Massachusetts, California, Minnesota, and Texas. They were already famous. Their dazzling smiles and those of other athletes had sold Pepsi cola, Hershey bars, and Wheaties cereal, the supposed breakfast of champions. The shortest was only four feet eight, yet they had stood for the nation. During international games, their team doctor had sexually assaulted each of them. One had been ousted for simply reporting the crime, her Olympic dreams shredded. Simone Biles, McKayla Maroney, Maggie Nichols, and Aly Raisman spoke on behalf of more than five hundred survivors.

Historians note that the modern Olympic Games coincided with the rise of nationalism. Since 1894, athletes had competed as their nations incarnate. That was certainly how the four gymnasts saw themselves. Their victories belonged to America. As McKayla Maroney explained, "My mother, who served in the United States Navy, instilled the importance of patriotism and sacrifice in me. More than anything, I wanted to one day win medals for Team USA." As one of eight gold medalists who had come forward, braving a leap more intimidating than the vault, Maroney sought assurance that her country would fulfill its side of the contract. "Enough is enough!" she said.[121]

Simone Biles expressed another sentiment they shared. "Please bear with me," the winner of twenty-five World Championships said before breaking into tears. Neither she nor her teammates had ever wanted to serve the nation in this way. "To be perfectly honest, I can imagine no place that I would be less comfortable right now than sitting here in front of you."[122]

Complaints against physician Larry Nassar, associate professor at Michigan State University, had accumulated for twenty years. His victims included collegiate athletes and children as young as six. Under the pretense of orthopedic treatment, Nassar digitally penetrated the vaginas and anuses of hundreds of Olympic aspirants and winners. He used their dearest hopes against them: they must submit for their own good, he implied, and if uncomfortable, they had only their own ambition to blame. Nasser appropriated their bodies, and then coaches told the girls to go out and smile for the judges. As Bessel van der Kolk shows in *The Body Keeps the Score,* trauma of this sort creates devastating, long-term damage.[123]

In 1996 Nassar began a second job for USA Gymnastics, the organization responsible for fielding athletes to international games. Olympic officials ignored allegations against the personable physician. Michigan State did, too. That began to change in 2015, the same year that Marie's conviction for false reporting came to light and Gretchen Carlson began assembling her evidence against Roger Ailes. A storm was brewing.

In June 2015, at the Olympic training camp run by Béla and Márta Károlyi, defectors from Romanian communism, seventeen-year-old Maggie Nichols privately asked her teammate Aly Raisman if the doctor who treated them daily put his fingers in her vagina too. Raisman, winner of three gold medals, confirmed that he did. It was the first time either had articulated an experience that haunted them both. A female coach overheard the conversation and reported it to her superior, who reported it to Steve Penny, president of USA Gymnastics. Maggie Nichols's mother contacted Penny directly, triggering the first formal investigation. Olympic policy was to ignore third-party allegations of child abuse without signed parental complaints.

Steve Penny had started in marketing. As he rose in the organization, he parlayed women's gymnastics into one of the US Olympic Committee's most valuable franchises. Unlike many countries, the United States gave no funds to its national teams; instead they raised money through corporate sponsorships. Cute gold medalists were a hot seller. Upon learning of Maggie Nichols's and Aly Raisman's allegations, Penny engaged an attorney to interview the young women, but he waited five weeks before reporting charges that might tarnish USA Gymnastics' pristine image. In July 2015, Penny finally contacted the Indianapolis field office of the FBI. He did not alert local police as required under new laws.

Over the next thirteen months, Maggie Nichols waited for the FBI to call. From a small suburb of Minneapolis, the outgoing brunette had studied gymnastics since age three. Nothing made her happier. As Maggie later told the Senate, "Since I was a child, I always had the dream of competing for my country in the World Championships and Olympic Games." In the months after reporting the abuse, she won a silver medal at the US National Championships, making her second only to Olympic-phenom Simone Biles.[124]

Yet she and her parents sensed a mood shift in the organization. When Maggie showed up to participate in a Hershey commercial with Simone,

Steve Penny phoned at the last minute to say that only Simone should be photographed. When Maggie's mother and father arrived at the July 2016 Olympic tryouts, a year after reporting Nassar's assault, they found that no one had reserved seats for them in the massive arena. Maggie still felt sure of making the team, despite recent knee surgery. In a purple and pink leotard sprinkled with silver glitter, she placed sixth. Steve Penny, however, announced to the roaring crowd of twenty thousand that only the top five would go to the games in Rio de Janeiro—then he invited three alternates who ranked below Maggie to accompany them.

Maggie Nichols did not know that the FBI had decided not to call her. Steve Penny had invited the agent in charge to discuss employment opportunities at USA Gymnastics over beer. Another agent met with Penny to discuss whether or not the crime fell within his geographic jurisdiction, and concluded it did not. Neither man reported the allegations to local authorities or FBI offices in relevant states. Maggie's parents did not call the police themselves because Steve Penny told them that doing so would jeopardize the FBI investigation.[125]

In the meantime, Penny allowed Larry Nassar to retire without a blemish on his record. While still employed by Michigan State University, Nassar assaulted at least seventy more girls over the next year. He counted on shame to keep them quiet. Nassar's abuse might never have come to light but for the courage of two other young women and the curiosity of a third.[126]

The year after Maggie Nichols reported Nassar, bronze-medalist Jamie Dantzscher, then retired from competitive gymnastics, approached a Los Angeles attorney who had won a lawsuit on behalf of boys abused by a priest. Nassar had assaulted Jamie from the age of twelve. The Sydney games in 2000 were one of countless occasions "all over the world." Heartsick, she "wasn't proud to be an Olympian." The Mormon athlete asked her attorney to file her plea in the spring of 2016 under the pseudonym "JD Doe."[127]

In Indianapolis, another young woman, a journalist, became interested in why schoolteachers remained slow to report child abuse. In March 2016 she got a tip about USA Gymnastics in Georgia. Marisa Kwiatkowski flew across the country that very night to retrieve court records. Reviewing them, she noticed that the organization shelved complaints against coaches unless a gymnast put them in writing. It was rare for traumatized children to report assault, which was why law required reporting by educators. USA Gymnastics made transparency even more unlikely by asking youngsters to risk their athletic careers. Kwiatkowski and two male colleagues at the *Indianapolis Star* began a four-month investigation. On the eve of the Rio Olympics, they published an article that was syndicated throughout the *USA Today* network.

Rachael Denhollander, a lawyer and former gymnast in Louisville, Kentucky, glimpsed the article on the internet. Larry Nassar had abused her in front of her own mother, cloaking his hand under a towel while pretending the medical procedure was normal. The embarrassed fifteen-year-old did not realize her mother could not see around the physician, who had positioned himself between them.

The day after reading the article, Denhollander emailed the Indiana journalists. "I have seen little hope that any light would be shed by coming forward, so I have remained quiet, " she wrote. "If there is a possibility that is changing, I will come forward as publicly as necessary." She knew that women who reported abuse "are mocked, they are questioned, they are blamed," as she told one reporter, "and that does incredible damage to the healing process." Sports fans might be angry that she had not kept quiet for the sake of the team. Athletes—and women—were supposed to put themselves last. But the *Star* convinced her she would not be alone. Rachael Denhollander became the first victim to call the police.[128]

She and the *Star* triggered a media blitz that brought the abuse to light. Female athletes across the nation corroborated the accusations, including Maggie Nichols and her teammates. At Nassar's trial in 2018, over one hundred gymnasts spoke, led by Rachael Denhollander, who asked the court, "How much is a little girl worth?" The court sentenced Nassar to three hundred years in prison based on testimony delivered with the fearlessness of Olympians.[129]

US marshals arrested Steve Penny that same year on felony charges of tampering with evidence. His case remained pending three years later, in 2021. Sitting in the Senate hearing room that fall, Simone Biles, McKayla Maroney, Maggie Nichols, and Aly Raisman wanted to know why. Government must be held accountable. "If we don't do all we can," Raisman warned, "we are deluding ourselves if we think other children will be spared the institutionalized tolerance and normalization of abuse that I, and so many, had to endure." Feminists had said it for years. Citizens must pull together when they recognize that their homeland has failed its people. Not to condemn, but to redeem.[130]

Members of the Judiciary Committee, half Democrats and half Republicans, were at odds over many issues, but they came together on behalf of the gymnasts. McKayla Maroney pointed out that the US Senate was "the only powerful institution that, from the beginning, has fought for us, rather than against us." Meanwhile, the athletes continued to push. Led by Rachael Denhollander, they won a $380 million settlement three months later from USA Gymnastics on behalf of five hundred survivors.[131]

Justice was piecemeal, however, as always. In 2022, a Texas district attorney dismissed the charges against Steve Penny for insufficient evidence. The FBI announced two months later that no agent would be charged with a crime, even though the US Office of the Inspector General identified multiple policy violations by the Indianapolis field office. Instead, one agent was fired, and another allowed to retire. In response, the gymnasts filed suit against the FBI this time, considering it a duty to hold the nation they loved accountable.[132]

+++

ANITA HILL'S TREATMENT by the US Senate helped to spark a third wave of feminism with an increasingly diverse cast of characters. By the time of the #MeToo Movement in 2017, some were calling for a fourth wave, others a fifth. One group of scholars, wondering if the metaphor was finally spent, argued against any "permanent waves." Feminism was no longer at sea but part of the American homeland. It had also, as Adichie reminded readers, become truly global.[133]

Other phenomena shaped the landscape, too. The election of a Black man as president of the United States in 2008, and of a multiracial woman as vice president in 2020, showed that the nation had narrowed the gap between its goals and practices. Yet the same elections provoked backlash, and conservatism gained followers as well. Economic uncertainty, global warming, internet bullying, political violence, racial conflict, rampant shootings, dystopian memes, and a global pandemic that compelled many working women to resume full-time childcare responsibilities made it hard for some to believe the nation had improved at all. One-fifth of all mothers raised children alone. One-third of them received no child support. Their families suffered the nation's highest poverty rate. Among Native single mothers, 43 percent struggled to feed their children. The United States remained the only member of the thirty-eight-nation Organization for Economic Cooperation and Development (OECD) that failed to provide paid maternal leave by law.[134]

Decades must pass before any historian can impartially assess the early twenty-first century. The country had changed to the point that a Black feminist artist was one of its most respected cultural icons. With better prosecution of sex crimes, reformers hoped to strengthen justice. At the same time, in 2022, the Catholic majority on the Supreme Court reversed *Roe v. Wade,* which had allowed women and girls to decide what happens within their own bodies. *Dobbs v. Jackson* guaranteed that many, especially the poor and very young, would endure unwanted pregnancies. Even some hoping to give birth would be harmed. For fear of prosecution under local law, a Texas hospital denied surgery to an expectant mother suffering a miscarriage, though such neglect can lead to infection and sterility. Louisiana denied an abortion to a woman carrying a nonviable fetus that lacked a skull. Notably, states with the most restrictive abortion laws also registered the nation's highest maternal and infant death rates.[135]

No one could know which aspects of progress would be sustained, advanced, or reversed. That is the next chapter, yet to be written.

Epilogue

WHY SUGGEST THAT GENDER EQUALITY can be seen as a patriotic value when many thoughtful readers do not identify with feminism and others do not identify with patriotism? The main reason is that common values can unite a diverse people. If this book helps Americans to agree that, despite divisions, they collectively aspire to advance the nation, and that equality between men and women helps them do so, it will have served its purpose.

Men were the first to challenge patriarchal systems of government in which one adult male, whether pope, emperor, or king, ruled everyone else. On behalf of the Continental Congress, a slaveowner who had history breathing down his neck—who knew that justice "cannot sleep forever"—penned the phrase, "We hold these truths to be self-evident, that all men are created equal." Thomas Jefferson and his generation established the first large, non-aristocratic republic. This sparked demands for women's rights from Abigail Adams, Charles Brockden Brown, and Judith Sargent Murray, as well as France's Olympe de Gouges and England's Mary

Wollstonecraft, who asserted that women were as fully human as men, and deserved the same natural rights.

Feminists sought to implement this idea. Progress was slow in the moment, but rapid compared with earlier millennia. Women entered secondary schools, formed benevolent organizations, spoke publicly on behalf of the enslaved, lobbied for the right to own property, petitioned to protect mental patients, and obtained the vote. They knitted the nation's safety net, overturned laws prohibiting birth control, won inclusion in the US Constitution, entered the economy on a competitive basis, claimed the freedom to express their sexuality, and demanded equal protection under the law.

They made America what it is. Educated women who became schoolteachers advanced the mass literacy that underwrote the Industrial Revolution. Susan B. Anthony paved the way for the Thirteenth Amendment outlawing slavery. Frances Perkins strengthened families through Social Security and unemployment insurance. Scholars cannot account for US history without these feminists—or for the economic growth of the twentieth century without the tripling of women's participation in the labor force. Or for the sixties without Pauli Murray, Ruth Bader Ginsburg, and Martha Cotera. Or for the rise of the New Right without Phyllis Schlafly. Feminism is not incidental to American history. It has been a powerful driver.

A few individuals devoted themselves to the cause full-time, but not most. Some activists today claim that genuine feminism is always and only "a conscious choice to be part of a movement" that involves a "commitment as well to intersectionality." If this definition were true, few individuals in US history could be considered feminists. Scholars would be unable to explain how women acquired property rights or won the ballot.[1]

In fact, the great majority of people who advanced gender equality were not activists. They were average Americans, women and men, who latched onto egalitarian sentiments. They were parents who sent their daughters to John Poor's Young Ladies Academy of Philadelphia. They were parishioners who crowded into churches to hear the Grimké sisters. They were farmwives who signed petitions for the Thirteenth Amendment, and congressmen who voted for the Susan B. Anthony bill. They were governors and presidents who invited women into their administrations. They were patriots who joined the armed forces in World Wars I and II.

They were girls who donned trousers, bikinis, and spacesuits. They included Republicans, Democrats, Progressives, Conservatives, Socialists, and Libertarians.

Orthodox factions within most world religions bucked the trend, reinforcing patriarchal customs even as government chipped away at patriarchal statutes. Women within them accepted the dogma that submission was ordained by God and yielded greater rewards than self-assertion. They believed that freedom undermined security and, ignoring the tug of democracy, covered their hair, deferred to their husbands, and eschewed birth control. In 2020, conservative writer Matthew Cochran praised religious women like Amy Coney Barrett, Ruth Bader Ginsburg's replacement on the court, who would still "submit to their husbands with joy."[2]

Yet these sects were in the minority. Patriarchy as a coherent, unquestioned set of laws and practices no longer existed, and the vast majority of citizens aspired to gender equality, with 91 percent of Americans in 2020 considering equality ideal. They modified their behavior to approximate it, in ways large and small. The majority of heterosexual couples called a fair division of household chores "very important" for a successful marriage, though most fell short of the goal. Fathers and mothers both increased the number of hours they spent with children between 1990 and 2015, with fathers doubling theirs, but mothers still averaging the most time overall. Gay and lesbian couples generally divided domestic chores more evenly, though the arrival of children typically led one person to shoulder greater responsibility. Research on transgender adults is still so new that the first surveys did not appear until 2020, revealing that approximately 19 percent had children. Nationwide, women made approximately eighty-one cents for every dollar a man earned in 2020, triple the rate of 1815, when women earned twenty-eight cents to a dollar. The pay gap was minimal for entry-level jobs, but widened as professionals with family responsibilities fell behind colleagues with none. In 2020, women held a quarter of seats in Congress, compared with zero a century earlier.[3]

Feminism has become a global phenomenon over the past two centuries, though gender equity varies widely by region. In 2021, the United States ranked twenty-first out of 170 countries on a number of measures, including female representation in government. (Scandinavian countries generally scored highest.) The United States also lagged in health care and maternity leave, and provided less support for childcare than thirty-nine other nations, a disparity compounded by the COVID-19 pandemic. It took another step away from the practice of most democratic nations when the Supreme Court invalidated *Roe v. Wade* and opened the door to restrictions on birth-control devices and medications.[4]

Viewed from the opposite angle, the United States outperformed 149 countries. In some, conditions remained as dismal as they had been in America hundreds of years earlier. One of the most recognizable faces of the century was Malala Yousafzai, a Pakistani who braved death threats to secure the right to learn. For her belief that girls should be able to attend secondary school, the Taliban shot the fifteen-year-old in the head. Malala recovered, and accepted the Nobel Peace Prize in 2014, but many girls still struggle for access to education despite the fact that for each year they attend school, infant mortality declines by 5 percent. Worldwide, girls who attend an additional three years enhance their children's survival rate by 18 percent. In the United States, infant mortality has fallen least wherever high school completion rates are low and teenage pregnancy common, particularly in the South.[5]

The situation for women tends to worsen whenever democratic governance suffers a setback. Political scientists have shown that women's rights typically decline when governments become more authoritarian. China's retreat from liberalism under President Xi Jinping prompted declines in women's pay. Under President Vladimir Putin, Russia repealed laws against wife beating. Bans against female genital mutilation, child marriage, and the killing of wives for adultery fell across the Middle East after the Islamic Revolution of 1979. History shows that any government can fail if subjected to enough pressure, so women have a particular stake in defending the democratic systems that have long favored them.[6]

Conditions within the United States itself vary widely. In 2020, the Georgetown Institute for Women, Peace, and Security found that on measures of inclusion, safety, and justice, women enjoyed circumstances four times more favorable in top-ranked Massachusetts than bottom-tier Louisiana. Nationwide, white women earned more college degrees, received better wages, and suffered less infant and maternal mortality than did women of color. Perhaps the gravest problem for all women remained the absence of affordable, high-quality daycare. The United States has not reckoned with the economic fact that both mothers and fathers now routinely work outside the home, yet someone must still mind the kids, the nation's only claim to a future.[7]

Given the country's vast territory, bifurcated sovereignty, religious heterogeneity, and record of ethnic strife, such deficits are unsurprising. The more remarkable comparison is with 1776. Some of the nation's ideals flourished more luxuriantly in sunnier global climes, but gender equality nonetheless advanced considerably. Patriotic feminism saved lives and helped citizens reclaim their dignity. Amy Post and Lydia Maria Child gave Harriet Jacobs the chance to document her victory over slavery. Susan B. Anthony rescued Phoebe Phelps from an insane asylum, and Elizabeth Packard rescued herself. Frances Perkins arranged police protection for Southern Black women migrating north, and Progressives in Chicago resuscitated half-frozen Rosa Cavalleri. Pauli Murray devised the argument that Ruth Bader Ginsburg used to win equal protection for women under the Constitution, and William Kunstler's law firm kept Yvonne Swan out of prison.

This book began with the reflection that all of us are born into a unique historical moment. A narrative that touches the present eventually reaches the storyteller, allowing me to give my final reason—more personal but still pertinent—for documenting this history. The lesson of the last decade has been that citizens can advance the nation by being transparent. Learning from them, I concede that feminism saved me, too.

Every person inhabits a time capsule that reveals the remarkable contrast between before and after. Our own lives are the stuff of history, as this book shows. I first recall my mother mentioning the "ancient battle of the sexes" when we lived down a two-mile dirt road in rural Southern California in the early 1960s. She had married my father at sixteen. His mother had married at thirteen. With three beloved brothers and three delightful sisters, I couldn't fathom the significance of her phrase.

The world had a shape I accepted as natural. My father was the highest authority in our family just as the male principal was the highest authority in our school, the male mayor the highest authority in our city, and the male president the highest authority in our country. Over time, I came to understand that this meant that men would make the big decisions, occupy the best jobs, and generally do what they liked. In the limited arena of my town and church, adult women groused, schemed, or drank when they were unhappy, but none had any solution beyond finding a good husband.

I learned that boys and girls were supposedly opposites. While adults bullied boys into acting like "real men," girls were reminded that they were "just girls." Each operated within preset boundaries, though girls' aspirations were confined to a smaller realm. I could run for class president because girls could vote in a democracy—something my generation took for granted. But teachers declined my requests to serve on safety patrol, operate audiovisual equipment, or play drums for the school orchestra because such activities were considered unsuitable for girls—something today's generation would find weird. We anticipated that boys would become fathers when they grew up, as one aspect of a multidimensional life, and we assumed that a girl's singular mission was to become a housewife. Those who did not have children would be pitied. An unenvied number might find positions in the newspaper section called "Jobs for Women."

By the time I entered high school in 1969, faint echoes of the national Civil Rights Movement had reached our dusty town. My oldest brother, taking a junior college course while fulfilling a construction apprenticeship, informed me that Marx was a philosopher, not a television comedian, and dubbed our panther-like house cat Eldridge Cleaver. A friend told me that a feminist was someone who believed in equality of the sexes.

The word made instinctive sense. *Of course* the sexes were equal, I thought; boys and girls were *created equal.* That was America's founding principle. Its patriotic creed. Energized by this novel application of the old self-evident truth, I was puzzled when friends and family resisted its logic. Boys might rebel without a cause in James Dean's America, but girls learned to sit still.

Some of these restrictions appear trivial, even quaint, in retrospect. What was so scandalous about playing the drums? Why whine about it now?

Small, inconsequential restrictions are the building blocks of mental prisons. As seen through this book's secondary characters, feminism has always confronted and combated some of the worst forms of suffering. Soon after I learned to distinguish Karl Marx from Groucho Marx, I left home to escape sexual abuse that my older sister and I had sequentially reported to eight adults, including two officials associated with the justice system, namely, a lawyer and the superior court. I was fourteen. In that era, no one thought to do anything further. The only ones who spent time in jail were me (three nights) and my sister (sixty days) for running away. Most Americans still considered women more or less the cause of any abuse that befell them. If not for Eve, Adam would have been an angel. Yet I happened, by sheerest chance, upon an alternative belief system. A high school friend introduced me to college students who had started the Women's Studies program at San Diego State. They possessed the curiously inalterable belief that women were not responsible for man's sins. Girls had an equal right to a place under the sun and to belong to themselves alone. This perspective helped me navigate hazards to which other young victims of abuse I knew succumbed—one murdered, one dead of a drug overdose, one a lifelong addict. Feminism gave me a normal life. Society gradually caught up. Three years later, in 1974, Senator Walter Mondale championed the first federal program to address child abuse. Mandatory reporting spread and America became a better country for it. Progress across a single lifetime, my very own, has been palpable. It has made me grateful, and motivates me to chart this trajectory now, when citizens obsess over the nation's failings and quail at its future.[8]

As one historian wisely points out, improvement is always "raggedy," with no unsullied victories. Yet history also allows observers to stand far back enough from the mess to see its hopeful contours. From a distance of nearly three centuries, the positive changes are extraordinary. No one should be shocked that the country has failed to fully realize its goals of liberty and justice for all. It would be more shocking if it had. The past shows that progress is a long slog, but also a worthwhile one.[9]

Like "democracy," a term once scorned, "feminism" gives Americans and other democratic peoples a common vocabulary. Susan B. Anthony considered failure impossible if citizens united around the nation's founding principles. Beyoncé Knowles-Carter shared her faith. Susan B. Anthony might have rubbed her wire-rimmed eyeglasses at the singer's get-up in "Run the World (Girls)," but she would have applauded its sentiment. "My persuasion can build a nation," Beyoncé sang.

Who wouldn't want to listen?

Notes

Works and persons frequently cited are referred to with the following abbreviations:

AP-MHS	Adams Family Correspondence, Adams Papers Digital Edition, Massachusetts Historical Society, Boston
BKC	Beyoncé Knowles-Carter
ECS	Elizabeth Cady Stanton
Gale	19th-Century US Newspapers, Gale News Vault
Gordon, *SP*	Ann D. Gordon, ed., *Selected Papers of Elizabeth Cady Stanton and Susan B. Anthony* (Rutgers University Press, 1997)
MCT	Mary Church Terrell
NYT	*New York Times*
SBA	Susan B. Anthony

Prologue

Epigraph: Roosevelt in Susan Ware, *Beyond Suffrage: Women in the New Deal* (Harvard University Press, 1981), 17.

1. Kyla Schuller, *The Trouble with White Women* (Bold Type Books, 2021), 9.

2. Richard Wike and Shannon Schumacher, "Democratic Rights Popular Globally," Pew Research, 2/27/2020: https://www.pewresearch.org/global/2020/02/27/democratic-rights-popular-globally-but-commitment-to-them-not-always-strong/.

3. Rebecca Clarren, "Fracking Is a Feminist Issue," *Ms. Magazine* (Spring 2013): 48; Josefin Dolsten, "Pro-Palestinian Activist: Support for Israel and Feminism Are Incompatible," *Jewish Telegraphic Agency,* 3/13/2017: https://www.jta.org/2017/03/13/united-states/pro-palestinian-activist-support-for-israel-and-feminism-are-incompatible.

4. *Oxford English Dictionary* online, OED.com, s.v. "patriot," accessed 6/22/2022.

5. Lady Bird Johnson Quotes, The Famous People: https://quotes.thefamouspeople.com/lady-bird-johnson-6642.php.

6. Lynn Sherr, *Failure Is Impossible: Susan B. Anthony in Her Own Words* (Times Books, 1995), 324.

7. Olive Logan in Elizabeth Cady Stanton, Susan B. Anthony, and Matilda Joslyn Gage, *History of Woman Suffrage,* 6 vols. (Fowler and Wells, 1882), vol. 2, 385.

8. Nancy Cott, *The Grounding of Modern Feminism* (Yale University Press, 1987), 4; Chimamanda Ngozi Adichie, "We Should All Be Feminists," TEDxEuston, 11/16/2015: https://singjupost.com/we-should-all-be-feminists-by-chimamanda-ngozi-adichie-full-transcript/; Kathleen Barry, *Susan B. Anthony, A Biography of a Singular Feminist* (Ballantine, 1988), 318.

9. Suzanne Venker and Phyllis Schlafly, *The Flipside of Feminism: What Conservative Women Know and Men Can't Say* (WND Books, 2011), 23; Clare Burton, *Subordination: Feminism and Social Theory* (George Allen & Unwin, 1985), xii–xiii; Roxane Gay, *Bad Feminist* (Harper, 2014), x.

10. *The Longest Revolution: News and Views of Progressive Feminism, December 1978–February/March 1982,* in Special Collections, Center for Women's Studies and Services Records, San Diego State University, box 18, folder 31.

1. The Right to Learn: 1776–1800

Epigraph: Gottlieb von Hippel in Susan Groag Bell and Karen Offen, *Women, the Family, and Freedom: The Debate in Documents,* 2 vols. (Stanford University Press, 1983), vol. 1, 116, emphasis mine.

1. *Diary of John Adams,* Summer 1759 (6/29/1759), AP-MHS.

2. Rosemary Keller, *Patriotism and the Female Sex: Abigail Adams and the American Revolution* (Carlson, 1994), 13; Watercolor, ca. 1800, in Woody Holton, *Abigail Adams, A Life* (Atria, 2009), 3.

3. Holton, *Abigail Adams,* 3; Abigail Adams to John Adams, 7/21/1776, AP-MHS.

4. Abigail Adams to Elizabeth Smith Shaw Peabody, 6/5/1809, Adams Papers, *Founders Online,* National Archives.

5. Nicole Eustace, "'The Cornerstone of a Copious Work': Love and Power in Eighteenth-Century Courtship," *Journal of Social History* 34, no. 3 (2001): 520–521; Philip Greven Jr., *Four Generations: Population, Land, and Family in Colonial Andover, Massachusetts* (Cornell University Press, 1970), 135; William Blackstone, *Commentaries on the Laws of England in Four Books* (Philadelphia, 1893), book 1, ch. 15, 441; Norma Basch, *In the Eyes of the Law: Women, Marriage, and Property in Nineteenth-Century New York* (Cornell University Press, 1982), 54.

6. Bradford in Keller, *Patriotism,* 93; Blackstone in Reva Siegel, "'The Rule of Love': Wife Beating as Prerogative and Privacy," *Yale Law Journal* 105, no. 8 (1996): 2124; Linda Kerber, *No Constitutional Right to Be Ladies: Women and the Obligations of Citizenship* (Hill and Wang, 1998), 26; David Bromfield, "Women and the Law of Property in Early America," *Michigan Law Review* 85, no. 1109 (1987): 1114.

7. John Winthrop, "Speech to Massachusetts General Court," 7/3/1645, in Owen Collins, ed., *Speeches That Changed the World: History in the Making* (Zondervan, 1998), 68; Basch, *In the Eyes of the Law,* 20–21.

8. *Pennsylvania Gazette,* 7/24/1732, Historical Society of Pennsylvania, Papers of Benjamin Franklin: https://franklinpapers.org/framedVolumes.jsp; Abigail Adams to Mary Smith Cranch, 1/31/1767, AP-MHS; Fordyce in Keller, *Patriotism,* 26.

9. John Gregory, *A Father's Legacy to His Daughters* (1834; Garland, 1974), 24, 26; John Adams to Abigail Adams, 11/4/1775, AP-MHS.

10. John Adams to Abigail Adams, 12/2/1778, AP-MHS; Jean-Jacques Rousseau, *Émile; or, On Education* (D. Appleton, 1911), 322, 324, 330, 332, 335.

11. Cabanis in Anne Vila, "Ambiguous Beings: Marginality, Melancholy, and the Femme Savant," in Sarah Knott and Barbara Taylor, eds., *Women, Gender, and Enlightenment* (Palgrave Macmillan, 2005), 55; Moreau in Joan Wallach Scott, "'A Woman Who Has Only Paradoxes to Offer': Olympe De Gouges Claims Rights for Women," in Sara Melzer and Leslie Rabine, eds., *Rebel Daughters: Women and the French Revolution* (Oxford University Press, 1992), 105; Susan Klepp, *Revolutionary Conceptions: Women, Fertility, and Family Limitation in America, 1760–1820* (University of North Carolina Press, 2009), 61; Gregory, *Father's Legacy,* 22; Rousseau, *Émile,* 345; Johnson in Karen Offen, *European Feminisms, 1700–1950* (Stanford University Press, 2000), 44.

12. David Fordyce in Barbara Knott, "Feminists vs. Gallants: Manners and Morals in Enlightenment Britain," in Sarah Knott and Barbara Taylor, eds., *Women, Gender, and Enlightenment* (New York, 2005), 39; *Chesterfield's Letters to His Son,* 9/5/1748, letter 49, 1776 edition, 246: https://www.gutenberg.org/files/3361/3361-h/3361-h.htm#link2H_4_0051.

13. Defoe and Swift in Sylvia Strauss, *Traitors to the Masculine Cause: The Men's Campaigns for Women's Rights* (Greenwood Press, 1982), 6–8.

14. For accuracy, I have not corrected misspellings or punctuation within quotes, and I use the Latin *sic* only when necessary to alert readers to read closely for intent.

15. Mary Beth Norton, *Liberty's Daughters: The Revolutionary Experience of American Women, 1750–1800* (Cornell University Press, 1996), 118; Abigail Adams to Isaac Smith Jr., 4/20/1771, AP-MHS; Abigail Adams to John Thaxter, 6/17/1782, AP-MHS.

16. *The Bible: Authorized King James Version,* Oxford World's Classics, eds. Robert Carrol and Stephen Prickett (Oxford University Press, 1997), vol. 3, 249, 219.

17. Jerome in David Gilmore, *Misogyny: The Male Malady* (University of Pennsylvania Press, 2001), 87–88; Tertullian in F. Forester Church, "Sex and Salvation in Tertullian," *Harvard Theological Review* 68, no. 2 (1975): 83.

18. Sherrin Marshall, ed., *Women in Reformation and Counter-Reformation Europe* (Indiana University Press, 1989), 7; Susan Karant-Nunn and Merry Wiesner-Hanks, eds., *Luther on Women: A Sourcebook* (Cambridge University Press, 2003), 18, 21, 23, 75; "A Sermon of Master John Calvin on the First Epistle of Paul to Timothy" (London, 1579): http://www.truecovenanter.com/calvin/calvin_19_on_Timothy.html.

19. Nachman Ben-Yehuda, "The European Witch Craze of the 14th to 17th Centuries: A Sociologist's Perspective," *American Journal of Sociology* 86, no. 1 (1980): 6, 11.

20. Abigail Adams to Isaac Smith Jr., 4/20/1771, AP-MHS.

21. Sharon Block, *Rape and Sexual Power in Early America* (University of North Carolina Press, 2006), 16, 44.

22. Block, *Rape,* 18, 20.

23. Abigail Adams to Isaac Smith Jr., 4/20/1771, AP-MHS.

24. Abigail Adams to John Adams, 4/17/1777, AP-MHS.

25. *Memoirs of Mrs. Abigail Bailey, Who Had Been the Wife of Major Asa Bailey* (Samuel Armstrong, 1815), 11.

26. Joel Perlmann, Silvana Siddali, and Keith Whitescarver, "Literacy, Schooling, and Teaching among New England Women, 1730–1820," *History of Education Quarterly* 37, no. 2 (1997): 126.

27. *Memoirs of Mrs. Abigail Bailey,* vii, x.

28. Philip Greven Jr., "Family Structure in Seventeenth Century Andover, Massachusetts," *William and Mary Quarterly* 23, no. 2 (1966): 241; *Memoirs of Mrs. Abigail Bailey,* 13; Eustace, "Cornerstone," 517–546.

29. *Memoirs of Mrs. Abigail Bailey,* 12.

30. *Memoirs of Mrs. Abigail Bailey,* 13.

31. *Memoirs of Mrs. Abigail Bailey,* 25–26, 147; paternity defendant in Trent MacNamara, *Birth Control and American Modernity: A History of Popular Ideas* (Cambridge University Press, 2018), 12. On mortality, see Klepp, *Revolutionary Conceptions,* 61.

32. OED online, s.v. "equal," www.oed.com, accessed 6/23/2022.

33. John Locke, *Two Treatises of Government,* ed. Thomas Hollis (London, 1764), 98: https://oll.libertyfund.org/titles/222.

34. Sir Robert Filmer, *Patriarcha; or the Natural Power of Kings. By the Learned Sir Robert Filmer Baronet,* facsimile (London, 1680), 4; John Clement Rager, *The Political Philosophy of St. Robert Bellarmine* (Indianapolis, 1926), 19: https://www.hedgeschool.com/Book_Content/07_Civics_Content/07_Civics_Content_Bellarmine.pdf.

35. Filmer, *Patriarcha,* 3, 7.

36. Filmer, *Patriarcha,* 12, 24, 38.

37. Locke, *Two Treatises,* 1–2.

38. John Locke, "Some Thoughts Concerning Education," in *The Works of John Locke in Nine Volumes,* 12th ed., vol. 8, facsimile (London, 1824), iii, 6.

39. Thomas Paine, *Common Sense* (1776), 86: https://www.gutenberg.org/files/147/147-h/147-h.htm.

40. Abigail Adams to John Adams, 4/10/1782, AP-MHS.

41. Abigail Adams to Mercy Otis Warren, 12/5/1773, AP-MHS; Edith Gelles, *Portia: The World of Abigail Adams* (Indiana University Press, 1992), 30, 31.

42. Abigail Adams to John Adams, 6/18/1775, AP-MHS.

43. John Quincy Adams to Joseph Sturge, Mar. 1846, AP-MHS, notes on Abigail Adams to John Adams, 6/18/1775. Also see Abigail Adams to John Adams, 7/16/1775, 3/31/1776, and 9/20/1776, AP-MHS.

44. Abigail Adams to John Adams, 3/31/1776, AP-MHS. For her commentary on slavery, see Abigail Adams to John Adams, 9/22/1774, AP-MHS. Also see Alice S. Rossi, ed., *The Feminist Papers: From Adams to de Beauvoir* (Columbia University Press, 1973), 10.

45. Abigail Adams to John Adams, 3/31/1776; John Adams to Abigail Adams, 11/4/1775; John Adams to Abigail Adams, 4/15/1776; and John Adams to Abigail Adams (Daughter), 4/18/1776, all in AP-MHS.

46. Abigail Adams to John Adams, 4/7/1776, AP-MHS; *Chesterfield's Letters,* 9/5/1748: https://www.gutenberg.org/files/3361/3361-h/3361-h.htm; Abigail Adams to John Adams, 4/21/1776, AP-MHS.

47. John Adams to Abigail Adams, 4/14/1776, AP-MHS.

48. John Adams to Abigail Adams, 4/14/1776, AP-MHS.

49. John Adams to James Sullivan, 5/26/1776, fn 2 on Sullivan's letter to Elbridge Gerry, AP-MHS.

50. John Adams to James Sullivan, 5/26/1776, AP-MHS.

51. "Result of the Convention of Delegates Holden at Ipswich in the County of Essex, Who Were Deputed to Take into Consideration the Constitution and the Form of Government Proposed by the Convention of the State of Massachusetts-Bay," *Memoir of Theophilus Parsons* (Boston, 1859), appendix, 376.

52. Abigail Adams to John Adams, 6/17/1782, AP-MHS.

53. Charles Brockden Brown, *Alcuin,* ed. Cynthia Kierner (New College and University Press, 1995), 13, 62, 63.

54. Judith Apter Klinghoffer and Lois Elkins, "'The Petticoat Electors': Women's Suffrage in New Jersey, 1776–1807," *Journal of the Early Republic* 12, no. 2 (1992): 173. The anonymous petition in the Burlington, NJ, *Advertiser* ran May 6, 1790.

55. Abigail Adams to Mary Smith Cranch, 11/15/1797, AP-MHS.

56. Abigail Adams to Mercy Otis Warren, 4/27/1776, AP-MHS.

57. Abigail Adams to John Adams, 5/7/1776, AP-MHS.

58. Abigail Adams to John Adams, 5/7/1776, AP-MHS. The last preceding occasion she used "Portia" was 10/22/1775.

59. Abigail Adams to John Adams, 9/20/1776, AP-MHS.

60. *Memoirs of Mrs. Abigail Bailey,* 21.

61. Gloria Main, "Gender, Work, and Wages in Colonial New England," *William and Mary Quarterly* 51, no. 1 (1994): 43–44.

62. *Memoirs of Mrs. Abigail Bailey,* 17.

63. *Memoirs of Mrs. Abigail Bailey,* 18.

64. *Memoirs of Mrs. Abigail Bailey,* 29.

65. *Memoirs of Mrs. Abigail Bailey,* 33.

66. *Memoirs of Mrs. Abigail Bailey,* 32–33, 42.

67. *Memoirs of Mrs. Abigail Bailey,* 34.

68. *Memoirs of Mrs. Abigail Bailey,* 34, 41; Block, *Rape and Sexual Power,* 75.

69. *Memoirs of Mrs. Abigail Bailey,* 44.

70. *Memoirs of Mrs. Abigail Bailey,* 51.

71. Quoted in Block, *Rape and Sexual Power,* 76. Also see Cornelia Hughes Dayton, *Women before the Bar: Gender, Law, and Society in Connecticut, 1639–1789* (University of North Carolina Press, 1995), 275–282.

72. Abigail Adams to Mercy Otis Warren, 4/24/1776, AP-MHS.

73. *Memoirs of Mrs. Abigail Bailey,* 82.

74. *Memoirs of Mrs. Abigail Bailey,* 81, 89, 91, 92.

75. See the stories of Deborah Sampson, Prudence Wright, and Grace and Rachel Martin in Susan Casey, *Women Heroes of the American Revolution* (Chicago Review Press, 2017).

76. Joel Perlman and Dennis Shirley, "When Did New England Women Acquire Literacy?" *William and Mary Quarterly* 48, no. 1 (1991): 51, 62–63; Gloria Main, "An Inquiry into When and Why Women Learned to Write in Colonial New England," *Journal of Social History* 24, no. 3 (1991): 583–584.

77. Eliza Love Shelton, "Edenton Tea Party," 7, 38, quoted in the *Virginia Gazette,* 11/3/1774: https://wams.nyhistory.org/settler-colonialism-and-revolution/the-american-revolution/edenton-tea-party/#.

78. Shelton, "Edenton Tea Party," 47, 52, 57, 59; quotation from Arthur Iredell, 1/31/1775, in *Papers of James Iredell,* ed. Don Higginbotham (Division of Archives and History of North Carolina, 1976), vol. 1, 282–284.

79. Emily Arendt, "'Ladies Going About for Money': Female Voluntary Associations and Civic Consciousness in the American Revolution," *Journal of the Early Republic* 34, no. 2 (2014): 172.

80. Linda Kerber, *Women of the Republic: Intellect and Ideology in Revolutionary America* (University of North Carolina Press, 1980), 11; Norton, *Liberty's Daughters,* 243, 248–249.

81. John Adams to Abigail Adams, 8/4/1776, AP-MHS.

82. Abigail Adams to John Adams, 8/14/1776, AP-MHS; Holton, *Abigail Adams,* 94.

83. Abigail Adams to John Adams, 6/30/1778; Abigail Adams to John Thaxter, 2/15/1778, AP-MHS.

84. Abigail Adams to Mary Smith Cranch, 4/26/1787, AP-MHS.

85. *Selected Writings of Judith Sargent Murray,* ed. Sharon Harris (Oxford University Press, 1995), xv, 4, 7.

86. Marion Savin and Harold Abrahams, "The Young Ladies Academy of Philadelphia," *History of Education Journal* 8, no. 2 (1957): 59; Ann Gordon, "The Young Ladies Academy of Philadelphia," in Carol Ruth Berkin and Mary Beth Norton, eds., *Women of America: A History* (Houghton Mifflin, 1979), 70; Anne Boylan, *The Origins of Women's Activism: New York and Boston, 1797–1840* (University of North Carolina Press, 2002), 100.

87. Benjamin Rush, *Thoughts upon Female Education, Accommodated to the Present State of Society, Manners, and Government, in the United States of America: Addressed to the Visitors of the Young Ladies' Academy in Philadelphia, 28 July 1787* (Boston, 1791), Evans Early American Imprint Collection, 8, 20, 26, 271.

88. Gerda Lerner, *The Creation of Feminist Consciousness: From the Middle Ages to 1870* (Oxford University Press, 1993), 30.

89. Judith Sargent Murray, *The Gleaner: A Miscellaneous Production in Three Volumes, by Constantia* (Boston, 1798), 188; Thomas Woody, *A History of Women's Education in the United States* (New York, 1929), vol. 1, 299, 395. Census takers began counting enslaved and free children in 1820, from which I have calculated a percentage for the early republic. See *Bicentennial Edition: Historical Statistics of the United States, Colonial Times to 1970* (US Census Bureau, 1975), 16, 18.

90. Rush, *Thoughts,* 19, emphasis mine; Margaret Nash, "Rethinking Republican Motherhood: Benjamin Rush and the Young Ladies' Academy of Philadelphia," *Journal of the Early Republic* 17, no. 2 (1997): 171–191.

91. Priscilla Mason, "Salutatorian Oration," in *Rise and Progress of the Young-Ladies Academy of Philadelphia* (Philadelphia, 1794), 90, 92, 93.

92. Mason, "Salutatorian Oration," front matter, 93–94; A. Kirsten Foster, *Moral Visions and Material Ambitions: Philadelphia Struggles to Define the Republic: 1776–1836* (Lexington Books, 2004), 156–158.

93. Wallace in Gordon, "Young Ladies Academy," 88.

94. Yuval Noah Harari, *Sapiens: A Brief History of Humankind* (New York, 2015), 165; Lafayette in André Maurois, *Adrienne: The Life of the Marquise de La Fayette* (McGraw-Hill, 1961), 64, 73, 142; Lafayette in *The Nation* 55, no. 1416 (1892): 124.

95. Susan Dunn, *Sister Revolutions: French Lightning, American Light* (Farrar, Straus & Giroux, 1999), 13.

96. Cynthia Bouton, *The Flour War: Gender, Class, and Community in Late Ancien Régime France* (Pennsylvania State University Press, 1993), 4, 17, 36; William Doyle, *Oxford History of the French Revolution* (Oxford University Press, 2002), 341–342; Yves Bessières and Patricia Niedzwiecki, "Women in the French Revolution: Bibliography," Commission of the European Communities, January 1991, 4: http://aei.pitt.edu/34003/1/A480.pdf.

97. David Garrioch, "The Everyday Lives of Parisian Women and the October Days of 1789," *Social History* 24, no. 3 (1999): 232.

98. Scott, "Woman Who Has Only Paradoxes," 105.

99. Darline Gay Levy and Harriet Applewhite, "Women and Militant Citizenship in Revolutionary Paris," and Claire Goldberg Moses, "'Equality' and 'Difference' in Historical Perspective: A Comparative Examination of the Feminisms of French Revolutionaries and Utopian Socialists," both in Sara Melzer and Leslie Rabine, eds., *Rebel Daughters: Women and the French Revolution* (Oxford University Press, 1992), 85, 234–235; Offen, *European Feminisms,* 56.

100. The quotation from Deputy-Cleric Abbé Sieyès (1789) is in Offen, *European Feminisms,* 52 (see p. 53 on the actions of the National Assembly); Marie-Jean-Antoine-Nicolas Caritat, Marquis de Condorcet, *The First Essay on the Political Rights of Women. A Translation of Condorcet's Essay "Sur l'admission des femmes aux droits de Cité" (On the Admission of Women to the Rights of Citizenship),"* trans. Alice Drysdale Vickery (Letchworth, 1912), 5: //oll.libertyfund.org/titles/1013.

101. Bell and Offen, *Women, the Family, and Freedom,* vol. 1, 98; Etta Palm D'Aelders, "Discourse on the Injustice of the Laws in Favor of Men," 12/30/1790: https://www.worldhistorycommons.org/etta-palm-d'aelders-discourse-injustice-laws-favor-men-expense-women-30-december-1790.

102. Mary Seidman Trouille, *Sexual Politics in the Enlightenment: Women Writers Read Rousseau* (SUNY Press, 1997), 272.

103. "Declaration of the Rights of Woman and of Citizen," trans. John R. Cole, in *Between the Queen and the Cabby: Olympe de Gouges's Rights of Woman* (McGill-Queen's University Press, 2011), 30, 32, 179.

104. Léon in Levy and Applewhite, "Women and Militant Citizenship," 88.

105. Sophie Mousset, *Women's Rights and the French Revolution: A Biography of Olympe de Gouges* (Routledge, 2007), 99; Edward Berenson, *The Trial of Madame Caillaux* (University of California Press, 1992), 105.

106. Chaumette in Trouille, *Sexual Politics,* 278–279.

107. Levy and Applewhite, "Women and Militant Citizenship," 95–96; Bessières and Niedzwiecki, "Women in the French Revolution," 8; Berenson, *Trial,* 105.

108. Abigail Adams to John Adams, 1/12/1794, AP-MHS; Thomas Jefferson, "Notes on John Adams and the French Revolution," 1/15/1793: https://founders.archives.gov.

109. Miriam Brody, *Mary Wollstonecraft: Mother of Women's Rights* (Oxford University Press, 2001), 68; R. M. Janes, "On the Reception of Mary Wollstonecraft's *A Vindication of the Rights of Woman," Journal of the History of Ideas* 39, no. 2 (1978): 293–302.

110. Judith Sargent Murray in Alice Rossi, *The Feminist Papers: From Adams to de Beauvoir* (Columbia University Press, 1973), 19; Macaulay in Catherine Gardner,

"Catharine Macaulay's 'Letters on Education': Odd but Equal," *Hypatia* 13, no. 1 (1998): 118.

111. Mary Wollstonecraft, *Thoughts on the Education of Daughters* (London, 1787), 38–39, and *Vindication of the Rights of Woman: With Strictures on Political and Moral Subjects* (London 1792), 3–4.

112. Wollstonecraft, *Vindication,* 3; Brody, *Mary Wollstonecraft,* 49.

113. Betsy Smith Peabody to Abigail Adams, 12/29/1793; John Adams to Abigail Adams, 1/22/1794, AP-MHS.

114. Abigail Adams to John Thaxter, 2/15/1778, AP-MHS.

115. Elias Boudinot, "An Oration Delivered at Elizabeth Town, New Jersey, Agreeably to a Resolution of the State Society of Cincinnati," 7/4/1793 (1893 printing), 21, courtesy of Special Collections and University Archives, Rutgers University Libraries, New Brunswick; "Wrongs of School Masters," Lexington, Kentucky, and "Reporter," *Raleigh Register* and *North-Carolina Weekly Advertiser,* 5/24/1811, issue 609, Gale.

116. Hannah More, *Strictures on the Modern System of Female Education,* 3rd American ed. (Boston, 1802), 167–168; Abigail Adams to Mary Smith Cranch, 7/6/1784, AP-MHS; Abigail Adams to Abigail Adams Smith, 5/18/1788, AP-MHS; Maxine Seller, "Boundaries, Bridges, and the History of Education," *History of Education Quarterly* 31, no. 2 (1991): 202.

117. More, *Strictures,* 167–168; More to Sir W. W. Pepys, 12/23/1820, in *Memoirs and Correspondence of Mrs. Hannah More,* ed. William Roberts (New York, 1837), vol. 2, 306.

118. Hannah More to the Earl of Oxford (Horace Walpole), 1793, in *Memoirs and Correspondence of Mrs. Hannah More,* vol. 1, 427.

119. More to the Earl of Oxford, 1793; Janes, "On the Reception of Wollstonecraft's *A Vindication,*" 294.

120. John Bennett, *Strictures on Female Education* (1795), Evans Early American Imprint Collection, 15, 84.

121. Abigail Adams to John Adams, 1/4/1795, AP-MHS.

122. John Adams to Abigail Adams, 12/18/1794, footnote, AP-MHS.

123. Thomas Jefferson to Nathaniel Burwell, 3/14/1818; Thomas Jefferson to Martha Jefferson, 12/22/1783: https://founders.archives.gov; Catherine Kerrison, "The French Education of Martha Jefferson Randolph," *Early American Studies* 11, no. 2 (2013): 351, 359.

124. Holton, *Abigail Adams,* 411–412.

125. *Memoirs of Mrs. Abigail Bailey,* 99, 112.

126. *Memoirs of Mrs. Abigail Bailey,* 113–114; Don Hagist, *Wives, Slaves, and Servant Girls: Advertisements for Female Runaways in American Newspapers, 1770–1783* (Westholme, 2016).

127. *Memoirs of Mrs. Abigail Bailey,* 116, 131.

128. *Memoirs of Mrs. Abigail Bailey,* 132, 134, 148, 156.

129. *Memoirs of Mrs. Abigail Bailey,* 157, 166, 185.

130. *Memoirs of Mrs. Abigail Bailey,* 189.

131. *Memoirs of Mrs. Abigail Bailey,* 189, 191, 194.

132. *Memoirs of Mrs. Abigail Bailey,* 194–195; Hendrick Hartog, *Man & Wife in America: A History* (Harvard University Press, 2000), 60.

2. The Right to Speak: 1800–1865

Epigraph: Angelina Grimké, *Walking by Faith: The Diary of Angelina Grimké, 1828–1835,* ed. Charles Wilbanks (University of South Carolina Press, 2003), 57.

1. Grimké, *Walking by Faith,* xxii, 2.

2. Catherine Birney, *The Grimké Sisters: Sarah and Angelina Grimké; the First American Women Advocates of Abolition and Woman's Rights* (Lee and Shepard, 1885), 18.

3. Grimké, *Walking by Faith,* 10; Katherine Du Pre Lumpkin, *The Emancipation of Angelina Grimké* (University of North Carolina Press, 1974), 12; Gerda Lerner, *The Grimké Sisters from South Carolina: Pioneers for Women's Rights and Abolition* (University of North Carolina Press, 2004), 48; James Leyburn, "Presbyterian Immigrants and the American Revolution," *Journal of Presbyterian History* 54, no. 1 (1976): 9.

4. Lerner, *Grimké Sisters,* 23; Lumpkin, *Emancipation,* 6; Conrad Edick Wright, *The Transformation of Charity in Postrevolutionary New England* (Northeastern University Press, 1992), 5, 63; Grimké, *Walking by Faith,* 9; Alexis De Tocqueville, *Democracy in America,* trans. Henry Reeve, 2nd ed. (Sever and Francis, 1863), vol. 2, 129.

5. Anne Boylan, *The Origins of Women's Activism: New York and Boston, 1797–1840* (University of North Carolina Press, 2002), 20–22.

6. Wright, *Transformation,* 190; Boylan, *Origins,* 27.

7. Benjamin Lynerd, *Republican Theology: The Civil Religion of American Evangelicals* (Oxford University Press, 2014), 104, 109; Mark Noll, *America's God: From Jonathan Edwards to Abraham Lincoln* (Oxford University Press, 2002), 5, 9; Boylan, *Origins,* 189.

8. Timothy L. Smith, "Christian Perfectionism and American Idealism, 1820–1900," *Asbury Seminarian,* 7–9: https://place.asburyseminary.edu/cgi/viewcontent.cgi?article=1735&context=asburyjournal.

9. James H. Moorhead, "Charles Finney and the Modernization of America," *Journal of Presbyterian History* 62, no. 2 (1984): 106; Charles G. Finney, *Lectures on the Revivals of Religion* (New York, 1835), 23; Noll, *America's God,* 307.

10. Grimké, *Walking by Faith,* 9, 20; Birney, *Grimké Sisters,* 82; Anna Speicher, *The Religious World of Anti-Slavery Women: Spirituality in the Lives of Five Abolitionist Lecturers* (Syracuse University Press, 2000), 75.

11. Lerner, *Grimké Sisters,* 18–19.

12. Mark Perry, *Lift Up Thy Voice: The Grimké Family's Journey from Slaveholders to Civil Rights Leaders* (Viking, 2001), 78.

13. Grimké, *Walking by Faith,* 58; Lerner, *Grimké Sisters,* 13, 27–28; Theodore Weld, *American Slavery as It Is* (American Anti-Slavery Society, 1839), 23; Nita Pyburn, "The Public School System of Charleston before 1860," *South Carolina Historical Magazine* 61, no. 2 (1960): 94; on the Work House, see Tiya Miles, *All That She Carried: The Journey of Ashley's Sack, A Black Family Keepsake* (Random House, 2021), 172.

14. Noll, *America's God,* 388–389, 392–393.

15. Edward Crowther, "Independent Black Baptist Congregations in Antebellum Alabama," *Journal of Negro History* 72, no. 2 (1987): 67, 74.

16. Brycchan Carey, *From Peace to Freedom: Quaker Rhetoric and the Birth of American Anti-Slavery, 1657–1761* (Yale University Press, 2012), 70; J. William Frost, "Quaker Anti-Slavery: From Dissidence to Sense of the Meeting," *Quaker History* 101, no. 1 (2012): 12.

17. Grimké, *Walking by Faith,* 57.

18. Grimké, *Walking by Faith,* 88, 99.

19. Grimké, *Walking by Faith,* 50–51, 57.

20. Grimké, *Walking by Faith,* 51, 131.

21. Deborah Gray White, *Ar'n't I a Woman: Female Slaves in the Plantation South* (Norton, 1999), 29–30.

22. Eliza Love Shelton, "The Edenton Tea Party, 25 October 1774: A Patriotic Female Community in Revolutionary North Carolina," master's thesis, East Tennessee State University, 2012, 37; Jeff Broadwater and Troy Kickler, eds., *North Carolina's Revolutionary Founders* (University of North Carolina Press, 2019), 27, 28; Jean Fagan Yellin, *Harriet Jacobs: A Life* (Basic Civitas, 2004), 10.

23. Harriet Jacobs (Linda Brent), *Incidents in the Life of a Slave Girl, Written by Herself,* ed. L. Maria Child (Boston, 1861), 11–12.

24. Jacobs, *Incidents,* 16, 121.

25. Yellin, *Harriet Jacobs,* 16–17.

26. Jacobs, *Incidents,* 24; Yellin, *Harriet Jacobs,* 17.

27. Mary Chesnut, *Mary Chesnut's Civil War,* ed. C. Vann Woodward (Yale University Press, 1981), 29; Yellin, *Harriet Jacobs,* 4, 7.

28. Jacobs, *Incidents,* 24, 55.

29. Jacobs, *Incidents,* 29.

30. Jean Fagan Yellin et al., eds., *The Harriet Jacobs Family Papers,* 2 vols. (University of North Carolina Press, 2008), vol. 1, 36; Jacobs, *Incidents,* 31.

31. Jacobs, *Incidents,* 46–47.

32. Jacobs, *Incidents,* 47.

33. Jacobs, *Incidents,* 61.

34. Jacobs, *Incidents,* 82, 85.

35. Barbara Welter, "Cult of True Womanhood, 1820–1860," *American Quarterly* 18, no. 2 (1966): 154, 157.

36. Jacobs, *Incidents,* 83.

37. Chesnut, *Mary Chesnut's Civil War,* 29; Jacobs, *Incidents,* 84–85.

38. Jacobs, *Incidents,* 85.

39. Jacobs, *Incidents,* 87, 89, 90.

40. Jacobs, *Incidents,* 117–119; Yellin, *Harriet Jacobs,* 39–40.

41. Jacobs, *Incidents,* 143.

42. Yellin, *Harriet Jacobs,* 41, 61; Jacobs, *Incidents,* 139; Cheryl Janifer LaRoche, *Free Black Communities and the Underground Railroad: The Geography of Resistance* (University of Illinois Press, 2014), 127.

43. Jacobs, *Incidents,* 134.

44. Jacobs, *Incidents,* 166.

45. Jacobs, *Incidents,* 175.

46. Grimké, *Walking by Faith,* 139, 142.

47. Carol Gold, "Fathers and Daughters: Copenhagen's Dottreskolen," *Scandinavian Studies* 65, no. 2 (1993): 213.

48. Chandler in Thomas Woody, *A History of Women's Education in the United States* (New York, 1929), vol. 2, 140, 142. Claudia Goldin and Lawrence Katz, *The Race between Technology and Education* (Harvard University Press, 2008), 130.

49. Florence Fleming Corley, "The Presbyterian Quest: Higher Education for Georgia Women," *American Presbyterians* 29, no. 2 (1991): 85; Maxine Seller, "Boundaries, Bridges, and the History of Education," *History of Education Quarterly* 31, no. 2 (1991): 205.

50. Catharine Beecher, *True Remedy for the Wrongs of Woman* (Phillips, Sampson, & Co., 1851), 52.

51. Kathryn Kish Sklar, *Catharine Beecher: A Study in American Domesticity* (Yale University Press, 1973), xiv; Julie Matthaei, *An Economic History of Women in America* (Schocken, 1982), 112; Rebecca Traister, *All The Single Ladies: Unmarried Women and the Rise of an Independent Nation* (Simon & Schuster, 2016), 45.

52. Grimké, *Walking by Faith,* 153–155, 170–171.

53. Grimké, *Walking by Faith,* 181.

54. *The Liberator,* 10/17/1835, 1; Lerner, *Grimké Sisters,* 84; Grimké, *Walking by Faith,* 209; Lumpkin, *Emancipation,* 73, 81–84; Andrew Jackson, Seventh Annual Message, 12/8/1835: https://www.presidency.ucsb.edu/documents/seventh-annual-message-2.

55. *The Liberator,* 9/19/1835; Lumpkin, *Emancipation,* 73, 81–82, 84.

56. Grimké, *Walking by Faith,* 212–213.

57. Jean Fagan Yellin and John Van Horne, eds., *The Abolitionist Sisterhood: Women's Political Culture in Antebellum America* (Cornell University Press, 1994), xv–xviii; Boylan, *Origins,* 183; A. E. Grimké, "Appeal to the Christian Women of the South," *Anti-Slavery Examiner* 1, no. 2 (September 1836): 23.

58. Susan Zaeske, *Signatures of Citizenship: Petitioning, Antislavery, and Women's Political Identity* (University of North Carolina Press, 2003), 54–59; Gerda Lerner, *The Feminist Thought of Sarah Grimké* (Oxford University Press, 1998), 181–184.

59. Lerner, *Grimké Sisters,* 89, 97.

60. Grimké, "Appeal," 5–6.

61. Grimké, "Appeal," 1, 21; Maria Stewart, "Farewell Address to Her Friends in the City of Boston," 9/21/1833: https://awpc.cattcenter.iastate.edu/2020/11/20/mrs-stewarts-farewell-address-to-her-friends-in-the-city-of-boston-sept-21-1833/.

62. "Communications," *Fayetteville Observer,* 9/29/1836, Gale.

63. Lerner, *Grimké Sisters,* 97, 99.

64. Lerner, *Grimké Sisters,* 108.

65. Angelina Grimké, *An Appeal to the Women of the Nominally Free States Issued by an Anti-Slavery Convention of American Women, Held by Adjournments from the 9th to the 12th of May, 1837* (Isaac Knapp, 1838), 5–6, 13, 21.

66. Grimké in Ira Brown, "Am I Not a Woman and a Sister?" The Anti-Slavery Convention of American Women, 1837–1839," *Pennsylvania History* 50, no. 1 (1983): 8.

67. Lucretia Mott to Elizabeth Cady Stanton, 3/16/1855, *Letters of Lucretia Coffin Mott,* ed. Beverly Wilson Palmer (University of Illinois Press, 2002), 233; Elizabeth Cady Stanton, Susan B. Anthony, and Matilda Joslyn Gage, *History of Woman Suffrage,* 6 vols. (Fowler and Wells, 1882), vol. 1, 342.

68. Phillips in Kathryn Kish Sklar, "'The Throne of My Heart:' Religion, Oratory, and Transatlantic Community in Angelina Grimké's Launching of Women's

Rights, 1828–1838," in Sklar and James Brewer Stewart, eds., *Women's Rights and Transatlantic Antislavery in the Era of Emancipation* (Yale University Press, 2007), 226; Child in Lumpkin, *Emancipation,* 137.

69. Phillips in Lerner, *Grimké Sisters,* 161; Stanton, Anthony, and Gage, *History of Woman Suffrage,* vol. 1, 396, 400.

70. Pastoral Letter (6/27/1837), reprinted in *The Liberator,* 8/11/1837; Grimké, *Appeal to the Women of the Nominally Free States,* 8.

71. John Greenleaf Whittier quoted in Lerner, *Grimké Sisters,* 143; Margaret Hope Bacon, "'The Double Curse of Sex and Color': Robert Purvis and Human Rights," *Pennsylvania Magazine of History and Biography* 121, nos. 1 / 2 (1997): 64.

72. Catharine Beecher, *An Essay on Slavery and Abolitionism, Addressed to Miss A. D. Grimké* (Henry Perkins, 1837), 38.

73. Beecher, *Essay on Slavery,* 101–102.

74. Beecher, *Essay on Slavery,* 107–108; Grimké, *Walking by Faith,* 154; "Fair against Fair," *Mississippi Free Trader,* 6/23/1837, no. 47, Gale.

75. *New Hampshire Patriot* in Lerner, *Grimké Sisters,* 100; Jonathan Walker to Garrison, 5/14/1848, in Yellin et al., *Jacobs Family Papers,* vol. 1, 98.

76. Angelina Grimké, *Letters to Catharine Beecher, in Reply to an Essay on Slavery and Abolitionism Addressed to A. E. Grimké* (Isaac Knapp, 1838), 108, 112, 114.

77. Lerner, *Feminist Thought,* 21.

78. Sarah M. Grimké, *Letters on the Equality of the Sexes and the Condition of Woman* (Isaac Knapp, 1838), 33–34, 37, 43, 45; Lydia Maria Child, *The History of the Condition of Women, in Various Ages and Nations* (John Allen & Co., 1835), 68.

79. Grimké, *Letters on the Equality of the Sexes,* 10, 71.

80. Alexander Keyssar, *The Right to Vote: The Contested History of Democracy in the United States* (Basic Books, 2000), 25, 42.

81. Holly Brewer, "Entailing Aristocracy in Colonial Virginia: 'Ancient Feudal Restraints' and Revolutionary Reform," *William and Mary Quarterly* 54, no. 2 (1997): 315, 345; Peggy Rabkin, *Fathers to Daughters: The Legal Foundations of Female Emancipation* (Praeger, 1980), 63, 68; George Haskins, "Beginnings of Partible Inheritance in the American Colonies," *Yale Law Journal* 51 (1942): 1280, fn4.

82. Thomas Hertell in Elizabeth Frost-Knappman and Kathryn Cullen-DuPont, *Women's Suffrage in America: Updated Edition* (Facts on File, 1995), 30; Rabkin, *Fathers to Daughters,* 87.

83. Rabkin, *Fathers to Daughters,* 82; Mattias Doepke, Michele Tertilt, and Alessandra Voena, "The Economics and Politics of Women's Rights," *Annual Review of Economics* 4 (2012): 356–357; "Rights of Women," *New-York Spectator,* 3/17/1837, Gale; "Rights of Women," *Cleveland Messenger,* reprinted in *The Liberator,* 6/9/1837, 96.

84. "An Act for the Protection and Preservation of the Rights and Property of Married Women," *The Globe,* 4/22/1837 (Washington, DC), 2, NewspaperArchive.com.

85. Norma Basch, "Invisible Women: The Legal Fiction of Marital Unity in Nineteenth Century America," *Feminist Studies* 5, no. 2 (1979): 360; Richard Chused, "Married Women's Property Law: 1800–1850," *Georgetown Law Journal* 71 (1982–1983): 1404; Angela Boswell, "Married Women's Property Rights and the Challenge to the Patriarchal Order," in Janet Coryell et al., *Negotiating Boundaries of Southern Womanhood* (University of Missouri, 2000), 2; Joseph Custer, "The Three Waves of Married Women's Property Acts in the Nineteenth Century with a Focus on Mississippi, New York, and Oregon," *Ohio Northern University Law Review* 40 (2014): 410, fn158.

86. Rabkin, *Fathers to Daughters,* 85; Elizabeth Cady Stanton, *Eighty Years and More* (T. Fisher Unwin, 1898), 150.

87. Rose in Frost-Knappman and Cullen-DuPont, *Women's Suffrage,* 30; and Rabkin, *Fathers to Daughters,* 111.

88. "Turn-out at Lowell," *Boston Evening Transcript,* 2/17/1834 and 2/18/1834: http://sites.fas.harvard.edu/~hsb41/course_resources/documents.html and http://sites.fas.harvard.edu/~hsb41/Documents/turnoutatlowell.pdf; "Rights of Women," *Daily National Intelligencer* (DC), 6/24/1835, Gale.

89. Claudia Goldin, *Understanding the Gender Gap: An Economic History of American Women* (Oxford University Press, 1990), 63.

90. "Rights of Women," *Morning Post,* 8/8/1832, Gale; Elisha P. Hurlbut, *Essays on Human Rights and Their Political Guarantees* (Greeley & McElrath, 1845), 117; "Petition to the Constitutional Convention of the State of New York," in Susan Ware, ed., *American Women's Suffrage: Voices from the Long Struggle for the Vote, 1776–1965* (Library of America, 2020), 35.

91. Elizabeth Cady Stanton to Amy K. Post, 9/24/1848, in Ann D. Gordon et al., *Selected Papers of Elizabeth Cady Stanton and Susan B. Anthony* (Rutgers University Press, 1997), vol. 1, 123; Otelia Cromwell, *Lucretia Mott* (Harvard University Press, 1958), 28–29.

92. "Declaration of Sentiments," July 19–20, 1848, http://utc.iath.virginia.edu/abolitn/abwmat.html.

93. *Proceedings of the Woman's Rights Convention Held at Worcester, October 23–24, 1850* (Prentiss & Sawyer, 1851), 4.

94. Quoted in Parker Pillsbury, *Acts of the Anti-Slavery Apostles* (Clague, Wegman, and Schlicht, 1883), 97–98.

95. Pillsbury, *Acts,* 98; Kelley in Speicher, *Religious World,* 49–50, 151.

96. Jacobs, *Incidents,* 175, 177, 183.

97. Jacobs, *Incidents,* 242.

98. Jacobs, *Incidents,* 245–247; Joshua Coffin to Lydia Maria Child, 6/25/1842, in Yellin et al., *Jacobs Family Papers,* vol. 1, 41–41.

99. Jacobs, *Incidents,* 244.

100. Jacobs, *Incidents,* 283.

101. Jacobs to Amy Kirby Post, 6/21/1857, in Yellin et al., *Jacobs Family Papers,* vol. 1, 236.

102. Martha Jones, *All Bound Up Together: The Woman Question in African American Public Culture, 1830–1900* (University of North Carolina Press, 2007), 60, 71.

103. Lydia Maria Child to Jacobs, 8/13/1860, in Yellin et al., *Jacobs Family Papers,* vol. 1, 277–278; Child in Jacobs, *Incidents,* 8; Child to E. Carpenter, 3/20/1838, in *Letters of Lydia Maria Child,* introduction by John Whittier Greenleaf (Houghton Mifflin, 1883), 43.

104. Jacobs, *Incidents,* 83–84.

105. Yellin, *Harriet Jacobs,* 152, 161.

106. Grimké to Child in Lerner, *Grimké Sisters,* 179; Grimké to Weld, 4/29/38, in Gilbert Barnes and Dwight Dumond, eds., *Letters of Theodore Dwight Weld, Angelina Grimké Weld, and Sarah Grimké, 1822–1844* (D. Appleton-Century, 1934), vol. 2, 649.

107. Janet Farrell Brody, *Contraception and Abortion in Nineteenth-Century America* (Cornell University Press, 1994), 164; Michael Haines, "Fertility and Mortality

in the United States," *Demography* 45, no. 2 (May 2008): 345–361: https://eh.net/encyclopedia/fertility-and-mortality-in-the-united-states/.

108. William D. Smyth, "O Death, Where Is Thy Sting?: Francis J. Grimké's Eulogy for Harriet Jacobs," *Journal of Negro History* 70, nos. 1 / 2 (1985): 37–38.

3. The Right to Lobby: 1865–1900

Epigraph: Kathleen Barry, *Susan B. Anthony, A Biography of a Singular Feminist* (Ballantine, 1988), 355.

1. *Alexander H. Stephens in Public and Private: With Letters and Speeches before, during, and since the War,* ed. Henry Cleveland (National Publishing, 1866), 721; Dan Doyle, *The Cause of All Nations: An International History of the American Civil War* (Basic Books, 2015).

2. Eric Foner, "Lincoln's Use of Politics for Noble Ends," *NYT,* 11/26/2012.

3. Ida Husted Harper, *The Life and Work of Susan B. Anthony, Including Public Addresses, Her Own Letters and Many from Her Contemporaries during Fifty Years,* 2 vols. (Bowen-Merrill, 1898), vol. 1, 35.

4. Harper, *Life and Work,* vol. 1, 43, 45; Barry, *Anthony,* 47.

5. Barry, *Anthony,* 10.

6. Harper, *Life and Work,* vol. 1, 39–40; Barry, *Anthony,* 41.

7. Harper, *Life and Work,* vol. 1, 43–44.

8. SBA, "Transactions of the National Council of Women of the United States: Assembled in Washington, D.C., February 22 to 25, 1891," 228, Library of Congress: https://www.loc.gov/item/15008748/; Speech to Daughters of Temperance, 3/2/1849, in Ann D. Gordon et al., *Selected Papers of Elizabeth Cady Stanton and Susan B. Anthony* (Rutgers University Press, 1997), vol. 1, 138. Also see "Appeal, Elizabeth Cady Stanton," 7/1/1852, in Gordon, *SP,* vol. 1, 201–203; SBA to the *Carson League,* 9/20/1852, in Gordon, *SP,* vol. 1, 206; Harper, *Life and Work,* vol. 1, 18.

9. Harper, *Life and Work,* vol. 1, 30, 46, 60, 126, 237; "Crown of Glory" from Mary Church Terrell, *A Colored Woman in a White World* (G. K. Hall, 1996 reprint), 374.

10. Harper, *Life and Work,* vol. 1, 52; Barry, *Anthony,* 54, 56.

11. Harper, *Life and Work,* vol. 1, 59, 172.

12. Harper, *Life and Work,* vol. 1, 65, 198.

13. Andrea Kerr, *Lucy Stone: Speaking Out for Equality* (Rutgers University Press, 1992), 5, 26; Harper, *Life and Work,* vol. 1, 95.

14. Harper, *Life and Work,* vol. 1, 99.

15. Harper, *Life and Work,* vol. 1, 89–91, 101–103.

16. Harper, *Life and Work,* vol. 1, 91.

17. Wendell Phillips to ECS, 4/25/1864, in Gordon, *SP,* vol. 1, 515; *Susan B. Anthony Diaries,* March 22–26, 1854, in Papers of Susan B. Anthony, Schlesinger Library, Radcliffe Institute, Harvard.

18. May in Harper, *Life and Work,* vol. 1, 148.

19. Harper, *Life and Work,* vol. 1, 201; SBA to ECS, 1/16/1861, in Gordon, *SP,* vol. 1, 456–457.

20. Harper, *Life and Work,* vol. 1, 202.

21. Garrison in Harper, *Life and Work,* vol. 1, 203–204.

22. Harper, *Life and Work,* vol. 1, 203–204.

23. Linda Carlisle, *Elizabeth Packard: A Noble Fight* (University of Illinois Press, 2010), 28, 36; Elizabeth Parsons Ware Packard, *Modern Persecution; or, Insane Asylums Unveiled,* 2 vols. (Case, Lockwood, and Brainard, 1873), vol. 2, 311.

24. Theophilus Packard in Myra Samuels Himelhoch and Arthur Shaffer, "Elizabeth Packard: Nineteenth-Century Crusader for the Rights of Mental Patients," *Journal of American Studies* 13, no. 3 (1979): 348; Elizabeth Parsons Ware Packard, *The Great Drama; or, The Millennial Harbinger,* 4 vols. (Elizabeth Parsons Ware Packard, 1878), vol. 4, 119, and appendix, "The Mystic Key," vol. 4, no. 24.

25. Carlisle, *Elizabeth Packard,* 20, 45; Packard, *Persecution,* vol. 1, 35, 37.

26. Kate Moore, *The Woman They Could Not Silence* (Sourcebooks, 2021), 63.

27. Packard, *Persecution,* vol. 1, 38.

28. Reva Siegel, "'The Rule of Love': Wife-Beating as Prerogative and Privacy," *Yale Law Journal* 105 (1996): 2146, 2150, 2154; Hendrik Hertog, "Mrs. Packard on Dependency," *Yale Journal of Law and the Humanities* 1, no. 1 (Jan. 1989): 90.

29. Packard, *Persecution,* vol. 1, 41; R. Richard Geddes and Sharon Tennyson, "Passage of the Married Women's Property Acts and Earnings Acts in the United States: 1850–1920," *Research in Economic History* 29 (2013): 153.

30. Packard, *Persecution,* vol. 1, 53–54, 146.

31. Carroll Smith-Rosenberg and Charles Rosenberg, "The Female Animal: Medical and Biological Views of Woman and Her Role in Nineteenth-Century America," *Journal of American History* 60, no. 2 (1973): 335; Elaine Showalter, *The Female Malady: Women, Madness, and Culture in England, 1830–1970* (Pantheon, 1985), 76–78; Katherine Pouba and Ashley Tianen, "Lunacy in the 19th Century: Women's Admission to Asylums in United States of America," *Oshkosh Scholar* 1 (Apr. 2006): 95, 100; Moore, *Woman They Could Not Silence,* 90.

32. Packard, *Persecution,* vol. 1, 56.

33. Barry, *Anthony,* 69–70.

34. SBA to Lydia Mott, ca. 4/10/1862, in Gordon, *SP,* vol. 1, 475; Sally McMillen, *Seneca Falls and the Origins of the Women's Rights Movement* (Oxford University Press, 2008), 157.

35. "Woman's Rights Meetings," *Liberator* (Boston), 7/6/1860, 106; Elizabeth Cady Stanton, Susan B. Anthony, and Matilda Joslyn Gage, *History of Woman Suffrage,* 6 vols. (Fowler and Wells, 1882), vol. 1, 276; Stephanie McCurry, *Women's War: Fighting and Surviving the American Civil War* (Harvard University Press, 2019), 39.

36. William Lloyd Garrison to Helen Garrison, 5/14/1863, in Walter Merrill, ed., *Letters of William Lloyd Garrison,* 6 vols. (Harvard University Press, 1971–), vol. 5, 154; Gordon, *SP,* vol. 1, 508; Eric Foner, *The Fiery Trial: Abraham Lincoln and American Slavery* (Norton, 2010), 291.

37. Rosalyn Terborg-Penn, *African-American Women in the Struggle for the Vote, 1850–1920* (Indiana University Press, 1998), 22; ECS, "To the Women of the Republic," 4/24/1863, in Gordon, *SP,* vol. 1, 484; "Meeting of the Loyal Women of the Republic," 5/14/1865, in Gordon, *SP,* vol. 1, 488; Elizabeth Cady Stanton, *Eighty Years and More* (T. Fisher Unwin, 1898), 237.

38. SBA in Barry, *Anthony,* 153; Merrill, *Letters of William Lloyd Garrison,* vol. 1, 154.

39. Harper, *Life and Work,* vol. 1, 230.

40. SBA to ECS, in Gordon, *SP,* vol. 1, 503; Barry, *Anthony,* 154.

41. Harper, *Life and Work,* vol. 1, 232, 316.

42. Harper, *Life and Work,* vol. 1, 235; SBA to Charles Sumner, 3/1/1864 and 3/6/1864, in Gordon, *SP,* vol. 1, 511–513.

43. Barry, *Anthony,* 162.

44. Phillips in Faye Dudden, *Fighting Chance: The Struggle over Woman Suffrage and Black Suffrage in Reconstruction America* (Oxford University Press, 2011), 62; ECS in Gordon, *SP,* vol. 1, 549.

45. Foner, *Fiery Trial,* 332; SBA, "Remarks at Memorial Service for Abraham Lincoln,"4/23/1865, in Gordon, *SP,* vol. 1, 546; Booth in Dudden, *Fighting Chance,* 61.

46. ECS to the Editor, *National Anti-Slavery Standard,* 12/26/1865, in Gordon, *SP,* vol. 1, 564.

47. ECS in Gordon, *SP,* vol. 1, 564. On Abigail Adams, see ECS in Gordon, *SP,* vol. 1, 483.

48. ECS to Wendell Phillips, 1/12/1866, in Gordon, *SP,* vol. 1, 570, and vol. 2, xxi. Also see ECS in Dudden, *Fighting Chance,* 166. On voting by noncitizens, see *Arguments of Counsel and Opinion of the Supreme Court of the District of Columbia on the Woman Suffrage Question* (Washington, 1871), 19, Library of Congress, National American Women's Suffrage Association Collection.

49. Douglass in Dudden, *Fighting Chance,* 188; Carol Bacon, "'The Double Curse of Sex and Color': Robert Purvis and Human Rights," *Pennsylvania Magazine of History and Biography* 121, nos. 1/2 (1997): 74; also see Purvis at the American Anti-Slavery Society, 5/9/1866, in Gordon, *SP,* vol. 1, 580; Stanton, Anthony, and Gage, *History of Woman Suffrage,* vol. 2, 265.

50. Dudden, *Fighting Chance,* 96. Also see Sojourner Truth on meeting Lincoln, 12/10/1864: https://dh.howard.edu/cgi/viewcontent.cgi?referer=https://www.google.com/&httpsredir=1&article=1025&context=og_slavery.

51. Norma Basch, *In The Eyes of the Law: Women, Marriage and Property in Nineteenth-Century New York* (Cornell University Press, 1982), 217; Reva Siegel, "The Modernization of Marital Status Law: Adjudicating Wives' Rights to Earnings, 1860–1930," *Georgetown Law Review* 82 (1993–1994): 2149–2150.

52. Dudden, *Fighting Chance,* 96; Hendrick Hartog, *Man & Wife in America: A History* (Harvard University Press, 2000), 193.

53. Dudden, *Fighting Chance,* 78–79; Stevens in *Congressional Globe,* 39th Cong., 1st sess., 537.

54. "Remarks by SBA at the Convention of Colored Citizens of New York," in Gordon, *SP,* vol. 1, 595; Dudden, *Fighting Chance,* 79.

55. Harper, *Life and Work,* vol. 1, 261; Barry, *Anthony,* 177.

56. Dudden, *Fighting Chance,* 123; SBA to ECS, *Yellin et al.,* vol. 2, 692.

57. Dudden, *Fighting Chance,* 115; Barry, *Anthony,* 180. On Anthony as racist, see Ellen DuBois, *Feminism and Suffrage: The Emergence of an Independent Women's Movement in America, 1848–1869* (Cornell University Press, 1978), 96. The quotation is from Cathleen Cahill, *Recasting the Vote: How Women of Color Transformed the Suffrage Movement* (University of North Carolina Press, 2020), 17.

58. SBA to Olympia Brown, 1/1/1868, in Gordon, *SP,* vol. 2, 121; Dudden, *Fighting Chance,* 129–130; DuBois, *Feminism and Suffrage,* 98.

59. "Prospectus of The Revolution for 1870," *The Revolution* 4, no. 20 (1869): 316.

60. Douglass in Lisa Tetrault, *The Myth of Seneca Falls: Memory and the Women's Suffrage Movement, 1848–1898* (University of North Carolina Press, 2017), 29;

Elaine Frantz Parsons, *Ku-Klux: The Birth of the Klan during Reconstruction* (University of North Carolina Press, 2015), 8.

61. SBA in Gordon, *SP,* vol. 2, 240.

62. Douglass in Gordon, *SP,* vol. 2, 181. Elizabeth Cady Stanton later eulogized him: see ECS, "Funeral of Frederick Douglass," 2/25/1895, in Gordon, *SP,* vol. 5, 681.

63. SBA in Gordon, *SP,* vol. 2, 240; Reva Siegel, "Home as Work: The First Woman's Rights Claims Concerning Wives' Household Labor, 1850–1880," *Yale Law Journal* 103 (1993–1994): 1128.

64. Dudden, *Fighting Chance,* 179; Eric Foner, *The Second Founding: How the Civil War and Reconstruction Remade the Constitution* (Norton, 2019), 114.

65. SBA to Sumner, 2/19/1872, in Gordon, *SP,* vol. 2, 483–484.

66. Woodhull in Barry, *Anthony,* 229.

67. Harper, *Life and Work,* vol. 1, 414; Barry, *Anthony,* 245–246.

68. SBA Diary, 5/11/1872, in Gordon, *SP,* vol. 2, 494; SBA to Wright, in Gordon, *SP,* vol. 2, 496.

69. Packard, *Persecution,* vol. 1, 79.

70. Packard, *Persecution,* vol. 1, 84–85.

71. Packard, *Persecution,* vol. 1, 87.

72. Packard, *Persecution,* vol. 1, 93; Hertog, "Mrs. Packard," 81.

73. Himelhoch, "Crusader," 344. For statistics, see Carlisle, *Elizabeth Packard,* 65.

74. Packard, *Persecution,* vol. 1, 97–98, 100–101, 142; Packard, *Great Drama,* vol. 4, 57.

75. Packard, *Persecution,* vol. 1, 112–114, 126, 130.

76. Packard, *Persecution,* vol. 1, 113.

77. Packard, *Persecution,* vol. 1, 116.

78. Packard, *Persecution,* vol. 1, 177–179, 201.

79. Packard, *Persecution,* vol. 1, 212.

80. Packard, *Persecution,* vol. 1, 241, 247, 340.

81. Packard, *Persecution,* vol. 1, 352.

82. Moore, *Woman,* 254.

83. Packard, *Persecution,* vol. 1, 354, and vol. 2, 187; Elizabeth Packard, *Great Disclosure of Spiritual Wickedness!! in High Places, with an Appeal to the Government to Protect the Inalienable Rights of Married Women* (Arno Press, 1974 reprint), 152; Himelhoch, "Crusader," 349; Carlisle, *Elizabeth Packard,* 16.

84. McFarland in Carlisle, *Elizabeth Packard,* 95; Packard, *Persecution,* vol. 1, 386, 389; Himelhoch, "Crusader," 356.

85. Packard, *Persecution,* vol. 2, 17.

86. Packard, *Persecution,* vol. 2, 20.

87. SBA in Barry, *Anthony,* 248; *Philadelphia Evening Telegraph,* 6/14/1872, in Gordon, *SP,* vol. 2, 508; Harper, *Life and Work,* vol. 1, 422.

88. Tetrault, *Myth,* 65; ECS to Isabella Beecher Hooker, 6/14/1872, in Gordon, *SP,* vol. 2, 511; Harper, *Life and Work,* vol. 1, 416.

89. Tetrault, *Myth,* 49, 59, 85; Albert Gallatin Riddle and Francie Miller in *Arguments of Counsel,* 72, in Gordon, *SP,* vol. 2, 526; Stanton, Anthony, and Gage, *History of Woman Suffrage,* vol. 2, 650.

90. Barry, *Anthony,* 250.

91. Barry, *Anthony,* 250.

92. Barry, *Anthony,* 250; SBA to Sarah Tucker Huntington, 11/11/1872, in Gordon, *SP,* vol. 2, 529–530; Harper, *Life and Work,* vol. 1, 424; Ann Gordon, "The Trial of Susan B. Anthony," Federal Judicial History Office (2005), 33: https://www.fjc.gov/sites/default/files/trials/susanbanthony.pdf.

93. SBA to ECS, 11/5/1872, in Gordon, *SP,* vol. 2, 524.

94. Harper, *Life and Work,* vol. 1, 426; Gordon, "Trial," 3.

95. Gordon, "Trial," 3.

96. Gordon, "Trial," 40; Harper, *Life and Work,* vol. 1, 433, 436.

97. Gordon, "Trial," 68; "Susan in Trouble," *Owyhee Avalanche* (Ruby City, ID), 6/28/1873, Gale.

98. Ariana Randolph Wormeley Curtis, *The Spirit of Seventy-Six; or, The Coming Woman, a Prophetic Drama,* 15th ed. (Little, Brown, 1873), 17–18; Emma Dassori, "Performing the Woman Question: The Emergence of Anti-Suffrage Dramas," *Transcendental Quarterly* 19, no. 4 (Dec. 2005): 302.

99. Stanton, Anthony, and Gage, *History of Woman Suffrage,* vol. 2, 630.

100. Henry Seldon in "An Account of the Proceedings of the Trail of Susan B. Anthony on the Charge of Illegal Voting" *Rochester Daily Democrat,* 1874, 19; Gordon, "Trial," 50.

101. Harper, *Life and Work,* vol. 1, 439; Stanton, Anthony, and Gage, *History of Woman Suffrage,* vol. 2, 682.

102. Stanton, Anthony, and Gage, *History of Woman Suffrage,* vol. 2, 686.

103. Stanton, Anthony, and Gage, *History of Woman Suffrage,* vol. 2, 687–689.

104. "States Rights Reasserted," *Georgia Weekly Telegraph and Georgia Journal & Messenger* (Macon, GA), 7/1/1873, Gale; Also see *Daily Arkansas Gazette* (Little Rock, AR), 6/22/1873, Gale.

105. George Hoar, "Woman Suffrage in the U.S. Senate, 1879, Argument for a Sixteenth Amendment": https://tile.loc.gov/storage-services/service/rbc/rbnawsa/n8360/n8360.pdf.

106. "The Sixteenth Amendment," *Milwaukee Daily Sentinel* (WI), 4/2/1877, Gale.

107. Francis Parkman, "The Woman Question," *North American Review* 129, no. 275 (Oct. 1879): 308, 310, 314, 321.

108. Barbara Sapinsley, *The Private War of Mrs. Packard* (Paragon House, 1991), 3; Moore, *Woman,* 23.

109. Sapinsley, *Private War,* 1; Packard, *Persecution,* vol. 2, 33, 40, 44.

110. Packard, *Persecution,* vol. 2, 23; Naomi Cahn, "Faithless Wives and Lazy Husbands: Gender Norms in Nineteenth-Century Divorce Law," *University of Illinois Law Review* (2002): 673, 676.

111. Jurors in "Packard v. Packard," *Great American Trials* (Visible Ink, 2003), 140; Packard, *Persecution,* vol. 2, 56–57; Kankakee *Gazette* (IL) quoted in "The Case of Mrs. Packard," *Chicago Tribune,* 1/28/1864, 2.

112. "Legal Disabilities of Married Women," *Chicago Tribune,* 11/13/1860, 2; "The Rights of Married Women," *Woodstock Sentinel,* 7/30/1868, 2; "Property Rights of Wives," *Chicago Evening Post,* 6/22/1869, 2.

113. Packard, *Persecution,* vol. 2, 68.

114. Himelhoch, "Crusader," 359, 369, 374; Ann Braden Johnson, *Out of Bedlam: The Truth about Deinstitutionalization* (Basic Books, 1990), 11; *Gerald Grob, The Mad among Us: A History of the Care of America's Mentally Ill* (Free Press, 1994); "Funeral of

Mrs. E. P. W. Packard," *Chicago Tribune,* 7/28/1897, 10; *Bangor Daily Whig and Courier* (ME), 2/7/1874, Gale.

115. Carlisle, *Elizabeth Packard,* 133, 141.

116. Mark Neely and Gerald McMurtry, *The Insanity File: The Case of Mary Todd Lincoln* (Southern Illinois University Press, 1986), 68; Carlisle, *Elizabeth Packard,* 179–180.

117. Packard, *Persecution,* vol. 2, 315.

118. Packard, *Persecution,* vol. 2, 194, 311, 313–314.

119. "Mrs. Packard's Work," *Chicago Tribune,* 7/22/1893, 14; Packard, *Persecution,* vol. 2, 311.

120. Packard, *Persecution,* vol. 2, 318; Himelhoch, "Crusader," 346, 374.

121. Lawrence Goldstone, *Inherently Unequal: The Betrayal of Civil Rights by the Supreme Court, 1865–1903* (Walker & Co., 2011).

122. SBA to Lepha Johnson Canfield, 1/2/1871, in Gordon, *SP,* vol. 2, 399; Diary of SBA, 1/20/1895, in Gordon, *SP,* vol. 5, 673; Lisa Tetrault, "The Incorporation of American Feminism: Suffragists and the Post-Bellum Lyceum," *Journal of American History* 96, no. 4 (2010): 1028.

123. "A Brave Lady," *Daily Rocky Mountain News* (Denver, Co.), 1/13/1877, Gale; "Mary Clemmer Says She Likes Susan B. Anthony," *Daily Evening Bulletin* (San Francisco), 2/17/1877; Harper, *Life and Work,* vol. 1, 340.

124. Emmeline Pankhurst, *My Own Story* (E. Nash, 1914), 37; Stanton, *Eighty Years,* 174.

125. SBA in Barry, *Anthony,* 351.

126. David Blight, *Race and Reunion: The Civil War in Memory* (Belknap Press of Harvard University Press, 2003), 9.

127. Harriot Stanton Blatch and Alma Lutz, *Challenging Years: The Memoirs of Harriot Stanton Blatch* (Putnam and Sons, 1940), 91–92.

4. The Right to Vote: 1900–1920

Epigraph: MCT, *A Colored Woman in a White World* (1940; G. K. Hall, 1996), 310.

1. "Mrs. Terrell's Triumph," *Washington Bee,* 7/25/1896, 4.

2. "Convention Notes," *Washington Bee,* 7/25/1896, 4.

3. Elizabeth Ewen, "City Lights: Immigrant Women and the Rise of the Movies," *Signs* 5, no. 3 (1980): S45.

4. To avoid confusion with more recent connotations, this book uses the word Progressive, capitalized, to refer solely to this era.

5. Nancy Cott, *The Grounding of Modern Feminism* (Yale University Press, 1987), 37.

6. MCT, *Colored Woman,* 8.

7. Alison Parker, *Unceasing Militant: The Life of Mary Church Terrell* (University of North Carolina Press, 2020), 12–13.

8. MCT, *Colored Woman,* 10–11.

9. MCT, *Colored Woman,* 20, 28.

10. MCT, *Colored Woman,* 15, 21, 28, 48.

11. MCT, *Colored Woman,* 15, 25.

12. Beverly Washington Jones, *Quest for Equality: The Life and Writings of Mary Church Terrell, 1863–1954* (Carlson, 1990), 72; MCT, *Colored Woman,* 50.

13. MCT, *Colored Woman,* 22; Brittney C. Cooper, *Beyond Respectability: The Intellectual Thought of Race Women* (University of Illinois Press, 2017), 55.

14. MCT, *Colored Woman,* 22–23.

15. MCT, *Colored Woman,* 39.

16. MCT, *Colored Woman,* 53.

17. MCT, *Colored Woman,* 144; Parker, *Unceasing Militant,* 122; Henry James in Marcia Jacobson, "Popular Fiction and Henry James's Unpopular 'Bostonians,'" *Modern Philology* 73, no. 3 (1976): 265.

18. Cott, *Grounding of Modern Feminism,* 219; Ellen DuBois, *Suffrage: Women's Long Battle for the Vote* (Simon & Schuster, 2020), 85.

19. Lynn Gordon, "The Gibson Girl Goes to College: Popular Culture and Women's Higher Education in the Progressive Era," *American Quarterly* 39, no. 2 (1987): 214; Abbe Carter Goodloe, *College Girls* (Charles Scribner's Sons, 1895), 31, 35, 98, 166.

20. Charlotte Perkins Stetson Gilman, *Women and Economics* (1898; Source Book Press, 1970), 71.

21. MCT, *Colored Woman,* 32.

22. Alice Freeman Palmer, *The Evolution of a New Woman: Ruth Bordin* (University of Michigan Press, 1993), 2; Vicki Howard, "The Courtship Letters of an African-American Couple: Race, Gender, Class, and the Cult of True Womanhood," *Southwestern Historical Quarterly* 100, no. 1 (1996): 77; MCT, *Colored Woman,* 41.

23. MCT, *Colored Woman,* 47.

24. MCT, *Colored Woman,* 47.

25. MCT, *Colored Woman,* 105, 108; Amy Wood, *Lynching and Spectacle: Witnessing Racial Violence in America* (University of North Carolina Press, 2009), 3.

26. MCT, *Colored Woman,* 62–63.

27. Parker, *Unceasing Militant,* 18.

28. MCT, *Colored Woman,* 102.

29. Parker, *Unceasing Militant,* 34, 38.

30. MCT, *Colored Woman,* 86, 88–89.

31. MCT, *Colored Woman,* 98–99.

32. Marie Hall Ets, *Rosa: The Life of an Italian Immigrant* (University of Wisconsin Press, 1999), 119. Rosa dictated her memoir to her friend Marie Hall Ets, a writer and settlement worker.

33. Ets, *Rosa,* 41, 109, 120.

34. Ets, *Rosa,* 86.

35. Ets, *Rosa,* 11, 33, 76.

36. Ets, *Rosa,* 77; Elizabeth Ewen, *Immigrant Women in the Land of Dollars: Life and Culture on the Lower East Side, 1890–1925* (Monthly Review Press, 1985), 51.

37. Ets, *Rosa,* 89.

38. Ets, *Rosa,* 98.

39. Ets, *Rosa,* 24, 154.

40. Ets, *Rosa,* 80–81, 157.

41. Ets, *Rosa,* 158–159.

42. Ets, *Rosa,* 160.

43. Ets, *Rosa,* 162; Vaneeta-marie D'Andrea, "The Life of Rosa Cavalleri: An Application of Abramson's Model of Rootedness / Rootlessness," in Rocco Caporale, ed., *The Italian Americans through the Generations* (Italian American Historical Association, 1986), 112.

44. Frances E. W. Harper, "Duty to Dependent Races," Transactions of the National Council of Women on the United States, Assembled in Washington, DC, February 22 to 25, 1891, 82; Library of Congress online: https://tile.loc.gov/storage-services/service/rbc/rbnawsa/n8748/n8748.pdf.

45. MCT, *Colored Woman,* 144.

46. MCT, *Colored Woman,* 144.

47. MCT, *Colored Woman,* 120; Martha Jones, *Vanguard: How Black Women Broke Barriers, Won the Vote, and Insisted on Equality for All* (Basic Books, 2020), 156; Mary Cookingham, "Bluestockings, Spinsters, and Pedagogues: Women College Graduates, 1865–1910," *Population Studies* 38, no. 3 (1984): 352.

48. MCT, *Colored Woman,* 125.

49. Parker, *Unceasing Militant,* 58.

50. MCT, *Colored Woman,* 148; Beverly Jones, "Mary Church Terrell and the National Association of Colored Women, 1896 to 1901," *Journal of Negro History* 67, no. 1 (1982): 22; DuBois, *Suffrage,* 102.

51. Parker, *Unceasing Militant,* 42, 44.

52. MCT, *Colored Woman,* 108, 120; Parker, *Unceasing Militant,* 48.

53. Sarah Silkey, *Black Woman Reformer Ida B. Wells: Lynching and Transatlantic Activism* (University of Georgia Press, 2018), 54. For Terrell's most famous writing on lynching, see MCT, "Lynching from a Negro's Point of View," *North American Review* 178, no. 571 (1904): 853–868.

54. Jacks is quoted in "Closing Day's Work," *St. Joseph Daily Herald,* 9/8/1895, 8.

55. Wells-Barnett in Parker, *Unceasing Militant,* 65.

56. Carrie Chapman Catt, "Mary Church Terrell: An Appreciation," *Oberlin Alumni Magazine* (June 1936): https://cdm15963.contentdm.oclc.org/digital/collection/p15963coll16/id/586; "Trustees in Petticoats," *Washington Times,* 4/6/1895, 1; Associated Press, "Women in Schools," *Semi-Weekly Interior Journal* (Stanford, KY), 6/28/1895.

57. Associated Press, "Women in Schools."

58. MCT, *Colored Woman,* 114, 129, 151; Parker, *Unceasing Militant,* 49.

59. "The Afro-American Women," *Washington Bee,* 7/25/1896, 4.

60. Shirley Carlson, "Black Ideals of Womanhood in the Late Victorian Era," *Journal of Negro History* 77, no. 2 (1992): 64.

61. "Mrs. Terrell's Triumph," *Washington Bee,* 7/25/1896, 4; Cooper, *Beyond Respectability,* 65.

62. Nancy Schrom Dye and Daniel Blake Smith, "Mother Love and Infant Death, 1750–1920," *Journal of American History* 73, no. 2 (1986): 349; MCT, *Colored Woman,* 107; Parker, *Unceasing Militant,* 51.

63. "First Presidential Address to NACW," in Jones, *Quest for Equality,* 134; "Colored Women Speak," *Indianapolis Journal,* 8/15/1899, 5; "Minutes of the Second Convention of the National Association of Colored Women; Held at Quinn Chapel, Chicago, August 14–16, 1899," 4: https://www.loc.gov/resource/lcrbmrp.t1616/?st=gallery.

64. Parker, *Unceasing Militant,* 70; MCT, *Colored Woman,* 152; Jones, *Vanguard,* 152.

65. Quoted in MCT, *Colored Woman,* 153–154; National Council of Women of the United States, *Report of Its Tenth Annual Executive and Its Third Triennial Session* (Hollenbeck Press, 1899), 49.

66. MCT, *Colored Woman,* 153–154; Edward Ayers, *The Promise of the New South,* 15th anniversary ed. (Oxford University Press, 2007), 132.

67. Washington quoted in Jones, *Vanguard,* 160.

68. Parker, *Unceasing Militant,* 332, n10; MCT, *Colored Woman,* 158; Laurie Kaiser, "The Black Madonna: Notions of True Woman from Jacobs to Hurston," *South Atlantic Review* 60, no. 1 (1995): 101; MCT, *Colored Woman,* 143; Kathleen Barry, *Susan B. Anthony: A Biography of a Singular Feminist* (Ballantine, 1988), 332, n8.

69. MCT, *Colored Woman,* 143; "To the Members of the State Societies Auxiliary to the National American Woman Suffrage Association" (n.d.), 2, MCT Papers, Howard University Archives, Moorland-Spingarn Research Center, box 102–13, folder 255.

70. Barry, *Anthony,* 347.

71. Barry, *Anthony,* 345–346.

72. Parker, *Unceasing Militant,* 53; MCT, *Colored Woman,* 111.

73. Parker, *Unceasing Militant,* 53; MCT, *Colored Woman,* 146.

74. George Washington to Phillis Wheatley, 2/28/1776: https://founders.archives.gov/documents/Washington/03-03-02-0281.

75. MCT, *Colored Woman,* 146; Program, "Thirty-Second Annual Convention of the National American Woman Suffrage Association at Church of Our Father, Washington," 2/8–14/1900, 4: www.loc.gov/resource/rbcmil.scrp1005902/?sp=10.

76. "Woman's Case in Equity," *Colored American,* 2/17/1900, 4.

77. "Woman's Case in Equity," 4.

78. "Woman's Case in Equity," 1, and "An Honored Tribute," *Colored American,* 7/7/1900, 8; MCT, *Colored Woman,* 146–147.

79. MCT to Robert Terrell, ca. August 1900, Mary Church Terrell Papers: Family Correspondence, 1890–1955, Library of Congress; MCT, *Colored Woman,* 145, 175; Parker, *Unceasing Militant,* 85.

80. MCT, *Colored Woman,* 167; Talitha LeFlouria, *Chained in Silence: Black Women and Convict Labor in the New South* (University of North Carolina Press, 2015), 99.

81. MCT, *Colored Woman,* 201.

82. "Deserves Fair Treatment," *The Orrville Courier* (Ohio), 8/12/1904, 2; *Washington Post* in MCT, *Colored Woman,* 205; Mary Church Terrell, "Address to Be Delivered at the International Congress of Women in Berlin, Germany," June 13, 1904, 4, Mary Church Terrell Papers, mss 42549, box 28, reel 1, Manuscripts Division, Library of Congress, http://hdl.loc.gov/loc.mss/ms009311.mss42549.0363.

83. MCT, "Susan B. Anthony, The Abolitionist," in Jones, *Quest for Equality,* 234–235; Robert Terrell, "Our Debt to Suffragists," *The Crisis* 10, no. 4 (August 1915): 181.

84. Ula Taylor, *The Veiled Garvey: The Life and Times of Amy Jacques Garvey* (University of North Carolina Press, 2002), 73.

85. Elna Green, "The Rest of the Story: Kate Gordon and the Opposition to the Nineteenth Amendment in the South," *Louisiana History* 33, no. 2 (1992): 176–177; Joel Williamson, *A Rage for Order: Black-White Relations in the American South since Emancipation* (Oxford University Press, 1986), 101, 103.

86. Jones, *Vanguard,* 181–182; Ira Katznelson, *Fear Itself: The New Deal and the Origins of Our Time* (Norton, 2003), 15; Campbell Gibson and Kay Jung, "Historical Census Statistics on Population Totals by Race, 1790–1990," US Census, Population Di-

vision, Working Paper 56, table A-12: https://www.census.gov/content/dam/Census/library/working-papers/2002/demo/POP-twps0056.pdf.

87. Parker, *Unceasing Militant,* 67; George Washington to Phillis Wheatley, 2/28/1776, in Founders Online, US National Archives: https://founders.archives.gov/documents/Washington/03-03-02-0281.

88. Descriptions of Rosa's experiences in this and the following paragraphs are from Ets, *Rosa,* 167–200.

89. Hendrick Hartog, *Man & Wife in America: A History* (Harvard University Press, 2000), 215, 293; Reva Siegel, "The Modernization of Marital Status Law: Adjudicating Wives' Rights to Earnings, 1860–1930," *Georgetown Law Review* 82 (1993–1994): 2129.

90. Ets, *Rosa,* 204.

91. Ets, *Rosa,* 205; Reva Siegel, "'The Rule of Love:' Wife-Beating as Prerogative and Privacy," *Yale Law Journal* 105 (1996): 2139; Elizabeth Pleck, "Wife Beating in Nineteenth-Century America," *Household Constitution and Family Relationships* (De Gruyter Saur, 1992), 189; Elizabeth Pleck, *Domestic Tyranny: The Making of Social Policy Against Family Violence from Colonial Times to the Present* (Oxford University Press, 1987), 97.

92. Ets, *Rosa,* 218–219; John Higham, *Strangers in the Land: Patterns in American Nativism, 1800–1925,* 2nd ed. (Rutgers University Press, 1988), 156; Rudolph Vecoli, "Are Italian Americans Just White Folks?" *Italian Americana* 13, no. 2 (1995): 156.

93. Ets, *Rosa,* 220.

94. George Martin, *Madam Secretary: Frances Perkins* (Houghton-Mifflin, 1976), 59; *Chicago Commons—Thirty Years and After* (Chicago Commons, 1924), 5, 23; Ets, *Rosa,* 225; Robyn Muncy, *Creating a Female Dominion in American Reform, 1890–1935* (Oxford University Press, 1991), 68. Also see Daniel Rodgers, *Atlantic Crossings: Social Politics in a Progressive Age* (Harvard University Press, 2000) and Clarke Chambers, *Seedtime of Reform: American Social Service and Social Action, 1918–1933* (University of Minnesota, 1963).

95. Jane Addams, *Twenty Years at Hull House* (Macmillan, 1910), 340; Melanie Gustafson, "'Good City Government Is Good Housekeeping': Women and Municipal Reform," *Pennsylvania Legacies* 11, no. 2 (2011): 17; "Women Must Register to Win Full Suffrage," *Chicago Examiner,* 1/29/1914, 4 (caption).

96. David M. Kennedy, *Birth Control in America: The Career of Margaret Sanger* (Yale University Press, 1970), 54, 57; Reva Siegel, "Reasoning from the Body: A Historical Perspective on Abortion Regulation Questions of Equal Protection," *Stanford Law Review* 44, no. 2 (1992): 282; Harriet Pilpel, "The Crazy Quilt of Our Birth Control Laws," *Journal of Sex Research* 1, no. 2 (1965): 137.

97. Kennedy, *Birth Control,* 16, 23, 84–85.

98. Trent MacNamara, *Birth Control and American Modernity: A History of Popular Ideas* (Cambridge University Press, 2018), 53–55; Eastman in Blanche Weisen Cook, ed., *Crystal Eastman on Women and Revolution* (Oxford University Press, 1978), 47.

99. Ellen Chesler, *Woman of Valor: Margaret Sanger and the Birth Control Movement in America* (Simon and Schuster, 1992), 149, 159–160, 201; Margaret Sanger, *Motherhood in Bondage* (Brentano's, 1928), 5–6, 411.

100. Quotations by Rosa in this paragraph and the rest of the section are from Ets, *Rosa,* 230–238.

101. MCT, *Colored Woman,* 316.

102. DuBois, *Suffrage,* 123; Marjorie Spruill Wheeler, *New Women of the New South: The Leaders of the Woman Suffrage Movement in the Southern United States* (Oxford University Press, 1993), 101.

103. George Frederickson, *White Supremacy: A Comparative Study of American and South African History* (Oxford University Press, 1981), 197.

104. Morton Sosna, "The South in the Saddle: Racial Politics during the Wilson Years," *Wisconsin Magazine of History* 54, no. 1 (1970): 31.

105. Sosna, "South in the Saddle," 34; Louis Harlan, *Booker T. Washington: The Wizard of Tuskegee, 1901–1915* (Oxford University Press, 1983), 17, 406–407, 409; Nancy Weiss, "The Negro and the New Freedom: Fighting Wilsonian Segregation," *Political Science Quarterly* 84, no. 1 (Mar. 1962): 62.

106. "A Discreditable Attempt," *Washington Herald,* 4/27/1914, 4; "Maurice Splain Is O.K. to Senate Committee," *Washington Evening Star,* 2/23/1914, 5; "Appointment of a Negro Stirs Senate," *Alaska Citizen,* 4/13/1914, 1; "News of the Day," *Alexandria Gazette,* 1/22/1914, 5; "Vardaman to Oppose Negroes and Whisky," *Washington Herald,* 6/29/1913, 3; Vardaman quoted in Jason Morgan Ward, *Hanging Bridge: Racial Violence and America's Civil Rights Century* (Oxford University Press, 2016), 63; MCT, *Colored Woman,* 262.

107. Booker T. Washington to US Attorney General George Wickersham, 12/3/1909, in Louis Harlan et al., eds., *Booker T. Washington Papers,* vol. 10 (University of Illinois Press, 1981), 239.

108. Parker, *Unceasing Militant,* 119; MCT, *Colored Woman,* 263–265.

109. Richard Thompson to Booker T. Washington, 3/14/1900, in Harlan et al., *Booker T. Washington Papers,* vol. 6, 463; Booker T. Washington to Robert H. Terrell, 4/27/1910, in Harlan et al., *Booker T. Washington Papers,* vol. 10, 323.

110. W. E. B. Du Bois, *The Crisis* 5, no. 6 (Apr. 1913): 267; Julius Taylor, "The Equal Suffrage Parade was Viewed by Many Thousand People from All Parts of the United States," *The Broad Ax,* 3/8/1913, 1.

111. DuBois, *Suffrage,* 113, 120.

112. "Notes Concerning Woman Suffrage," *Whitesville Alleghany County News* (NY), 2/26/1914, 4.

113. *Congressional Record,* 63rd Cong., 2nd sess., 51, part 5, 3/19/1914, 5088, 5096; "Women Denied Right to Ballot by Senate Vote," *Indianapolis Star,* 3/20/1914, 6.

114. "Complicates Things," *Kokomo Tribune,* 3/6/1914, 3; Jones, *Vanguard,* 168; *Congressional Record, Senate,* vol. 51, part 5, 3/19/1914, 5094, 5097.

115. Jones, *Vanguard,* 171; *The Shelby Republican* (TN), 4/23/1914, 6; MCT, *Colored Woman,* 264.

116. Susan Goodier, *No Votes for Women: The New York State Anti-Suffrage Movement* (University of Illinois Press, 2012), 30.

117. Ida Tarbell, *The Business of Being a Woman* (Macmillan, 1912), 4, 9–10.

118. Thomas Jablonsky, *The Home, Heaven, and Mother Party: Female Anti-Suffragists in the United States* (Carlson, 1994), 13; Ernest Bernbaum, ed., *Anti-Suffrage Essays by Massachusetts Women* (Forum, 1916).

119. "Reasons against Woman Suffrage," *The Remonstrance* (Boston) (Jan. 1908), 2, Massachusetts Historical Society, Records of the Massachusetts Association

Opposed to the Further Extension of Suffrage to Women: https://www.masshist.org/database/viewer.php?item_id=3381&mode=large&img_step=1#page1.

120. "Reasons," 2.

121. Victoria Bissell Brown, "Did Woodrow Wilson's Gender Politics Matter?," in John Milton Cooper Jr., ed., *Reconsidering Woodrow Wilson* (Woodrow Wilson Center, 2008), 129, 134; Lynn Dumenil, *Second Line of Defense: American Women and World War I* (University of North Carolina Press, 2017), 78.

122. Deborah Thom, *Nice Girls and Rude Girls: Women Workers in World War I* (L. B. Tauris, 1998), 146.

123. Beth A. Behn, "Woodrow Wilson's Conversion Experience: The President and the Federal Woman Suffrage Amendment," PhD diss., University of Amherst, 2012, 181–182, 228.

124. Gary Gerstle, "Race and Nation in the Thought and Politics of Woodrow Wilson," in Cooper, *Reconsidering,* 93.

125. "Wilson Backs Amendment for Woman Suffrage," *NYT,* 1/10/1918, 1, 3; Elizabeth Cobbs, *The Hello Girls: America's First Women Soldiers* (Harvard University Press, 2017), 118, 210; Woodrow Wilson, "Address to the Senate on the Nineteenth Amendment," 9/30/1918: https://www.presidency.ucsb.edu/node/329326.

126. Cott, *Grounding of Modern Feminism,* 15, 37.

127. Cott, *Grounding of Modern Feminism,*14, 60.

128. Cott, *Grounding of Modern Feminism,* 61; Mrs. Horace Davis, "The True Function of the Normal Woman," in Ernest Bernbaum, ed., *Anti-Suffrage Essays by Massachusetts Women* (Forum, 1916), 124; Lily Rice Foxcroft, "Suffrage a Step toward Feminism," in Bernbaum, *Anti-Suffrage Essays,* 152.

129. Catt quoted in Jacqueline Van Voris, *Carrie Chapman Catt: A Public Life* (Feminist Press at City University of New York, 1996), 72; President Woodrow Wilson, "Address to the Senate on the Nineteenth Amendment," 9/30/1918: https://www.presidency.ucsb.edu/node/329326.

130. MCT, *Colored Woman,* 212; Cathleen Cahill, *Recasting the Vote: How Women of Color Transformed the Suffrage Movement* (University of North Carolina Press, 2020).

131. MCT, *Colored Woman,* 410.

132. Borah in *Congressional Record,* 66th Cong., 1st sess. (1919), 564.

133. McKellar in *Congressional Record,* 65th Cong., 2nd sess. (1918), 10779, 10783.

134. Katznelson, *Fear Itself,* 8, 160, 312; "Suffrage Wins in Senate," *NYT,* 6/5/1919, 1.

135. Elaine Weiss, *The Woman's Hour: The Great Fight to Win the Vote* (Viking, 2018), 260–261.

136. Weiss, *Woman's Hour,* 209, 266; MCT, *Colored Woman,* 145.

137. Weiss, *Woman's Hour,* 209, 306.

138. Carrie Chapman Catt and Nellie Rogers Shuler, *Woman Suffrage and Politics: The Inner Story of the Suffrage Movement* (Charles Scribner's Sons, 1923), 107–108.

139. Carrie Chapman Catt, "Mary Church Terrell: An Appreciation," *Oberlin Magazine,* July 1936: https://ohio5.contentdm.oclc.org/digital/collection/p15963coll16/id/586/.

140. Carrie Chapman Catt to MCT, 3/15/1939, MCT Papers, Howard University Archives, Moorland-Spingarn Research Center, box 102–1, f23; MCT, "Colored Women and World Peace," 2 (1932), MCT Papers, box 102–13, f263.

141. Parker, *Unceasing Militant,* 130–131.

142. Estele Davis quoted in Sandra VanBurkleo, *"Belonging to the World": Women's Rights and American Constitutional Culture* (Oxford University Press, 2001), 195; Evelyn Brooks Higginbotham, "Clubwomen and Electoral Politics in the 1920s," in Ann Gordon and Bettye Collier-Thomas, eds., *African American Women and the Vote, 1837–1965* (University of Massachusetts Press, 1977), 138.

143. MCT, *Colored Woman,* 310; Parker, *Unceasing Militant,* 230, 280; Paula Giddings, *When and Where I Enter: The Impact of Black Women on Race and Sex in America* (Bantam, 1984), 219.

144. Parker, *Unceasing Militant,* 278, 282, 284.

145. Kim Nielsen, *Un-American Womanhood: Anti-Radicalism, Anti-Feminism, and the First Red Scare* (Ohio State University Press, 2001), 135.

5. The Right to Earn: 1920–1960

Epigraph: "Help Wanted," *NYT,* 3/2/1933, 36.

1. Robert Gordon, *The Rise and Fall of American Growth: The U.S. Standard of Living since the Civil War* (Princeton University Press, 2016), 18.

2. Ann Marie Low [née Riebe], *Dust Bowl Diary* (University of Nebraska Press, 1984), prologue. This memoir was published under the author's married name, but all the events described herein took place under her maiden name. To convey the spirit of the times, I use the last name "Riebe" throughout.

3. Kirstin Downey, *The Woman behind the New Deal: The Life and Legacy of Frances Perkins—Social Security, Unemployment Insurance, and the Minimum Wage* (Anchor Books, 2010), 125.

4. Frances Perkins, *The Reminiscences of Frances Perkins,* Columbia University Oral History Research Office, 9 vols. (Microfilming Corp. of America, 1977), vol. 1, 183, 185. The entire collection is at http://www.columbia.edu/cu/lweb/digital/collections/nny/perkinsf/transcripts/perkinsf_1_1_1.html.

5. Perkins, *Reminiscences,* vol. 1, 183.

6. Perkins, *Reminiscences,* vol. 1, 183; Edmund Morris, *The Rise of Theodore Roosevelt* (Coward, McCann, & Geoghegan, 1979), 487.

7. *Historical Statistics of the United States, Colonial Times to 1970* (Government Printing Office, 1975), part 1, 379; Downey, *Woman,* 11.

8. Kathryn Kish-Sklar, *Florence Kelley and the Nation's Work: The Rise of Women's Political Culture, 1830–1900* (Yale University Press, 1997), 223.

9. Alice Kessler-Harris, *In Pursuit of Equity: Women, Men, and the Quest for Economic Citizenship in 20th-Century America* (Oxford University Press, 2001), 30.

10. Gompers in Kessler-Harris, *Pursuit,* 68.

11. Perkins, *Reminiscences,* vol. 1, 201; George Martin, *Madame Secretary, Frances Perkins: A Biography of America's First Woman Cabinet Member* (Houghton-Mifflin, 1983), 117.

12. Perkins, *Reminiscences,* vol. 1, 18, 58.

13. Perkins in Downey, *Woman,* 15; Jerry Klutz and Herbert Asbury, "The Woman Nobody Knows," *Collier's Magazine,* 8/5/1944, 30.

14. Martin, *Madame,* 55.

15. Gordon, *Rise and Fall,* 68.

16. Perkins, *Reminiscences,* vol. 1, 11.

17. Perkins, *Reminiscences,* vol. 1, 11–12; Martin, *Madame,* 61.

18. Inaugural Address of Theodore Roosevelt, 3/4/1905, Avalon Project, Yale Law School: https://avalon.law.yale.edu/20th_century/troos.asp.

19. Perkins, *Reminiscences,* vol. 1, 186.

20. Perkins, *Reminiscences,* vol. 1, 23.

21. Perkins, *Reminiscences,* vol. 1, 30–32; Kareema Gray, "Social Change for Social Betterment: African-Americans in Nineteenth Century Philadelphia," *Journal of African American Studies* 18, no. 4 (2014): 440.

22. Perkins, *Reminiscences,* vol. 1, 34.

23. Perkins, *Reminiscences,* vol. 1, 36; Kessler-Harris, *Pursuit,* 69.

24. Frankfurter in Kessler-Harris, *Pursuit,* 30.

25. *Muller v. Oregon* in Kessler-Harris, *Pursuit,* 30–31, and in Claudia Goldin, *Understanding the Gender Gap: An Economic History of American Women* (Oxford University Press, 1990), 255.

26. Goldin, *Understanding the Gender Gap,* 60, 111–112, 17, 178.

27. Downey, *Woman,* 43.

28. Downey, *Woman,* 48, 53; Martin, *Madame,* 103, 108.

29. Perkins, *Reminiscences,* vol. 1, 231–232.

30. Perkins, *Reminiscences,* vol. 1, 232; Wilson quoted in Martin, *Madame,* 125.

31. Downey, *Woman,* 56.

32. Christina Simmons, *Making Marriage Modern: Women's Sexuality from the Progressive Era to World War II* (Oxford University Press, 2009), 106; Eric Rauchway, *The Refuge of Affections: Family and American Reform Politics: 1900–1920* (Columbia University Press, 2001), 12.

33. Perkins, *Reminiscences,* vol. 1, 197, 201, 244; Downey, *Woman,* 59.

34. Claudia Goldin, *Career & Family: Women's Century-Long Journey toward Equity* (Princeton University Press, 2021), 54.

35. Perkins, *Reminiscences,* vol. 3, 643.

36. Martin, *Madame,* 136, 233, 469.

37. Jo Freeman, *A Room at a Time: How Women Entered Party Politics* (Rowman and Littlefield, 2000), 214–215.

38. Kelley in Downey, *Woman,* 77; "Perkins Appointment Held Up in Senate," *NYT,* 1/29/1919, 13.

39. Low, *Dust Bowl Diary,* 182.

40. Low, *Dust Bowl Diary,* 7–8.

41. Willa Cather, *Not under Forty* (Alfred Knopf, 1936), prefatory note. Ann Marie Riebe Low changed the names of her sister Elinor and brother John in the published version of her diary. This book continues that convention for the sake of consistency. For the original names, see North Dakota State Library, Digital Horizons, Pingree: 1880–1980: http://www.digitalhorizonsonline.org/digital/collection/ndsl-books/id/43804/.

42. Low, *Dust Bowl Diary,* 1.

43. Letter to the Editor, *Daily Illini,* 4/20/1922, quoted in Paula Fass, *The Damned and the Beautiful: American Youth in the 1920s* (Oxford University Press 1971), 291;

quotation is from "Fighting for 'Feminism,'" *Washington Evening Star,* 2/17/1921, 6. Also see "Woman's Party to Hold Meet in Colorado," *Bismarck Tribune,* 6/22/1927, 8; "Women of the World Weigh the Future of Feminism," *Bismarck Tribune,* 7/31/1933, 5.

44. "Memorial Statue for Pioneers of Ballot Unveiled," *Mobile News-Item* (AL), 2/16/1921, 2; "3 Suffragists (in Marble) to Move up to the Capitol," *NYT,* 9/27/1996, A18.

45. "Three Old Ladies in a Bathtub," 4/6/1928, *Muscatine Journal and News Tribune* (IA), 9; "Inscription Erasure Rouses Women's Ire," *Wisconsin State Journal,* 10/17/1921, 17; Herbert Plummer, "A Washington Daybook," *Beatrice Daily Sun* (NE), 1/17/1921, 4.

46. Low, *Dust Bowl Diary,* 37; *Historical Statistics,* part 1, 379.

47. Low, *Dust Bowl Diary,* 13, 17, 118.

48. Low, *Dust Bowl Diary,* 8.

49. Low, *Dust Bowl Diary,* 15.

50. Joseph Warren, "Husband's Right to Wife's Services," *Harvard Law Review* 38, no. 4 (1925): 433.

51. Low, *Dust Bowl Diary,* 15.

52. David Hamilton, "The Causes of the Banking Panic of 1930," *Journal of Southern History* 51, no. 4 (1985): 585, 588.

53. Low, *Dust Bowl Diary,* 15.

54. Low, *Dust Bowl Diary,* 17.

55. Low, *Dust Bowl Diary,* 19.

56. Low, *Dust Bowl Diary,* 37.

57. Low, *Dust Bowl Diary,* 48.

58. Low, *Dust Bowl Diary,* 26.

59. Low, *Dust Bowl Diary,* 23, 26, 37.

60. Low, *Dust Bowl Diary,* 33.

61. Harold James, "1929: The New York Stock Market Crash," *Representations,* 110, no. 1 (2010): 135–137; Charles Calomiris and Joseph Mason, "Fundamentals, Panic, and Bank Distress during the Great Depression," *American Economic Review* 93, no. 5 (2003): 1616.

62. Low, *Dust Bowl Diary,* 33.

63. Low, *Dust Bowl Diary,* 36–37, 42.

64. Low, *Dust Bowl Diary,* 38, 41.

65. Low, *Dust Bowl Diary,* 41, 43.

66. Frances Perkins, *The Roosevelt I Knew* (Penguin, 2011), 24–25.

67. Perkins in Downey, *Woman,* 105.

68. Perkins, *Roosevelt,* 99.

69. Perkins, *Roosevelt,* 109.

70. Downey, *Woman,* 115.

71. Martin, *Madame,* 236–237.

72. Martin, *Madame,* 237–238; Associated Press, "A.F. of L. Head Disappointed in in Miss Perkins' Selection," *Atchison Daily Globe* (KS), 3/1/1933, 1.

73. Downey, *Woman,* 89; Perkins, *Reminiscences,* vol. 1, 209.

74. Perkins, *Roosevelt,* 44–45; Martin, *Madame,* 524.

75. Associated Press, "Eyewitness Tells Story of Shooting," *Oakland Tribune,* 2/16/1933, 1–2; "Hitler Reassures Industrial Chiefs," *NYT,* 2/22/1933, 9; "Sixty Year Plan for Italy: Mussolini Says 21st Century Will Be Blackshirt Era," *NYT,* 3/19/1934, 9.

76. Martin, *Madame,* 239–240; Perkins, *Roosevelt,* 144.

77. "Report to the President of the Committee on Economic Security," Jan. 1935: https://www.ssa.gov/history/reports/ces/ces5.html.

78. Martin, *Madame,* 240–241.

79. Martin, *Madame,* 241.

80. Perkins, *Reminiscences,* vol. 3, 639.

81. Martin, *Madame,* 232, 241, 289; Nellie Webb, "Wreaths and Wallops for Women," *Atchison Globe Daily* (KS), 3/7/1933, 6; Downey, *Woman,* xiii, 279.

82. Perkins, *Reminiscences,* vol. 4, 178.

83. Perkins, *Reminiscences,* vol. 4, 179–180.

84. Perkins, *Reminiscences,* vol. 4, 180–181.

85. Perkins, *Roosevelt,* 145–146.

86. "Police Dog Bites Senator Caraway at White House Party," *Sunday Star* (DC), 4/30/1933, 1.

87. Anna Eleanor Roosevelt, *It's Up to the Women* (Frederick Stokes, 1933), ix; Susan Ware, *Beyond Suffrage: Women in the New Deal* (Harvard University Press, 1981), 8–10, 17; Joseph Lash, *Eleanor and Franklin* (Norton, 1971), 485.

88. Perkins, *Reminiscences,* vol. 4, 100.

89. Perkins, *Reminiscences,* vol. 4, 102–103.

90. Perkins, *Reminiscences,* vol. 4, 87.

91. Perkins, *Reminiscences,* vol. 4, 480–481.

92. "Miss Perkins Defends Plan," *Abilene Morning News* (TX), 3/24/1933, 4; Perkins, *Reminiscences,* vol. 4, 483, 491.

93. Perkins, *Reminiscences,* vol. 4, 492.

94. Perkins, *Reminiscences,* vol. 4, 492.

95. Martin, *Madame,* 275.

96. Kessler-Harris, *Pursuit,* 77; Dorothy Sue Cobble, *For the Many: American Feminists and the Global Fight for Democratic Equality* (Princeton University Press, 2021), 70; on Bismarck, see Social Security History, https://www.ssa.gov/history/ottob.html, accessed 6/18/2021.

97. Martin, *Madame,* 98; Perkins, *Reminiscences,* vol. 1, 179, 182–183.

98. Martin, *Madame,* 341, 356; Downey, *Woman,* 237, 244; Robyn Muncy, *Creating a Female Dominion in American Reform, 1890–1935* (Oxford University Press, 1991), 139.

99. David M. Kennedy, "What the New Deal Did," *Political Science Quarterly* 124, no. 2 (2009): 253.

100. Downey, *Woman,* 244.

101. Downey, *Woman,* 236.

102. Kessler-Harris, *Pursuit,* 120.

103. Cobble, *For the Many,* 174.

104. Kessler-Harris, *Pursuit,* 96.

105. Goldin, *Understanding the Gender Gap,* 117; Kessler-Harris, *Pursuit,* 106; Cobble, *For the Many,* 352; Congressman Martin Dies to Carl Huhndorff, 5/27/1938, 2, Dies Papers, box 4, file 10, Sam Houston Regional Library and Research Center, Texas State Archives; Howard D. Samuel, "Troubled Passage: The Labor Movement and the Fair Labor Standards Act," *Monthly Labor Review* (Dec. 2000), 32: https://www.bls.gov/opub/mlr/2000/12/art3full.pdf.

106. On state minimum-wage laws, see US Department of Labor, "Minimum Wages for Tipped Employees": https://www.dol.gov/agencies/whd/state/minimum-wage/tipped, accessed 6/18/2022.

107. US Department of Labor, *Handbook of Labor Statistics,* 1941 ed., vol. 2 (Government Printing Office, 1942), 384.

108. Author's search of NewspaperArchive.com, using the word "feminist," for 1930 and 1945.

109. Julia Blanshard, "Women Learned Equality in 1932 and Won Honors Despite Adverse Times," *Port Arthur News* (TX), 1/3/1933, 5; Goldin, *Understanding the Gender Gap,* 117, 147.

110. Simone de Beauvoir, *The Second Sex,* trans. H. M. Parshley (Vintage, 1989), xix. Ferdinand Lundberg and Marynia Farnham, *Modern Woman: The Lost Sex* (Harper & Brothers, 1947), 143, 175.

111. Martin, *Madame,* 356.

112. Low, *Dust Bowl Diary,* 76.

113. Low, *Dust Bowl Diary,* 65, 80, 84, 90.

114. Low, *Dust Bowl Diary,* 60, 65, 67.

115. Low, *Dust Bowl Diary,* 61.

116. Low, *Dust Bowl Diary,* 37, 91.

117. Low, *Dust Bowl Diary,* 175; *Historical Statistics,* vol. 1, 386.

118. Low, *Dust Bowl Diary,* 49, 52, 56; Benjamin Cook et al., "The Worst North American Drought of the Last Millennium: 1934," *Geophysical Research Letters* 41, no. 30 (2014): https://agupubs.onlinelibrary.wiley.com/doi/full/10.1002/2014GL061661.

119. Low, *Dust Bowl Diary,* 68–69.

120. Richard Hornbeck, "Enduring Impact of the American Dust Bowl," *American Economic Review* 102, no. 4 (2012): 1478.

121. For the descriptions of Ann's experiences in this and the following paragraphs, see Low, *Dust Bowl Diary,* 95–114.

122. Blanche Coll, *Safety Net: Welfare and Social Security, 1929–1979* (Rutgers University Press, 1995), 104.

123. Low, *Dust Bowl Diary,* 174.

124. Low, *Dust Bowl Diary,* 122.

125. Low, *Dust Bowl Diary,* 127, 135, 149.

126. "Notes," *Abilene Morning Reporter-News* (TX), 3/5/1933, 15.

127. Downey, *Woman,* 197; Martin, *Madame,* 405.

128. Martin, *Madame,* 403.

129. Perkins, *Reminiscences,* vol. 6, 112; AP, "Perkins Writes about Dispute of Labor Groups," *Reno Evening Gazette,* 8/29/1941, 6; "Byrd Begs Mme. Perkins to Resign," *Wisconsin State Journal,* 4/25/1941, 2; Tulsa, Asheville, and Detroit in "Perkins, Ickes and Hopkins," *Daily Hawk-Eye Gazette* (Burlington, IA), 4/30/1941, 4.

130. Harold Ickes, *The Secret Diary of Harold Ickes,* vol. 1 (Simon and Schuster, 1954), 531; Martin, *Madame,* 530.

131. "Frances Perkins Denies Propaganda Charges of Jewish Ancestry," *Southern Israelite* (Atlanta), 4/10/1936, 1; Martin, *Madame,* 398–399.

132. Joseph Alsop and Robert Kintner, "The Capital Parade: Communist Prober Martin Dies," *Washington Evening Star,* 8/22/1938, 9.

133. "Impeachment of Secretary of Labor, Frances Perkins, Threatened by Texas Solon," *Montana Standard,* 9/9/1939, 1.

134. Kim Nielsen, *Un-American Womanhood: Anti-Radicalism, Anti-Feminism, and the First Red Scare* (Ohio State University Press, 2001), 31, 76; Dies in Martin, *Madame,* 410. Also see "Sec. Perkins Is Accused by Dies of Aiding Bridges," *Wilson Daily Times* (NC), 10/31/1938, 1.

135. AP, "Threaten Life of Secretary," *Beatrice Daily Sun* (NE), 4/19/1933, 6; Martin, *Madame,* 410.

136. Perkins, *Reminiscences,* vol. 6, 478.

137. Perkins, *Reminiscences,* vol. 6, 481.

138. Perkins, *Reminiscences,* vol. 6, 484.

139. Perkins, *Reminiscences,* vol. 6, 482; AP, "Fight on Renewal of Dies Probe Led by 3 Legislators," *Washington Evening Star,* 2/1/1939, 4.

140. Perkins, *Reminiscences,* vol. 6, 519.

141. Perkins, *Reminiscences,* vol. 6, 494; Frances Perkins, "Statement before the House Judiciary Committee in Reply to House Resolution 67, Impeachment of Frances Perkins," 2/8/1939, 2: https://exhibitions.library.columbia.edu/exhibits/show/perkins/item/443.

142. Downey, *Woman,* 311, 338.

143. Carolyn Dimitri et al., "The 20th Century Transformation of U.S. Agriculture and Farm Policy," USDA, *Economic Information Bulletin* 3 (June 2005): 2: https://www.ers.usda.gov/webdocs/publications/44197/13566_eib3_1_.pdf.

144. Low, *Dust Bowl Diary,* 143, 150.

145. Low, *Dust Bowl Diary,* 134, 150, 160; Online Etymology Dictionary, "Ball and Chain," 1920: https://www.etymonline.com/word/ball%20and%20chain.

146. Low, *Dust Bowl Diary,* 179, 182.

147. "Dorothy Dix Says—Wife Must be Helpmate in Way Most Suited to Conditions," *Washington Star,* 2/1/1939, B8.

148. Low, *Dust Bowl Diary,* 134, 176.

149. Low, *Dust Bowl Diary,* 178.

150. "Anne Riebe a Bride: North Dakota Girl Married to S. H. Low, Harvard Graduate," *NYT,* 10/6/1937, 22; US Department of Labor, *Handbook of Labor Statistics,* vol. 2, 118.

151. Tom Levitt, *Courage to Meddle: The Belief of Frances Perkins* (Tom Levitt, 2020), xvi; DeLysa Burnier, "Frances Perkins' Disappearance from American Public Administration: A Genealogy of Marginalization," *Administrative Theory and Practice* 30, no. 4 (Dec. 2008): 418.

152. Low, *Dust Bowl Diary,* 185; Obituary, "Seth Haskell Low," *Eastern Birding Banding Association News* 25, no. 3 (May–June 1962): https://sora.unm.edu/node/147483; Col. William E. Williams et al., *Buchenwald and Beyond: 120th Evac* (ca. 1947), unnumbered pages, see "Directory" appendix: https://digicom.bpl.lib.me.us/cgi/view content.cgi?article=1171&context=ww_reg_his.

153. Goldin, *Understanding the Gender Gap,* 176; Lynn Dumenil, *American Working Women in World War II: A Brief History with Documents* (Bedford / St. Martin's, 2020), 117–127.

154. Blanche Crozier, "Constitutionality of Discrimination Based on Sex," *Boston University Law Review* 15, no. 4 (Nov. 1935): 723; Hendrick Hartog, *Man & Wife in*

America: A History (Harvard University Press, 2000), 306; Brief for Appellant, *Reed v. Reed,* US Supreme Court (Oct. term, 1970), 32, 35; *American Women: The Report of the President's Commission on the Status of Women and Other Publications of the Commission* (Charles Scribner's Sons, 1965), 46.

6. The Right to Equal Treatment: 1960–1975

Epigraph: Shulamith Firestone, *The Dialectic of Sex: The Case for Feminist Revolution* (William Morrow, 1970), 3.

1. Newspaperarchive.com and the *NYT* both show articles on the topic from twenty states in 1969. Prior to 1969, "sexism" appeared only once, in a nationally syndicated column where the meaning was ambiguous. See George Adams, "Today's Talk: The Best 'Ism,'" *Wichita Falls Times* (TX), 1/2/1963, B6; Marguerite Michaels, "Woman Power Is Deep in the Heart of Texas," *Parade,* in *Austin American-Statesman,* 3/5/1978, SM9.

2. Benita Roth, *Separate Roads to Feminism: Black, Chicana, and White Feminist Movements in America's Second Wave* (Cambridge University Press, 2004), 7.

3. Maylei Blackwell, *¡Chicana Power!: Contested Histories of Feminism in the Chicano Movement* (University of Texas Press, 2015), 21; author's oral history interview with Martha P. Cotera, Austin, TX, 7/29–30/2021.

4. Kimberly Springer, *Living for the Revolution: Black Feminist Organizations, 1968–1980* (Duke University Press, 2005), 4; Sherna Gluck, "Whose Feminism, Whose History?," in Nancy Naples, ed., *Community Activism and Feminist Politics: Organizing across Race, Class, and Gender* (Routledge, 1998).

5. Cotera interview (Cobbs). Also see "Testimony from a Tejana Feminist," in Vicki Ruiz, ed., *Las Obreras: Chicana Politics of Work and Family* (1993; UCLA Chicano Studies Research Center Publications, 2000), 275.

6. Cotera interview (Cobbs).

7. Ruiz, *Las Obreras,* 275–276; "Oral Memoirs of Martha P. Cotera," interview by Joyce Langenegger, Mar. 3 and Apr. 6, 1973, 4, Baylor University Institute for Oral History interviews, Digital Collections, Baylor University Libraries, https://digitalcollections-baylor.quartexcollections.com/Documents/Detail/oral-memoirs-of-martha-p.-cotera transcript/1575027?item=1575035.

8. Cotera interview (Cobbs).

9. Joan Kahn and Leslie Whittington, "The Labor Supply of Latinas in the USA: Comparing Labor Force Participation, Wages, and Hours Worked with Anglo and Black Women," *Population Research and Policy Review* 15, no. 1 (1996): 45, 48; Roth, *Separate Roads,* 34; Cotera interview (Cobbs).

10. Cotera interview (Cobbs).

11. Gloria Steinem also cared for a single mother—see Steinem, *My Life on the Road* (Random House, 2015), 12; Cotera interview (Cobbs); Cotera oral memoirs (Langenegger), 7.

12. Ryan Abt, "Defining Nazism and the Holocaust in American Public Schools, 1933–1964," PhD diss., Texas A&M University, 2021, 141–143, 145; Zoe Burkholder, *Color in the Classroom: How American Schools Taught Race, 1900–1954* (Oxford University Press, 2011), 147, 168, 174.

13. Kennedy on YouTube: https://www.youtube.com/watch?v=SLILjDx0SO0, accessed 6/30/2022.

14. Cotera interview (Cobbs).

15. Cotera interview (Cobbs); Cotera oral memoirs (Langenegger), 18; Ruiz, *Las Obreras,* 278–279.

16. Claudia Goldin, *Career & Family: Women's Century-Long Journey toward Equity* (Princeton University Press, 2021), 54, 96, 99, 103–104.

17. Calvin Holder, "Racism toward Black African Diplomats during the Kennedy Administration, *Journal of Black Studies* 14, no. 1 (1983): 39; "We, the American Hispanics," US Bureau of the Census (September 1993), 2: https://www.census.gov/history/pdf/we-the-americans-hispanics-092020.pdf.

18. Alice Rivlin and June O'Neill, "Growth and Change in Higher Education," *Proceedings of the Academy of Political Science* 30, no. 1 (1970): 66; Patricia Gándara, *Over the Ivory Walls: The Educational Mobility of Low-Income Chicanos* (SUNY Press, 1995), 10.

19. Cotera oral memoirs (Langenegger), 21.

20. Cotera interview (Cobbs); David Frum, *How We Got Here: The 70s* (Basic Books, 2000), 244.

21. Ernesto Chávez, *"¡Mi Raza Primero!": Nationalism, Identity, and Insurgency in the Chicano Movement in Los Angeles, 1966–1978* (University of California Press, 2002), 5; also see Anna Nieto-Gómez, "Francisca Flores, the League of Mexican American Women, and the Comisión Feminil Mexicana Nacional, 1958–1975," in Dionne Espinoza, María E. Cotera, and Maylei Blackwell, eds., *Chicana Movidas: New Narratives of Activism and Feminism in the Movement Era* (University of Texas Press, 2018), 33.

22. Frantz Fanon, *The Wretched of the Earth,* trans. Constance Farrington (Grove, 1963), 86, 94.

23. David Montejano, *Quixote's Soldiers: A Local History of the Chicano Movement, 1966–1981* (University of Texas Press, 2010), 59, 109, 118; "Gun-Barrel Politics: The Black Panther Party, 1966–1971," Report by the Committee on Internal Security, House of Representatives (Government Printing Office, 1971), 14–15, 22.

24. Ana Raquel Minian, "'Indiscriminate and Shameless Sex': The Strategic Use of Sexuality by the United Farm Workers," *American Quarterly* 65, no. 1 (2013): 67; Ula Taylor, *The Promise of Patriarchy: Women and the Nation of Islam* (University of North Carolina Press, 2017), 107, 182.

25. Cotera interview (Cobbs); Ruiz, *Las Obreras,* 283; Alma Garcia, "The Development of Chicana Feminist Discourse, 1970–1980," *Gender and Society* 3, no. 2 (1989): 222; Alma Garcia, ed., *Chicana Feminist Thought: The Basic Historical Writings* (Routledge, 2014), 1.

26. Vera Glaser, "Women's Rights Groups Growing Tired of Waiting," *Lubbock-Avalanche Journal* (TX), 3/20/1969, 71; "Governor's Committee Sites Case of Discrimination," *Lubbock-Avalanche Journal,* 2/13/1969, B2; Cotera interview (Cobbs); Montejano, *Quixote's Soldiers,* 156.

27. Ruiz, *Las Obreras,* 283.

28. Roth, *Separate Roads,* 60; Robin Morgan, ed., *Sisterhood Is Powerful: An Anthology of Writings from the Women's Liberation Movement* (Vintage, 1970), 35; Belinda

Robnett, *How Long? How Long? African-American Women in the Struggle for Civil Rights* (Oxford University Press, 1997), 159; Rosalind Rosenberg, *Jane Crow: The Life of Pauli Murray* (Oxford University Press, 2017), 267; Nik Heynen, "Bending the Bars of Empire from Every Ghetto for Survival: The Black Panther Party's Radical Antihunger Politics of Social Reproduction and Scale," *Annals of the Association of American Geographers* 99, no. 2 (2009): 412; Baraka in Winifred Breines, *The Trouble between Us: An Uneasy History of White and Black Women in the Feminist Movement* (Oxford University Press, 2006), 57; Beal in Sara Evans, *Tidal Wave: How Women Changed America at Century's End* (Free Press, 2003), 36.

29. Taylor, *Promise,* 161; Beal in Evans, *Tidal Wave,* 36.

30. Montejano, *Quixote's Soldiers,* 157.

31. Nieto-Gómez, "Francisca Flores," 46.

32. Cotera interview (Cobbs); Enriqueta Longauex y Vasquez, "The Mexican-American Woman," in Robin Morgan, ed., *Sisterhood Is Powerful: An Anthology of Writings from the Women's Liberation Movement* (Vintage, 1970), 379; Bernice Rincón, "La Chicana: Her Role in the Past and Her Search for a New Role in the Future" (1971), in Garcia, *Chicana Feminist Thought,* 28.

33. Katie Gibson, *Ruth Bader Ginsburg's Legacy of Dissent: Feminist Rhetoric and the Law* (University of Alabama Press, 2018), 9, 36, 38; transcript of interview of US Supreme Court Associate Judge Ruth Bader Ginsburg, 4/10/2009, *Ohio State Law Journal* 805, no. 70 (2009): 812.

34. Author's interview with Yvonne Swan, 7/7/2021–7/8/2021, Inchelium, WA.

35. Louise Erdrich, *The Night Watchman* (HarperCollins, 2020), 201. Swan interview (Cobbs); Donna Hightower Langston, "American Indian Women's Activism in the 1960s and 1070s," *Hypatia* 18, no. 2 (2003): 116; Michael Walch, "Terminating the Indian Termination Policy," *Stanford Law Review* 35, no. 6 (1983): 1185; Clayton Koppes, "From New Deal to Termination: Liberalism and Indian Policy, 1933–1953," *Pacific Historical Review* 46, no. 4 (1977): 556.

36. Swan interview (Cobbs).

37. Swan interview (Cobbs); Estelle Fuchs, "A National Study of American Indian Education," *Council on Anthropology and Education Newsletter* 2, no. 2 (1971): 13: http://www.jstor.org/stable/3219547.

38. Swan interview (Cobbs).

39. Swan interview (Cobbs).

40. Antonia Abbey et al., "Alcohol and Sexual Assault," *Alcohol Research and Health* 25 (2001): 43: https://pubs.niaaa.nih.gov/publications/arh25-1/43-51.

41. Swan interview (Cobbs).

42. Pagan Kennedy, "The Rape Kit's Secret History," *NYT,* 1/17/2020; Diana Russell, *The Politics of Rape: The Victim's Perspective* (Stein and Day, 1974); Susan Brownmiller, *Against Our Will: Men, Women, and Rape* (Simon and Schuster, 1975); Louise Armstrong, *Kiss Daddy Goodnight: A Speak-Out on Incest* (Pocket Books, 1978); I. B. Weiner, "On Incest: A Survey," *Abstracts on Criminology and Penology* 4 (1964): 137; R. J. Barry, "Incest: The Last Taboo (Part I)," *FBI Law Enforcement Bulletin* 53, no. 1 (1984), 2: https://www.ojp.gov/pdffiles1/Digitization/93130NCJRS.pdf; Diana Russell, *The Secret Trauma: Incest in the Lives of Girls and Women* (1986; Basic Books, 1999), 10, 216–217.

43. Patricia Tjaden and Nancy Thoennes, "Prevalence, Incidence, and Consequences of Violence against Women: Findings from the National Violence against Women Survey," in National Institute of Justice, *Research in Brief* (Nov. 1998), 2–3, 5: https://www.ojp.gov/pdffiles/172837.pdf.

44. Swan interview (Cobbs).

45. Nancy Hicks, "Demands for Daycare Are Outrunning Growth," *NYT,* 11/30/1970, 1.

46. Swan interview (Cobbs); Donna Coker and Lindsay Harrison, "The Story of *Wanrow:* The Reasonable Woman and the Law of Self-Defense," in Donna Coker and Robert Weisberg, eds., *Criminal Law Stories* (Foundation Press, 2013), 217.

47. M. L. Aldridge and K. D. Browne, "Perpetrators of Spousal Homicide: A Review," *Trauma, Violence, & Abuse* 4, no. 3 (2003): 265–276; Tina Hotton, "Spousal Violence after Marital Separation," *Juristat* (Canadian Centre for Justice Statistics) 21, no. 7: https://publications.gc.ca/Collection-R/Statcan/85-002-XIE/0070185-002-XIE.pdf.

48. Swan interview (Cobbs).

49. Roth, *Separate Roads,* 211.

50. Ruiz, *Las Obreras,* 283.

51. Ruiz, *Las Obreras,* 278.

52. Cotera oral memoirs (Langenegger), 60; Martha P. Cotera, "Feminism: The Chicana and Anglo Versions," in Margarita Melville, ed., *Twice a Minority: Mexican American Women* (C.V. Mosby, 1980), 229; Dionne Espinosa, "The Partido Belongs to Those Who Will Work for It: Chicana Organizing and Leadership in the Texas La Raza Unida Party," *Aztlán: A Journal of Chicano Studies* 36, no. 1 (2011): 198.

53. Blackwell, *¡Chicana Power!,* 62–63.

54. Blackwell, *¡Chicana Power!,* 63; Laura Garcia et al., *Teatro Chicana: A Collective Memoir and Selected Plays* (University of Texas Press, 2008), 177; Alan Braid, "Why I Violated Texas's Extreme Abortion Ban," *Washington Post,* 9/18/2021; "Achievements in Public Health, 1900–1999: Healthier Mothers and Babies," Centers for Disease Control, 10/1/1999: https://www.cdc.gov/mmwr/preview/mmwrhtml/mm4838a2.htm.

55. Blackwell, *¡Chicana Power!,* 70; Heynen, "Bending the Bars of Empire," 413; Roth, *Separate Roads,* 139.

56. Mirta Vidal, *Women: New Voice of La Raza* (Pathfinder Press, 1971), 4; Jennie Chavez, "Women of the Mexican American Movement," in Garcia, *Chicana Feminist Thought,* 22, 36–37; poet Inés Hernández, "Testimonio de Memoria," Charles Tatum, ed., *New Chicana / Chicano Writing 2,* (University of Arizona Press, 1992), 15.

57. Michele Wallace, *Black Macho and the Myth of the Superwoman* (1979; Verso Classics, 1999), 11; Akasha Gloria Hull, Patricia Bell-Scott, and Barbara Smith, *All the Women Are White, All the Men Are Black, But Some of Us Are Brave* (Feminist Press, 1982); Marilyn Boxer, "Women's Studies as Women's History," *Women's Studies Quarterly* 30, nos. 3 / 4 (2002): 44.

58. Martha P. Cotera, *The Chicana Feminist* (Information Systems Development, 1977), 26; Martha P. Cotera, "Mujeres Bravas: How Chicanas Shaped the Feminist Agenda at the National IWY Conference in Houston, 1977," in Espinoza, Cotera, and Blackwell, *Chicana Movidas,* 52.

59. Blackwell, *¡Chicana Power!,* 161, 178; Montejano, *Quixote's Soldiers,* 145; Shelley Savren, "Ofelia Gonzalez on Chicana Organizing," *Longest Revolution: News and Views of Progressive Feminism* 1, no. 3 (1977), 1: Special Collections, San Diego State University, Center for Women's Studies and Services Records.

60. Blackwell, *¡Chicana Power!,* 166, 172–173; Ruiz, *Las Obreras,* 287.

61. Vidal, *Women,* 4.

62. Vidal, *Women,* 9.

63. Blackwell, *¡Chicana Power!,* 175–176.

64. Blackwell, *¡Chicana Power!,* 177; Vidal, *Women,* 7.

65. Cotera interview (Cobbs); Blackwell, *¡Chicana Power!,* 181. Indian women faced the same accusations. See Renya Ramirez, "Race, Tribal Nation, and Gender: A Native Feminist Approach to Belonging," *Meridians* 7, no. 2 (2007): 25.

66. Cotera, *Chicana Feminist,* 12; Blackwell, *¡Chicana Power!,* 185.

67. Martha Cotera, "Raza Unida Women," paper for Professor David Montejano, Borderlands History 101, University of Texas, Austin (5/11/1991), 1, courtesy of the author.

68. "Women's Action Program, Chicana Meeting," 2, and Memorandum, Secretary Eliot Richardson, 6/4/1971, "Affirmative Action Plans for Women," 2, in box 1, folder 28, Enriqueta Chavez Papers, Special Collections, San Diego State University; Deluvina Hernández and Cecilia Cota-Robles Suárez, *Low Income Women Who Head Households* (National Chicana Foundation, 1978); Cecilia Cota-Robles Suárez and Lupe Anguiano, eds., *Every Woman's Right: The Right to Quality Education and Economic Independence* (National Chicana Foundation, 1981); Cotera, "Feminism," 229.

69. "Chicanas in Profile: Diosa y Hembra," *Austin American Statesman,* 11/1/1976, C1; Teresa Palomo Acosta and Ruthe Winegarten, *Las Tejanas: 300 Years of History* (University of Texas Press, 2003), 225; Martha P. Cotera, *Profile of the Mexican American Woman* (Information Systems Development, 1976) and *Diosa y Hembra* (Statehouse Printing, 1976), 33–34.

70. Firestone, *Dialectic of Sex,* 42; Ursula Le Guin, *Left Hand of Darkness* (Walker and Company, 1969), 100, 106.

71. Anna Costain, "The Struggle for a National Women's Lobby," *Western Political Quarterly* 33, no. 4 (Dec. 1980): 477.

72. Cotera oral memoirs (Langenegger), 26; Linda Garcia Merchant, "Chicana Diasporic: An Introduction," *Chicana Por Mi Vida:* http://chicanadiasporic.org/journey/chicana/chicana-diasporic-an-introduction?path=index, accessed 8/22/2021.

73. Cotera, *Chicana Feminist,* 18–19.

74. Cotera, "Feminism"; Melville, *Twice a Minority,* 232; Terry Mason, "Symbolic Strategies for Change: A Discussion of the Chicana Women's Movement," in Melville, *Twice a Minority,* 100.

75. Evans, *Tidal Wave,* 36.

76. Cotera interview (Cobbs).

77. Swan interview (Cobbs).

78. Department of Police, Spokane, Report by Shirley Hooper, 8/11/1972, 1, courtesy of Donna Coker; Sue Lasbury, "Ruling Ends Seven Year Ordeal for Y. Wanrow," *Longest Revolution: News and Views of Progressive Feminism* 3, no. 5 (1979): 6, available

in Special Collections, Center for Women's Studies and Services Records, San Diego State University; "*Washington State v. Wanrow,*" Justicia US Law: https://law.justia.com/cases/washington/supreme-court/1977/43949-1.html.

79. Department of Police, Spokane, Report 438565, Sgt. Leahy, 12/16/1969, courtesy of Donna Coker.

80. Coker and Harrison, "The Story," 227; *Washington v. Wanrow,* 88 Wash.2d 221, 559 P.2d 548 (1977), transcript, 278, courtesy of Donna Coker.

81. Swan interview (Cobbs).

82. Swan interview (Cobbs).

83. Coker and Harrison, "The Story," 229.

84. Swan interview (Cobbs).

85. Coker and Harrison, "The Story," 230; Department of Police, Spokane, 911 report, 8/12/1972, and Police Report 7254656, Sgt. Harding, "Additional Information," 8/12/1972, courtesy of Donna Coker; *Washington v. Wanrow,* transcript, 13–14.

86. Diana E. H. Russell and Nicole Van de Ven, ed., *Proceedings of the International Tribune on Crimes against Women* (Frog in the Well, 1984), 95.

87. Coker and Harrison, "The Story," 230; Swan interview (Cobbs).

88. *Washington v. Wanrow,* transcript, 302.

89. Coker and Harrison, "The Story," 230.

90. *Washington v. Wanrow,* transcript, "Plaintiff's' Closing Argument," 5/12/1973, 21.

91. Swan interview (Cobbs).

92. Coker and Harrison, "The Story," 231–232; Department of Police, Spokane, 8/12/1972, 911 report, 8/12/1972, and Police Report 7254656, Sgt. Harding, "Additional Information," 8/12/1972.

93. Coker and Harrison, "The Story," 232.

94. *Washington v. Wanrow,* transcript, 24, 477; Coker and Harrison, "The Story," 233–234.

95. Marjorie Spruill, *Divided We Stand: The Battle over Women's Rights and Family Values That Polarized American Politics* (Bloomsbury, 2017), 36; Richard Nixon, "Proclamation 4217, Mother's Day, 1973": https://www.govinfo.gov/content/pkg/STATUTE-87/pdf/STATUTE-87-Pg1209.pdf.

96. Coker and Harrison, "The Story," 255; Deborah McBride, "Wanrow Plea Not a Cop-Out," *Spokesman-Review* (Spokane, WA), 4/28/1979, 14.

97. Jo Freeman, "The Tyranny of Structurelessness," *Berkeley Journal of Sociology* 17 (1972–1973): 158; Ben Zimmer, "Ms.," *NYT Magazine,* 10/23/2009, 16; Frum, *How We Got Here,* 446.

98. Diana Camacho in Espinoza, Cotera, and Blackwell, *Chicana Movidas,* 59; Montejano, *Quixote's Soldiers,* 154; Cotera interview (Cobbs).

99. Cotera, *Chicana Feminist,* 16.

100. Rosemary Beales and Nancy Neff, "Women's Conference: Turn-on or Sham?" *Austin American Statesman,* 11/16/1975, B1; "The Many Faces of Women in Public Life," *Austin American Statesman* 11/9/1975, H1.

101. Cotera, *Chicana Feminist,* 30–31; Mary Dudley, "Chicana Liberation Goals, Ideas Discussed," *Austin American Statesman* (11/23/1975), G5.

102. Irene Dominguez and Martha P. Cotera, *¡Doña Doormat No Está Aquí! Assertion and Communication Techniques for Hispanic Women* (Chicana Research and Learning Center, ca. 1982), 1; Blackwell, *¡Chicana Power!*, 198–202.

103. National Commission on the Observance of International Women's Year, *To Form a More Perfect Union . . . Justice for American Women* (Government Printing Office, 1976), ii.

104. *To Form a More Perfect Union*, iv; Catherine Rymph, *Republican Women: Feminism and Conservatism from Suffrage through the Rise of the New Right* (University of North Carolina Press, 2006), 81, 210.

105. Spruill, *Divided*, 124; Doreen Mattingly, *Feminist in the White House: Midge Costanza, the Carter Years, and America's Culture Wars* (Oxford University Press, 2016), 146–148, 252.

106. Mark Daniels et al., "The ERA Won. At Least in the Opinion Polls," *PS* 15, no. 4 (1982): 579–580.

107. Espinoza, Cotera, and Blackwell, *Chicana Movidas*, 56, 62; Texas Coordinating Committee, *Texas Women's Meeting: Summary of the Final Report to the National Commission on the Observance of the International Women's Year*, eds. Claudia Stravato and Owanah Anderson, Sept. 1977, Marjorie Randal National Women's Conference Collection, 1996-007, box 2, folder 11, OCLC 3679387, University of Houston Libraries Special Collections: https://digitalcollections.lib.uh.edu/concern/texts/mk61rh69c?locale=en.

108. Ruiz, *Las Obreras*, 287.

109. Evans, *Tidal Wave*, 3; Mattingly, *Feminist in the White House*,151.

110. Donald Critchlow, *Phyllis Schlafly and Grassroots Conservatism: A Woman's Crusade* (Princeton University Press, 2005), 244–245.

111. Jane Dougherty, "You Have to Do It with Style, Sensitivity—Martha Cotera," *Austin American Statesman*, 11/13/1977, C4; Espinoza, Cotera, and Blackwell, *Chicana Movidas*, 58; Stravato and Anderson, *Texas Women's Meeting*, ii.

112. Stravato and Anderson, *Texas Women's Meeting*, iii, 107; Espinoza, Cotera, and Blackwell, *Chicana Movidas*, 66, 71.

113. Letter from Diana Camacho to Pat Vasquez (ca. June 1977), reproduced in Espinoza, Cotera, and Blackwell, *Chicana Movidas*, 58.

114. Spruill, *Divided*, 168, 174, 188.

115. Anna Quindlen, "Women Relay the Movement's Torch from Seneca Falls to Houston," *NYT*, 10/7/1977, 53.

116. Dorothy Sue Cobble, *For the Many: American Feminists and the Global Fight for Democratic Equality* (Princeton University Press, 2021), 342; Margaret Mead, ed., *American Women: The Report of the President's Commission on the Status of Women* (Charles Scribner's Sons, 1965), 51.

117. Rosenberg, *Jane Crow*, 2, 137, 241–242, 250.

118. Becker, "The Sixties Shift to Formal Equality and the Courts," *William and Mary Law Review* 40, no. 1 (October 1998), 227; Kimberlé Crenshaw, "Mapping the Margins: Intersectionality, Identity Politics, and Violence against Women of Color," *Stanford Law Review* 43, no. 6 (July 1991).

119. Rosenberg, *Jane Crow*, 254, 257–258, 261; Serena Mayeri, *Reasoning from Race: Feminism, Law, and the Civil Rights Revolution* (Harvard University Press, 2011), 14.

120. Gibson, *Ruth Bader Ginsburg's Legacy,* 42; "Ruth Bader Ginsburg Shares How Legal Pioneer Pauli Murray Shaped Her Work," *Time Magazine,* 10/16/2020: https://time.com/5896410/ruth-bader-ginsburg-pauli-murray/.

121. Swan interview (Cobbs).

122. "Wounded Knee Trial Opens with Revolt Warning," *NYT,* 2/13/1974, 14; Swan interview (Cobbs).

123. Coker and Harrison, "The Story," 235; Emily Thuma, *All Our Trials: Prisons, Policing, and the Feminist Fight to End Violence* (University of Illinois Press, 2019), 16, 35.

124. Robert Post and Reva Siegel, "Legislative Constitutionalism and Section Five Power, *Yale Law Journal* 112, no. 1943 (2002–2003): 1991.

125. Fred Strebeigh, *Equal: Women Reshape American Law* (Norton, 2009), x; Coker and Harrison, "The Story," 222.

126. Thuma, *All Our Trials,* 31.

127. Elizabeth Schneider, *Battered Women and Feminist Lawmaking* (Yale University Press, 2000), 31; Coker and Harrison, "The Story," 238.

128. Russell and Van de Ven, *Proceedings,* 94, 99, 100.

129. Coker and Harrison, "The Story," 242.

130. Coker and Harrison, "The Story," 252.

131. Coker and Harrison, "The Story," 241.

132. Elizabeth Bochnak, *Women's Self-Defense Cases: Theory and Practice* (Women's Self-Defense Law Project, 1981), 261; V. Fuster, A. Jerez, and A. Ortega, "Anthropometry and Strength Relationship: Male-Female Differences," *Anthropologischer Anzeiger* 56, no. 1 (Mar. 1998): 49.

133. "150 Best Places to Live in America in 2021–2022," *U.S. News and World Report:* https://realestate.usnews.com/places/rankings/best-places-to-live, accessed 8/15/2021.

134. Pamela Cochran, *Evangelical Feminism: A History* (New York University Press, 2005), 33, 36; Scott Billingsley, *It's a New Day: Race and Gender in the Modern Charismatic Movement* (University of Alabama Press, 2008), 53.

7. The Right to Compete: 1975–2000

Epigraph: Schlafly in Catherine Rymph, *Republican Women: Feminism and Conservatism from Suffrage through the Rise of the New Right* (University of North Carolina Press, 2006), 22.

1. Harris and Roper Polls in Leonie Huddy et al., "Support for the Women's Movement," *Public Opinion Quarterly* 64, no. 3 (2000): 322; Morris Fiorina, *Culture War? The Myth of a Polarized America,* 3rd ed. (Longman, 2011), 92.

2. Jo Freeman, *A Room at a Time: How Women Entered Party Politics* (Rowman and Littlefield, 2000), 128; Rymph, *Republican Women,* 17; Judy Klemesrud, "Opponent of ERA Confident of its Defeat," *NYT,* 12/15/1975, 53; Bill Morlin, "Phyllis Schlafly Leaves a Legacy Tied to Conspiracy Theories," Southern Poverty Law Center, 9/7/2016: https://www.splcenter.org/hatewatch/2016/09/07/eagle-forums-phyllis-schlafly-leaves-legacy-tied-conspiracy-theories.

3. Huddy et al., "Support," 323, 326; Richard Wike and Shannon Schumacher, "Democratic Rights Popular Globally, Pew, 2/27/2020: https://www.pewresearch.org

/global/2020/02/27/democratic-rights-popular-globally-but-commitment-to-them -not-always-strong/; Laura Silber, "Where Americans and Europeans Agree and Differ," Pew, 10/16/2019: https://www.pewresearch.org/fact-tank/2019/10/16/where -americans-and-europeans-agree-and-differ-in-the-values-they-see-as-important/; Jamie Ballard, "How Many Americans Call Themselves Feminists?," YouGovAmerica, 8/9/2018: https://today.yougov.com/topics/lifestyle/articles-reports/2018/08/09/feminism -american-women-2018, accessed 6/15/2022.

4. Muriel Siebert with Aimee Lee Ball, *Changing the Rules: Adventures of a Wall Street Maverick* (Free Press, 2002), 128; Susan Ware, *Game, Set, Match: Billy Jean King and the Revolution of Women's Sports* (University of North Carolina Press, 2011).

5. Carol Felsenthal, *The Sweetheart of the Silent Majority: The Biography of Phyllis Schlafly* (Doubleday, 1981), 10.

6. Charles Mohr, "Goldwater Favors Raising Social Security Benefits," *NYT*, 8/22/1964, 1.

7. Felsenthal, *Sweetheart*, 13.

8. Felsenthal, *Sweetheart*, 24–25.

9. Felsenthal, *Sweetheart*, 31; Norman Rockwell Museum: https://www.nrm .org/rosie-the-riveter/.

10. Felsenthal, *Sweetheart*, 56.

11. Felsenthal, *Sweetheart*, 71.

12. Felsenthal, *Sweetheart*, 78.

13. Felsenthal, *Sweetheart*, 80; Anthony Leviero, "Truman Says G.O.P. Uses 'The Big Lie'; Asserts Eisenhower Condones Technique and Party Runs on McCarthy Coattails," *NYT*, 10/31/1952, 1.

14. Felsenthal, *Sweetheart*, 86–87.

15. Samuel Fomon, "Infant Feeding in the 20th Century," *Journal of Nutrition* 131, no. 2 (2001), 411S; Lynn Weiner, "Reconstructing Motherhood: The La Leche League in Postwar America," *Journal of American History* 80, no. 4 (1994): 1359.

16. Felsenthal, *Sweetheart*, 123.

17. Donald Critchlow, *Phyllis Schlafly and Grassroots Conservatism: A Woman's Crusade* (Princeton University Press, 2005), 48.

18. Critchlow, *Schlafly*, 75.

19. Felsenthal, *Sweetheart*, 172; Rymph, *Republican Women*, 176.

20. Critchlow, *Schlafly*, 134.

21. Critchlow, *Schlafly*, 136; Fiorina, *Culture War?*, 28; "Goldwater's 1964 Acceptance Speech," *Washington Post* archives: https://www.washingtonpost.com/wp -srv/politics/daily/may98/goldwaterspeech.htm.

22. Felsenthal, *Sweetheart*, 183.

23. Felsenthal, *Sweetheart*, 185; Rymph, *Republican Women*, 184, 179.

24. Felsenthal, *Sweetheart*, 194; Marie Smith, "Two GOP Rivals Unbutton Gloves," *Washington Post*, 5/3/1967, D1.

25. Felsenthal, *Sweetheart*, 187.

26. Rymph, *Republican Women*, 182.

27. L. Allen Klope, "GOP Women Plot Strategy: Schlafly's Eagles Cold to Rocky," *Alton Evening Telegraph* (IL), 2/16/1968, 1; Felsenthal, *Sweetheart*, 267.

28. Felsenthal, *Sweetheart*, 196.

29. Felsenthal, *Sweetheart*, 204.

30. Felsenthal, *Sweetheart,* 204; "Tribune's Choices for Congress," *Chicago Tribune,* 11/1/1970, 3.

31. Felsenthal, *Sweetheart,* 212; "Phony Economic Facts Blamed by Schlafly," *Alton Evening Telegraph,* 11/7/1970, A2; "Traditional Party Balance Continues in Illinois House Delegation Race," *Daily Illini,* 11/4/1970, 2.

32. Siebert, *Changing,* 5.

33. Muriel Siebert, Application for Admission, 9/25/1945, 4, Case Western Reserve University Archives; "First Woman to Join the Big Board Finds 'Grand' Reception," *NYT,* 1/1/1968, 24.

34. Siebert, *Changing,* 5; Sue Herera, *Women of the Street: Making It on Wall Street—The World's Toughest Business* (John Wiley and Sons, 1997), 85.

35. Melissa Fisher, *Wall Street Women* (Duke University Press, 2012), 33; Jonathan Brown and Harold Bronson, "New York Stock Exchange Program Research Program on Stock Ownership," *Journal of Finance* 8, no. 2 (1953); 131.

36. Siebert, *Changing,* 2.

37. Siebert, *Changing,* 7.

38. Siebert, *Changing,* 5, 13.

39. Siebert, *Changing,* 13.

40. Siebert, *Changing,* 23.

41. Siebert, *Changing,* 16.

42. "Yule Fete Dec. 24 for Settlement: Annual Christmas Cotillion at the Waldorf Will Assist Henry Street Group," *NYT,* 12/12/1956, 48; Author's interview with Jane H. Macon (San Antonio, TX), 9/16/2021.

43. Siebert, *Changing,* 17.

44. Siebert, *Changing,* 19.

45. Siebert, *Changing,* 19; "Muriel Siebert: First Lady of Wall Street," video: https://www.youtube.com/watch?v=Izx0NAD45gc, accessed 6/15/2022.

46. Siebert, *Changing,* 62.

47. "Muriel Siebert: First Lady of Wall Street."

48. Louise Marie Roth, *Selling Women Short: Gender and Money on Wall Street* (Princeton University Press, 2006), 59.

49. Siebert, *Changing,* 29.

50. Gregg Jarrell, "Change at the Exchange: The Causes and Effects of Deregulation," *Journal of Law and Economics* 27, no. 4 (Oct. 1984): 275.

51. Siebert, *Changing,* 31; Mirra Komarovsky, *Women in the Modern World: Their Education and Their Dilemmas* (Little, Brown, 1953), 9, 31.

52. Siebert, *Changing,* 30–31.

53. Siebert, *Changing,* 31; "Law Career Led Him to Big Board Position," *Daily News,* 1/10/1965, B36.

54. Siebert, *Changing,* 34; "Muriel Siebert: First Lady of Wall Street."

55. Siebert, *Changing,* 29.

56. Siebert, *Changing,* 35.

57. Siebert, *Changing,* 35.

58. "Woman Marks First Year on N.Y. Stock Exchange," *Williamsport Sunday Grit* (PA), 3/2/1969, 19; Siebert, *Changing,* 37–38.

59. Vartanig Vartan, "Miss Siebert's Memorable Day," *NYT,* 1/1/1968, 23.

60. Felsenthal, *Sweetheart,* 232.

61. Nixon in Lee Stout, *A Matter of Simple Justice: The Untold Story of Barbara Hackman Franklin and a Few Good Women* (Penn State University Libraries, 2020), 83; Felsenthal, *Sweetheart,* 240.

62. Critchlow, *Schlafly,* 206, 207, 209.

63. Felsenthal, *Sweetheart,* 240.

64. Mary Frances Berry, *Why the ERA Failed: Politics, Women's Rights, and the Amending Process of the Constitution* (Indiana University Press, 1986), 90–94.

65. Phyllis Schlafly, "What's Wrong with 'Equal Rights' for Women?," *Phyllis Schlafly Report* 5, no. 7 (Feb. 1972): 2: https://eagleforum.org/publications/psr/feb1972.html.

66. Dorothy Sue Cobble, *The Other Women's Movement: Workplace Justice and Social Rights in Modern* America (Princeton University Press, 2004), 62, 191, 192.

67. Ruth Bader Ginsburg, "The Need for an Equal Rights Amendment," *Journal of the American Bar Association* 59 (Sept. 1973): 1014.

68. Felsenthal, *Sweetheart,* 271.

69. Felsenthal, *Sweetheart,* 244.

70. Schlafly, "What's Wrong," 3.

71. Phyllis Schlafly, "The Right to Be a Woman," *Phyllis Schlafly Report* 6, no. 4 (Nov. 1972): 4: https://eagleforum.org/publications/psr/nov1972.html; Rosemary Thomson, *The Price of LIBerty* (Creation House, 1978), 64.

72. Berry, *Why the ERA Failed,* 3.

73. Phyllis Schlafly, *The Power of the Positive Woman* (Arlington House, 1977), 30; Schlafly, "What's Wrong," 3; Marguerite Sullivan, "ERA's Vigorous Foe," *The Times* (San Mateo, CA), 2/27/1976, 15.

74. Schlafly, *Power,* 50.

75. Marjorie Spruill, *Divided We Stand: The Battle over Women's Rights and Family Values That Polarized American Politics* (Bloomsbury, 2017), 97.

76. Marabel Morgan, *The Total Woman* (1973; Pocket Books, 1975), 96–97.

77. Sheela Kennedy and Steven Ruggles, "The Rise of Divorce in the United States," *Demography* 51, no. 2 (2014): 595.

78. Thomson, *Price,* 66, 106, 132.

79. Schlafly, *Power,* 74–76; Schlafly, "What's Wrong," 2.

80. Ula Taylor, *The Promise of Patriarchy: Women and the Nation of Islam* (University of North Carolina Press, 2017), 5, 89.

81. Schlafly, "What's Wrong," 2–4.

82. Felsenthal, *Sweetheart,* 322.

83. Felsenthal, *Sweetheart,* 301; Critchlow, *Schlafly,* 253.

84. Phyllis Schlafly, *Feminist Fantasies,* foreword by Ann Coulter (Spence, 2003), 31.

85. Berry, *Why the ERA Failed,* 83.

86. Robert McCrae, "Social Consequences of Experiential Openness," *Psychological Bulletin* 120, no. 3 (1996): 325.

87. Critchlow, *Schlafly,* 280; Mark Daniels, Robert Darcy, and Joseph Westphal, "The ERA Won. At Least in the Opinion Polls," *PS* 15, no. 4 (1982): 579, 580; Chelsea Ball, "From Red Dirt to Red State: Oklahoma and the Equal Rights Amendment, 1972–1982," master's thesis, University of Oklahoma, 2016, 2, 85.

88. Siebert, *Changing,* 40, 61.

89. Siebert, *Changing,* 155.

90. Siebert, *Changing,* 49.

91. Siebert, *Changing,* 28, 45.

92. Elizabeth Fowler, "Women Crowd Harvard Club for Talks on Investing," *NYT,* 3/23/1961, 47, 52.

93. Siebert, *Changing,* 41–42.

94. Phyllis Battelle, "Muriel Siebert: Wall Street's Wonder Woman," *Austin Herald* (Minnesota), 7/30/1974, 6.

95. High Water Women, Financial Literacy Education: https://highwaterwomen.org/our-programs/financial-literacy-education/, and testimony of Muriel Siebert, Securities and Exchange Commission (undated): https://www.sec.gov/comments/4-645/4645-10.pdf.

96. "Securities Acts Amendments of 1975," Senate Hearings, Committee on Banking, Housing and Urban Affairs, (Feb. 19–21, 1975), 2.

97. Siebert, *Changing,* 63, 69.

98. Aharon Ofer and Arie Melnick, "Deregulation in the Brokerage Industry: An Empirical Analysis," *Bell Journal of Economics* 9, no. 2 (1978): 634; Macon interview (Cobbs); Siebert, *Changing,* 65.

99. Siebert, *Changing,* 202; Enid Nemy, "The Women's Forum—'Coming to Terms With Power,'" *NYT,* 9/24/1974, 36; Macon interview (Cobbs).

100. Battelle, "Muriel Siebert," 6; author's interview with Chris Myers, New York, 4/21/2022. Myers, who worked for Siebert for more than a decade, even took the wheel of her car when they attended functions.

101. Siebert, *Changing,* 76.

102. Siebert, *Changing,* 76; Dean Kotlowski, "Richard Nixon and the Origins of Affirmative Action," *Historian* 60, no. 3 (1998): 529.

103. Siebert, *Changing,* 76.

104. Siebert, *Changing,* 109; Shamin Asghari, "Early Marriage in Iran: A Pragmatic Approach," *Journal of Human Rights Practice* 11 (Dec. 2019): 578.

105. Siebert, *Changing,* 130.

106. Toril Moi, "I Am Not a Feminist, But . . . : How Feminism Became the 'F' Word," *PMLA* 121, no. 5 (2006): 1736.

107. Spruill, *Divided,* 92.

108. "Sex Discrimination in the Workplace," Hearings before the Committee on Labor and Human Resources, US Senate (Government Printing Office, 1981), 400–403, 416–417.

109. Matthew Lassiter, "Inventing Family Values," in Bruce Schulman and Julian Zelizer, eds., *Rightward Bound: Making America Conservative in the 1970s* (Harvard University Press, 2008), 13.

110. Robert Self, *All in the Family: The Realignment of American Democracy since the 1960s* (Hill and Wang, 2012), 8; Critchlow, *Schlafly,* 8.

111. Critchlow, *Schlafly,* 42; Schlafly, *Power,* 46; Schlafly, *Feminist Fantasies,* 34, 42; Phyllis Schlafly, "How the Feminists Want to Change Our Laws," *Stanford Law and Policy Review* (Spring 1994): 65; Suzanne Venker and Phyllis Schlafly, *The Flipside of Feminism: What Conservative Women Know and Men Can't Say* (WND Books, 2011), 26–27, 36.

112. Spruill, *Divided,* 20.

113. Elaine Hall and Marnie Rodriguez, "The Myth of Postfeminism," *Gender and Society* 17, no. 6 (2003): 888–889.

114. Fiorina, *Culture War?,* 19, 49; Hall and Rodriguez, "Myth," 886, 889; Steve Crabtree, "New Poll Gauges Americans' General Knowledge Levels," Gallup, 7/6/1999: https://news.gallup.com/poll/3742/new-poll-gauges-americans-general-knowledge-levels.aspx.

115. Siebert, *Changing,* 129.

116. Siebert, *Changing,* 129.

117. Donald Critchlow, *Intended Consequences: Birth Control, Abortion, and the Federal Government in Modern America* (Oxford University Press, 1999), 176, 185, 195.

118. Frank Lynn, "Muriel Siebert Joins Race for U.S. Senate," *NYT,* 5/26/1982, B1.

119. Lynn, "Muriel Siebert."

120. Sara Diamond, *Not by Politics Alone: The Enduring Influence of the Christian Right* (Guilford Press, 1998), 144.

121. Critchlow, *Intended Consequences,* 200, 202, 212, 216, 220. On the Catholic role in antiabortion, see Kristin Luker, *Abortion and the Politics of Motherhood* (University of California Press, 1984), 128.

122. Fiorina, *Culture War?,* 89; Siebert, *Changing,* 133, 142.

123. UPI, "Siebert Finances Ahead of GOP Foes," *Syracuse Post-Standard,* 9/17/1982, A12.

124. Maurice Carroll, "2 G.O.P. Primary Losers May Sue Conservative Party," *NYT,* 11/9/1982, B3.

125. Maurice Carroll, "Moynihan Wins Overwhelming Victory," *NYT,* 11/3/1982, B5.

126. Siebert, *Changing,* 143.

127. Schlafly, *Power,* 180.

128. Deborah Charles / Reuters, "Schlafly's Son, 41, Tells Newspaper That He Is Gay," *Buffalo News,* 9/19/1992.

129. Alessandra Stanley, "The 1992 Campaign: Barbara Bush, First Lady on Abortion: Not a Platform Issue," *NYT,* 8/14/1992, 1; Will Dunham, "Barbara Bush, Wife and Mother of Presidents, Dies at 92," Reuters, 4/17/2018: https://www.reuters.com/article/us-people-barbarabush/barbara-bush-wife-and-mother-of-u-s-presidents-dies-at-92-idUSKBN1HO3HG.

130. Siebert, *Changing,* 199.

131. Siebert, *Changing,* 40; Christopher Mahoney, "Women Equal Bathroom Access the NYSE," Famous Daily, n.d.: http://www.famousdaily.com/history/women-equal-bathroom-access-nyse.html, accessed 6/15/2022.

132. John Paul II, "Letter of Pope John Paul II to Women," 6/29/1995: https://www.vatican.va/content/john-paul-ii/en/letters/1995/documents/hf_jp-ii_let_29061995_women.html; Sue Ellen Browder, *Sex and the Catholic Feminist* (Ignatius Press, 2020), 14.

133. Siebert, *Changing,* 212.

134. George Washington, "Farewell Address," 9/17/1796, American Presidency Project: https://www.presidency.ucsb.edu/node/200675; Phyllis Schlafly, *How the Re-*

publican Party Became Pro-Life (Dunrobin, 2016), 27; Jill Lepore, *These Truths: A History of the United States* (Norton, 2018), 658.

8. The Right to Physical Safety: 2000 to the Present

Epigraph: Testimony, Simone Biles, Senate Judiciary Committee Meeting, 9/21/2021, 1: https://www.judiciary.senate.gov/imo/media/doc/Biles%20Testimony1.pdf.

1. Claudia Goldin, *Career & Family: Women's Century-Long Journey toward Equity* (Princeton University Press, 2021), 224.

2. Janell Hobson, "Beyoncé's Fierce Feminism," *Ms.* 23, no. 2 (2013): 44; Meredith Evans and Chris Bobel, "I Am a Contradiction: Feminism and Feminist Identity in the Third Wave," *New England Journal of Public Policy* 22, no. 1 (2007): 211, 213; Hadera McKay, "Is Taylor Swift Revolutionary or Is She Just White?," *Berkeley Beacon,* 11/11/2021: https://berkeleybeacon.com/is-taylor-swift-revolutionary-or-is-she-just-white/; Victoria Dawson Hoff, "Beyoncé Just Released a Very Personal Short Film on Feminism, Body Image, and Life," *Elle,* 12/12/2014: https://www.elle.com/culture/movies-tv/news/a19631/beyonce-yours-and-mine-video/.

3. Kinitra Brooks and Kameelah Martin, eds., *The Lemonade Reader* (Routledge 2020), 3.

4. bell hooks, "Beyoncé's Lemonade Is Capitalist Money-Making at Its Best," *The Guardian,* 5/11/2016; Hobson, "Beyoncé's Fierce Feminism," 42, 44; Sandra Song, "bell hooks Critiques Beyoncé's Depictions of Feminism and Race," *Paper,* 5/10/2016: https://www.papermag.com/beyonce-bell-hooks-lemonade-1789047140.html. Also see Christina Baade, Marquita Smith, and Kristin McGee, "Introduction: Beyoncé Studies," in Baade and McGee, eds., *Beyoncé and the World* (Wesleyan University Press, 2021), 7; Eliana Dockterman, "Flawless: 5 Lessons in Modern Feminism from Beyoncé," *Time,* 12/17/2013.

5. Noreen Malone, "'I'm No Longer Afraid:' 35 Women Tell Their Stories about Being Assaulted by Bill Cosby and the Culture That Wouldn't Listen," *The Cut,* 7/26/2015: https://www.thecut.com/2015/07/bill-cosbys-accusers-speak-out.html#kaya-thompson2.

6. J. Randy Taraborrelli, *Becoming Beyoncé: The Untold Story* (Grand Central, 2015), 14, 41.

7. BKC, Kelly Rowland, and Michelle Williams with James Patrick Herman, *Soul Survivors: The Official Autobiography of Destiny's Child* (Regan Books, 2002), 10; Michael Eric Dyson, "The King of Pop and the Queen of Everything," in Veronica Chambers, ed., *Queen Bey: A Celebration of the Power and Creativity of Beyoncé Knowles-Carter* (St. Martin's, 2019), 118; Kiersten Willis, "Mathew Knowles Says Colorism Made Him Initially Attracted to Ex-Wife Tina Lawson," *Atlanta Black Star,* 2/2/2018: https://atlantablackstar.com/2018/02/02/mathew-knowles-says-colorism-made-initially-attracted-ex-wife-tina-lawson-thought-white/.

8. BKC et al., *Soul Survivors,* 13, 37; Don Merten, "The Meaning of Meanness: Popularity, Competition, and Conflict among Junior High School Girls," *Sociology of Education* 70, no. 1 (1997): 177; Maisie Ghoulson and Danny Martin, "Smart Girls, Black Girls, Mean Girls, and Bullies: At the Intersection of Identities and the Mediating Role

of Young Girls' Social Network in Mathematical Communities of Practice," *Journal of Education* 194, no. 1 (2014): 19.

9. Taraborrelli, *Becoming,* 31; BKC et al., *Soul Survivors,* 9.

10. BKC et al., *Soul Survivors,* 13.

11. BKC et al., *Soul Survivors,* 14.

12. Taraborrelli, *Becoming,* 33; "Beyoncé at Age 7," YouTube: https://www.youtube.com/watch?v=9OeqgtpOYGU, accessed 6/13/2022; BKC et al., *Soul Survivors,* 15.

13. A. R. Riverol, "Myth America and Other Misses: A Second Look at the Miss America Beauty Contest," *ETC: A Review of General Semantics* 40, no. 2 (1983): 214.

14. BKC et al., *Soul Survivors,* 15; BKC, "Pretty Hurts," Columbia Records (2013).

15. BKC et al., *Soul Survivors,* 15–16.

16. Taraborrelli, *Becoming,* 40, 53.

17. Taraborrelli, *Becoming,* 41.

18. BKC et al., *Soul Survivors,* 194.

19. Taraborrelli, *Becoming,* 70.

20. Taraborrelli, *Becoming,* 72–73.

21. Taraborrelli, *Becoming,* 61, 73.

22. Taraborrelli, *Becoming,* 7.

23. Taraborrelli, *Becoming,* 76, 305.

24. Taraborrelli, *Becoming,* 182.

25. BKC et al., *Soul Survivors,* 121; Hoff, "Beyoncé Just Released."

26. BKC et al., *Soul Survivors,* 95; Taraborrelli, *Becoming,* 223, 268.

27. BKC et al., *Soul Survivors,* 96–98; Brittney Cooper, *Eloquent Rage: A Black Feminist Discovers Her Superpower* (St. Martin's, 2019), 27; Taraborrelli, *Becoming,* 282.

28. Taraborrelli, *Becoming,* 241.

29. Taraborrelli, *Becoming,* 274; BKC, "Survivor" (Columbia, 2001); Rowland in BKC et al., *Soul Survivors,* 93. Please note that for simplicity this book lists BKC as the sole author of her songs, though she listed collaborators on most.

30. Ann Powers, "Music: In Tune with the New Feminism," *NYT,* 4/29/2001, 2:1; Destiny's Child, "The Story of Beauty" (Columbia, 2001).

31. Taraborrelli, *Becoming,* 263.

32. Deborah Solomon, "Pop Goes the Feminist," *NYT,* 8/6/2006; Jennifer Baumgardner and Amy Richards, *Manifesta* (Farrar, Straus and Giroux, 2000), 185.

33. Emma Green, "The Feisty Feminism of 'Girls Just Want to Have Fun,' Thirty Years Later," *Atlantic,* 4/1/2014; Justin Moyer and Sarah Kaplan, "Cyndi Lauper: The Secret Feminist History of 'Girls Just Want to Have Fun,'" *Washington Post,* 4/30/2015.

34. Veronica Chambers, "Introduction," in Chambers, *Queen Bey,* 2.

35. Leora Tanenbaum, *Slut! Growing Up Female with a Bad Reputation* (Seven Stories Press, 1999), 18; Vice News, 9/21/2018: https://www.youtube.com/watch?v=4oPnd911FcM; Rebecca Walker, "I Am the Third Wave," *Ms.* (1992): https://teachrock.org/wp-content/uploads/Handout-1-Rebecca-Walker-"I-Am-the-Third-Wave".pdf?x96081.

36. Anna Clark, "11,431 Rape Kits Were Collected and Forgotten in Detroit," *Elle* (June 2016): https://www.elle.com/culture/a37255/forgotten-rape-kits-detroit/.

37. T. Christian Miller and Ken Armstrong, *A False Report: A True Story of Rape in America* (Crown, 2018), 99.

38. Emily Winslow, "The Saga of My Rape Kit," *NYT,* 5/19/2016, A27; Russ McQuaid, "IMPD Possesses More Than 5000 Untested Rape Kits," 9/20/2021, Fox 59: https://fox59.com/news/indycrime/impd-possess-more-than-5000-untested-rape-kits/, accessed 6/ 15 / 2022. For state figures, see "End the Backlog": https://www.endthebacklog.org/backlog/where-backlog-exists-and-whats-happening-end-it, accessed 6/15/2022.

39. James P. McClure and J. Jefferson Looney, *The Papers of Thomas Jefferson* (University of Virginia Press, 2008–2021); Tamara Rice Lave, "The Prosecutor's Duty to 'Imperfect' Rape Victims" *Texas Tech Law Review* 49, no. 1 (2016): 231; Miller and Armstrong, *False,* 38, 208–209; Kimberly Lonsway, Joanne Archambault, and David Lisak, "False Reports: Moving beyond the Issue to Successfully Investigate and Prosecute Non-Stranger Sexual Assault," *The Voice* (National Center for the Prosecution of Violence against Women), 2: https://evawintl.org/wp-content/uploads/FalseReports-Movingbeyondtheissue.pdf.

40. Deborah Tuerkheimer, "Incredible Women: Sexual Violence and the Credibility Discount," *University of Pennsylvania Law Review* 166, no. 1 (2017): 3; Andrew Van Dam, "Less Than 1% of Rapes Lead to Felony Convictions, *Washington Post,* 10/6/2018.

41. Miller and Armstrong, *False,* 22.

42. Miller and Armstrong, *False,* 32, 196.

43. Miller and Armstrong, *False,* 79, 252.

44. Miller and Armstrong, *False,* 110.

45. Regina Schuller, Blake McKimmie, Barbara Masser, and Marc Klippenstine, "Judgements of Sexual Assault: The Impact of Complainant Emotional Demeanor," *New Criminal Law Review* 13, no. 4 (2010): 760, 761. On reported statistics by country in 2021, see *World Population Review:* https://worldpopulationreview.com/country-rankings/rape-statistics-by-country.

46. Schuller et al., "Judgements," 767.

47. Miller and Armstrong, *False,* 115, 118.

48. Miller and Armstrong, *False,* 245.

49. Bill Leuders, *Cry Rape: The True Story of One Woman's Harrowing Quest for Justice* (University of Wisconsin Press, 2006), 58; Miller and Armstrong, *False,* 207; Joanna Walters, "Sara Reedy: The Rape Victim Accused of Lying and Jailed by U.S. Police, *The Guardian,* 12/15/2021.

50. Sandy C., "'Unbelievable' Watched by 32 Million Households on Netflix," *Netflix Life,* 10/16/2019: https://netflixlife.com/2019/10/16/unbelievable-netflix-32-million-viewers/, accessed 6/15/2022.

51. Taraborrelli, *Becoming,* 331.

52. Hoff, "Beyoncé Just Released"; *Beyoncé: Life Is But a Dream,* film (Parkwood Entertainment, 2013).

53. Marquis Bey, "Close-Up: Beyoncé: Media and Cultural Icon," *Black Camera* 9, no. 1 (2017): 169.

54. BKC et al., *Soul Survivors,* 131–132, 266.

55. "Bills, Bills, Bills," music video (Columbia, 1999): https://www.youtube.com/watch?v=NiF6-0UTqtc.

56. BKC, "Independent Women—Part I" (Columbia, 2000).

57. BKC, "Single Ladies, Put a Ring On It" (Columbia, 2008).

58. BKC, "Run the World (Girls)," (Columbia, Parkwood, 2011).

59. Catherine Traywick, "Beyoncé's New Album Got FP Global Thinker Chimamanda Adichie All Wrong," *Foreign Policy,* 12/13/2013.

60. Taraborrelli, *Becoming,* 372.

61. Aisha Harris, "Who Run the World? Husbands?" *Slate,* 2/4/2013: https://slate.com/culture/2013/02/beyonces-mrs-carter-show-world-tour-why-use-her-married-name.html; Hobson, "Beyoncé's Fierce Feminism," 44.

62. BKC, "Pretty Hurts" (Columbia, 2014): https://www.youtube.com/watch?v=LXXQLa-5n5w.

63. BKC et al., *Soul Survivors,* 231; Taraborrelli, *Becoming,* 269.

64. BKC, "Bootylicious" (Columbia, 2001); Taraborrelli, *Becoming,* 268–269; Quinci LeGardye, "Beyoncé Wrote Bootylicious in Response to Criticism about Her Weight," *Harper's Bazaar,* 8/16/2021: https://www.harpersbazaar.com/celebrity/latest/a37318391/beyonce-wrote-bootylicious-response-criticism-weight/.

65. Taraborrelli, *Becoming,* 327.

66. Elahe Izadi, "Beyoncé Performs at the Grammys as a Pregnant Golden Goddess," *Washington Post,* 2/12/2017.

67. Traywick, "Beyoncé's New Album"; BKC, "Flawless" (Parkwood and Columbia, 2013); Spencer Kornhaber, "Beyoncé's 'Flawless': The Full Story," *Atlantic,* 6/26/2014.

68. Bonnie Fuller, "Hollywood Life" blog, 3/18/2013: https://www.youtube.com/watch?v=XomRUVzCzuE, accessed 6/16/2022.

69. Chimamanda Ngozi Adichie, *We Should All Be Feminists* (Random House, 2014).

70. BKC, "Flawless."

71. Tammy Wynette, "Stand by Your Man" (Epic, 1968); BKC, "Me, Myself, and I" (Columbia, 2003).

72. BKC, "Irreplaceable" (Columbia, 2006).

73. BC Jean, "If I Were a Boy," sung by BKC (Columbia, 2008).

74. Hollywood Reporter, "Beyoncé Fired Dad Amid Accusations of Theft, Legal Documents Show," *Billboard,* 7/12/2011: https://www.billboard.com/music/music-news/beyonce-fired-dad-amid-accusations-of-theft-legal-documents-show-report-1177143/; "Beyonce Parts Ways with Her Manager Father," BBC News, 3/29/2011: https://www.bbc.com/news/newsbeat-12890866.

75. BKC, "Life Is But a Dream" (Parkwood, 2013).

76. Jenny Stevens, "Beyoncé Takes Part in Feminist Campaign to Ban the Word Bossy," *NME News,* 3/12/2014: https://www.nme.com/news/music/beyonce-137-1247109, video: https://www.youtube.com/watch?v=6dynbzMlCcw, accessed 6/16/2022; BKC, "Gender Equality Is a Myth!," in Maria Shriver et al., eds., *The Shriver Report: A Woman's Nation Pushes Back from the Brink* (Palgrave Macmillan, 2014), 34.

77. Robert Lee and Paul Greenlaw, "The Legal Evolution of Sexual Harassment," *Public Administration Review* 55, no. 4 (1995): 358; Steve Duin, "The Women Oregon Senator Robert Packard Preyed On," *Oregonian,* 9/6/2020; Jessica Guynn, "Sexual Harassment Used to Cost Women Their Careers," *USA Today,* 12/4/2017.

78. Megyn Kelly, *Settle for More* (Harper Collins, 2017), 307.

79. Gretchen Carlson, *Getting Real* (Viking, 2015), 17.

80. Carlson, *Getting Real,* 26.

81. Carlson, *Getting Real,* 76.

82. Carlson, *Getting Real,* 3, 81, 97, 99; William Goldman, *Hype and Glory* (Villard, 1990), 213, 287.

83. Gretchen Carlson, "This Year Has Changed Me," *Parade Magazine,* 9/10/1989, 5.

84. Carlson, *Getting Real,* 133.

85. Carlson, *Getting Real,* 143, 216.

86. Lee and Greenlaw, "Legal Evolution," 358, 360.

87. "Why We Fail to Report Sexual Harassment," *Harvard Business Review,* 10/4/2016; Caroline Criado Perez, *Invisible Women: Data Bias in a World Designed for Men* (Abrams, 2019), 138.

88. Carlson, *Getting Real,* 213.

89. Martin Williams, "Fox News Presenters Mock Female Pilot," *The Guardian,* 9/25/2104.

90. "Fox & Friends," 6/14/2012: https://www.youtube.com/watch?v=z_vqfRvcjrs.

91. Jennifer Berdahl, "Harassment Based on Sex: Protecting Social Status in the Context of Gender Hierarchy," *Academy of Management Review* 32, no. 2 (2007): 642; Tony Maglio, "Gretchen Carlson Is Objectified Over and Over Again on Fox News," *The Wrap,* 7/7/2016: https://www.thewrap.com/gretchen-carlson-fox-friends-roger-ailes-sexual-harassment/; Carlson, *Getting Real,* 217; Gabriel Sherman, *The Loudest Voice in the Room: How the Brilliant, Bombastic Roger Ailes Built Fox News and Divided a Country* (Random House, 2017), 298.

92. Gretchen Carlson v. Roger Ailes, Superior Court of New Jersey, 7/6/2016, 3: https://www.documentcloud.org/documents/2941030-Carlson-Complaint-Filed.

93. Sherman, *Loudest,* 398; John Koblin, "Gretchen Carlson, Former Fox Anchor, Speaks Publicly about Sexual Harassment Lawsuit," *NYT,* 7/13/2016, B1; Sarah Ellison, "After Ailes, Fox News Has a New Crisis," *Vanity Fair,* 8/25/2016.

94. Sherman, *Loudest,* 114, 115; Gabriel Sherman, "6 More Women Alleged That Roger Ailes Sexually Harassed Them," *New York Magazine,* 7/9/2016.

95. Carlson, *Getting Real,* 213.

96. Matt Ford, "After Cosby, California Changes Its Rape Laws," *Atlantic,* 9/29/2016; "Spurred by Brock Turner Case, Gov. Jerry Brown Signs Laws to Toughen Laws against Rape," *Los Angeles Times,* 9/30/2016.

97. Paul Solotaroff, "Trump Seriously: On the Trail of the GOP's Tough Guy," *Rolling Stone,* 9/9/2015.

98. Malone, "I'm No Longer Afraid"; Michael Barbaro and Megan Twohey, "Crossing the Line: Trump's Private Conduct with Women, *NYT,* 5/14/2016, A1; Jodi Kantor and Megan Twohey, *She Said: Breaking the Sexual Harassment Story That Helped Ignite a Movement* (Penguin, 2019), 17.

99. Kelly, *Settle for More,* 301.

100. Holly Yan, "Donald Trump's 'Blood' Comment about Megyn Kelly Draws Outrage," CNN, 8/8/2015: https://www.cnn.com/2015/08/08/politics/donald-trump-cnn-megyn-kelly-comment/index.html.

101. Kelly, *Settle for More,* 262, 283.

102. Kelly, *Settle for More,* 300, 304, 306.

103. Kelly, *Settle for More,* 194; Christopher Rosen, "Megyn Kelly: Feminist Definition Discussed with Stephen Colbert," *Entertainment Weekly,* 2/8/2016: https://ew.com/article/2016/02/08/megyn-kelly-feminist-stephen-colbert/.

104. Kelly, *Settle for More,* 309.

105. Audrey Carlsen et al., "#MeToo Brought Down 201 Powerful Men," *NYT,* 10/29/2018.

106. Gretchen Carlson, *Be Fierce: Stop Harassment and Take Your Power Back* (Center Street, 2017), 4; Kate Arthur, "Gretchen Carlson: Five Years after Her Lawsuit Brought Down Roger Ailes," *Variety,* 7/6/2021: https://variety.com/2021/tv/news/gretchen-carlson-sexual-harassment-lawsuit-five-year-anniversary-1235010908/; "Former Fox News Anchor Gretchen Carlson Speaks Out," YouTube, 11/17/2016: https://www.youtube.com/watch?v=h7Zb8NbiDT0.

107. Carlson, *Getting Real,* 6.

108. Evette Dionne Brown, "BDSM, Gazes and Wedding Rings," in Adrienne Trier-Bieniek, ed., *The Beyoncé Effect: Essays on Sexuality, Race and Feminism* (McFarland, 2016), 189; Lindsey Stewart, "Something Akin to Freedom: Sexual Love, Political Agency, and *Lemonade,*" in Brooks and Martin, *Lemonade Reader,* 25.

109. Riley Cardoza, "Jay-Z Shares 'the Most Important' Part of Parenting His and Beyoncé's 3 Kids," *Us Magazine,* 4/27/2021.

110. "Jay-Z Physically Attacked by Beyoncé's Sister," TMZ.com, 5/12/2014: http://www.tmz.com/2014/05/12/jay-z-solange-fight-elevator-video-beyonce-met-gala/.

111. Taraborrelli, *Becoming,* 446.

112. For lyrics, see "Lemonade film (script), annotated," Genius, https://genius.com/Beyonce-lemonade-film-script-annotated; on Shire, see Patricia Garcia, "Warsan Shire is the Next Beyoncé-Backed Literary Sensation," *Vogue,* 4/25/2016: https://www.vogue.com/article/warsan-shire-lemonade-poet.

113. BKC, "Sorry" (Parkwood and Columbia, 2016).

114. Morgan Baila, "The 19 Most Controversial Lyrics on Beyoncé's Lemonade," *Refinery29,* 4/25/2016: https://www.refinery29.com/en-us/2016/04/109139/controversial-lyrics-beyonce-lemonade-album; Kyra Gaunt, "Beyoncé's Lemonade and the Black Swan Effect," in Brooks and Martin, *Lemonade Reader,* 215.

115. Birgitta Johnson, "She Gave You Lemonade, Stop Trying to Say It's Tang," in Brooks and Martin, *Lemonade Reader,* 235.

116. Jay-Z, "4:44" (Roc Nation, 2017).

117. Dean Baquet, "Jay-Z and Dean Baquet," *NYT,* 11/29/2017; Travis Andrews, "Jay-Z Opens Up to David Letterman about Cheating on Beyoncé and His Mother's Sexuality," *Washington Post,* 4/6/2018. For streaming numbers, see https://genius.com/albums/Beyonce/Lemonade and https://genius.com/albums/Jay-z/4-44.

118. Carmen Perez, "Beyoncé's Radical Ways," in Chambers, *Queen Bey,* 142.

119. BKC, "Beyoncé in Her Own Words: Her Life, Her Body, Her Heritage," *Vogue,* 8/6/2018: https://www.vogue.com/article/beyonce-september-issue-2018.

120. Dyson in Chambers, *Queen Bey,* 114; BKC, *Beyoncé: Year of Four* (Parkwood, 2011): https://www.youtube.com/watch?v=3vXXiku0580.

121. Toby Rider and Matthew Llewellyn, "The Five Rings and the 'Imagined Community': Nationalism and the Modern Olympic Games," *SAIS Review of Interna-*

tional Affairs 35, no. 2 (2015): 22; Testimony, McKayla Maroney, Senate Judiciary Committee Meeting, 9/21/2021, 2: https://www.judiciary.senate.gov/imo/media/doc/Maroney%20Testimony.pdf. For the full hearing, see https://www.judiciary.senate.gov/meetings/dereliction-of-duty-examining-the-inspector-generals-report-on-the-fbis-handling-of-the-larry-nassar-investigation.

122. Testimony, Simone Biles, Senate Judiciary Committee Meeting, 9/21/2021, 1: https://www.judiciary.senate.gov/imo/media/doc/Biles%20Testimony1.pdf.

123. Bessel van der Kolk, *The Body Keeps the Score: Brain, Mind, and Body in the Healing of Trauma* (Penguin, 2015).

124. Testimony, Maggie Nichols, Senate Judiciary Committee Meeting, 9/21/2021, 1: https://www.judiciary.senate.gov/imo/media/doc/Nichols%20Testimony.pdf; Kati Breazeal, "Friday Focus: The Magnificent Maggie Nichols," *FloGymnastics,* 9/29/2014: https://www.flogymnastics.com/articles/5039468-friday-focus-the-magnificent-maggie-nichols, accessed 6/15/2022.

125. Testimony, Aly Raisman, Senate Judiciary Committee Meeting, 9/21/2021, 1: https://www.judiciary.senate.gov/imo/media/doc/Raisman%20Testimony.pdf.

126. Office of the Inspector General, Department of Justice, "Investigation and Review of the Federal Bureau of Investigation's Handling of Allegations of Sexual Abuse by Former USA Gymnastics Physician Lawrence Gerard Nassar" (July 2012), ii, 17–18: https://oig.justice.gov/sites/default/files/reports/21-093.pdf.

127. Bonni Cohen and Jon Shenk, *Athlete A* (Actual Films / Netflix, 2020); "Former Olympic Gymnast Says Doctor Abused Her 'All Over the World,' *Washington Post,* 3/28/2017.

128. Tim Evans, "'Athlete A' Tells Part of the Larry Nassar Investigation: This Is the Part You Didn't See," *Indianapolis Star,* 6/24/2020.

129. BBC News, "How Much Is a Little Girl Worth?," 1/24/2018: https://www.bbc.com/news/av/world-us-canada-42810609; Juliet Macur, "In Larry Nassar's Case, a Single Voice Eventually Raised an Army," *NYT,* 1/24/2018.

130. Office of the Inspector General, "Investigation," iv; Raisman testimony, 5.

131. Maroney testimony, 2.

132. John Barr and Dan Murphy, "Evidence-Tampering Charges Dismissed against Former USA Gymnastics CEO Steve Penny," *ESPN,* 4/26/2022: https://www.espn.com/olympics/gymnastics/story/_/id/33811363/evidence-tampering-charges-dismissed-former-usa-gymnastics-ceo-steve-penny; Matt Bonesteel and Cindy Boren, "Gymnasts Sue FBI for $1 Billion Over Mishandling of Larry Nassar Case," *Washington Post,* 6/8/2022.

133. Nancy Hewitt, ed., *No Permanent Waves: Recasting Histories of U.S. Feminism* (Rutgers University Press, 2010). On the fifth wave, see Perez, "Beyoncé's Radical Ways," 142.

134. John Creamer and Abinash Mohanty, "U.S. Poverty Rate Drops to 11.8% in 2018," 9/10/2019: https://www.census.gov/library/stories/2019/09/poverty-rate-for-people-in-female-householder-families-lowest-on-record.html; Lori Pace, "Single Mother Household Statistics in 2022," Single Mothers, 9/17/2021: https://singlemothers.us/single-mother-statistics/, accessed 6/15/2022; Beth Bovino et al., "The Key to Unlocking U.S. GDP Growth? Women," *S&P Global* (2017), 1: https://www.spglobal.com/_Media/Documents/03651.00_Women_at_Work_Doc.8.5x11-R4.pdf.

135. Trent MacNamara, *Birth Control and American Modernity: A History of Popular Ideas* (Cambridge University Press, 2018), 55; "They Had Miscarriages and New Abortion Laws Obstructed Treatment," *NYT,* 7/17/2022; "I'm Carrying This Baby Just to Bury It," *NYT,* 8/19/22; "Study Finds Higher Maternal Mortality Rates in States with More Abortion Restrictions," Tulane University News, 8/23/2021: https://sph.tulane.edu/news/study-finds-higher-maternal-mortality-rates-states-more-abortion-restrictions; Roman Pabayo et al., "Laws Restricting Access to Abortion Service and Infant Mortality Risk in the United States," *International Journal of Environmental Research and Public Health,* 5/26/2020: https://www.ncbi.nlm.nih.gov/pmc/articles/PMC7312072/.

Epilogue

1. Allie Long, "Why Does the Right Co-Opt the Language of Feminism?," *The Medium,* 6/10/2017: https://medium.com/@allielong/how-did-the-right-co-opt-the-language-of-feminism-549be44a802c.

2. Matthew Cochran, "How Strong Women Like Amy Coney Barrett Submit to Their Husbands with Joy," *The Federalist,* 10/5/2020: https://thefederalist.com/2020/10/05/how-strong-women-like-amy-coney-barrett-submit-to-their-husbands-with-joy/.

3. "One-in-Five U.S. Adults Were Raised in Interfaith Homes," Pew, 10/26/2016: https://www.pewforum.org/2016/10/26/one-in-five-u-s-adults-were-raised-in-interfaith-homes/#religion-seen-as-less-important-for-successful-marriage-than-shared-interests-satisfying-sex-fair-division-of-household-labor; Claudia Goldin, *Career & Family: Women's Century-Long Journey toward Equity* (Princeton University Press, 2021), 158, 207; Claire Cain Miller, "How Same-Sex Couples Divide Chores and What It Reveals about Modern Parenting," *NYT,* 5/18/2018; "19% of Transgender Adults in the US Are Parents," UCLA School of Law, 10/5/2020: https://williamsinstitute.law.ucla.edu/press/trans-parents-press-release/.

4. Georgetown Institute for Women, Peace, and Security, *Inclusion, Justice, Security: Women, Peace, and Security Index, 2021/2022* (Georgetown Institute, 2021), 76; Anna Gromada and Dominic Richardson, *Where Do Rich Countries Stand on Childcare? A National Ranking of National Childcare Policies in Wealthy Countries* (UNICEF Office of Research, 2021), 7; Aria Bendix, "Birth Control Restrictions Could Follow Abortion Bans, Experts Say," NBC News, 6/24/22: https://www.nbcnews.com/health/health-news/birth-control-restrictions-may-follow-abortion-bans-roe-rcna35289.

5. Malala Yousafzai, Nobel Lecture, 12/10/2014: https://www.nobelprize.org/uploads/2018/06/yousafzai-lecture_en.pdf; Regina Fuchs, Elsie Pamuk, and Wolfgang Lutz, "Education or Wealth: Which Matters More for Reducing Child Mortality in Developing Countries," *Vienna Yearbook of Population Research* 8 (2010): 176; Charles Menifield and Jacob Dawson, "Infant Mortality in Southern States: A Bureaucratic Nightmare," *Journal of Health and Human Services Administration* 31, no. 3 (2008): 395.

6. Peter Beinart, "The New Authoritarians Are Waging War on Women," *Atlantic* (Jan. / Feb. 2019); Amy Qin, "A Prosperous China Says 'Men Preferred,' and Women Lose," *NYT,* 7/16/2019; Amy Ferris-Rotman, "Putin's War on Women," *Foreign Policy,* 4/9/2018; Ann Louise Bardach, "Tearing Off the Veil," *Vanity Fair,* 3/4/2015; Valerie

Hudson et al., *The First Political Order: How Sex Shapes Governance and National Security Worldwide* (Columbia University Press, 2020).

7. Georgetown Institute for Women, Peace, and Security, *The Best and Worst States to Be a Woman* (Georgetown Institute, 2020), 20, 32.

8. "Notes on People: Young Award Winner," *NYT,* 1/12/1980, 22; Elizabeth Cobbs, Rockefeller Award Winner Interview, *Today Show,* 4/6/1980: http://elizabethcobbs.com/time-capsule.

9. Robyn Muncy, "Partial Victories, All! America Women and the Vote," 11/30/2020, webinar, Vassar College: https://www.youtube.com/watch?v=RKOxufZeqII&t=724s, accessed 7/12/2022.

Acknowledgments

I am grateful for all the kind input that has advanced this project. Many people have given help with both hands, and I am humbled by their generosity. Some are fellow historians who guided me away from mistakes and enriched my understanding. Myra Burton, Victoria Bynum, Donna Coker, Donald Critchlow, Lynn Dumenil, David Kennedy, Robyn Muncy, Allison Parker, Bruce Schulman, and Susan Ware deserve much credit—and no blame—for the work herein. I wish to thank my agent, Don Fehr of Trident Literary, and the dedicated team from Harvard University Press, including Julie Carlson and Emeralde Jensen-Roberts. Legendary editor Joy de Menil, who christened this book "Fearless," was relentless in her quest to understand the subject, stretching my ability to explain it. Publicist Gretchen Crary of February Media has been my unerring guide for five books, and I have promised never to leave home without her. I would also like to acknowledge the spiffy detective assistance of History Works, particularly Terry Fife, Elizabeth Trantowski, and Kyle Wolfe, who put me in touch with the family of Grace Banker during my research on *The Hello Girls* and helped me plumb Illinois records on Elizabeth Packard for this book.

Martha Cotera and Yvonne Swan paid me the honor of placing their stories in my hands. It is rare for a historian to meet her subjects, and I hope I have merited their trust. Friends who are writers or editors gave canny advice about storytelling, particularly Gabrielle Glaser, Nigel Quinney, and Alexandra Shelley. Two other friends, Deborah Dewise and Sue Morris, provided their woman-on-the-street perspective, helping me feel it was all worthwhile. They were unfailingly gracious, as was Ryan Abt, who included me in a perspicacious student writers' group at Texas A&M University. (They also know I usually disparage ten-dollar words like "perspicacious," so this is for them, since it genuinely applies.)

Lucia Hodgson gave marvelous suggestions on biographical possibilities, and Charlotte Shaw did crackerjack newspaper research. The History Department of Texas A&M University, and Melbern and Susanne Glasscock, gave me funds and time to produce this book. My sharp-eyed friend Tina Lewis Abernethy kindly proofread it. Kelly Cook and Margaret Gregory expertly helped me organize a conference on "Revolutionary Women of Color" in the midst of it all. Did I mention Catherine Clinton, a patron saint of women's history? Catherine has fed me, put a roof over my head, and given me ingenious suggestions for almost a dozen years. I also wish to thank my long-ago companions in the women's movement, particularly Joyce Lane and Sue Kirk.

Last but far from least is my family. My generous children, Gregory and Victoria Shelby, asked questions and made suggestions that improved each chapter, as they have for every book I've written since they could read. Their perspective as young feminists kept me sharp (I hope). My husband, James Shelley, who brought the inimitable Muriel Siebert to my attention, absorbed each word and shared every tear. When we married, I suggested that we vow to put each other's needs ahead of our own, whereupon he suggested that we vow to treat each other's needs like our own. As a woman who placed her family first when very young, at a high cost, I am still learning how to do this. I cannot thank him enough for his love and companionship.

Index